WINNIPEG
WI
D0440979

Cruise ships against the Montreal skyline at night
© Stéphan Poulin / Tourisme Montréal

THE GREEN GUIDE

Montreal & Quebec City

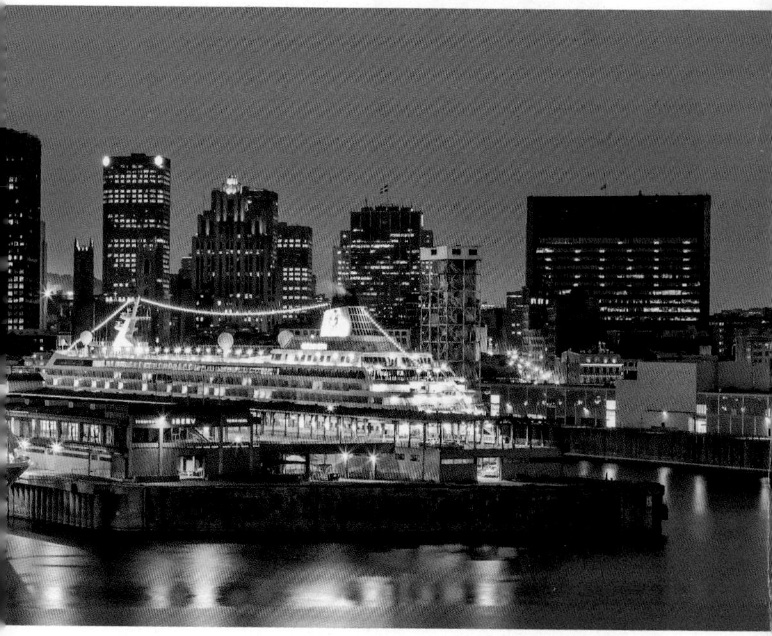

How to...

Plan Your Trip

Understand Montreal & Quebec City

Discover Montreal & Quebec City

Green Guides - Discover the Destination

Main sections

PLANNING YOUR TRIP
The blue-tabbed section gives you **ideas for your trip** and **practical information.**

INTRODUCTION
The orange-tabbed section explores **Nature, History, Art and Culture** and the **Region Today.**

DISCOVERING
The green-tabbed section features Principal Sights by region, **Sights, Walking Tours, Excursions,** and **Driving Tours.**

Region intros

At the start of each region in the Discovering section is a brief introduction. Accompanied by the region maps, these provide an overview of the main tourism areas and their background.

Region maps

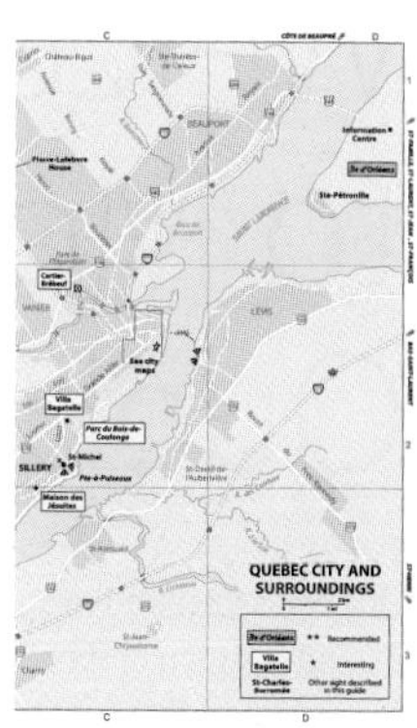

Star ratings

Michelin has given star ratings for more than 100 years. If you're pressed for time, we recommend you visit the three or two star sights first:

- ★★★ **Highly Recommended**
- ★★ **Recommended**
- ★ **Interesting**

Tours

We've selected driving and walking tours that show you the best of each town or region. Step by step directions are accompanied by detailed maps with marked routes. If you are short on time, you can follow the star ratings to decide where to stop. Selected addresses give you options for accommodation and dining en route.

Addresses

We've selected the best hotels, restaurants, cafés, shops, nightlife and entertainment to fit all budgets. See the Legend on the cover flap for an explanation of the price categories. See the back of the guide for an index of where to find hotels and restaurants.

Other reading

- Green Guide Canada
- Green Guide New York City
- Must Sees Boston
- Must Sees Vancouver
- Michelin Northeastern USA/ Eastern Canada Regional Map

Welcome to Montreal & Quebec City

Quebec's vast and rugged landscape—an area three times the size of France—provides much of its tourist appeal. Visitors will find sea-swept coastlines, snow-covered mountains, deep forests and pastoral farms, in a climate of cold winters, mild summers with long hours of daylight, and an autumn that arrives in a fiery blaze of color. Culturally, Quebec owes much to France, the source of its language, its main religion, and most of its art and architecture, though many other influences are at work, including a home-grown generosity of spirit that provides a warm welcome to immigrants and visitors alike.

Parc national de l'Île-Bonaventure-et-du-Rocher-Percé © Tourisme Gaspésie, ATRG

Planning Your Trip

Introducing Montreal & Quebec City

Discovering Montreal & Quebec City

Regions of Montreal & Quebec City

Montreal and Surroundings (pp106–285)

Located on the busy St. Lawrence River, Montreal has long been a commercial crossroads and a magnet for newcomers, and it retains that role today. Visitors will find a cosmopolitan hub that is rich in history but forward-looking, and flanked by tourist delights. To the West are the resorts and parks of the Laurentian Mountains, plus Canada's most-visited museum, while to the East are peaceful villages, rich farmland, maple forests, and the ski areas and hiking trails of the Appalachian Mountains.

Quebec City
© Luc-Antoine Couturier / Québec City Tourism

Montreal
© Stéphan Poulin / Tourisme Montréal

Quebec City and Surroundings (pp290–387)

The original capital of New France, Quebec City is a beautifully preserved slice of the old continent, but in a new-country setting, a combination that is unlike any other city in North America. But the city is more than a refreshing antidote to an increasingly homogenous world: it's also temptingly close to the inspiring land-meets-sea attractions of the Côte de Charlevoix and Saguenay Fjord to the Northwest, and the cliffs and lighthouses of the Gaspé Peninsula to the Northeast.

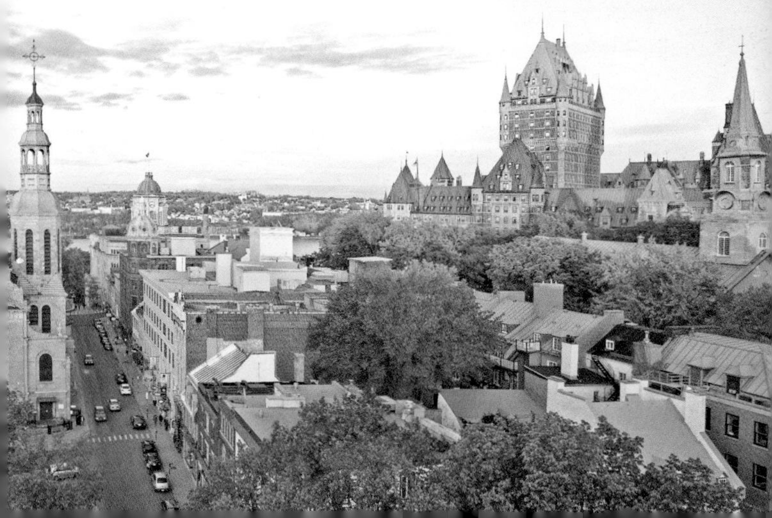

Baskatong Reservoir, Laurentides
© Guillaume Pouliot / Marleyne Babin / Tourisme Laurentides / laurentians.com

Outer Quebec (pp432–483)

Montreal and Quebec City are the urban gateways to an immense landscape of forest and mountain, a terrain of proudly preserved sights and rural charm that evokes a bygone era, yet is filled with ferries, cable cars, historic hotels, renovated inns, thrilling excursions, and visitor-friendly parks. The remote Côte-Nord is home to the pristine Mingan Archipelago and Île d'Anticosti, while the distant Northern and Western areas, featuring James Bay and the evocative landscapes of Nunavik, appeal to travelers who share the same sense of adventure that has been a hallmark of the region since time immemorial.

Grand Basque Island, Côte-Nord
© Tourisme Sept-Îles

Canyon Sainte-Anne, Côte de Charlevoix
© Canyon Sainte-Anne

Planning Your Trip

Porte Saint-Louis, Quebec City
© Tibor Bognar / Photononstop

Planning Your Trip

Canoeing in Jacques-Cartier National Park
© Jean Pierre Huard - SÉPAQ / Québec City Tourism

Inspiration

WHAT'S HOT

– The **Old Port of Montreal** has added new attractions, including a labyrinth and a zipline, to its already-rich slate of tourist offerings (p130).

– **Quebec City**'s Augustine Museum has unveiled its newly renovated museum with state-of-the-art displays (p 318).

– **Far northern Nunavik**, a land of strong winds and snowy winters, now offers the high-adrenaline sport of kite-skiing, through Arctic Wind Riders (p483).

– Visitors to **Pointe-au-Père Lighthouse National Historic Site**, on the Gaspé Peninsula near Rimouski, can now tour the remarkable 90m/295ft *Onondaga* submarine (p406).

– **Port-Menier**, in the far northeast corner of Quebec, will open a new Discovery and Visitor Center, complete with restaurant, bar, gift shop, and museum dedicated to Anticosti National Park, in 2015 (p456).

– Visitors to **Mont-Tremblant National Park** can clip themselves onto a steel cable and climb 200m up a cliff face, with built-in steps, beams and bridges, on the new Via Ferrata du Diable (p208).

Pointe-à-Callière, Montréal Museum of Archaeology and History

© Caroline Bergeron / Pointe-à-Callière / Tourisme Montréal

Visiting Montreal & Quebec City

Quebec is a year-round destination that offers an unparalleled combination of urban culture, visible history, and natural beauty.

IDEAS FOR YOUR VISIT

There is more to Quebec than long driving tours in the countryside, expeditions in the woods and fantastic urban festivals, although these are among the province's best features. The following ideas are designed to help you appreciate Quebec in unusual yet accessible ways.

SHORT BREAKS (3–4 DAYS)

Île Saint-Bernard
Just south of the Island of Montreal, this former nun's retreat is now the site of an inexpensive resort and nature reserve.

Laurentians
The Laurentian Autoroute heads north into a rare mountain paradise.

Quebec City & Île d'Orleans
Take the train, book a hotel, and sign up for local tours of Old Town and the island.

Tour Cantons-de-l'Est
Head east along the Eastern Townships Autoroute and let serendipity carry you away.

LONG BREAKS (1–2 WEEKS)

Cruise to Îles de la Madeleine
This eight-day cruise is the best-kept secret in the province. Try cruising one-way and flying back.

Gaspé
Take a train or a plane, or drive your car, to this remote community for summertime sightseeing, seafood and local hospitality.

Cruise the North Shore Mingan Archipelago
For something completely exotic, yet without leaving the continent, try this epic trip.

Saguenay Fjord
No other destination on the continent offers as much biodiversity as this remarkable fjord.

P'tit Train du Nord
A 400km/240mi cycling, walking and skiing circuit that features villages, restaurants, galleries and quaint inns along the way.

USEFUL WEBSITES

www.bonjourquebec.com – Official government tourist board.
www.quebecregion.com – Events, accommodations, and other useful information.
www.hihostels.ca – Hosteling information.
www.tourisme-montreal.org – Travel, accommodations, and travel advice.
skicentral.com/quebec.html – Ski resort directory, lodging, ski runs, pistes, etc.
www.pc.gc.ca – National Parks of Canada.
www.sepaq.com – Provincial Parks of Quebec.

CYCLING IN AND AROUND MONTREAL

Surrounded by water, and featuring an extensive network of safe cycling routes, **Montreal** (*see MONTREAL*) is an excellent city to experience the pleasures of urban cycling, especially on a quiet Sunday morning. Ride along the peaceful **Canal de l'Aqueduc** in the Lachine District and have a refined picnic purchased at the gourmet **Atwater Market**.

Cycling in Montreal
© Fitz and Follwell Co. / Tourisme Montréal

More ambitious riders might like the challenge of crossing the St. Lawrence River on the **Champlain Bridge** before touring the small islands lining the **St. Lawrence Seaway**. Another option is to take a small ferry (no space for cars) with your bike from Old Montreal to Longueuil. www.velo.qc.ca.

TRAIN TOURS AROUND MONTREAL

Some trains that transport stressed-out commuters to downtown Montreal also carry relaxed day-trippers on package tours in the summer, on weekends and sometimes on weekdays. This clever idea has been very successful, so reserve tickets in advance if you want to enjoy the countryside without having to drive; choose from among the day trips offered by the *Agence métropolitain de transport*. You can sample maple liqueur in Mirabel, cheese and rabbit specialties in Saint-Sophie and apples in a Lower Laurentians orchard. If you prefer a taste of history, you can visit the Trestler House in Vaudreuil-Soulange, the Canadian Train Museum in Saint-Constant or **Île Perrot,** with its natural and historical features. Many of these tours include lunch at a local restaurant. Some also go to **Laval**, north of Montreal, home of the Cosmodôme Space Camp. **For further information**: 514-287-8726 or 1-888-702-8726 (toll-free). www.amt.qc.ca/escapades.

GHOST TOURS OF QUEBEC CITY

What qualifications landed an applicant the job of Executioner in the 1600s in Quebec City? How did the French execute criminals before the invention of the guillotine? You'll have these answers and more, as 400 years of murders, executions, mysterious ghost sightings, tragedies and hauntings will be imprinted in your mind forever. This is a highly rated ghost tour, well-researched and expertly guided. Tours in English or

Trois-Rivières

© Masci Giuseppe / age fotostock

French, from May to October. And if it rains? The tour is even better and scarier, say the organizers. ℘418-692-9770 or 855-692-9770. www.ghosttoursofquebec.com.

CULTURAL AND HISTORICAL TOURS IN TROIS-RIVIÈRES

The city of **Trois-Rivières** *(see TROIS-RIVIÈRES)*, between Montreal and Quebec City on the St. Lawrence River, has a vibrant cultural scene, thanks to its favored geographic position and the low cost of making a living as an artist there. Visitors can easily tour the beautiful downtown **art galleries**, such as illico, Maistre, St-Antoine and L'Oeil Tactile.

Old Trois-Rivières is very compact, yet as old as the historic parts of Quebec City. This makes it pleasant and easy to walk around Old Trois-Rivières, armed with a **self-guided tour** leaflet from the city tourism office, accompanied by constant, soothing views of the river.

REGIONAL TOURIST OFFICES

Contact the regional offices listed below for information on points of interest, seasonal events and accommodation, and road and city maps. Regional offices, which distribute maps, brochures and other travel information free of charge, extend their operating hours during summertime.

IN QUEBEC

Tourisme Québec
1255 rue Peel, bureau 400, Montreal (QC) H3B 4V4; www.bonjourquebec.com. ℘514-873-7977 or, toll free at 1-877-266-5687

Abitibi-Témiscamingue
155 Ave. Dallaire, bureau 100, Rouyn-Noranda (QC) J9X 4T3; www.abitibi-temiscamingue tourism.org. ℘819-762-8181 or 1-800-808-0706

Bas-Saint-Laurent
148 rue Fraser, 2nd floor, Rivière-du-Loup (QC) G5R 1C8; www.tourismebas-st-laurent.com. ℘418-867-1272 or 1-800-563-5268

Centre-du-Québec
20 Blvd Carignan Ouest, Princeville (QC) G6L 4M4; www.tourismecentreduquebec.com. ℘819-364-7177 or 1-888-816-4007

Charlevoix
495 Blvd de Comporté, La Malbaie (QC) G5A 3G3;

www.tourisme-charlevoix.com. ✆418-665-4454 or 1-800-667-2276

Chaudière-Appalaches
800 Autoroute Jean-Lesage, Lévis (QC) G7A 1E3; www.chaudiereappalaches.com. ✆418-831-4411 or 1-888-831-4411

Duplessis (Lower North Shore)
312 Ave. Brochu, Sept-Îles (QC) G4R 2W6; www.tourismecote-nord.com. ✆418-962-0808 or 1-888-463-0808

Eastern Townships/Cantons-de-l'Est
20 rue Don-Bosco Sud, Sherbrooke (QC) J1L 1W4; www.easterntownships.org. ✆819-820-2020 or 1-800-355-5755

Gaspésie
1020 Blvd Jacques-Cartier, Mont-Joli (Quebec) G5H 0B1; www.tourisme-gaspesie.com; ✆418-775-2223 or 1-800-463-0323

Lanaudière
3568 rue Church, Rawdon (QC) J0K 1S0; www.lanaudiere.ca. ✆450-834-2535 or 1-800-363-2788

Laurentides
14142 rue de la Chapelle, Mirabel (QC) J7J 2C8; www.laurentides.com. ✆450-224-7007 or 1-800-561-6673

Laval
480 Promenade du Centropolis, Laval (QC) H7T 3C2; www.tourismelaval.qc.ca. ✆450-682-5522 or 1-877-465-2825

Magdalen Islands/Îles de la Madeleine
128 chemin Principal, Cap-aux-Meules (QC) G4T 1C5; www.tourismeilesdelamadeleine.com. ✆418-986-2245 or 1-877-624-4437

Manicouagan (Upper North Shore)
337 Blvd La Salle, bureau 304, Baie-Comeau (QC) G4Z 2Z1; www.cotenord-manicouagan.com or www.routedesbaleines.net. ✆418-294-2876 or 1-888-463-5319

Mauricie
1882 rue Cascade, C.P. 100, Shawinigan (Quebec) G9N 8S1; www.tourismemauricie.com. ✆819-536-3334 or 1-800-567-7603

Montérégie
8940 Blvd Leduc, bureau 10, Brossard (Quebec) J4Y 0G4; www.tourisme-monteregie.qc.ca. ✆450-466-4666 or 1-866-469-0069

Montreal
1255 rue Peel, Suite 100, Montreal (QC) H3B 4V4; www.tourisme-montreal.org. ✆514-844-5400 or 1-877-266-5687

NORTHERN QUEBEC

James Bay/Baie-James
1252 Rte. 167 Sud, C.P. 134, Chibougamau (QC) G8P 2K6; www.tourismebaiejames.com. ✆418-748-8140 or 1-888-748-8140

Eeyou Istchee
203 Opemiska Meskino, C.P. 1167, Oujé-Bougoumou (QC) G0W 3C0; www.creetourism.ca. ✆418-745-2220 or 1-888-268-2682

Nunavik Tourism Association
P.O. Box 779, Kuujjuaq (QC) J0M 1C0; www.nunavik-tourism.com. ✆819-964-2876 or 1-888-594-3424

Outaouais
103 rue Laurier, Gatineau (QC) J8X 3V8; www.tourismeoutaouais.com. ✆819-778-2222 or 1-800-265-7822

Quebec City and Area
835 Ave. Wilfrid-Laurier, Quebec (QC) G1R 2L3; www.quebecregion.com. ✆418-641-6290 or 1-877-783-1608

Saguenay–Lac-Saint-Jean
412 Blvd Saguenay Est, bureau 100, Chicoutimi District (QC) G7H 7Y8; www.saguenaylacsaintjean.ca. ✆418-543-9778 or 1-877-253-8387

FROM OVERSEAS

Tourisme Québec
www.bonjourquebec.com. ✆1-514-873-2015

Baie Sainte-Marguerite, Parc national du Fjord-du-Saguenay

© Luc Rousseau / Tourisme Saguenay - Lac-Saint-Jean

INTERNATIONAL VISITORS

CANADIAN EMBASSIES AND CONSULATES ABROAD

Atlanta
1175 Peachtree St., 100 Colony Square, Suite 1700, Atlanta GA 30361-6205; ☏404-532-2000

Chicago
Two Prudential Plaza, 180 North Stetson Ave., Suite 2400, Chicago IL 60601; ☏312-616-1860

Los Angeles
550 S. Hope St., 9th Floor, Los Angeles CA 90071-2627; ☏213-346-2700

New York
1251 Avenue of the Americas, New York NY 10020-1175; ☏212-596-1759

Washington DC
501 Pennsylvania Ave., NW, Washington DC 20001-2114; ☏202-682-1740

Australia
Level 5, Quay West Building, 111 Harrington St., Sydney, N.S.W. 2000; ☏9364-3000

Germany
Leipziger Platz 17, 10117 Berlin; ☏30 20 31 20

United Kingdom:
Canada House, Trafalgar Square, London SW1Y 5BJ; ☏20 7004 6000

FOREIGN EMBASSIES AND CONSULATES IN QUEBEC

Consulates of most foreign countries are located in Montreal. Embassies are located in Ottawa, the capital of Canada.

Germany
1250 Blvd René-Lévesque Ouest, Suite 4315, Montréal (QC) H4B 4X1, ☏514-931-2277

Japan
600 rue de la Gauchetière Ouest, Suite 2120, Montréal (QC) H3B 4W8; ☏514-866-3429

United Kingdom
1000 rue de la Gauchetière Ouest, Suite 4200, Montréal (QC) H3B 4W5; ☏514-866-5863

United States
1155 rue Saint-Alexandre, Place Félix-Martin, Montréal (QC) H3B 3Z1; ☏514-398-9695

Michelin Driving Tours

The following is a selection of the driving tours featured in this guide. Allow enough time to enjoy the sights and make unexpected stops.

LOCAL DRIVES

FROM TADOUSSAC TO SEPT-ÎLES

450km/279mi by Rte. 138.

See CÔTE-NORD.

Starting at the marine park, this mythical route encompasses a long stretch of seaside communities and ancient geologic formations, and has a deep historical relevance for the entire North American continent. Highlights include Les Escoumins, Jardins des Glaciers in Baie-Comeau, and Musée Amérindien in Godbout.

ROUND TRIP FROM COWANSVILLE

159km/98.7mi.

See CANTONS-DE-L'EST.

Cruise through the idyllic regions near the US border, along rolling backroads like Rte. 202 in the heart of Loyalist country. Route includes Stanbridge, Frelighsburg, and the resort town of Sutton, plus the round barns near Mansonville, ski hills of Owl's Head, and the abbey at Lake Memphremagog. It continues to Knowlton and Lac-Brome, then takes Rte. 104 back to Cowansville.

SCENIC MAURICIE PARK

62km/38.5mi between the two Mauricie national park entrances.

See MAURICIE.

This route takes in the pink Canadian Shield rock along Lac Wapizagonke, with cliffs, sandy beaches at Lac Edouard, and a spectacular view from the deck at Le Passage. See the powerful Mauricie River and view indigenous wildlife from a maze of perspectives along this pristine route.

SAINT-JÉRÔME TO ST-DONAT

Circuit of 177km/110mi.

See LAURENTIDES.

This "Gateway to the Laurentians" begins just north of Montreal and explores the foothills and mountains which Hermann "Jackrabbit" Johanssen made famous as the best ski area in the northeast. Tour the famous Mont Sainte-Saveur, Sainte-Adèle and Sainte-Agathe-des-Monts surroundings, and enjoy the remarkable P'tit Train du Nord cycling and walking path.

ÎLE D'ORLÉANS

67km/41.6mi. *See QUEBEC CITY.*

Leave Quebec City on Rte. 440 or 138 and cross Île d'Orleans Bridge. Stop at the tourist information on Rte 368 and begin your tour of six quaint communities. Stop in Sainte-Pétronille to admire the chapel (1871) and one of the oldest golf courses in North America, have a meal at La Goeliche, and visit the villages of Saint-Laurent, Saint-Jean, Sainte-Famille, and L'Éspace Félix Leclerc in Saint-Pierre, which is near your starting point.

FROM BEAUPRÉ TO BAIE-SAINTE-CATHERINE

220km/136mi. *See CÔTE DE CHARLEVOIX.*

This majestic route unveils the splendor of the Charlevoix coast east of Quebec City. Breathtaking vistas convince travelers they are looking at the sea, and it is easy to see why this route is one of the best on the continent. Extending from the urban landscape of Beaupré through rolling hills to the marine sanctuary of the Saguenay Fjord, this spectacular drive is not to be missed.

THEMED TOURS

WINE TOUR (EASTERN TOWNSHIPS)

140km/87mi.

Linking nine communities in Cantons-de-l'Est, the Wine Route zigzags throughout the Brome-Missisquoi region visiting vineyards, from Farnham to Saint-Armand and on up to Lac-Brome and the village of Knowlton.

WHALE TOUR (MANICOUAGAN/ DUPLESSIS)

900km/560mi.

Follow the largest mammals on earth along this epic whale-watching route from Tadoussac at the mouth of the Saguenay River east through the marine park and whaling villages, and on to Natashquan and the end of Rte. 138.

NAVIGATOR'S ROUTE

470km/290mi.

This historic route traces the paths of the early European explorers. Rte. 138 east from Baie-du-Febvre to Sainte-Luce links three centuries of navigation, boat-building and architecture along the shore of the Saint Lawrence River.

FARMLANDS ROUTE

226km/140mi.

Loop through a farmgrowers' paradise southwest of the Laurentides, from Lac des Deux Montagnes along the Ottawa River west. Visitors will see a beekeeping center, apple orchards, maple producers, and makers of artisinal cheese.

PATRIOTS' ROAD

78km/48.4mi.

See VALLÉE DU RICHELIEU.

The Richelieu Route extends along the entire length of the west bank of this famous waterway, and this tour covers part of the east bank between the municipalities of Saint-Jean-sur-Richelieu and Sorel-Tracy, crossing the Chambly Canal and the Saint Ours Canal.

Richelieu River, Montérégie Region

© Yves Marcoux / age fotostock

COUNTRYMAN'S TOUR

197km/122mi.

This delicious agricultural outing criss-crosses the southwestern Montérégie Region, forming a loop that includes a drive along the US border at the foot of the Adirondacks. Access from Napierville, 28km/17.4mi southwest of Saint-Jean-sur-Richelieu (*see VALLÉE DU RICHELIEU*).

FJORD ROUTE (FROM TADOUSSAC TO L'ANSE-SAINT-JEAN)

250km/155mi.

See FJORD DU SAGUENAY.

Unique in North America, this tour circumnavigates the dramatic fjord, from Tadoussac via Cap Trinité to Chicoutimi, the city of Saguenay, Rivière Éternité, L'Anse-Saint-Jean, and the village of Petit-Saguenay. This natural amphitheatre is sometimes called the "Valley of Biodiversity."

THE KING'S ROAD (CHEMIN DU ROY)

260km/160mi.

This is the oldest road in Canada, and many driving tours in this guide feature it, and for good reason. Rte. 138 begins at Repentigny, in the Lanaudière region, and proceeds to Old Quebec City, passing through the pretty Mauricie region along the way.

Outdoor Activities

For further information regarding the activities listed below, contact Regroupement Loisir Québec (RLQ), 4545 Ave. Pierre-de-Coubertin, Montréal (QC) H1V 3R2 ℘514-252-3126 or 1-800-932-3735, www.loisirquebec.qc.ca, or contact the appropriate organizations directly.

WINTER ACTIVITIES

Due to abundant snowfall, a variety of winter sports attracts both Quebecers and visitors from afar. The winter sports season begins in mid-November and ends around mid-April, although some northern regions have good snow conditions through mid-May. Popular ski areas are easily accessible from most major cities. National and provincial parks feature winter sports, and many communities have skating rinks for ice hockey and recreational skating. **For further information** on winter activities, contact regional tourist offices, the ski resorts themselves, or Tourisme Québec.

ALPINE SKIING

Quebec boasts four major ski regions: Charlevoix, Cantons-de-l'Est (also called Eastern Townships, or Estrie), the Laurentians, and the Quebec City region. One of the largest concentrations of ski resorts is in the Laurentians, less than an hour's drive from Montreal, which attracts a considerable number of Ontario skiers. The Laurentians offer reliable snow conditions (average snowfall of almost 300cm/118in), renowned ski schools, night skiing and excellent slope-side accommodations. The imposing Appalachian Mountains stretch across the Eastern Townships region and have long been favored by Americans and Quebecers for their cross-country trails and alpine ski slopes. Snowmaking equipment guarantees good skiing conditions all winter, although average snowfall is well above 350cm/138in. Four main resorts, located 60 minutes from

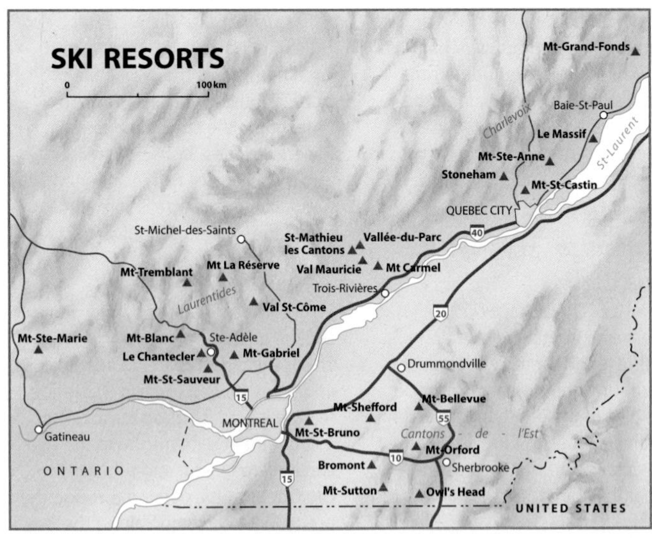

	Info ✆	Vertical Drop		Total Runs	Runs			Total Lifts	Rooms
		M	ft		B	I	E		
Bromont	450-534-2200	**385**	1263	111	35	50	26	9	400
Le Chantecler	450-229-1404	**201**	663	17	3	6	8	3	179
Le Massif	418-632-5876	**770**	2525	52	8	16	28	5	20
Mont-Bellevue	819-821-5872	**81**	266	6	3	3		3	
Mont-Blanc	819-688-2444	**300**	985	41	7	13	24	7	72
Mont-Gabriel	450-227-4671	**200**	655	18	2	6	10	5	
Mont-Grand-Fonds	418-665-0095	**335**	1095	18	4	6	8	3	
Mont-Orford	819-843-6548	**589**	1945	62	21	16	25	8	1,100
Mont-St-Bruno	450-653-3441	**134**	440	15	5	5	5	8	
Mont-St-Sauveur	450-227-4671	**213**	700	38	8	9	21	8	
Mont-Ste-Anne	418-827-4561	**625**	2050	71	15	31	22	8	1,500
Mont-Ste-Marie	819-467-5200	**381**	1250	20	5	7	8	3	40
Mont-Sutton	450-538-2545	**460**	1500	60	15	18	27	9	75
Owl's Head	450-292-3342	**540**	1770	52	14	16	15	8	60
Stoneham	418-848-2411	**345**	1131	42	7	7	25	7	160
Tremblant	819-681-2000	**645**	2116	96	18	30	47	14	1,200
Val St-Côme	450-883-0701	**300**	984	35	9	13	15	5	66

Runs: B = *Beginner;* **I** = *Intermediate;* **E** = *Expert + Extreme*

Quebec City, provide slopes certified by the International Ski Federation. Snowfall averages 375cm/147in.
For further information, contact the Association des stations de ski du Québec, 1347 rue Nationale Terrebonne (QC) J6W 6H8 ✆450-765-2012; www.maneige.com.

CROSS-COUNTRY SKIING

Quebec is renowned for its cross-country skiing, and offers a well-maintained network of trails totaling several thousand kilometers. Trails for every level of difficulty are patrolled, and many have heated cabins. Lessons, guided tours and ski rentals are available in many areas.
For further information on cross-country ski trails, maps and services offered along trails, contact the Fédération québécoise de ski: ✆514-252-3089, www.skiquebec.qc.ca.

SNOWMOBILING

Some 210 local clubs belong to the Fédération des clubs de motoneigistes du Québec (✆514-252-3076, www.fcmq.qc.ca), which maintains 33,500km/20,938mi of marked trails crisscrossing the province. Heated cabins, other accommodations and repair services can be found along the Trans-Quebec trail network.
It is important to follow safety rules: exercise caution before crossing public roads, keep headlights on at all times, and travel with at least one other snowmobile.
A **registration card**, obtained by contacting the Federation, is required to operate a snowmobile. It is also

Cross-country skiing, Laurentides

advisable to acquire snowmobile liability insurance. The Federation publishes a yearly snowmobiler's guide to the Trans-Quebec trails, listing locations of service areas, repair shops, snowmobile dealers offering equipment rentals, and organized excursions. The Trans-Quebec Snowmobile Trail Network Map can be obtained by contacting Tourisme Québec or at www.fcmq.qc.ca.

SUMMER ACTIVITIES

Blessed with innumerable lakes, rivers, parks and mountains, Quebec features a wonderful variety of outdoor recreation. A few are listed below.

CANOEING AND KAYAKING

These activities are enjoyed on many lakes and rivers across the province, and visitors can also canoe or kayak in parks and rivers near cities. Canoe-camping trips are organized by several organizations, including the Fédération québécoise du canot et du kayak: ✆514-252-3001, www.canot-kayak.qc.ca.

CYCLING

Quebec is a model province in terms of its tourism cycling routes. Many parks include well-maintained cycling trails and offer bike rentals. Most cities have developed cycling networks. **For further information**, contact Vélo-Québec: 1251 rue Rachel Est, Montreal (QC) H2J 2J9 ✆514-521-8356 or 1-800-567-8356, www.velo.qc.ca.

GOLF

Golfers can choose from nearly 300 courses in Quebec, most of them located in Cantons-de-l'Est (Estrie), the Laurentians, and the Montérégie, Mauricie–Bois-Francs and Outaouais regions. Advance reservation is recommended. For a list of courses, contact Golf Québec: 4545, Pierre-de-Coubertin, H1V 0B2 ✆514-252-3345, www.golfquebec.org. Publications by the regional tourist offices also give detailed information on courses, travel directions, facilities offered, availability to non-members, and rates.

HIKING

Nature lovers can escape the hustle and bustle of the city by walking on well-marked trails over mountains, through dense forests or along windy seashores. Adventurous hikers can enjoy off-the-beaten-path trails through undisturbed wilderness. **For further information**, contact the Fédération québécoise de la marche: ✆514-252-3157 and 1-866-252-2065, www.fqmarche.qc.ca. To obtain topographic maps, contact Natural Resources Canada in Ottawa, Ontario: ✆ 1-800-465-6277, maps.nrcan.gc.ca.

HORSEBACK RIDING

Many reputable stables can be found in the Cantons-de-l'Est, **Gaspésie** and **Bas-Saint-Laurent** regions. Farms specializing in ranch vacations often offer accommodations and riding lessons. Horseback riding is also available in most Canada and Quebec national parks. **For further information**, contact Québec à cheval (in Blainville, north of Montreal): 450-434-1433, www.cheval.qc.ca.

SAILING

Enthusiasts can choose from a wealth of lakes in the Duplessis, Charlevoix, Laurentides, Manicouagan and Montreal regions. A sail on the challenging St. Lawrence River should be on every serious sailor's list.
For further information, contact the Fédération de voile du Québec 514-252-3097, voile.qc.ca.

SCUBA DIVING

Popular diving spots include the coast of Parc national du Canada Forillon and around Île Bonaventure (*see GASPÉSIE)* and the Magdalen Islands (*see ÎLES DE LA MADELEINE)*, as well as Côte-Nord (*see CÔTE-NORD)*. **For further information**, contact the Fédération des activités subaquatiques Québecoise: 514-252-3009 or 1-866-391-8835, www.fqas.qc.ca.

ROCK CLIMBING

Many regions of Quebec offer excellent climbing. Charlevoix, Côte-Nord, Cantons-de-l'Est, Gaspésie, the Laurentians, and the Saguenay Fjord area have walls with drops from 30 to 300m (99 to 990ft). Rock-climbing season lasts from early May to late October. Ice climbing is also popular in these areas during the winter.
For further information, contact the Fédération québécoise de la montagne et de l'escalade 514-252-3004, www.fqme.qc.ca.

WINDSURFING

This sport is popular on lakes, in parks and around the shores of the Gaspé Peninsula and the Magdalen Islands. The season runs from mid-June through the end of August.
For further information, contact the Fédération de voile de Québec 514-252-3097, voile.qc.ca.

HUNTING AND FISHING

Southern Quebec boasts plentiful reserves of fish and game. Renowned for salmon fishing, the rivers of the Gaspé Peninsula also teem with speckled trout and small-mouth bass. The central Quebec region abounds in moose, black bear, grouse and white-tailed deer among other types of game, and is also well known for its variety of fish species. Anticosti Island is a favorite

Hiking near Chic-Chocs Mountain Lodge in Parc national de la Gaspésie

© Mathieu Charland / Auberge de montagne des Chic-Chocs / Société des établissements de plein air du Québec (Sépaq)

HUNTING AND FISHING REGULATIONS

Hunting is prohibited in the parks; however, the wildlife reserves are open to hunters with permits, except in areas where hunting is subject to quotas. Fishing is permitted in most parks and reserves. Hunting and fishing **permits** (required for freshwater fishing) can be obtained from most local sporting goods stores and outfitters. The price varies according to season, location and type of game or fish. You are required by law to **register** your game within 48 hours after leaving the hunting area. Registration centers are generally found along major roads and in the airports of more isolated regions. Strict **safety regulations** are enforced and every hunter is asked to help fight poaching. **For additional information** contact the Ministère des Ressources naturelles et Faune du Québec, 880 chemin Sainte-Foy, RC 120-C, Quebec (QC) G1X 4X4 ✆418-627-8600 or 1-866-248-6936, www.mern.gouv.qc.ca.

sport fishing hotspot. In northern Quebec, above the 52nd parallel, non-residents are required to hire the services of an outfitter. Big game here includes caribou and moose. Regions known for their excellent hunting and fishing include Abitibi-Témiscamingue, Côte-Nord, Mauricie-Bois-Francs, Outaouais, Saguenay-Lac-Saint-Jean and Nunavik.

OUTFITTERS

Outfitters' lodges are easy to reach by land or air and offer packages for experienced sports enthusiasts as well as novices. There are two types of outfitters, or *pourvoiries*: some have leased territories, while others escort their expeditions onto government-owned land. In addition to making all arrangements, including air transportation to remote locations, they provide accommodations and equipment needed to ensure a safe and carefree expedition. Some outfitters offer fish and game storage, refrigeration and transport. **Registration Centers** are located along main roads and at airports in remote areas. A publication of **outfitters' lodges** is available at information kiosks or through the Fédération des pourvoyeurs du Québec, 5237 Blvd Wilfrid-Hamel, Suite 270 Quebec (QC) G2E 2H2; ✆418-877-5191 and 1-800-567-9009, www.pourvoiries.com.

SIGHTSEEING

The options for touring and discovering nature in Quebec are plentiful. Tourisme Québec's regional tourist guides are helpful when planning an itinerary, and there are a variety of escorted tours by bus, private car or on foot.

ORGANIZED NATURE TOURS

Organized nature tours are popular. The Zoological Society of Montreal arranges a variety of field trips that involve visiting different regions throughout the Montreal area. Trips are usually one or two days. **For further information** on reservations and available trips, contact the Zoological Society, 1117 Ste-Catherine Street West, Suite 525, Montreal (QC) H3B 1H9 ✆514-845-8317, www.zoologicalsocietymtl.org. Visitors may also participate in organized observation tours of whales and other marine mammals near Tadoussac in the Saguenay-St. Lawrence Marine Park. All-inclusive three-day excursions are led by expert guides. It is advisable to make reservations well in advance due to limited group size. The whale-watching tour begins early Friday morning; the group travels by bus and stays at the famous Hotel Tadoussac, before returning to Montreal late Sunday. Tour is $680 for non-members.

ADVENTURE TRAVEL

Sports enthusiasts can choose from a variety of adventure trips, including ski-mountaineering, dogsledding, snowmobiling, ice- and rock-climbing, canoeing and kayaking trips. These expeditions into the hinterlands of Quebec require careful planning; it is advisable to employ the services of experienced guides. **For further information** on adventure travel, contact **Ecole Escalade** (ice- and rock-climbing only): 2374 rue Bastien, Val-David (QC) J0T 2N0 ☏819-323-6987, www.ecole-escalade.com; **Randonnée Aventure**, Box 26541, RPO Queen Mary, Montreal (QC) H3X 4B1 ☏514-359-6781, www.randonnee.ca.

NATIONAL PARKS OF CANADA

Parks Canada, the Canadian parks service, operates three national parks in Quebec. **For further information**, trail maps and brochures, contact Parks Canada National Office, 30 rue Victoria, Gatineau (QC) JBX 0B3; ☏1-888-773-8888 (enquiries from US and Canada); www.pc.gc.ca.

All parks offer interpretation programs, some of which include guided hikes, slide and video presentations, exhibits and seasonal lecture programs that help visitors understand the natural environments. Visitors are asked to respect wildlife and park rules. Most parks have camping facilities operated on a first-come-first-served basis. Camping facilities fill quickly during the summer; **for reservations** to any National Park of Canada in Quebec, call ☏1-877-737-3783, or use the website. Entrance fees vary from park to park, as do the fees charged for camping, fishing, or other activities. Contact the park service for opening season dates.

- **Parc national du Canada Forillon** (*see GASPÉSIE*) ☏418-368-5505. Activities: hiking, backpacking, nature programs, biking trails, camping, swimming, sailing, scuba diving, boat tours, fishing, cross-country skiing.
- **Parc national du Mauricie** (*see MAURICIE*) ☏819-538-3232. Activities: hiking, backpacking, camping, canoeing, sailing, scuba diving, swimming, fishing, cross-country skiing.
- **Mingan Archipelago** 1340 rue de la Digue, Havre-Saint-Pierre (QC) G0G 1P0. ☏418-538-3285 (in season) or ☏418-538-3331 (off-season). Activities: hiking, backpacking, camping, sailing, boat tours.

PROVINCIAL PARKS AND NATURE RESERVES OF QUEBEC

In the parks operated by **Parcs Québec**, visitors can enjoy wildlife and forestry reserves year-round. Hiking, climbing, cycling, canoeing, fishing and hunting, cross-country or alpine skiing, and snowmobiling are just some of the activities awaiting the outdoor enthusiast. A comprehensive guide (free) entitled *Découvrez votre vraie nature* (English version also available) covers the entire list of parks and their activities as well as detailed maps of park areas. Parcs Québec also operates **nature reserves.** Please note that some of these parks are closed off-season. Also, please note that provincial parks are often called national parks by the province of Quebec, which can be confusing.

For further information on provincial parks, contact **SÉPAQ** (Société des établissements de plein air du Québec): Place de la Cité, Tour Cominar, 2640 Blvd Laurier, Suite 1300 (13th floor), Quebec City (QC) G1V 5C2, ☏418-890-6527 or 1-800-665-6527, www.sepaq.com.

- **Aiguebelle** *(Abitibi-Témiscamingue)* Mont-Brun Visitor Center ☏819-637-7322.
- **Anticosti** *(Duplessis)* Information Center ☏418-535-0289.
- **Bic** *(Bas-Saint-Laurent)* Interpretation Center ☏418-736-5035.
- **Fjord-du-Saguenay** *(Saguenay-Lac-Saint-Jean)* Interpretation Center ☏418-272-1566.

- **Frontenac** *(Cantons-de-l"Est)* Interpretation Center: ✆418-486-2300 ext 221.
- **Gaspésie** *(Gaspésie)* Interpretation Center ✆418-763-7494.
- **Grands-Jardins** *(Charlevoix)* Interpretation Center Château-Beaumont ✆418-439-1227.
- **Hautes-Gorges-de-la-Rivière-Malbaie** *(Charlevoix)* Interpretation Center ✆418-439-1227.
- **Île-Bonaventure-et-Rocher-Percé** *(Gaspésie)* Interpretation Center ✆418-782-2240.
- **Îles-de-Boucherville** *(Montérégie)* Reception Center ✆450-928-5088.
- **Jacques-Cartier** *(Quebec)* Reception Center ✆418-848-3169.
- **Kuururjuag** *(Nunavik)* Park Office ✆819-337-5454.
- **Lac-Temiscouata** *(Bas-Saint-Laurent)* Reception Center ✆418-855-5508.
- **Miguasha** *(Gaspésie)* Reception Center ✆418-794-2475.
- **Mont-Mégantic** *(Cantons-de-l'Est)* Reception Center ✆819-888-2941.
- **Mont-Orford** *(Cantons-de-l'Est)* Reception Center ✆819-843-9855.
- **Mont-Saint-Bruno** *(Montérégie)* Reception Center ✆450-653-7544.
- **Mont-Tremblant** *(Laurentians)* Reception Center ✆819-688-2281.
- **Monts-Valin** *(Saguenay–Lac-Saint-Jean)* Information ✆418-674-1200.
- **Oka** *(Laurentians)* Reception Center ✆450-479-8365.
- **Plaisance** *(Laurentians)* Reception Center ✆819-427-5334.
- **Pointe-Taillon** *(Saguenay–Lac-Saint-Jean)* Interpretation Center ✆418-347-5371.
- **Saguenay** *(Saguenay–Lac-Saint-Jean)* Interpretation and Observation Centers ✆418-237-4383; Parc Marin du Saguenay–Saint-Laurent ✆418-235-4703, Ext. 0.
- **Yamaska** *(Cantons-de-l'Est)* Reception Center ✆450-776-7182.

Activities for Kids

Sights of particular interest to children, such as the Aquarium in Quebec City or the Zoo in Saint-Félicien, are indicated with the Michelin Green Guide Kids symbol (👪). Most attractions offer discount fees for children and teenagers.

Quebec is an excellent place to travel with children. Hotel rooms are large and hotels often have swimming pools. Outdoor activities that appeal to children, such as hiking, canoeing and fishing, are cheap and easily accessible. And the Quebec woods are relatively safe, with no killer insects or poisonous plants lurking in the bush. The only predator to watch for is the black bear, which is generally afraid of humans, and for good reason.

La TOHU (in Montreal, ✆514 376-8648 or 1-888-376-8648, www.tohu.ca) is one of the world's largest gathering places for circus arts training, creation, production and performance. It was created in 2004 by the Quebec association of circus arts, the National Circus School and Cirque du Soleil. The adjoining circus exhibition is also fascinating.

The **Canadian Children's Museum** *(in Gatineau, just across from Ottawa, ✆819-776-7000 and 1-800-555-5621, www.historymuseum.ca/childrens-museum)* achieves the rare feat of entertaining and educating children at the highest levels possible. It is part of the Canadian Museum of History, the most popular museum in Canada, so families can't go wrong here.

Rue du Petit-Champlain shop, Quebec City

Shopping

Native arts and crafts are the most sought-after souvenirs, while maple products, jeans, and winter clothing are also popular with shoppers.

NATIVE ART

In Quebec, the most popular souvenir items are **Native crafts**. There are no First Nations in China, so watch for "made in China" bow and arrow sets. However, there are plenty of authentic Native crafts in Quebec, even in tourist areas, that are worth purchasing.

The best experience is to buy these items on First Nations reserves. This way you know exactly where the item was made, its significance and its cultural value. This buying experience also allows for a genuine interaction. Buying in Indian reserves also brings better prices. This is particularly true with **fur apparel**. A beaver hat costing $100 in an Indian reserve will cost double that in a Montreal department store.

OTHER WARES

Quebec is traditionally a land of apparel making and so it is logical that some of the best **winter clothing** in the world can be found there. The Kanuk™ brand is the benchmark of design, fabric and quality.

Traditional winter coats *(canadiennes)*, wool scarfs, hats and heavy bed sheets can be found at the Hudson's Bay Company flagship store in downtown Montreal. The store uses its historical stature to sell modern versions of apparel used by Metis "voyageurs" and frontier pioneers.

Winter sports gear is a Canadian specialty. Hockey players around the world use Quebec-made equipment. Snowshoes are also a good buy; the traditional snowshoes used for trapping fur animals make an outstanding discussion topic.

Jeans are consistently cheaper in Quebec than in Europe. The relative strength of the Canadian dollar greatly influences the cost of goods in Canada that are available elsewhere.

Maple products are always a worthwhile purchase. You can buy maple syrup practically anywhere in the world, but in Quebec the variety of maple products is unparalleled.

During the last few decades, Quebec has become famous for its outstanding cheeses, meats, sweets and fine liqueurs, ice ciders, and Belgian-style beers. Some 7,000 of these artisanal products and more can be found at the **Marché des Saveurs** (Market of Flavors) at Montreal's Marché Jean-Talon in the north end of town (at the corner of Saint-Laurent and Jean-Talon Streets).

Entertainment

The International Jazz Festival in Montreal is the signature event, but there are music, theater and dance options to suit every taste.

MUSIC

There are 13 professional symphony orchestras in the province of Quebec. Montreal alone boasts several, with the most renowned being the Montreal Symphony Orchestra (**Orchestre Symphonique de Montréal** ℘514-842-9951), under the direction of Kent Nagano, and l'**Orchestre métropolitain** (℘514-598-0870), under the direction of Yannick Nézet-Séguin. Canada's oldest symphony orchestra, **Orchestre Symphonique de Québec** (℘418-643-8131), plays under the direction of Fabien Gabel. Also in Quebec City, Bernard Labadie conducts chamber orchestra **Les Violons du Roy** (℘418-692-3026). In Montreal, chamber orchestra **I Musici** (℘514-982-6038) is conducted by Jean-Marie Zeitouni. The other professional symphony orchestras of the province are in Laval, Trois-Rivières, Sherbrooke, Drummondville, Saguenay, Longueuil and Rimouski. Classical music lovers traveling to Quebec in the summer can also enjoy numerous festivals featuring symphony orchestras from around the world, the most important being **Le Festival de Lanaudière** (℘450-759-4343 or 1-800-561-4343), **Le Domaine Forget** (℘418-452-3535 or 1-888-336-7438) and **Le Festival Orford** (℘819-843-3981 or 1-800-567-6155). The prestigious **Place des Arts** performing arts complex (tickets ℘514-842-2112 or 1-866-842-2112) has five multi-purpose concert halls where the Montreal Opera Company (**Opéra de Montréal** ℘514-985-2258) and McGill University's **McGill Chamber Orchestra** (℘514-487-5190) perform. Also on the McGill campus, **Pollack Concert Hall** (℘514-398-4547) hosts classical, jazz and chamber music. The immensely popular **International Jazz Festival** (℘514-871-1881 or 1-855-299-3378; www.montrealjazzfest.com) held in June has become Montreal's flagship festival and musical event since its inception in 1977. The music goes well beyond jazz, embracing world-

Les Grands Ballets Canadiens de Montréal

Place des Arts, Montreal

beat, reggae, folk, and rock, and the action is hot both indoors and out as music-lovers gather at concert venues, and in the streets of the Quartier des spectacles.

The 21,000-seat **Bell Center** (✆514-790-2525 or 1-877-668-8269) also offers a variety of performances throughout the year, including pop and rock concerts.

DANCE

Montreal's **Les Grands Ballets Canadiens** (✆514-849-8681), famous for its classical repertoire, performs nationally and abroad. Les Grands Ballets is one of the top three classical dance companies in Canada, along with The National Ballet of Canada (Toronto) and the Royal Winnipeg Ballet.

Montreal is the capital of modern dance in Canada, with a number of prestigious, innovative dance troupes such as **O Vertigo** (✆514-251-9177) and **La La La Human Steps** (✆514-277-9090) leading the way.

Quebec dance luminaries from the present and recent past include Ginette Laurin, Édouard Lock, Louise Lecavalier, Gilles Maheu, Paul-André Fortier and Marie Chouinard.

THEATER

Internationally renowned playwright/actor/director, Robert Lepage, was raised in a bilingual household in Quebec City. His dark, daring body of work is paradoxically appealing to people who generally dislike theater. In 2004, the Conseil des Arts et des Lettres de Quebec (Quebec's arts and literature council) officially recognized the top seven theater companies in Quebec. The list includes Théâtre du Nouveau Monde, Théâtre d'Aujourd'hui, Théâtre du Rideau Vert, Théâtre Espace Go and Théâtre de la Manufacture, all French-language theaters from Montreal, as well as Quebec City's Théâtre du Trident. The only English-language theater in the elite group is Montreal's **Centaur Theater Company** (✆514-288-3161). The Centaur Company bills itself as "the voice of English-speaking Montreal." Many of its plays are Montreal-based, and written by Montreal playwrights. Respected Québécois playwrights, such as Michel Tremblay, are translated into English and their plays are showcased at the Centaur.

Summer theaters are popular and can be enjoyed throughout the province. Repertory theaters and dinner theaters perform in both French and English. **For schedules**, see the arts and entertainment supplements in local newspapers (weekend editions) or free brochures distributed at hotels.

Books and Films

SUGGESTED READING

20C Literature

Home Truths, Selected Canadian Stories by Mavis Gallant (*Stoddart, 1956*)

The Watch that Ends the Night by Hugh MacLennan (*General Paperbacks, 1958*)

The Apprenticeship of Duddy Kravitz by Mordecai Richler (*McClelland & Stewart, 1959*)

The Favorite Game by Leonard Cohen (*McClelland & Stewart, 1963*)

Beautiful Losers by Leonard Cohen (*McClelland & Stewart, 1966*)

St. Urbain's Horseman by Mordecai Richler (*McClelland & Stewart, 1966*)

A North American Education by Clark Blaise (*General Paperbacks, 1973*)

Joshua Then and Now by Mordecai Richler (*McClelland & Stewart, 1980*)

Voices in Time by Hugh MacLennan (*Stoddart, 1980*)

Montréal mon amour, Short stories from Montreal ed. Michael Benazon (*Penguin, 1989*)

Solomon Gursky was Here by Mordecai Richler (*Penguin, 1989*)

Across the Bridge by Mavis Gallant (*McClelland & Stewart, 1993*)

Evil Eye by Ann Diamond (*Véhicule Press, 1994*)

Sonia and Jack by David Homel (*Harper Collins, 1995*)

The Tragedy Queen by Linda Leith (*NuAge Editions, 1995*)

True Copies by Monique LaRue (*NuAge Editions, 1996*)

Two Solitudes by Hugh MacLennan (*Fitzhenry & Whiteside Ltd., 1996*)

Myths, Memory and Lies by Esther Delisle (*Studio 9 Books, 1998*)

7 Waves: Quebec Women Writers by Clare Braux (*Morgaine House, 1999*)

Life of Pi by Yann Martel (*Knopf Canada, 2002*)

Quebec Authors in Translation

Maria Chapdelaine by Louis Hémon (*1916/Tundra Books, 2004*)

The Town Below by Roger Lemelin (*McClelland & Stewart, 1944*)

The Outlander by Germaine Guèvremont (*McClelland & Stewart, 1945*)

The Tin Flute by Gabrielle Roy (*McClelland & Stewart, 1945*)

The Madman, the Kite and the Island by Félix Leclerc (*Oberon Press, 1958*)

A Season in the Life of Emmanuel by Marie-Claire Blais (*McClelland & Stewart, 1965*)

Kamouraska by Anne Hébert (*General Paperbacks, 1970*)

The Alley Cat by Yves Beauchemin (*McClelland & Stewart, 1981*)

The Beothuk Saga by Bernard Assiniwi (*McClelland & Stewart, 2000*)

Thunder and Light by Marie-Claire Blais (*House Of Anansi, 2004*)

History and Architecture

Children of Aataentsic by Bruce Trigger (*McGill-Queen's University Press, 1976*)

Canada-Québec Synthèse Historique by Jacques Lacoursière and Denis Vaugeois (*Éditions du Renouveau Pédagogique, 1978*)

Inuit Stories by Nungak and Arima (*University of Toronto Press, 1988*)

Montreal Architecture, A Guide to Styles and Buildings by Francois Rémillard and Brian Merrett (*Méridian Press, 1990*)

Sauver Montréal, Chroniques d'architecture et d'urbanisme by Jean-Claude Marsan (*Boréal, 1990*)
The Living Past of Montreal by R.O. Wilson and Eric McLean (*McGill-Queen's University Press, 1993*)
A Short History of Quebec, 3rd ed. by John A. Dickinson and Brian J. Young (*McGill-Queen's University Press, 2003*)
Loin du Soleil: Architectural Practice in Quebec City during the French Regime by Marc Grignon (*Peter Lang, 1995*)
Making History in Twentieth-Century Quebec by Ronald Rudin (*University of Toronto Press, 1997*)
Canada and Quebec: One Country, Two Histories by Robert Bothwell (*University of British Columbia Press, 1998*)
Sacré Blues: An Unsentimental Journey Through Quebec by Taras Grescoe (*McFarlane Walter & Ross, 2000*)

Photographic Essays
Wide Landscapes of Quebec (*Libre Expression, 1991*)
Montréal: a Scent of the Islands by François Poche (*Stanké, 1994*)
Les croix de chemin au temps du Bon Dieu by Vanessa-Oliver Lloyd (*Éditions du Passage, 2007*)

SELECTED FILMS

Titles listed below represent Quebec filmmaking highlights from 1970 through the present. The list also features international films set in the province.

I Confess (1953) Alfred Hitchcock
The Act of the Heart (1970) Paul Almond
The Apprenticeship of Duddy Kravitz (1974) Ted Kotcheff
Lies My Father Told Me (1975) Jan Kadar
The Street (1976) Caroline Leaf
Joshua Then and Now (1985) Ted Kotcheff
The Decline of the American Empire (1986) Denys Arcand
The Man Who Planted Trees (1988) Frédéric Back
Night Zoo (1987) Jean-Claude Lauzon
Train of Dreams (1987) John N. Smith
Jesus of Montréal (1989) Denys Arcand
Bethune, the Making of a Hero (1990) Phillip Borsos
The Company of Strangers (1990) Cynthia Scott
An Imaginary Tale (1990) André Fournier
Léolo (1992) Jean-Claude Lauzon
Love and Human Remains (1993) Denys Arcand
The Confessional (1995) Robert Lepage
Thirty-two short films about Glenn Gould (1995) François Girard
The Boys (1997) Louis Saia
The Red Violin (1998) François Girard
Un crabe dans la tête (2001) André Turpin
15 février 1839 (2001) Pierre Falardeau
The Score (2001) Frank Oz
The Far Side of the Moon (2003) Robert Lepage
Les invasions barbares (2003) Denys Arcand
Seducing Doctor Lewis (2003) Jean-François Pouliot
C.R.A.Z.Y. (2005) Jean-Marc Vallée
Congorama (2006) Pierre Falardeau
Good Cop, Bad Cop (2006) Erik Canuel
L'âge des ténèbres (2007) Denis Arcand
Borderline (2008) Lyne Charlebois
Barney's Version (2010) Richard J. Lewis
The High Cost of Living (2010) Deborah Chow
Louis Cyr (2013) Daniel Roby
Le règne de la beauté (2014) Denys Arcand

Festivals & Events

Following is a selection of Quebec's popular annual events. Dates and duration of certain events may vary from year to year. For further information, contact Festivals et Événements Québec and the Société des Attractions Touristiques: 4545 Pierre-De-Courbertin Ave., C.P. 1000, Succursale M, Montreal (PQ) H1V 0B2 ℘514-252-3037 and 1-800-361-7688, www.attractonsevents.com; the regional tourist offices; or Tourisme Québec via its website at www.bonjourquebec.com.

SPRING

MAR

Festival beauceron de l'érable (maple sugar festival of music, sports, and cuisine), Saint-Georges, (Chaudière-Appalaches *see BEAUCE*), *www.festivalbeaucerondelerable.com*

MID-MAY

Festival des harmonies et orchestres symphoniques du Québec (classical music), Sherbrooke (*see SHERBROOKE*), *www.festivaldesharmonies.com*

LATE MAY

Montreal Bike Fest (cycling race and festival), Montreal (*see MONTREAL*), *www.velo.qc.ca*

MAY: Montreal Bike Fest

© Gaétan Fontaine / Tourisme Montréal

SUMMER

EARLY JUN

Grand Prix Montréal (F1 car racing), Île Notre-Dame (*MONTREAL*), *www.grandprixmontreal.com*

MID-JUN

Festival de la chanson (Quebec song festival), Tadoussac (*see CÔTE-NORD*), *www.chansontadoussac.com*

Francofolies de Montréal (French music festival) (*see MONTREAL*), *www.francofolies.com*

MID TO LATE JUN

James Bay Walleye Fishing Tournament *www.festivaldudore.com*

LATE JUN–EARLY JUL

Festival en chanson de Petite-Vallée (singing), Petite-Vallée (*GASPÉSIE*), *www.festivalenchanson.com*

Festival International de Jazz de Montréal (*see MONTREAL*), *www.montrealjazzfest.com*

LATE JUN – AUG

Festival Orford (music festival) Magog (*see CANTONS DE L'EST*), *www.arts-orford.org*

Festival international du Domaine Forget (classical music and jazz), Saint-Irénée (*see CÔTE-DE-CHARLEVOIX*), *www.domaineforget.com*

EARLY JUL

Festirame, Alma (*see LAKESAINT-JEAN), www.sagamie.org/alma/festivalma*

Just for Laughs Festival/ Festival Juste pour rire (world's largest and most prestigious comedy festival), Montreal (*see MONTREAL), www.hahaha.com*

EARLY TO MID-JUL

Festival d'été de Québec du Maurier (international summer festival), Quebec City (*see QUEBEC CITY), www.infofestival.com*

Mondial des cultures de Drummondville (*see DRUMMONDVILLE), www. mondialdescultures.com*

EARLY JUL – EARLY AUG

Festival de Lanaudière, Joliette (*see LANAUDIÈRE), www.lanaudiere.org*

L'International des feux Loto-Québec (fireworks), Six Flags Amusement Park, Île Sainte-Hélène (*see MONTREAL), www.internationaldesfeuxlotoquebec.com*

MID-JUL

Les Grands Feux Loto-Québec (international fireworks competition), Quebec City, over the Montmorency Falls (*see QUEBEC CITY), www.lesgrandsfeux.com*

LATE JUL–EARLY AUG

Exposition agricole, Saint-Hyacinthe (*see VALLÉE DU RICHELIEU), www.expo-agricole.com*

Grand Prix de Trois-Rivières (F3 automobile racing), Trois-Rivières (*see TROIS-RIVIÈRES), www.gp3r.com*

Traversée internationale du lac Saint-Jean, Roberval (*Lake Saint-Jean), www.traversee.qc.ca*

Traversée internationale du lac Memphrémagog (international swim marathon), Magog (*see CANTONS-DE-L'EST), www.tilm.ca*

Festival Innu Nikamu (First Nations music festival), Réserve de Maliotenam (*see ÎLE D'ANTICOSTI), innunikamu.net*

EARLY AUG

Festival du bleuet de Dolbeau-Mistassini, *Mistassini* (*see LAKE SAINT-JEAN), www.festivaldubleuet.com*

Fêtes de la Nouvelle-France (heritage festival) Quebec City (*see QUEBEC CITY), www.nouvellefrance.qc.ca*

MID-AUG

Maski-Courons Festival International (marathon), Saint-Gabriel-de-Brandon, *www.lanaudiere.ca*

AUGUST: Fêtes de la Nouvelle-France, Quebec City

© Xavier Dachez / Québec City Tourism

JANUARY-FEBRUARY: Carnaval de Québec, Quebec City

Concours de châteaux de sable (sandcastle-building contest), Havre-Aubert (*see ÎLES DE LA MADELEINE*), *www.chateauxdesable.com*

Rogers Cup (Tier 1 tennis tournament, men's or women's, depending on the year), Montreal, at Uniprix Stadium *(see MONTREAL)*, *www.rogerscup.com*

Festival de montgolfières, St-Jean-sur-Richelieu (*see VALLÉE SUR RICHELIEU*), *www.montgolfieres.com*

LATE AUG–EARLY SEPT

Festival des films du monde (film festival), Montreal *(see MONTREAL)*, *www.ffm-montreal.org*

FALL

EARLY SEPT

Festival de montgolfières (hot-air balloon festival), Gatineau (*see OUTAOUAIS*), *www.montgolfieresgatineau.com*

MID-SEPT

Festival western de Saint-Tite (cowboy and Western music festival), Saint-Tite, *www.festivalwestern.com*

Tennis Challenge Bell (a women's indoor tournament), Quebec City, at Université Laval *(see QUEBEC CITY)*, *www.challengebell.com*

EARLY TO MID-OCT

Festival de l'oie blanche (snow goose festival), Montmagny *(See BAS-ST-LAURENT)*, *www.festivaldeloie.qc.ca*

WINTER

LATE JAN–FEB

Festival des petits poissons des chenaux (Tomcod ice fishing festival), Sainte-Anne-de-la-Pérade *(see TROIS-RIVIÈRES)*, *www.tourismemauricie.com*

Carnaval de Québec (winter carnival), Quebec City *(see QUEBEC CITY)*, *www.carnaval.qc.ca*

Bal de Neige/Winterlude, Gatineau *(see OUTAOUAIS)*, *www.winterlude.ca*

LATE FEB

Grand Prix Ski-Doo de Valcourt (snowmobile festival), Valcourt (*see CANTONS-DE-L'EST*), *www.grandprixvalcourt.com*

Festival de montgolfières, Gatineau

Practical Info

TOP TIPS

Best time to go: A legitimate four-season destination.

Best way around: By car or rail.

Best for sightseeing: Quebec City; Fjord du Saguenay.

Most authentic accommodation: Chic-Chocs Mountain Lodge.

Need to know: Most road signs are in French. (see Road Regulations p45).

Need to taste: Sagamite, a First Nations specialty.

Bell Centre, Montreal © Matthias Berthet / Tourisme Montréal

Before You Go

WHEN TO GO

Quebec is a year-round vacation destination for sports enthusiasts, nature lovers, hunters and anglers.

CLIMATE

Northern Quebec is subject to Arctic temperatures, while the regions around the St. Lawrence are more temperate. *See the temperature chart below for an idea of temperature and seasonal variations by areas throughout the province.*

Most cultural attractions are open from mid-May (Fete des Patriotes) through the first weekend in September (Labor Day). *Sight descriptions contain more specific information.*

SEASONS

In March and April, the harvesting of maple syrup signals the coming of **spring** with sugaring-off parties. This season is brief with pleasant days and chilly evenings. In the southern part of Quebec, **summer**, extending from mid-June through mid-September, is hot and humid. Light, loose-fitting clothes are best for hot weather, but it is advisable to have a light jacket for cool evenings and excursions on lakes and rivers. Late May through June is mosquito and black fly season and insect repellent is a must, and virtually indispensable for those planning to camp or hike.

In **fall**, beginning in early October, visitors can enjoy the many forest colors of the "Indian Summer." **Winter** can begin as early as November, with an abundance of snow. Temperatures often fall below freezing and during January and February can drop below 0°F (-17°C). Plenty of warm clothing will protect visitors from the cold. The Saint Lawrence Valley is warmer but more humid, so may feel just as cold.

GETTING THERE

BY PLANE

In the province of Quebec, most international and domestic flights arrive at Montreal's **Pierre Elliott Trudeau International (YUL)** airport (in the Dorval district) 514-394-7377. Some domestic and international flights land in Quebec City's **Jean-Lesage International (YQB)** airport 418-640-3300. The **Mont-Tremblant International** airport (in the Laurentians Region) 819-275-9099 receives flights from Toronto and New York City. Canada's national airline, **Air Canada** (a Star Alliance member), serves major European cities, the Caribbean, Asia and the Pacific, and provides service to most destinations within Canada and the US. Quebec is also serviced by a network of regional airlines (*see chart next page*).

Canada's low-cost airline, **WestJet**, is an excellent option for the more than

SEASONAL TEMPERATURES (°F/°C)

	April		July		October		January	
	min.	max.	min.	max.	min.	max.	min.	max.
Chicoutimi	25/-4	45/7	54/12	75/24	34/1	48/9	-9/-23	14/-10
Gaspé	27/-3	41/5	52/11	73/23	34/1	52/11	3/-16	21/-6
Kuujjuarapik	9/-13	28/-2	41/5	51/15	30/-1	41/5	-13/-25	0/-18
Montreal	34/1	52/11	61/16	79/26	39/4	55/13	5/-15	21/-6
Quebec City	28/-2	19/7	55/13	77/25	36/2	52/11	0/-17	18/-8
Sherbrooke	28/-2	50/10	52/11	77/25	32/0	54/12	0/-17	21/-6

AIRLINE	Local ✆	Toll-free ✆	Website
Air Canada and Air Canada Jazz	514-393-3333	1-888-247-2262	www.aircanada.com
Air Inuit	514-631-0883	1-800-361-2965	www.airinuit.com
First Air	613-254-6200	1-800-267-1247	www.firstair.ca
WestJet	403-539-7070	1-888-937-8538	www.westjet.com

100 destinations it serves in North America and the Caribbean.

Service to remote areas, provided by charter companies, may be offered once or twice a week only.

For telephone numbers of local air carriers, consult your travel agent or contact the appropriate provincial or regional tourist office.

BY SHIP

The Quebec government operates an extensive ferry boat system.

For further information and schedules, contact the regional tourist office or Tourisme Québec, or the Société des Traversiers du Québec, 250 rue Saint-Paul, Québec (QC) G1K 9K9; ✆418-643-2019 or 1-877-562-6560; www.traversiers.gouv.qc.ca.

ENTRY REQUIREMENTS

United States citizens must show a US passport to visit Quebec and return to the US by air. A visa is not required for US citizens for a stay up to 180 days. Permanent **US residents** who are not citizens must carry their Alien Registration Cards.

European Union citizens and all other international visitors to Canada (not US citizens or US permanent residents) must carry a valid passport and, if required, a visa. Citizens from the UK, France, Germany, Mexico, Japan, the Republic of Korea, Australia and others do not require a visa to enter Canada. Visit the Citizenship and Immigration Canada website (www.cic.gc.ca/english/visit/visas.asp) for a complete list of countries whose citizens require visas to enter Canada. You can also check with the Canadian embassy or consulate in your country regarding entry regulations. No vaccinations are necessary when entering Canada. All visitors admitted to Canada will be permitted to stay for a maximum of six months, unless otherwise notified in writing by an examining officer.

Persons **under 18** who are not accompanied by an adult must have a letter from a parent or guardian stating the traveler's name and duration of the trip. Students should carry a student ID; senior citizens (over 65) are required to present proof of age when requesting discounts at many attractions.

For further information on all Canadian embassies and consulates abroad, contact the website of the Canadian Department of Foreign Affairs, Trade and Development: www.dfait-maeci.gc.ca.

CUSTOMS REGULATIONS

The import of **tobacco** is limited to 50 cigars or 200 cigarettes per adult. The limit for **alcoholic beverages** is 1.14 liters of spirits, two 750ml bottles of wine, or 24 350ml bottles of beer. Visitors to Canada can bring in personal goods without paying duty or tax, as long as they do not leave them in Canada. Visitors can bring in gifts without paying duty or tax, if they have a value of less than C$60 per gift. Gifts with a value over $60 are subject to duty and tax on the amount over $60.

Since Quebec has strict laws concerning narcotics and other drugs, all prescription drugs should

be identified; it is advisable to carry a copy of the prescription or a letter from your doctor.
Bringing **handguns** into Quebec is prohibited. Non-residents must declare all firearms.
For further information on firearms contact the Canada Firearms Center, Ottawa (ON) K1A 1M6 ✆1-800-731-4000 or www.rcmp.grc.gc.ca.
Pets must be accompanied by a certificate of vaccination against rabies (within last 3 years).
For further information contact the Canadian Food Inspection Agency, 2001 Blvd Robert-Buorassa, Montréal (QC) H3A 3N2; ✆514-283-8888, www.inspection.gc.ca.

HEALTH

Before leaving your country, it is advisable to check with your medical insurance provider to determine whether you are covered for doctor visits, medication and hospital stays while visiting Quebec. A visitor insurance policy can be purchased either before leaving or within 30 days following the arrival in Canada ($3.50–$15 per day or more depending on age and insurance limit). However, Blue Cross recommends purchase to be made prior to arrival. If purchased after the arrival in Canada, the contract will be effective 72 hours after the purchase. Maximum coverage period is 180 days. Purchase of coverage can be made online. For more details contact Blue Cross of Quebec, 550 rue Sherbrooke Ouest, Suite B-9, Montréal (QC) H3A 3S3 ✆514-286-7686 or 1-877-909-7686, www.qc.croixbleue.ca. US visitors traveling by car must have proof of automobile insurance with a liability coverage of at least $50,000 (*see p46*).

♿ ACCESSIBILITY

Sights accessible to disabled travelers are indicated by the ♿ symbol in this guide. Most public buildings, churches, restaurants and hotels provide wheelchair access. Parking spaces reserved for the disabled are strictly enforced. Passes issued by the International Transport Forum and by US authorities are recognized in Quebec and allow for parking in designated parking spaces for the disabled.
For further information or to obtain *The Accessible Road (downloadable free of charge on the Kéroul website)*, contact Kéroul, 4545 Ave. Pierre-de-Coubertin, C.P. 1000, Station M, Montréal (QC) H1V 0B2 ✆514-252-3104 and www.keroul.qc.ca. More information, including an online guide "Take Charge of Your Travel: A Guide for Persons with Disabilities," is available from the Canadian Transportation Agency, Ottawa K1A 0N9, ✆1-888-222-2592, www.cta-otc.qc.ca/eng/accessibility. The **Autocars Orléans Express** inter-city bus line offers transportation for persons with reduced mobility.

Pierre Elliott Trudeau International Airport, Montreal

On Arrival

GETTING AROUND

BY TRAIN

Rail service within the province of Quebec and the rest of Canada is provided by **VIA Rail Canada.**

Trains are relatively slow but fares are reasonable, service is good and the trains are comfortable. A foreign visitor should be aware of the great distances within Quebec (travel time between Montreal and the Gaspé Peninsula, for example, is 19 hours). **For further information** and schedules, contact VIA Rail Canada, P.O. Box 8116, Station A, Montréal (QC) H3C 3N3; ✆1-888-842-7245 (from anywhere in Canada and the US), www.viarail.ca.

Significant discounts are offered for advance purchase, youth and senior citizens; students of all ages obtain good rates if they can show an ISIC (International Student Identification Card). Reservations should be made well in advance in summer.

A **Canrailpass - System Unlimited** *($1,169.10)* buys you 12 days of unlimited travel in Comfort class (Economy) during a 60-day period. Just show your Canrailpass each time you obtain a ticket for a trip during this 60-day period.

The card can be used anywhere that VIA goes, from the Atlantic to the Pacific, and up to Hudson Bay. You can make as many stops as you like during your journey. You can add up to three extra days' travel, which you can buy in advance or at any time during the 60-day validity period.

The United States train passenger service, **Amtrak**, provides daily service from Washington DC via New York City to Montreal; rates are excellent, but trains on the Montreal route are very slow.

For further information and schedules in the US and Canada, call ✆1-800-872-7245 or visit www.amtrak.com.

BY CAR

Foreign **driver's licenses** are valid in Quebec for six months. Drivers must carry the **vehicle registration** information and rental contract at all times.

The price of **gasoline**, sold in liters (3.78 liters to a US gallon), varies from province to province and is higher than in the US. **Service stations** are plentiful, except in isolated areas, and are usually full-service. Caution and lower speeds are recommended when driving on gravel and dust roads—common outside the main road network. Special precautions should be taken when driving in winter. Since 2008, **winter tires** on all wheels are compulsory for Quebec vehicles from November 15 to April 1. Except during winter storms, most highways are cleared and open for traffic, but it is always advisable to check traffic conditions before leaving. For up-to-date reports on road conditions, call Transport Québec's "info-roads line" ✆1-888-355-0511 or check webcams at www.quebec511.info.

Road Regulations

Transport Quebec maintains a network of four-lane, divided, controlled access expressways (called motorways in the UK, freeways in the US, and autoroutes in Quebec), of numbered provincial highways, and of secondary roads (often unpaved in remote areas). Most road signs are in French (some are also in English near borders with the US, Ontario, New Brunswick, and around Montreal) and distances are posted in meters or kilometers. The speed limit on inter-city expressways is usually 100km/h (60mph), 90km/h (55mph) on highways and 50km/h (30mph) within city limits, unless otherwise posted. Turning right at a red light is prohibited in Montreal, but allowed in the rest of the province, unless posted otherwise. The law requires that traffic in both directions halt for a stopped school bus. Seat belts are mandatory for all vehicle occupants. The possession or use of radar detection devices is illegal. Approach railroad crossings with caution; most do not have barriers, but are signaled with flashing lights and sound. Blue road signs indicate services and points of interest for tourists, and brown signs indicate national parks.

Canadian Automobile Association (CAA)
CAA Québec, ✆514-861-7575, 1-800-686-9243, www.caaquebec.com. All member services of this national motorclub are offered to US tourists upon presentation of the membership card of the American Automobile Association (AAA). The CAA is also affiliated with the Alliance Internationale de Tourisme (AIT), the Fédération Internationale de l'Automobile (FIA), the Federation of Interamerican Touring & Automobile Clubs (FITAC) and the Commonwealth Motoring Conference (CMC). CAA provides helpful travel information, insurance coverage and emergency road service: **24-hour emergency road service** ✆514-861-1313 or 1-800-222-4357.

Car Rental
The chart *(see above)* presents a selection of rental car agencies operating in Quebec. The numbers listed are toll-free within Quebec: Major car rental companies operate offices in airports, train stations and larger cities. More favorable rates can usually be obtained with advance reservations. Minimum age for renting a car is 21; reservation and payment are easiest by credit card. Some agencies offer special packages, but be aware of drop-off charges if you return the car to a location other than the place you rented it. The rental price does not include collision coverage. Liability coverage is mandatory.

RENTAL CAR AGENCY	Info ✆
Avis	1-800-331-1084
Budget	1-800-472-3325
Hertz	1-800-263-0678
Thrifty	1-800-367-2277
National	1-800-227-7368

For any other information about car insurance or coverage while in Quebec, contact the Insurance Bureau of Canada: ✆514-288-1563 or 1-844-227-5432, www.ibc.ca; or Société de l'assurance automobile du Québec: ✆514 873-7620 or1-800-361-7620, www.saaq.gouv.qc.ca.

Camper Rental
Families or groups of four to six people may prefer to rent a camper with amenities (beds, kitchenette, shower, toilet, and so on) to travel around Quebec. Many campgrounds are operated by **Parks Canada** (pccamping.ca, 1-877-737-3783), and private campgrounds abound as well. **For further information**, see campsource.ca.
Be aware that traveling with a camper is very popular; it is best to make reservations at least six months in advance. Minimum age to rent or drive a camper is 21, with a valid driver's license or international driver's permit. Check with your local travel agent for information; in Quebec, camper rentals are listed under *"Véhicules Récréatifs."*

In case of accident
First-aid stations are well marked on the major roads. Non-residents sustaining vehicular damage and/or bodily injury should contact the local police and stay at the scene until an officer has completed an inspection. In certain cases, non-residents may be entitled to compensation

under the Quebec automobile insurance plan. Société de l'assurance automobile du Québec ✆514 873-7620 or 1-800-361-7620, www.saaq.gouv.qc.ca.

BY COACH/BUS

Orléans Express serves the Montreal-Quebec City-Gaspésie corridor. The Société de transport de Montréal (✆1-514-786-4636) offers a Tourist Card that allows unlimited travel for 1 to 3 consecutive days. The rest of Quebec is served by regional bus companies.

For further information contact: Orléans Express ✆514-842-2281 or 1-888-999-3977, www.orleansexpress.com; Intercar ✆418-525-3000, www.intercar.qc.ca; or Limocar ✆1-866-692-8899, limocar.ca/en. No reservation is necessary.

PLACES TO STAY AND EAT

STAY

Hotels and Restaurants are located in the Address Books throughout the *Discovering Quebec* section of this guide.

For coin ranges and for a description of the symbols used in the Addresses, see the Legend on the cover flap.

Hôtel Place d'Armes, Montreal

© Bertrand Rieger / hemis.fr

Quebec offers a wide range of accommodation, from luxurious hotels to campgrounds. Reservations should be made well in advance during the peak tourist season (late Jun–Sept). However, you can usually find a bed/roof combination without reservations, though it may not always be what you pictured. It is advisable to guarantee reservations with a credit card. In remote areas, hotels often close during some months of the year. Lower weekend rates may be available and many hotels offer packages that include some or all meals.

Travelers should be aware that there is a 14.5 percent tax on food in restaurants, and 14.5 percent tax on accommodation; additional accommodation taxes apply in some areas.

Hotels

The large hotel chains can be found in most big cities. The accompanying telephone numbers are toll-free within Canada and the US.

For further information on hotels, contact Tourisme Québec, 1255 rue Peel, Suite 100, Montréal; ✆514-873-2015 or 1-877-266-5687; www.bonjourquebec.com.

Small hotels, known for their ambiance and excellent regional cuisine, are plentiful in urban areas and in the countryside. Quality accommodations at moderate prices are offered by **Comfort Inn, Quality Hotels & Suites** (reservations through Choice Hotels ✆1-877-424-6423; www.choicehotels.com) or **Days Inn** (✆1-800-329-7466, www.daysinn.com). Family-owned motels and guesthouses provide basic accommodations, often without a restaurant.

Youth Hostels

In Quebec, Hosteling International Canada (✆1-800-663-5777, www.hihostels.ca) has 12 youth hostels

HOTEL	INFO	WEBSITE
Best Western International	1-800-780-7234	www.bestwestern.com
Fairmont	1-800-257-7544	www.fairmont.com
Hilton	1-800-445-8667	www.hilton.com
Holiday Inn	1-888-465-4329	www.holidayinn.com
Hôtel des Gouverneurs	1-888-910-1111	www.gouverneur.com
Radisson	1-800-967-9033	www.radisson.com
Ramada Inn	1-800-854-9517	www.ramada.com
Sheraton	1-800-325-3535	www.sheraton.com

that offer clean, reliable, inexpensive lodging. Youth hostels are now designed and operated with all age groups in mind. Shared rooms (from $15/night, $25/night for non HI members) are the mainstay of "hosteling," but private rooms are increasingly available. Private rooms (for couples and families) in hostels are cheaper than similar rooms in hotels. Hostels are centrally located in cities, towns and villages, generally near tourist attractions and transportation terminals. Some "rustic" hostels provide affordable access to nature areas. Hosteling International membership also translates into discounts on attractions, activities, food and travel gear.

Bed & Breakfasts and Country Inns

An alternative to small hotels, bed & breakfasts ***(gîtes du passant)*** and country inns provide a welcoming atmosphere and range from elaborate to modest. Usually family-owned, they may consist of an extra room in a Victorian house, a backyard cottage, a converted lighthouse, or a lovely town house on a quaint city street. Rates average $85/night (breakfast included), though not all provide private bathrooms. Farm holidays, for a day, a week or longer, are a good option for families with children who can participate in farm activities. The website of the Association de L'Agrotourisme et du Tourisme Gourmand du Québec

Fishing huts, Lac Saint-Jean, Fjord du Saguenay

lists establishments and provides detailed information on facilities and locations (4545 Pierre-de-Coubertin Ave., C.P. 1000, Succursale M, Montreal (QC) H1V 0B2; ✆514-252-3138, www.terroirsetsaveurs.com). For further information on the Quebec association of resorts and country inns: Hôtellerie Champêtre, 467 Rue Notre-Dame, Suite 208, Repentigny (QC) J6A 2T3; ✆514-861-4024, 1-800-861-4024, www.hotelleriechampetre.com.

Camping

Government-operated and private campground rates range from $22–$48/night depending on services offered. Situated in scenic locations, federal and provincial government campgrounds (operated by Parks Canada and Parcs Québec) are generally better maintained, situated in nicer natural environments, and more popular.

For further information on camping, caravanning, and canoeing, or to order the annually published *Quebec Campground Guide* (free), contact Camping Québec ✆450-651-7396 or 1-800-363-0457, www.campingquebec.com.

Universities and Colleges

Some universities and colleges rent dormitory space when school is out *(May–Aug)* at moderate rates. Contact Tourisme Québec or the institution's housing department. In Montreal: McGill University ✆514-398-6368; Université de Montréal ✆514-343-4455; Concordia University ✆514-848-2424. In Trois-Rivières: Université du Québec ✆819-376-5011. In Rimouski: Université du Québec ✆418-723-1986.

Ski Resorts

Major ski resorts in Charlevoix, Cantons-de-l'Est, the Laurentians and the Outaouais regions offer a complete range of accommodations, including on-site lodgings, deluxe hotels and bed and breakfasts. as well as condominium and chalet rentals. Some hotels offer their own ski schools and provide complete vacation packages. **For more information,** contact the Association des stations de ski du Québec ✆450-765-2012, www.maneige.com/en/.

EAT

Certain sections of **Montreal**, including Old Montreal, Plateau Mt-Royal, Blvd St-Laurent and downtown, are known for their restaurants. Yet the most pleasant, reasonably priced restaurants are often on small streets, hidden away (like the intimate restaurants of rue Marie-Anne, running parallel to Ave. Mt-Royal in the Plateau). These memorable restaurants often cannot afford to advertise in tourist publications.

Quebec City also boasts a wide assortment of fine restaurants, mostly along rue Sainte-Anne, rue Saint-Jean, rue Saint-Louis, Ave. Cartier and the Grande-Allée in the Upper Town, and along the rue du Petit-Champlain area and rue Saint-Paul in the Lower Town. **French food** (high class and bistro style) provides the most satisfying experience. Service and décor are often better than in Montreal because Quebec City is so tourism-oriented, but beware the widespread "tourist food," which is international fare made to please the average tourist at an average price, with below-average results.

Many regions, including **Outaouais**, **Montérégie**, **Lanaudière**, **Charlevoix**, **Gaspésie** and **Saguenay-Lac-Saint-Jean** have developed modern regional *spécialités*. You could easily miss this gastronomic bounty if you stick to chain restaurants. ☺Some regional food producers have arrangements with specific restaurants, so look out for these places.

Practical A-Z

BUSINESS HOURS

Regular business hours are Monday to Friday 9am–5pm. Retail stores are usually open Monday to Friday 9am–6pm (until 9pm Thursday and Friday). Saturday hours are 10am–5pm, and in the larger towns, stores are usually open Sundays noon–5pm.

COMMUNICATIONS

Quebec Province is divided into four telephone area codes: 514 (Montreal), 450 (Laval, North & South Shores, Laurentides, Vallée du Richelieu), 418 (Quebec City, Gaspé Peninsula and Eastern Quebec), and 819 (Cantons-de-l'Est, Gatineau, and northern Quebec). All numbers beginning with 1-800, 1-888 and 1-877 are toll-free. To call long distance within Canada and to the US, dial 1 + Area Code followed by the 7-digit number. For overseas calls, dial 011 + country code, or dial 0 for operator assistance, available in both English and French. Directory assistance can be reached by dialing 411; for numbers outside the local area dial 1 + Area Code + 555-1212. A local call at a public phone booth costs 50 cents. Credit card calls and collect calls can be made from public pay phones. You can also purchase calling cards virtually anywhere, which allow you to call from telephone booths without using coins or a credit card. Cell phone service is sporadic in the most remote areas of the province, and, depending upon your provider, roaming charges may apply.

ELECTRICITY

110 volts, 60 cycles. Electrical appliances from the US can be used in Quebec. European appliances require plug adapters and current transformers. However, things can get complicated if you try to use appliances designed for 220 volts on a 110-volt outlet; electrical appliances may work poorly and electronic appliances may not work at all, and might get damaged. It is best to stick to chargers and appliances that are designed to operate at 110 volts or at both 110 and 220 volts.

911 EMERGENCIES

Anywhere in Quebec and in the rest of Canada, call 911 to report life-threatening emergency situations requiring the intervention of ambulance/paramedics, a fire department and/or the police. If dialing 911 does not allow you to reach emergency services, just dial "0" and press "0" again to ask an operator to connect you to the proper emergency number.

LANGUAGES

The official language of the province of Quebec is French, spoken by 80 percent of the population. The second language is English. Visitors can expect Quebecers in urban areas and in Southern Quebec to be bilingual. In much of the rest of the province, however, don't expect everyone to understand basic English. With some exceptions near borders and in the Montreal area, all road signs are in French. Tourist information is generally available in both languages. In Nunavik a majority of the Inuit speak Inuktitut, but English and French have become more common in schools and public life.

LIQUOR LAWS

The minimum drinking age in Quebec is 18 (lower than in many Canadian provinces and parts of the US). The provincial government regulates the sale of wine and liquor sold in ***"Société des Alcools du Québec"*** or S.A.Q.

stores. In Montreal and Quebec City, selected wine and liquor are also sold at Maisons des Vins. Stores are open during regular store hours, including on Sundays. Mainstream beers and lesser-quality wines are also sold in grocery stores. When driving, the legal blood alcohol limit is 0.08 percent. Drinking alcohol or walking around with an open bottle of alcoholic beverage is prohibited everywhere except on private property (including camping sites), or on a licensed site, restaurant or bar.

MAIL/POST

Post offices are open Monday to Friday 8am–5:30pm. Some sample rates for first-class mail (letter or postcard):

- within Canada, 85 cents (up to 30 grams);
- to the US, $1.20 (up to 30 grams);
- international mail, $2.50 (up to 30 grams).

Mail service for all but regional deliveries is by air. Postal facilities are located at regular post offices and other retailers (generally pharmacies and convenience stores) throughout the province.

For further information regarding postal codes or locations of facilities call ✆1-866-607-6301 (within Canada) or 416-979-3033 (outside Canada); www.canadapost.ca.

When writing to Quebec, use the following format:

Company or Name
Street Address
City
Postal Code
CANADA

MEDIA

In large cities, international newspapers are generally available at airports, major hotels and newsstands. The English-language paper, ***The Gazette***, published daily in Montreal, is available in other towns throughout Quebec, as is the ***Chronicle-Telegraph*** published each Wednesday in Quebec City.

The Canadian Broadcasting Corporation (CBC) broadcasts in English and French throughout the Quebec territory, on the radio and on television.

METRIC SYSTEM

In 1980, Canada adopted the metric system. All distances and speed limits are posted in kilometers (multiply by 0.625 to obtain the equivalent in miles). Gasoline is sold in liters. However, proximity to the US, which still uses the Imperial measure system, brought about a form of "measurement bilingualism" to the Quebec population. Quebecers know their height and weight in feet, inches and pounds better than in meters, centimeters and kilograms. They still buy pounds of meat at the grocery store, and they measure their apartments in square feet.

- **1 kilometer (km)** = 0.6 mile
- **1 meter (m)** = 3.3 feet
- **1 kilogram (kg)** = 1,000 grams (g) = 2.2 lbs
- **1 liter (l) = 33.8 fl.oz.** = 1 quart = 0.26 gallons
- **Celsius to Fahrenheit:** *multiply °C by 9, divide by 5, and add 32 = °F*

MONEY

The basic unit of currency is the Canadian dollar: one dollar = 100 cents. Bills (notes) are issued in denominations of $5, $10, $20, $50 and $100. Coins are 5 cents, 10 cents, 25 cents, $1 and $2. Major credit cards (mainly Visa®, MasterCard® and American Express®) are widely accepted. Travelers' checks (mainly American Express®) are still generally accepted but are becoming a rarity. Visitors may also use their credit cards or bank cards 24hrs/day to withdraw cash from automatic teller machines (ATMs, ***guichets automatiques***).

If necessary, it is also possible to receive cash sent to Canada through Western Union®.
The Canadian dollar fluctuates with the international money market. Exchange facilities tend to be limited in rural or remote areas. It is generally recommended to exchange money in an area where exchange offices compete for customers, in order to receive the most favorable exchange rate.

Banks
Banks are generally open Monday to Friday 10am–3pm, and often offer extended hours on Thursday, Friday and Saturday. Banks and foreign exchange counters at international airports have extended hours. Banks with ATMs, affiliated with American or European banking institutions, will allow withdrawal of Canadian funds. Some banks charge a fee for cashing travelers' checks.
In Canada, as in the US, **tax** is not usually included in the purchase price, but is added at the time of payment. In addition to the national tax (Goods and Services Tax, or GST) of 5 percent, there is a 9.975 percent provincial sales tax (*taxe de vente du Québec*, or TVQ) in Quebec.

PUBLIC HOLIDAYS	
New Year's Day	January 1
Good Friday	Friday before Easter Sunday
Easter Monday	Day following Easter Sunday
Fête des Patriotes	3rd Monday in May
Québec National Holiday	June 24
Canada Day	July 1
Labor Day	1st Monday in September
Thanksgiving Day	2nd Monday in October
Christmas Day	December 25

Reduced Rates
Reductions are omnipresent. Students (with ID, the ISIC card is best), children and youths (under 25), and seniors (over 60 or 65) get significant discounts. Sometimes couples get concessions for train tickets for example. Always look and ask for reductions.
Discount-coupons booklets are also distributed massively.

PUBLIC HOLIDAYS
Most banks, government offices and schools are closed on the legal holidays shown in the chart.

SMOKING
Quebec used to be facetiously called "Canada's smoking zone." But not anymore: smoking is most positively prohibited in every indoor venue (including bars), and there are no designated smoking rooms (in airports, etc.). If no police officer tells you to put out your cigarette, people around you will. Smoking is even prohibited outdoors, near the entrance of public buildings and in bus shelters.

TIME ZONES
Quebec is located in the Eastern Standard Time (EST) zone (like Toronto and New York City), with the exception of the Magdalen Islands, which are in the Atlantic Time zone (one hour ahead of the rest of Quebec). Daylight Saving Time (time advances one hour) is observed in Quebec (as in the US) from the second Sunday in March to the first Sunday in November.

TIPPING
Tips are not included in restaurant bills. It is customary to leave 10–15 percent of the total as a tip for good service. Taxi drivers, bellboys and hairdressers are usually tipped at the customer's discretion, although the 10–15 percent rule seems to apply here as well.

Parc national de la Mauricie

© San Hoyano / age fotostock

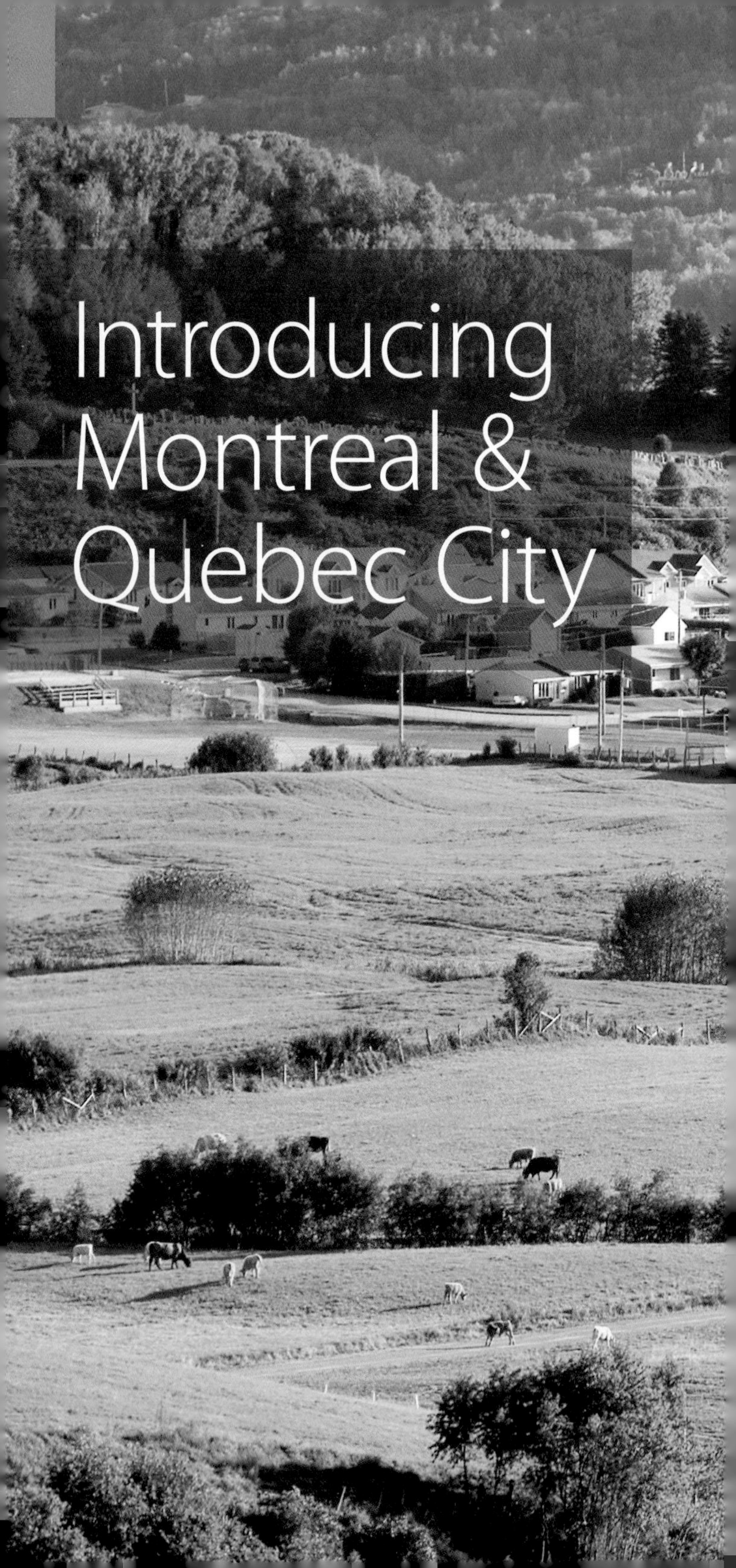

Introducing Montreal & Quebec City

La Malbaie, Charlevoix

© Robert Chiasson / age fotostock

Features

Statue on Montreal's Basilique-Cathédrale Marie-Reine-du-Monde with skyscraper of 1000 de la Gauchetière in the background

© Philippe Renault / hemis.fr

Montreal & Quebec City Today

After a period of soul-searching, Quebec has forged a lasting identity within Canada.

Old Montreal and Old Port of Montreal © Tourisme Montréal

Quebec Today

A refreshing cosmopolitan spirit has pervaded the province, as contemporary attitudes continue to redefine the cultural landscape. Thanks in part to the popularity of such home-grown icons as *Cirque du Soleil, Montreal International Jazz Festival,* and *Arcade Fire*, Quebec has announced itself as a major player on the international stage.

GOVERNMENT

Quebec's political system derives from the Canadian Constitution of 1867, which defines the jurisdiction of the provincial and federal governments.

Legislative power rests with the unicameral **National Assembly of Québec**, created in 1968 to replace the Legislative Assembly. The 125 members of "l'Assemblée nationale du Québec" are elected by universal suffrage for a maximum of five years (elections are generally held every four years). The members belong to a range of parties reflecting the various political tendencies among the electorate. The **Lieutenant-Governor**, the official representative of the British Crown, joins with the National Assembly to form the **Parliament**.

The government is headed by the party that obtains the most seats in the National Assembly. The leader of this majority party—who is designated the **Premier**—appoints his or her **Executive Council** from among the National Assembly members. This council, which constitutes the government's **executive branch**, is responsible for introducing bills to the Assembly. Much of the Assembly's work is carried out by parliamentary committees, which review and investigate various matters brought before the legislative body.

Quebec's **judicial branch** is composed of two levels: the lower courts and the Court of Appeal. The first level is made up of the municipal courts, the Quebec Court and the Superior Court. The Quebec Court (1988), comprising the Provincial Court, the Courts of Sessions of the Peace, and the Juvenile Court, is responsible for certain civil, criminal and penal issues. Judges serving on the Quebec Court are appointed by the provincial government. Its judges appointed by the federal government, the Superior Court rules on all cases outside the jurisdiction of the other courts and acts as a court of appeal for offenses concerning penal law. The federally appointed Court of Appeal is the general appellate court for the entire province.

Quebec City, Parliament Building

©Doug Rogers/Michelin

The Supreme Court of Canada, with nine judges appointed by the federal government, is the highest court in the land and can hear appeals on decisions reached by Quebec's Court of Appeal.

The Electoral System

The principle of universal suffrage applies to all citizens 18 years of age and older. The plurality single-member electoral system is based on the concept of territorial representation. Each of the 125 Quebec members of Parliament represents the population of one constituency or "riding."

Since 1963, Quebec electoral law stipulates that all parties must file financial statements and sets a limit on expenses, while at the same time providing state contributions for the financing of standard administrative and electoral expenses of parties that obtain a minimum level of electoral success. For the purposes of public administration, Quebec is divided into 17 administrative regions.

Federal Government

Quebecers also elect members to the Canadian House of Commons in Ottawa, and are represented in the Canadian Senate by legislators appointed by the federal government. Representation in Ottawa is usually proportional to a province's population. In 2015, Quebec was represented by 75 of the 308 federal members of Parliament and 24 of the 105 senators.

International Relations

Under the Canadian Constitution, international relations fall within federal jurisdiction. However, since the 1960s, Quebec has obtained permission to institute its own foreign delegations and economic development offices and created a Ministry of International Affairs, using the principle of international extension of internal powers, in an effort to fully assume its responsibilities in matters of immigration, foreign loans, the environment and, above all, culture.

With an increasingly prominent role in the French-speaking world, including former French colonies in Africa, Quebec has achieved a unique status at international French-language events. Quebec City hosted the *Second Sommet de la Francophonie* (1987), as well as the First World Forum of the French Language (2012). The eighth Francophonie summit was held in Moncton, New Brunswick (officially the only bilingual province in Canada), in 1999, attended by 52 government officials and heads of state. Currently 80 countries are represented in the Francophonie group, accounting for over 220 million French-speakers.

Since 1988 Quebec and Canada have both participated in TV5, the international French-language television network. In the 2011 census, some seven million Canadians—nearly six million of them in Quebec— reported French as their mother tongue, second in the world after France.

ECONOMY

Historically, Quebec's abundant natural resources have constituted its primary economic base. These industries are becoming increasingly important and lucrative in a world that is hungry for commodities. Meanwhile, industrial giant **Bombardier**, a world leader in the manufacture of public transportation equipment and business and passenger planes, started in Quebec as a snowmobile maker, and continues to prosper. Quebec is also a leader in pharmaceuticals (Apotex Inc.) and a number of knowledge-based industries. Countries like China, India and Mexico may attract clothing brands abroad, but firms like **Ubisoft** lead the gaming craze in Quebec, and industry leaders like **Warner Brothers Games** have set up studios because of the educated workforce and government tax incentives.

The Fur Industry

A driving force in the settlement of northern Quebec and a traditional activity of the First Nations populations, trapping is now a marginal activity. Nonetheless, Canada remains a major fur producer—it is known worldwide as the producer of the world's finest furs— and Montreal is the center of its industry. Native trappers and breeders are now grouped into cooperatives, and Quebec trappers kill and skin mostly beaver, muskrat, lynx and marten. Increasingly, furs are produced on farms, rather than by trapping.

Agriculture

Until the 1920s, agriculture was a cornerstone of the Quebec economy, beginning in the 1880s with the marketing of milk and dairy products, but today it accounts for less than two percent of the province's gross domestic product.

The principal farming areas developed in the fertile regions bordering the St. Lawrence River, including Bas-Saint-Laurent, Beauce, and the Gaspé Peninsula. Quebec's modern agricultural industry is primarily based on animal products (milk, pork, poultry and cattle), and large-scale cultivation of cereal products (corn, barley, oats and wheat), as well as vegetable and fruit farming. The main seasonal fruits are apples, strawberries, raspberries and blueberries. Quebec is also at the forefront of small-scale, organic production of fruits and vegetables, and is home to a fast-growing boutique wine industry.

Forestry

Quebec's extensive forests have generated considerable revenue since the colonial period. In many regions, farmers turned to forestry to supplement their livelihood during the long winter months. Early in Quebec's history, shipbuilding, construction and heating created a great demand for wood in the domestic market as well as in England, where much of Quebec's timber was exported to supply the wood-hungry British navy. In the early 1900s, new technologies and an increasing demand for newsprint fueled a massive market for **pulp and paper**. Commercial forest land remains essential to the regional economy and is located mainly in Abitibi-Témiscamingue, Côte-Nord and Saguenay-Lac-Saint-Jean. Sawmills and workshops generate half the jobs and products in the lumber industry. One-third of Canada's pulp and paper originates in Quebec, particularly in the Mauricie Region, and Canada remains the world's top producer of newsprint.

Fisheries

Quebec's major fishing centers are on the Gaspé Peninsula, the Magdalen Islands and Côte-Nord. In recent years, annual catches brought in by Quebec fishing fleets have contributed relatively little to the gross domestic product (approximately $145 million in 2007). Once treated, these catches generate products worth about $320 million.

Ocean catches generally include cod, Greenland halibut, rockfish, mackerel and herring. The proportion of revenue coming from shellfish and crustaceans (crab, shrimp, lobster and scallops) now represents more than 90 percent of the total, as fish stocks are decreasing.

Inland, most commercial fishing is concentrated to the west of Cape Tourmente and particularly in the region of Lake Saint-Pierre (Yamaska, Maskinongé, Nicolet and Sorel). The

Vineyard on île d'Orléans

© Camirand Photo / Québec City Tourism

main catches are sturgeon, perch and eel, but freshwater fish stocks are also a cause for concern.

Mines

The history of Quebec's mining industry is closely linked to three eras and three regions: asbestos mining started in the last quarter of the 19C in the Cantons-de-l'Est; in the 1920s gold and copper were discovered in the Abitibi region; and starting in 1945, iron ore was mined in the Côte-Nord area in Fermont and Schefferville (Duplessis region).
Two-thirds of Quebec's mineral production involves metallic minerals (gold, silver, iron, copper, lead, zinc), while the other third involves non-metallic (asbestos) and other minerals. The Côte-Nord produces nearly half of Quebec's minerals. One quarter of the province's minerals and virtually all its gold production emanate from the mines of Abitibi. Quebec is the world's largest exporter of asbestos, and although proven to be highly toxic, new licenses to mine it are regularly reviewed by the Quebec authorities.
Although mining remains the principal activity in several regions, total production accounts for only about 2 percent of the gross domestic product.

Hydroelectric power

Quebec imports oil and natural gas but produces and exports hydroelectric power. The province's industrialization remains closely linked to its hydroelectric resources which, as early as 1900, provided low-cost energy for the lumber, petrochemical and metal industries, particularly aluminum plants (Rio Tinto Alcan, Reynolds).
Proponents of economic nationalism soon demanded the nationalization of the province's hydroelectric industry, a step already taken by Ontario at the beginning of the 20C. From the days of the Shawinigan Water and Power Co. (1902) to the creation of **Hydro-Québec** (first nationalization in 1944 to be followed by large-scale nationalizations in 1962–63 on the initiative of René Lévesque, as minister in the government of Jean Lesage), hydroelectricity became a key element of Quebec's economic policy. The first hydroelectric dams on the Manicouagan River reflected the will of Quebecers to take charge of their economy and develop an engineering expertise that is now in demand worldwide.
Most of the province's electricity is produced by its hydroelectric plants, though there are also a few thermal plants, and a growing number of biomass plants and wind farms. The province sells some of its electricity to other Canadian provinces and to the US. The James Bay project, a mammoth hydropower development in central Quebec that dammed and diverted nine rivers and flooded a region the size of Belgium, has caused enormous controversy over the environmental and cultural consequences of such massive hydropower developments. Yet generally Quebecers are proud of their hydroelectric industry and see it as less damaging than non-renewable forms of energy.

New Directions

The **Quiet Revolution** (*Révolution tranquille*) of the 1960s was characterized by increased Quebec government involvement in education, social affairs and the economy. Viewed in the North American context, Quebec's political economy has distinct characteristics reflected in its nationalization programs (asbestos and hydroelectricity), corporate aid and investment institutions, large-scale infrastructure projects (Expo '67, Montreal subway opening in 1966, Montreal's 1976 Summer Olympic Games, massive hydropower projects) and linguistic policies that promote the role of francophones in key business sectors.
Montreal, the headquarters of many Canadian banks and insurance companies and of the Montreal Stock Exchange, suffered a large exodus of companies and business talent in the wake of the francophone unrest, and its role as Canada's main financial center was eclipsed by Toronto in the 1970s. Greater

Vieux-Port, Montreal

Montreal still dominates the provincial economy, and the metropolitan area contains about one-half of Quebec's manufacturing companies and jobs.

In recent years traditional sectors of the Quebec economy have suffered, and in some places disappeared, owing to increased competition from China and other countries in Asia, but the province has found markets for its high-tech expertise in aeronautics, telecoms and engineering. The **service industry** has been the stronghold of the economy since the 1950s.

Since the establishment of a north–south railway network in 1850, the opening of the **St. Lawrence Seaway** (1959), which enabled ships to sail into the heart of North America by way of the Great Lakes, the completion of an extensive network of expressways, and the North American Free Trade Agreement (1994), the economies of Quebec and the US have become closely integrated, and more than 70 percent of Quebec's foreign exports are bound for the US.

POPULATION AND LANGUAGE

Quebec's current population totals some 7,903,000 people, out of Canada's total population of about 35,540,000. Quebec ranks as the second-most populous province behind Ontario (population 12,861,940). More than four out of every five Quebecers reside in urban areas, and the "exode rurale" is continuing, as cities are growing and rural areas are becoming less and less inhabited.

Earliest Inhabitants

In 2006, 108,425 Quebecers (less than two percent) claimed native ancestry, a demographic that includes, in descending order of population numbers, the Mohawk, Cree, Montagnais, Algonquin, Atikamekw, Mi'kmaq, Huron-Wendat, Naskapi and Abenaki.

Currently, the main languages spoken by Native families in Quebec are Iroquoian (Mohawk and Huron dialects) and Algonquian (Cree, Montagnais/Naskapi, Mi'kmaq and Abenaki dialects). Today the majority of Quebec's Native population lives in the communities of Pointe-du-Buisson, Mashteuiatsh, Odanak, Lorette and Kahnawake. A large Cree-speaking population (around 17,500) is concentrated in the villages of the James Bay region.

The Inuit, inhabitants of Quebec's subarctic regions, number approximately 12,000. The province's Inuit population lives primarily in the coastal villages of Nunavik, the vast region occupying Quebec's northernmost territory; their language is Inuktitut.

Non-indigenous People

In the 2006 census, 5,877,660 Quebecers declared that French was their mother tongue, and 575,555 declared that English was their mother tongue. Interestingly, 939,350 people declared that neither French nor English was their mother tongue. Italians, Greeks and Eastern Europeans represented the largest waves of immigration in the early and mid-20C, and more recently,

Asian, Black, Hispanic and Arabic immigration has increased. Most immigrants settle in the Montreal area, where they often have family ties.

Nearly half of Quebec's population resides in Montreal's metropolitan area. Since World War II, and especially between 1965 and 1980, when Quebec's nationalistic fervor was rising, the anglophone population that settled in Quebec City, Montreal and the Cantons-de-l'Est during the early 1800s wave of immigration declined, as many departed for Toronto and other destinations. In the early 1900s many Italian and Eastern European immigrants settled in Quebec, and after 1945 immigration intensified again, mainly Mediterranean countries. In the 1970s southeast Asians, mostly French-speaking Vietnamese (and some Cambodians), emigrated to Quebec in large numbers, as did Latin Americans (particularly Chileans) in the following decade, all to escape political strife. Since the early 1990s, Asians have been the largest immigrant group, while policies to encourage French-speaking immigration resulted in an influx of people from France, Algeria, Morocco and Haiti. More than half the immigrant population has some knowledge of French.

The Language Debate

Three factors gave rise to the language controversy that climaxed in the 1960s and 1970s: a vivid awareness of the fragility of French culture in North America, which first led Quebecers to perceive and refer to themselves as "Quebecois" rather than "French Canadians"; the first signs of a decrease in fertility (the birth rate declined by 50 percent between 1951 and 1986); and lastly, an acute awareness of the consequences of heavy postwar immigration (immigrants overwhelmingly integrated into the English minority rather than the French majority).

In Quebec, the language problem initially focused on the issue of education. Conscious of the role of schools in the development of cultural identity, the Government of Quebec passed laws (Bill 63 in 1969, Bill 22 in 1974) establishing restrictions on the admission of immigrants into English schools. The pro-sovereignty Parti Québécois, elected for the first time in 1976, passed the landmark **Bill 101** in the following year. Bill 101 is a form of charter defining the status of the French language and regulating its use. In the field of education, current legislation allows children of parents who completed an English elementary school curriculum anywhere in Canada to attend English public elementary and secondary schools. In 1988 the government passed **Bill 178**, amending Bill 101's stipulation that commercial signs appear only in French. The new law required businesses to post French signs outdoors, while allowing the use of bilingual signs indoors, provided that the French-language wording appears more prominently. The law was further amended in 1993 with the passage of Bill 86 permitting bilingual exterior signage, again under the condition that the French wording clearly predominates.

Today, the language debate persists, but the actual separation of Quebec from Canada appears increasingly improbable. In turn, Quebec seems to have developed a unique identity within the confines of the Canadian Confederation. In any case, it is remarkable that the descendants of the 60,000 French-speaking inhabitants of New France, at the time of the British Conquest in 1759, have not only resisted assimilation to the English language in North America, but have developed and nurtured a distinct, vibrant French-speaking culture.

CUSTOMS AND TRADITIONS

Quebec's customs and traditions reflect the values of a rural people whose everyday life was greatly influenced by the Catholic Church and the rigors imposed by the natural environment. The oral and material heritage of Quebec is permeated with reminders of harsh winters, the era of the *coureurs des bois,* the settlement of forest regions and the predominance of the Church.

The Catholic Church long remained the focus of Quebecers' social and cultural

A LIFESTYLE LINKED TO THE SEASONS

The traditions and festivities that have developed over the centuries in the southern part of the province are intimately linked to the four seasons. In late March the maple sap starts to rise, heralding the return of **spring** and the celebrations associated with the making of maple syrup. This sweet "water" was traditionally collected in pails hung on spouts inserted into the trunks of maple trees. The water was then boiled down to the proper consistency, producing maple syrup. This tradition, known as sugaring-off, is still very much a part of Quebec culture, but the pails have for the most part disappeared; today, maple water is collected in plastic tubing that brings the sap directly to a central evaporator. For the traditional sugaring-off parties, families and friends congregate in large wooden cabins known as sugar shacks, built at the edge of maple groves. Inside, long picnic tables are laden with a variety of hearty dishes and desserts cooked or covered in maple syrup. Hot syrup is also poured over fresh snow to form a taffy-like substance known as *tire d'érable,* which is deftly rolled onto a stick. The 24th of June is dedicated to St. John the Baptist, but it is also Quebec's national holiday, and heralds the arrival of **summer**. As a religious and national holiday, "la Saint-Jean-Baptiste", as it is commonly called, is a major event, celebrated throughout the province as a sign of Quebec's cultural and linguistic distinctiveness. Floats, flag parades, bonfires and live shows by some of Quebec's major entertainers are typically part of the celebrations. The hot, humid summer is followed by Quebec's most beautiful season, **fall**. As the nights grow cooler, maple trees display their fall finery: vivid reds, rusty oranges and golden yellows. This is the best time to visit the Laurentians and the Cantons-de-l'Est, and it is also harvest time in apple-growing country. Many orchards are open to the public and resound with the sounds of families and friends who turn apple-picking into a pleasant outing. The snow usually starts falling in late November or early December and melts in March or April. Although the days are cold and short, the **winter** months are generally sunny and very bright because of the sparkling snow. Quebecers celebrate winter with carnivals, the most famous of which is the **Carnaval de Québec** (Quebec City Carnival), with its famous parades, giant ice castle and ice sculpting contests. Other popular winter activities include ice fishing on the frozen lakes and rivers, skiing, and snowmobiling.

life. Although the role of this institution has sharply diminished since the mid-20C, reminders of its once powerful presence are everywhere, in countless churches with silver-colored steeples, tiny processional chapels and wayside crosses.

Industrialization and urbanization have radically transformed the traditional Quebec lifestyle. In the city and countryside, many old customs have given way to the 21C, while others endure.

Legends

The numerous stories, childhood tales, legends and proverbs of Quebec are of French inspiration, and often feature the devil. Long winter nights were ideal for the telling of fantastic tales. A favorite is the legend of the *chasse galerie* or "wild chase." As winter approached, young men often joined logging camps to supplement their income. Life was harsh in these camps, and the men's dreams sometimes drifted to a wife or girlfriend back home. On New Year's Eve, the devil appeared with a tempting offer: he would take the lovelorn men to their sweethearts in a special canoe capable of traveling through the air at great speed. In exchange, the men would promise to refrain from using swear words during the entire trip lest they be eternally damned. The men stood by their word on the way home, but on the return trip, they would sometimes forget their promise and speak the forbidden words. The flying canoe would come crashing to earth and the souls of the unfortunate passengers would plunge into hell.

Another popular tale is the story of Rose Latulippe, the girl who danced with the devil. One night, during a dance, the door opened and a handsome stranger strolled in. Taken by his charm, Rose left her partner to dance with the newcomer. After several hours of dancing, the exhausted young girl tried to stop, but discovered she could not. Her partner continued to whirl and twirl her around the dance floor until she thought this hour must surely be her last. Just as she despaired, the village priest appeared. Recognizing the the devil, he chased him off with prayers and a few drops of holy water. Poor Rose was exorcized and vowed never again to dance with any other than her appointed beau.

Like many Quebec tales, these two classic folk stories—Rose and chasse galerie—feature many variations, as the storytellers try to wow their listeners with clever variations.

...and Folk Heroes

Logger **Louis Cyr** (1863–1912) was a legend in his own time. Weighing in at 165kg/364lb, he acquired a reputation as the world's strongest man by lifting a platform on which 18 people stood, weighing 1,967kg/4,336lb. His record still stands.

Born in the Lake Saint-Jean region, **Alexis Lapointe** owed his nickname "Alexis le trotteur" (Alexis the runner) to his amazing speed. He could run 240km/149mi in a single day and often raced horses and even trains. It is said that the autopsy performed on him revealed double joints, bones and muscles akin to those of horses.

Vernacular Objects

Quebecers' appreciation of beauty and form is reflected in the design and decoration of buildings, furniture and everyday objects. Even the most functional items were decorated with symbols and motifs that are still visible in the countryside, such as wooden maple-sugar molds in the shape of hearts and leaves, weather vanes with animal motifs, barn doors and shutters with floral motifs.

From the earliest days of the colony, clothing was designed to protect Quebecers from the bitterly cold winters. Tuques, mittens, woolen scarves and boots are still essential. A hooded coat known as a "canadienne," and fur coats made of fox, raccoon and mink where traditionally popular winter gear. They have been replaced by "technical apparel" made with modern fabrics, often produced in Quebec.

Culinary Tradition

Perhaps the most tangible changes in the province over the past couple of decades are the ones experienced at the dining table. There are many wonderful eateries, and an international food festival has been created to celebrate this bounty. The **Montréal en Lumière** festival focuses everyone's mid-winter attention on cuisine, both local and imported. An international food star hosts each festival, with other global chefs invited to perform in duet with local colleagues. The results bring residents out of the weather doldrums, and into almost two weeks of tastings, workshops, launches, and local deals at a bevy of restaurants.

Food also holds sway in daily conversations throughout the province. The Beauce region is famous for syrup, taffy, maple sugar, pie, yogurt, ice cream and liqueur. The Saguenay-Lac-Saint-Jean region serves heavy but delicious culinary delights such as *cipaille,* a six-layer meat pie with shortened crust, and *soupe aux gourganne,* a soup made with a type of large bean. Other traditional dishes include a thick stew known as *ragoût*, and a meat pie called *tourtière.* Fish and all kinds of seafood abound in many regions: fresh or smoked salmon from the Côte-Nord, lobster from the Magdalen Islands, different fish from the Gaspé Peninsula, shrimp from Matane and winkles from Bas-Saint-Laurent. For dessert, sugar pie and maple treats are traditional favorites.

Montreal & Quebec City History

Quebec's vivid history—from French rule to British, and now a strong state within Canada—has given it a unique perspective.

Hôtel de Ville, Montreal © A. Carpentier / Tourisme Montréal

Key Events

Key dates, events, characters, politics, society and cultural shifts in Montreal & Quebec's history: from Pre-Colonial Period to Contemporary Quebec

PRE-COLONIAL PERIOD

BC

c. 20,000–15,000	Earliest human migration into North America from Asia during the last ice age.
c. 5000– 1000	Nomadic hunters of the Archaic culture occupy most of the continent.
c. 1,000	Development of the Woodland culture: appearance of pottery and agriculture.

AD

c. 1000	Norse sailors reach the shores of present-day Newfoundland.
c. 1100	The Thule people, ancestors of the Inuit, migrate into the Ungava Peninsula.
1492	Christopher Columbus lands on the island of San Salvador in the Caribbean.

NEW FRANCE

1534	In the Gaspésie region, **Jacques Cartier** claims Canada in the name of François 1, King of France.
1534–1608	The Huron and the Algonquin force the Iroquois out of the St. Lawrence Valley.
1535	On his second voyage, Cartier travels upstream on the St. Lawrence to Hochelaga, the site of present-day Montreal.
1608	**Samuel de Champlain** founds **Quebec City**, the first permanent European establishment in North America after Jamestown.
1609–1633	French and Hurons form an alliance against the Iroquois and British.
1610	British navigator **Henry Hudson** discovers the strait and bay that today bear his name, in his quest for the Northwest Passage.

Statue of Samuel de Champlain, Quebec City

© Tibor Bognar / age fotostock

1627	The Company of One Hundred Associates is founded.
1642	**Maisonneuve** founds Ville-Marie, later renamed **Montreal. Iroquois Wars** begin.
1648–1649	Iroquois destroy Huronia (in present-day Southern Ontario) and regain control of the St. Lawrence Valley.
1670	The **Hudson's Bay Company** is founded; it operates in North America but its headquarters are in London, England.
1673	Father Marquette and Louis Jolliet explore the Mississippi.
1701	Montreal Peace Treaty (*La Grande Paix de Montréal*) marks the end of the Iroquois Wars.
1730s–1750s	La Vérendrye family explores the Canadian West.
1744	Pierre-François-Xavier de Charlevoix publishes *History and General Description of New France.*
1755	Acadian deportation begins.
1756	Beginning of the Seven Years' War, in which Austria, Russia, France and Spain oppose Great Britain and Prussia.
1759	British defeat the French at the **Battle of the Plains of Abraham** (Quebec City) on September 13. On September 18, Quebec City surrenders to the British.
1760	Montreal surrenders to the British.
1763	The **Treaty of Paris** marks the end of the Seven Years' War. New France is ceded to Great Britain.

BRITISH REGIME

1774	**Quebec Act** recognizes the French social system and civil laws and grants the freedom to practice the Roman Catholic religion.
1775–1776	American invasion and occupation of Montreal; American defeat in Quebec City.
1783	American Independence is recognized by Great Britain. Americans loyal to Britain begin emigrating to Canada, with many settling in Quebec.
1789	French Revolution and spreading of new ideas. Counter-revolutionary current after the death of Louis XVI.
1791	Constitutional Act divides the country into Lower (Quebec) and Upper (Ontario) Canada; each province is granted a legislative assembly.
1806	*Le Canadien,* the first Francophone newspaper, is founded in Montreal.
1812–1814	War of 1812; second American invasion; French Canadians and Indians win victory for the British at the Battle of the Châteauguay, under the command of Salaberry.
1837–1838	**Patriots' Rebellion** in the Montreal region and the Richelieu Valley. Suspension of the Constitution of 1791.
1841	**Act of Union** creates the United Canadas.

1845–1848	François-Xavier Garneau publishes *History of Canada*. Major wave of Irish immigration.
1852	Laval University, first francophone university in North America, is founded in Quebec City.
1854	Seigneurial regime is abolished.

CANADIAN CONFEDERATION

1867	British North America Act (later renamed **Constitution Act of 1867**) creates the Canadian Confederation.
1870	Rupert's Land is sold to the Canadian Confederation.
1892	Construction of the **Château Frontenac** begins in Quebec City.
1900	Creation of the first cooperative savings and loan company *(caisse populaire)* by Alphonse Desjardins.
1910	Montreal newspaper *Le Devoir* is founded by Henri Bourassa.
1912	Canadian government gives Quebec province a portion of Rupert's Land, thereafter known as Nouveau-Québec.
1918	Quebec women obtain the right to vote in federal elections; right to vote in provincial affairs is granted in 1940.
1927	After years of dispute, the territorial limit between Quebec and Labrador is established; Quebec does not officially recognize the border.
1939–1945	World War II brings a large wave of immigration from southern Europe.

CONTEMPORARY QUEBEC

1948	Quebec adopts its provincial flag.
1959	Opening of the **St. Lawrence Seaway**, enabling ships to navigate from the Atlantic to the Great Lakes.
1960	Government of Prime Minister Jean Lesage heralds the beginning of the **Quiet Revolution** *(Révolution tranquille)*.
1967	Expo 67 world's fair in Montreal; publication of the Report of the Royal Commission on Bilingualism and Biculturalism in Canada.
1968	Parti Québécois is founded.
1969	Passage of Bill 63, the first law promoting the use of the French language in Quebec.
1970	Hostage-taking by the Quebec Liberation Front (Front de libération du Québec) leads to the October Crisis and the enactment of the War Measures Act.
1973	Construction of phase 1 of the controversial James Bay hydroelectric project begins.
1976	**Summer Olympic Games** in Montreal; the Parti Québécois, under the leadership of **René Lévesque**, becomes the first nationalist-sovereign party to be elected.

1977	**Bill 101**, the charter on the French language, is passed.
1980	Referendum on sovereignty is rejected by 59.96 percent of the voters.
1982	The Canadian Constitution of 1867 is repatriated from London. The **Constitution Act, 1982** calls for a new constitution. Quebec is the only Canadian province that refuses to sign the new constitution.
1985	Historic Quebec City becomes the first urban center in North America to be inscribed on UNESCO's World Heritage List.
1987–1990	**Meech Lake Accord:** Quebec sets five conditions upon which it will adhere to the Constitution of 1982.
1988	The socio-cultural region of Nunavik is recognized by the provincial government as homeland of Quebec's Inuit.
1990	Two provinces (Newfoundland and Manitoba) refuse to sign the Meech Lake Accord by the June 23 deadline. Quebec refuses to sign the 1982 Constitution. First Nations crisis at Oka.
1992	Montreal celebrates the 350th anniversary of its founding.
1993	The Bloc Québécois becomes the official Opposition in the Canadian House of Commons.
1995	A second referendum on Quebec sovereignty is rejected by 50.6 percent of the voters.
1996	Severe floods devastate the Saguenay region.
1998	The worst ice storm in the region's history slams into southwestern Quebec, damaging the hydroelectric system and leaving millions without electrical power.

THE NEW MILLENNIUM

2000	Montreal becomes the home of the first NASDAQ stock exchange satellite market in Canada.
2001	A nationwide **census** confirmed a population of 30 million in Canada. Federal and Quebec elections renew debate about Quebec sovereignty. Famous hockey franchise the Montreal Canadiens is sold to an American businessman, but remains in Montreal. Lucien Bouchard resigns as premier and is replaced by Bernard Landry.
2003	A court ruling legalizes same-sex marriage in Quebec. In a general election, the Liberals, headed by federalist Jean Charest, defeat the Parti Québécois.
2005	Bernard Landry resigns as leader of the Parti Québécois, and is replaced by André Boisclair.
2006	The federal Conservative Party forms a minority government and wins 10 new seats in Quebec.
2007	The Liberal Party of Quebec barely escapes defeat, and forms a minority provincial government. Official Opposition becomes grassroots, right-wing Action

	Démocratique. Parti Québécois' third place reflects a loss of momentum for the sovereignty option.
2008	400th anniversary of the founding of Quebec City. According to the Canadian government, it "reminds us that French is Canada's founding language."
2011	The Bloc Québeçois, Quebec's national political party, loses 92 percent of its seats in the Federal election, being replaced largely by the New Democratic Party.
2012	The Parti Québécois is elected once again in Quebec; its leader, Pauline Marois, becomes the first woman to head the Quebec government.
2014	In a snap election in which the central issues are sovereignty, the business climate, and divisive language and cultural issues, the Liberals overcome an early Parti Québécois lead, and Philippe Couillard becomes Premier.

PEOPLE AND EVENTS

EARLY SETTLEMENT

According to recent excavations and interpretations, the earliest migration of humans into the North American continent may have occurred some 15,000 years ago. The first settlers are believed to have journeyed from Asia, crossing over the land bridge that joined Siberia and Alaska during the last glacial period. After a few thousand years, the ice sheet retreated from the central part of present-day Canada, clearing the way for human occupation.

Two principal cultures mark the many centuries separating the initial settlement of central Canada and the arrival of the Europeans in the 11C. The first, known as the "Archaic" culture (5000 to 1000 BC), were nomadic peoples, who relied on hunting and gathering for sustenance. During the subsequent cultural era known as "Woodland" period, (1000 BC to AD 1500), native peoples adopted a sedentary lifestyle characterized by the production of pottery and the development of agriculture (particularly corn) to complement their diet of fish and game. It is thought that at least three million people inhabited the North American continent immediately prior to the arrival of Columbus.

For centuries after the short-lived Viking settlements on the coast of present-day Newfoundland in AD 1000, Europe appeared to have forgotten about the existence of the North American continent. It wasn't until the 16C that Quebec's indigenous peoples first came into contact with Europeans—primarily the cod fishermen who had ventured up the St. Lawrence beyond the famous breeding grounds of Newfoundland's Great Banks.

The arrival of European missionaries and fur traders had a profound effect on indigenous cultures, bringing about changes in their lifestyle and political alliances. However, Native people largely resisted the Church's attempts to convert them to the Catholic faith, as described in Relations, the Jesuits' historic account of their missionary work in New France. In fact, the native cultures already had their own elaborate systems of beliefs and customs. Nonetheless, the modification of intertribal political relations and traditional trade routes, devastating wars, zealous colonization and endemic diseases brought to the New World by Europeans eventually brought about the permanent disruption of First Nations lifestyles.

NEW FRANCE

In the 15C, European explorers set sail in hopes of finding a route to India and China. Among these was Christopher Columbus who, in 1492, claimed the island of San Salvador for the Spanish Crown. Although French explorer **Jacques Cartier** (1491–1557) sailed to the New World between 1534 and 1542, France did not establish a firm presence on the North American continent until 1608, when **Samuel de Champlain** (c.1570–1636) founded Quebec City. Shortly after, Europeans began exploring the continent in search of beaver and mink, the mainstays of the lucrative **fur trade** that played a decisive role in Quebec's history. In the early 17C, the administration and development of the colony was entrusted to private companies such as the Company of One Hundred Associates (Compagnie des Cent-Associés, 1627), composed of merchants and aristocrats intent on colonizing New France for commercial gain. However, settlement progressed slowly; by 1663, there were approximately 3,000 inhabitants, fewer than half of whom were born in the New World. The Jesuits' attempts at evangelization had little success, and the fur trade led to alliances and to the Iroquois Wars. Between 1627 and 1701, the Iroquois nations repeatedly raided Algonquian-speaking nations, notably the Huron, Montagnais and Algonquin, who had allied themselves with the French settlers. Beginning in 1642, the French retaliated by building a series of forts and providing their allies with firearms. However, the attacks continued until 1701, when the Iroquois signed the Montreal Peace Treaty and established their neutrality.

A ROYAL COLONY (1663–1763)

Under the reign of Louis XIV (1643–1715), the administration of New France mirrored that of other French colonies. A governor conducted the colony's military and external affairs; another appointed official ruled over judicial and financial matters, and landlords, or ***seigneurs,*** performed various local administrative functions. The seigneurs also enforced the law, erected mills, collected dues (tithes, annuities and grain taxes) and could, at will, subject their tenants to forced labor. *Seigneurs*, military personnel and religious communities allocated land plots to tenant farmers under a mode of land distribution and occupation known as the **seigneurial system**. These land plots, known as rangs, formed long, narrow rectangles perpendicular to a body of water or a road. Farmers comprised 80 percent of the early population, which stood at 20,000 at the beginning of the 18C and at approximately 70,000 in 1760.
In a truly epic adventure, explorers pushed back the geographical boundaries of New France. In the 1730s, the La Vérendryes engaged in an extensive exploration of North American waterways, traveling as far as Manitoba, Saskatchewan, Wyoming, Montana and the Dakotas. They built forts and opened a fur trade route that was used by their successors.

THE BRITISH CONQUEST

The traditional rivalry between France and England, exacerbated by conflicting interests in the fur trade, led to recurring wars between New France and the surrounding British colonies, ultimately resulting in the capture of Quebec City in 1629. In 1632 the city returned to the French following the signing of the Treaty of Saint-Germain. The Treaty of Utrecht (1713) brought about a temporary peace that lasted until the Seven Years' War (1756–1763), in which France, Austria, Spain and Russia opposed Great Britain and Prussia. On September 13, 1759, British General Wolfe defeated French General Montcalm on the Plains of Abraham, heralding the end of the French colony. Montreal surrendered to the British on September 8, 1760, and the colony was ceded to England in 1763, by the Treaty of Paris.

THE ERA OF CONSTITUTIONS (1760–1791)

The late-18C is known as the "era of constitutions." The military conquest had placed English Protestants, governed by a constitutional monarchy, in opposition with French Catholics, subjects of an absolute monarchy. The constitution of 1774 (known as the Quebec Act) gave the great majority of francophones the right to maintain the seigneurial system and French civil laws, and the freedom to practice the Roman Catholic religion.

The inhabitants of the 13 American colonies won their independence from England in 1776, trying in vain to convince Canadians to join them during an invasion that was finally crushed at Quebec City. Loyalists—American citizens faithful to the British Crown—made their way north, and many of them settled in the area now known as Cantons-de-l'Est, or Eastern Townships.

Quebec remained sympathetic to the French Revolution of 1789 until the regicide of Louis XVI in 1793. British colonial authorities looked unfavorably upon the abolition of monarchy and the execution of its royal representative, and the Catholic Church, witnessing the overthrow of royal and ecclesiastical authority, fostered a counter-revolutionary current through its sermons and editorials. Despite attempts to maintain the status quo, a liberal-minded middle class was gradually taking shape. In 1791 the British parliament gave its North American colonies a new constitution, granting a separate legislative assembly to Quebec (Lower Canada) and Ontario (Upper Canada). This was Quebec's first experience of parliamentary democracy.

FROM CONSTITUTIONAL DEBATES TO POPULAR UPRISINGS (1791–1840)

French Canadians grew accustomed to British institutions and, by the turn of the century, they constituted a majority in the elected assembly, and began to draw attention to their grievances. Led by **Louis-Joseph Papineau** (1786–1871), the Patriot Party (*Parti patriote*), also known as the *Parti canadien* until 1826, was hindered by a British governor and legislative council that frequently defeated bills submitted by the peoples' representatives.

The constitutional impasse and British colonial policies eventually led to several uprisings known as the **Patriots' Rebellion**, particularly in the region of Montreal (Saint-Denis-sur-Richelieu, Saint-Charles-sur-Richelieu, Saint-Eustache). Various beliefs and convictions were reflected in this rebellion of 1837–38: a democratic ideology that valued the supremacy of the House of Assembly, an anti-British and anti-colonial sentiment based on a belief in the right to self-government, and a movement away from the power held by the ***seigneurs*** and the clergy. After the failure of the rebellions, Governor-General Lord Durham was sent to assess the state of the colony; in 1839, he submitted a report recommending the union of the two Canadas, in order to assimilate French Canadians.

THE ACT OF UNION (1840–1867)

Passed in 1841, the Act of Union joined Lower and Upper Canada into one province. At the time, Lower Canada's population stood at 750,000 (510,000 French Canadians) and Upper Canada numbered 480,000 inhabitants. Although Upper Canada's debt was far greater, the two public debts were consolidated, and the Legislative Assembly adopted English as the language of the Province of Canada. By the mid-19C, the extremely high birth rate of the seigneurial era had led to overpopulation in Lower Canada, and large numbers of people moved to new settlements in the Mauricie, Saguenay–Lac-Saint-Jean and Bas-Saint-Laurent regions or to the industrial towns of New England. Although vast new regions were opened to colonization in Quebec, nearly one million French-Canadians emigrated to the US between 1850 and 1930.

Weakened by its lack of clergy and official recognition, the Catholic Church proved staunchly loyal to the British government from 1763 to 1840, even during the Patriots' Rebellion; it was rewarded for its good faith after 1840, when it received a special legal status that allowed it to retain its assets. As it became more involved in the political scene and forged close ties to the party led by **Louis-Hippolyte Lafontaine** (1807–64), the Church gained control over public education. Working with Upper Canada Reformists, Lafontaine secured the right to a "responsible government" formed by the parliamentary majority. Although the Union began in a period of renewed political liberalism, it ended with the emergence of an ideological and political conservatism. Frequent political crises finally led to a new political system of government known as Confederation, which French-Canadian Liberals opposed in vain.

CANADIAN CONFEDERATION

Ratified by the British Parliament in 1867, the **British North America Act** (today known as the Constitution Act, 1867) established the Canadian Confederation—a new political entity that included Quebec among its four founding provinces (along with Ontario, Nova Scotia and New Brunswick). The Confederation's **Constitution of 1867** called for a parliamentary system of government and a separation of federal and provincial powers. Education was among the key areas of jurisdiction granted to the provinces. To guarantee the rights of the Protestant minority in Quebec and the Catholic minority elsewhere in Canada, the controversial **Article 93** created a school system divided along religious rather than linguistic lines.

The Constitution used the term French Canada to refer to francophones living in Quebec, New Brunswick, Ontario and Manitoba. In the following decades, when British imperialism reached its peak, **Wilfrid Laurier** (1841–1919) became the first French prime minister of Canada (1896–1911). Between 1870 and 1917, francophone Catholic minorities outside Quebec gradually lost a number of educational and linguistic rights. Among the transformative events of the early 1900s was Quebec's opposition to the draft imposed by the federal government.

A NATIONALIST REVIVAL

This progressive loss of rights as well as the issue of autonomy, and the threat to the French language stemming from industrialization, gave rise to two nationalist trends. The first, embodied by **Henri Bourassa** (1868–1952), founder of Montreal's francophone daily *Le Devoir* (1910), advocated greater autonomy for Canada within the British empire, and greater autonomy for each province within the Confederation. Historian **Lionel Groulx** (1878–1967) promoted a nationalist ideology based on the threefold identity of French Canadians: Catholic, francophone and rural. Groulx's campaign began just as Quebec's rural culture was weakening and ended as the role of Catholicism in Quebec society was fading.

In Quebec the economic crisis of 1929, coupled with turmoil wrought by World War II, lasted into the 1940s; both these events led to economic and social interventions primarily backed by the federal government. So began an era of federal centralization vividly opposed by **Maurice Duplessis,** Premier of Quebec from 1944 to 1959.

NEW IDENTITY

THE QUIET REVOLUTION

In the 1960s there appeared a climate of social and economic change that contrasted sharply with the staunch conservatism of successive Duplessis governments. Among the events that led to the so-called Quiet Revolution of

1960–66 (*la Révolution tranquille*) were the economic prosperity engendered by the mining industry of the Côte-Nord region, Quebecers' introduction to consumerism through the automobile and television (1952), and the strengthening of the labor movement during the miners' strike (1949) in Asbestos.

The Quebec government launched a series of economic and social programs aimed at gaining economic leverage for Quebec. In 1962 it nationalized its hydroelectric industry (Hydro-Québec was first nationalized in 1944); in 1965 it created the ***Caisse de dépôt et placement*** to manage the assets of a new pension plan, and it helped promote francophone business in Quebec. The government also intervened in social and cultural matters by taking over the management of health and social services from the Church, administering public education and creating the Ministry of Cultural Affairs (1961). By taking charge of the educational and cultural sectors, the provincial government was finally realizing an objective first set by Liberals in the 19C.

A SOVEREIGN STATE?

The increasing role of the provincial government paralleled the rise of a nationalist political ideology. The issue of Quebec's sovereignty became a hotly debated topic between supporters of a federalism—personified by **Pierre Elliot Trudeau**, Prime Minister of Canada from 1968 to 1979 and 1980 to 1984—and partisans of Quebec sovereignty, embodied by **René Lévesque**, former popular journalist, leader of the Parti Québécois, and Premier of Quebec from 1976 to 1985. Lévesque (1922–87) transformed what was primarily a cultural nationalism into a political ideology. Nonetheless, on May 20, 1980, Lévesque's Parti Québécois lost a referendum on Quebec sovereignty when 59.6 percent of Quebecers voted against separation. The tension between the provincial and federal governments reached new heights when Quebec declined to sign the new **Canadian Constitution of 1982** and the Charter of Rights and Freedoms. Pierre Elliot Trudeau left politics in 1984 as the Progressive-Conservative Party of Quebec-born Brian Mulroney took power in Ottawa.

René Lévesque retired from the political scene in 1985. Six months later, the Parti Québécois was defeated by the Quebec Liberal Party, headed by Robert Bourassa. The Liberal government announced it would sign the 1982 Constitution provided five conditions were met. At a meeting held at Meech Lake, near Ottawa, the Canadian Prime Minister and the 10 provincial premiers tentatively agreed to these conditions. The **Meech Lake Accord** (April 30, 1987), which provided a special status for Quebec as a "distinct society," had to be ratified by the federal government and all 10 provinces before June 23, 1990. However, a consensus was not reached and the failure of the Meech Lake Accord once again renewed doubts about Quebec's adherence to the Canadian constitution.

No solution to this thorny issue has yet been reached. The narrow failure of a second referendum on Quebec sovereignty, held in October 1995 (50.6 percent of Quebecers voted "no"), seemed to indicate that the questions of sovereignty and Quebec's relationship with other Canadian provinces would continue to influence the political scene. But maybe not, as in the 2011 federal election the Bloc Québécois was all but destroyed, being replaced largely by the New Democratic Party. The young and educated Quebecer is connected to a growing global identity, and does not seem to feel the same fear as former generations. Quebec has arrived on the international stage with a political and cultural entity all its own.

Montreal & Quebec City Art and Culture

From church-inspired paintings to modern jazz, the art scene has grown up with the province.

McCord Museum, Montreal © McCord Museum / Tourisme Montréal

Architecture

Marked by French, British and American influences, and set in a Nordic climate, Quebec's rich and varied architecture constitutes a cultural heritage that is unlike anything else in North America.

17C

Due to the ephemeral nature of Native constructions, very little remains from the period preceding the arrival of Europeans. The earliest European structures found in Quebec date from the late 17C. Erected by craftsmen and architects imported from France, these simple buildings bear the influence of various regional styles, in particular those of Brittany and Normandy. With a view to defending and protecting the strategic location of both Quebec City and Montreal, the colonial administration encouraged the building of fortifications around the early settlements. The villages that grew inside the fortified walls provided a model for the urban centers that subsequently developed. Among fortification ruins, only the old powder magazine and redoubt of the Quebec Citadel remain as examples of the French Regime's military design.

A lack of trained craftsmen and tools gave rise to domestic architecture characterized by simplicity of design and lack of ornamentation. Illustrating the austerity of these early constructions, the Jacquet House (1699), in Quebec City, was built of rough fieldstone and topped by a steep roof. Toward the end of the century, the principal urban areas were embellished by impressive administrative and religious edifices, erected by the French-born architects **Claude Baillif** and **François de la Joüe**. The Château Saint-Louis and the Quebec Basilica-Cathedral figured among those imposing monuments; unfortunately, neither of the original structures has survived intact. The arrival of religious orders (Ursuline, Augustine and Jesuit) gave rise to an institutional style that reflected the influence of French classicism. Noteworthy buildings from this period are Quebec City's Ursuline convent, with an interior courtyard reminiscent of a 16C French châteaux, and Montreal's Old Sulpician Seminary. These and other opulent residences were erected with stone vaulting.

EARLY–MID-18C

Following several devastating fires, such as the one in Quebec City's Lower Town, local administrators established new ordinances that "Canadianized" the architecture. Constructions were adapted to the North American context, giving rise to a vernacular style that later evolved into the "maison québécoise" (previously "maison canadienne"). Strict regulations required the use of slate roofs and stone vaults, while prohibiting decorative elements liable to help spread fire. Erected in 1798, the Calvet House in Montreal exemplifies this common building type by its simple fieldstone walls, firebreaks (the part of the wall extending beyond the roof as a shield against flying sparks), corner consoles, wide chimney stacks, and gabled roof.

The Baillairgé Family

The 18C saw the emergence of this dynasty of prolific architects, painters and sculptors. **Jean Baillairgé** (1726–1805) left France to work on new Canadian projects under the renowned military engineer **Chaussegros de Léry** (1682–1756). Shortly after landing in Quebec, he was selected to draw up plans for several buildings, including the Quebec City cathedral. After studying in France at the Académie royale de peinture et de sculpture, his son, **François** (1759–1830), returned to

ARCHITECTURAL TERMS

Apse	The rounded or polygonal termination of a church, in which the altar is housed.
Baldachin	An ornamental canopy over an altar supported by columns.
Barrel vaulting	Continuous arched vault of semicircular cross section.
Bas-relief	Low relief. A form of sculpture in which figures or shapes project slightly from the background plane.
Bastion	In military architecture, a masonry structure projecting from the outer wall of a fortification.
Battlement	The uppermost portion of a fortified wall with alternate solid elements and openings (embrasures or crenels).
Blockhouse	In 18C and 19C military architecture, a fortified structure, commonly of wood, with a square floor plan and an overhanging upper floor.
Buttress	A masonry structure built against a wall to add support or strength.
Capital	Crowning feature of a column or pilaster.
Cornice	A molded projection crowning the top of a building or wall.
Curtain wall	In modern architecture, a non-weight-bearing exterior wall suspended on the face of a building like a curtain.
Dormer window	A small window projecting from a sloped roof.
Embrasures	A series of crenels or intervals cut into the top portion of a battlement, often used as openings for weapons.
Fanlight	A semicircular window over a door or window.
Gable	The vertical triangular section of wall closing the end of a double-sloped roof.
Mansard roof	A roof with two slopes on all four sides, the lower slope being the steeper of the two (named after the 17C French architect, François Mansart).
Nave	The central main body of a church designed to accommodate the congregation.
Pediment	Any triangular or semicircular crowning element used over doors, windows or niches.
Pilaster	An engaged pier or pillar projecting slightly from a wall surface, generally with base and capital.
Portal	A monumental entrance or gate.
Porte-cochere	A large covered entrance porch.
Portico	A porch or covered walk consisting of a roof supported by columns.
Quoin	A cornerstone often distinguished from the adjoining masonry by a special surface treatment.
Redoubt	A small free-standing fortification.
Reredos	A decorative screen or wall behind an altar sometimes forming part of the retable.
Retable	A decorative screen placed above and behind an altar and generally containing a work of art.
Rose window	A large circular stained-glass window dissected by stone members or mullions arranged like the spokes of a wheel.
Turret	A small tower generally placed at the corner of a building.

Quebec City and elaborated designs for the cathedral's interior. **Thomas Baillairgé** (1791–1859), Quebec's pre-eminent 18C architect, studied sculpture with his father, François, and with the Montreal woodcarver and sculptor Louis-Amable Quévillon (1749–1823), known especially for his interior decoration of the church at Sault-au-Récollet. Thomas contributed to the Quebec cathedral and later supervised the construction of churches throughout the province. Drawing on British architectural trends, Thomas developed an original style, which combined Neoclassical influences and Quebec's mixed architectural heritage. Thomas and his father collaborated on the elaborate interior of the Saint-Joachim church between 1815 and 1825. The son of a cousin of Thomas, **Charles** Baillairgé (1826–1906) was trained as an architect and engineer. He became Quebec City's engineer in 1866, beautifying the city with monumental edifices, such as the main pavilion of Université Laval, public spaces and imposing staircases.

Late 18C

Following the British Conquest, the province's urban areas and the villages east of Quebec City along the St. Lawrence River lay in ruins. Though post-French Regime architecture still dominated until 1800, British influence drastically altered the architectural landscape in the early-19C. The Neoclassical style, in particular Palladianism, bore a determining influence on constructions. Transformed into single-family homes, domestic structures of this period, based on the British model, occupied a relatively small area of land, but were built with two or three storeys. Massive chimneys rising from a four-sided gently sloped roof replaced the characteristic steeply pitched roof of the French Regime constructions.

The development of commerce and a relatively prosperous economy fostered the growth of new urban areas around nascent industries, such as Sherbrooke and Saint-Hyacinthe. Small cities also sprung up around military fortifications (Chambly, Sorel and Vaudreuil). Beginning in the 1780s, resort areas along the banks of the St. Lawrence attracted a wealthy British bourgeoisie, who developed a taste for the "picturesque style" imported from Great Britain.

19C

Palladianism continued to dominate the early part of the century. This popular style, inspired by the works of the 16C Italian architect Andrea Palladio, is characterized by austerity and symmetry of design and employs elements from classical antiquity, including pediments, pilasters, Doric and Ionic columns, cornices and quoins. In addition, the structures designed in this style were often faced with a smooth layer of cut stone. The Holy Trinity Anglican Cathedral in Quebec City represents a colonial version of Palladianism. A more resolutely Classical style appeared about 1830, as exemplified by the large yet elegant Bonsecours Market in Montreal.

The **maison québécoise**, the Quebec equivalent of the rustic English cottage, came into vogue in the 1830s and 40s. Offering a harmonious synthesis between the French heritage and British influence, this type of building is embel-

Centre Canadien d'Architecture in Montreal

lished by picturesque ornaments and incorporates amenities such as large windows, balconies, reception rooms and heating systems.

The mid- to late-19C reflected an eclectic mix of more exuberant revival styles, inspired by architectural trends of the past and made possible by new materials and building techniques developed in the 19C. Numeous churches in Quebec City were erected in the **Gothic Revival style** popularized by the French architect and restorer Viollet-le-Duc, who is credited with resurrecting the prevailing style of the Middle Ages. Catholic churches were generally based on French Gothic architecture, while Protestant places of worship adopted the British model. Victor Bourgeau's Notre-Dame Basilica in Montreal and the Chalmers-Wesley Church, by John Wells, in Quebec City, exemplify two variants of this style.

Modeled on Italian palaces and villas, the **Renaissance Revival style** was associated with the wealthy British elite and therefore used mainly for commercial buildings. The Ritz-Carlton in Montreal exemplifies this style, characterized by wide cornices, exuberant ornamentation and rustication.

The **Second Empire style**, in fashion during Napoleon III's reign, gained prominence in the 1870s under the Quebec architect **Eugène-Étienne Taché** (1836–1912). In search of a unified architecture for governmental buildings of the new province following the Confederation of 1867, Taché drew on this style for his plans of the Parliament Building in Quebec City. Recognizable by its distinctive double-sloped mansard roof pierced by dormer windows, the style also introduced arched lintel windows, a profusion of columns, and wrought-iron roof cresting, as seen in the Shaughnessy House in Montreal.

After creating several works in Gothic Revival, the architect **Victor Bourgeau** (1809–88) became a proponent of the **Baroque Revival style**. His masterpiece, Montreal's Mary Queen of the World Basilica-Cathedral, a small-scale replica of St. Peter's Basilica in Rome, illustrates the tenets of this style with its massive proportions, enormous dome, and elaborate interior embellished by an imposing baldachin.

While striving to adapt the Second Empire style to the Canadian environment, Eugène-Étienne Taché proposed structures that would reflect the era of New France's discoverers, Cartier and Champlain. Inspired by the French châteaux of the Loire valley, Taché designed monumental edifices, complete with towers and turrets, conical roofs and machicolation. The most famous example of the **Château style** remains the Château Frontenac, erected by **Bruce Price** (1843–1903) in 1892–1893.

In the late-19C, another interpretation of Medieval architecture, the **Romanesque Revival**, was mainly used for religious buildings. This style was appropriated by H.H. Richardson, the prominent American architect who later modified it into the Richardsonian Romanesque style, characterized by rounded arches and buttresses, squat columns, arcades and deep-set windows. Montreal's Windsor Station is an excellent example of this distinctly North American style.

20C and Beyond

The early 1900s saw a wave of architects turning to the École des Beaux-Arts in Paris for inspiration. The exuberant **Beaux-Arts style**, which employs a Classical vocabulary in monumental compositions, became the preferred institutional style and proliferated under the government of Louis-Alexandre Taschereau. Montreal's Museum of Fine Arts, boasting an imposing staircase and portico colonnade, illustrates this style, which relies on monumentality and symmetry. Introduced to the province at a time of economic prosperity, the Beaux-Arts style also symbolized wealth and power. Near the Olympic Stadium in Montreal, the Château Dufresne with its elegant coupled columns, balustrades and elaborate ornaments reflects the tastes of the opulent French Canadian bourgeoisie of the day.

The invention of steel-frame constructions heralded the beginning of the first

Habitat '67, Montreal

skyscrapers, or buildings with more than 10 storeys. Influenced by the Chicago School, these structures reveal a complete break with past architectural trends. New techniques and building materials, such as reinforced concrete, provided architects with many new possibilities.

Introduced at a Paris Exposition in 1925, the **Art Deco style** soon made its appearance in Quebec's large corporation buildings. Hallmarks of the style include clean vertical lines, stepped forms, a pronounced axial symmetry, and often, geometric ornaments carved on marble, bronze, stainless steel, and other expensive materials. The Price Building in old Quebec City is a stunning example of the Art Deco style.

After a period of artistic stagnation, the late 1950s marked the beginning of urban renewal and the growth of modern architecture. Modern architecture embodied practical and functional thinking, developed in the works of Le Corbusier and Gropius. Simple, geometric lines, devoid of ornamentation, typified a style that did not rely on any past tenets of architecture. The influential architect Mies van der Rohe, proponent of the **International style**, made use of glass curtain walls, black metal and reinforced concrete, as seen in Montreal's Westmount Square and the Fairmont Queen Elizabeth hotel. The city's Place Ville-Marie, erected by I.M. Pei, and Habitat '67, designed by **Moshe Safdie**, also illustrate these modern trends that profoundly changed the image of Quebec's largest city.

Ecclesiastical architecture experienced a renaissance under **Dom Paul Bellot** (1876–1944), a Benedictine monk, who drew inspiration from Viollet-le-Duc's works and introduced modern church architecture into Quebec. Known as "modern Gothic," his style is best illustrated by St. Benedict's Abbey in Cantons-de-l'Est, and St. Joseph's Oratory, in Montreal.

In recent years, **Post-Modern** currents have presented an eloquent reply to the anonymity of the architecture of the 1960s. Post-Modernism often incorporates existing structures and uses elements from previous styles, such as pointed arches, fanlights and other embellishments, to produce a harmonious ensemble that blends with its environment. Montreal's La Place de la Cathédrale, Maison Alcan and the Canadian Center for Architecture, by **Peter Rose** and **Phyllis Lambert**, all exemplify this trend. The up-and-coming Quartier International (International District), located northwest of Old Montreal, provides a vision of how the future can be built while respecting a city's architectural inheritance.

Art and Culture

A renaissance of art is evident throughout "La belle province," and it is visible in city and countryside alike. New galleries, museums, and workshops bear witness to this vigorous revival. Hotels feature local paintings, and some boast tiny museums, while it is common to see original local artworks hanging in restaurants, bookstores and shops.

FIRST NATIONS ART

Through the centuries Quebec's Native peoples have developed diverse modes of artistic expression that bear witness to their distinctive lifestyles and beliefs.

Traditional Art

Most Algonquian-speaking Natives (namely Abenaki, Algonquin, Cree, Mi'kmaq, Montagnais and Naskapi) are descendants of nomadic peoples who excelled in the art of beadwork (shell, bone, rock or seed) and embroidery (porcupine quills and moose or caribou hair). Caribou-hide vests and moccasins, and various birchbark objects were often decorated with geometric incisions and drawings. Red, the symbol of continuity and renewal, was the dominant color. Elaborate belts of **wampum** (beads made from shells) feature motifs illustrating the main events in Native history. Wampum was exchanged at peace ceremonies and during the signing of treaties.

The smaller, more sedentary, Iroquoian-speaking groups included Hurons, Mohawks, Onondagas and Senecas. As agricultural societies, they formed semi-permanent villages and built multi-family dwellings known as longhouses; out of their sedentary lifestyle evolved an artistic repertoire free from the constraints of nomadism. Among their most beautiful works are exquisite moosehair embroideries that gradually began incorporating floral motifs under European influence. Huron women were the most adept at this delicate art; the complex techniques they applied with

Musée d'art contemporain, Montreal

© Atlantide SNC / age fotostock

remarkable skill have never been replicated. Also of interest are the wooden masks known as "False Faces" that represented mythological figures associated with traditional healing practices.

The Contemporary Scene

First Nations art has undergone a profound transformation in the past 20 years. Whereas artists traditionally relied on natural materials such as hide and bark, today they are exploring new media such as canvas, acrylics and charcoal, and new techniques have emerged although inspiration is still drawn from social and cultural traditions. The result is a new, contemporary vision of aboriginal art that keeps alive the memory of the past.

INUIT ART

Art forms developed over centuries have brought no small renown to the inhabitants of North America's Arctic regions.

Origins

The earliest-known artifacts produced by the Inuit are small stone projectile points attributed to the Pre-Dorset and Dorset cultures, which developed in the first millennium BC. Petroglyphs or rock carvings attributed to these cultures have been found in the steatite hills of Kangiqsujuaq.

The Thule people, generally considered to be the ancestors of the present-day Inuit, crafted more refined objects including combs and figurines. Generally small in size, these early artifacts were closely associated with religious beliefs and practices.

Beginning in the 19C, many miniature sculptures made of stone, ivory (walrus tusks) and whalebone were traded for staples such as salt, and firearms, provided by Europeans. With the decline of traditional lifestyles resulting from increased contact with non-indigenous peoples, sculpture and other forms of arts and crafts gradually lost their magical or religious significance, but provided a new source of income for the Inuit population.

Inuit Art Today

Today the term "Inuit art" evokes images of steatite carvings. Abundant in the north, **steatite** (known as soapstone) is a soft rock ranging from greyish green to brown. Other harder rocks commonly used include green serpentine, argillite, dolomite and quartz. Modern Inuit sculptures, which can reach impressive dimensions, represent local fauna, life in the northern regions and other arctic themes popular with the public. Other art forms include printmaking, sculpted caribou antlers, rock engravings and tapestries. The art trade has become a lucrative economic activity for the Inuit population.

In order to prevent the exploitation of Inuit artists by retailers from the south, local **cooperatives** were created in the 1960s and have since been brought together under the umbrella of "la Fédération des Coopératives du Nouveau-Québec," which controls the marketing of artworks. The most renowned centers for Inuit sculpture are the villages of Povungnituk and Inukjuak, located on the shores of Hudson Bay. Salluit and Ivujivik are also well-known artistic communities. Three artists had a profound effect on the development of modern Inuit sculpture: Joe Talirunili (1893–1976), Alasua Amittuq Davidialuk (1910–76) and Charlie Sivuarapik (1911–68). Among the foremost sculptors of the current generation are Joanassie and Peter Ittukalak, from Povungnituk, and Eli Elijassiapik, Lukassie Echaluk and Abraham Pov of Inukjuak.

PAINTING AND SCULPTURE

17C–18C

The arrival of French colonists in the early 17C introduced European esthetics and forms to Quebec's artistic landscape.

Religious Art

Religion was the very fabric of life in New France. Each village had its own Catholic church and great pains were taken to decorate its interior. As most canvases were imported from France, very few local religious paintings were executed in this early period. The works of Brother Luc (1614–85), a member of the Récollets order, were a notable exception.

In early colonial times, altars, retables, baldachins and statues were all imported from France. The transportation of such large objects proved problematic, however, and eventually craftsmen were trained locally. Sculptures, always made of wood, were carved in relief and gilded. The Baroque style, very much in fashion in France at that time, remained the preferred style until the mid-19C among Quebec sculptors. The art of church decoration was handed down through generations, and certain families became famous for their artistic accomplishments. In the 1650s brothers **Jean and Pierre Levasseur** became the first of a dynasty of sculptors that continued into the 18C with Noël and Pierre-Noël Levasseur. Although they were best known for their religious artwork, they also sculpted ships' figureheads and other naval ornaments.

In the years following the British Conquest (1759–60), religious art came to a near-standstill. But in the late 18C, church building resumed at a rapid pace. In Quebec City, the **Baillairgé** family was gaining wide recognition for its wood sculptures; three generations, represented by Jean (1726–1805), François (1759–1830) and Thomas (1791–1859), would perpetuate the tradition. At the same time, **Philippe Liébert** (1733–1804) was winning acclaim in Montreal, particularly for his decoration of the church at Sault-au-Récollet, which also contains sculptures by his student **Louis-Amable Quévillon** (1749–1823). This renowned sculptor and designer developed a distinctive style inspired by Louis XV decoration, with foliage, arabesque and finely adorned vaults. Throughout the early 19C, the so-called Quévillon school embellished the interiors of numerous churches throughout Quebec.

Later in the century, a new form of religious statuary made with plaster casts appeared, and eventually led to the decline of traditional wood sculpting. While most artists were turning to new art forms, sculptor **Louis Jobin** (1845–1928) was an exception. In 1881 he created the monumental wood-and-metal statue known as **Notre-Dame-du-Saguenay**, which overlooks the Saguenay from high atop a cliff. In the Church of Saint-Georges-de-Beauce, Jobin's equestrian sculpture of **Saint-Georges** (1912) was the last work created by a traditional wood sculptor. The craft of woodcarving has survived in certain areas of Quebec, such as Saint-Jean-Port-Joli, but it is largely a popular folk art, with no connection to the religious art that adorns many Quebec churches.

Military Topographic Art

In the period following the Conquest, British army officers were sent to Quebec to paint topographic views of the colony for military purposes. Some of this artwork, inspired by the romantic ideals of late-18C England, is best exemplified by the carefully executed watercolors of officer Thomas Davies (1737–1812) and the equally remarkable works of George Heriot (1766–1844) and James Cockburn (1778–1847).

Late 18C and 19C

Quebec art entered its Golden Age in the late-18C, at a time of economic prosperity. The primarily European-trained artists began producing works focusing on such popular subjects as **landscapes** and, above all, **portraits**, commissioned by an emerging bourgeoisie. The work of self-taught painters like Louis Dulongpré (1754–1843), François Beaucourt (1740–94) and **Jean-Baptiste Roy-Audy** (1778–1848) may seem somewhat naive by European standards, but the next generation of portraitists was trained in France where they acquired a more Classical style. The best known of these is **Antoine Plamondon** (1802–95), who also painted religious themes. **Théophile Hamel** (1817–70) gained recognition as a leading portraitist of his day, while **Joseph Légaré** (1795–1855) created paintings that depicted contemporary events against dramatic backgrounds, such as *L'incendie du quartier Saint-Roch*.

Throughout the 19C, the arrival of European artists had a decisive impact on Quebec painting. Paul Kane (1810–71), born in Ireland, came to Canada as a child, before perfecting his skills as a painter in Europe. His splendid portraits of Native peoples are now of great historical interest. Among the painters who developed a marked interest in regional themes was **Cornelius Krieghoff** (1815–72); this Dutch-born painter produced superb landscapes, as well as scenes of daily life in the Montreal region, in unprecedented detail.

By the mid-19C Montreal had evolved into a sophisticated city, prosperous enough to lend financial assistance to an association whose goals were to promote the arts, organize exhibitions and mount a permanent collection.

The oldest art gallery in Quebec was opened by the **Art Association of Montreal** in 1879; its operations were eventually taken over by the present-day **Montreal Museum of Fine Arts,** featuring the inspiring Claire and Marc Bourgie Pavilion (inside a renovated 1894 heritage church).

The late-19C was also marked by the emergence of photography. Acclaimed for his portraits and his renditions of the increasingly urban landscape of Montreal, Scottish-born **William Notman** (1826–91) was one of Canada's most prominent photographers.

20C

At the onset of the 20C, the influence of the so-called Paris school was already visible in Quebec art, particularly in the works of Wyatt Eaton (1849–96) and Montreal art professor William Brymner (1855–1925). Their followers include Impressionist-style painters **Marc-Aurèle de Foy Suzor-Côté** (1869–1937), Maurice Cullen (1866–1934), Clarence Gagnon (1881–1942) and Modernist-Fauvist **James Wilson Morrice** (1865–1924).

Although a contemporary of these artists, **Ozias Leduc** (1864–1955), a native of Mont-Saint-Hilaire, stood apart from the rest with his deeply mystical, luminous paintings. His still-lifes and landscapes reveal a spiritual symbolism that goes far beyond their subjects, reflecting the long-lived union of art and religion in Quebec. In addition to the frescoes adorning the church of Mont-Saint-Hilaire, Leduc's works can be viewed in the Notre-Dame Basilica in Montreal, and in several public collections.

Sculpture

As the 20C began, Quebec sculpture lost much of its religious character, while an era of great commemorative monuments dawned. Among the most notable sculptors were artist-architect **Napoléon Bourassa** (1827–1916) and the celebrated **Louis-Philippe Hébert** (1850–1917). Applying the techniques of French Realism to his art, Hébert created, among others, the famous Maisonneuve monument, and the statues of Jeanne Mance and Monsignor Ignace Bourget, all located in Montreal. **Alfred Laliberté** (1878–1953) fashioned sculptures along the fluid lines of Art Nouveau while maintaining an academic approach. One of his best-known works

Statue of Maisonneuve, Place des Armes.

is a monument dedicated to Dollard des Ormeaux. Marc-Aurèle de Foy Suzor-Côté, a close friend of Laliberté, used the same Art Nouveau techniques to create a series of bronze works. His *Femmes de Caughnawaga*, showing a group of First Nations women fighting against the wind, is so brilliantly executed that it seems the wind itself has sculpted the silhouettes.

Contemporary Arts Society

In the 1930s Montreal artists began to rebel against the "wild landscape nationalism" of the "Group of Seven" English-Canadian painters, most of them from Toronto, who claimed sole authorship of a typically Canadian style of painting. A staunch critic of the Group, **John Lyman** (1886–1967), attempted to redirect Canadian art according to the precepts of the Paris school of thought. In 1939 he created the Contemporary Arts Society and organized a group known as the Modernists. Its members included André Biéler, **Marc-Aurèle Fortin** (1888–1970), Goodridge Roberts (1904–74), Stanley Cosgrove and **Paul-Émile Borduas** (1905–60).

Automatists and Plasticists

World War II marked a turning point in the evolution of Quebec art. In 1940 **Alfred Pellan** (1906–88) returned to Quebec after an extended stay in France, to exhibit paintings strongly influenced by Picasso and other proponents of Cubism. Paul-Émile Borduas and several fellow artists, including **Jean-Paul Riopelle** (1923–2002), Pierre Gauvreau, Fernand Leduc and Jean-Paul Mousseau, founded the group called **les Automatistes**, whose paintings reflected the goal of Surrealism to transfer onto canvas the creative impulses of the psyche. In 1948, the Automatists published the **Refus Global**, a manifesto whose virulent attacks on the established, fossilized order of Quebec society had a far-reaching impact that went far beyond the artistic milieu.

As a response to the lyricism and spontaneity of the Automatists, Guido Molinari and Claude Tousignant founded the **Plasticist** group (1955), freeing painting from the Surrealist idiom through the use of an abstract geometric vocabulary. Form and color were the key elements of their work. However, no single school of thought prevailed over the inspirational and creative effervescence of contemporary art, although several Montreal painters such as Charles Gagnon, Yves Gaucher, Ulysse Comtois and sculptors Armand Vaillancourt, Charles Daudelin and Robert Roussil developed their own highly personal styles.

CURRENT ART SCENE IN QUEBEC

The Montreal World Exposition of 1967 renewed interest in public art.

Under a provincial law passed in 1978, building constructors must allocate one percent of construction costs for all new public buildings erected in the province to artwork. Sculptors often collaborate with architects to integrate their art into the building design. The most remarkable example of this can be seen in Montreal's subway system: each station is designed by different architects and incorporates art and sculptures. The work of Marcelle Ferron, at the Champ-de-Mars station in Old Montreal, and Jordi Bonet (1932–76), at the Pie-IX station near the Olympic Stadium, are among the best.

In recent years, Quebec art has evolved alongside major international trends; it has distanced itself from traditional painting while emphasizing diverse forms and techniques, including "installation," a primarily sculptural idiom that also includes other art forms such as painting and photography. Among its proponents are Betty Goodwin, Barbara Steinman, Geneviève Cadieux, Jocelyne Alloucherie and Dominique Blain.

Michel Goulet and Roland Poulin have made important contributions to the field of sculpture, and Melvin Charney, an architect and urban planner, has also produced remarkable works; his most important creation is the garden of Montreal's celebrated Canadian Center for Architecture.

Popular Culture

Montreal's new symphony house leads a robust roster of popular culture events throughout the province. World-premiere Cirque du Soleil shows regularly launch in Quebec City and Montreal, while Quebec-inspired literature, cinema, theater and music continue to evolve and prosper, providing visitors with a remarkable array of entertainment choices.

LITERATURE

Throughout the era of exploration and colonization, the literature of New France was limited to travel memoirs (Cartier, Champlain), stories, descriptive writings (Sagard, Charlevoix), and historical missives known as the **Relations**, written by Jesuit missionaries recording their life and work in the New World.

Emergence of Quebec Literature

Two newspapers, *Le Canadien,* founded in 1806 in Quebec City, and *La Minerve,* founded in 1826 in Montreal, were instrumental in the development of French-Canadian literature.

In 1837 the young Philippe Aubert de Gaspé published the first French-Canadian novel, entitled *L'influence d'un livre,* inspired by legends. The first fiction novels were influenced mainly by rural traditions, as evidenced in *The Canadians of Old* (*Les Anciens Canadiens*), written in 1863 by **Philippe Aubert de Gaspé** senior.

Nationalist and conservative ideologies were also a source of inspiration, as in Pierre Joseph Olivier Chauveau's novel *Charles Guérin* (1846–53). Indeed, Quebec literature was long influenced by a conservative ideology that arose in the 1860s, promoting the moral values and precepts of the Catholic Church.

Historical novels, inspired by **François-Xavier Garneau's** *History of Canada (Histoire du Canada),* published in the 1840s, became very popular in the mid-1800s, as did the romantic poetry of Octave Crémazie (1827–79). Louis-Honoré Fréchette (1839–1908) published his popular work, *The Story of a People* (*Légende d'un peuple),* in 1887.

20C

The early-20C was dominated by the nationalist works of writer and historian **Lionel Groulx** (1878–1967), leader of the "Action française," and by the poet Émile Nelligan (1879–1941), who produced his entire work between the ages of 17 and 20, before being confined to a mental asylum. In 1916 French-born **Louis Hémon**'s novel *Maria Chapdelaine,* depicting life in rural Quebec, was published posthumously, and has been translated into more than 20 languages. In 1933 **Claude-Henri Grignon** wrote his celebrated novel *The Woman and the Miser* (*Un homme et son péché*), which has been the core subject of the immensely popular television series and movie, *Séraphin.* Urbanization and the trauma of World War II resulted in greater introspection among Quebec writers, as they questioned the established order. The end of World War II marked the end of the dominance of rural life, which formed the basis of traditional French Canadian society. Novelist **Robert Charbonneau** abandoned his tales of rural life for psychological novels. Quebec poetry was redefined through the works of **Alain Grandbois** (1900–75) and **Hector de Saint-Denys Garneau** (1912–43). **Roger Lemelin**'s *The Town Below* (*Au Pied de la Pente Douce,* 1944) was the first novel to explore the lifestyle of the urban working class. The theme of city life also permeated the works of **Gabrielle Roy**, such as *The Tin Flute* (*Bonheur d'occasion*), published in 1945. Roy was born and raised in rural Manitoba (Western Canada), and thus her take on Montreal's poor, industrial neighborhoods was particularly poignant.

The Quiet Revolution (*la Révolution tranquille*) of the 1960s reflected Quebecers' growing awareness of their distinct cultural identity and their reappraisal of traditional values and institutions. The literature of the day faithfully reflected this period of upheaval as writers explored a rich variety of subjects and styles. It was the poets, however, who instilled the most strength and energy into Quebec literature at that time: **Gaston Miron** (1928–96), Gatien Lapointe, Jacques Brault and Fernand Ouellette. The 1960s witnessed the rise of new novelists to prominence, while already well-known writers became associated with the finest of Quebec letters, among them **Hubert Aquin** (*Hamlet's Twin/Neige noire*), **Marie-Claire Blais** (*A Season in the Life of Emmanuel/Une Saison dans la vie d'Emmanuel*), **Roch Carrier** (*La guerre, yes sir!*), **Réjean Ducharme** (*The Swallower Swallowed/L'avalée des avalés*), **Jacques Ferron** (*The Juneberry Tree/L'amélanchier*), **Jacques Godbout** (*Knife on the Table/Le couteau sur la table*), **Anne Hébert** (*Kamouraska and In the Shadow of the Wind/Les fous de Bassan*) and **Yves Thériault** (*Agaguk*). Also during the 1960s, playwright **Michel Tremblay** made a resounding entrance onto the literary scene with *Les Belles-Sœurs*. In the 1960s and 70s, poet-singer-novelist **Leonard Cohen** (b.1934, in Montreal) wrote of the sexual revolution and resistance to the Vietnam War. Two of the best-known anglophone novelists are **Hugh MacLennan** (1907–90) and Montreal-born **Mordecai Richler** (1931–2001), who won numerous literary prizes including the prestigious Governor General's Performing Arts Award. Nova Scotia-born MacLennan, a professor at Montreal's McGill University, confronted the issue of Quebec's relationship to the rest of Canada in his *Two Solitudes* (1945). Following the trend of the 1960s, the early 1970s were characterized by a broad diversity of styles, most notably the "psychological" novel. Prominent authors from this prolific period of Quebec literature include Louis Hamelin (*La rage*), Suzanne Jacob (*Laura Laur*), Claude Jasmin (*Mario/La sablière*), Sergio Kokis (*Le pavillon des miroirs*), Marie Laberge (*Julliet*), Robert Lalond (*Le petit aigle à tête blanche*) and Monique Larue (*True Copies/Copies conformes*). In 2002, Yann Martel won the Booker Prize for Fiction for his Life of Pi, while the Hollywood feature film production of Barney's Version in 2010 brought new readers to the works of Mordecai Richler.

THEATER

The theatrical arts were introduced fairly late in Quebec: the first permanent French theater companies appeared in the 1880s. But in the late-1940s to early-1950s the foundations of an enduring tradition were laid. At that time, an original repertoire and several theater institutions took shape, as a generation of actors, trained for the most part with Father Legault's Les Compagnons de Saint-Laurent, paved the way for their successors. Professional theater companies were created: The Théâtre du Rideau Vert (1949), the Théâtre du Nouveau Monde (1951), the Quat'Sous (1954) and the avant-garde Apprentis-Sorciers and Égregore.

Gratien Gélinas created *Tit-Coq* (1948), a play based on a popular character whose deceptively naive demeanor hid a mind capable of astute social criticism. In 1959 Gélinas wrote *Bousille et les justes* while heading the Comédie-Canadienne, a name that reflected the will to create a truly French-Canadian theatrical repertoire. A friend of Jean Anouilh and Arthur Miller, **Marcel Dubé** staged *Un simple soldat* at the Comédie-Canadienne in 1958; his ability to explore universal themes won wide recognition. The Compagnie Jean Duceppe was founded by the comedian **Jean Duceppe** (1923–90) in 1973, and earned an excellent reputation for its contemporary repertoire.

Michel Tremblay, whose plays have had more international exposure than those of any other Quebec playwright, pursued his predecessors' exploration of city life. From *Les Belles-Sœurs* (1968), which is considered a milestone in the development of Quebec theater, to *The Real World?* (*Le vrai monde?*, 1987), Tremblay has created a true human comedy, with a cast of characters who speak the street slang heard in the working-class neighborhoods of Quebec City and Montreal. The strength and originality of Quebec's modern theater lie in the **experimental works** of authors like Jean-Pierre Ronfard (*Vie et mort du roi boiteux,* 1981) at the Théâtre Expérimental de Montréal, and Gilles Maheu at Carbone 14. Playwright Normand Chaurette came on the scene in the 1980s with such pieces as *Provincetown Playhouse and Fragments of a Farewell Letter Read by Geologists* (*Fragments d'une lettre d'adieu lus par des géologues,* 1986); in 1996, his *Le passage de l'Indiana* gained wide acclaim at the Avignon Festival, and garnered a prestigious Governor General's Performing Arts Award.

Other renowned names of Quebec theater include Michel Marc Bouchard (*The Orphan Muses/Les muses orphelines,* 1989), René-Daniel Dubois (*Don't Blame the Bedouins/Ne blâmez jamais les Bédouins,* 1985) and Marie Laberge (*Night/L'homme gris,* 1986).

Lebanese-Canadian writer, actor, and director Wajdi Mouawad rose to prominence In the 1990s, and his grand spectacle Women (Des femmes) was presented at Avignon in 2011.

In Quebec's Ligue nationale d'improvisation, famous in the French-speaking world, actors improvise dialogue in the context of a competitive, rough ice hockey game, by far Quebec's best-loved sport. The widely acclaimed **Cirque du Soleil** (Circus of the Sun) has delighted audiences around the world with its innovative and enchanting blend of traditional circus entertainment, music, theater and dance, embellished with stunning costumes.

TOHU is a world-renowned circus arts center located in Quartier Saint-Michel. Housing the world HQ for Cirque du Soleil, as well as a circus arts training facility, this center offers workshops for performers, and venues featuring international, national and local shows for the whole family.

MUSIC

The Montreal Symphony Orchestra, conducted by Californian Kent Nagano, is widely acclaimed, and under his inspiration Montreal's new Symphony House attracts new generations to a state-of-the-art facility, featuring a massive new Casavant Fréres pipe organ. Since 1963 the Montreal International Music Competition (Concours international de Montréal) has welcomed young musicians from all over the world. Both the Mount Orford and Lanaudière music camps are vibrant training centers. The Festival de Lanaudière, a summer music festival in Joliette, has earned international recognition.

Composers, Conductors and Musicians

The authors of Canada's national anthem, *Ô Canada,* are two French-Canadians: Adolphe-Basile Routhier (1839–1920) wrote the lyrics and Calixa Lavallée (1842–91) composed the music. Conductor Wilfrid Pelletier (1896–1982) launched Montreal's dynamic music scene while Claude Champagne (1891–1965), composer of the *Symphonie gaspésienne,* opened the way for numerous other composers. Among the foremost are Alexander Brott (founder of the McGill Chamber Orchestra), Jean Papineau-Couture and Jean Vallerand. The Contemporary Music Society of Quebec (Société de musique contemporaine du Québec), founded in 1966, includes composers such as Serge Garant, Pierre Mercure, Gilles Tremblay and André Prévost.

Pianists Henri Brassard, André Laplante and Louis Lortie have all triumphed in international music competitions, while violinist Angèle Dubeau and pianist Marc-André Hamelin have carved brilliant careers at home as well as abroad Kenneth Gilbert is known for his research and remarkable renditions of 17C and 18C harpsichord music. Raymond Daveluy, Mireille and Bernard Lagacé are famous for their mastery of the pipe organ. Founded in 1879, the Casavant Frères company of Saint-Hyacinthe has maintained its reputation as one of the world's foremost organ manufacturers.

Opera

Since the days of Chambly's Emma Lajeunesse (1885–1958), better known as **Albani**, several Quebec voices have been heard in Milan, New York, Paris and London: Soprano Pierrette Alarie, contralto **Maureen Forrester**, tenors Raoul Jobin and Leopold Simoneau, bass Joseph Rouleau and baritones Louis and Gino Quilico.

The Montreal Opera has staged several well-received productions each year since its creation in 1980.

Traditional and Popular Music

Music is the heart and soul of Quebec's oral tradition. From the songs of the "voyageurs" to *Un Canadien errant* (1842), popularized by Nana Mouskouri, Quebec's folk repertoire, inspired by traditional French songs, was part of everyday life.

Félix Leclerc (1914–88) was Quebec's pre-eminent folk musician. A raconteur and poet, he introduced Quebec culture to France after World War II, leading the way for many other Quebec folk singers or *chansonniers*.

In the late-1950s, several chansonniers and musicians formed a group known as "les Bozos," named after one of Leclerc's songs. They included Raymond Lévesque, Clémence Desrochers, André Gagnon, Claude Léveillé (*Frédéric*)—who worked with Edith Piaf—and Jean-Pierre Ferland (*Je reviens chez nous*). Joining this talented new generation of singers and songwriters was **Gilles Vigneault**, the poet of Natashquan. His song *Gens de mon pays* accompanied the rise to power of the Québécois Party. Pauline Julien and Renée Claude are known today for their renditions of works by Quebec's great folk singers.

The rock music of **Robert Charlebois** reflected a more critical social outlook typical of the 1960s. At that time, large-scale shows and a recording industry heavily influenced by American culture were adding a whole new dimension to Quebec music. The California counterculture was echoed in the music of highly creative groups such as Harmonium and Beau Dommage.

Diane Dufresne created a personal and dramatic style that has won her numerous awards at home and in France. She often sang compositions by **Luc Plamondon**, one of the most famous Quebec songwriters. Plamondon founded the Quebec Society of Professional Authors and Composers (Société professionnelle des auteurs et compositeurs du Québec) and worked on the rock opera *Starmania* in 1976.

The late Sylvain Lelièvre, whose musical career took shape in the early 1970s, is considered among Quebec's finest singer-songwriters. Richard and Marie-Claire Séguin, the rock group Offenbach, and Claude Dubois also rose to prominence in the 1970s, and Ginette Reno's powerful voice made her one of Quebec's most acclaimed pop singers. Such singers and composers as Richard Desjardins, Luc de Larochelière and Paul Piché appeared on Quebec's musical scene during the 1980s. The 1990s witnessed the phenomenal rise of songstress **Céline Dion**, whose fame extends worldwide. Other musical stars of note include Laurence Jalbert, Isabelle Boulay,

Orchestre symphonique de Montréal

© Jean Buithieu/Orchestre symphonique de Montréal/Tourisme Montréal

Bruno Pelletier and Garou, who were all celebrated in France as well as in Quebec. Jazz legend **Oscar Peterson** was born in Montreal's Little Burgundy community to West Indian parents in 1925. Icon composer/bandleader Duke Ellington called him the "Maharaja of the keyboard." International jazz impresario Norman Granz was on his way out of Montreal in the 1940s when he heard a live broadcast on his cab's radio. He immediately had the car turn around, found the pianist and signed him to his famous "Jazz at the Philharmonic" touring group. "O.P," as Peterson's friends and family called the virtuoso, would make his international concert debut at Carnegie Hall at age 24. The eventual winner of seven Grammy Awards, Peterson recorded 200 albums over 60 years of performances worldwide. He is considered one of the greatest jazz pianists of all time.

In 2004, Montreal-based anglophone artist **Sam Roberts** won both Artist and Album of the Year Juno Awards (the annual Canadian music awards) for his *We were born in a flame* recording. His success marked the beginning of an enduring series of English-speaking bands, like **Arcade Fire,** who find inspiration and creative synergy in Montreal, mainly in the Mile End, the multi-ethnic, western portion of trendy Plateau Mont-Royal.

Considered by legions of music aficionados as a global hub for the hip-hop/house DJ music style of contemporary music, Montreal has spawned such acts as **DJ Champion, Mole of Soul,** and many others feeding the rave dance audiences worldwide.

Béatrice Martin, better known by her stage name Couer de pirate (Pirate Heart), has conquered the public on both sides of the Atlantic, and is credited for reviving and bringing French chanson music to a new generation.

CINEMA

Since 1895 most of the films shown in Quebec were imported from the US. The first feature films were produced in the province between 1944 and the introduction of television in 1952. But the birth of the Quebec film industry really dates back to the 1960s.

Several executive directors and directors of photography were trained at the National Film Board of Canada, a federal institution (1939) based in Montreal since 1956. The NFB has acquired an international reputation for its animation films, especially those of Frédéric Back (two-time Oscar winner), and its documentary tradition, which evolved into a genre known as "cinéma-vérité," a widely recognized trend in the Quebec film industry, best reflected in the works of **Pierre Perrault** (*The Moontrap,* 1963; *Wake up, mes bons amis!,* 1970) and Michel Brault (*Les Ordres,* 1974).

Claude Jutra won international fame for *Mon Oncle Antoine* (1971) and *Kamouraska* (1973), based on a novel by Anne Hébert. Jean Beaudin's movie *J.A. Martin, photographe* (1975) won an award at the Cannes Film Festival.

Denys Arcand reached the European and American public with his films *The Decline of the American Empire* (1986) and *Jesus of Montreal* (1989); the latter was nominated at Cannes and Hollywood. Jean-Claude Lauzon's *Night Zoo* won 13 of the 17 Genies awarded during the Canadian film industry's annual gala awards celebration in 1987. Robert Lepage's 1995 movie *The Confessional (Le confessionnal)* won the Prix Claude-Jutra.

In 2003, Denys Arcand's ultimate recognition came about with *Les invasions barbares* (sequel to *The Decline of the American Empire*). The movie won the foreign film Oscar, as well as two awards in Cannes.

Various movies by Quebec directors have been successful, including *Seducing Doctor Lewis* (Jean-François Pouliot) and *C.R.A.Z.Y.* (Jean-Marc Vallée).

Since 2010, three Quebec films have been nominated for Best Foreign Language Film Academy Awards: *Scorched* (2010) by Denis Villeneuve; *Monsieur Lazhar* (2011), by Philippe Falardeau and *War Witch* (2012), by Kim Nguyen.

See Films in Planning your Trip for a selection of Quebec's films.

Nature

Long winters and mild summers, plus an inspiring but rugged landscape, have shaped the soul of the province.

Colors of the Indian summer © Alain Evrard GPA / age fotostock

Landscape

Quebec is Canada's largest province, occupying about 15 percent of the country's land mass. With a total area of 1,542,056sq km/595,391sq mi, Quebec is bigger than Alaska, and nearly three times the size of France. At its largest point, the province stretches nearly 1,500km/930mi from east to west and 2,000km/1,240mi from north to south. Only Canada's newest territory, Nunavut, is larger.

REGIONAL LANDSCAPES

The province boasts a striking range of landscapes and climates, from the often-steep shores of the mighty St. Lawrence River, to the cultivated terraces of the Appalachian valleys, to the wide-open spaces of the northern tundra. From the air, Quebec's most striking feature is the sheer number of lakes, rivers and streams that decorate its vast geographic mass.

The Canadian Shield

The granitic and gneissic rocks of this immense craton, which covers over 80 percent of Quebec's territory, are the roots of ancestral mountain ranges that were repeatedly uplifted and eroded over billions of years. During the Paleozoic era, much of the ancient Shield surface was covered by shallow seas and buried under thick marine sediments. Today this expanse is generally flat, rising no higher than 600m/1,968ft above sea level. The landforms of the Shield consist of extensive plateaus interrupted by a few mountain massifs. Only near the rim of the Shield is the land deeply incised by rivers flowing towards the surrounding lowlands. Within the Canadian Shield, the following subregions are commonly identified.

The Northern Plateau

Known for its many lakes, this was the only area in Quebec still glaciated during the final stages of the last ice age, approximately 6,000 years ago. The Otish Mountain massif and its summits of over 1,000m/3,280ft dominate the plateau's southern half. Located to the southeast of the Otish Mountains, the Manicouagan Reservoir now fills the impact crater of a meteor. Westerly winds from Hudson Bay deposit more than 1m/39in of precipitation per year, nearly half of it as snow—a remarkable total for this high latitude. Separating Ungava Bay from the Labrador Sea, the Torngat Mountains rise to Mt. Iberville (1,652m/5,420ft), the highest summit in Quebec.

Abitibi-Témiscamingue

This part of the Shield lies along the border with Ontario between the Ottawa River and the Eastmain Plain, south of James Bay. To the south, the recurving upper Ottawa River frames the region of Témiscamingue, noted for its dairy farms nestled among spruce-covered hills.

The Laurentides

When viewed from a high vantage point, the sea of well-rounded crests is remarkably even in elevation (600m/1,968ft–800m/2,624ft).

On the other side of the Saguenay Fjord lies the sparsely inhabited expanse of Côte-Nord, the north shore of the Gulf of St. Lawrence. More than 1,000km/620mi of wind-buffeted coast, this spruce-covered coastal plain lies in front of the Laurentian escarpment into which tumultuous rivers have cut narrow rock-strewn valleys. Mont-Tremblant, one of the most popular downhill ski destinations in the province, continues to attract year-round outdoor enthusiasts. The massive Mont-Tremblant Park nearby forms an extensive additional network of lakes and rivers, highlighted by mountainous regions and populated by a wide range of wildlife, such as beaver, black bear, deer, fox, wolf and otter.

Saguenay–Lac-Saint-Jean

The Saguenay–Lac-Saint-Jean Region owes much of its economic dynamism to its oasis-like situation within the Laurentian Plateau (or Canadian Shield). The basin has an extensive cover of fertile soils, a notably warm, if brief, summer as compared with the coastal areas farther south, and tremendous industrial power potential stored in the region's numerous rivers. From depths of 275m/902ft, the sheer rock faces of Cape Éternité and Cape Trinité form canyon-like walls, soaring many feet above the surface of Saguenay Fjord.

The St. Lawrence Lowlands

Shaped like a triangle with its apex near Quebec City, the lowlands are lodged between the Canadian Shield to the north, and the Appalachian Mountains to the southeast. The lowlands rise gradually to the northeast so that the area around Quebec City has a higher elevation (100m/328ft above sea level) than the Montreal plain, which rarely surpasses the 70m/230ft mark.

Between Montreal and the first Appalachian ridges to the east, a string of isolated, massive outcrops known as the **Monteregian Hills** looms above an otherwise uniformly flat landscape. Graced with fertile soils and a moderate climate, the lowlands support a variety of agricultural activities.

The Appalachian Mountains

Separated from the St. Lawrence lowlands by **Logan's Line**, the Appalachian Mountains cross into Quebec from Vermont and New Hampshire and run to the northeast along the boundary with the US and the province of New Brunswick.

Broadleaf forests cover the higher elevations and ridges, while mixed agriculture occupies the larger valleys. Towards the northeast and the Gaspé Peninsula, agriculture becomes increasingly marginal and forests of coniferous trees predominate.

The Cantons-de-l'Est and Beauce

These two regions are the most populated areas in Appalachian Quebec. The Cantons-de-l'Est occupy the southwestern portion of the Appalachian region between the US border and the Chaudière River basin, while the Beauce region is centered on the upper Chaudière River. While fruit orchards and even vineyards can be found among the pastures and dairy farms along the western margin of this region, forests of sugar maple predominate in the Beauce area.

The similarity in landscape between the Cantons-de-l'Est and northern New England is unmistakable. Vermont's Green Mountains continue north of the border as the Sutton Mountains which, in turn, are followed by a ridge of low hills in the upper Bécancour basin near Thetford Mines.

The Lower St. Lawrence and the Gaspé Peninsula

To the northeast of the Chaudière River, the Green Mountains-Sutton Mountains belt is known as the Notre-Dame Mountains, whose northern slopes descend to a narrow coastal plain along the

Parc national de la Gaspésie

© Tourisme Gaspésie / ATRG

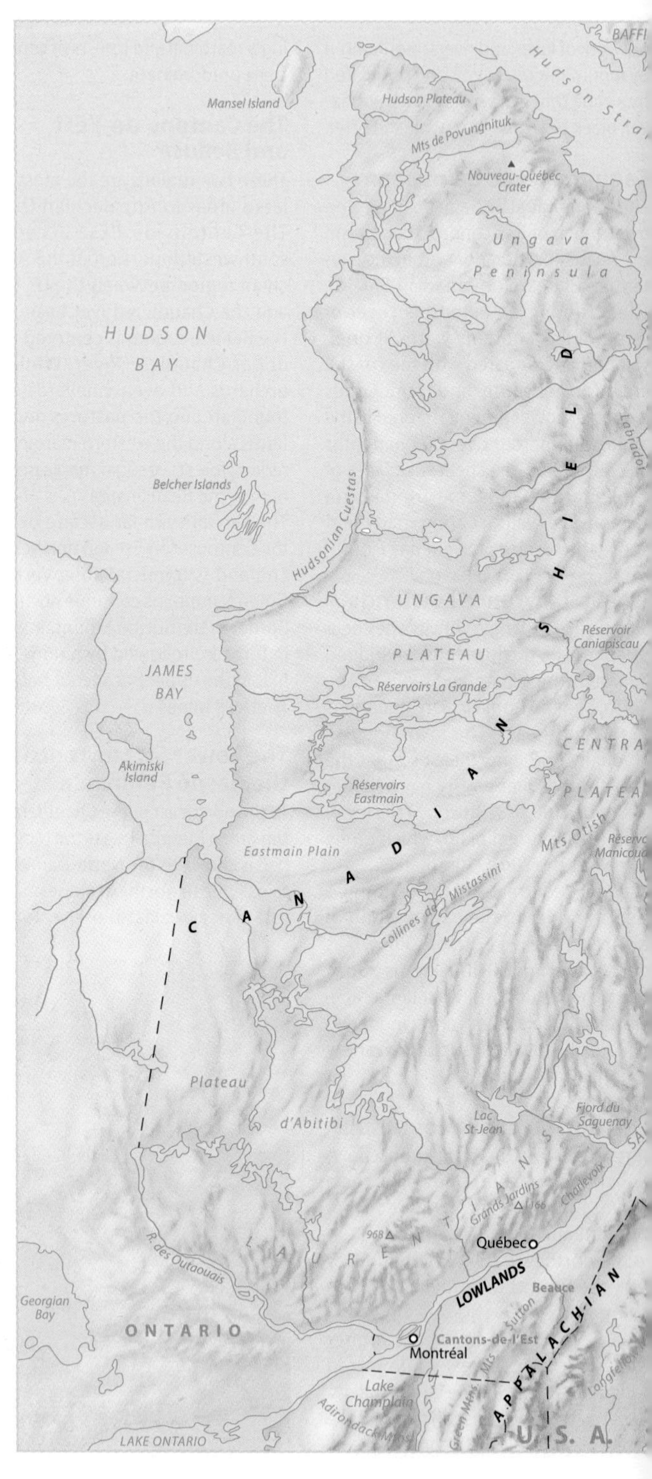

Mansel Island
Hudson Plateau
Hudson Strait
Mts de Povungnituk
Nouveau-Québec Crater
Ungava Peninsula
HUDSON BAY
Belcher Islands
Hudsonian Cuestas
Labrador
UNGAVA PLATEAU
Réservoir Caniapiscau
JAMES BAY
Réservoirs La Grande
CENTRAL PLATEAU
Akimiski Island
Réservoirs Eastmain
Mts Otish
Eastmain Plain
Collines de Mistassini
CANADIAN SHIELD
Plateau d'Abitibi
Lac St-Jean
Fjord du Saguenay
Grands Jardins
Charlevoix
1166
968
LAURENTIAN
Québec
LOWLANDS
Beauce
R. des Outaouais
Georgian Bay
ONTARIO
Sutton
Cantons-de-l'Est
Montréal
APPALACHIAN
Lake Champlain
Adirondack Mts
Green Mts
U.S.A.
LAKE ONTARIO

REGIONAL LANDSCAPES
ISLAND
Akpatok Island
UNGAVA BAY
LABRADOR SEA
MONTS TORNGAT
1622
Whale River Plateau
Hills
NEWFOUNDLAND
Smallwood Reservoir
Labrador
Les Groulx
NORD
Long Range Mtns.
Île d'Anticosti
LAURENT
Mts Chic-Chocs
1268
Gaspé Peninsula
GULFE DU SAINT-LAURENT
MTNS.
Chaleur Bay
Îles de la Madeleine
NEW BRUNSWICK
PRINCE EDWARD ISLAND
ATLANTIC OCEAN
NOVA SCOTIA
0
400 km

Fjord du Saguenay

lower St. Lawrence River. Shielded by the Chic-Choc Mountains from Arctic north winds, this area, once called "Quebec's Mediterranean," is known for its favorable microclimate.

To the south and east of the Gaspé Peninsula, the Appalachian zone includes mostly flat-lying red sandstone and schist strata that underlie the Magdalen Islands and the province of Prince Edward Island in the Gulf of St. Lawrence.

The St. Lawrence River

Known in Mohawk as *Kaniatarowanenneh* ("big waterway") and in French as *fleuve Saint-Laurent*, the St. Lawrence River (1,197km/744mi long) connects the Great Lakes with the Atlantic Ocean, and forms a boundary between New York, Ontario and Quebec. The Saguenay-St.Lawrence Marine Park features fifteen species of marine mammals in an explosion of biodiversity running from La Malbaie east of Quebec City to Les Escoumins east of Tadoussac (the oldest European settlement in North America). From May to October it is possible to book whale-watching tours into this marine protectorate, where sightings of harbor seals, minke, fin, beluga, and humpback whales are common. Ferry-style boats as well as the smaller zodiacs run through the bountiful waters of this unique environment. Statistics reveal that more than 1,100 individual whales visit this zone, including 11 blue whales, the largest animals on the planet.

CLIMATE

Because of its high latitude and location at the eastern margin of the continent, Quebec undergoes extreme fluctuations in temperature. Very cold winters and surprisingly warm periods during the summer months are the hallmarks of a continental climate. Of course, with increasing northern latitude, summers become cooler and winters are frigid, but the sizable gap in seasonal temperatures remains. For example, Montreal's average summer temperature is 22°C/72°F, and its winter averages -9°C/16°F.

For Kuujjuarapik, an Inuit settlement on the eastern shore of Hudson Bay, the equivalent figures are 11°C/52°F and -23°C/-9°F. Precipitation is abundant, augmented by the nearby open seas of the Atlantic Ocean and Hudson Bay. Annual totals average between 35cm/13in and 110cm/43in. The amount of annual rainfall generally decreases inland and northward, and is fairly evenly divided between summer rains and winter snows.

FLORA

Latitude is an important factor in the distribution of plant cover, since it largely determines the length and average temperatures of the growing season. In Quebec's far northern reaches, the nominal growing season is less than 40 days as compared to more than 180 days around Montreal. Elevation above sea level and proximity to the ocean as well as local microclimates that develop in response to particular landforms, such as the Lake Saint-Jean basin, are additional factors modifying the latitudinal pattern of plant cover.

Most common in the southern part of Quebec, the mainly broadleaf hardwood or **deciduous forest** is dominated by maple species mixed with beech, hickory, basswood, ash and oak. Stretching from the southern Laurentians to the coastal areas of the Gaspé Peninsula, this forest persists in mostly hilly and mountainous areas. As latitude and altitude increase, it gradually mixes with balsam fir and yellow or white birch.

Covering the Côte-Nord, Abitibi and Saguenay–Lac-Saint-Jean regions, the dense **boreal forest** is dominated by straight-trunked, coniferous (cone-bearing) trees. Extending broadly in homogeneous stands, these needle-leaf softwood forests are better adapted to the shorter growing season. Common associations include fir stands with white birch or black spruce, and lichen-spruce woodlands, as well as Jack pine and birch-aspen stands. The boreal forest constitutes the largest reserve of wood fiber in Quebec. An ongoing reforestation program, launched by the government of Quebec in the 1980s, aims to protect this valuable resource by the planting of several million saplings each year.

Farther north, at the fringes of the high-latitude boreal forest, is the **taiga**. An extensive forest of softwood species, it is controlled by the subarctic climate and grows increasingly sparse as latitudes increase. Well-spaced clusters of trees—mainly black spruce, white birch, or tamarack—already stunted in growth, decrease in height to shrub-like forms and eventually give way to ground cover such as lichens and Arctic mosses. The tree line marks the northern limit of the taiga. Two factors—low average summer temperatures and lack of available water—limit the growth and reproduction of trees. The brief summer period melts only a shallow layer of soil on top of the solidly frozen permafrost.

The northernmost vegetation zone, the **tundra**, has been called a cold desert. Interspersed by bedrock outcrops and fields of shattered rocks, a thin carpet of grasses, mosses, lichens and flowering herbs clings tenuously to the soil. Widely scattered low shrubs of willow and birch manage to survive only in sheltered pockets. In the tundra, year-round moisture is scarce and summers are too short and cold to support the growth of trees. The ground is perennially frozen and impermeable, and this inadequate surface drainage creates the tundra's characteristic landscape of bogs, or "muskeg." During the few long summer days, the grassy tundra hastily completes its annual flowering cycle, spectacular in both color and intensity.

FAUNA

Considering the size of Quebec, the variety of animal life is relatively limited. Slightly more than 50 species of mammals, such as beaver, deer and bear (brown, black and polar); 350 bird species, of which 5 to 7 percent winter in the area; and 120 species of fish have been identified.

From south to north, animal diversity decreases, from 50 mammal species in the Ottawa River Valley to some 20 near the Ungava Peninsula. In southern Quebec, white-tailed deer and moose (Laurentians and Chic-Chocs) predominate, contributing to Quebec's reputation as a hunter's paradise. Indeed, Quebec offers 15 wildlife reserves abounding in popular game animals, such as moose, caribou, white-tailed deer and black bear. This area also contains harder-to-view species like cougar, coyote and bobcat.

Farther north, the taiga provides habitat to herds of **caribou**, such as the George River herd, which roams the area south of Ungava Bay and numbers 14,000 head (2014 census). Seven smaller herds are found along the transitional zone between taiga and tundra. The area is punctuated by lakes and waterways teeming with salmon, smelt, pike and trout. Fishermen come from around the world to fish Quebec's remarkable number of waterways, and among the most popular targets are the large-mouthed bass, walleye and pickerel. Among animal species indigenous to the rugged tundra are the arctic hare, fox and polar bear, as well as the gyrfalcon and snowy owl (Quebec's provincial bird) and the musk ox.

Many species of **marine mammals** travel up the St. Lawrence River on their migratory routes. They include the common seal as well as the beluga, humpback, blue, fin and minke **whales**. Whale watching is a popular attraction, especially in the Saguenay fjord and Côte-Nord regions, where the Saguenay-St.Lawrence Marine Park zone has fascinated scientists for decades. The confluence of the fresh water runoff coming through the Saguenay fjord empties into the salty St. Lawrence River, providing a dense food source for marine mammals. As whale populations remain threatened worldwide, Quebec's leadership in protecting this rare marine environment becomes more critical.

Birders abound throughout the province. Birds of prey include the red-tailed hawk, merlin, kestrel and great horned owl. Quebec is on the flyway of millions of migrating Canada and snow geese. Several areas on the St. Lawrence shores are renowned for birdwatching in spring and fall, led by **Cap Tourmente** east of Quebec City, and Baie-de-Febvre on the south shore of the St.Lawrence River between Montreal and Quebec City. Even ruby-throated hummingbird flocks can be seen, along with peregrine falcon groups, and many species of ducks. There's a **Snow Goose Festival** every October in Montmagny near Quebec City, where visitors ride a wagon to the flocks' resting areas and enjoy other activities, including tasting sessions. Double-crested cormorants may also be seen regularly throughout the lakes of the province, along with the distinctively Canadian sight and song of the great northern loon. The great blue heron, with its massive wingspan, has an island named after it near Montreal, and together with its cousin the night heron, makes for dramatic sightings during summer in the cities. The sandhill crane makes Quebec home during fair weather, as do the northern gannet, European herring gull, and the always popular Atlantic puffin.

Quebec may not have an enormous number of wildlife species, but because of its enthralling landscape, together with an ever-ready populace that likes to get outdoors and have fun, Quebec exhilarates and entertains anyone who is willing to visit and explore.

Whale watching, Tadoussac

Snow Geese at Cap Tourmente
© Luc-Antoine Couturier / Québec City Tourism

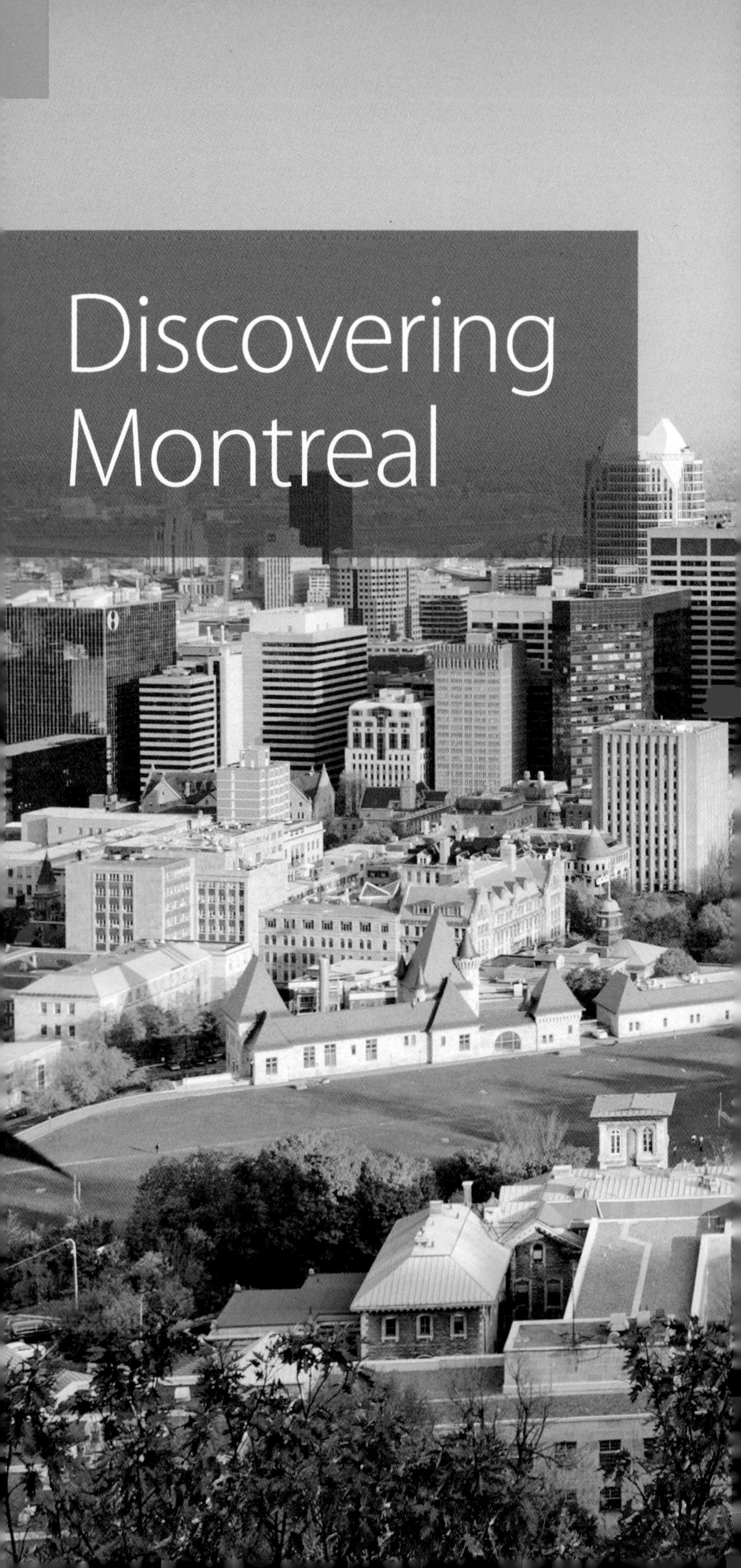

Discovering Montreal

Montreal skyline from Parc du Mont-Royal

© Jon Arnold / hemis.fr

Montreal

Basilique Notre-Dame

© SuperStock / age fotostock

Montreal and Surroundings

Few cities can match the multiple charms of Montreal, an historic island city dominated by a towering mountain preserve, surrounded by idyllic waterfront communities, and located just 90 minutes from Mont-Tremblant, a year-round outdoor playground. Home to the innovative Cirque du Soleil, and host to the largest jazz festival on earth (Festival International de Jazz de Montréal), the city's heady mix of visible history, vibrant culture, international cuisine, and playful nightlife make it one of the top destinations in Canada.

Highlights

1. **Place d'Armes**, site of lofty and important buildings (p119)
2. The grandeur and serenity of the **Basilique Notre-Dame** (p122)
3. New arts and entertainment district, the **Quartier des spectacles** (p143)
4. The **Jardin Botanique de Montréal**, considered one of the finest in the world (p162)
5. The wildlife haven and nature retreat of **Île Saint-Bernard** (p175)

Clean, safe and proud of its diversity, Montreal is the largest French-speaking community outside of Paris, and and the first UNESCO Design City in North America. An intimate city of distinct neighborhoods, such as the trendy Griffintown, it is also in the global spotlight as headquarters for 70 international organizations and the site of many global conferences world leaders. An historic city where cobblestone streets date to the early 1600s, it also has a progessive, contemporary outlook, as seen in its high-tech companies, and the vibrant new entertainment district, the Quartier des spectacles.

Culture and Family

Greater Montreal is home to nearly 4 million residents, mostly of French-Quebec origin, but with strong showings of the historic English community and successive waves of newcomers from around the world.

For visitors, Montreal's signature lifestyle is evident throughout, as fashion, music, art, cuisine, and family dominate in a metropolis once called "Canada's Cultural Capital."

Ville-Marie, or City of Mary as Montreal was originally called, sits on a heart-shaped island about 50km/31mi by 16km/9.9mi. Mount Royal dominates the cityscape, rising to a height of 233m/ 764 ft.

A glimpse of local life can be enjoyed at Mount Royal Park on any given weekend, no matter the season. There visitors will find

Jardin Botanique de Montréal

BIXI

www.bixi.com

© BIXI Montréal

This public bicycle sharing service combines the words bicycle and taxi.

For $5 for 24 hours, customers rent sturdy, multi-gear street bikes (with useful baskets), picking up and stopping off at any of 460 stands set up throughout the city core and beyond.

Currently available from Apr 15–Nov 15, service extends west to Verdun, north around the Metropolitan Expressway (Highway 40), and east past Parc Maisonneuve at the Olympic Complex, a massive area that includes plenty of urban bike paths, and many sites for travelers.

Customers can also purchase tickets for longer periods of use, such as $12 for three full days, or $85 for a full year subscription. Some promotions are also available for BIXI users, such as a discount at CommunAuto, the public car-share company.

Originally created by the city as a public system, BIXI is now a private company, but the original municipal model has spread to other cities including Québec City, Toronto, Ottawa/Gatineau, New York, Boston, Minneapolis, Washington, and London, England, with more expected.

© BIXI Montréal

Montreal and Surroundings

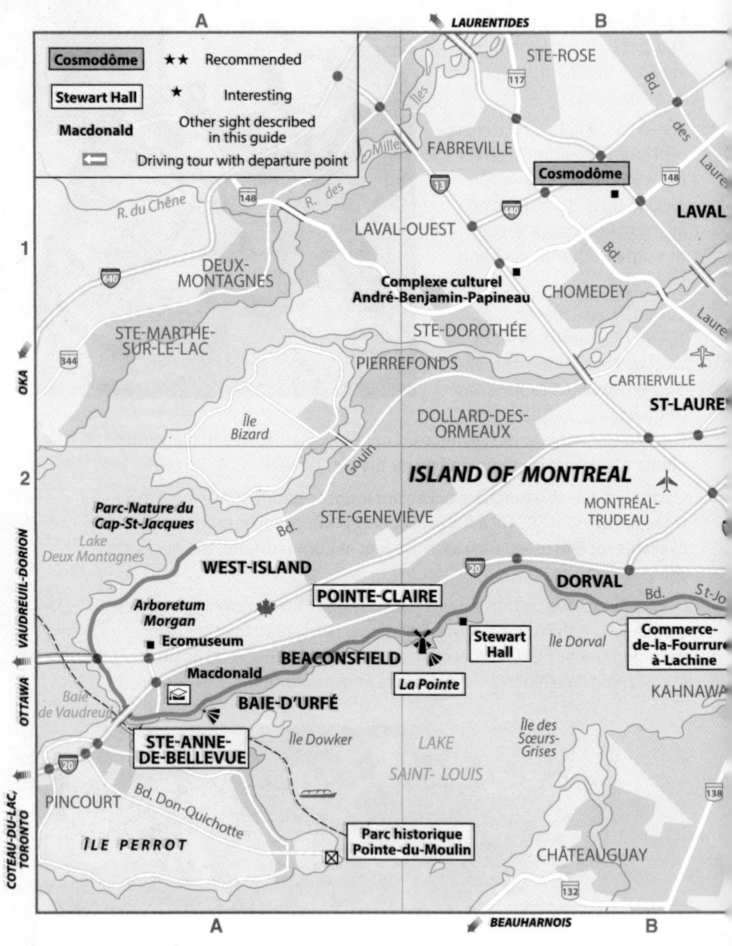

families, couples, and friends walking to the lookouts, cycling, and enjoying the abundant green space. Group picnics abound in fair weather; and in winter Nordic skiing, tobogganing, and skating at Beaver Lake are the favorite pastimes. It's infectious, as everyone is welcomed into the extended outdoor conviviality à la québeçois.

Industry and Tourism

During the four decades when the threat of separation from Canada dominated the political scene, many businesses fled to other cities across North America, but those times are now a distant memory. Montreal's nine universities and 12 junior colleges are producing students who are clearly focused on a global agenda, and are savvy in the ways of technology, performing arts, and business leadership.

Because of these scholarly standards, led by McGill University, Université de Montréal, Concordia University, and Université du Québec à Montréal, international companies are eager to set up shop in the city. Major entertainment companies such as WB Games and THQ Inc. have opened production studios to create video games, while

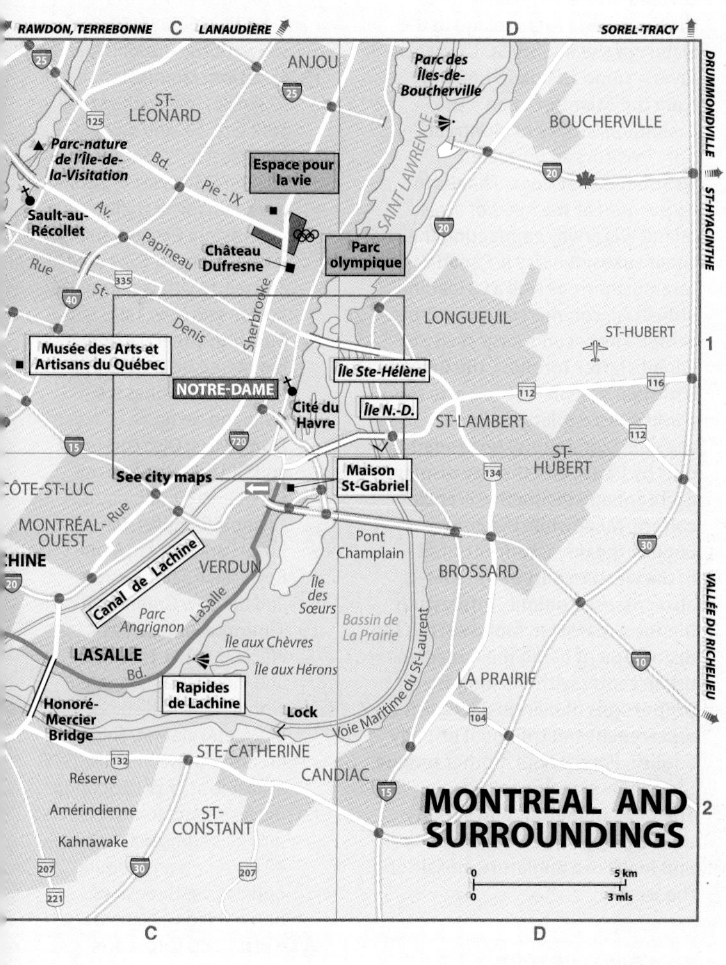

pharmaceutical, aerospace, and apparel companies continue to expand, as do transportation, telecommunications, and tourism firms.

The Formula 1 Grand-Prix has returned to the city, and so has the royalty, with Prince William and Kate Middleton touring the city, and taking cooking classes at the **Institut de tourisme et d'hotellerie du Québec**.

Bridges and Discoveries

A pleasant byproduct of Montreal's renaissance is the rich cornucopia of delights found across any bridge off the island. Visitors will be impressed by the extensive entertainment options awaiting them within an hour's drive of downtown.

From Laval's Cosmodôme Space Science Centre, to apple-picking at Saint-Joseph-du-Lac, Rigaud's sugar shacks, Arbraska zip-line forest adventures, and Île Saint-Bernard, featuring the Marguerite D'Youville Wildlife Refuge, a rich bounty of discoveries awaits travelers and locals alike. This rich spirit of discovery—a heritage that is many centuries old—is what sets Montreal apart from all other cities.

Montreal★★★

Located on the largest island of the Hochelaga Archipelago in the waters of the mighty St. Lawrence River – some 1,600km/1,000mi from the Atlantic Ocean – the cosmopolitan city of Montreal offers visitors an unrivaled wealth of attractions. Thanks to its position at the head of a vast inland waterway connecting the Great Lakes, the city is Canada's foremost port as well as a leading industrial, commercial and cultural center. The second-largest city in Canada (after Toronto), the Greater Montreal Region (GMR) is also the world's second-largest French-speaking community (exceeded only by Paris), and the city displays a vibrant and distinctive French culture. Meanwhile the city's English speakers, concentrated in the western part of the Island, also possess a unique, interesting, blended character. Montreal has the distinction of being the Canadian urban center with the highest proportions of bilingual (English and French) and trilingual (usually English, French, and mother tongue of an immigrant) speakers. The city's numerous and varied ethnic groups often make it look and feel like a miniature mosaic of the world.

- **Population:** 3.9 million.
- **Info:** 514-873-2015 & 1-877-266-5687. www.tourisme-montreal.org.
- **Location:** Montreal is 533km/331mi north of New York City, 509km/316mi northeast of Toronto and 200km/124mi east of Ottawa. It is a hub for air traffic into Eastern Canada, and is well-connected, by road and rail, to Ottawa, Toronto, Boston and New York.
- **Parking:** Street parking is metered, so watch for signs— fines are swift and costly.
- **Don't Miss:** Old Montreal and Old Port, the Lachine Canal-area cycling paths, Olympic Complex, Mount Royal Park, Plateau Mont-Royal, Blvd Saint-Laurent and the new Griffintown.
- **Timing:** Montreal has efficient public transit, and most attractions are within walking distance of a Metro station. The Montreal Museums Pass ($75) available at 17 participating museums and tourist centers, provides admission to nearly 40 museums and cultural outlets over three days, plus guided walking tours.
- **Kids:** TOHU (circus arts center), Théatre Maison (children's live theater in French), Insectarium, new Planetarium, Montreal Science Center (IMAX cinema) at the Old Port, La Ronde, and Parc Jean-Drapeau with its beach and water sports. Calèche rides in Old Montreal in summer and in winter on Mount Royal, Cosmodome Space Camp, and the Exporail Canadian Railway Museum.

A BIT OF HISTORY

Montreal Island was inhabited by Mohawks of the Iroquois nation long before Europeans set foot in North America. In 1535, **Jacques Cartier** landed on the island while searching for gold and a route to the Orient, and encountered the Mohawk village of **Hochelaga** at the foot of Mount Royal. Legend has it that Cartier, having climbed the mountain, was so taken by the view that he exclaimed "It's a royal mountain!" (*C'est un mont réal!*) In a more believable story, and according respected historian Gustave

Lanctot, Montreal was named by Cartier in honor of Cardinal de Medici, bishop of the Sicilian town of Monreale.
When **Samuel de Champlain**, the "Father of New France," sailed up the river from his newly established settlement of Kebec (Quebec City) in 1611, Hochelaga had ceased to exist. Champlain considered founding a new community on Île Sainte-Hélène, but his project never materialized.

The City of Mary – The 17C was a period of zealous evangelization on the island, as the Roman Catholic Church, hoping to regain the ground lost during the Protestant Reformation, viewed colonization as a means of spreading the faith. During this period, two Frenchmen decided to establish a mission on Montreal Island: **Jérôme Le Royer de la Dauversière** and **Jean-Jacques Olier**. The latter had founded the Sulpician Order in Paris in 1641. They raised money and chose **Paul de Chomedey, Sieur de Maisonneuve** to lead their mission, which they called **Ville-Marie** (City of Mary).
Maisonneuve and about 40 companions crossed the Atlantic in 1641, and after wintering in Quebec City, they arrived on the island in May 1642. Despite their high-minded zeal, the Catholic missionaries inevitably came into conflict with the peoples they had hoped to convert. The hostilities continued until peace with the Iroquois was established by an historic treaty, the Grande paix de *Montréal*, in 1701.

18C – After the failure of evangelization, Ville-Marie (soon renamed Montreal) began to grow as a center of the fur trade. Explorers set off across the Great Lakes and their attendant waterways, returning loaded with pelts. The furs were prized in Europe, where they were transformed into luxurious apparel, mainly hats. The fur trade became Montreal's principal commercial activity, one strong enough to spawn other businesses and farms all over the island. By the time of the **British Conquest**, the city of Montreal was firmly established. After the surrender of the French in Quebec City in 1759, British troops commanded by Gen. Jeffery Amherst marched on Montreal. In 1760 Chevalier de Lévis prepared a gallant defense of the city, but Montreal's governor, Marquis de Vaudreuil, ordered him to surrender without a fight.
Following the Conquest of Canada, most of the French nobility returned

A City of Islands and Rivers

Lying at the confluence of the Ottawa and St. Lawrence rivers, the island of Montreal measures 50km/31mi in length and 17km/10.5mi at its widest point. The island is connected to the mainland by a tunnel and fifteen road bridges, six of which span the St. Lawrence. Since 2006, the City of Montreal has been divided into boroughs, occupying most of Montreal Island, which is dominated by a 233m/764ft hill, known as **Mount Royal**. Nicknamed "the Mountain," Mount Royal is one of the Monteregian Hills, a series of eight peaks in the St. Lawrence Valley.

The sun rises in the . . . south?

Travelers accustomed to determining their geographical orientation by the position of the sun will have to make an adjustment in Montreal. The St. Lawrence River is considered to flow from west to east, a correct assumption for the most part. However, as it approaches the downtown area, the river makes an abrupt northward swing, and thus flows almost due north as it passes the city. Montreal streets at right angles to the St. Lawrence are thereby considered to be oriented north–south (when actually they extend east–west), and streets parallel to the river are designated east–west, though in reality they run north–south. "Québec ça faire" as they say: "that's how it's done in Québec."

Fresco depicting the history of Quebec, Plateau Mont-Royal district

to France. The first English-speaking people to settle in the city were Scots, attracted by the fur trade.

In 1775–76, Montreal was again occupied. American troops under General Richard Montgomery invaded the city in an attempt to persuade Montrealers to join the thirteen colonies in revolt against the British Crown. During the seven-month occupation, many leading Americans, including **Benjamin Franklin**, visited Montreal.

Early in 1776, the occupying troops departed for Quebec City, where they were defeated by the British Army. After the American Revolution, an influx of Loyalists from the US swelled Montreal's anglophone population.

19C – The fur trade in Montreal reached its heyday in the late 18C and early 19C. Trading posts, where the local indigenous population brought furs to exchange for a wide range of goods, were established all over Canada. The furs were subsequently transported to Montreal by canoe. The **North West Company**, a partnership between some of the great figures in Montreal history, including Fraser, Frobisher, Mackenzie, McGill, McGillivray, McTavish, and Thompson, was created in 1783. These men and others founded the **Beaver Club**, an association of important, prosperous traders.

In 1821, the merger of the North West Company with its more successful rival, the **Hudson's Bay Company (HBC)**, marked the decline of Montreal's dominance in the fur trade, as the HBC exported its furs to Europe via Hudson Bay, bypassing Montreal. Fortunes had nonetheless been made in Montreal, and the profits were invested in other sectors of activity as the 19C progressed.

Even though Montreal did not participate in the American Revolution, the city and its region were the center of revolts against British rule in 1837 and 1838. The colony was administered by a Crown-appointed governor and his council. The assembly elected by the Canadian people lacked the power to enforce its decisions. Many leading French-Canadians, among them **Louis-Joseph Papineau** and **George-Étienne Cartier**, raised their voices in protest. The motivations behind the **Rébellion des Patriotes** were not lost on the vastly outnumbered British, who subsequently granted full representative government to French Canada. After several years of exile, Papineau briefly returned to politics before retiring to Montebello; Cartier went on to become a great Quebec politician and one of the Fathers of Canadian Confederation (1867).

An Expanding Economy – About 1820, Montreal's economy experienced a conversion to commerce and import-export activities. The anglophone business community established St. James Street (today renamed rue Saint-Jacques) as a financial center, and founded the Bank of Montreal (1817) and the Board of Trade (1822), institutions whose investment activities promoted development in the city and throughout Quebec and Canada. Today, rue Saint-Jacques is home to the Montreal Stock Exchange as well as the city's dominant financial and banking institutions.

After 1815 the anglophone community's economy was fueled by additional British immigrants, coming mainly from Ireland. In the 1860s Montreal experienced an influx of rural French-Canadians, who restored its francophone character. In about 1840, the enlargement of the **Lachine Canal**, which had enabled vessels to circumvent the Lachine rapids since its completion in 1824, spurred further industrialization. A new system of canals, on the St. Lawrence River as far as the Great Lakes and on the Richelieu River as far as New York via Lake Champlain and the Hudson River, opened new commercial routes, which were quickly supplemented by railroad lines. The first short-line railroad (1836) linked La Prairie to Saint-Jean-sur-Richelieu.

Montreal rapidly became the headquarters of financing, construction, employment, and maintenance for the rail system. The opening of the Victoria Bridge in 1860 brought rail traffic across the river, establishing a continuous, north–south railroad link between Montreal and Vermont. It was the longest bridge in the world at the time, and the first to cross the formidable St. Lawrence River. Montreal's **port** grew with the construction, in the 1880s, of the Canadian Pacific railway linking the nation's Atlantic and Pacific coasts. Development of the Prairie provinces created new markets for Montreal: Inland grain made its way by rail to the port's storage silos before being exported across the Atlantic, and products manufactured in the city were transported west in wagons.

20C – The period of growth that followed World War I came to a halt during the Great Depression. Lack of funds led to widespread unemployment, and the skeletal outlines of unfinished projects marked the cityscape. The post-World War II years brought renewed prosperity and dynamism to the city. Under the leadership of Mayor Jean Drapeau, the downtown and eastern areas of Montreal underwent a major modernization, while the city hosted the **Expo '67** World's Fair, which marked the centennial of Canada's Confederation, and in 1976, the **Summer Olympic Games**.

During the 1970s, francophone unrest caused many companies to move their headquarters to Toronto, and Montreal was relegated to the status of second-largest metropolis in Canada. City fathers responded by securing the 1976 Summer Olympic games, and decided to capitalize on the games by selecting the Hochelaga-Maisonneuve District in which to build the Olympic Park Complex, rejuvenating the east-end working-class neighborhood in the process.

Montreal continues to evolve, develop, and attract new business investment from abroad. One unusual aspect of this island-city is the sprinkling of business zones throughout all neighborhoods, resulting in a unique mix of "quartiers" and a boost in tax revenues.

The steady influx of new residents from all corners of the world continues to enrich the cultural weave of a vibrant metropolis. Montreal is also an adaptable city; Vieux-Montreal's cobblestone streets, waterfront perch and heritage architecture often act as doubles for European and American locations in feature film productions. It is a medium-sized metropolis built on a human scale, compared to many of its North American contemporaries: Plateau Mont-Royal, for example, has one of the highest concentration of residents in North America who do not

GETTING THERE

BY AIR – Montréal-Pierre Elliott Trudeau International Airport in Dorval: 22km/13.6mi *(approximately 30min)* west of downtown by Service 747 Express bus *($10 in coins only)* or taxi *($40)*; free shuttle minibuses to Dorval hotels. Information: *℘514-394-7377 and 1-800-465-1213 or www.admtl.com.*

BY TRAIN – VIA Rail Canada Central Station (Gare centrale): *895 rue de la Gauchetière Ouest* (Bonaventure). *Information & reservations: ℘1-888-842-7245 or www.viarail.ca.*

BY BUS – Montreal Bus Central Station (Orléans Express, Greyhound, Vermont Transit, etc.): *505 Blvd de Maisonneuve Est* (Berri-UQAM). *Information: ℘1-888-999-3977 or 514-842-2281 or www.orleans express.com and www.greyhound.ca.*

GETTING AROUND

Métro & Bus – Local métro and bus service provided by Société de Transport de Montréal (STM) *(℘514-786-4636; www.stm.info).* The Métro generally operates from 5:30am–12:30am. Each metro line is designated by a number and a color; the direction is indicated by the name of the station at the end of the line in that direction. Métro and bus tickets (they are interchangeable) are available at Métro stations and some convenience stores (dépanneurs), and may be purchased individually *($3.25)*, or in booklets *(lisière)* of six *($14.25)*, or in tourist passes *($10/24 hours or $18 for three consecutive days)*.

Car Rental – Major rental companies are located at the airport, at Central Station (train), and throughout the city: Avis (Namur) *℘514-387-2847*; Budget (Gare Centrale / Central Station Bonaventure) *℘514-866-7675*; Discount (2250 Guy St. Guy) *℘514-798-7235;* Hertz (1475 Aylmer St.) *℘514-842-8537*; and Thrifty (1155 Guy St. Guy) *℘514-989-7100.*

Taxis – **Good to know:** Montreal taxi fares include all taxes, are regulated, and the fare must be visible on the meter for customer to see. It's $40 from central downtown to the airport. Co-op *℘514-725-9885*; Pontiac *℘514-931-6666* (providing tours). The deluxe Allante Limousine is more expensive *℘514-643-0262.*

VISITOR INFORMATION

Tourist Information – Centre Infotouriste de Montréal (part of Tourisme Québec): *1255 rue Peel* (Peel). *Hours might vary. Apr 1–Jun 20 and Sep 1–Oct 9, 9am–6pm, Jun 21–Aug 31 9am–7pm, Nov 1–Mar 31 9am-5pm. ℘514-873-2015 & 1-877-266-5687. www.tourisme-montreal.org.*

Accommodations – Staff at Infotouriste office will make hotel reservations for you, in person or on the phone. *For specific listings of hotels, see Addresses.*

Montreal Daily Newspapers – English: *The Gazette.* French: *Le Journal de Montréal, Le Devoir, La Presse.* Each has e-editions for web, tablets and phones.

Post Office – Postal facilities are located in pharmacies throughout the city; look for the red *Canada Post* sign. Full-service post office at 800 Blvd René Lévesque, corner of rue Université (Bonaventure or Peel) *℘514-395-4909 or 1-866-607-6301. www.canadapost.ca.*

CURRENCY EXCHANGE OFFICES

Montréal-Pierre Elliott Trudeau International Airport – ICE Currency Exchange (counters in Arrivals & Departures buildings, open daily) *℘514-394-7377.* Calforex, 1230 rue Peel (Peel) ℘514-392-9100 (across from the main Infotouriste office).

USEFUL NUMBERS

Police–Ambulance–Fire (emergency calls only): *℘911*
Montreal Telephone Area Code: *℘514*
Directory Assistance *℘411*
Tourisme Québec/Montréal: *℘514-873-2015*
Canadian Automobile Association (**CAA/AAA**) *℘514-861-7575*
Road conditions *℘1-888-355-0511* or dial 611 and follow prompts in French.
Weather (24hr/day) *℘514-283-4006*

Artworks Turn 'Le Métro' into an Attraction

Inaugurated in 1966 in time for Expo '67, the four lines of the Métro now extend over 90km/50mi with some 70 stations. It was designed according to the Parisian Métro "tire on rail" technology and is completely underground to remain undisturbed by winter storms. In places the tunnel is close to the surface, but sinks to a maximum of 55m/180ft as it passes under the St. Lawrence River to Longueuil. The decor of each metro station was conceived by a different architect, in relation to its surroundings, and enhanced by so many works of art that "Le Métro" is, in itself, a tourist attraction. Some of the more noteworthy stations in the system include Place-des-Arts, Peel, Place-Saint-Henri, Outremont, Acadie, du Collège and de la Concorde. Some stations, like McGill, Berri-UQAM, and Bonaventure, open to bustling subterranean malls with shops and food courts connecting to hotels, cinemas and theaters.

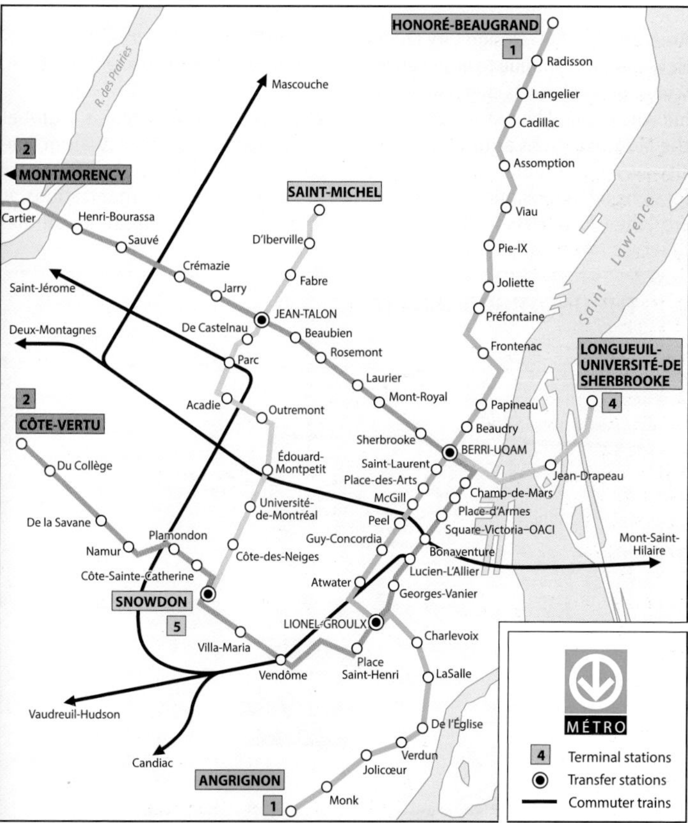

own an automobile. Visitors will see the home-grown BIXI bike rental facilities throughout the city, and the maze of one-way streets inspires travelers to breathe in the creativity of this imaginative city from the seat of a rental bike, or by walking its neighborhoods.

The artistic milieu extends into all areas of the Montreal lifestyle, confirmed by the city being chosen as the first North

The Underground City (Ville Souterraine)

Temperatures in Montreal change dramatically from season to season, but pedestrians can move throughout most of the downtown shopping district without undue exposure via the "the underground city." Montreal's underground walking city began in the 1960s with the construction of the landmark skyscraper, **Place Ville-Marie**. Remarkable for the spaciousness of its corridors and for its esthetically "landscaped" atmosphere, the system connects the principal downtown hotels and office buildings; major department stores; hundreds of boutiques; several cinemas, including an IMAX theater; hundreds of restaurants, bistros, and cafés; Central Station (trains); the bus terminal; the city's major cultural center, **Place des Arts**; and two major convention centers, **Place Bonaventure** and **Palais des Congrès**, plus the new Montreal Symphony Hall. *See the map below which helps to simplify the route, highlighting relevant sights along the way.*

American UNESCO Design City (2006). New eateries continue to arrive on the scene, joining famous chef Daniel Boulud who opened his Maison Boulud in the Montreal Ritz-Carlton Hotel. The city even has a sound of its own, and for some this is romantic crooner Leonard Cohen, for others the contemporary Arcade Fire band, jazz icon Oscar Peterson, or even recording star Celine Dion.

21C – Modern Montreal is a global city prized for its intellectualism, joie de vivre and creativity. Headquarters to 70 international organizations, it also hosts C2 Montréal, an annual

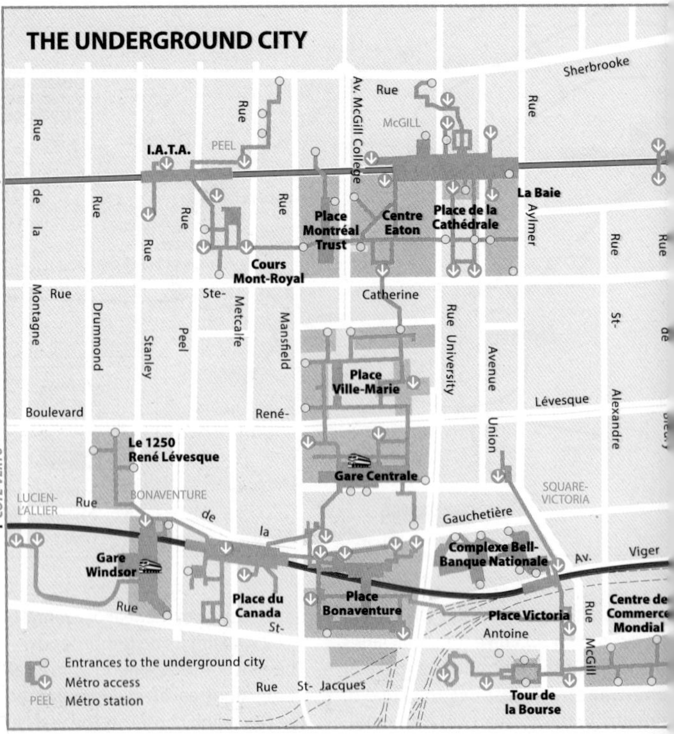

THE UNDERGROUND CITY

Entrances to the underground city
Métro access
PEEL Métro station

three-day business event that brings together influential speakers from various areas of modern culture. More traditional, but equally recognized, is the annual Conference of Montreal of the International Economic Forum of The Americas, which hosts world leaders in a multiday think tank that addresses key global issues. The Montréal Fashion and Design Festival reflects the city's passion for fashion: it is one of the top centers for apparel manufacturing in North America, and has a long-standing reputation for being a famously fashionable city.

The environment is in the forefront at Space For Life, Canada's largest natural science museum, which is made up of the Rio Tinto Alcan Montreal Planetarium, Biodôme, Insectarium and Botanical Garden, creating a vast and enjoyable resource near Olympic Park.

Culture thrives; Montreal is home to almost 150 theater companies, including the National Theatre School of Canada, and more than 100 professional dance companies, including Les Grands Ballets Canadiens de Montréal. They are joined by about 500 film and TV related companies, 71 museums that attract nearly 6.2 million visitors annually, and 100 arts, cuisine and performance festivals, including the ultra-cool MuralFestival, which showcases street art and graffiti on a section of Blvd Saint-Laurent every year in June.

WALKING TOURS

1 OLD MONTREAL★★★ TO THE CITÉ MULTIMÉDIA

See Central Montreal map, pp120–121.

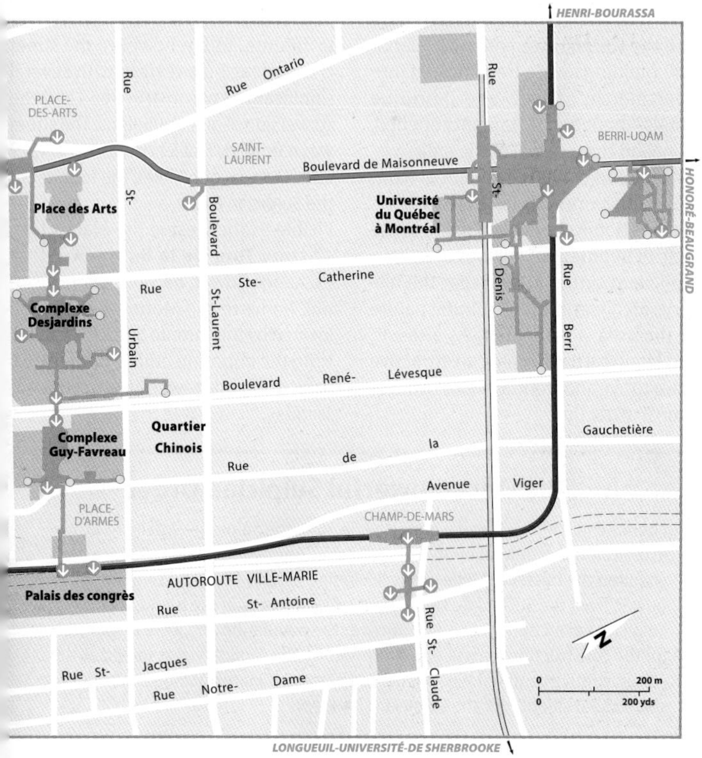

This walking tour encompasses four major areas—Old Montreal, Vieux-Port, Place d'Youville and Cité Multmédia. You could choose to break up the walk and spend a morning or an afternoon in each region.

OLD MONTREAL

Square-*Victoria.*

The term "Old Montreal" refers to the section of the city formerly surrounded by fortifications. The imposing stone walls (5m/18ft high and 1m/3ft thick) were built early in the 18C and removed a century later. They contained the area today bounded by rue McGill to the west, rue Berri to the east, rue de la Commune beside the river to the south and a line between rues Saint-Jacques and Saint-Antoine to the north.

During the 18C and 19C, the city gradually expanded beyond the old walls. Montrealers built their houses farther from the river, and businesses were established in what became the downtown area. Warehouses sprang up where homes and gardens had previously flourished and the older Montreal fell into decline. By the 1960s, however, interest in Old Montreal revived. The surviving 18C homes were renovated and the warehouses and more elaborate buildings were transformed into apartments, offices, and boutique hotels. Shops and restaurants opened, signaling the renewal of the area.

Since the mid 1990s, residential (condos) and commercial investments (several hotels) have been made to the tune of hundreds of millions of dollars, while authorities ensure that the historic, architectural and cultural nature of the area is respected. As a result, Old Montreal has become an attractive place to live and work, as well as a major tourist attraction.

Good to know – *Horse-drawn carriages (calèches) depart from Rue Notre-Dame at Place d'Armes, and rue de la Commune at Place Jacques-Cartier, enabling visitors to discover Old Montreal in the manner of bygone eras.*

Rue Saint-Jacques★

Once the "Wall Street of Canada," rue Saint-Jacques is lined with a stately ensemble of 19C and early 20C stone buildings and still retains much of its former grandeur. Note in particular the **Canada Life Building** (*no. 275*), Montreal's first steel-framework skyscraper (1895), and the **Banque de Commerce Impériale (CIBC)**, where HMS Titanic tickets were sold when it housed the White Star Line, and whose façade is adorned with fluted Corinthian columns. The former bank, which now is the Théâtre St-James reception hall, features a monumental interior **banking hall.** The decline of rue Saint-Jacques was accelerated during the mid-1970s when several major financial institutions moved their headquarters to the downtown area or to Toronto. Today, however, the street is experiencing a revival, with several significant new constructions and the conversion of older buildings. The street was named by Dollier de Casson in 1672 after Jean-Jacques Olier, the founder of the Sulpician Order.

Visible to the west is the black glass, 47-story **Tour de la Bourse★** (Stock Exchange Tower, *no. 800 Square Victoria*), home to the Montréal Exchange (owned by the Toronto Stock Exchange). Note the imposing edifice of the Royal Bank of Canada tower, at 360 rue Saint-Jacques.

The Once-Powerful Sulpician Order

Founded in Paris by Jean-Jacques Olier in 1641, the Sulpician Order was firmly established in Montreal by 1657. In 1663 the Compagnie de Saint-Sulpice acquired the mission of Ville-Marie, including its land titles and seigneurial power, from the Société de Notre-Dame. As seigneurs of the island, the Sulpicians exercised great authority over the population and were responsible for the construction of Basilique Notre-Dame. The seminary also served as the administrative center of Ville-Marie. Today the seminary building continues to serve as a residence for the Sulpicians (*see p124*).

Banque Royale du Canada★ (Royal Bank Building)

360 rue Saint-Jacques. Open year-round Mon–Fri 10am–4pm. Closed major holidays. ♿ ✆514-845-5261.

The Royal Bank Building (1928) was the first structure erected in Montreal after a 1924 modification of zoning regulations, which allowed buildings of more than 10 storeys on the condition that setbacks be incorporated into their designs. Inspired by the "Setback Law" of New York, the new regulation left more latitude to architects. The 23-story Royal Bank Building was, at the time, the tallest in the British Empire. The bottom tier—of Renaissance Revival design—is a severe composition influenced by the Teatro San Carlo in Naples. The entire tower, whose traditional roof has long dominated the skyline of Montreal's financial district, is best viewed from the opposite side of rue Saint-Jacques. The bank's headquarters were located here until the 1962 completion of the Royal Bank of Canada Tower at Place Ville-Marie, and the ground floor of the building served as a Royal Bank branch until 2012.

Place d'Armes

© Philippe Renault / hemis.fr

Tribute to an Artist

Ⓜ *Square-Victoria.* Just west of the new wing of the Montreal Convention Centre (Palais des Congrès), between Ave. Viger and rue Saint-Antoine, this small square pays tribute to a courageous Quebec artist, Jean-Paul Riopelle (1923–2002), with one of his sculptures, *La Joute.* It is circled at night with fire, showing Riopelle's vision of life.

Interior

The bronze main entry doors open onto a vast vestibule adorned with a coffered, richly ornamented, vaulted ceiling. A blue, pink, and gold color scheme enlivens the ground floor, from which four arched doorways give access to the wings and elevators. A magnificent marble staircase leads to the immense **banking hall**, which is 45m/148ft long, 14m/46ft wide and 14m/46ft tall.

▶ Walk eastward on rue Saint-Jacques. Turn right on rue Saint-Jean.

DHC/ART – Fondation pour l'Art contemporain

451 & 465 rue Saint-Jean. Open Wed–Fri noon–7pm, Sat–Sun 11am–6pm. No charge. ✆514-849-3742, 1-888-934-2278. www.dhc-art.org.

Inaugurated in 2007, the mandate for this set of spaces is the promotion of visual arts. Photography, video, installations and films invite the visitor to enter into the universe of the artists.

▶ Return to rue Saint-Jacques and continue walking east.

Place d'Armes★

As superior of the Sulpician Order (see panel, opposite) in 1670, Dollier de Casson devised a city plan for Montreal, outlining new streets north of rue Saint-Paul and a large open square in the center, later to become the site of the Notre Dame Basilica. According to

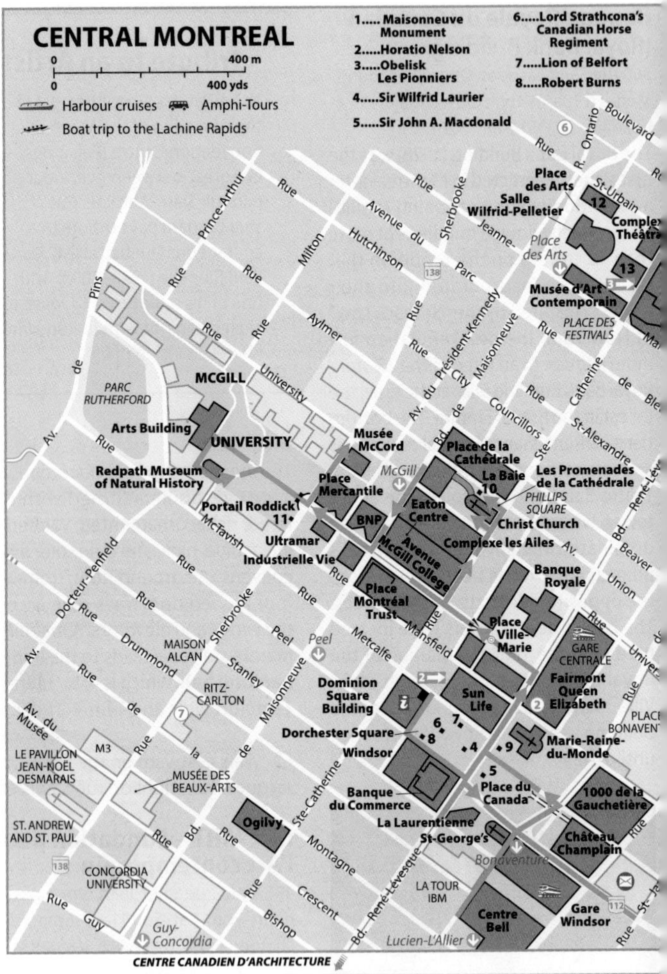

CENTRAL MONTREAL

0 400 m
0 400 yds

Harbour cruises · Amphi-Tours
Boat trip to the Lachine Rapids

1.....Maisonneuve Monument
2.....Horatio Nelson
3.....Obelisk Les Pionniers
4.....Sir Wilfrid Laurier
5.....Sir John A. Macdonald
6.....Lord Strathcona's Canadian Horse Regiment
7.....Lion of Belfort
8.....Robert Burns

CENTRE CANADIEN D'ARCHITECTURE

WHERE TO STAY

- Hôtel ALT ①
- Fairmont Le Reine Elizabeth ②
- Hostellerie Pierre du Calvet ③
- Nelligan (Hôtel) ④
- Place d'Armes (Hôtel) ⑤
- Résidences Universitaires UQAM ⑥
- Ritz-Carlton Montréal ⑦

legend, Casson's central square occupied the site of the 1644 battle during which the founder of Montreal, Paul de Chomedey, Sieur de Maisonneuve (1612–76), killed the local Indian chief, causing 200 of the chief's followers to flee the settlement. Place d'Armes, as the square has been called since 1723, traditionally served as drill grounds where troops presented arms to the sovereign or his representative, in this case, the Messieurs de Saint-Sulpice, seigneurs of the island.

In 1775–76, during the American occupation, vandals trashed the bust of George III, which stood at the center of the square. Rediscovered in an old well on the site, the bust is now part of

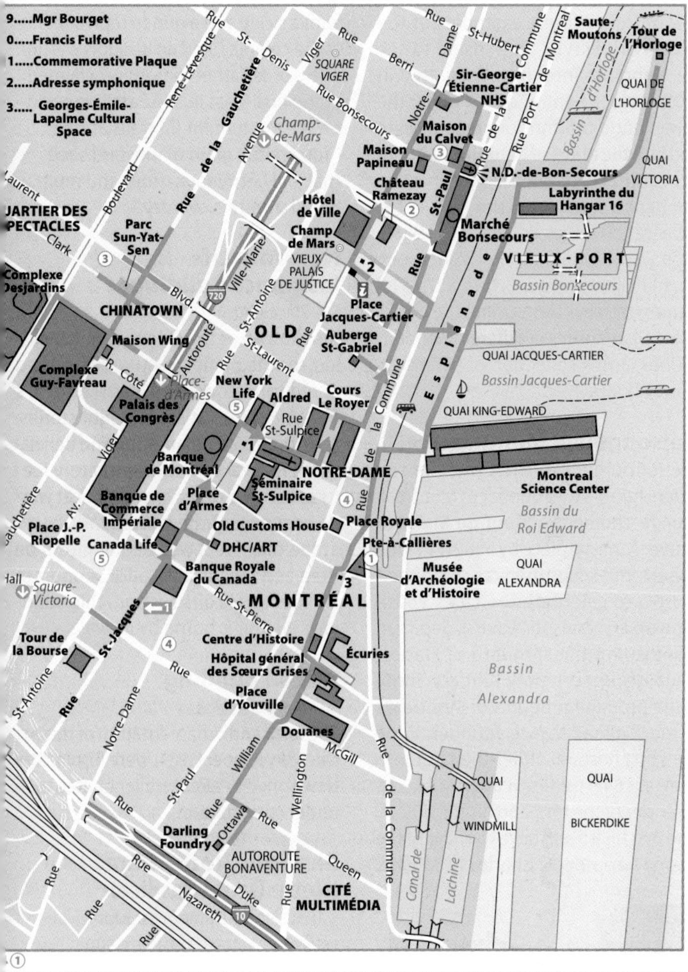

9.....Mgr Bourget
0.....Francis Fulford
1.....Commemorative Plaque
2.....Adresse symphonique
3..... Georges-Émile-Lapalme Cultural Space

WHERE TO EAT

Arrivage (L')..... ①
Club Chasse et Pêche (Le)..... ②
Cafe Saigon..... ③
Tapas24..... ④
Toqué!..... ⑤

the collection of the McCord Museum. In 1832 the square was the site of an electoral riot against the Tories, led by the legendary Patriot **Jos Montferrand**, who is immortalized in the songs of Gilles Vigneault.

Today, Place d'Armes is home to some of the most prestigious buildings in the city.

Banque de Montréal★ (Bank of Montreal)

119 rue Saint-Jacques.

Dominating the north side of the vast square, Montreal's main branch of Canada's oldest bank presents an imposing façade, evoking the Pantheon in Rome. Along with the Bonsecours market further east, the edifice (1847) is one

of Montreal's finest examples of the Neoclassical style. Step inside to see the elaborate interior redecorated in 1905. From the entrance hall under the dome, huge columns of green granite lead into the massive **banking hall** with its beautiful coffered ceiling.
The bank's small **museum** (turn left at entrance and go through revolving doors; open year-round Mon–Fri 10am–4pm; closed major holidays; ✆514-877-6810) features displays showcasing the bank's history, banknotes of different denominations, and a collection of whimsical money boxes.

Maisonneuve Monument★(1)

The monument in the center of the square honors the founder of Montreal, Paul de Chomedey, **Sieur de Maisonneuve**. A masterpiece by Louis-Philippe Hébert, the sculpture was completed in 1895 to celebrate the city's 250th anniversary. Maisonneuve is depicted brandishing the standard of France, while grouped below him are some of the prominent figures of Montreal's history: Jeanne Mance, founder of the city's first hospital, Hôtel-Dieu de Montréal, in 1645; General Lambert Closse, defender of the fort, and his dog Pilote, who first heard and gave warning of the enemy's approach; Charles Le Moyne, with a sickle and a gun to represent life in the colonies; and an Iroquois warrior. The words Father Vimont proclaimed at the first Mass in 1642 are engraved on the monument (in translation): "You are the grain of mustard seed that will germinate, grow, and multiply all over this country."

Banque de Montréal
© Philippe Renault / hemis.fr

New York Life Insurance Building

511 Place d'Armes.
Also known as the Quebec Bank Building, the magnetic structure is sheathed in red sandstone, and was Montreal's first skyscraper at a lofty eight stories. A synthesis of Romanesque and Renaissance Revival styles, the structure features corner towers, arched-lancet windows and rough-hewn stone. Although at the time steel was beginning to be used as a means of interior support in architectural construction, this building's weight is borne by its walls.

Aldred Building

507 Place d'Armes.
The form and ornamentation of this Art Deco skyscraper (1931) were inspired by New York City's Rockefeller Center, then under construction.

Basilique Notre-Dame★★★ (Notre Dame Basilica)

110 rue Notre-Dame West. Open year-round Mon–Fri 8am–4:30pm, Sat 8am–4pm, Sun 12:30–4pm (also Jun 24–Sept 7 Tue–Fri 8am–7pm, Sat 8am–4pm, 6pm–7pm) $5 (including 20min guided tour). Mass Sat 5pm. ♿ ✆514-842-2925. www.basiliquenddm.org.
The twin towers of Montreal's most famous religious edifice rise over 69m/226ft on the southern edge of Place d'Armes. At the time of the basilica's construction, they dominated the entire city but have since been overshadowed by the taller structures housing Montreal's financial institutions.
Rulers of Montreal Island, the **Sulpician** seigneurs long opposed the division of their territory into small parishes administered by the bishop of Quebec. To impede such a division, and a lessening

© Juliane Martini / MICHELIN
Basilique Notre-Dame

of their power, the Sulpicians decided to erect this church, large enough to accommodate the entire community at worship (seating capacity of 2,800). Despite the Sulpicians' efforts, the Diocese of Montreal was established in 1830 and the island subsequently divided into parishes.

The basilica, Quebec's first major building in the Gothic Revival style, was designed by James O'Donnell (1774–1829), an Irish architect from New York, who supervised its construction from 1824 through 1829. A Catholic convert, O'Donnell is buried in the basilica's basement crypt. John Ostell finished the towers in 1843 according to the original plans. Lack of funds halted progress on the interior until after 1870, when it was finally completed under the direction of Victor Bourgeau.

Notre-Dame was Montreal's first large-scale limestone edifice. Its construction required the opening of new quarries (Griffintown and Eastern Townships), and stonecutters had to be hired and trained to work the stone, thus leading to its widespread application as a sheathing material. The three Baccirini statues adorning the façade were purchased in Italy and represent the Virgin Mary, St. Joseph and St. John the Baptist. The east tower, named Temperance, contains a ten-bell carillon (set of bells), while the west tower, known as Perseverance, houses "Jean-Baptiste," a magnificent, 10,900kg/24,030lb brass bell, cast in London and rung only on special occasions.

Interior

The church's central nave is flanked by two side aisles surmounted by deep-set double galleries. Without deviating from this basic plan, Victor Bourgeau reappointed and enriched the interior décor between 1872 and 1880, embellishing it with the sculptures, wainscoting and giltwork typical of provincial religious architecture. Notre-Dame's Gothic Revival style is distinguishable from that of non-Catholic churches by the interior furnishings and ornamentation, inspired by the French Gothic style. The magnificent interior is a veritable gallery of religious art in hand-carved white pine, painted and gilded with 22-carat gold. The nave, measuring 68m/223ft long, 21m/69ft wide and 25m/82ft high, follows the natural slope of the terrain from the entrance to the altar, and the interior space is illuminated by three rose windows piercing the polychromed vaulted ceiling. Designed by Bourgeau and carved by Henri Bouriché, the altar and **reredos** (ornamental screens) incorporate white-oak statues, which stand out against the background's soft blue hues. The massive black-walnut **pulpit** was designed by Henri Bouriché; note Louis-Philippe Hébert's statues of Ezekiel and Jeremiah at its base.

The **stained-glass windows** of the lower level were designed by Jean-Baptiste Lagacé and produced at the Chigot studio in Limoges, France. Commissioned at the basilica's 1929 centenary and installed in 1931, the

windows depict scenes from the history of Montreal.
The massive **organ**, one of the world's largest, was produced in 1887 by Casavant Brothers of Saint-Hyacinthe, and has 7,000 pipes, 97 stops, four manual keyboards, and a pedal-board. To the right of the entrance, note the baptistry, decorated by Ozias Leduc in 1927. Because of its fine acoustics, Notre-Dame is often the setting for organ recitals and Montreal Symphony Orchestra concerts.

Our Lady of the Sacred Heart Chapel (Chapelle Notre-Dame du Sacré-Cœur)

Entrance behind the choir.
Added to the church in 1891, the original chapel was intended mainly for intimate celebrations and weddings. It was completely destroyed by arson in 1978 and reconsecrated in 1982. Its ornamentation combines elements from the original chapel with contemporary additions. The vault is of steel sheathed in linden wood, and side skylights permit daylight to filter into the interior. Dominating the whole is an impressive **bronze reredos**, the work of Charles Daudelin. Measuring 17m/56ft high by 6m/20ft wide and weighing 20 tonnes, its 32 panels were cast in England.

Vieux Séminaire de Saint-Sulpice★ (Old Sulpician Seminary)

116 rue Notre-Dame Ouest.
Located west of the Notre Dame Basilica, the freestone building is the oldest structure in Montreal. It was built in 1685 as a residence and training center by **Dollier de Casson** (1636–1701), Superior of the Messieurs de Saint-Sulpice and Montreal's first historian.
Like numerous other structures in Montreal, the architecture of the seminary bears traits of 17C French classicism. Its palatial, U-shaped plan was adopted by all of the island's religious orders.
The main building, topped by a mansard roof, was enlarged in 1704 and 1712, under the direction of the Sulpician Vachon de Belmont (1654–1732). Lateral wings around a court of honor give way to staircase turrets at the juncture of the main buildings. The seminary building conceals an immense garden which, until the 19C, overlooked the St. Lawrence River. Take note of the antique clock over the front doorway.
This façade **clock,** created in Paris, was installed in 1701. Its face was engraved by Paul Labrosse and gilded by the Sisters of the Congregation. Believed to be the oldest public timepiece in North America, the clock's original movement

Rue Saint-Paul

Place Jacques-Cartier

was made entirely of wood. It was replaced by an electric mechanism in 1966.

Walk east and turn right down rue Saint-Sulpice.

Cours Le Royer (Le Royer Courtyard)

Bounded by rues Saint-Dizier, de Brésoles, Le Royer, and Saint-Paul.

After 1861, a series of warehouses designed by Victor Bourgeau was constructed on the former site of the Montreal General Hospital. These buildings were renovated into housing units during the 1980s in a large-scale project that began to transform Old Montreal into a residential area. The structures overlook a charming courtyard, dotted with flower-filled planters. The rue Saint-Paul side is home to art galleries, offices, and boutiques.

Follow rue Saint-Dizier to rue Saint-Paul and turn left.

Rue Saint-Paul★★

Along with rue Notre-Dame, this narrow street is one of the oldest in Montreal. Its curves and dips are explained by its origins as a footpath along the riverbanks between the fort and the hospital. In 1672, Dollier de Casson straightened the street somewhat in his formal plan of the city, and named it in honor of Paul de Chomedey, Sieur de Maisonneuve.

Lovely, well-proportioned 19C buildings line modern rue Saint-Paul. The section between Blvd Saint-Laurent and Place Jacques-Cartier incorporates former warehouses, now transformed into shops and artists' studios, and is a pedestrian-only zone in the summer.

Pop-Art sensation Johanne Corno operates a gallery on rue Saint-Paul *(no. 51 west)* called AKA Gallery, and continues to sell her work worldwide.

Take a short detour north (left) up rue Saint-Gabriel *(one east of Blvd Saint-Laurent)* to admire the **Auberge Saint-Gabriel** *(no. 426)*, built in 1688 as the first inn in North America, and now a restaurant. Today, the stately building has been respectfully and creatively renovated. Interior designer Bruno Braën conducted research into Quebec history and maintained the original architecture, while creating his own signature combination of compelling elements and artifacts.

Place Jacques-Cartier★★

With its outdoor cafés, street performers and flower vendors, this cobblestone square is lively all summer, especially in the evenings. The public square was created in 1847 by the city council and named for the famous explorer who, according to tradition, docked his ship at its foot in 1535. During the early 18C,

the Marquis de Vaudreuil erected his château on the spot now covered in gardens; the building was destroyed by fire in 1803. A bustling fruit, vegetable, and flower market operated on the square for over 40 years, until the construction of Bonsecours Market.

The numerous early 19C buildings surrounding Place Jacques-Cartier today house hotels, restaurants, clubs, boutiques, art galleries, and offices. Montreal's City Hall stands on the north side of the square, and the Old Port is accessible from its southern end.

A statue of **Horatio Nelson** (**2**) crowns a 15m/49ft column at the top of the square. Erected in 1809, this monument was the first to honor Nelson (1758–1805), who defeated French and Spanish forces at the battle of Trafalgar in 1805 (a similar, more renowned monument in London's Trafalgar Square dates from 1842).

The **Tourist Welcome Office in Old Montreal**, at the southwest corner of Place Jacques-Cartier and rue Notre-Dame (daily May 9am–6pm, Jun–Sept 9am–7pm, Oct 10am–6pm. ✆1-877-266-5687. www.tourism-montreal.org) occupies the site of the former Silver Dollar Saloon. Named for the 300 American silver dollars embedded in the floor, the saloon attracted clients who "walked on top of a fortune."

A tiny side street off Place Jacques-Cartier, **rue Saint-Amable,** is renowned for the artists who, during the summer, draw caricatures on the spot, and show and sell works depicting Montreal and the quarter. The street is named for the wife of Jacques Viger, first mayor of Montreal.

Infamous Resident

Pierre du Calvet (1735–86), who came to Montreal from France in 1758, was the house's most infamous resident. He offered his services to the British in 1760 and to the Americans in 1775, and as a result, he was imprisoned for treason in 1780. After his release in 1784, he set sail to London to appeal his punishment, but when the ship sank on the dangerous crossing, the controversial du Calvet was drowned.

Hôtel de Ville★ (City Hall)

275 rue Notre-Dame Est. Main hall open Mon–Fri 8:30am–5pm; hourly without reservation, Jun 24–Sept 7. Closed major holidays. ♿ ✆514-872-0311. ville.montreal.qc.ca.

The first important building in Quebec to adopt the Second Empire style was originally built in the 1870s. After a fire in 1922, it was rebuilt by Joseph-Omer Marchand, who preserved the original walls but added a storey.

General Charles de Gaulle delivered his bombastic "Vive le Québec... vive le Québec libre!" speech in 1967 from the balcony overlooking the main entrance. Just inside the main door stand two sculptures, recast from the original bronze works, *The Sower and Woman with Bucket,* by Alfred Laliberté. The elegant **main hall** (*hall d'honneur*) is 31m/102ft long by 12m/40ft wide and features a marbled floor and walls, and a huge bronze chandelier weighing over one tonne. The **Council Chamber** can be visited if there is no session in progress (*access from the door under the clock*). Its stained-glass windows represent various aspects of city life during the 1920s. Walk to the back of City Hall for a beautiful view of downtown Montreal. Excavation of the **Champ-de-Mars**, now a vast expanse of lawn, has revealed the base of a section of the old stone fortification wall, and has been preserved.

Musée du Château Ramezay★

280 rue Notre-Dame Est. Open Jun–early Oct daily 9:30am–6pm; rest of the year Tue–Sun 10am–4:30pm. Closed holidays. $10. ✕ ♿ ✆514-861-3708. www.chateauramezay.qc.ca.

Across from the City Hall stands one of Montreal's finest examples of early 18C domestic architecture (1705) and the first building classified as an his-

torical monument in the province. Constructed for Claude de Ramezay (1659–1724), 11th governor of Montreal during the French Regime, the building underwent numerous transformations, always emerging relatively unchanged in appearance but for the tower, which was added in the early 20C. The building's walls are formed of stone fragments and topped with a lead-covered copper roof pierced by dormers. In 1745, Ramezay's heirs sold the house to the **West India Company**, and master builder Paul Tessier (also known as Lavigne) was hired to rebuild it in 1756. The original structure was doubled in size, allowing for the addition of an "apartment," imposing vaults and firebreak walls.

The house became known as a "château" after the Conquest, when British governors resided in it from 1764 through 1849. For seven months in 1775–76, during the American occupation, it served as the headquarters of Richard Montgomery's army. Benjamin Franklin lodged here during this period while on a diplomatic mission.

Museum

The Château Ramezay, restored and transformed into a museum in 1895, presents Montreal's economic, political, and social history. Several rooms on the main level house long-term temporary exhibits using objects drawn from the permanent collection, including furniture, paintings, newspapers, letters, costumes, and manuscripts. Note especially the room embellished with hand-carved mahogany paneling. Produced in 1725 in Nantes, France, for the headquarters of the West India Company, this remarkable woodwork is attributed to the French architect, Germain Boffrand (1667–1754), a proponent of the Louis-XV style. Shipped to Montreal for display in the French pavilion during Expo '67, the **paneling** was ultimately presented to the Château Ramezay because of the latter's connection with the company.

The basement, with its huge vaults, houses the museum's permanent exhibits, a series of rooms designed to resemble a common room. Other displays here present traditional arts and crafts and furniture.

Continue east on rue Notre-Dame to its intersection with rue Berri.

Maison Papineau (Papineau House)

440 rue Bonsecours.

This large edifice was erected in 1785 by Jean-Baptist Cérat, also known as Coquillard. With its steeply pitched roof pierced by two rows of dormer windows and carriage door leading to a rear courtyard, the structure represents a typical French Regime house. During a reconstruction in 1831, the original stone walls were covered in wood, sculpted and painted to resemble limestone. This modification lent a Neoclassical appearance to the traditional-style structure. The house was owned by six generations of the Papineau family, including **Louis-Joseph Papineau** (1786–1871), leader of the Patriot party, who lived in it periodically between 1814 and 1837.

The charming **view** down rue Bonsecours to the little church of Our Lady of Good Help is one of the most photographed perspectives in the city.

Retrace your steps back to the corner of rue Berri.

Lieu historique national du Canada de Sir-George-Étienne-Cartier★ (Sir George-Étienne Cartier National Historic Site of Canada)

458 rue Notre-Dame Est. Open Jun 20–Sept 7 Wed–Sun 10am–5pm, Sept 11–Dec 20 10am–5pm. $3.90. ♿ ☎514-283-2282. www.pc.gc.ca/cartier.

This limestone, mansard-roofed landmark consists of two houses, linked by a covered passage, that feature rare Victorian home interiors. From 1848 through 1872, the structure was the sometime home and legal office of the renowned statesman, **George-Étienne Cartier**

(1814–73). An influential member of the Sir John A. Macdonald cabinet until his death, Cartier was a prominent figure in Canadian politics during the 19C.

The visit begins on the ground floor of the building's eastern section, where colorful signs, mannequins and panels introduce visitors to 19C Montreal society. The second level illustrates Cartier's life and work, highlighting his role as one of the proponents of Canada's railway development, and as a Father of Canadian Confederation.

The meticulously restored western half sends visitors back in time to the Victorian era. Period furnishings and recorded voices evoke the lifestyles of upper-class Montrealers during the late-19C. Guided tours by actors in costume take place during summer.

Walk south down rue Berri and turn right going west along rue Saint-Paul.

Maison Pierre du Calvet (Pierre du Calvet House)

401 rue Bonsecours at corner of rue Saint-Paul Est. 514-282-1725. www.pierreducalvet.ca.

Constructed in 1725 on a lot belonging to French Protestant merchant, Pierre du Calvet (*see box, p126*), this structure is Montreal's finest existing example of a traditional urban residence (it is now a hotel-restaurant). Typical elements include unadorned fieldstone walls, firebreaks (the part of the wall extending beyond the roof as a shield against flying sparks), corner consoles, tall chimneys incorporated into large gables, and a pitched roof unrelieved by dormers. The third level, with three small windows, evokes the mansard roofs introduced by the Loyalists. The interior, today renovated as an inn, offers a greenhouse bar, library, and public dining room, and also features the Montreal Bronze Museum, as well as an art workshop and gallery. Fireplaces in winter make this an amazing accommodation in which to unwind, use as a base for touring the city, or even as a long-stay abode. Note the beamed woodwork characteristic of the 18C, and the handcrafted finishings so uniquely characteristic of the French woodcarvers in every corner of the province.

Chapelle Notre-Dame-de-Bon-Secours★

400 rue Saint-Paul East. Open Tue–Sun 11am–4pm. $12. 514-282-8670. www.marguerite-bourgeoys.com.

The small **Chapelle Notre-Dame-de-Bon-Secours** is distinguished by its copper steeple, and by a 9m/30ft statue of the Virgin with arms outstretched toward the river, created by Philippe Laperle. Commissioned by Marguerite Bourgeoys in 1657, and dedicated in 1678, the original chapel burned in 1754, and the present structure dates from the mid-18C.

The façade and interior decoration were added in the late 19C. The tower was constructed over the apse between 1892 and 1894 to house the statue of the Virgin. Also added at this time were an "aerial chapel" and an observatory accessible from the tower (climb of 100 steps). From here, the **panorama★** extends over the St. Lawrence River, St. Helen's Island, the Jacques-Cartier Bridge and the Old Port.

The chapel, nicknamed "the Sailors' Church," was hung with small carved

Chapelle Notre-Dame-de-Bon-Secours

ships offered to the Virgin by devout seamen. Some of these votive offerings can still be seen today in the chapel. The oak statue of the Virgin, located in the chapel to the left of the altar, is the focus of special devotion, having been recovered intact after fire and theft. Beneath the nave of the chapel, the foundation walls of the original building have been uncovered, along with the traces of a wood palisade and indications of a Native presence here as early as 400 BC.
Musée Marguerite-Bourgeoys – A former school next to the chapel as well as the tower and crypt house a museum dedicated to the life and work of **Marguerite Bourgeoys** (1620–1700). This legendary woman arrived in Ville-Marie with Maisonneuve in 1653, opened the first school and founded the first non-cloistered religious community of women on the continent, the **Congregation of Notre Dame**. For many years, Sister Bourgeoys sheltered the **Filles du Roy** (the "King's wards"), young women who came from France with dowries provided by Louis XIV to marry the first settlers. A special feature of the museum is its collection of charming figurines, dressed in regional and period costume and displayed in 58 scenes that relate the extraordinary life of this famed Montreal nun. Marguerite Bourgeoys was canonized in 1982.

Walk west on the rue Saint-Paul Est.

Marché Bonsecours (Bonsecours Market)

350 rue Saint-Paul Est. Champ-de-Mars. Open daily from 10am. ℘514-872-7730. www.marchebonsecours.qc.ca.
Originally built to house Montreal's first interior market, this building (1845) occupies the former site of the Intendant's Palace, destroyed in 1796. With its 163m/535ft freestone façade and lofty dome, the elegantly ornamented structure is best viewed from the riverside. The ground-floor merchant stalls were accessible from the outside through large bays. After fire destroyed the Parliament Buildings in 1849, the market became the seat of the Legislature of the United Canadas. From 1852 through 1878, it served as the City Hall, and is now leased to 15 shops, boutiques, and exhibitions. The amusing **Cabaret du Roi** is a pirate-themed dinner theater with actors in the costumes of New France (363 rue de la Commune; open from 6 pm Fri–Sun mid-Oct–mid-May; open from 11:30am for lunch and dinner mid-May–mid-Oct. ℘514-907-9000; www.oyez.ca).

At this point, you could decide to finish your tour and have coffee or lunch in the market. To extend your tour, continue W on rue Saint-Paul Est to the foot of Place Jacques-Cartier. Turn left, and cross rue de la Commune.

VIEUX-PORT★ (OLD PORT)

Place-d'Armes or Champ-de-Mars.
In Montreal's early years, barges and canoes were hauled by hand onto the muddy St. Lawrence banks. In the mid-18C, several wooden quays were built on the site of the present port. These were replaced in 1830 by stone piers, loading ramps and a breakwater, constructed by the newly created Harbor Commission. Concrete piers, steel sheds, docks, jetties, and a huge grain elevator (demolished in 1978) were erected in 1898. During the 1920s Montreal had become the largest grain port on the continent, with a traffic volume second only to New York, even though at the time, ice forced an annual shutdown of several months.
Today, much of the maritime traffic bypasses Montreal on the St. Lawrence Seaway, and the port's principal activities center on the handling of shipping containers. The older section of the port has been converted into a park.

Esplanade du Vieux-Port

Entrances at rue Berri, Place Jacques-Cartier, Blvd Saint-Laurent, and rue McGill.
With its sunny, breeze-swept spaces and paths for walking, skating or biking, this immense waterfront park is pleasurable in any weather, espe-

Clock Tower Beach

cially during summer. The esplanade boasts excellent **views** of the city and river, boat trips, bike rentals, and **iSci/IMAX**—the Montreal Interactive Science Center *(see below)*.

Walking from one end of the esplanade to the other (the western tip is at rue McGill) is quite easy; note the new Bota-Bota spa located on a barge dockside, and the curious-looking Habitat-67 structure, where the residences are in pre-fabricated cubes. Retrace your steps heading back towards Marché Bonsecours, but then veer south (right) to explore the marina/beach area.

At the eastern end of the Quai de l'Horloge, note the **Tour de l'Horloge** (Clock Tower). Completed in 1922, the 45m/148ft tower honors the sailors who perished during World War I. You can climb the 192 steps to the top for the best available panorama of the city *(donation requested)*.

The new **Clock Tower Beach** is Montreal's latest summertime urban playground. This stretch of sand along the Old Port waterfront promenade has beach umbrellas, sun chairs, a refreshment stand along a wooden boardwalk, and to cool down, showers and mist stations. The most thrilling 45 seconds of any Old Port visit would be the new Tyrolienne Montréal Urban Zipline. With great views of the city and river, it costs about $20, and is usually open from 10am–10pm daily, and until 11:30pm on fireworks nights (minimum age 7 years).

Saute Moutons Jet Boat Trips on the Lachine Rapids★★ (Expéditions dans les rapides de Lachine)

Departs from quai de l'Horloge (Champ-de-Mars). 1hr round-trip. Runs May–Oct at 10am, noon, 2pm, 4pm and 6pm. $65; children (ages 13–18) $57 (ages 6–12) $47. 514-284-9607. www.jetboatingmontreal.com.

For those who can handle the excitement, be prepared to have the ride of your life. These powerful boats ride in and around the Lachine white-water rapids, maximizing on the driver's ability to ride the waves. Everyone gets splashed, and everyone has a memorable time. During the ride out to Lachine the view of the Mount Royal, the Old Port, downtown, and the bridges is amazing, especially at sunset.

Return to the esplanade.

Montreal Science Center★

Quai King Edward at Blvd St. Laurent and Rue de la Commune. Parking available. Open Mon–Fri 9am–4pm, Sat–Sun 10am–5pm; summer hours are usually longer. $15.00, children $8.50.

℘514-496-4724. www.montreal sciencecentre.com.
Major **interactive science exhibitions** change periodically, while temporary and permanent educational exhibitions are produced interactively with an energetic sense of wonder and participation. Science 26 permits your tiny Einsteins to test no fewer than 26 mechanical devices; imagine being projected into space. Meanwhile, idTVa invites visitors become science journalists and report the scientific news of the day. The **IMAX-Telus Theatre** (open 10am; last film at 8 or 9pm, reservations advised; $11.50) continues to thrill viewers with its 3D sensations.

Harbor Cruises★

Depart from Quai King Edward. May–Oct daily 11:30am, 2pm and 4pm; round-trip 1hr 30min, commentary, reservations required. $29, $16 children. Dancing and dinner cruises available, departing at 7pm, round-trip 4hr, commentary, reservations required; $104 for 5-course dinner cruise without wine. **Croisières AML:** ℘1-800-563-4643 or www.croisieresaml.com.
Cruises of various lengths offer visitors a new perspective on Montreal from the river. The port installations, bridges, islands, the St. Lawrence Seaway, and the Olympic Stadium are among the highlights.

Amphi-Tours

Depart from the corner of Blvd Saint-Laurent & rue de la Commune. Jun 21–Sept 1, 11am–8pm every hour; May 1–Jun 20 & Sept 2–Oct 31, daily noon, 2pm, 4pm, 6pm. Round-trip 70min. Commentary. Reservations advised in high season. $35. ℘514-849-5181. www.oldportofmontreal.com.
The "Kamada," an amphibious bus, tours Old Montreal before sailing onto the St. Lawrence River for a cruise around Cité du Havre.

Leave the quai to rejoin the rue de la Commune and turn left in the direction of Place d'Youville.

A Life of Devotion

Quebecer Marie Marguerite Dufrost of Lajemmerais (1701–71), widow of François d'Youville, in 1737 established a secular order devoted to the city's elderly, paupers, and sick. This order gave birth to the Sisters of Charity Congregation, known as the Grey Nuns. Her life of devotion was officially recognized in 1959, when Marguerite of Youville was beatified, and was later canonized as a saint by Pope John Paul II.

AROUND PLACE D'YOUVILLE

Place-d'Armes.
The St. Pierre River ran along this square to join the St. Lawrence River at Pointe-à-Callière, until it was channeled underground in the 19C.

Place Royale

In 1645, Maisonneuve erected his dwelling on this square, originally known as the Place d'Armes. By 1706, it had become the public market place, the popular setting for official announcements by the town crier, criminal punishments including whippings and hangings, and occasional duels. The square was officially named Place Royale in 1892.

Cross rue de la Commune to enter the compelling building housing the *Pointe-à-Callière* Museum of Archaeology and History.

Pointe-à-Callières, Montreal Museum of Archeology and History

350 Place Royale. Open late Jun–Labor Day Mon–Fri 10am–6pm and Sat–Sun 11am–6pm; rest of the year Tue–Fri 10am–5pm, weekends 11am–5pm. Closed major holidays. $20. ℘514-872-9150. www.pacmuseum.qc.ca.
Opened in 1992, this museum complex brings alive the fascinating history of

Montreal from its beginnings at Callière Point. In the striking, contemporary Éperon Building, visitors can view an absorbing multimedia presentation (*16min*) on the evolution of Montreal. Temporary exhibits are mounted on the second floor, and from the third-floor belvedere a lovely **view** extends over the Old Port Esplanade.

An underground passage leads from the Éperon Building to the **archeological crypt** located directly beneath Place Royale. Artifacts on display here bear witness to Montreal's many centuries of human occupation. In the crypt, visitors can see the actual vestiges of early Montreal, foundations and even walls of structures uncovered in the course of archeological excavations. Scale models of the city illustrate its appearance during various periods, and interactive monitors allow visitors to interact with the images of some of Montreal's early inhabitants.

The underground passage ends at the **Old Customs House** (1838, John Ostell). Above ground, the edifice's Neoclassical façade dominates the Place Royale. Today transformed into an interpretation center, the dignified building houses exhibits on the history of Montreal as a center of trade and commerce.

Place d'Youville

The square was named after **Marguerite d'Youville**, who founded the Grey Nuns in 1737. In 1849 it was the site of the Colonial Legislature created after the Patriots' Rebellion of 1837 with representatives from Lower Canada (Quebec) and Upper Canada (Ontario). Tories burned the building to the ground to show their objection to a law compensating anyone whose land had been damaged during the Rebellions (including rebels). The Legislature moved briefly to Bonsecours Market and then left for Kingston, Quebec, and finally Ottawa; it would never again meet in Montreal.

The buildings surrounding the pleasant square represent different epochs in the city's history, from the 17C Grey Nuns Hospital to the 19C warehouses and the immense, Beaux-Arts style **Édifice des Douanes** (Customs House), erected between 1912 and 1936. Today, numerous residences are renovating, adding to the charm of this up-and-coming area. Montreal was born on this small triangle of land, where the St. Pierre River joined the St. Lawrence, in May 1642. The spot had already been cleared in 1611 by Samuel de Champlain, who deemed it an excellent location for a harbor. Thirty-one years later, Paul de Chomedey, Sieur de Maisonneuve, established the settlement of Ville-Marie on the site, surrounding it with a wooden stockade. A 10m/33ft **obelisk** (**3**), *Les Pionniers*, commemorates de Maisonneuve's landing. Callière Point is named for Louis-Hector de Callière, Governor of Montreal from 1684 through 1698, whose home formerly occupied the site.

Centre d'histoire de Montréal★ (Montreal History Centre)

335 Place d'Youville. Open Wed–Sun 10am–5pm. $6. 514-872-3207. www.ville.montreal.qc.ca/chm.

Restored in 1981, this red brick building (1903), a former fire station, features elements of Dutch Baroque architecture: An elegantly gabled roof, an imposing dormer and sculpted ornamentation. The rear tower was used to hang the water hoses to dry, and stone arches at the front provided access for firefighting vehicles.

Today the building houses a delightful interpretation center dedicated to Montreal's history from 1535 to the present. Audio tracks, murals and original objects illustrate the economic, social, and urban trends that influenced the city's colorful past.

Écuries d'Youville (Youville Stables)

298–300 Place d'Youville.

Enclosing a pleasant garden courtyard, these low stone structures (1828) were built as warehouses for the Grey Nuns, and later used to store grain. The complex never actually served as a shelter for animals; however, it is thought that

its present name derives from 19C stables that were located nearby. Restored in 1967, the complex currently houses offices and a restaurant, and the surrounding buildings have been renovated as condominiums. Visitors enter the courtyard through the central carriage door.

Hôpital général des Sœurs Grises (Grey Nuns' Hospital)

Bounded by rue Saint-Pierre, rue d'Youville, rue Normand and Place d'Youville.

In 1680, the Sulpicians ceded the marshland near the St. Pierre River to François Charron de la Barre and his brothers, who constructed a hospital on the site in 1694. In 1747, Marguerite d'Youville and the Grey Nuns assumed direction of the hospital, rebuilding it after it was largely destroyed by fire in 1765.

In 1871, due to frequent flooding of the site and increased activity in the adjacent port, the Grey Nuns left the area for a quieter location to the west of the center. Their chapel on rue Saint-Pierre was demolished, the street was extended to the river, and warehouses were erected.

In 1980, the convent building was renovated to house a novitiate and the general administration offices for the Grey Nuns. The oldest section of the convent can be seen from Rue Normand.

CITÉ MULTIMÉDIA

The southwestern sector of Old Montreal is now called Multimedia City. It occupies the former Récollets seigneurie property in a neighborhood that was once an Irish immigration zone. The first Irishmen to live and work in this area were tasked with the challenge of digging the Lachine Canal after 1820, and then building the Victoria and Jacques Cartier bridges. Warehouses and metallurgical industries, plus a number of foundries, were built at the same time, transforming the area until the Stock Market Crash of 1929. This dramatic event marked the beginning of the neighborhood's decline, and continued until the World War II years (1940–45), when many locals enlisted. Twenty years after the war, the construction of the Bonaventure Expressway (1966), together with the development of Expo 67 World's Fair kept the boys working, until the closing of the Lachine Canal in 1969. Today, the former industrial buildings have been renovated into condominiums or demolished in favor of new housing, or recommissioned as offices and workshops.

A good example is the visual arts center, the **Darling Foundry**, (745 rue Ottawa; open Wed–Sun noon–7pm, Thu until 10pm; $5 514-392-1554; www.fonderiedarling.org). The Darling brothers opened this foundry in 1880, making metal pieces, heaters, pumps and elevators, until it became the second-busiest foundry in the city. Through the hard times and drastic changes to the neighborhood, the plant survived, but finally closed in 1991. This period corresponded with an artistic need for a place to house contemporary visual artistic expression, and a new population made the Darling Foundry their new home. Brick walls, original underpinnings and historical touches fitted the needs of the creatives like a glove. There are two exhibition rooms, and the mandate of the Darling Foundry continues to promote and support the visual arts.

2 FROM DORCHESTER SQUARE TO MCGILL UNIVERSITY★

See Central Montreal map, pp120–121.
Peel.

This walk through the commercial heart of present-day Montreal leads past some of the city's landmark skyscrapers. The high-rises along Avenue McGill College illustrate the diverging tendencies that mark the post-Modern movement.

Dorchester Square

Surrounded by a group of remarkable buildings, this pleasant green square has long been considered the heart of the city, though more recent skyscrap-

ers have stolen some of the limelight. Formerly known as Dominion Square, it was renamed in 1988 to commemorate Lord Dorchester, Governor of British North America from 1768 through 1778 and from 1786 through 1795. Situated outside city limits prior to 1855, the area originally served as a cemetery, especially for the many victims of the 1832 cholera epidemic. The cemetery was eventually moved to Mt. Royal, and the second bishop of Montreal, **Monsignor Ignace Bourget** (1799–1885), decided to erect a cathedral on the site, much to the chagrin of his parishioners, residents of the old town who objected to having to walk so far to church.

The square contains several notable memorials, including a statue of **Sir Wilfrid Laurier** (**4**) by Émile Brunet. Laurier (1841–1919) was the first French-Canadian Prime Minister of Canada; his famous words carved on the pedestal read (in translation): "The governing motive of my life has been to harmonize the different elements which compose our country." The monument to Laurier faces one of **Sir John A. Macdonald** (**5**) across the street in Place du Canada. The monument to **Lord Strathcona's Canadian Horse Regiment** (**6**), honoring the Canadians killed in the Boer War (1899–1901), is the work of George Hill, who also sculpted the nearby lion commemorating **Queen Victoria's Jubilee** (**7**). The statue of **Robert Burns** (**8**) was erected by devotees of the renowned Scottish poet (1759–96).

Dorchester Square

©Gregory B. Gallagher / Michelin

Dominion Square Building

On northern side of Dorchester Square between rue Peel and rue Metcalfe.

This imposing Renaissance Revival structure (1929) evokes the grandeur of 15C Florentine palaces. Reputed to be the "largest commercial building in Canada," the edifice displayed several features considered innovative for the time: an underground parking area and two-level shopping mall, and the first wooden escalators to appear in Montreal. Also considered novel was the fact that the building housed both offices and boutiques.

The **Quebec Tourism** office (which has information on Montreal) is on the ground floor (entrance on rue du Square-Dorchester) between rue Peel and rue Metcalfe (Hours might vary; Apr–Jun 20 and Sept–Oct 9, 9am–6pm; Jun 21–Aug 9am–7pm; Nov–Mar 9am–5pm; ♿ P ✆514-873-2015 & 1-877-266-5687 www.tourisme-montreal.org). Visitors will find many tourist services here, including an information desk, guided tours (👣) of the city, a bookstore, currency exchange, hotel reservations, car rentals, phones, internet access, and washrooms.

Le Windsor

1170 rue Peel.

Today one of Montreal's most distinctive office buildings, the Windsor Hotel was inaugurated in 1878 with a ball honoring the Marquis de Lorne (then Governor-General) and his wife Louise, daughter of Queen Victoria. Seriously damaged by fire in 1906 and destroyed in 1957, the structure's main wing was replaced by the Canadian Imperial Bank of Commerce. The hotel continued to operate in the remaining wing until 1981. The stone and brick façade is

The Origins of Ice Hockey

A winter preoccupation for more than 150 years, ice hockey is Canada's national game. The enthusiasm is not limited to the big leagues: more than 580,000 young Canadians on some 25,000 teams participate in organized minor-league hockey tournaments, and community rinks are ubiquitous.

Derived from the French *hoquet* ("shepherd's crook") for the shape of the stick, hockey originated from variations of stick and ball games brought to Canada by English soldiers in the 1850s. In 1875, Montreal student J.G. Creighton formalized the rules and replaced the ball with a flat rubber disk (puck) to give better control on ice.

The fast and often rough play appealed to spectators, the game spread quickly, and rivalries among college amateur teams intensified. Professional teams soon followed: Formed in 1917, the National Hockey League has added franchises over the years and now consists of 30 teams, including seven in Canada, with the addition of a team in Winnipeg. A trophy donated by Governor General Lord Stanley in 1893 is still awarded to the winner of the Stanley Cup Championships held each June. The original silver cup is on display in Toronto's Hockey Hall of Fame (*see The Green Guide Canada*). The *Montreal Canadiens* have won the Stanley Cup a record 24 times.

:opped by a mansard roof decorated with dormers and œil-de-bœuf (round) windows. The renovation of the hotel nterior into office space preserved the Adamesque décor of the ground floor, exemplified in the sumptuous ballroom.

Sun Life Building

155 rue Metcalfe.

This magnificent Beaux-Arts edifice 1913), built of steel sheathed in white granite and adorned with colossal olonnades on its four façades, occupies the entire east side of Dorchester Square. Headquarters of the Sun ife Insurance Company, the building ould accommodate 2,500 employees nd was touted as the "tallest building n the British Empire." Its construction nd subsequent expansions (1923–33) ontributed to Montreal's status as anada's most important financial city uring those years. During World War , the British government stored its reasury bonds and gold reserves in his building. Today it houses the Sun ife administrative headquarters and ther prestigious insurance and brokerge firms.

Cross Blvd René-Lévesque and ontinue down rue Peel.

Place du Canada

Several high-rises tower over this green plaza, facing Dorchester Square. The elongated **Banque du Commerce** (Canadian Imperial Bank of Commerce, 1962) presents an unusual contrast between the slate window frames and the glass and stainless-steel façade. Across the street rises the post-Modern, copper and glass **La Laurentienne** (Laurentian Building, 1986). Popularly known as the "cheese-grater," the **Marriott Château Champlain Hotel** stands on the south side of the square. The slender building (1967), marked by convex, half-moon windows, bears the influence of Frank Lloyd Wright, mentor of architect Roger d'Astous. The prevailing architectural tastes of the 1990s are reflected in the **1000 de la Gauchetière** office building dominating the southeast corner of the square; it was once Montreal's tallest structure at 205m/672ft, since replaced by the nearby La Tour IBM/Marathon building at 222m/741ft.

St. George's Anglican Church★

Entrance on rue de la Gauchetière.
Open year-round, Tue–Sun 9am–4pm.
♿ ✆514-866-7113. www.st-georges.org.

Erected in 1870, this charming Gothic Revival church is the oldest building on Place du Canada. The well-proportioned interior features a striking double hammer-beam vaulted **ceiling** of red pine and spruce. The side screens and sculptures, also of oak, were produced by the Casavant Company of Saint-Hyacinthe, who installed the organ in 1896.

Gare Windsor

© David Chapman / age fotostock

Gare Windsor (Windsor Station)

Corner of rue Peel and rue de la Gauchetière.

Designed by Bruce Price, famed architect of Quebec City's Château Frontenac, this distinctive former railway station (1889) is one of Montreal's finest examples of the Richardsonian Romanesque style, characterized by towers, turrets, and round arches. The splendid concourse has both sky-lit and outdoor courtyard spaces, and is one of Montreal's few grand reception venues that can hold more than 5,000 guests.

Centre Bell

Guided visits. Open for National Hockey League games as scheduled. ℘514-989-2841. www.centrebell.ca and www.temple.canadiens.com.

Connected to the Windsor Station on l'Avenue des Canadiens-de-Montréal is a hockey mecca, and is home to one of the winningest sports franchises on the planet, the **Montreal Canadiens Hockey Club**, established in 1909. Seeing a hockey game here is a rite of passage for many visitors. More than 850,000 people pass through the turnstiles each year to see "Les Habs" play. Outside, take some time to examine the marvelous statues of Howie Morenz, Maurice "Rocket" Richard, Jean Beliveau, Hector "Toe" Blake, and other team immortals on Centennial Plaza. The Bell Center is also host to major concerts and events, but of course, not on hockey nights.

▶ Return to Place du Canada.

Basilique-Cathédrale Marie-Reine-du-Monde★★ (Mary Queen of the World Basilica-Cathedral)

Main entrance on Blvd René-Lévesque, at rue de la Cathédrale. Open year-round, except for some religious events, Mon–Fri 7am–6:15pm, Sat–Sun 7:30am–6:15pm. ♿ ℘514-866-1661.

Designed by Victor Bourgeau, this monumental edifice is distinguished by large Greek columns, ornate decoration and a row of statues lining the cornice.

After a fire destroyed St. James Cathedral (Cathédrale Saint-Jacques) located on the east side of Montreal, Monsignor Ignace Bourget decided to erect a new cathedral in the west quarter to reinforce the importance of the Catholic Church in this Anglophone, Protestant district. A proponent of papal supremacy, the bishop of Montreal selected as a model St. Peter's in Rome, the mother church of Roman Catholicism. The scale of this Baroque Revival replica was reduced to one-third the size of the 16C Italian basilica. The church was consecrated in 1894. Originally dedicated to St. James the Major, the structure was recognized as a minor basilica in 1919 and adopted its present name in 1955. Alphonse Longpré (1881–1938) carved the cornice figures, representing patron saints from parishes comprising the Montreal diocese in 1890. The copper dome was added in 1886; its original iron cross was replaced by an

Le Village

Montreal has a vibrant, inexpensive, and happy clubbing scene (mainly downtown and on rue Saint-Laurent), highlighted by Le Village, a gay community area (Beaudry, on Rue Sainte-Catherine, east of the downtown core). Le Village is colorful, fun and arty, and its shops and restaurants possess a special flair. On warm summer nights, the neighborhood explodes with energy, music, and lively street life. The Cabaret Mado *(1115 Rue Catherine Est, corner of Rue Amherst; 514-525-7566, www.mado.qc.ca)* drag queen show is a famous tourist attraction.

aluminum version in 1958. The **statue (9)** of Monsignor Bourget, standing to the right of the cathedral, is the work of Louis-Philippe Hébert. The bishop also appears on the statue's pedestal in the company of the architect of the cathedral, Victor Bourgeau.

Interior

In the entrance vestibule hang the portraits of all the bishops of Montreal, among them the late Paul Grégoire, appointed Cardinal in 1989. Cast in copper covered with gold leaf, the magnificent **baldachin** (ornamental canopy) designed in 1900 by Victor Vincent dominates the nave; it replicates the 16C masterpiece that Italian sculptor Bernini created for St. Peter's Basilica. The interior is decorated with large paintings by Georges Delfosse representing episodes in the history of Canada, including the martyrdoms of the Jesuit priest Jean de Brébeuf and Gabriel Lalement; and the drowning of Nicolas Viel, the first Canadian martyr, and Ahuntsic, his Native disciple. In the chapel behind the altar stands a delicate statue of the Virgin by Sylvia Daoust, the renowned 20C Canadian sculptor.

Interior, Basilique-Cathédrale Marie-Reine-du-Monde

©Gregory B. Gallagher / Michelin

Located on the left side of the nave, a **mortuary chapel** (1933) contains the tombs of several archbishops and bishops. The Italian marble walls and floor are embellished with beautiful mosaics. In the center, note Bourget's mausoleum, executed in Rome. Above the altar in the back of the chapel, a magnificent bronze bas-relief represents St. Peter's of Rome.

Cross Blvd René-Lévesque and continue east.

Montreal's largest hotel, **Fairmont Queen Elizabeth Hotel** (1958), occupies the block of Blvd René-Lévesque between rue Mansfield and rue Université. The Central train station (Gare Centrale), terminus for VIA Rail and Amtrak trains, is located beneath the hotel.

Place Ville-Marie★★

Corner of Ave. McGill College and rue Cathcart.

The original centerpiece of the Underground City, Place Ville-Marie initiated the rebirth of Montreal's downtown and has become the forerunner of many such developments across the country. Inspired by New York City's Rockefeller Center (*consult The Green Guide New York City*), Place Ville-Marie is a landmark building that symbolizes Montreal.

The **Banque Royale Tower★** (1962; I.M. Pei, Affleck and Assoc.) dominates the complex. The cruciform structure, sheathed in aluminum, boasts 3,534sq m/38,000sq ft of office space on each of its 42 stories. The Banque Royale and the three other buildings making up the complex enclose a concrete esplanade that is especially lively in summertime. From this raised vantage point, an unparalleled **vista★** extends to the north of the city, down Ave. McGill College to the McGill University campus, dominated by the bulk of Mt. Royal. Gerald Gladstone's bronze fountain, entitled *Female Landscape* (1972), stands in the foreground. From the shopping center beneath the esplanade, large skylights afford intriguing views of the surrounding towers.

Good to know – Access to Underground City (open during business hours) via glass pavilions in front of the Banque Royale Tower.

From Place Ville-Marie, proceed northward on Ave. McGill College.

Extending from Place Ville-Marie to the gates of McGill University, **Avenue McGill College** has become a showplace for post-Modern architecture. Planned in 1857 as an extension of the main campus axis toward the downtown area, the avenue is now home to several important architectural projects initiated during the 1980s and 1990s. The avenue is beautifully lit during the Christmas season, and it displays outdoor photo exhibitions year-round.

Rue Sainte-Catherine

© Philippe Renault / hemis.fr

Place Montréal Trust★★

1500 Ave. McGill College.

This enormous edifice (1989) of rose marble blocks partitioned by sheets of pastel blue glass occupies the entire left side of the block between rue Sainte-Catherine and Blvd de Maisonneuve. Conceived by the architects **E. Zeidler**, **E. Argun** and **P. Rose**, the tower's bold design features a cylinder encased in a square base. The glass-walled **atrium** rises five floors from the Mètro level; a panoramic elevator permits visitors to admire the three-tiered central bronze fountain. With more than a hundred boutiques, a restaurant and numerous exotic food vendors, the atrium is a popular lunchtime spot.

Walk east on rue Sainte-Catherine.

Montreal's main retail artery, **rue Sainte-Catherine** is lined with such major department stores as **Ogilvy** (soon to be rebuilt and incorporated into a new Holt, Renfrew department store) and **La Baie**; huge commercial centers, including Centre Eaton; and numerous boutiques and restaurants. After business hours, this thoroughfare is a popular place for eating, strolling and window-shopping.

Complexe les Ailes

677 Sainte-Catherine Street West. Open Mon–Tue and Sat 10am–6pm, Wed–Fri 10am–9pm, Sun 11am–5pm. 514-288-3759.

Famous for generations as Eaton's Department Store, established in 186[illegible] by Irish immigrant Timothy Eaton in St. Mary's, Ontario, Eaton's went on to become a national chain before its bankruptcy in 1999. Considerably modified and enlarged from its former days of glory into the Eaton Centre, it is now

Place Montréal Trust

a huge quadrilateral complex running between rue University and rue Sainte-Catherine, Ave. McGill College, and the Blvd de Maisonneuve.

Christ Church Cathedral★

Entrance from rue Sainte-Catherine between rue University and Ave. Union. Open year-round, daily 8am–6pm. ♿ ✆514-843-6577. www.montreal.anglican.org/cathedral.

Distinguished by its triple portico, this graceful structure (1859) reflects the Gothic Revival style. The limestone edifice, topped by a slender central spire, was erected as Montreal's second Anglican cathedral, after the first one burned in 1856. During the 1980s, the base of the church was discovered to be sinking. In response, the Anglican Church of Canada leased the land to a development company, which saved the church by shoring up the founda-ions and building an underground ommercial complex beneath it.

Before entering, note the **monument 10**) (*to the right of the church*) dedicated o Francis Fulford (1803–68), the Angli-an bishop at the time of the cathedral's onstruction. A pointed arched nave nd windows decorated with trefoil nd quatrefoil (three-and four-lobed) lements distinguish the interior. The hancel features a beautifully carved tone **reredos**. The William Morris tudio of London, England, produced many of the magnificent stained-glass windows. Note the organ below the rose window at the south end—of North German inspiration, it was built in 1980 by Karl Wilhelm of Mont-Saint-Hilaire. *Organ recitals are regularly held in the cathedral.*

▶ Enter Les Promenades de la Cathédrale by the doors on either side of the cathedral's main entrance.

Les Promenades de la Cathédrale

Open Mon–Wed 10am–6pm, Thu–Fri 10am–9pm, Sat 10am–5pm, Sun 11am–5pm. Closed for major holidays. ✆514-845-8230. www.promenadescathedrale.com.

Linking Eaton Centre and La Baie department store, Les Promenades (1988) is the result of one of Montreal's most spectacular feats of engineering. Excavation and construction occurred beneath La Cathédrale for several months, during which the structure's weight was borne only by slim pylons. Ogive (arched) ornamentation in the underground concourses is a reminder of the presence of the religious monument above.

▶ Ascend to the street level "cloister," a tiny green space located between the cathedral and the office tower, Place de la Cathédrale.

Place de la Cathédrale★

600 Blvd de Maisonneuve Ouest.

Post-Modern in design, this distinctive, 34-story office tower (1988; Webb, Zerafa, Menkès, and Houdsen) reveals the influence of the adjacent cathedral, as much by its pointed arched entrances, colonnades and deep embrasures (openings) as by its pitched roof and tall, arched windows. A prominent landmark among Montreal's downtown skyscrapers, the building is sheathed in copper-colored reflecting glass. Step into the nave-like **foyer** for the sight of Christ Church Cathedral and its steeple through the five-story glass wall.

▶ Exit to Blvd de Maisonneuve and walk west to Ave. McGill College.

Tours de la Banque Nationale de Paris/Banque Laurentienne★ (National Bank of Paris Laurentian Bank Towers)

1981 Ave. McGill College.

Completed in 1981, the sprawling, twin-towered structure is designed in a play of angles and shapes. The metallic-blue glass exterior of the office complex camouflages the actual number of stories within (16 and 20 stories) and reflects the neighboring buildings. Its jagged, abstract form surrounds a small forecourt highlighted by La foule illuminée, a fiberglass group sculpture by the French artist, Raymond Masson. The "blue building," as it is called by many Montrealers, symbolizes the economic growth experienced by the city during the early 1980s.

Tour l'Industrielle Vie (Industrial Life Tower)

2000 Ave. McGill College.

This granite-clad tower (1986) features a rather conventional exterior enlivened by post-Modern ornamentation. The huge fanlight window at its entrance is repeated at the top of the building. On the sidewalk, note the delightful bronze **sculpture** *Le banc du secret* by Léa Vivot, of two children on a bench. The work bears numerous bilingual inscriptions, poems, and sentiments, all anonymous but for one: "Montreal, a secret to share," signed Jean Doré, former Mayor of Montreal.

Maison Ultramar (Ultramar Building)

2200 Ave. McGill College.

This edifice (1990) successfully integrates the former University Club (*892 Rue Sherbrooke*) and the Molson House (*2047 Rue Mansfield*). The building's recessed entranceway surmounted by a rounded glass façade displays the architect's skillful handling of a corner lot.

Place Mercantile

Across from the Ultramar Building; entrance at 770 rue Sherbrooke Ouest.

This aluminum and glass complex (1982) incorporates, on the rue Sherbrooke side, the façades of a row of greystones dating from 1872. One of these, Strathcona Hall (1904), was sold by McGill University with the stipulation that the hall be preserved. It collapsed during construction of Place Mercantile but was entirely rebuilt.

▶ Turn right on rue Sherbrooke.

Musée McCord ★★ (McCord Museum)

690 rue Sherbrooke Ouest. Open year-round Tue and Thu–Fri 10am–6pm, Wed 10am–9pm, Sat–Sun 10am–5pm. (Jun 29–Aug, Mon 10am–6pm). $14, free Wed eve. 514-398-7100. www.mccord-museum.qc.ca.

Founded in 1921, the McCord figures prominently among Canada's foremost historical museums.

With a view to founding a museum dedicated to Canada's social history, David Ross McCord (1844–1930) donated his extensive personal collections to McGill University in 1919. Today the collection features more than 1.4 million objects, images, photographs and manuscripts including the Notman Photographic Archives, all offering insight into various facets of Canadian history.

3uilding

n 1968, the museum moved its collections to this sober structure of gray imestone, originally a social center for McGill University students. Erected in 1906 by Percy E. Nobbs, the edifice is ighlighted by an elaborate portal lanked by Tuscan pilasters (false colımns). An extension (1992) has been ıdded to the south of the structure, ›ermitting additional exhibit space, :onservation laboratories, a library, ınd various amenities. The new building's façade reflects the elegant style of he original structure. Galleries on two loors showcase the museum's permaıent and temporary exhibits.

:ollections

magnificent Haida façade pole made rom Queen Charlotte Islands (British :olumbia) red cedar in the stairwell eads to the second floor. This level ouses the permanent exhibit "Monréal: Points of View." This presentation ighlights 10 significant aspects of the istory of Montreal, from before the rrival of the Europeans, to the conemporary metropolis of the 21C, with ubway system, skyscrapers, and urban ridlock. Visitors will discover Montrel's mystery through the background tories, key moments in its history, nd the people who had a hand in eveloping this global city. The exhibi·on also uses new media techniques, uch as touch-screen stations, audio ıstallations and podcasts, which will rovide visitors with minutiae about ıe selected objects on display. Also lustrating the Canadian lifestyle are xamples from the museum's extenive costumes and textiles collection s well as selections from the **Notman hotographic Archives**. This out:anding collection of negatives and hotographs, 400,000 of which were ιot by master photographer William otman (1826–91), portrays historical gures, events, and Canadian sites over 78-year period and constitutes a comrehensive chronicle of Canadian life in ıe 19C and early 20C.

▶ Cross rue Sherbrooke to main entrance of the campus.

McGill University★

End of Ave. McGill College at Sherbrooke St. ☎514-398-4455. www.mcgill.ca.

Graced with an attractive downtown campus, Canada's oldest university originated when its benefactor, the Scottish fur trader James McGill (1744–1813), bequeathed Burnside, his country estate, and £10,000 for the foundation of an English-speaking university. Granted a Royal Charter by George IV in 1821, McGill's first classes (in medicine) were held in 1829, following the incorporation of the Montreal Medical Institute. In the years since, the university has witnessed enormous growth and today has an enrollment of nearly 40,000 students at the 32ha/79-acre downtown campus and at the Macdonald College campus located at Sainte-Anne-de-Bellevue, in the West Island.

Campus

Enter the campus by the Greek Revival **Portail Roddick** (Roddick Gate, 1924), erected in memory of Sir Thomas Roddick, dean of the Medical School; embedded in the gate is a clock, the gift of Lady Roddick in honor of her husband's extreme punctuality. The more than 70 buildings located on the university's downtown campus reflect a wide variety of architectural styles. Ornate façades, towers, and turrets embellish early 19C limestone structures. Executed in an eclectic 19C style, they contrast with the unadorned concrete of more recent buildings. To the west of the main campus avenue, note the beautiful stone fountain (1930), attributed to Gertrude Vanderbilt Whitney.

Arts Building

At the end of the main campus avenue.

The central and east sections of the campus's oldest structure were designed by John Ostell between 1839 and 1843. The west pavilion (Molson Hall) and the wings linking the three sections date from between 1861 and 1880. The Doric

portico and interior were rebuilt in 1924, in the austere Neoclassical style. From the steps of the portico there is a good **view** of downtown through the trees of the campus. The tomb of the university's founder, James McGill, stands in front of the building.

Redpath Museum of Natural History ★

To the west of the Arts Building. Open Mon–Fri 9am–5pm, Sun 1–5pm (opens Sun 11am in summer). Closed holidays. P 514-398-4086, ext. 4092. www.mcgill.ca/redpath.

This building (1882) was the first in Canada designed to hold a natural history museum. Its generous benefactor was Peter Redpath, industrialist and founder of the nation's first sugar refinery. The building's Greek and Renaissance façade evokes an antique temple. Inside, visitors can see an incredible array of treasures, including Egyptian mummies and the skeleton of an Albertosaurus. The first floor houses offices and classrooms, as well as a selection of objects drawn from the museum's zoology, paleontology, and mineral collections. The upper floors re-create the charming, studious atmosphere of Victorian-era museums, and house an amazing number of invertebrate and vertebrate fossils, minerals and other zoological artifacts, as well as Egyptiar antiquities.

▶ Exit the campus by the Roddick Gate and turn right.

Located on the edge of campus border ing rue Sherbrooke, just west of the Roddick Gate, a **plaque** (**11**) commem orates the Indian village of Hochelaga which (as was supposed in the 19C stood on this spot at the time of Jacques Cartier's arrival in 1535.

3 FROM QUARTIER DES SPECTACLES TO CHINATOWN★

See Central Montreal map, p120–121.
Place des Arts.

Long neglected by city leaders, this are experienced a renaissance during an after the 1960s French counterculture movement. The decision to erect th modern Place des Arts Complex in th eastern part of the city, made by th municipal administration under mayo Jean Drapeau, reflected a growing inte est in francophone culture and marke the beginning of a series of investment in the then neglected French sector c Montreal. The inception of Place de Arts engendered other projects suc as the Desjardins Complex, the Univer sity of Quebec at Montreal, the Olympi

Concert, Quartier des Spectacles

Place des Arts

© Philippe Renault / hemis.fr

·tadium, the Guy-Favreau Complex and ·he Convention Center.

·UARTIER DES ·PECTACLES★★

·his newly designated quarter runs ·etween rue City Councillors on the ·est, rue Saint-Hubert on the east, rue ·herbrooke northside, to Blvd René-·évesque on the southern boundary. ·he Quartier des Spectacles contains ·ne premier venues for live perfor-·ances, and includes Place des Arts ·which is renovating its esplanade ·ith new gardens and fountains, and ·n outdoor stage), Symphony Hall, ·heatre de Nouveau Monde, Metropo-·s Club, Maison du Festival Jazz Rio ·into Alcan, Club Soda, Musée d'art ·ontemporain, Théatre Saint-Denis, ·héatre Telus, Monument National (one ·f the homes of the National Theater ·chool of Canada), Les Ateliers de danse ·oderne de Montréal, Cinemathéque ·uébeçois, Grande Bibliothèque, and ·e Society for Arts and Technology ·AT); plus other venues, galleries, and ·aces. Throughout this arts zone runs ·n installation called Luminous Pathway ·hich works on three levels: common ·ghting, architectural and stage light-·g, and vibrant elements that highlight ·vents of the day.

Place des Arts★★

North side of rue Sainte-Catherine between rue Jeanne-Mance, and rue Saint-Urbain. Open year-round, daily. Ticket Office Mon–Sat noon–8:30pm. ✆514-842-2112 & 1-866-842-2112. www.laplacedesarts.com.

Montreal's premier cultural complex for the visual and performing arts is undergoing a major overhaul to its esplanade, which will be completed by 2018; the esplanade will serve as an outdoor stage surrounded by gardens, pools, fountains, and trees. Place des Arts consists of three structures bordering a central square. The imposing concert hall (1963) is flanked by a theater building (1967) and the Montreal Contemporary Art Museum (1992). Now also included on-site is La Vitrine ticket outlet, which sells last-minute tickets to events throughout the city, as well as Symphony Hall, the new home for the Montreal Symphony Orchestra **(12)**, Symphony Hall, plus the Georges-Émile Lapalme Cultural Space **(13)** where concerts, readings, and performances are free. The buildings of Place des Arts are situated around the esplanade where lively crowds gather in good weather. Several annual festivals and events take place here, among them the International Jazz Festival.

A Taste of the East

While Montreal's Chinatown is not large, it boasts an abundance of shops and restaurants, especially vegetable stands and barbecue eateries with glazed ducks and barbecue pork hanging in the windows. To whet your appetite, explore Kim Phat *(1059 Blvd Saint-Laurent)*, which is stocked with a variety of exotic foods including octopus, bamboo shoots, jackfruit, dried seaweed, Oriental candies, and fragrant spices, while the restrained yet attractive dining room at Le Pavillon Nanpic *(75A Rue de la Gauchetière Ouest; ℘514-395-8106)* specializes in Canadian-Chinese dishes, including a tasty General Tao chicken.

The building and its hall

Highlighted by an elliptical façade of windows and slim concrete columns, the building was home to the prestigious Orchestre Symphonique de Montréal prior to the opening of the new Symphony Hall adjacent. Les Grands Ballets Canadiens and l'Opéra de Montréal continue to base their productions here. The main auditorium (Salle Wilfrid-Pelletier) has a seating capacity of 2,982. The interior central hall, called the Piano Nobile, features works of art by renowned Canadian artists: Flamboyant tapestries by Robert Lapalme and Micheline Beauchemin, an imposing sculpture by Anne Kahane, and Louis Archambault's brass-leaf *Anges radieux* (Radiant Angels), which dominates the hall's main staircase. On the lower level, note the aluminum mural by Julien Hébert, ceramic panels by Jordi Bonnet, a marble swan by Hans Schleech and a sculpture by the Inuit artist Innukpuk. Jean-Paul Riopelle's *La Bolduc* and a painting by Fernand Toupin also decorate the hall.

Complexe Théâtral (Theater Building)

The complex's theaters are housed in this imposing building situated on the corner of Rues Sainte-Catherine and Saint-Urbain. The Théâtre Jean-Duceppe is designed exclusively for plays and musicals. Directly above it is the Maisonneuve Theater, of Italian inspiration. These "stacked" performance spaces are separated by an ingenious system of springs which acts as a floating floor for the Maisonneuve, above, or as a suspended ceiling for the Jean-Duceppe below. A complete soundproofing system permits separate productions to occur in the two theaters simultaneously. The smaller and more intimate Studio Theater is on the metro level.

Musée d'art contemporain de Montréal★★ (Contemporary Art Museum)

185 rue Sainte-Catherine Ouest. Tue 11am–6pm, Wed–Fri until 9pm, Sat–Sun 10am–6pm. $14. ℘514-847-6226. www.macm.org.

Rising to the west of the Place des Arts this imposing edifice houses spacious well-lit galleries that display work selected from the permanent collection of more than 5,000 paintings, sculptures, prints, drawings, photographs and large-scale installations. More than 60 percent of the pieces are by Quebec artists, enabling the museum to showcase major trends in Quebec contemporary art with the work of Paul-Émile Borduas, Jean-Paul Riopelle, Guido Molinari, Claude Tousignant, Alfred Pellan, Ulysses Comtois, and Armand Vaillancourt. International contemporary artists are also represented. **sculpture garden** is accessible from the second floor (*closed in winter*); from here extends a view of the Place des Arts. Situated in the public space between by the Place des Arts complex and the Contemporary Art Museum is the **Cinquième Salle** (the "fifth auditorium") a smaller, multipurpose theater space.

Take the underground passageway leading to the Complexe Desjardins.

SOUTH OF LA PLACE DES ARTS

Complexe Desjardins★

South side of rue Sainte-Catherine between rues Jeanne-Mance and Saint-Urbain.

Opened in 1976, this complex appears heavy and austere from the outside. The vast interior plaza, better suited to the Montreal climate than an outdoor plaza, consists of four towers embracing an immense polygonal atrium lined with three levels of shops. This layout is reminiscent of an amphitheater, in which passersby are both spectators and players. The atrium is the site of exhibits and popular cultural activities, like television shows, in contrast to the Place des Arts, which during the 1970s acquired a reputation as a symbol of highbrow culture.

Follow the passage under Blvd René-Lévesque to the Guy-Favreau Complex.

Complexe Guy-Favreau

200 Blvd René-Lévesque.

Completed in 1984, this complex was named for **Guy Favreau** (1917–67), a lawyer, politician, public prosecutor and minister of justice in prime minister John Diefenbaker's Cabinet (1957–63). Consisting of six interconnected structures, it contains Montreal's federal administration offices (including the all-important passport office) and numerous apartments, as well as a mall. The red brick exterior complements the handsome stainless steel and brick interior atrium. Exhibits are regularly organized in the main hall and in the mall. Offering a respite from the downtown bustle, the tranquil exterior **garden** is dotted with fountains and sculptures.

Exit on rue de la Gauchetière for Chinatown.

The massive concrete and glass construction (1983) that forms a bridge over the Ville-Marie Expressway is the original **Palais des Congrès de Montréal★** (Montreal Convention Center). Erected in 1983, this mammoth building, capable of accommodating up to 10,000 people, hosts conventions, trade shows, and exhibits throughout the year. A new wing opened in 2002, with a multi-colored glass exterior that has become one of the architectural symbols of 21C Montreal.

The colorful glass wall is in front of the new Place Jean-Paul-Riopelle, another fresh element in Montreal's urban landscape. On the first floor at the western end of the building, take a look at the *Lipstick Forest* installation by architect Claude Cormier, always good for a conversation starter.

CHINATOWN★ (QUARTIER CHINOIS)

Along rue de la Gauchetière between rue Jeanne-Mance and Blvd Saint-Laurent, and on cross streets.

Montreal's Chinatown developed during the 1860s, with the arrival of immigrants who worked on the railroads and in the gold mines of the American West. Like many immigrants, the Chinese originally grouped in their own neighborhoods, but the Chinese population in the area slowly declined in the 1950s, and Asians now reside throughout the city, though some retirees and newly arrived immigrants still live in Chinatown. On Sundays, however, families gather in the area, and shops are open. Restricted to and frequently jammed with pedestrians, these few blocks of rues de la Gauchetière and Blvd Saint-Laurent have become the social hub of Montreal's Asian community, with numerous Chinese and Vietnamese restaurants and grocery stores. Two large Chinese-style arches (1963) span rue de la Gauchetière, and a series of bronze medallions on the ground represents Chinese virtues. Murals along rue Saint-Urbain depict Chinese legends such as the Monkey King. On rue Clark, erected in 1826, the **Maison Wing** *(Wing House, 1009 rue Côté)*, one of the oldest houses in the neighborhood, is now a bakery supplying fortune cookies for restaurants throughout the city.

Rue Crescent Revelry

Crescent Street was Montreal's first nightlife hotspot decades ago and it is still going strong. No one does it better than **Thursday's**, *(1449 Crescent St. 514-288-5656, www.thursdaysmontreal.com)*, an institution since 1973 that is packed with drinkers, diners and dancers at its four spaces, on four levels: the bistro, the bar, the club and the summer-time terrace. Watch for daily specials such as duck magret, all-you-can eat leg of lamb, surf n' turf or bouillabaisse. One street over from Crescent, meat on skewers and gyrating dancers are the order of the day at **le Milsa** *(1445 Rue Bishop; ℘514-985-0777; www.lemilsa.com)*, which specializes in traditional Brazilian barbecue.

Rue Saint-Urbain – On the left as you head south, note the wonderful wall mural depicting a Chinese legend.

Rue de la Gauchetière – Among the curiosities to notice along this pedestrian pathway are the arches built in 1963, north of rue de la Gauchetiere at Blvd René-Lé vesque. They feature bronze medallions telling stories from the Chinese homeland.

Parc Sun Yat-Sen – A small park is dedicated to **Sun Yat-Sen** (1866–1925), who helped overthrow the Qing Dynasty and establish the short-lived Republic of China on the mainland.

4 RUE SHERBROOKE OUEST★★

Map rue Sherbrooke Ouest, p147.

Peel. Begin the walking tour at the corner of rue Sherbrooke Ouest and rue Peel. All addresses are on rue Sherbrooke Ouest, unless otherwise indicated.

One of the city's busiest and most prestigious downtown arteries, rue Sherbrooke combines a bustling retail sector with some of Montreal's choicest residences. Flamboyant Victorian, Gothic, and Romanesque-style structures combine with less decorative 1950s office buildings to form the city's most architecturally diverse district. Rue Sherbrooke marks the southern border of the historic **Mille Carré Doré** (Golden Square Mile), bound on the other sides by Ave. des Pins, rue Université and the junction of rue Guy and chemin de la Côte-des-Neiges (approximately 2.6sq km/1sq mi).

Originally part of the Sulpician seigneury, the area fell into the hands of English and Scottish fur traders after the British Conquest. Successful landowners such as James McGill built country estates near the renowned orchards on the slopes of Mt. Royal, followed in 1885 by an affluent bourgeoisie reaping the benefits of the newly completed Canadian Pacific Railway.

At the turn of the 20C, the residents of the Golden Square Mile held seventy percent of Canada's wealth. To the west of the Golden Square Mile lies the town of **Westmount**, home to the island's most expensive residential real estate.

Rue Peel

This elegant street was named for Sir Robert Peel (1788–1850), the British prime minister who founded the Conservative Party (the Tories) and facilitated England's transition to the industrial era by promoting various economic and financial legislation. Peel also created the London police force, nicknamed "Bobbies" in his honor. To the north, rue Peel is lined with elegant mansions, many belonging to McGill University.

Return to and continue on rue Sherbrooke Ouest.

Rue Stanley was named for the former Canadian Governor General who donated the famous Stanley Cup, trophy of the National Hockey League's prestigious championship.

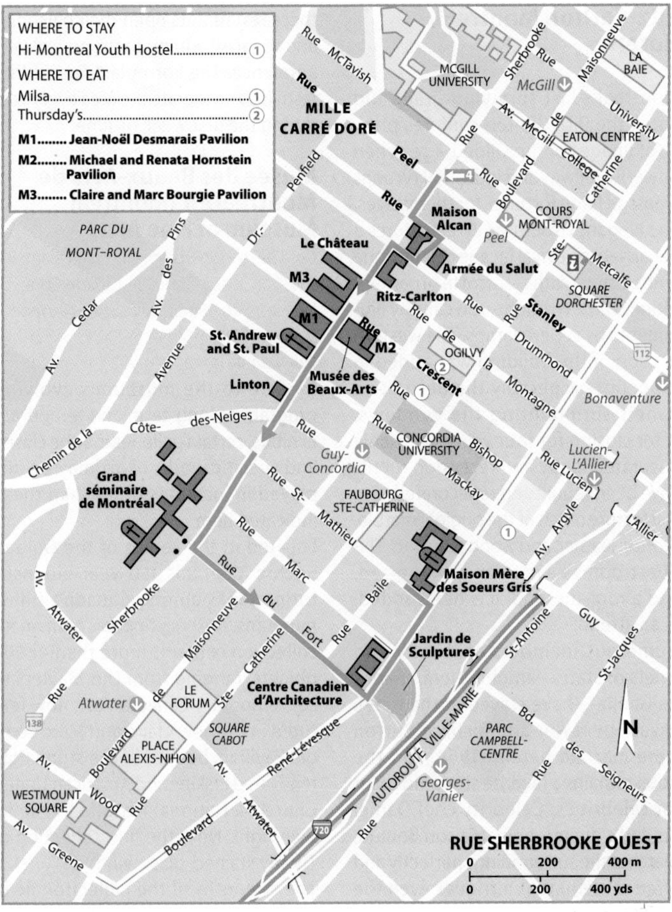

WHERE TO STAY
Hi-Montreal Youth Hostel........................ ①
WHERE TO EAT
Milsa.. ①
Thursday's... ②
M1........ Jean-Noël Desmarais Pavilion
M2........ Michael and Renata Hornstein Pavilion
M3........ Claire and Marc Bourgie Pavilion

RUE SHERBROOKE OUEST
0 200 400 m
0 200 400 yds

Maison Alcan★

No. 1188; main entrance at 2200 rue Stanley.

The headquarters of Alcan Limited, a major aluminum producer, features an innovative mix of old and new. Designers of the structure (1983) successfully followed preservation regulations by integrating into its façade the five 19C buildings on the south side of rue Sherbrooke between rues Stanley and Drummond.

At the far left, the **Atholstan House** (*no. 1172*) was commissioned by Lord Atholstan (1848–1938), famed philanthropist and founder of the now-defunct Montreal Star. Built in 1895 in the Beaux-Arts style then associated with the wealthy elite, the limestone building features an Adamesque interior and presently houses the offices of Alcan's president. A superb glass-roofed **atrium** links the five structures to the Davis Building, a modern aluminum-sheathed edifice located at the rear. Worth noting here are several works of art, including colorful textile panels, Inuit soapstone sculptures, and *Paolo et Francesca*, a 1985 sculpture by Esther Wertheimer. Stroll down the pleasant pedestrian walkway linking rues Stanley and Drummond behind the Maison Alcan building to see the massive, gray **Armée du Salut** (Salvation Army Citadel, *2050 rue Stanley*), erected in 1884 in the style of an Ionic temple.

▶ Return to rue Sherbrooke Ouest.

Ritz-Carlton Montréal Hotel★

No. 1228.

Montreal's last surviving grand old hotel, the Ritz-Carlton conjures powerful images of the Gilded Age, when powerful railway and industrial tycoons amassed large fortunes for themselves. The elegant structure (1912) features a Renaissance Revival façade of limestone embellished with terracotta ornamentation, and a wrought-iron canopy illuminated by superb lamps. The western section of the building was added in 1956; note especially the decorative panels surmounting the windows. After closing for four years, the richly decorated lobby and reception rooms have been rebuilt and redecorated, and still feature much of the original marble, bronze, leather, and wood paneling. The guestrooms have been modernized, and a roof-top pool has been added, in an atrium.

Numerous members of royalty and chiefs of state—among them Charles de Gaulle—have stayed at the hotel. Elizabeth Taylor and Richard Burton were married here in 1964, and the hotel remains a favorite stopping point for celebrities. Celebrity chef Daniel Boulud's dining room, Maison Boulud, matches the surroundings perfectly and offers a menu that intrigues even the most experienced culinary savant.

On the other side of the street at number 1321, stand the condo-apartments of **Le Château** (1925), featuring an ornate sloping roof, with crenels and stone turrets. The building was constructed with Tyndall limestone, which was also used for the interiors of the Parliament Buildings in Ottawa.

Walk on rue Sherbrooke until you reach rue Crescent.

Rue Crescent

The two blocks of this street between rues Sherbrooke and Sainte-Catherine are lined with charming Victorian structures, today occupied by fashionable boutiques, nightclubs, and restaurants. During the summer months, many of these restaurants open their balconies and terraces, adding to the area's lively ambiance. The Formula 1 Grand-Prix festivities invigorate the area every year during the first week of June.

Musée des Beaux-Arts de Montréal★★ (Montreal Museum of Fine Arts)

No. 1380 rue Sherbrooke Ouest. Open Tue–Sun 10am–5pm, Wed 10am–9pm. Free last Sun of month. $20, $10 Wed 5–9pm. 514-285-2000. www.mmfa.qc.ca.

Due to the museum's evolving program of long-term and temporary exhibits, certain galleries may be closed and specific works of art may be displayed in locations other than those indicated here.

Located in the center of the Golden Square Mile, this 150-year-old institution ranks among Canada's finest museums. The encyclopedic permanent collection contains more than 41,000 objects, ranging from Old Masters to contemporary Canadian art, now featured in the new Claire and Marc Bourgie Pavilion, housed in the stunningly renovated Erskine and American United Church, a National Historic Site in its own right. Note the fine collection of Tiffany stained-glass windows.

The strengths of the collection lie in the areas of Canadian and Inuit art, its prints and drawings, and decorative arts ranging from old Chinese bronzes to 20C glassware, and the world's largest collection of Japanese incense boxes (more than 3,000 pieces).

The Buildings

First established in 1860 as the Art Association of Montreal, the museum moved into the current North Pavilion (also known as the Michael and Renata Hornstein Pavilion) half a century later, with a small collection of just 467 works. With its majestic staircase, portico colonnade of white Vermont marble, and solid, massive doors, the 1912 edifice exemplifies the Beaux-Arts style commonly employed in museum buildings of the period.

Enlarged twice, in 1939 and 1977, the museum underwent a third major expansion, onto the south side of Rue Sherbrooke in 1991 with the addition of the South Pavilion **(M2)**—also known as the Jean-Noël Desmarais Pavilion. A series of underground galleries connects the two pavilions. The new annex, which provided much-needed additional space, is the work of the architect **Moshe Safdie**, renowned for such prestigious commissions as Habitat '67, Ottawa's National Gallery of Canada, and Quebec City's Museum of Civilization. Adorned with a monumental entry portal, the building incorporates the Renaissance Revival brick façade of the New Sherbrooke apartment complex (1905), the site's former occupant. The large windows and skylights afford expansive views of the city. Facing rue Bishop, a set of five large vaulted galleries, devoted to temporary exhibits, opens onto a skylit interior.

Michael and Renata Hornstein Pavilion (M1)

North side of rue Sherbrooke.

On the second floor, paintings, sculpture, furniture, and decorative arts cover the sweep of Canadian art from the 18C through 1945. Works on view may include sculptures by Louis Archambault and Robert Roussil, and paintings by Antoine Plamondon and Cornelius Krieghoff. Visitors may also find paintings by Paul Kane (1810–71) and Suzor-Côté (1869–1937), as well as canvases by the Group of Seven and works of Montreal artists James Wilson Morrice (1865–1924), Ozias Leduc (1864–1955) and Alfred Laliberté (1878–1953). The museum possesses stunning examples of 18C–20C Quebec **sacred silverware**, featuring pieces by François Ranvoyzé (1739–1819).

Galleries of Ancient Cultures★

The underground galleries linking the Hornstein Pavilion to the Jean-Noël Desmarais Pavilion house African and Oceanic art featuring sculpted masks and other striking ritual objects, while the Asiatic art section houses porcelains, funerary objects of Chinese antiquity and sculptures from India and Pakistan. The **Islamic art** section offers a large number of ceramics, from Persian pieces of the Sassanian period (3C–7C AD) to Spanish and Moorish wares.

Claire and Marc Bourgie Pavilion (M3)

This new home for Canadian and Quebec art is on the same side of Sherbrooke Street as the original Museum building. This new house presents some 600 works, divided on six levels, including Inuit art and pieces created up until 1970. It is attached to the Erskine and American United Church, itself a beautiful example of the Neo-Roman "Richardsonian" style and built in 1894. The interior offers many items of interest: the 24 Tiffany stained-glass biblical works, a painted dome, finely chiseled molding, and more. The new pavilion features a concert hall as well.

Jean-Noël Desmarais Pavilion

The new building on the south side of rue Sherbrooke.

The fourth floor is devoted exclusively to **European art** from the Middle Ages to the 19C. Polychromed wood sculptures, triptychs (three-panel sets), frescoes, and stained-glass windows beautifully illustrate the artistic richness of the medieval era. Renaissance art includes the superb Judith and Didon by Andrea Mantegna, and Flemish artists are represented by Peter Brueghel the Younger's *Return from the Inn*, as well as *Portrait of a Young Man* by Hans Memling. European art of the 17C and 18C includes masterpieces by Rembrandt (*Portrait of a Young Woman, around 1665*), El Greco, Ruysdael, Canaletto and Gainsborough (*Portrait of Mrs. George Drummond*). The 19C section features painters of the Barbizon school, Impressionists and post-Impressionists. Two additional galleries present the museum's impressive collection of prints and drawings, including several works by Albrecht Dürer. *For conservation purposes, prints and drawings are occasionally removed from view.*

The Collections

The **Canadian art** collection is outstanding. You can trace the course of Canadian history from the struggling colony of 17C France to the present day through decorative arts, paintings, and sculptures. Traditional furniture and religious and domestic silverware by silversmiths such as Paul Lambert, Samuel Payne, and François Ranvoyzé can be found next to early portraits of the bourgeoisie by Jean-Baptiste Roy-Audy and Paul Kane's paintings of Native Canadians. Landscapes range from vistas of the Canadian shield by members of the famous Group of Seven to a large collection of paintings by James Wilson Morrice.

The steady progress of Canadian painting into modernism can be traced through major works by Paul-Émile Borduas and the Automatistes, such as the landmark *Black Star* (1957) and Jean-Paul Riopelle's vibrant *Austria* (1954).

Since 2007, a gallery space has been devoted to painter Marc-Aurèle Fortin. From the body of work that established his reputation there are two signature canvases: his famous tall trees in Sainte-Rose and a Charlevoix landscape. Many more works were donated to the museum when the artist's own museum closed recently in Old Montreal.

The museum also has a rich collection of **European art**, with paintings, sculptures, and objects from the Middle Ages to the present day.

Most of the works in the 19C collection were gifts or bequests from prominent Montreal families and reflect their preference for painters of the Barbizon School such as Corot and Daubigny. A magnificent Daumier (*Nymphs Pursued by Satyrs*), and the striking Tissot painting *October* are included with Impressionist and Post-Impressionist works by Renoir, Sisley, Pissarro, Monet and Cézanne. The collection of early 20C art includes Pablo Picasso, Henri Matisse, Lyonel Feininger, Georges Rouault, Salvador Dalí and Otto Dix, and a fine collection of small bronzes.

The **Ancient cultures** collection of antiquities spans most of the entire Ancient world with objects from Africa, Oceania, Central and South America, as well as China, Korea, Japan and India. It also reveals Islamic art, including a 13C bowl inlaid with silver.

The **Mediterranean archeology** collection has expanded and contains Greek, Roman, Egyptian, and Anatolian objects. Several aspects of the Central and East Mediterranean cultures are represented.

The **decorative arts** section of the museum displays a spectacular design collection in the new **Liliane and David M. Stewart Pavilion** (2001). In total, 700 decorative art objects covering six centuries of design are presented.

The museum's rich collection of **20C** art and international and Canadian **contemporary art** (since 1960) features works by Picasso, Sam Francis, Christian Boltansky, Alexander Calder, Gerhard Richter, Rebecca Horn, and others, as well as works by renowned Canadian contemporary artists Jean-Paul Riopelle, Paul-Émile Borduas, Betty Goodwin, and Geneviève Cadieux. The Magic Realism of Canadian Alex Colville's *Church and Horse* is also featured.

Church of St. Andrew and St. Paul

No. 1431. Open year-round, Mon–Fri 9am–5pm. ♿ ✆514-842-3431. www.standrewstpaul.com

Erected in 1932, this Gothic cathedral-like edifice is home to the Black Watch (Royal Highland) Regiment of Canada. Made of steel and reinforced concrete sheathed in Indiana limestone, the Presbyterian church features an immense stained-glass window above the altar, commemorating victims of World War I. The church also boasts the largest organ in Montreal and a fifty-member choir. The first two windows in the left nave were designed by **Edwin Burne-Jones** of the William Morris Studio, an early practitioner of the Arts and Crafts style. At the northwest corner with rue Simpson stands the ornate, Beaux-Arts **Linton** apartment complex (*no. 1509*), one

of the largest buildings of its type at the time of its construction (1907). Its brick exterior is richly embellished with terracotta ornamentation.

Across the street, an attractive row of gray town houses (*nos. 1400–1460*) contains some of Montreal's most prestigious art galleries. At no. 1460, the **Guilde canadienne des métiers d'art** (Canadian Guild of Crafts), houses a superb collection of **Inuit sculpture** and First Nations art and fine crafts. (open year-round Tue–Fri 10am–6pm, Sat 10am–5pm; ℘514-849-6091; www.canadianguild.com).

Grand séminaire de Montréal (Sulpician Seminary)

No. 2065 at junction with rue du Fort.

Two **towers** with "pepper-box" roofs mark the former site of a small fort constructed by the Sulpicians in 1685 to protect their mission and its First Nations converts. The fort was built in stone with four towers and a defending wall to protect the chapel, the priests' residence and a barn. The two north towers were destroyed in 1854 to make room for the construction of the seminary (1857). The remaining towers are, along with the Sulpician Seminary on rue Notre-Dame, among the oldest structures on the island of Montreal. Now restored, the towers are supplemented by a small outdoor panel display illustrating the history of the fort and of the Sulpician congregation.

Inside the main building, the striking seminary **chapel★** was designed by Joseph-Omer Marchand in 1904 and completed in 1907 (open year-round, daily 9am–4:30pm; ♿ P ℘514-935-1169; www.gsdm.qc.ca). The monumental interior features a large nave reminiscent of early Christian architecture, spanned by cedar beam vaulting. Note the mosaics adorning the floor, the exquisitely carved oak stalls facing each other in the manner of collegiate chapels, and, in the portico, Descente de la Croix, an enormous painting by Napoléon Bourrassa. In 1991 the chapel acquired its superb Guilbault-Thérien organ, manufactured in the classical French tradition of the 18C.

▶ Follow rue du Fort to its intersection with rue Baile.

Centre Canadien d'Architecture★ (Canadian Centre for Architecture)

1920 rue Baile. Open year-round Wed–Sun 11am–6pm (Thu 9pm). Closed some holidays. ⊛$10. ♿ P ℘514-939-7026. www.cca.qc.ca.

Thanks to **Phyllis Lambert**—architect, noted preservationist and heiress to the Seagram fortune—this center was inaugurated in 1989. Lambert collaborated with Canadian architect Peter Rose to restore **Shaughnessy House** (1874), a Second Empire mansion, and to incorporate it into a new construction. A comprehensive reference and research facility, the center also features temporary exhibits, a conservation laboratory and a bookstore.

Trenton limestone, black granite, maple paneling and flooring and aluminum fittings grace the interior of the main building. Located on the first floor, seven galleries display temporary exhibits on architectural themes. Also open to the public are the Shaughnessy House reception rooms and the delightful **conservatory**, restored to 19C splendor and furnished with works of contemporary design.

Jardin de sculptures (sculpture garden)

Located across Blvd René-Lévesque, this unusual outdoor space designed by architect Melvin Charney was conceived as a tribute to the buildings of the neighborhood and to the architectural heritage of the Western world. Among the pieces on display in the esplanade overlooking a maze of highways are ten raised sculptures, or "allegorical columns," depicting various architectural elements.

▶ Turn right on Blvd René-Levesque and left onto rue Saint-Mathieu.

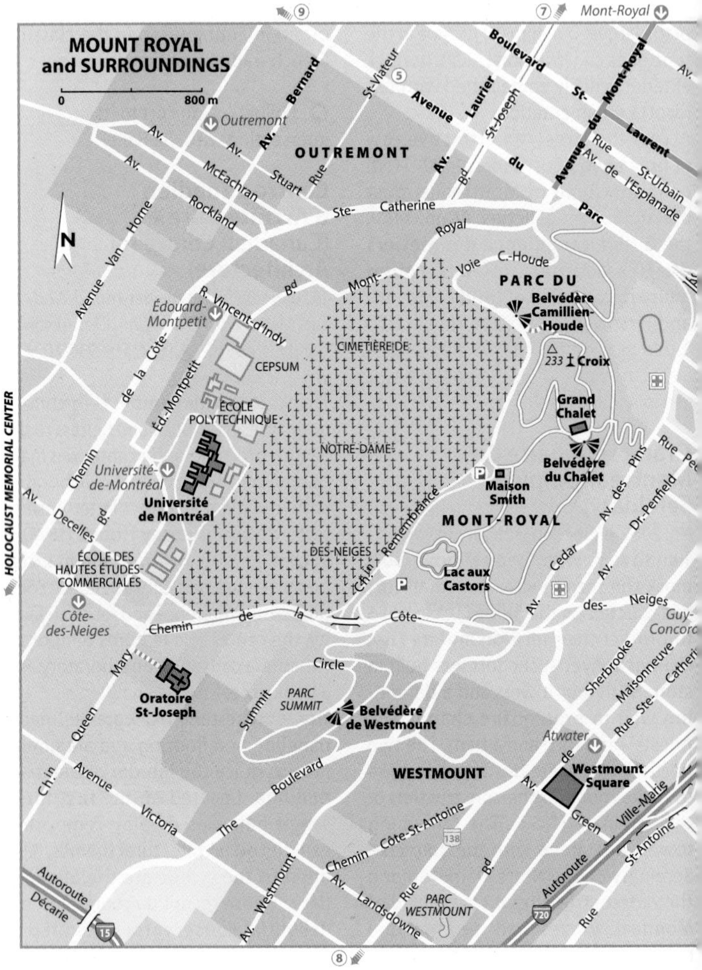

MOUNT ROYAL and SURROUNDINGS

Maison Mère des Sœurs Grises

North side of Blvd René-Lévesque between rue Guy and rue Saint-Mathieu. Entrance for visitors at 1185 rue Saint-Mathieu. P. The interior of the convent is now open to the public and accommodations are available during summer. The historic heritage chapel can be visited during the guided tour of the Marguerite d'Youville Centre.

See box on Marguerite d'Youville, p131.

Designed in the Neoclassical style, this elegant building (1869–1903) housed the Grey Nuns after their departure from Old Montreal in 1871. The plan is typical of 19C convent architecture. To highlight the chapel at the center of the building, the architect Victor Bourgeau adopted the Romanesque style of medieval French abbeys.

The slender steeple, one of the tallest in the city, was added in 1890. Concordia University's Faculty of Fine Arts lives here now.

MOUNT-ROYAL AND SURROUNDINGS★★

See Mount Royal map, above.

Nicknamed "the Mountain," Mount-Royal rises some 233m/764.4ft over the center of downtown Montreal. Residents and visitors alike flock to

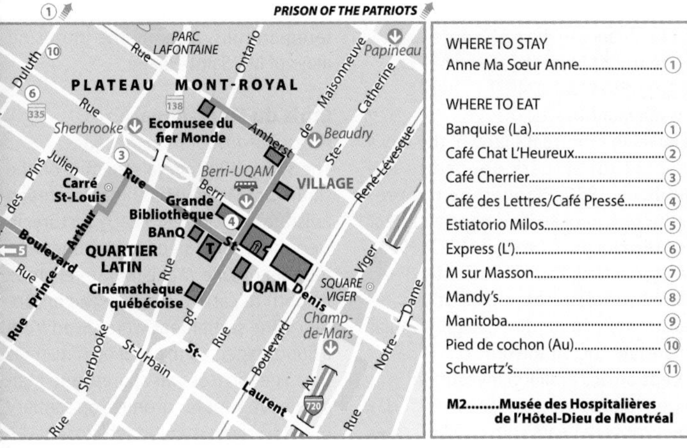

Mount-Royal Park, a popular leisure spot located on the highest of the mountain's three peaks.

Historically an anglophone district, the town of **Westmount** (founded 1874), situated on the western flank of the mountain overlooking downtown and the St. Lawrence River, is one of Montreal's choicest residential areas.

Westmount's steeply sloping streets are bordered with imposing 19C mansions of brick and stone interspersed with modern residences surrounded by manicured gardens. From the **Westmount Belvedere** (*between nos. 18 and 36 Summit Circle*), the **view★** plunges over the rooftops of lovely residences to the three towers of **Westmount Square★** (*corner of rue Sainte-Catherine and Ave. Green*), designed by Mies van der Rohe in 1966. The glass and black metal towers house elegant apartments, offices and shops. The Victoria Bridge is visible in the distance. The community of **Outremont**, founded in 1875 on the mountain's eastern flank, is the enclave of Montreal's francophone bourgeoisie and is Westmount's counterpart for beautiful homes, private mansions and green lawns and parks.

Two cemeteries are located on Mount-Royal, in addition to several reservoirs for drinking water, and the Canadian Broadcasting Corporation/Radio-Canada transmission tower (1963).

Below are the main sights of the area followed by a smaller walking tour of the Latin Quarter.

Parc du Mont-Royal★★ (Mount-Royal Park)

Access **on foot:** 30min climb from downtown. Walk to top of rue Peel at Ave. des Pins and take the path with small flights of steps to a steep flight of 204 steps. **By car:** Drive up Voie Camillien-Houde or chemin

Parc du Mont-Royal

© Philippe Renault / hemis.fr

Remembrance to the parking areas.
By metro: Ⓜ Mont-Royal, and bus 11.
✕♿🅿 ✆514-843-8240.
www.lemontroyal.qc.ca.

A jewel in Montreal's crown, the city's premier urban park opened to the public in 1876. Planned by the pre-eminent American landscape architect **Frederick Law Olmsted** (1822–1903), creator of New York City's Central Park, Mount-Royal Park exemplifies the naturalistic style of garden design popular in the late 19C. At the time of the park's inception, a $1 million investment was required to appropriate the land. Today the property bears some 60,000 trees and 650 species of plants and flowers, and is home to a proliferation of wildlife including foxes, raccoons, gray squirrels, and birds. The park also features a lake, two excellent lookout points, three chalets, a towering illuminated cross, and numerous walking paths through the forest.

Belvédère du Chalet (Chalet Lookout)

From the parking lot, take the footpath to this historic chalet (7min) and the broad terrace and lookout with telescopes for better views of the St. Lawrence River and downtown.

Another chalet, Maison Smith, is a cozy stop for a light lunch indoors, or on the terrace in the summer, and also offers an exhibition about the history of the mountain.

The splendid **view★★★** from the front of the small chalet here encompasses the bustling downtown. Below the lookout lies the campus of McGill University, notably the distinctive, cylindrical form of the McIntyre Medical Sciences Building. The downtown skyscrapers are prominent, especially the IBM Marathon Building, Bank of Commerce Tower, 1000 de la Gauchetière, the cruciform structure of Place Ville-Marie, and Place de la Cathédrale, with its double-sloped roof and copper-colored exterior. From this vantage point, the St. Lawrence River appears as a silver ribbon stretching away to the distance, and looming on the horizon are the shadowy Monteregian Hills, notably the imposing mass of Mt. Saint-Hilaire.

Croix du Mont-Royal (Cross)

Accessible on foot from the chalet.

The 36.6m/120ft metal structure on the summit of Mt. Royal commemorates an episode in Montreal's early history. In December 1642, Sieur de Maisonneuve, founder of Ville-Marie (Montreal), took an oath to carry a cross up the mountain if the settlement were saved from a flood, expected to occur on Christmas Day. The fortress was spared, and Maisonneuve kept his promise on January 6, 1643, erecting a wooden cross at the summit. Today's metal cross dates from 1924. Illuminated at night, it is visible from as far away as 100km/62mi.

Belvédère Camillien-Houde (Camillien Houde Lookout)

Accessible by car on the Voie Camillien-Houde.

From this popular vantage point, the **view★★** of eastern Montreal is dominated by the Olympic Stadium. To the south, several of the Monteregian Hills are visible. The foothills of the Laurentian Mountains rise to the north. Camillien Houde (1889–1958), the namesake of the viewpoint, served as Montreal's mayor for several nonconsecutive terms between 1928 and 1954.

Université de Montréal

Entrance on Blvd Édouard-Montpetit at its intersection with Ave. Louis-Colin.
Ⓜ Université de Montréal.

Created in 1878 as a branch of Laval University in Quebec City, the university became an independent institution by papal decree in 1919. Originally located on rue Saint-Denis in what is currently the UQAM area, the university moved to its present site in 1942.

Construction of the main pavilion began in 1928, but was interrupted by the Great Depression in 1930 and not resumed until 1941. Designed by Ernest Cormier, the building consists of a central section topped by a lofty tower, with perpendicular wings branching toward the front. Replete with stylized

ornamentation, geometric surfaces, and setbacks, this striking edifice exemplifies the Art Deco style. The central hall and the large auditorium have retained their original Art Deco interiors.
With an enrollment of more than 60,000 students, it is the largest francophone university in the world outside Paris. Its 13 departments are supplemented by the École Polytechnique (*northeast of main building*) and the École des Hautes Études Commerciales (*Ave. Decelles*).

Oratoire Saint-Joseph★★ (St. Joseph's Oratory)

Entrance on chemin Queen Mary.
Côte-des-Neiges. Open year-round, 7am–evening. $3. 514-733-8211. www.saint-joseph.org.
Set on the northwest slope of Mount-Royal, this renowned Roman Catholic shrine is visited yearly by millions of pilgrims. Its enormous dome dominates northern Montreal.

Oratoire Saint-Joseph
© All Canada photo / hemis.fr

The Basilica★

Towering 154m/505ft over the city, this colossal structure was 43 years in the making. Construction of the ambitious project began in 1924, but it was repeatedly interrupted by lack of funds, the great depression, and technical difficulties. In 1936 the renowned Benedictine monk-architect, **Dom Paul Bellot**, was called upon to act as chief architect of the oratory. He selected concrete rather than granite for the construction of the dome, and revised the interior plans in a modern style. The monument was finally completed in 1967, and visitors will immediately notice its towering, octagonal, copper-clad dome. Built of concrete sheathed in granite, the basilica is 104m/341ft long, 64m/210ft wide and 112m/367ft high.
Rising 44.5m/146ft above the roof of the basilica, the dome has a diameter of 38m/125ft. The cross crowning the structure is 8m/26ft high.
The visitor is struck by the immensity and austerity of the basilica's **interior**. Henri Charlier carved the stone main altar, the crucifix and the tall wooden carvings of the apostles (*in the transept*); the stained-glass windows were designed by Marius Plamondon. Roger Prévost executed the bronze grilles and Roger de Villiers the life-size Stations of

André the Healer

Alfred Bessette (1845–1937) entered the Congregation of Holy Cross in 1870 and took the name Brother André. During 40 years as a doorkeeper at Notre-Dame College *(across from the Oratory)*, he preached the healing power of devotion to St. Joseph. In 1904 he erected a small chapel on the path which led from the college to Mt. Royal. Many afflicted people who came to pray with him left the chapel cured, abandoning their crutches, canes, and wheelchairs as testament to their recovery, and spreading the lay brother's reputation as a healer. By the early 20C, the crowds of pilgrims had grown to such proportions that the present basilica was built to receive them.

the Cross statues (*around the nave*). The altar in the Chapel of the Blessed Sacrament (*behind the choir*) is the work of Jean-Charles Charuest, and the mosaic of the life of St. Joseph was produced at the Labouret Studio in Paris. During the summer, organ recitals are held here on Wednesday evenings at 8pm (514-337-4622). Within the main edifice are a **votive chapel** enshrining the remains of Brother André; a 56-bell **carillon**, originally cast in Paris for installation on the Eiffel Tower; the **crypt**, where daily Masses are held; and the **Musée du Frère André** (*Brother André Museum; same hours as the Oratory*), displaying a collection of photographs and mementos tracing the friar's history. The **chapelle du Frère André** (Brother André's **original chapel**) is located outside the main structure. The **Stations of the Cross★** statues built into the hillside were designed by Louis Parent and executed in Indiana buff stone by the Italian sculptor, Ercolo Barbieri, in 1960. Outside the basilica, the wide terrace affords a superb **view** of northern Montreal and of the Laurentian Mountains rising on the horizon.

Montreal Holocaust Memorial Centre

5151, Côte-Ste-Catherine (Côte-Ste-Catherine). Mon–Tue and Thu 10am–5pm, Fri and Sun 10am–4pm, Wed 10am–9pm. $8. 514-345-2605. www.mhmc.ca.

Between 5,000 and 8,000 survivors of the Holocaust settled in Montreal, and their testimonies and memories constitute the basis of this museum. The museum details the rise of the Nazis, anti-Semitic laws, the effects of popular journalism in Germany, and the horror of the death camps. This journey also allows the visitor to assess the official position of Canada with respect to the Jewish question during and after the war, the impact of anti-Semitism lobbies, and the effect on Jews of refugee policies. Videos of survivors relating their stories punctuate the journey, while memorabilia is introduced through exhibition panels.

5 LE QUARTIER LATIN★

Outlined in green on the map p152–153.

Musée des Hospitalières de l'Hôtel-Dieu de Montréal (Hospitallers Museum) (M2)

201 Ave. des Pins Ouest. Entrance at rue Saint-Urbain and Ave. des Pins. Open mid-Jun–mid-Oct Tue–Fri 10am–5pm, Sat–Sun 1–5pm; rest of the year Wed–Sun 1–5pm. Closed 25 Dec. $6. 514-849-2919. www.museedeshospitalieres.qc.ca.

Housed in a former chaplain's residence (1925), this museum traces the history of the Hospitallers of St. Joseph (a religious order devoted to caring for the sick) and its role in the development of Montreal. In addition to temporary exhibits, the museum displays a selection of some 400 objects (historic documents, medical instruments, sacred art) drawn from its permanent collection of more than 19,000 artifacts.

A massive oak staircase (17C) from the Hôtel-Dieu hospital in La Flèche, France, dominates the entrance hall of the museum's new addition (1992). The ground floor presents the history of Montreal and of the Hospitaller order, and boasts a magnificent gold-leafed retable (altar backdrop) sculpted in 1777 by Philippe Liébert. Exhibits here illustrate the cloistered life of the Hospitaller nuns from the 19C and the early 20C. Displays on the second floor focus on the Hospitallers' nursing vocation. A fine collection of historic medical instruments offers an excellent glimpse at the evolution of medical techniques. The visit ends with a video presentation (*15min*) about the Hospitaller order throughout the world.

Head towards Sherbrooke (south), turning right on Blvd Saint-Laurent, then left (east) along rue Prince Arthur.

Rue Prince-Arthur

From Blvd Saint-Laurent, east to St-Louis Square.

This small pedestrian street, named for Prince Arthur, third son of Queen Victoria and Governor-General of Canada

The Many Attractions of La Rue Saint-Denis

The bakery-café **La Brioche Lyonnaise** *(1593 rue Saint-Denis, ℘514-842-7017)* is charming, with stone walls and lace curtains, along with light meals, melt-in-your-mouth croissants, and sumptuous pastries. **Juliette et Chocolat** *(1615 rue Saint-Denis, ℘514-287-3555)* brings artistic passion to crepes, waffles, fondues, and sundaes, with ingredients from around the world, while **Café Cherrier** *(3635 rue Saint-Denis, ℘514-843-4308)* serves up tasty meals from breakfast to dinner; take a seat on the terrace and watch the world pass by. Visit the elegant showroom of renowned florist/horticulturist **Marcel Proulx** *(3835 rue Saint-Denis, ℘514-849-1344)* to admire the glorious dried arrangements, rare flowers, and pieces of decorative art. **L'Express** *(3927 rue Saint-Denis, ℘514-845-5333)* is one of the most popular bistros in Montreal, thanks to its fine wine list, faultless service, and consistently excellent cuisine, while across the street is the exquisite **Arthur Quentin** boutique, which has fine tableware, bedding, bathrobes and gifts *(3960 rue Saint-Denis, ℘514-843-7513)*.

Rue Prince-Arthur

© Philippe Renault / hemis.fr

from 1911 to 1916, was a popular center of the counterculture movement during the 1960s. Today the area is home to Italian, French, Polish and Greek restaurants, and is populated in fine weather by musicians, magicians, acrobats, portrait painters and other street performers.

Carré Saint-Louis★ (Saint-Louis Square)

Rue Saint-Denis between rue Sherbrooke and Ave. des Pins.

Named for Emmanuel and Jean-Baptiste Saint-Louis, two eminent local businessmen, this picturesque, tree-shaded square is surrounded by attractive Victorian structures featuring whimsical rooflines and gables. The district became a select neighborhood during the late 19C, when the francophone bourgeoisie began moving to the area, attracted by its tranquil atmosphere. Long popular with Quebec artists and poets (Louis Fréchette, Quebec's Poet Laureate Émile Nelligan whose bronze statue is in the square, and, more recently, Gaston Miron), the square was the center of the nationalist movement during the 1970s. Although the fleur-de-lys is still in evidence, today the square is more likely to resound with American folk songs than with separatist chants. It is still considered a Francophone bastion for Quebec writers, musicians, filmmakers, and actors.

Rue Saint-Denis★

This avenue is lined with attractive town houses, today occupied by restaurants, art galleries, and fashionable stores. Named after Denis-Benjamin Viger, an affluent landowner during the mid-19C, the street was frequented by wealthy francophones who erected charming Victorian homes. The area became known as Montreal's **Quartier Latin** (Latin Quarter) when several institutions of higher education were established here during the early 20C. The polytechnical institute opened in

1905, followed by the École des Hautes Études Commerciales (*Viger Square*) and the Université de Montréal. The **Saint-Denis Theatre** (**T**) (Théâtre Saint-Denis) was erected during this period, followed in 1912 by the Saint-Sulpice Building (*no. 1700*), now home to the **Bibliothèque et Archives nationales de Québec** or **BAnQ** (National Library and Archives of Quebec). The houses were divided into smaller apartments to accommodate the many students attending these institutions.

The area's economic stability suffered when the Université de Montréal moved to its present campus on the north slope of Mt. Royal, and the street only regained its original vibrancy during the 1960s. Cafés, intimate restaurants, small boutiques, and bookstores proliferated, drawing a young crowd back to the area.

Today, rue Saint-Denis is a favorite with Montrealers and tourists alike. The section between rue Sainte-Catherine and rue Duluth is extremely popular during the summer months, when bars and cafés put tables and chairs onto the street. The entire Quartier-Latin experienced a huge lift when the Grande Bibliothèque built its contemporary structure at the corner of Blvd de Maisonneuve and rue Berri in the heart of the quarter (www.banq.qc.ca).

Cinémathèque québécoise

335 Blvd de Maisonneuve East. Exhibitions: Tue noon–6pm, Wed–Fri noon–9pm, Sat–Sun 1pm–9pm. $10. 514-842-9768. www.cinematheque.qc.ca.

Founded in 1963, this Quebec public archive allows the public to enjoy feature and documentary films, from local, national, and international directors. For example, the works by Moses Znaimer, a legend in both Canadian television and film production, can be seen here in their entirety. This collection allows viewers a unique perspective on the visual medium dating back to the period called "Between-the-two-Wars." Rare memorabilia such as television sets are on display, including the Komet made by the Kuba Corporation (1957–62), one of the first portable TVs. The history of the industry's inventors, people like John L. Baird (1888–1946) and Allan B. DuMont (1901–65), is also celebrated. Retrace your steps and go east on Blvd de Maisonneuve heading for Métro Berri-UQAM at the corner of rue Berri. See the breathtaking Grande Bibliothèque (www.banq.qc.ca), Québec's national library. Stunning architecture, millions of books, documents, films, and discs are available in an atmosphere unlike any other. There is an entire level for kids called Espace Jeunes. There is even an amazing dining room called Café des Lettres/Presse Café, featuring market-fresh cuisine, wine, and delectables (*see Addresses, p170*).

Université du Québec à Montréal (University of Quebec at Montreal, UQAM)

Traversed by rue Saint-Denis, the main section of the campus extends between Blvd René-Lévesque and Blvd de Maisonneuve.

Founded in 1969, this university (known as UQAM) is housed in a series of contemporary brick buildings integrated with older structures. One of these occupies the former site of Église Saint-Jacques (St. James Church), designed in the Gothic Revival style by John Ostell in 1852. All that remains of the church today are the façade of the south transept facing rue Sainte-Catherine and the bell tower on rue Saint-Denis. This spire, which was added to the church about 1880, is the tallest in Montreal at 98m/321ft. With an ever-increasing enrollment of more than 40,000 students, the institution is expanding, and now occupies some of the buildings that once housed the polytechnical institute. A second campus between Place des Arts and rue Sherbrooke features an enormous complex for the study of the sciences.

Return to rue de la Maisonneuve and turn left onto rue Amherst.

Ecomusée du Fier-Monde

2050 rue Amherst (corner Ontario). Open Wed 11am–8pm, Thu–Fri 9:30am–4pm, Sat–Sun 10:30am–5pm. $8 (children $6). 514-528-8444. www.ecomusee.qc.ca

This collection of photos and artifacts reflects the industrial revolution of the late 19C and the lives of the working-class people of south-central Montreal. Farther east (a short cab ride away) is the **Prison des Patriotes** at 903 avenue De Lorimier *(east of rue Papineau; 450-787-3623; www.mndp.qc.ca. Closed Mon–Tue)*. Visitors will see a heritage stone structure almost immediately under the Jacques-Cartier Bride; locals gather here in summer to watch fireworks from La Ronde across the water. Today, this fascinating building is occupied by the SAQ, the provincial government alcohol corporation. The former prison (1831–40) has been completely preserved, including its original façade facing the St. Lawrence River. Tours take visitors to one of the preserved prison cells, a reminder of the turbulent side of Canadian history, as some 1300 Patriotes were imprisoned here between 1837 and 1838. Various historical panels speak of the struggle for independence against British rule.

LE PLATEAU MONT-ROYAL

North of rue Sherbrooke to rue Mont-Royal, between rue Papineau and Blvd Saint-Laurent.

Known as Le Plateau, this up-and-coming residential neighborhood has the highest concentration of residents who do not own a car in North America. You must be vigilant here when crossing streets as a pedestrian. While there are designated bike paths, many riders like to do their own thing, creating a confusing protocol among walkers, cyclists, and drivers. Le Plateau runs north of Sherbrooke to Mont-Royal, between Papineau and Saint-Laurent, and is renowned for its creative population. Artists, musicians, writers, and new media creators live and work in this area. Jammed with neighborhood cafés, grocery stores, bistros, clubs, and boutiques, a popular trend for travelers is simply to walk up and down the streets, stopping at eateries and window-shopping, or hanging out in the evenings to dance and meet locals.

Boulevard St-Laurent

This lively thoroughfare is the starting point for the numbering of east–west streets. Traditionally, it represented the linguistic border between the anglophone west and the francophone east, although this limit is not as clear as before. Established in 1672 during the formal planning of the city, and extended to the Prairies River, near Sault-au-Récollet, the artery long formed Montreal's principal passageway, hence its nickname "the Main." After a devastating fire in 1852, the road was extended to the city's new limit at Mile End; it became a boulevard in 1905. For more than a century, the Main has welcomed immigrants who have in various ways affected its development. Chinese immigrants settled in the southern section during the 19C, while Jewish merchants arriving around 1880 concentrated in the northern section as far as rue Sainte-Catherine and established a textile industry (now largely defunct). Greek immigrants moved into the area during the early 20C, but many left after 1940 to relocate on Avenue du Parc. More recently, Slavs, Portuguese, and Hispanics have settled in the area. Although its popularity diminished between 1960 and 1980, the boulevard still attracts a diverse crowd to its shops and restaurants (many of which are unchanged since the 1940s) and to the newer cafés and boutiques. A wide range of specialty stores manifests the area's ethnic diversity, and its sidewalk sales remain popular.

Exit at Métro station Mont-Royal.

Avenue du Mont-Royal

On this street, you can immerse yourself in French culture in an area popular with newly arrived French-speaking

immigrants. The scent of strong coffee wafts out of cafés, and bakeries, bistros, and independent bookstores line the street. To the south is another main artery through this neighborhood called rue Rachel that runs east/west; at its northern limit is Park Lafontaine, known for its lake, fountain, and outside theater. If you follow rue Rachel west, you will run directly into Jeanne Mance Park at the foot of Mount Royal. Every Sunday, from May through November, Les Tam-Tams unfolds; these irrepressible summertime festivals are weekly mini-Woodstocks, freestyle outdoor parties that take place on Sundays from noon to sunset on the eastern flank of the mountain, along ave du Parc. Visitors can enjoy the legions of drummers, musicians, dancers, and craftspeople who gather for a day of music, food and family celebration.

Go back to Blvd St-Laurent, turn left (north) and proceed to the Mile End neighborhood.

A dynamic area filled with European immigrants, this is also a popular quarter for students and others looking for cheaper rentals. Media production companies have also taken over the former light industrial buildings which made the area such an attractive location to new residents at the turn of the 20C. Don't miss stopping on rue Fairmont, at the **Fairmont Bagel** shop (*see Addresses*), open 24/7, to sample some of the legendary bagels cooked fresh on site. And take note of the many religious buildings throughout this area, starting with Saint-Michael's dome on rue Saint-Urban at the core of Mile End. The exterior spiral staircases attached to the buildings are a unique architectural element, and make for challenging descents in winter. The quaint streets are packed with children, so drive slowly, and take note of the limited parking zones, many restricted to residents only.

Follow Blvd St-Laurent and go under the viaduct at rue Van Horne. Heading north, you are now entering Little Italy. Speckled with storefront trattorias, sports cafés, bistros, pizzerias, and shops, the area surrounds the **Marché Jean-Talon,** where Montrealers in the know shop for their fresh fruit and vegetables throughout the year. Flower vendors mix here with purveyors of fruit, vegetables, cheeses, fresh pasta, breads, fish, meats, and more. Bring your appetite, because you will want to sample the food—it's a Montreal tradition.

OLYMPIC PARK AREA★★

See Regional Map pp108–109.

Viau or Pie-IX, or by car (entrance to the parking lot from 3200 rue Viau). Information desk and ticket office at base of tower. Shuttle service (free) to and from the park, the Montreal Botanical Garden and the Biodôme.

Situated in the heart of Montreal's growing Hochelaga-Maisonneuve District (east end), this vast recreational area is dominated by the striking silhouette of the Olympic Stadium. Visiting the many sites contained here is a must for the Biodôme, Botanical Gardens, Insectarium, and more.

To accommodate the 1976 summer Olympic Games, a gigantic sports complex covering 55ha/136 acres was erected at the heart of Montreal's East End, in the former City of Maisonneuve. The city's most controversial public project, the Olympic complex is nonetheless a stunning architectural achievement, and is particularly beautiful at night. The various constructions present a harmonious synthesis of form and function, their lines evoking movement and activity in a concrete monument to the glory of sport and nature. The park includes the stadium and tower complex (ride the funicular to the top); a sports center with six pools for swimming, diving and recreation; a concrete esplanade stretching above the largest underground parking garage in Canada; the Pierre Charbonneau Center and Maurice Richard Arena. Long idle, the former Velodrome has

been converted into the Biodôme, a living museum of natural sciences, and the city's professional soccer team, the Montreal Impact, has built the new Saputo Stadium (2008) where the former Olympic practice grounds were.

A Controversial Project

Excavation work in the park began in 1973, but only the stadium, velodrome, aquatic complex and Olympic Village were completed in time for the 1976 Games. Tremendously expensive ($1.2 billion), the park installations remained incomplete for many years. A series of technical difficulties delayed construction of the stadium tower until 1979. When it was discovered the tower would be too heavy if erected as planned, a moratorium was imposed for four years. Completion of the tower and the roof in 1987 was followed by a series of innovations and adaptations destined to turn the park into a profitable venture. Although the stadium still faces financial difficulties, it has made valiant efforts to remain relevant.

Created in 1975, a government organization, the Régie des installations olympiques (RIO), has been in charge of completing, managing, and transforming the complex as a recreational and tourist center. The park hosts sports and cultural events.

Olympic Stadium

Visit by guided tour of the tower via funicular (30min). Hours vary. Mon 1pm–5pm (except closed Mon, mid-Oct–Dec 23) Tue–Sun 9am–5pm or 6pm; Jul–Aug open until 8pm. Closed early Jan–Feb. $22.50. 514-252-4737. www.parcolympique.qc.ca.

The tour of the park installations does not include ascent to the top of the tower ($15). Conceived by the French architect Roger Taillibert, the concrete structure consists of 34 enormous cantilevered ribs crowned by a structural ring containing lighting and ventilation systems. The stadium is dominated by the world's tallest inclined **tower**. From the top of the tower, 26 suspension cables descend to the roof, made of Kevlar, an ultra-thin synthetic fiber with the strength of steel. At the time of its construction, it was the largest mobile roof in the world. When the cables were retracted by means of the 46 winches anchored at the tower's base, the entire roof was hoisted into a niche at the summit of the tower. The stadium could then be closed by redeploying the roof like a parachute over the opening. Despite its strong material, the roof has been subject to deterioration and tears owing to the city's harsh weather conditions, and it is no longer retractable.

With a seating capacity of 55,147, the interior space is large enough (18,950sq m/203,763sq ft) to accommodate Rome's Colosseum. Spectators seated in the terraces enjoy unobstructed views of the playing surface. Intended as a complex for sporting events, the stadium also hosts rock concerts, operatic productions, conventions, and religious meetings during summer.

A good perspective of the stadium's exterior can be seen from the footbridge leading from the Pie-IX metro station to the esplanade; in the foreground is *La Joute*, a bronze sculpture-fountain by the Quebec artist Jean-Paul Riopelle.

Tower Observatory

Completed in 1987, the 175m/574ft tower is composed of two parts: The lower concrete base bears the brunt of the weight, acting as the tower's center of gravity. The steel upper section hovers over the stadium at a 45° angle. The tower belongs to the prestigious World Federation of Great Towers. The spine of the stadium's tower can be mounted by a **funicular** elevator that travels up 266m/872ft of rails in two minutes. Though the angle of the climb ranges from 23° to 63.7°, a gyroscope-controlled levelling system ensures that the cabin, which can hold up to 76 people, is always horizontal. The view during the ascent is spectacular: It encompasses the stadium and Montreal's East End. From the observa-

Concert in Maisonneuve Park beneath the Olympic stadium tower

tion deck, the panoramic **view★★★** can extend as far as 80km/49.7mi, weather permitting. Three large skylights offer a breathtaking vertical view of the stadium. The windows lining the three sides of the triangular deck command expansive views of downtown Montreal, the Laurentian Mountains to the north and the Monteregian Hills to the south. The Botanical Garden is visible directly to the north.

Below the observation deck, a hands-on interpretation center presents exhibits revolving around different themes: the park's conception and history, the technological innovations involved in its construction, and the materials used.

Village olympique (Olympic Village)

On north side of rue Sherbrooke, east of rue Viau.

Nicknamed "the Olympic Pyramids," these twin 19-story buildings (1976) were constructed to house 11,000 athletes for the Olympic Games. Inspired by the complex at Baie-des-Anges in southern France, the buildings now contain a residential complex.

Rio Tinto Alcan Montreal Planetarium

4801 Ave. Pierre de Coubertin. ✆514-872-4530. www.planetarium.montreal.qc.ca. Open year-round daily 9am–5pm (until 6pm in summer).

The planetarium (2013), together with the Biodôme, Insectarium and Botanical Garden, make up the **Space For Life★★**. Now Canada's largest natural science museum, it is a unique combined attraction that invites visitors to reconnect with nature and cultivate a new way of living, in harmony with the natural world. The planetarium features two theaters, multimedia shows, and interactive exhibitions, plus workshop space, and it gives visitors a unique look at our universe from millions of miles away.

Jardin botanique de Montréal★★ (Montreal Botanical Garden)

4101 rue Sherbrooke Est. Ⓜ Pie-IX. Open mid-May–Oct daily 9am–6pm; Nov–mid-May Tue–Sun 9am–5pm. $16 (including guided tours). ✕♿🅿 ($8). Shuttle service (free) to and from the Biodôme, Olympic Park and the Botanical Garden. ✆514-872-1400. www.museumsnature.ca.

Covering 75ha/185 acres, the Montreal Garden is located across from the Olympic Park and the Biodôme. Ranked among the world's finest horticultural facilities, the garden was founded in 1931 by Brother Marie-Victorin (1885–1944). The garden contains more than 21,000 species from all over the world, including 10,000 tree specimens, 1,500 types of orchids and an extensive collection of bonsais. Since 1939, the Research

The Maisonneuve Renaissance

In 1883, leading French Canadian businessmen established the community of Maisonneuve 10km/6.2mi outside downtown Montreal in an attempt to rival the Anglophone economic domination of the city. After 1896, Maisonneuve experienced a significant economic boom, becoming a major center for the manufacture of shoes, textiles, baked goods and candy. A shipbuilding industry also took root. To emphasize its prosperity, the city launched a program of aesthetic and structural development based on the tenets of the American "City Beautiful" movement, building the immense **Maisonneuve Park**, grand boulevards and prestigious buildings, including Château Dufresne. However, the exorbitant cost of development, combined with the postwar recession, gradually drove Maisonneuve into bankruptcy; by 1918, the government of Quebec decreed that the city be annexed by Montreal.

Covering 204ha/504 acres, the Maisonneuve Park today encompasses the **Botanical Garden**, Insectarium, Blodiversity Centre, an extensive bike trail, picnic grounds, and a snack bar with healthy options. Families flock here during the summer to enjoy walks and picnics in this pleasant, natural setting. During the winter, sports enthusiasts can partake of the five cross-country ski trails lacing the park, and skate on the floodlit ice rink. Situated across from the Botanical Garden on rue Sherbrooke, the **Olympic Park** has contributed greatly to the economic boom experienced by Eastern Montreal in the past decade.

Institute on Plant Biology has been housed in the Art Deco-style administration building. Not far from the building lies the **reception garden**, which displays vividly colored annual flowers from April through October. Nearby, the **reception center** leads to the Molson greenhouse, where visitors can get a first glimpse into the plant kingdom before exploring the ten greenhouses and some 30 thematic gardens that make up the Botanical Garden.

Serres d'exposition★ (Conservatories)

A stroll through the garden's ten magnificent exhibition greenhouses leads through reproduced botanical environments from around the world. From the Main Greenhouse, where temporary exhibits change seasonally, continue on to the Chinese Greenhouse, also known as the Jardin céleste. Here you'll find the wonderful **Wu Collection** of *penjing*, given to the Botanical Gardens in 1984 by Wu Yee-Sun, a Hong Kong banker who mastered the art of penjing, or "landscape in a pot." Following is a re-created Mexican hacienda, its courtyard and walls covered with cacti and succulent plants. Plants from arid regions occupy the next greenhouse, and the next features over 100 species of begonia and gesneriads. Tropical flora occupies two greenhouses, one devoted to rainforest vegetation, the other to **tropical plants** destined for export, such as banana, cocoa, coffee, teak, mahogany, palm, mango, and bamboo, while orchids and aroids thrive in the last conservatory.

Jardin de Chine★ (Chinese Garden)

Opened in 1991, this enchanting landscape is a replica of a typical Ming-dynasty (14–17C) garden from central China, near the Yangtze River. Architect Le Wei Zhong combined the key elements of Chinese gardens, mountains and water, to encourage peaceful contemplation.

The seven pavilions, with their steeply curving grey roofs, were built in Shanghai and assembled on site. The ornate main pavilion—called the "Friendship Pavilion"—hosts temporary exhibits. The large terrace affords sweeping views over the lakes and gardens. Across the lake rises a jagged rock

mountain (9m/29.5ft), with a stone stairway, cave and tumbling waterfall. Don't miss the Chinese Lantern Exhibition each fall from September through end of October.

Jardin japonais (Japanese Garden)

Designed by the Japanese landscape architect Ken Nakajima, this 2.5ha/6.2-acre garden (1988) presents a wonderful juxtaposition of water, boulders and plants—including a pond and a waterfall—in the traditional Japanese style, creating an atmosphere of peace and harmony that attracts visitors year-round. The unusual green rocks are peridotites from the Eastern Townships. Exhibit spaces in the **Japanese pavilion** (1989), styled as a traditional family home, offer visitors a glimpse into Japanese artistic and cultural expression. The pavilion complex includes a Zen garden, composed of raked pebbles and stones. The Japanese garden also features a garden of **bonsais** cultivated according to the Japanese tradition (*on view seasonally*).

First Nations Garden

Since 2001, this 2.5ha/6-acre area of maples, ash, elms and herbs allows non-Natives to explore the original environment of the resident eleven First Nations tribes living in this place before the Europeans arrived. Discover the farming methods of the Algonquin Nation, or a fall camp in the middle of 5,000 trees.

University of Montreal Biodiversity Center

This glass, wood and steel structure brings together three levels of study. Temporary exhibitions cover a wide swath of biodiversity topics; another level is dedicated to botanist Marie-Victorin and is filled with plants, mushrooms and insects (visits by appointment). Research laboratories occupy the third level (no visits permitted). Together, these three facets of the building highlight the three guiding principles of the Botanical garden site: conservation, organization and research.

The Botanical Garden offers a wealth of other points of interest to delight plant lovers. The seasonal **Exhibition Garden** (arranged in traditional French patterns) features shrubs, plants of Quebec, toxic plants, medicinal plants, trial vegetables and hardy perennials. In the **Rose Garden**, visitors can admire over 10,000 specimens planted among the trees and shrubs. Ornamental plants indigenous to aquatic environments, such as lotuses, water lilies and water hyacinths, grow in the **Marsh and Bog Garden**'s 110 pools. In the **Shade Garden**, 1,000 species of primulas and begonias are shaded beneath lime, maple and ash

Jardin de Chine, Jardin botanique de Montréal, during Halloween

© Philippe Renault / hemis.fr

St. Lawrence River and Biosphère Canada on Île Ste-Hélène

trees; and the **Flowery Brook** features irises, peonies, asters and other flowers arranged in a traditional English garden. Not to be missed are the **Alpine Garden**, with plants from the world's major mountain ranges displayed in a rock garden setting; the **Leslie Hancock Garden** of azaleas and rhododendrons; and the **Arboretum**, which covers more than half of the total area with over 10,000 specimens of about 3,000 different species.

Montreal Insectarium

North side of rue Sherbrooke in the Botanical Garden. Open Tue–Sun Jan–mid-May 9am–5pm; mid-May–Aug until 6pm; Sept–Oct until 9pm. www.museumsnature.ca.

Built in the shape of a giant bug, this unusual and fascinating museum (1990) displays a vast selection of insects from all over the world (approximately 150,000 specimens). Most of the insects on exhibit are preserved, although some living specimens can be observed (including a beehive). The collections are presented as thematic exhibits that highlight the fascinating world of entomology and the role insects play in our environment. The insectarium also features a fine collection of monarch butterflies. Renovated in 2011, the permanent exhibition "We are the Insects" unveils the fascinating universe of the many tiny species that dominate the globe through sheer numbers.

Biodôme★

Open Jun 24–Labor Day, daily 9am–6pm; rest of the year daily 9am–5pm. $16.50 (Biodôme only, or $28 for Biodôme, Botanical Gardens and Insectarium). 514-868-3000. www.museumsnature.ca. Shuttle service (free) to and from the Biodôme, Olympic Park and the Botanical Garden.

Originally used as the Velodrome for the Olympic cycling events, this imaginative **building★** resembles a cyclist's racing helmet. Its vast, scalloped roof spans 160m/526ft and is supported by four "feet." The ceiling's six ribs are composed of 144 jointed sections, each one weighing between 50 and 100 tonnes. These six arches are linked by transverse bands, forming a trellis to support the skylights, which admit natural light to the interior.

Lack of interest in indoor cycling led to the velodrome's conversion into the Biodôme, an innovative museum of environmental and natural sciences. The museum, which opened its doors in 1992, re-creates the habitats of four "ecosystems." Equipped with sophisticated climatic regulators, the habitats support thousands of plants and animals indigenous to the ecosystem. Luxuriant vegetation and a variety of wildlife characterize the torrid **Tropical Forest,** inspired by the Amazonian jungle. Lynx, beaver, and otter frolic in the **Laurentian Forest**, domain of maple trees, pines birches and spruce.

Austere granite cliffs rise above the **St. Lawrence Marine Ecosystem**, where visitors can contemplate many types of fish and marine invertebrates.

The frozen banks of the **Polar World** harbor penguins and other water birds, illustrating the rigors of life in the Arctic and Antarctic regions. In the discovery room, visitors can observe the mechanisms by which plants and animals adapt to cold, heat, drought, or darkness. An "environment place" offering films and video completes the installation.

Musée du Château Dufresne

Southwest corner of rue Sherbrooke and Blvd Pie-IX; entrance at 2929 Avenue Jean-d'Arc just west of the building. Métro Pie-IX. Open year-round, Wed–Sun 10am–5pm. $14. 514-259-9201. www.chateaudufresne.com.

The Château Dufresne was constructed between 1915 and 1918 for two eminent figures of the French Canadian bourgeoisie—the brothers Oscar (a shoe industrialist) and Marius (architect and civil engineer) Dufresne. The symmetrical façade, with eight monumental Ionic columns and a dentiled cornice surmounted by a balustraded terrace, illustrates the tenets of the Beaux-Arts style in vogue at the time of construction. One of the most luxurious homes in the city of Maisonneuve, the reinforced concrete building reflected the grandiose aspirations that eventually led the city into bankruptcy and its subsequent annexation to Montreal.

Interior

Two identical wings, one for each brother, contained a total of 44 rooms decorated with mahogany paneling, ornamentation, and furnishings evoking the lifestyle of Montreal's moneyed class in the 1920s and 1930s. An innovation of the period, many of the decorative elements were prefabricated, ordered from catalogues.

The **rooms of Marius Dufresne** (*west side*), are characterized by abundant use of oak and Neoclassical woodwork. Mahogany paneling, Italian marble, and French wall coverings characterize the **rooms of Oscar Dufresne** (*east side*), which feature delicately tinted **mural panels★** by Guido Nincheri (1885–1973) in the parlor. Coffered ceilings, mahogany embellished with gilded foliage, Renaissance-style mural wall coverings; Each room here reveals perfection in its myriad details.

ADDITIONAL SIGHTS

ÎLE STE-HÉLÈNE ★

Métro Jean-Drapeau. By car: cross the Jacques-Cartier Bridge or the Concorde Bridge.

In 1611, Samuel de Champlain named the small island in the St. Lawrence, east of the main island of Montreal, after his wife, **Hélène Boulé**. Prior to 1665, when it became part of the Longueuil seigneury, the island served as a strategic defense point for the First Nations in their battles against the European newcomers. After Canadian Confederation in 1867, the island became the property of the federal government until

Hidden Culinary Gems

An unassuming location in the business district belies culinary riches at **Le Grand Comptoir** *(1225 Square Phillips; 514-393-3295)*, where classic bistro dishes like *ris de veau* (calf's sweetbread) and *bavette à l'échalotte* (flank steak with shallots) are easy on palate and wallet. Looking for a quick, tasty meal, especially in the wee hours? Try the famous smoked-meat sandwiches at **Dunn's** *(1249 rue Metcalfe, just south of rue Sainte-Catherine; 514-395-1927)*. Or if you find yourself in Old Montreal and want to try one of the city's leading home-grown chefs, look opposite Marché Bonsecour for Chuck Hughes' homey and inventive soul food downstairs at **Le Bremner** *(361 rue Saint-Paul Est, 514-544-0446)*. *See Addresses for more recommended restaurant options.*

Parc Jean-Drapeau

© Philippe Renault / hemis.fr

the city purchased it as a park early in the 20C. In 1967, Île Sainte-Hélène was extended to cover 138ha/341 acres, in order to host a major World's Fair, Expo '67, along with neighboring Île Notre-Dame. Together, these islands form the **Parc Jean-Drapeau**.

Today, most of the island is a public park; the road skirting the west side of the island provides excellent **views★** of the city skyline and port installations.

Stewart Museum (Old Fort)★

Open year-round Wed–Sun 11am–5pm. ⊛$10. ✗🅿 ✆514-861-6701. www.stewart-museum.org.

St. Helen's Island was sold in 1818 to the British government, which subsequently erected a citadel. Now affiliated with the McCord Museum, the Old Fort houses the **Musée David M. Stewart★** (David M. Stewart Museum), devoted to the history of European settlement in Quebec. The museum proudly presents displays covering two floors, on the early discoverers and first settlers, their explorations across the continent, the British Conquest, the effects of the American Revolution, the War of 1812 and the Patriote Rebellion. Note also the wonderful collection of maps and globes, ship models, kitchen utensils, weapons and navigation instruments and many archival documents. The newest exhibition "History and Memory" brings visitors from the earliest Native settlements to the present day through more than 500 artifacts.

Biosphère, Environment Museum★

Open Jun–Oct daily 10am–5pm; rest of the year Wed–Sun 10am–5pm ⊛$12. ✗♿🅿 ✆514-283-5000. www.ec.gc.ca/biosphere.

This geodesic dome designed by Buckminster Fuller for Expo '67 reveals the form the future was expected to take in the 1960s. Erected to house the US Pavilion for the World's Fair, the immense structure (76.2m/250ft in diameter) was originally covered with an acrylic sheath that was destroyed by fire in 1976. Since 1995 the Biosphère has housed Canada's first museum devoted to the conservation of water and the ecosystems of the St. Lawrence River and the Great Lakes, now expanded to include the entire environment. In the **Water Delights Hall** (*1st floor*), interactive consoles and hands-on exhibits highlight the nature of water and the crucial role it plays in the survival of living things. In **Connexions Hall** (*2nd floor*), visitors can view a multimedia presentation (*25min*), then participate in discussions designed to increase awareness of the fragility of our natural environment. The **Visions Hall** (*top floor*) affords glorious views of the St. Lawrence via telescopes; monitors simulate a helicopter flight over the river. From this level, step onto

Casino de Montréal

© Mathieu Dupuis / Tourisme Montréal

the balcony for a **view★** of Longueuil, the Victoria Bridge and downtown Montreal through the dome's skeleton of interconnecting tubes. In 2015, the museum began a large-scale renovation of its exhibition galleries.

La Ronde (Six Flags family)

Open mid-May–mid-Jun daily 10am–8pm; mid-Jun–early Sept daily 10am–10:30pm; early Sept–late Sept daily noon–7pm; Oct, Sat noon–9pm, Sun noon–8pm (ticket office closes 1hr before closing time). $38. 514-397-2000. www.laronde.com.

Montreal's major amusement park enjoys a wonderful site at the east end of St. Helen's Island. During summer, the park hosts the International Fireworks Competition.

ÎLE NOTRE-DAME★ (NOTRE DAME ISLAND)

By car: Bonaventure Highway and Concord Bridge. **By public transportation:** Free bus service from the Jean-Drapeau Métro station.

An artificial construction, Notre Dame Island was created for the St. Lawrence Seaway in 1959. Enlarged for Expo '67 with landfill excavated from the Métro, the island now extends over 116ha/286 acres. In 1978, a Formula 1 racetrack, the **Gilles Villeneuve Circuit**, was built. It now hosts the Formula 1 race, le **Grand Prix du Canada**, the biggest sporting event in Quebec.

The Expo '67 French Pavilion, formerly known as the Palais de la Civilization, is the island's most prominent edifice. Designed by the French architect Jean Faugeron, the striking structure adorned with aluminum spikes today houses the **Casino de Montréal**.

In summer, **Lac Notre-Dame** (*west side of the island*), lined by a sandy 600m/1,968ft beach, has canoes for rent, and welcomes sailing enthusiasts, swimmers and windsurfers. A company called KSF offers paddle-board rentals and lessons, and this protected little lake is a great place to learn (514-595-7873. www.ksf.ca).

Les Jardins des Floralies (floral garden, open year-round daily 6:30am–midnight; ($10) 514-872-6120; www.parcjeandrapeau.com) features superb gardens created for the International Floralies of 1980 and 2000.

CITÉ DU HAVRE

Constructed to protect the port, this peninsula links the city to St. Helen's Island via the Concorde Bridge. Among the structures remaining from Expo '67 is **Habitat '67★**, a futuristic, modular apartment complex, which launched the international career of the architect **Moshe Safdie**, also known for the National Gallery in Ottawa and the Musée de la civilisation à Québec.

ADDRESSES

STAY

HI-Montreal Youth Hostel – *1030, rue Mackay, Métro Lucién-Allier. 514-843-3317 or 1-866-843-3317. www.hostellingmontreal.com. 217 beds.* Organized into private rooms and small dorms that accommodate between four and 10 people, this Hostelling International youth hostel is located a few minutes from downtown and the train station.

Hôtel ALT – *12 rue Peel (ê Peel or Square-Victoria). 514-375-0220 or 1-855-823-8120. www.montreal.althotels.ca. 154 rooms.* ALT – a hip, hot brand from boutique specialists Groupe Germain Hospitalité of Quebec City – is a cornerstone of Griffintown, a trendy Montreal neighborhood. A young-in-spirit, contemporary concept, ALT features minimalist décor and comforts such as Egyptian cotton sheets, down duvets, pod coffee machines and glass spa showers.

Hôtel Anne ma soeur Anne – *4119 rue Saint-Denis (Mount Royal or Sherbrooke). 514-281-3187 or 1-877-281-3187. www.annemasoeuranne.com. 17 rooms and suites.* An unusual residential experience in a vintage two-storey house in the Plateau district. Rooms and studios have micro-kitchens and some have murphy beds and access to terraces. Breakfast croissants included.

Résidences Universitaires UQAM Ouest – *2100 rue Saint-Urbain. 514-987-7747, www.residences-uqam.qc.ca. Open May 15–Aug 15. Hundreds of rooms available when school is out.* Why not spend some time in a university residence? Situated at the edge of the Quartier des spectacles, this residence offers bargain rates for studios, and has apartments with kitchens and two to eight bedrooms.

Le Germain Montréal *2050 rue Mansfield (Peel or McGill). 514-849-2050 or 1-877-333-2050. www.germainmontreal.com. 101 rooms and suites.* An upscale boutique hotel that stands out for its chic interiors and personal service, Le Germain has a petite lobby with fresh flowers, a fireplace lounge and well-equipped rooms decorated in smart black and white with color pops. Rates include all-day coffee bar and continental breakfast at Laurie Raphaël, a gourmet restaurant that also sells Quebec food products. Pet-friendly.

Hôtel de l'Institut – *3535 rue Saint-Denis (Sherbrooke), 514-282-5120 or 855-229-8189. www.ithq.qc.ca.* 40 rooms and two suites. The hotel section of the well-known hospitality school is a good buy at the heart of the Bohemian action of Saint-Denis Street, facing the park, Carré Saint-Louis. The front desk is staffed by advanced students. Attractive, modern rooms and fine food can be had at the formal Restaurant de l'Institut, where students assist professional chefs and servers, and at the lower-priced Restaurant-école Paul-Émile-Lévesque, which is a student production. Breakfast included.

Hôtel Nelligan – *106 rue Saint-Paul Ouest (Place-d'Armes). 514-788-2040 or 1-877-788-2040 (free). www.hotelnelligan.com. 52 rooms and 53 suites.* Boutique design, heritage stone, poetry framed on the walls (Nelligan was the Poet Laureate of Quebec), chocolates on your pillows, and a location in one of the liveliest dining/drinking locales in the city. Lush trappings, great service, an attractive roof-top lounge in summertime, plus a gym and massage room, add up to a pleasurable experience. Two upscale eateries on site: the casual **Le Méchant Boeuf** *(www.mechantboeuf.com)* and the gourmet **Verses** *(514-788-4000; www.versesrestaurant.com).* Reservations at both are recommended.

Hostellerie Pierre du Calvet *– 405 rue Bonsecours Champ-de-Mars. 514-282-1725 and 1-866-544-1725.*

House of Jazz

2060 Rue Aylmer. 514-842-8656. Jazz lovers in the mood for excellent live music and a laid-back ambiance should keep this famed hangout in mind when planning an evening on the town. Stop in for a set or two and sample tasty barbecued chicken or ribs, either inside or on the outdoor summer terrace.

Bring Your Own Wine

Restaurants that don't have a liquor licenses can allow patrons to bring in their own favorite vintages. Most BYOW eateries are located in the Plateau Mont-Royal, Quartier des spectacles, Vieux-Montréal and Quartier Latin districts. There is no corkage fee.

www.pierreducalvet.ca. 9 rooms. *See Maison Pierre du Calvet, p109. Restaurant* ⊜⊜⊜⊜. Step back in time at the oldest home open to public accommodation in Montreal. The 18C structure has been restored as an elegant European house decorated with family heirlooms, antiques, and Oriental rugs. Enjoy breakfast in the airy, plant-filled Victorian greenhouse. Dinner is served nightly to the public in **Les Filles du Roy**. Greenhouse for cocktails, library for tranquility, fireplace for ambiance, and Museum of Bronze for something different.

⊜⊜⊜⊜ **Hôtel Place d'Armes** – *701 Côte de la Place d'Armes, Place-d'Armes. 514-842-1887 or 1-888-450-1887. www.hotelplacedarmes.com. 80 rooms and 53 suites.* This charming boutique hotel is strategically located on Place d'Armes in the center of Old Montreal. Calming colors and rich mahogany furnishings characterize the elegant rooms; amenities include bathrobes, down comforters, whirlpool baths, and Internet access. Large windows afford nice views of Chinatown, downtown Montreal, and Notre-Dame Basilica.

EAT

Good to know: Montreal's top chefs also operate baby bistros that are more casual and affordable than their main restaurants, but maintain the same high standards; call it gourmet comfort food. Check out Brasserie T!, sister to the Relais & Châteaux member Toqué!; and Taverne F, a fun spinoff of Café Ferreira, both in the Quartier des spectacles. Le Filet in Le Plateau is an epicurean affiliate of the excellent Le Club Chasse et Pêche. And another distinguished Relais & Châteaux Grand Chef, Jérôme Ferrer of Europea, also runs Birks Café in an historic jewellery store. Martin Picard, who made foie gras poutine famous at Au Pied du Cochon, goes country-style at Cabane à Sucre, his maple sugar shack.

⊜ **L'Arrivage** – *350 Place Royale. 514-872-9128. Mon 11:30am–2pm; Tue–Sun 11:30am–4pm.* This pleasant lunch spot in Old Montreal, located within the Pointe-à-Callière Montreal Museum of Archaeology and History, serves delightful creations in an airy space with a view of the Old Port. It is particularly nice in summer, when the terrace is open.

⊜ **Sumac** – *3618 rue Notre-Dame Ouest, Saint-Henri (Place Saint-Henri). 514-935-1444. www.sumacrestaurant.com. Open Tue–Thu 11:30am-9pm, Fri until 10pm, Sat 3pm–10pm.* This is the place for a homespun Middle Eastern feast—babaganoush, hummus, beef kefta in pita, and crisp cool salads of cucumber and cabbage—served in a cozy neighborhood atmosphere.

⊜⊜ **La Banquise** – *994 rue Rachel Est. 514-525-2415. www.restolabanquise.com. Open noon–12am.* This is the Temple of Poutine, and after a night on the town, you will understand what this signature Quebec dish is all about. Try the Classic, the Inferno, or the Elvis, or have a burger or hot dog instead. Serves good microbrews as well.

⊜⊜ **Café des Lettres/Presse Café** – *475 blvd de Maisonneuve Est, inside the Grande Bibliothèque (main library). 514-499-2999. www.banq.qc.ca. Open library hrs Tue–Sun 10am–10pm, Café des Lettres open Tue–Fri 11am–3pm.* Hip music, an awesome structure, and friendly service top an informal lunch menu highlighted by salade niçoise, croque-monsieur, pizza with arugula and proscuitto, and Quebec pecan pie. Enjoy this gem.

⊜⊜ **M sur Masson** – *2876 rue Masson est. 514-678-2999, www.msurmasson.com. Mon–Fri 11:30am–5pm, Mon–Sat 5:30pm–11, Sun 10am–3pm.* Delicious fare in a stylish, contemporary tavern-bistro, with chalkboard daily specials, good wine and local beer. The menu includes tartares, kale salad, onion soup, braised veal cheeks, steak-frites, black pudding and cassoulet.

⊜⊜ **Café Saigon** – *1280 rue Saint-André (Berri-UQAM). 514-849-0429. BYOW. Open daily Mon–Fri 11:30am–2:30pm, and*

5pm–9. Sat opens at 5pm. Cash only, but there is an ATM. A family-run pan-Asian original, serving Vietnamese soups, General Tau chicken, peanut butter dumplings, Imperial rolls, and generous shrimp and scallop plates, topped with home-made soy sauce. Recent renovations have made this Gay Village institution popular, although the surrounding area remains scruffy.

⊖⊜⊜ **Au Pied de Cochon** – *536 rue Duluth East, Le Plateau (Ⓜ Mount Royal or Sherbrooke). ✆514-281-1114. www.restaurantaupieddecochon.ca. Open 5pm–midnight. Closed Mon–Tue.* Chef Martin Picard has gone global with his foie gras poutine, and Au Pied has made its reputation on rich and hearty dishes such as duck carpaccio, bison tartare, cassoulet and roast pork, and maple syrup pie. A tribute to Quebec ingredients and techniques; park your calorie-counter at the door when you enter this temple to calorific cuisine.

⊖⊜⊜ **Le Club Chasse et Pêche** – *423 rue Saint-Claude, Old Montreal (ⓂChamp-de-Mars). ✆514-861-1112. leclubchasseetpeche.com. Open Tue–Sat 6pm–10:30pm.* An original kitchen, extensive wine cellar, great service and warm ambiance make this one of Montreal's most appealing French restaurants. Delicacies include bison ravioli, veal cheeks with daikon, risotto with braised pork and foie gras, and duck with blood oranges and wagyu beef.

⊖⊜⊜ **L'Express** – *3927 rue Saint-Denis. Le Plateau (Ⓜ Mont-Royal or Sherbrooke). ✆514-845-5333. www.restaurantlexpress.ca Open Mon–Fri 8am–2am, Sat 10am–2am, Sun 10am–1am. Closed Dec 25.* This quintessential bistro has good service, a popular bar and traditional French comfort dishes such as celery remoulade, pot-au-feu, fish soup, kidneys in mustard sauce, roast quail and duck confit. Very Montreal.

⊖⊜⊜ **Manitoba** – *271 Saint-Zotique Ouest, Rosemont. ⓂParc. ✆514-270-8000. Open Tue–Fri 11am–4pm, Tue–Sat 6–12pm, Sun 10am–3pm. www.restaurantmanitoba.com.* One of the city's top new restaurants has a hunter-gatherer theme, with cuisine sauvage (wild, foraged ingredients) and a First Nations accent. You'll dine on quail, sagamite croquettes, elk, rabbit, local fish and venison.

Music and Ambiance

When in the city for the evening, be sure to stop by **Les Deux Pierrots** *(104 Rue Saint-Paul Est; ✆514-861-1270).* A Montreal institution, this nightclub is the perfect place to discover traditional Quebec music in a very convivial setting.

⊖⊜⊜ **Tapas24** – *420 Notre-Dame Ouest, Old Montreal. (ⓂSquare-Victoria-ICAO). ✆514-849-4424. wwwtapas24.ca. Mon–Fri 11:30am–11pm, Sat 5pm–11.* Authentic Barcelona-style tapas in a striking contemporary space of natural wood and black walls. Flounder ceviche, tortillas with chorizo sausage, garlic gambas (shrimp), Iberian ham, mussels, cod croquettes and sweets like Catalan flan, from the country that made small plates famous.

⊖⊜⊜⊜ **Estiatorio Milos** – *5357 ave du Parc, Le Plateau. Ⓜ Mont-Royal. ✆514-272-3522. Lunch Mon–Fri 12–2:45pm, dinner Sun–Fri from 5:30pm. www.milos.ca/restaurants/montreal.* The wildly successful Montreal Milos, which has the look of a seaside Greek tavern, is the flagship of a group of gourmet restaurants now operating in New York, Athens, Miami, Las Vegas and London. This is the restaurant of choice for power brokers and visiting celebrities who are fans of its crab cakes, grilled octopus, tomato and feta salad, aged rib-eye, lamb and market-fresh fish. These delicacies are pricey at night, but there are $25 specials at lunch-time and after 10pm.

⊖⊜⊜⊜ **Toqué!** – *900 Place Jean-Paul-Riopelle, Old Montreal. ⓂSquare-Victoria or Place-d'Armes. Open Tue–Sat 5:30pm–10pm and Tue–Fri 11:30am–1:45pm. Closed Sun–Mon. ✆514-499-2084. www.restaurant-toque.com.* One of Montreal's best-known chefs, Normand Laprise, artfully presents contemporary French cuisine using fresh, and often unusual, local ingredients. Signature dishes include veal carpaccio, octopus with merguez, venison chop, duck magret, and halibut with fennel and pancetta, followed by dreamy desserts like maple pannacotta.

TAKING A BREAK

Good to know: In multi-cultural Montreal, you can sip your coffee with croissants, baklava, pastilles, bagels or biscotti. Tea shops are blossoming with aromatic brews, and the city's top bagel bakeries have been dueling for decades. Food trucks, the latest trend in fabulous fast food, pop up every summer. And, if you miss your pets back home, the newest places to chill out are cat cafés. Pass the cream, please.

Le Bilboquet – *1311 rue Bernard Ouest. (Outremont). 514-276-0414. Closed Jan–Feb. Opens daily at 11am; closes anytime between 9pm and midnight.* A dreamy artisanal ice-cream shop that opened in 1983, Bilboquet has set the standard for all followers. Favorites include chocolate-orange, maple, and chocolate-cashew ice creams, and raspberry, mango and strawberry sorbet. Has branches on Sherbrooke in Westmount, and in Laval.

Café Chat L'Heureux – *172 ave Duluth Est (Mont Royal). 438-333-1505. www.cafechatlheureux.com. Tue–Thu 11am–8pm, Fri–Sat 10am–10pm, Sun 10am–8pm. Closed Mon.* Cat cafés are the latest rage and if you left Sylvester or Muffin at home, you will find cuddles here, with alumni from the SPCA. Cat Lady Sandwich and Cat-Puccino are simply purr-fect.

Caffé Italia – *6840 Blvd Saint-Laurent (de Castelnau, Little Italy). 514-495-0059. Daily 6am–11pm.* An authentic old-school café in Little Italy with bracing espresso, cappucino and latte. Recent renovations have preserved most of the 1950s retro simplicity. A five-minute walk from Jean-Talon Market.

Mandy's – *5033 rue Sherbrooke Ouest, Westmount. (Vendome). 514-227-1640. Open Mon–Sat 11am–9pm. www.mandys.ca. Branches at 2067 rue Crescent and 203 ave Laurier Ouest. Plateau. (Laurier). 514-670-7820.* This tiny take-out spot with a few tables and a summer-time patio tosses great, made-to-order salads. You can choose fresh baby greens and add cranberries, tomatoes, blue cheese, tuna, chicken, tofu or nuts, plus zingy dressings such as Asian sesame, honey-mustard and cilantro. Call ahead to skip the line.

Schwartz's Hebrew Deli – *3895 blvd Saint-Laurent (Sherbrooke). 514-842-4813. www.schwartzsdeli.com. Open Sun–Thu 9am–12:30am, Fri 9am–1am, Sat 9am–2:00am.* Opened in 1928, Schwartz's is part of Montreal lore, famous for hand-cut smoked meat and grilled steaks with signature spices. Communal tables, a frenetic ambiance and outdoor line-ups add to the atmosphere. Don't expect fast service; waiting in line is part of the charm.

St-Viateur Bagel Shop – *263 rue Saint-Viateur Ouest (Laurier). 514-276-8044. www.stviateurbagel.com. Open 24hrs.* Open since 1957, St-Viateur bakes about 12,000 hand-rolled bagels a day in its wood-fired oven. You can buy cream cheese and smoked salmon to make your own bagel-and-lox, and head over to Mount Royal for a picnic. A similar formula exists two blocks away at **Fairmont Bagel** – *74 rue Fairmount Ouest (Laurier). 514-272-0667. www.fairmountbagel.com. Open 24hrs.*

Le Duc de Lorraine – *5002 chemin de la Côte-des-Neiges (Côte-des-Neiges, near the western side of Mount Royal). 514-731-4128. www.ducdelorraine.ca. Mon–Fri 7am–7:30pm, Sat–Sun 7am–6:30pm.* Renowned for their quality French breads and pastries, this charming, windowed tearoom is a fine spot to sample quiche, croque-monsieur, café au lait, éclairs, cakes and macaroons.

Olive + Gourmando – *351 rue Saint-Paul Ouest (Square-Victoria). 514-350-1083. oliveetgourmando.com. Tue–Sat 8am–5pm.* This venerable neighborhood bakery and café serves salads, gourmet sandwiches with pancetta, goat cheese and vegetables, along with brownies, brioches and espresso. A welcome break if you are touring Old Montreal.

Palm Court Bar, Ritz-Carlton Montréal – *1228 rue Sherbrooke West (Peel). 514-842-4212. www.ritz carlton.com. Two seatings daily 1:00pm and 4:30pm.* The Palm Court is a splendidly restored 1912 salon off the lobby and the formal tea service ($32) is the real English deal: finger sandwiches, petits-fours and scones with Devonshire cream and strawberry jam.

SHOPPING

Good to know: A variety of boutiques, clothing stores, art galleries, and fashionable and fast-food restaurants can be found along Sainte-Catherine, Sherbrooke, Peel, Crescent and de la Montagne streets. Multi-cultural and trendy, Blvd Saint-Laurent is alive with an intriguing selection of grocery stores and clothing outlets.

Underground City – About 2,000 mostly chain stores, movie theaters and food courts in various indoor malls are connected via the Métro's station network. Opening hours vary for each building. Stores might open at 9:30 or 10am Mon–Sat and 11am or noon on Sundays, and close at 5, 6 or 9pm.

Complexe Desjardins – *150 rue Sainte-Catherine Ouest* (Place-des-Arts or Place-d'Armes) *514-281-1870.*

Centre Eaton – *705 rue Sainte-Catherine Ouest* (McGill) *514-288-3708.*

Place Montréal Trust – *1500 McGill College Ave.* (McGill or Peel) *514-843-8000.*

Place Ville-Marie – *1 Place Ville-Marie* (Bonaventure or McGill) *514-866-6666.*

Promenades de la Cathédrale – *625 rue Sainte-Catherine Ouest* (McGill) *514-845-8230.*

MILE-END

Drawn & Quarterly – *211 rue Bernard Ouest, Outremont. 514-279-2224. www.drawnandquarterly.com. Open Sun–Tue 11am–7pm, Wed–Fri 11am–9pm, Sat 10am–8pm.* This is a temple to alternative comic books, fiction and art books from around the world; Quebec authors and artists in particular are well-represented here.

PLATEAU

Kanuk – *2485 rue Rachel Est, Mont-Royal, 514-284-4494. www.kanuk.com.* A specialist outdoors shop whose signature items are chic and durable parkas, in all shapes, sizes and colors. Every Quebecer has at least one piece from this store – it's the perfect antidote to a cold Canadian winter.

DRINKS

Le Cheval Blanc – *809 rue Ontario Ouest (Berri-UQAM ou Sherbrooke). 514-522-0211. www.lechevalblanc.ca. Daily from 3pm.* One of the undisputed champions of the microbrewery scene, Cheval has 11 local brews on tap, and it also offers a lineup of live music, art exhibitions and book and record launches.

Bily Kun/O Patro Vys – *354/356 rue Mont-Royal Est (Mont-Royal). 514-845-5392. www.bilykun.com.* Starting each day at 3pm, this combo cocktail bar and live music venue attracts a steady following. Jazz, hip-hop, house, reggae and beyond, the DJs and musicians hold court with gusto; an inviting place to hang out, listen to music, or have an intimate conversation.

Brasserie T! – *1425 rue Jeanne-Mance (Place-des-Arts). 514-282-0808. Open daily from 11:30am. www.brasserie-t.com.* The younger partner of the famous eatery TOQUÉ offers an appealing range of fresh seasonal products including homemade charcuteries, tartars, and fresh fish. An ideal spot to meet for cocktails after work. Try their pan-seared foie-gras.

Café du Nouveau-Monde – *84 rue Sainte-Catherine Ouest (Place-des-Arts). 514-866-8669. Mon 11:30am–8pm, Tue–Fri 11:30am–midnight, Sat 5pm–midnight.* This café/bistro/restaurant is located inside the theater, and is a great meeting place for a pre-play drink or snack, or just to watch the passers-by.

Plateau Lounge – *901 sq. Victoria (Square-Victoria). 514-395-3195. www.wunderbarmontreal.com. Mon–Sat 4pm until closing, Sun 5pm until closing.* This is the cocktail bar inside the Hotel "W" facing Place Victoria in Old Montreal. A crossroads for legions of high-tech workers, as well as traders from the Montreal Exchange, this bar has earned a name for itself by inventing drinks like Saraswatini, Milton's Hope, and more.

ENTERTAINMENT

Tickets for major events can be purchased at the venue or through the following: **Admission** *514-790-1245 and 1-800-361-4595, www.admission.com.* **La Voitrine** at 145 rue Sainte-Catherine Ouest (inside Place des Arts) offers last-minute tickets to events. *℘514-285-4545 or www.lavitrine.com.* For local entertainment and sport schedules check out *www.montrealplus.ca.*

MUSIC

The complex at Place des Arts offers eight spaces for performing in one central zone, including the prestigious Opéra de Montréal. *www.operademontreal.com.*

McGill University fosters the widely respected McGill Chamber Orchestra *(℘514-487-5190)*, which often performs at Place des Arts. McGill University's **Pollack Hall** *(℘514-398-8993)* presents a full calendar of classical and jazz concerts. Centre Bell *(www.centrebell.ca)*, home of the Montreal Canadiens Hockey Club, also presents touring acts, mega rock concerts and special events throughout the year *(℘514-989-2841).*

In the Bohemian Mile End district, **Casa del Popolo** and **Salla Rosa** *(4848 blvd St-Laurent; ℘514-284-0122; www.casadelpopolo.com)* are temples of independent, contemporary music. **Cabaret Mile End** also has jazz and hip-hop on its roster, in the same part of town *(5240 avenue Parc; ℘514-563-1395; www.lemileend.org).* Avenue Mont-Royal boasts the **Orange Divan** *(4234 blvd Saint Lawrence; ℘514-840-9090; www.divanorange.org)*, where a high level of enthusiasm is presented for electro and emerging local musicians.

SPORTS

Montreal is home to several professional sports teams. **Ice hockey:** Montreal Canadiens (National Hockey League), from Oct–Mar at the Bell Center (ⓜLucien-L'Allier) *℘514-989-2841.* **Canadian football:** Montreal Alouettes (Canadian Football League), from mid-Jun–early Nov at Percival Molson Stadium (ⓜMcGill) *℘514-871-2255.* **Soccer:** Montreal Impact (Major League Soccer), from Apr–Sept, at Saputo Stadium (ⓜPie-IX and Viau) *℘514-328-3668.*

Recreation – Year-round indoor ice skating ($7.50) and rentals at the Patinoire de l'Atrium Le1000, *1000 rue de la Gauchetière* (ⓜBonaventure) *℘514-395-0555, www.le1000.com.* IMAX-Telus Theatre in Old Montreal (at the Montreal Science Center) *℘514-496-4724, www.oldportofmontreal.com.* Casino de Montréal (ⓜJean-Drapeau) *℘514-392-2746, www.casino-de-montreal.com.*

EVENTS

Montréal en Lumière – *www.montreal enlumiere.com. Last two weeks of February.* This international culinary/performance festival offers workshops, tastings, fireworks, and concerts, promoting the traditions of a different country each year. For dining out, visiting chefs team with locals to create specials at eateries throughout the city. The popular **Festival All Nighter** closes the event; a few downtown businesses stay open all night, and a mammoth breakfast is served free of charge to all who are still standing.

Grand Prix Week – *www.grandprix montreal.com.* The largest event of the year in Montreal: for one week in early June the city pulses to the rhythms of Formula 1 racing at the Circuit Gilles-Villeneuve on Île Notre-Dame, near downtown. The week features parties, clubbing, street scenes and celebrities, and peaks with the two-hour race.

Francofolies – *www.francofolies.com.* In June, performers of French music converge for a celebration of all things Gallic.

Montreal International Jazz Festival – *www.montrealjazzfest.com.* An exuberant celebration of world-class jazz plus a selection of musical styles beyond the definition of jazz, on indoor and outdoor stages throughout the city. This famous festival is a can't miss for aficionados and newcomers alike.

Just For Laughs Festival – *Mid to late July, after the jazz fest.* French and English humorists, featuring some of the best acts in the world.

Film Festival – *www.ffm-montreal.org.* Late August into September. Recognized internationally for its artistic integrity and high-quality screenings.

Montreal Festival de nouveau cinema – *www.nouveaucinema.ca.* 10 days in October. For more than 40 years this festival of new cinema has been a leader in all formats.

ÎLE SAINT-BERNARD: A TRAVELER'S WONDERLAND

Cross any bridge to Montreal's south shore, head west to the community of Châteauguay, and in about 20 minutes (depending on traffic) you will arrive at a traveler's wonderland called Île Saint-Bernard. In summertime, you can park the car at the Lachine Marina just southwest of the city, and take the one-hour shuttle boat, enjoying a waterside tour in the process.

Formerly a religious retreat operated by the Grey Nuns, the entire 404ha/1,000-acre island was recently sold to the town of Châteauguay. The non-profit organization Héritage Saint-Bernard *(www.heritagestbernard.qc.ca)* operates a modest hotel, restaurant, bistro, and live theater *(Pavilion de l'Ile)*, and the **Marguerite-D'Youville Wildlife Refuge** *(open daily sunrise to sunset)*.

It is a perfect day trip from Montreal to explore the reserve. You could stay overnight at the **Manoir d'Youville**; with about 120 sparse but comfortable rooms, the Manoir includes three meals per day and two snacks, at surprisingly modest rates.

There is nothing sparse about the location however, with over 300 apple trees immediately within view, the oldest grain mill in North America (1631), and a million-dollar view across to the Island of Montreal and beyond. Adirondack chairs are lined up along the resort's waterfront, and trails through the property extend in all directions. Île Saint-Bernard's bevy of wildlife will appeal to any nature enthusiast—marshland stocked with bird species, and open fields and forest, where deer, turtles, otters and other species happily coexist. If you are lucky, you might even see the rare night heron, or the more common pileated woodpecker, both known to reside here.

For an utterly tranquil perch on the water, home-made cuisine, entertaining live theater, activity programs for the kids and a wildlife refuge surprisingly robust, this new/old resort is the place to visit. A warm welcome is to be expected from the staff and guides. Ask about their audioguide.

℘450-698-3133. www.ilesaintbernard.com.

Île Saint-Bernard

© Xavier de Belle / Michelin

The Island of Montreal

The City of Montreal occupies the center of its namesake island, and contains 19 boroughs, which include many former small towns and neighborhoods around the island. Dominating the landscape is the green space of Mount Royal, a perpetual magnet for residents in any season. Boating is also popular, and, with its considerable shoreline, it is common to see families and amateur fishermen enjoying one of the continent's great waterways, the St. Lawrence River, which flows from the Great Lakes to the Atlantic Ocean. The Lachine Canal leads from downtown around the Lachine Rapids and on to the West Island bedroom communities, and residents on the north side of the island, at the east end, enjoy the outdoors in Parc de la Visitation, cycling, running, or walking along the rich green waterside.

- **Population:** 3.9 million for Greater Montreal.
- **Michelin Map:** pp108–109.
- **Info:** 514-873-2015 & 1-877-266-5687 or www.tourisme-montreal.com.
- **Location:** Southwest in Province of Quebec. The city core covers most of the Island of Montreal where the St. Lawrence and Ottawa rivers meet at Lake of Two Mountains in the western tip. Montreal lies between the St. Lawrence River on its south, and the Rivière des Prairies on the north. The city is named for its dominant feature, a three-headed hill called Mount-Royal, which rises 232m/773ft above sea level.
- **Kids:** The Parc-nature de l'île-de-la-Visitation in Sault-au-Récollet is a fantastic urban park with plenty of activities on offer.
- **Timing:** Montreal is in the Eastern Standard Time zone. Every season offers a new experience.

THE NORTHEAST

SAINT-LAURENT

28km/17mi from Sainte-Anne-de-Bellevue or about 10km/6.2mi north of downtown by rue Sherbrooke Est (Rte. 138), Rte. 15 Nord, and Blvd Décarie.

This industrial-residential suburb of Montreal was founded about 1687, when the brothers Paul, Michel and Louis Descarie arrived to farm the land they called the Côte Saint-Laurent.

Le Musée des maîtres et artisans du Québec★

On the grounds of Cégep Saint-Laurent, at 615 Ave. Sainte-Croix. From Blvd Décarie, turn right on rue du Collège. The college is straight ahead at the junction with ave. Sainte-Croix. Du Collège. Open Wed–Sun noon–5pm. $7. 514-747-7367.

This small museum is located in the Presbyterian Church of St. Andrew and St. Paul (1867), and was moved from Dorchester Boulevard to this site in 1931. The striking Gothic Revival structure served as a chapel until 1975 when it was converted into a museum. Inside, the intricately carved wooden vault and luminous stained-glass windows can still be seen.

The museum owns an impressive collection of French-Canadian artifacts, including the remnants of the legendary glassblower's (Jean Vallières) shop Verrière la Mailloche from Quebec City. Displayed in exhibits concentrating on particular themes, the objects illustrate such trades as tin smithing, textile fabrication, ceramic making, furniture making, silver and gold smithing and wood sculpting. Of particular interest is the authentic reconstruction of a silversmith's shop. A large collection of religious sculpture and some fine pieces of furniture complement the exhibits. The museum also mounts temporary exhibits on the area's cultural and artistic heritage.

SAULT-AU-RÉCOLLET

Located about 12km/7.4mi north of downtown Montreal by rue Sherbrooke Est (Rte. 138), rue Cartier, rue Rachel, and Ave. Papineau.

Today part of the City of Montreal, Sault-au-Récollet is one of the oldest communities on Montreal Island. Set beside rapids on Rivières-des-Prairies, it was visited by both Jacques Cartier, in 1535, and Samuel de Champlain, in 1615. It was named for a Récollet brother, Nicolas Viel, who drowned in the rapids in 1625 while returning from the Huron country with his Native companion, Ahuntsic. The Sulpicians founded a mission here in 1696, and the parish came into existence in 1736. Sault-au-Récollet was a separate municipality until 1916 when it was annexed by Montreal. Since 1930, the rapids have been harnessed by Hydro-Québec for electricity.

Église de la Visitation-de-la-Bienheureuse-Vierge-Marie★ (Church of the Visitation of the Blessed Virgin Mary)

1847 Blvd Gouin Est. From Ave. Papineau turn left on Blvd Henri-Bourassa and left on rue des Jésuites. Henri-Bourassa. Open year-round, Mon–Wed and Fri 9am –11:30am, 1:30pm–3pm. Closed Thu and some holidays. 514-388-4050.

Built between 1749 and 1752, this edifice is the oldest church on Montreal Island. Its large nave and absence of lateral chapels are in keeping with the style of Récollet churches in New France. The stone **façade** (1850, John Ostell), flanked by two tall towers, was inspired by the church of Sainte-Geneviève de Pierrefonds (northwest of Montreal), designed a few years earlier by Thomas Baillairgé. Victor Bourgeau later used this same design throughout the region, notably for the Church of St. Rose, in Laval. The **interior★★** illustrates the esthetic principles of the Quévillon school. The turquoise and gold vault, adorned with diamond-shaped barrels, is of rare quality; like the sculpted décor in the chancel, it was installed by David Fleury-David about 1820. Fashioned by Vincent Chartrand of the Quévillon studio, the magnificent **pulpit★** (1837), with its finely decorated sound reflector, is one of the most beautiful pieces of liturgical furniture sculpted in Quebec. The tabernacle above the main altar is attributed to Philippe Liébert (1732–1804); the main altar and side altars were designed by Louis-Amable Quévillon (1749–1823). The portals (1820) leading to the sacristy are embellished with polychrome bas-reliefs inscribed into Louis XV-style panels.

Parc-nature de l'Île-de-la-Visitation

Henri-Bourassa, 2425 Blvd Gouin Est. Open year-round, daily sunrise–sunset. Closed to vehicles. Reception center open late May–mid-Aug daily 9:30am–6pm; rest of year daily 9:30am–4:30pm. $7. 514-280-6733. www.ville.montreal.qc.ca/grandsparcs.

L'île-de-la-Visitation is one of six nature parks operated by the Montreal Urban Community. Its 33ha/82 rolling acres are laced with paths for biking and skiing. Several mills have occupied the strip of land connecting the island to the banks of the Prairies River since the 18C. The last one operated until 1970. Before reaching the island, the attractive, early-19C **Maison du Pressoir** (Cider Press House) can be visited. The original cider-pressing mechanism is exposed here, and displays illustrate the cider-making process. This is a great place to enjoy lunch and a drink overlooking the water (514-850-4222 open late May–late Oct, daily noon–6pm).

DRIVING TOUR

THE WEST END★★

See Map Montreal and Surroundings, p108–109.

This shoreline drive offers visitors a pleasant break from the bustle of Montreal city. Beginning on the southwestern outskirts of the city of Montreal, a **panoramic road★** leads to the western tip of the island.

The meandering lakeshore drive hugs the St. Lawrence River and Lake Saint-Louis shores and borders affluent residential districts interspersed with numerous parks, equipped with picnic spots and playgrounds. First named Blvd LaSalle in LaSalle, the street becomes Blvd Saint-Joseph in Lachine, then chemin du Bord-du-Lac (or chemin Lakeshore) between Dorval and Sainte-Anne-de-Bellevue.

Maison Saint-Gabriel★ (Saint-Gabriel House)

2146 Place Dublin (Metro Charlevoix then bus no. 57) in the borough of Pointe-Saint-Charles, 4km/2.5mi from downtown Montreal by rue Wellington. Turn left at Parc Marguerite-Bourgeoys, and follow signs. Open Tue–Sun 1pm–5pm, guided tours hourly. $10 for admission and tour, $15 Jun 21–Sept 6, which includes outdoor activities. P 514-935-8136. www.maisonsaint-gabriel.qc.ca.

In 1668 **Marguerite Bourgeoys** built a house here to care for the filles du roy, the king's wards. Destroyed by fire in 1693, the structure was rebuilt five years later on the old foundations. Restored in 1965 and today considered one of the oldest structures on Montreal Island, the house serves as a historical museum, and features a boutique, events area, patio, and dining hall.

Maison Saint-Gabriel

© Gregory B. Gallagher / Michelin

Located on the first floor, the community and reception rooms contain much of the original 18C furniture and present displays on Marguerite Bourgeoys and her order. Domestic equipment and utensils are on display in the kitchen. A dormitory and the bedroom of one of the *filles du roy* can be seen on the upper floors. Still joined by the original wooden pegs (1698), the rafters and beams of the attic attest to the house's solid construction.

Return to rue Wellington and continue to Blvd LaSalle.

LaSalle

5km/3mi.

Named for Robert Cavelier de La Salle (1643–87), this community was formerly part of Lachine, but became independent in 1912. At the end of 6th Avenue, take the path across the old hydro dam (1895) to enjoy superb **views★** of the Lachine Rapids. Offshore lies Île aux Hérons, an island designated as a nature reserve to protect herons. The long-necked wading birds fish in the rapids and can often be spotted along both banks of the river.

Blvd LaSalle passes under the double span of the **Honoré-Mercier Bridge** before entering Lachine. Opened in 1934, the bridge was named for Mercier, Premier of Quebec from 1887 through 1891.

Parc René-Lévesque (René Lévesque Park)

From Blvd LaSalle, turn left onto chemin du Canal.

Formerly called Grande-Jetée, this park is situated on a peninsula jutting out into Lake Saint-Louis. The peninsula was built up on land reclaimed from the river between 1873 and 1884 to shelter the third entrance to the Lachine Canal. The park was renamed after René Lévesque (1922–87), premier of Quebec from 1976 through 1985. Foot and cycle paths lead to the tip of the peninsula past 12 pieces of contemporary sculpture created for various symposia held every two years in the borough's

parks. Note in particular Georges Dyens' work, *Les forces vives du Québec* (Quebec's Vital Forces), unveiled in 1988 to honor Lévesque.
The park affords views of the St. Lawrence as it leaves Lake Saint-Louis, of the borough of Lachine and, downstream, of the bridges spanning the river. A ferry operates between the tip of the peninsula and Saint Louis Park in summer.

Lachine

7.5km/5mi.
Lachine has a rich history that is closely linked to the development of the French colony and to the commercial and industrial evolution of the province. In 1667 Robert Cavelier de La Salle was granted a seigneury by the Sulpicians at the point where the St. Lawrence empties into Lake Saint-Louis. As La Salle was forever in search of the elusive "passage" to the East, his seigneury was facetiously nicknamed "La Chine" (French for China).
Lachine soon became an outpost for the city of Ville-Marie, the original French name of Montreal (The First Nations name was Hochelaga).
On August 4, 1689, the community was the site of a brutal massacre, as some 1,500 Iroquois attacked and burned the village to the ground, killing more than 200 people and taking more than 100 prisoners.
Lachine became a borough of the city of Montreal in January 2006.

Pôles des Rapides Tourist Reception Centre – Lachine. ✆514-364-4490. www.poledesrapides.com. Open end Jun–mid-Oct daily 10am–5pm.
Created at the sluice of Dock No 5 of the canal of Lachine, this site is the official gateway to the entire region, and from where you can pick up information on how best to explore the best of the West island areas. Walking trails, bike paths, kayak rentals, and boat rides (ferries, tours, rentals, etc) are available, and there's also an onsite boutique and cafeteria.

Lachine Rapids and Canal

© M. Sanchez / Michelin

Lachine Rapids and Canal★

Beyond Lake Saint-Louis, the level of the St. Lawrence drops 2m/6.5ft over a distance of 2km/1.2mi. In 1603, from the top of Mt. Royal, Champlain had noted the existence of "the most impetuous rapids one is likely to see." These impressive rapids presented a considerable obstacle to the various explorers wishing to travel upriver.
As early as 1680, Dollier de Casson, superior of the Saint-Sulpice seminary, proposed the construction of a canal to bypass the rapids. The project was not undertaken, however, until 1821. Completed in 1824, the 13.6km/8.5mi channel linked Lake Saint-Louis and the Port of Montreal; seven locks raised ships a total of 14m/49ft. The canal was enlarged twice, from 1843 through 1849 and from 1873 through 1884. It remained the only passage around the rapids until the opening of the St. Lawrence Seaway in 1959.
No longer used for travel, the canal today forms a recreational corridor about 15km/9.3mi long. Pleasure boats large and small cruise the waters, and a pleasant bike path borders the old docks of Montreal and Verdun and connects the Old Port to Lachine. In winter it becomes a trail for cross-country skiers.
The rapids are visible from Blvd LaSalle in the borough of LaSalle.

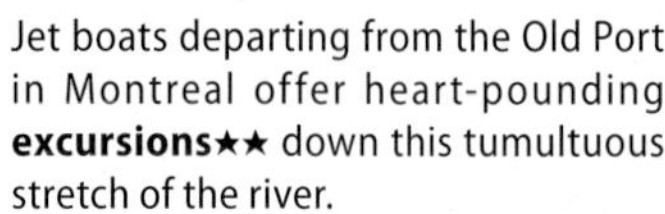

Jet boats departing from the Old Port in Montreal offer heart-pounding **excursions★★** down this tumultuous stretch of the river.

Musée de Lachine (Lachine Museum)

On Blvd LaSalle, turn left before crossing the canal. Ⓜ Angringon; bus 110. Open Apr–Nov noon–5pm, Closed Mon in summer, and Mon–Tue in spring and fall. 🅿 ☏514-634-3478.

This museum is set around an old stone house built 1669–85 by Charles Le Moyne and Jacques Le Ber, two of the first merchants to settle in Lachine. The house is now known as the Maison Le Ber-Le Moyne. Displays of period furniture and tools complement the exhibits on historical themes and handicrafts. An adjacent modern structure, called Benoît-Verdickt Pavillon, houses furniture dating from the 1850s to the present, as well as contemporary art exhibits.

Outside the museum, the church in Kahnawake can be seen across the lake. Begin your visit of one of the largest outdoor museums in Canada by viewing the visible works of art installed around the Old Lachine Museum stone structure. This open-air museum occupies some 4km/2.5mi beside the banks of Lake Saint-Louis. You will see more than 50 contemporary sculptures as you head west.

Go to the furthest point of land to admire the mighty Saint Lawrence River. You can see ocean-going ships traveling in either direction as they travel between the Atlantic and the Great Lakes.

Commerce-de-la-Fourrure-à-Lachine (Fur Trade at Lachine National Historic Site of Canada)★

1255 Blvd Saint-Joseph, across from 12e Ave. and from the Sainte-Anne College. Ⓜ Angrignon, then bus 195 West. Open Jun 20–Sept 7, daily 10am–5pm. ⊛$4. ✗♿🅿 ☏514-637-7433. www.pc.gc.ca/fourrure.

This majestic stone warehouse immediately beside the canal was used to store furs and trade goods from 1803 through 1859, and contains an interesting and evocative display on Montreal's fur trade. Strolling among bundles of fur and boxes of merchandise, visitors can identify the different stages of the industry's history. On display are maps of the fur country showing the trading posts of both the North West Company and the Hudson's Bay Company, plus interactive installations making history come alive for kids and adults alike. Before the North West Company merged with the Hudson's Bay in 1821, nearly 80 percent of the furs exported to Europe passed through Lachine. Self-guided and animator-guided tours available.

Promenade Père-Marquette (Father Marquette Walk)

Main access on Blvd Saint-Joseph, across from 18e Ave.

The walk along Lake Saint-Louis was named for Father Jacques Marquette (1637–75), who discovered the Mississippi River with Louis Jolliet in 1673. It affords views of the Couvent des Sœurs de Sainte-Anne (Sisters of St. Anne Convent), who run the Sainte-Anne College (1861), across from the warehouse, and of the Église des Saints-Anges-Gardiens (Church of the Guardian Angels), erected in 1919.

Les Berges cycle path is a linear park that stretches for 21km/13mi along the banks of the St. Lawrence River. Bicycles are not the only way to enjoy nice views of the wide river and the Lachine Rapids: the Les Berges path is also open to rollerblades and walking shoes, and in winter, cross-country skis. There are rest areas on the trail.

WEST ISLAND

West of Lachine, the communities on Montreal Island are collectively known as the **West Island**. Lined with opulent residences boasting their private boat docks, yacht clubs and lush parks, the "island's" communities are home to most of Montreal's English-speaking residents. The first suburb, **Dorval** *(4.5km/2.7mi)*, was named for Jean-

Baptiste Bouchard, a native of Orval, France, who acquired land here in 1691. Today, Dorval is best known for its international airport.

Pointe-Claire★

6km/3.7mi.

This middle-class, traditionally anglophone suburb on the shore of Lake Saint-Louis was named for the fine and clear (*claire*) **views★** available from the strip of land that extends into the lake.

Stewart Hall★

On left side of chemin du Bord-du-Lac (Lakeshore); follow signs. Pointe-Claire Cultural Centre open Mon–Thu 8:30am–8pm, Fri 8:30am–4:30pm, Sat 9:30am–3:30pm, Sun 1pm–5pm. Closed holidays. ♿ P ☎514-630-1220.

Built in 1915, this copper-roofed stone mansion is a half-scale model of a castle located on the Isle of Mull in Scotland. In 1963 Mr. and Mrs. Walter Stewart purchased the property and donated it to the City of Pointe-Claire as a cultural center. Today the building contains a library, an art gallery with changing displays, and a beautiful wood-paneled reception room. Meetings, plays, concerts, and other activities organized by the Cultural Center are held here. The lovely garden offers magnificent **views★** of the lake.

La Pointe★

Turn left off chemin du Bord-du-Lac (Lakeshore) onto rue Sainte-Anne and park beside the church.

Located at the end of this peninsula jutting into Lake Saint-Louis, the convent (1867) belongs to the Congregation of Our Lady. Behind it, an old stone **windmill** dates from 1709 *(access on foot only)*. Once an outer fortification for Montreal, this structure served as a retreat in case of a Native attack.

Topped by a single steeple, the Église Saint-Joachim (Church of St. Joachim) was built in 1882. Adjacent to it stands the presbytery with its wraparound porch and distinctive roofline, enlivened by numerous pyramidal forms. The **views** from this site are superb.

After Pointe-Claire, the chemin du Bord-du-Lac becomes Blvd Beaconsfield. It traverses the affluent suburb of **Beaconsfield** *(5km/3mi)*, named for the British prime minister Benjamin Disraeli (1804–80), who was conferred the title of Lord Beaconsfield by Queen Victoria on his retirement.

The road returns to being called chemin du Bord-du-Lac as it passes through **Baie-d'Urfé** *(6km/3.7mi)*, named for François-Saturnin Lascaris d'Urfé, who founded a mission here in 1686.

Sainte-Anne-de-Bellevue

© AGE / Photononstop

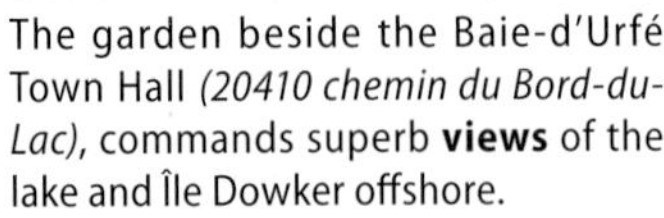

The garden beside the Baie-d'Urfé Town Hall *(20410 chemin du Bord-du-Lac)*, commands superb **views** of the lake and Île Dowker offshore.

Sainte-Anne-de-Bellevue★

3km/1.8mi.

Located at the western tip of Montreal Island, this university community was part of the Bellevue seigneury granted in 1670. Dedicated to St. Anne in 1714, the parish took its present name in 1878. The main street *(rue Sainte-Anne)* runs beside the Ottawa River, whose rushing waters join the St. Lawrence in Lake Saint-Louis after passing through a lock. Above the lock, the twin spans of Highway 20 and cross to Île Perrot.

Macdonald Campus

Located on rue Sainte-Anne, at entrance of the community.

In 1907 Sir William Macdonald (1831–1917), Chancellor of McGill University and founder of the Macdonald Tobacco Company, donated 650ha/1,605 acres to the university. Distinctive red brick buildings were erected on the site, today home to McGill's Faculty of Agriculture and Environmental Sciences. Especially popular with children, the campus' **experimental farm** *(open May–Jul 9am–5pm; 514-398-7701)* features a dairy barn and an animal farm where sheep, goats, pigs, rabbits, and other animals thrive. Covering 245ha/600 acres, the **Morgan Arboretum** (open daily 9am–4pm; $6 for trails; 514-398-7811) boasts Canada's most complete collection of indigenous tree species. This is a great place for cross-country skiing in winter, and walking in summer.

Ecomuseum (zoo)

21125 chemin Sainte-Marie. Open daily 9am–5pm. $15, children (age 3-15) $9. 514-457-9449. www.ecomuseum.ca.

Follow the same road for the Morgan Arboretum, but instead of going through "The Pines," turn right on rue Sainte-Marie. For close to 20 years, this amazing site, independent of Macdonald College, has offered the public interaction with over 115 species living in Quebec, like river otters, Arctic fox, black bear, eagles, and so on. Reptiles and amphibians are on display in vivariums. Even night animals like possums, raccoon and owl can be seen and appreciated. Their exterior facilities are home to coyote, caribou, wolf, and many other species. Spend a day visiting, or volunteer to help with animal care.

From Sainte-Anne-de-Bellevue, follow the rue Sainte-Anne through the upscale community of Senneville. As you travel, the road begins to veer northeast and Lake of the Two Mountains will be visible on your left. Bois-de-la-Roche farms are on your right, and you will pass Blvd l'Anse-à-l'Orme on your right as well. Keep going straight. On your left, just before the big turn, you will see the entrance to the largest park on the entire Island of Montreal.

Parc Cap-Saint-Jacques

20009 Blvd Gouin West, Pierrefonds. Welcome Chalet. Hours vary, from 10 or 11am to 5 or 7pm. $6 for two hours or $9 for the day. 514-280-6871.

Over 288ha/711 acres of mixed bush, sandy waterfront and farmland offer visitors a unique chance to connect with the island's outdoor highlights. Take a picnic, visit the boutique, pet the farm animals, and walk the idyllic trails through sugar maple, birch, and many other species of trees. 5.7km (over 3mi) of paths are marked and maintained, with 8km/4.8mi for bikes. The farm employs troubled teens, who help grow organic vegetables, which are then sold through a food-basket system. In winter, the park has cross-country skiing, snowshoeing, and hiking. The interpretation trail includes details of 142 species of birds (herons, hawks, hummingbirds, and more), plus plants, mammals, and marine life. Follow Blvd Goiun east to rue Saint-Charles, then turn right (south) to Rte. 40 (direction Montreal), or retrace your route back along the waterfront.

Laval

The Laval community enjoys a privileged position. Since 2007, direct subway access to downtown Montreal has been available, and residents are only a short car ride from the Laurentian Mountains. Residents of this fast-growing area enjoy outdoor sports, and the community is als[…] its cultural life. Le Co[…] is a local tourism gem […] nothing else like it in […]

- **Population:** 420,870.
- **Michelin Map:** p108–109: B1.
- **Info:** ℘450-682-5522 & 1-877-465-2825. www.tourismelaval.com.
- **Location:** The island of Laval is located 12km/7.4mi north of downtown Montreal. Laval is accessible by three […] and is […]rt than […]eal. […] street […] days and […]s (fees). […]lf day or full […]ve to the […] to visit the […] Fleur, then follow Rte. 440 back to the Cosmodôme. The parks and old village along the Rivière Mille-Îles on Boulevard Ste-Rose make a pleasant place to take kids to unwind.
- **Kids:** The Cosmodôme (enquire about the Space Camp).

SIGHTS

Cosmodôme★★

2150 Autoroute des Lau[…] *(Chomedey)*. From Mont[…] *(Exit 9)* and follow signs.

The Cosmodôme opened in 1994 with a mission to "promote the study and practice of space science and technology." A three-quarter-scale scale replica of an Ariane rocket stands in front of the ultramodern complex, making it easy to spot from afar.

Space Science Centre

Open daily Jun 24–Labor Day 9am–5pm, rest of year 10am–5pm. $15.50. ℘450-978-3600. www.cosmodome.org.

Interactive consoles, mural panels, scale models, large-scale replicas, simulators and videos make for a fascinating, hands-on exploration of space. A path through the exhibits traverses six different thematic sections, introducing visitors to the wonders of the universe. In the first section, a multimedia show *(20min)* traces the history of human space exploration. In the second section, various scientific instruments of yesteryear bring home the incredible technological strides achieved in human knowledge of the universe. The third section focuses on the history of telecommunications. Earth is next—the importance of water, continental drift, undersea mountains, and other aspects of our planet are examined. Don't miss the magnificent mural representation of the continents as viewed from space. The fifth section boasts two themes: teledetection and its various roles, ranging from meteorology to espionage; and human exploration of the moon, including a space rock donated by NASA. The last section offers the chance to explore the solar system; note in particular a holographic image of the Hubble space telescope surrounded by meteor fragments. The final exhibit ("Are We Alone?") details historic efforts to communicate across the universe.

Space Camp Canada

Reservations required.
For information ℘450-978-3600.

Modeled after similar programs in the US, the camp offers an array of space-oriented educational activities for kids and adults. Programs of varying length, some necessitating overnight stays and

From L'Île de Jésus to Laval

In the 17C the Jesuits gave the name **Île de Jésus** to this large island just to the north of Montreal. The first parish, Saint-François-de-Sales, was created in 1702 and the fertile land was quickly settled.

A master sculptor and principal designer of church interiors in Quebec in the early 19C, **Louis-Amable Quévillon** (1749–1823) was born and lived in the small parish of Saint-Vincent-de-Paul. With the help of apprentices, friends and associates, he created what historians labeled the "Quévillon school."

In the 20C the advent of the automobile, together with the building of bridges and highways, rapidly changed Île Jésus, transforming it into the main industrial and residential suburb of Montreal. In 1965 the 14 municipalities on the island merged and selected their new name in honor of Monsignor Laval, former *seigneur* of Île Jésus. Today Laval is the third most populous city in Quebec province after Montreal and Quebec City.

all run by specially trained counselors, initiate campers to the life and work of real astronauts through workshops, exercises, training programs, and mission simulations.

Good to know – Vieux (Old) Sainte-Rose is a charming district on the north shore of the island of Laval facing the Milles-Îles River, a 20-minute drive north of the Sheraton Laval. It was settled in the 1700s and many of its original stone and clapboard houses come alive in summer with sidewalk cafés, ice cream parlors and art galleries, all fanning out from the impressive church, l'Église Sainte-Rose-de-Lima, which is a heritage site. You can spend a day at the riverfront Parc des Milles Îles, which has watercraft for rent for cruising through an island wildlife sanctuary. Artists set up easels and sketch along Blvd Sainte-Rose, and the passion culminates in the annual Rose-Art Symposium at Galerie d'Art La Vieille Caserne *(annually in July, 450-625-7925. www.roseart.ca).*

ADDRESSES

STAY

Hôtel Sheraton Laval – *2440 Autoroute des Laurentides. 450-687-2440. www.sheraton-laval.com.* Spa. *244 rooms.* A large, reliable, comfortable hotel near the Cosmodôme, with plenty of shopping and near several Laval attractions.Convenient access to Montreal's airport and downtown core, except in rush-hour traffic. Amerispa, part of a respected chain, is the in-hotel spa. (*450-682-3365 & 1-866-263-7477; www.amerispa.ca*).

EAT

Le Saint-Christophe – *94 Blvd Sainte-Rose, on the northern shore of Laval. 450-622-7963. Dinner from 6pm Tue–Sat. www.restosaintchristophe.ca.* Le Saint-Christophe serves fine French fare in the formal surroundings of a Victorian manor house in Vieux (Old) Sainte-Rose, a historic waterfront district. Chef Gérard Jalby and his wife Josy left Toulouse, France, 25 years ago but remain true to classics like foie gras, sweetbreads, rack of lamb, lobster, filet mignon and apple-tarte-tatin for dessert.

Île Perrot

Montérégie region

Located at the confluence of the Ottawa and St. Lawrence rivers, this tranquil island is 11km/6.8mi long by 5km/3mi wide. Today the island is a pleasant stopover on the route from Montreal to Toronto or Ottawa.

- **Population:** 10,800.
- **Michelin Map:** p108: A2.
- **Info:** Seasonal tourist centre 190 Blvd Métropolitain. ℘1-800-378-7648. www.tourisme-monteregie.qc.ca. www.ile-perrot.qc.ca.
- **Location:** Île Perrot sits about 45km/28mi west of downtown Montreal by Rte. 20 (Exit 38), between Lac Saint-Louis and Lac des Deux-Montagnes.
- **Don't Miss:** Camping at Parc Historique Pointe-du-Moulin during the Perseids meteor showers in August.
- **Kids:** Kids' days at Parc Historique Pointe-du-Moulin include musicians and magicians.

A BIT OF HISTORY

In 1672 it was granted to **François-Marie Perrot**, Governor of Montreal and a captain in the Auvergne Regiment, who had married a niece of Intendant Jean Talon a few years earlier. Perrot used the island's strategic location as a base for illegal trade in liquor and furs with the Native Canadians.

It was not until 1703, when Joseph Trottier, Sieur Desruisseaux, acquired the land, that clearing and tilling began. Trottier built a manor house and a windmill *(moulin)* on the estate, known thenceforth as the Domain of Pointe-du-Moulin.

VISIT

Notre-Dame-de-l' Île-Perrot Église Sainte-Jeanne-de-Chantal★

Rue de l'Église. Open Mon–Fri or Sun 8am–noon, by appointment only. ℘514-453-2125.

Completed in 1786, this little stone church stands on the southern half of the island, in the Village-sur-le-Lac secteur. The view of the church's exterior from the cemetery evokes an image of old and rural Quebec. The elegant interior was decorated between 1812 and 1830 by Joseph Turcaut and Louis-Xavier Leprohon, two sculptors of the Quévillon school. From the church, the **view** over Lake Saint-Louis is splendid.

Parc historique Pointe-du-Moulin★

2500 Blvd Don-Quichotte.

Open May 17–Oct 13, daily 9:30am–5pm, except Jun 23–Aug 24 9:30am–8pm. $6 Wed–Fri, $8 Sat–Sun, free Mon–Tue. ℘514-453-5936. www.pointedumoulin.com

This park, at the eastern end of Île Perrot, covers about 12ha/30 acres and encompasses the location of Joseph Trottier's manor house (now destroyed). The lovely site juts out into the water, offering sweeping **views** of Lake Saint-Louis and of Montreal in the distance. On clear days, the Adirondacks are visible to the southwest. Picnic sites dot the grounds, amid winding paths.

An **interpretation center** *(same hours as the park)* near the park entrance features displays and films *(15min)* tracing the history of the estate, and describing the seigneurial system and traditional 18C farming methods. Activities such as crafts demonstrations, theatrical productions, and concerts are offered on weekends in summer.

At the extreme tip of the park stands Trottier's stone **windmill** (c.1705), which has been rebuilt and is in full working order. The entire upper section of the mill can be revolved with a pole, enabling the broad sails to catch the wind from any direction. On windy summer Sundays, the mechanisms are put into operation, offering an extraordinary view of the ingenious 18C processes involved in harnessing the wind to mill grain. The stone walls are pierced with loopholes, as the mill also served as a fortification in the 18C. The **miller's house** stands nearby. Built about 1785, it contains displays on traditional family life in New France (cooking and baking, dress, furniture, and architecture).

EXCURSIONS

Vaudreuil-Dorion

15km/9mi N of l'Île Perrot.

Located just west of the island of Montreal, the seigneury of Vaudreuil was granted to Philippe Rigaud de Vaudreuil, Governor of Montreal, in 1702. Barely developed under the French Regime, the community was acquired in 1763 by Michel Chartier de Lotbinière, who established a parish. On October 25, 1783, he proposed a town plan in which a church and market place in the center would be surrounded by a set of perpendicular streets. The 18C design was never carried out and the village kept its rural character. Engulfed by the Montreal suburbs during the 1970s, the twin communities of Vaudreuil and Dorion were eventually absorbed, and today form the municipality of Vaudreuil-Dorion.

Maison Trestler★ (Trestler House)

85 chemin de la Commune. From Rte. 20, turn right on Blvd Saint-Henri, and right on Ave. Trestler. Open year-round Mon–Fri 10am–noon, 1pm–4pm; Sun 1–4pm. Closed Sat and mid-Dec–early Jan. $4. 450-455-6290. www.trestler.qc.ca

This enormous stone house stands on a beautiful site overlooking Lake Deux Montagnes. It measures an impressive 44m/144ft long by 13m/42ft wide, and has a total of 14 dormer windows protruding from its wood shingle roof. The center section dates from 1798 and was built by **Jean-Joseph Trestler**, a German (his original name was Johann Joshef Tröstler) who made his fortune in the fur trade. The wings were added in 1805 and 1806. Several rooms in the house are furnished with exemplary pieces of 18C and 19C furniture. The tour passes through the beautiful curved-ceiling vault, where furs were hung to dry and displayed for purchasers. During the summer, classical and jazz concerts are held in the house.

Maison Valois (Valois House)

331 Ave. Saint-Charles, 1km/.6mi from the Trestler House. From Ave. Trestler, turn right onto Blvd Saint-Henri, then bear right on Blvd Saint-Charles. Open late Jun–late Aug, daily; hours vary depending on the exhibit. 450-455-7202.

Set in a pleasant park overlooking Lake Deux Montagnes, this edifice (1796) is typical of local residences, with its stone base and wooden walls. Note its steep roof, which measures about half the height of the structure and has no overhang. Restored by the municipality, it is used as an art gallery and hosts temporary exhibits.

Musée régional de Vaudreuil-Soulanges

431 Ave. St-Charles. Open Tue–Fri 9.30am–noon 1:30–4:30pm, Sat–Sun 1pm–4:30pm. Closed late Dec–early Jan. $5. 450-455-2092 & 1-877-455-2092. www.mrvs.qc.ca.

This Old Vaudreuil museum is located in a stone school building (1859), where **Lionel Groulx** (1878–1967), the great French-Canadian historian, studied. Typical of religious architecture of the period, it features a windowed mansard roof topped by a small lantern. The museum contains ethnographic objects used in various facets of domestic and artisanal life. In addition, the museum presents thematic and traveling exhibits.

Église Saint-Michel

On Blvd Roche, near the museum. Open mid-Jun–late Aug, Sun–Fri 10am–4pm; rest of year by appointment. Donation for guided tour. 450-455-4282.

Completed in 1789, this church—one of the oldest in the Montreal region—was declared a historic monument in 1957. A new façade was added in 1856, while inside, note the liturgical pieces sculpted by Philippe Liébert in the late 18C: the main altar with its tabernacle the side tabernacles and the pulpit. The choir paneling and stalls are by Louis-Amable Quévillon. The sculpted décor is complemented by an astonishingly realistic trompe-l'œil (visual deception) by F. E. Meloche, a student of the 19C artist Napoléon Bourassa. The painting of St. Michael above the altar was executed by William Von Moll Berczy. Jean-Joseph Trestler *(see opposite)* is buried in the crypt.

Pointe-des-Cascades

Take Rte. 338 from Vaudreuil-Dorion. The village is 7km/4.3mi from the intersection with Rte. 20.

Ancres Park lies near the point where the waters of the St. Lawrence and Ottawa rivers meet, just upstream from Lake Saint-Louis. The park is next to an old lock on the Soulanges Canal, one of the many canal systems that predated the St. Lawrence Seaway.

Lieu historique national du Canada de Coteau-du-Lac★

Open Jun 20–Sept 7 10am–5pm. $4. 450-763-5631. www.pc.gc.ca.

A National Historic Site of Canada, Coteau-du-Lac is located on the northern bank of the St. Lawrence River at the point where it leaves Lake Saint-François. The history of this community is closely linked to the presence of turbulent rapids nearby. Over the years, various canal systems were built to avoid the rapids and facilitate navigation. The problem was finally resolved by the construction of the St. Lawrence Seaway (*see INTRODUCTION*).

Vestiges of one of the first canal lock systems in North America are located on a pleasant **site**. Visitors get an idea of how pioneers lived and solved the difficulties of trade and transportation on the St. Lawrence River.

Until the early 20C, these rapids were the most treacherous between Montreal and Kingston. The construction of the **Beauharnois Canal** and hydroelectric plant in the 1920s necessitated a system of dams and waterworks to divert water into the hydroelectric station. The river level thus dropped 2.5m/8ft, and the rapids lost much of their force.

Archeology Findings

Archeological excavations have uncovered various parts of the warehouses and barracks built during the American Revolution and the War of 1812.

Octagonal Blockhouse

Built during the War of 1812, this unusual eight-sided blockhouse was burned down in 1837 to prevent its falling into the hands of the Patriots. The log exterior and stone foundations were rebuilt by Parks Canada in 1967. The interior includes a first floor and an overhanging upper floor. The walls are pierced by gun embrasures, while inside, informative displays describe the transport of goods on the canal.

Conquering the Rapids

When traveling downriver, the indigenous people who first settled the area "portaged" their canoes around the most dangerous parts of the rapids. Fur trade, however, brought trappers with heavier canoes and more goods to transport. In 1750 the French at Coteau-du-Lac solved the problem by building a *rigolet* canal, actually a stone dike, to facilitate passage to the Great Lakes. The remains of this dike are still visible from the park's walkways.

After the American Revolution (1776–1778), the British army established outposts along the St. Lawrence River and the Great Lakes. The *rigolet* canal proved too small for their large boats, so the British built a new **canal** in 1779. Approximately 300m/984ft long and 2.5m/8ft deep, the canal incorporated three locks which raised boats 2.7m/9ft. It remained in service until 1845, when the first Beauharnois canal opened. A boardwalk runs through the old, now dry, canal.

Sunset over the St. Lawrence River, Coteau-du-Lac
© Patrick Di Fruscia / age fotostock

West of Montreal

This diverse and sprawling area includes sights on the west side of the Saint Lawrence river north to Quebec City, along with southern areas including Hull and the Gatineau region. Whatever the season, and whatever the region— from Rivière du Diable and Chûtes Croches in winter, to St-Donat or Sainte-Agathe in summer—visitors will find an abundance of memorable highlights.

Rivers That Lead the Way

The Ottawa and St. Lawrence Rivers served as the main fur-trading routes from 1500 to 1850, bringing riches to merchants and traders in Montreal and eventually throughout Europe. The St. Lawrence River led Europeans deep into the continent to discover the Great Lakes, Mississippi River, Louisiana, and the west. The Ottawa River forms the natural border between the provinces of Ontario and Quebec.

The Bridges

At least nine bridges exit the Island of Montreal. Two lead west: Galipeault Bridge on Route 20, and Île aux Tourtes Bridge via Route 40 west to Ottawa and the Outaouais.

Reaching the Laurentians

When heading for the mountains, follow Rte. 15 north across the Médéric Martin Bridge through Laval, or Rte. 40 east across the Charles De Gaulle Bridge to Trois-Rivières, the Mauricie, and Quebec City. If crossing the Île aux Tourtes Bridge west, and passing through Vaudreuil-Dorion suburbs, take Rte. 40 west towards Ottawa.

Regional Hospitality

If you wish to explore, cross the Île aux Tourtes Bridge, and turn off at Exit 28 on to Boulevard Harwood. Continue west for two streets, turning right on rue Bellevue. This road ends at **Como** (turn right for ferry to Oka and Quebec routes 344 and 148 to Montebello and Ottawa, or left to Hudson and Rigaud). These smaller roads offer a chance to meet locals and savor regional hospitality, such as **Sucrerie de la Montagne** (*www.sucreriedelamontagne.com*) one of Quebec's legendary maple syrup domains, and a great place to enjoy traditional foods. **Auberge des Gallant** (*www.gallant.qc.ca*) offers an upscale overnight stay with gourmet food, fine wine, and a spa.

Highlights

1. Discover the delightful **Parc de la Gatineau** (p199)
2. Fish, hunt and listen to beautiful music in the **Laurentides** (p202)
3. Stroll along the river in the **Trois-Rivières** region (p220)
4. Immerse yourself in local culture at the **Musée québécois de culture populaire** in Trois-Rivières (p224)
5. Explore the landscape of **Parc National de la Mauricie** (p233)

The Historic Route

Local residents head "up north" to the Laurentian Mountains via Rte. 15, exiting anywhere between Sainte-Agathe and Mont-Tremblant. These mountains are appealing in all seasons. Head east on Route 40 to Lanaudière and Mauricie to explore nature in the massive Parc Mauricie, and history on the quaint chemin du Roy (King's Road), including old prisons, churches and mills. In the 19C, horse-drawn carriages took up to six days to travel between Montreal and Quebec City, making 30 stops on the way.

Music festival in Saint-Sauveur-des-Monts, Laurentides

© Chambre de commerce de la Vallee de Saint-Sauveur / Tourism Laurentians / laurentians.com

West of Montreal

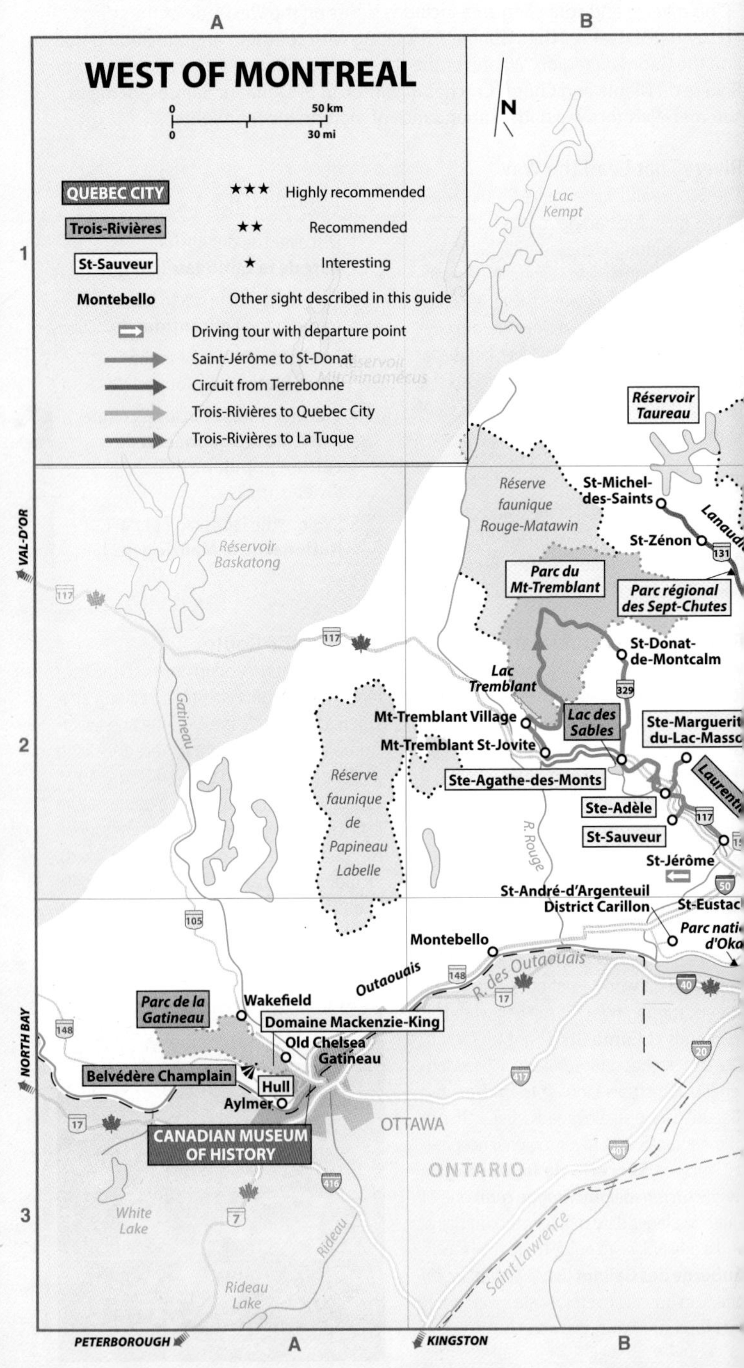

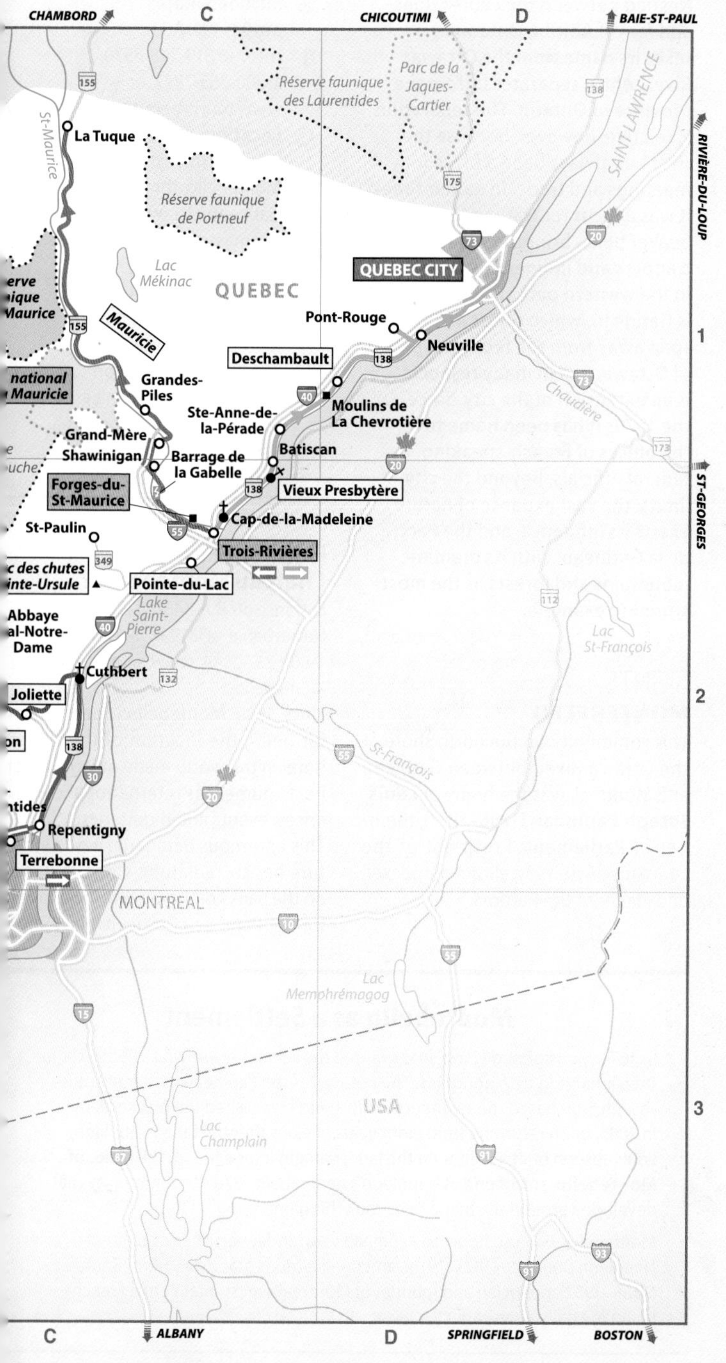
CHAMBORD
C
CHICOUTIMI
D
BAIE-ST-PAUL
RIVIÈRE-DU-LOUP
ST-GEORGES
Réserve faunique des Laurentides
Parc de la Jaques-Cartier
SAINT LAWRENCE
La Tuque
St-Maurice
Réserve faunique de Portneuf
Lac Mékinac
QUEBEC
QUEBEC CITY
Pont-Rouge
Neuville
Mauricie
Deschambault
Grandes-Piles
Moulins de La Chevrotière
Ste-Anne-de-la-Pérade
Chaudière
Grand-Mère
Shawinigan
Barrage de la Gabelle
Batiscan
Forges-du-St-Maurice
Vieux Presbytère
Cap-de-la-Madeleine
St-Paulin
Trois-Rivières
Pointe-du-Lac
Lake Saint-Pierre
Lac St-François
Abbaye
Cuthbert
Joliette
St-François
Repentigny
Terrebonne
MONTREAL
Lac Memphrémagog
USA
Lac Champlain
1
2
3
C
ALBANY
D
SPRINGFIELD
BOSTON

Outaouais

Nestled between the Laurentides and far-off Abitibi, Outaouais takes its name from the Ottawa River, which separates it from the province of Ontario. The separation is relative, however, because the river has always been a place for meetings and trade. In earlier times, it was a focus for trading in precious beaver pelts, bringing together trappers and indigenous people. In the western part of Outaouais is Gatineau, which is just a bridge span away from the federal capital of Ottawa, and in many respects is an extension of the city. Since the 1970s it has been home to the offices of French-speaking federal officials. Beyond the city limits, the vast expanse of nature exerts its influence, and the Parc de la Gatineau, with its dramatic mountains and forests, is the most stunning example.

- **Population:** 351,000.
- **Michelin Map:** pp190–191: AB3.
- **Info:** ℘819-778-2530, 1-800-265-7822, or www.tourismeoutaouais.com.
- **Location:** Running west/northwest from Montebello, through Gatineau/Ottawa, and into the massive wilderness of western Quebec.
- **Kids:** Canadian Museum of History, plus Children's Museum on same site.
- **Timing:** A four-season destination that offers a year-around selection of sites, events, and activities.

SIGHTS

MONTEBELLO

This community on the north shore of the Ottawa River, between Gatineau and Montreal, was the home of **Louis-Joseph Papineau** (1786–1871), member of Parliament, President of the Legislative Assembly, eloquent speaker, and leader of the Patriots.

Fairmont Le Château Montebello★

Entrance off Rte. 148, 392 rue Notre-Dame. ℘819-423-6341 or 1-800-257-7544. www.fairmont.com/Montebello.

Since 1930, Montebello is best known for being the location of the largest hotel in the world made of logs, which hosts numerous international conferences, events and dignitaries.

This enormous octagonal wood structure has six radiating wings. It stands on the banks of the Ottawa River on the former Papineau Estate. It was built in

Montebello as a Settlement

In 1674, Monsignor de Laval was granted the seigneury known as Petite-Nation, then inhabited by Algonquins. The notary, Joseph Papineau, father of Louis-Joseph, purchased the seigneury in 1801 and established the first settlement. In 1845, upon returning from eight years of exile after the failed Rebellion, Louis-Joseph built a manor on the land, naming it for a friend, the **Duke of Montebello**, son of one of Napoleon's generals. In 1878 the community that developed around the manor also took this name.

Montebello was also home to Papineau's son-in-law, artist and architect Napoléon Bourassa (1827–1916), and his illustrious grandson, Henri Bourassa (1868–1952), politician and founder of Montreal's most intellectual French-language daily newspaper *Le Devoir*.

1930 in 90 days by the Montreal architect, Harold Lawson, for the exclusive Seigniory Club, and the massive hunting and fishing property is still accessible as the Kenauk Nature (www.kenauk.com), a nearby resort complex. Ten thousand red cedar logs from British Columbia were used in its construction. Today an exclusive hotel, the building has hosted many international events, and the main hall boasts one of the largest fireplaces in the world.

Lieu historique national du Canada du Manoir-Papineau★ (Papineau Manor National Historic Site of Canada)

Visit by guided tour (45min) only, Jun 19–Sept 7, daily 10am–5pm; May 16–Jun 18 and Sept 8–Oct 12 Fri–Sun and holidays only. $7.80. 819-423-6965. www.pc.gc.ca/manoirpapineau.

The manor, an extraordinary structure with castle-like towers, was built between 1848 and 1850 by Louis-Joseph Papineau.

The main floor of the manor has been restored to reflect the period of the Papineau family's residence. A fireproof library built in a four-story tower once held Papineau's volumes. Visitors can see the funeral chapel where Louis-Joseph Papineau was laid to rest, the estate's original granary and several outbuildings.

GATINEAU AND HULL★

Across the wide waters of the Ottawa River, Gatineau is the Quebec section of the National Capital Region (NCR). The core district of Gatineau is Hull, where you will find the **Canadian Museum of History**, Canada's most popular museum. Gatineau is Quebec's fourth-largest urban area, behind Montreal, Quebec City and Laval, yet beautiful natural settings are never far away. Visitors will notice that the contrast between French-speaking Gatineau and English-speaking Ottawa is striking.

Hull was founded by Loyalist settler **Philemon Wright** in 1800, some 26 years prior to the establishment of Bytown (Ottawa) across the river. Wright built a mill beside the Chaudière Falls and named his community Hull after the Yorkshire town from which his parents had emigrated. Logging activities developed quickly at the small farming settlement, made possible by the region's abundance of red and white pine trees, which were well suited for shipbuilding. Wright and his fellow settlers rafted the long, straight trunks down the river to Montreal and from there to Quebec City, where they sold them to the British Navy, thus beginning an industry that continued throughout the 19C.

In 1851 an American, **Ezra Butler Eddy**, arrived in Hull. He started a clothespin business and a match factory that acquired national fame, and "Eddy lites" are still sold throughout the continent. Eddy's pulp mill dominates part of the Gatineau waterfront, but the downtown economy is now focused on two large federal government complexes (Place du Portage and Les Terrasses de la Chaudière).

Not unlike Ottawa, Gatineau has laid out bike paths along the river. Not far from here, gamblers head for the enormous (23,400sq m/251,878sq ft) avant-garde structure on the banks of Lake Leamy that houses the **Casino du Lac-Leamy**. The Jacques Cartier Park (*off rue Laurier*) affords particularly good **views★** of Ottawa on the opposite bank of the Ottawa River, including Parliament Hill, the Fairmont Château Laurier and the National Gallery of Canada (*see The Green Guide Canada*).

Maison du Citoyen (City Hall)

25 rue Laurier between rue Victoria and rue Hôtel-de-Ville. Open Jun 24–Labor Day, Mon–Fri 8:30am–4pm, closed noon–1pm; rest of the year 8:30am–4:30pm. 819-595-2002.

Gatineau's City Hall is called "la Maison du Citoyen" (Citizen's House) to reflect a will to open the doors to a beautiful, brightly lit brick structure (1980) encompassing an art gallery, the city library, a performance hall, conference rooms, and office space, all of which are

THE OUTAOUAIS REGION

History

Ten thousand years of First Nations oral tradition gave way to written history when explorer Samuel de Champlain arrived in the "Land of the Algonquins" in 1613. Today, only two major Algonquin communities remain, in Maniwaki and La Verendrye, both in the northern area of the Outaouais. Long-standing traditions of hunting, fishing, and collaborating with nature continue in this pristine environment, but co-exist with modern technologies, such as snowmobiles and cellphones. The area is named for Chief Pontiac, who had an Odawa mother and an Ojibway father.

Champlain's first trip was up the Ottawa River from Montreal, crossing the Gatineau River, then Rideau River, to Chaudière Falls. Modern travelers coming from Montreal will follow this same route up the Ottawa River on Route 344 from Oka, and will officially enter the immense collection of rivers, lakes, mountains and forests called the Outaouais at Montebello, on Rte. 148 (Rte. 344 ends at Grenville).

The legendary "coureur du bois" traveled with Champlain, as the main cultural link with the First Nations Peoples. Fur traders, trappers and interpreters, they opened the region and the country to European development and trade. After the fur trade, forestry products made this area a magnate for entrepreneurs seeking their riches, like Ezra Eddy, maker of the wooden match and legions of other paper and wood products. Construction of dams, sawmills, hotels, and new towns along the rivers established this geography as key to the development of both the pulp and paper industry worldwide, and the formation of Canada as a nation.

Key political figures in this story include William Lyon Mackenzie King, Canada's tenth Prime Minister, who bequeathed his massive Gatineau Hills estate to the "People of Canada" (*see Domaine Mackenzie-King*), and Louis-Joseph Papineau, firebrand Member of Parliament and fighter for the rights and freedoms of francophones throughout Quebec.

Geography

Western Quebec is bounded by Abitibi-Témiscamingue to the northwest, the Laurentians to the north and east, and Ontario and the City of Ottawa to the west. Urbanites will gravitate towards Gatineau/Ottawa, while the call of the wild will keep others heading for Gatineau Park and numerous outdoor possibilities beyond.

Gatineau is Quebec's fourth-largest city (an amalgam of Hull, Aylmer, Gatineau, Buckingham, and Masson-Angers), with over 260,000 residents and counting. Meanwhile, Gatineau/Ottawa is Canada's fourth-largest metropolis.

Gatineau by itself covers 340 sq km/216 sq mi, and sits at the gateway to a remarkable frontier for campers, fishing enthusiasts, hunters, and nature trekkers coming here throughout the year. Of course, it also has all the urban offerings of a modern city, and kid-friendly options exist both in town and out-of-town; whether it's museums, train rides, water parks, bike paths, ziplines, or animal sanctuaries, Gatineau and the five territories making up the Outaouais are simply some of the world's best for the smaller citizens.

Sprawling over 33,000 sq. km/19,800 sq.mi, the Outaouais boasts over 20,000 lakes and many rivers, and is considered the whitewater capital of Canada. Gatineau Park, the Parc national de Plaisance and the Forêt de l'Aigle, along

© Yves Marcoux / age fotostock

Chutes de Plaisance on the Petite-Nation River

with the Réserves fauniques de Papineau-Labelle and La Vérendrye, draw adventurous travelers for their beautiful scenery.

Geologically part of the 570 million-year-old Canadian Shield, the core of the territory is defined east/west by the Ottawa River, and from north to south by the Dumoine, Noire, Coulonge, Gatineau, du Lièvre, La Blanche, and Petite-Nation rivers.

Great Outdoors

The Outaouais Region extends into a massive zone of sheer isolated wilderness, hardly changed since the early explorers plied the river waters. The National Capital Region in and around Ottawa/Gatineau is flush with urban activities, services, and fun, but it is the nearness of the wild outdoors which equally draws growing numbers of enthusiasts.

From driving Siberian huskies across rolling winter snow trails, to spelunking world-class caves, to the best whitewater rafting in the country, or a gentle paddle in a rabaska or kayak along one of the thousands of waterways here, the Outaouais delivers memories in the making for outdoor fans. Mountain biking or cycling hundreds of kilometers of backroads, hot-air ballooning, skating, Nordic skiing, boarding, equestrian tours, water parks, or even riding a pedal boat through a 6km/3.6mi maze, are among the many outdoor activities the region has to offer.

Culture

Heritage treasures contained in this fascinating part of the province include churches and covered bridges; many are considered architectural masterpieces. More than 1,000 covered bridges have been constructed here, and while no longer practical, these quaint creations speak of the talents of the local woodworking tradition. Take note of the numerous wood handicrafts on sale throughout the province at gift stores, boutiques, and museums reflecting this woodworking heritage.

Wintertime Fun

If you've never tobogganed down a steep wintery hill on a simple sled, this is the place for you. **Les Glissades Sur Tubes Edelweiss** *(www.skiedelweiss.com)* offers pure adrenaline to all visitors. Faint-of-heart riders may wish to try a double-seater, so they are not sliding alone. Edelweiss also offers ski slopes with four lifts, snowmaking, and a ski school.

For another taste of winter sport, try ice-fishing with an expert. Traditional huts, some more elaborate than others, are set up when the ice thickens in January. Test the winter waters for bluegill, perch, northern pike, muskie, and sturgeon, until March.

Summertime offers its pleasures as well. Fishing vacations on the region's many lakes range from a day's outing to expeditions to remote sites. Contact The Quebec Outfitters' Federation www.pourvoiries.com, ✆418-877-5191 or 1-800-567-9009 or Outaouais tourism at tourismeoutaouais.com, ✆1-800-265-7822.

set around a large glassed-in atrium called the **Agora**.

The **Hall of Nations** displays art objects given by numerous countries throughout the years. See artifacts from the US, China, Czech Republic, Turkey, Greece, Brazil, and many others. Meanwhile the city offers a generous grouping of fine art galleries boasting the talented works of local and international artists. Outside the building is a pleasant park used as a skating rink in winter. La Maison du Citoyen is connected to a conference center (Palais des Congrès), a hotel and a shopping center.

On the same site is the **Galerie Montcalm**, (120 rue Principale, ✆819-685-5033), a museum that presents many exhibits throughout the year, as well as educational workshops.

Canadian Museum of History★★★

100 rue Laurier, between Interprovincial Bridge and rue Victoria. Open Jul–Labor Day, daily 9:30am–6pm (Thu until 8pm); rest of the year, 9:30am–5pm (Thu until 8pm) Closed Dec 24–25 and first week of Jan. $13 (free Thu 4–8pm, and Jul 1 and Nov 11). ($12.50 or $2.50/30min). ✆819-776-7000 & 1-800-555-5621. www.historymuseum.ca.

Directly across the Ottawa River from Parliament Hill are the remarkable buildings of the Canadian Museum of History, formerly called the Canadian Museum of Civilization.

The museum is dedicated to the history of Canada since the arrival of the Vikings, and to the art and traditions of indigenous peoples and various ethnic groups who have established themselves in Canada throughout the centuries.

Through its impressive collection of five million artifacts and the use of innovative and interactive displays, dioramas, and high-tech projection systems, the museum seeks to promote intercultural understanding among the 275 different peoples who call Canada home, and to preserve their cultural heritage.

Architecture

The two museum buildings represent architect Douglas Cardinal's breathtaking vision of the Canadian landscape. Using computer-assisted design techniques, Cardinal was able to create the sweeping curves that evoke the emergence of the North American continent and its subsequent molding by the wind, water and glaciers. Fossil impressions are visible in the Tyndall limestone sheathing the exterior walls. The building to the left of the main entrance, the **Canadian Shield Wing**, houses storage space, administrative offices and laboratories for conservation and restoration. On the right, the vast **Glacier Wing** (16,500sq m/19,734sq yd) contains the museum's exhibit halls. Some 3,300sq m/3,947sq yd of space is reserved for temporary exhib-

Grand Hall, Canadian Museum of History

© Jean-Pierre De Mann / age fotostock

its organized by the museum or other institutions, while the remainder houses permanent exhibits.

IMAX Cinema

Main level. Features change periodically, and films are shown alternately in English and French. Tickets are available at main entrance booth or at ℘819-776-7010, or 1-800-555-5261. Advance purchase recommended. $11 (children $7). Films and screening times at www.historymuseum.ca/imax.

Two seven-storey IMAX screens (10 times the size of conventional movie screens) provide unparalleled viewing opportunities for a maximum of 295 spectators (*latecomers not admitted*). The seats in the steeply inclined auditorium tilt backward for greater viewing ease and comfort. IMAX is a Canadian technology, and there are now more than 300 IMAX theaters in 40 countries. The theater is the only one in North America that shows both 3D on the IMAX screen and 2D in the Dôme IMAX.

Canadian Children's Museum

Main level (Level 2).

This delightful place for "hands on" learning encourages children to discover the world by participating in activities they enjoy, either individually or aided by supervisors. Near the museum entrance, the **Kaleidoscope** features temporary exhibits specially created for children. In the **Crossroads** area, children can climb aboard a Pakistani bus for an imaginary trip to eight different countries, and the **Great Adventure** offers a superlative opportunity to get to know other countries and cultures by way of the International Village, a microcosm of the planet Earth. Here, kids can embark on exciting adventures, including a trip across the desert with a mysterious pyramid looming in the background.

A costume room, puppet theater, toys, and games section and an art studio complete the indoor activities. Weather permitting, **Adventure World**, an enclosed outdoor exhibition park, invites visitors to climb on a real tugboat, play a life-size game of chess, or get into the cockpit of a Cessna 150.

Canadian Stamp Collection

Main level (Level 2).

This exhibit, opened in 2014, displays every stamp ever issued in Canada, some 3,000 of them, along with historical and technical information. The Canadian Postal Museum formerly housed here closed in 2012, and its artifacts have been moved to other exhibits.

Grand Hall

Lower level (Level 1).

This immense elliptical space houses a stunning exhibition that displays the rich cultural and artistic heritage of the Native peoples of Canada's west coast. Looking down across the wide expanse of the hall, visitors will see the façades of six chieftains' houses, symbolizing a traditional First Nations village erected between the coastal rainforests (represented here by an enormous mural photograph) and the Pacific Ocean (evoked by a smoothly polished gray granite floor). Built on-site by native artisans using ancestral techniques, each façade reveals a distinct culture: Coast Salish, Nuu-chah-Nulth (Nootka), Kwakwaka'wakw (Kwakiutl), Nuxalk, Haida and Tshimshian. Most of the artifacts incorporated into the façades date from the second half of the 19C. Majestic totem poles (some original) illustrate the artistic talent of the Pacific Coast peoples. Worth noting is the openwork Wakas pole (1893), a 12m/39ft masterpiece that stood in Vancouver's Stanley Park for 60 years. Floor-to-ceiling windows on the left open onto the Ottawa River and Parliament Hill, flooding the hall with natural light.

First Peoples Hall

Lower level.

Dedicated mainly to the arts and cultures of Canada's indigenous populations as well as their long history and their role in present-day society, this hall presents the richness and diversity of the First Nations through a wide variety of permanent and temporary exhibits. Comprising some 10,000 paintings, carvings, sculptures, photographs, and diverse craft objects, the permanent collection of contemporary indigenous art—shown on a rotating basis—features works by established artists (Norval Morrisseau, Bill Reid, Alex Janvier, Kenojuak Ashevak, Pudlo Pudlat, Jessie Oonark) as well as rising talents (Edward Poitras, Shelley Niro, Arthur Renwick, David Ruben Piqtoukun, Toonoo Sharky, James Ungalaq).

Canada Hall

Upper level (Level 3).

This enormous exposition hall, with its 17m/56ft vaulted ceiling, as well as Level 4, will re-open in 2017 as the Canadian History Hall, and will tell the story of Canada's settlement from the first human inhabitants to the present day. Among those collaborating on the project is architect Douglas Cardinal, who designed the Museum building. The new space will eventually cover 4,000sq m, or about half the Museum's permanent exhibition space.

The former Face to Face exhibition, in which visitors became acquainted with 27 fascinating and influential Canadian men and women, will become part of the Canadian History Hall.

Inuit Ublumi (1974) Sculpture by Pierre Karlik

ADDITIONAL SIGHTS

Gatineau Sector

4km/2.5mi northeast on Rte. 148.

The Pointe-Gatineau sector, where the Gatineau River meets the Ottawa River, is where Philemon Wright, the founder of the former city of Hull, assembled his vast rafts of floating wood in the 19C.

Aylmer Sector

12km/7.5mi west on Rte. 148.

In the mid-19C, the Aylmer sector was the capital of the canton of the former city of Hull. Charles Symmes, the nephew of Philemon Wright, was one of the first to settle here, on the shore of Lac Deschênes. The place was first known as Symmes Landing, then later renamed Aylmer as a tribute to the fifth Baron Aylmer, Governor General of British North America from 1831 to 1835. Auberge Symmes (1832), the inn built by Charles Symmes, has been magnificently restored as a local museum, and overlooks the lake. Its imposing stone structure inspired the painter Cornelius Krieghoff. Today, the rue Principale (main street) is lined with opulent homes and golf courses.

Old Chelsea

From Gatineau, take Rte. 5 north for 8km/5mi to Exit 12 (Old Chelsea/ Gatineau Park); turn west (left) onto chemin Old Chelsea.

By the early 19C this tranquil village was a stopping place for lumbermen traveling into backcountry forests. Settlers recognized that picturesque Chelsea Creek could provide power for saw- and gristmills, and the hamlet grew, eventually becoming a service center. By the 1870s, four hotels—all owned by Irishmen—prospered as well-frequented watering holes. Old Chelsea is home to the **Gatineau Park Visitor Centre,** at 33 Scott Road, and has shops, art galleries, cozy restaurants, and rental stores catering to outdoor enthusiasts. New England pioneers, attracted to the area's timber and agriculture, are buried in the **Old Protestant Burial Ground**. Look for the grave of Asa Meech, minister, doctor, teacher and farmer, for whom nearby Meech Lake (of the Meech Lake Accord) is named. Genealogists especially will enjoy St. Stephen's Church and cemetery, where headstones date from the 18C.

Wakefield

From Old Chelsea, take Rte. 5 north for 10km/6.2mi, then continue on Rte. 105 to Wakefield for another 10km/6.2mi. From Gatineau, take Rte. 5 and Rte. 105 for 32km/19.8mi.

Wakefield occupies a beautiful **site★** on the banks of the wide Gatineau River. In the early 19C, the first British settlers arrived from Britain and named the village for a town in Yorkshire, England.

PARC DE LA GATINEAU★★

Park open daily year-round. Certain parkways closed from first snowfall until early May. Visitor Center open May 1–Nov 1, and Dec 26–Jan 4 daily 9am–5pm, rest of the year Mon–Fri 10am–4pm, Sat–Sun 9am–5pm. Closed Christmas. $11/car. 819-827-2020 & 1-866-456-3016. www.ncc-ccn.gc.ca/places-to-visit/gatineau-park.

Covering 356sq km/137sq mi of lovely rolling hills interspersed with lakes, Gatineau Park lies nestled between the valleys of the Ottawa and Gatineau rivers. This enchanting place is named for the French fur trader from Trois-Rivières, **Nicolas Gatineau**, who disappeared in 1683 during a trip up the river that now bears his name. Gatineau is also the namesake of the community, located at the junction of both rivers, and of the surrounding range of hills, part of which is included in the park. William Lyon Mackenzie King, tenth Prime Minister of Canada, helped create Gatineau Park in 1938. Formerly part of an Algonquin and Iroquois territory, the park is now administered by the National Capital Commission.

Within its boundaries lie several federal government buildings, notably the Prime Minister's summer residence on Lac Mousseau (Harrington Lake), and the official meeting center on Meech Lake, the Willson House.

DRIVING TOUR

PARKWAY ROUTE

51km/31.6mi round-trip from Gatineau on Rte. 148.

Start on the Gatineau Parkway.

This beautiful drive skirts high walls of pink granite rock, then winds its way through the dense hardwood forests of the Gatineau Hills. Rounded by glaciers, these hills end in an abrupt slope, the Eardley escarpment, which demarcates the Canadian Shield. Several viewpoints afford superb views of the Ottawa River valley with its productive farms and sparkling lakes.

Belvédère Champlain★★ (Champlain Lookout)

6km/3.7mi round-trip from the intersection of the Champlain Parkway and the Lac Fortune Parkway.

The edge of the Eardley escarpment, at an altitude of 335m/1,098ft, offers a superb **panorama** of the Ottawa valley, where the Canadian Shield meets

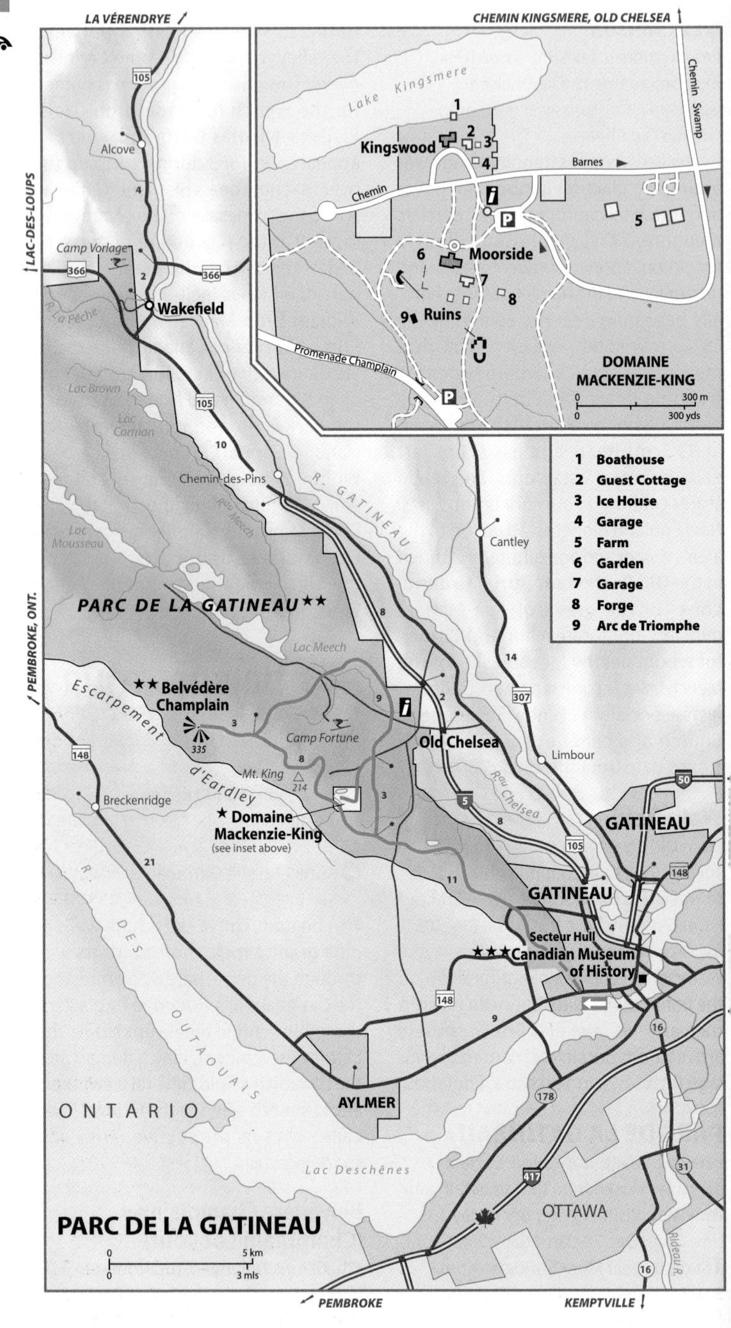
LA VÉRENDRYE
CHEMIN KINGSMERE, OLD CHELSEA
LAC-DES-LOUPS
PEMBROKE, ONT.
PEMBROKE
KEMPTVILLE
Lake Kingsmere
Kingswood
Chemin Barnes
Chemin Swamp
Moorside
Ruins
Promenade Champlain
DOMAINE MACKENZIE-KING
0 300 m
0 300 yds
1 Boathouse
2 Guest Cottage
3 Ice House
4 Garage
5 Farm
6 Garden
7 Garage
8 Forge
9 Arc de Triomphe
Alcove
Camp Vorlage
Wakefield
R. La Pêche
Lac Brown
Lac Carman
Chemin-des-Pins
Rau Meech
R. GATINEAU
Cantley
Lac Mousseau
PARC DE LA GATINEAU ★★
Lac Meech
★★ Belvédère Champlain
335
Escarpement d'Eardley
Camp Fortune
Old Chelsea
Limbour
Mt. King
214
★ Domaine Mackenzie-King
(see inset above)
Rau Chelsea
GATINEAU
Breckenridge
GATINEAU
Secteur Hull
★★★ Canadian Museum of History
R. DES OUTAOUAIS
ONTARIO
AYLMER
Lac Deschênes
OTTAWA
Rideau R.
PARC DE LA GATINEAU
0 5 km
0 3 mls

the St. Lawrence Lowlands. Below the lookout, a nature trail is dotted with eight observation stations, where various hardwood trees and other vegetation in the park are identified for visitors.

Domaine Mackenzie-King★ (Mackenzie King Estate)

3km/1.8mi round-trip from the Gatineau Parkway; take Kingsmere Rd. Open mid-May–mid-Oct, Mon–Fri 10am–5pm, Sat–Sun 11am–6pm (museums closed Tue). $9/car 819-827-2020.

At the heart of Gatineau Park lies the estate of the man who held power in Canada for a total of 22 years, the longest of any Prime Minister. **William Lyon Mackenzie King** was Canada's Prime Minister from 1921 to 1930 and 1935 to 1948. During these years, he retreated to the park to escape the pressures of power. When he died in 1950, he left his personal estate of 231ha/5,701 acres to the Canadian people. The estate comprises several houses and is criss-crossed by walks landscaped by Mr. King himself.

Kingswood – This rustic cottage was the first summer home built by Mr. King in 1903. He enlarged the house in 1924 and continued to live here until 1928. A pleasant walk to the lake offers a view of the **boathouse (1)**.

Moorside – This attractive clapboard house was purchased by King in 1924, and he lived here from 1928 to 1943. The upper-floor rooms have remained intact; the first floor now houses a delightful tea and lunch room. In the former **garage (4)**, an audiovisual presentation (*15min*) explains the life and career of former Prime Minister King. The simple, utilitarian **forge (8)** sits nestled among the trees at Moorside.

The Ruins – Mr. King salvaged pillars, stones and other architectural features from buildings slated for demolition and had them installed on his estate as a means of landscaping his property. A few sections of the former Parliament Building, destroyed by fire in 1916, can be found, as well as some stones from the British Parliament bombed in 1941. The **Arc de Triomphe (9)**, dating from 1936, is a salvaged front entrance from the demolished Bank of North America building. A third house, **The Farm (5)**, where King lived from 1943 until his death, is now the official residence of the Speaker of the House of Commons (*closed to the public*).

Fun and Games For All Ages

If the wilderness doesn't appeal, there are many other outdoor activities in the region. Go-kart lovers can meet at the **Amigo Recreational Complex** (*1870 Blvd. Maloney Est*) which has a 1.1km/0.68mi lighted track for regular or high-performance vehicles (kiddy cars too), as well as climbing walls, trampolines, and other amusements. Golfers can play the 6,164-yard par 72 **Club de Golf Tecumseh** (*475 rue Saint-Louis, www.golftecumseh.ca*), while beach-lovers can visit **Parc Lac-Leamy** (www.ncc-ccn.gc.ca), on the shores of Lake Leamy, which has archaeological sites that date back 6,000 years.

ADDRESSES

EAT

Les Saisons Cafe – *232 Old Chelsea Rd, Chelsea. 819-827-3303. www.lessaisonscoffee.com. Open Mon–Fri 7am–6pm, Sat–Sun 8am–6pm, closed Tue.* A charming café in an old red house set in a garden, serving sandwiches, light fare, and gourmet coffee. A nice place to relax and linger.

Chelsea Pub – *238 Old Chelsea Rd, Chelsea. 819-827-5300. www.chelseapub.ca. Mon–Fri 11am–midnight, Sat 11am–midnight, Sun 11am–11pm.* A traditional, wood-paneled Canadian pub, set in a hotel dating to 1875, serving pub cuisine and craft beers.

⊖⊖ **Les Fougères** – *783 Rte 105, Tenaga-Chelsea, Parc de la Gatineau. ℘819-827-8942. www.fougeres.ca. Mon–Fri 11am–8:30pm, Sat–Sun 10am–8:30pm. Sometimes closed Mon.* The hands-on chef-proprietors at this dining spot favored by residents offer locally smoked fish (from La Boucanerie Chelsea Smokehouse) and other specialties. Try the fish of the day or the confit de canard (roasted, salted duck), a Quebec favorite. A pleasant patio is open in spring and summer, and an attached store offers gourmet specialties.

ACTIVITIES

Greg Christie's – *148 chemin Old Chelsea (Old Chelsea District). ℘819-827-5340. www.gregchristies.com. Mon, Wed, Fri 10:30am–6pm, Thu 10:30am–8pm, Sat–Sun 9am–5pm, closed Tue.* This venerable establishment has been selling and renting bikes, skis and other outdoor equipment for many years.

Galerie Old Chelsea – *783 Rte. 105. Open Wed–Sat 10am–6pm, Sun 11am–5pm (hours may vary, call to check). ℘819-827-4945. www.galerieoldchelsea.ca.* Upstairs from Les Fougères restaurant (***see opposite***), you will find this co-op, which displays and sells the works of many local artists.

Laurentides★★

This region of Quebec is home to much of the Laurentian Mountain range (the "Laurentians"), a scenic highland that extends east to west across the province of Quebec. Formed more than one billion years ago in the Precambrian era, they are among the oldest mountains in the world, and form part of the Canadian Shield, a vast plateau in the shape of a horseshoe that nearly encircles Hudson Bay. The range of low, rounded mountains rises to a maximum altitude of 968m/3,175ft at Mont-Tremblant. To Montrealers, the Laurentians are a haven for recreational retreats, and on weekends, city dwellers rush northward on Rte. 15 to enjoy this vast summer and winter playground.

- **Population:** 511, 273.
- **Michelin Map:** p190–191 AB:2-3.
- **Info:** Maison du tourisme des Laurentides at La Porte du Nord, Exit 51 from Autoroute 15 Nord. ℘1-800-561-6673. www.laurentides.com.
- **Location:** The Laurentian region extends north from the Ottawa River and Laval. Autoroute 15 takes you north from Montreal into the Laurentian Mountains, then becomes Rte. 117 shortly after Ste-Agathe, extending northwest to Mont-Laurier. Rte. 344 follows the Ottawa River west towards Gatineau and Ottawa.
- **Timing:** The roads going north can be very busy on weekends—especially during winter, but also during the fall colors. Mont-Tremblant has become a very popular all-season resort, and offers a wide range of activities.
- **Kids:** Saint-Sauveur Waterpark, Santa's Village in Val-David, or Jungle Magic Play Park in Sainte-Faustain–Lac-Carré.

A BIT OF HISTORY

Few people inhabited this area before the arrival of the legendary **Father Antoine Labelle** (1833–91). Deputy minister of agriculture and colonization, Father Labelle—better-known as Curé Labelle—devoted his entire life to persuading his fellow French-Canadians to settle in the wilderness. He traveled by canoe and on foot to select sites for new settlements and was responsible for the

Kayaking, Laurentides

© Parc régional du Poisson Blanc / Tourism Laurentians / laurentians.com

establishment of more than 20 parishes in the Laurentians. Today many of these communities still bear the names of their parish saints, particularly in the area just north of Montreal. Thus the name **Valley of the Saints** has been given to the area beside the Nord River where Saint-Jérôme, Saint-Sauveur, Sainte-Adèle, and Sainte-Agathe are located.

Despite Curé Labelle's efforts to establish agriculture, farming proved unprofitable in the Laurentians. However, a new source of wealth developed in the 20C, when the ever-increasing population of Montreal began to retreat to the Laurentians in search of recreation, and today boaters, swimmers, and anglers enjoy the many lakes of the region, while the surrounding hills are the domain of hikers, horseback riders, and golfers.

In summer, several renowned theaters open their doors to visitors, while during the fall season, the mountains display a dazzling array of fire-red, orange, and gold foliage. In winter, the area attracts downhill and cross-country skiers and offers a wide range of *après-ski* activities. The Laurentians have the highest concentration of alpine ski centers in North America. Small chalets and luxurious homes are nestled in the mountains and along lakesides, and the region's principal resorts cater to an international clientele.

DRIVING TOUR

ST-JÉRÔME TO ST-DONAT

Circuit of 177km/110mi shown on the driving tour map, above.

Saint-Jérôme

51km/31.6mi from Montreal by Rte. 15 (Exit 43, rue de Martigny Est).

Founded in 1830, this city grew rapidly, primarily through the efforts of Curé Labelle. Known as the "Gateway to the Laurentians," it is an important administrative center located on a pleasant site beside the River of the North (Parc du rivière du nord is Exit no. 45 from Rte. 15).

Cathédrale Saint-Jérome

355 rue Saint-Georges. Opens 30min before every Mass; call for times. On request, a sacristan will accompany your visit. Contribution requested. 450-432-9741.

The tall spires of this imposing stone church (1900) tower above the community of Saint-Jérôme. The rounded forms of its portico and pinnacles, and the monumental treatment of the décor are hallmarks of the Romano-Byzantine style. Inside, note the stained glass by D.A. Beaulieu of Montreal.

Across from the cathedral, a bronze **statue** of Curé Labelle, by Alfred Laliberté, stands in a pleasant square. The

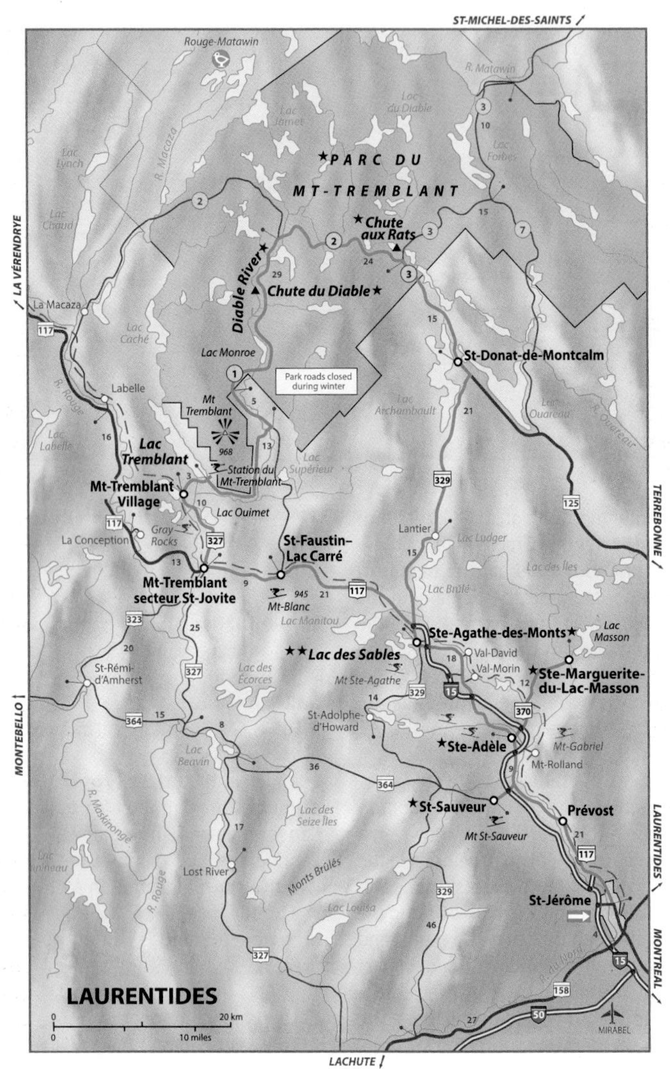

former courthouse (palais de justice), on the north side of the square, has been converted into an exhibition center focusing on contemporary visual arts.

Promenade

Located between rue de Martigny and rue Saint-Joseph, this walk (*610m/667yd*) is lined with descriptive panels that recount the history of this community. The walkway also affords fine views of the Nord River.

From the center of Saint-Jérôme, take rue de Martigny Est to Rte. 117 (blvd. Labelle) and continue north.

Traveling north, ski centers come into view from the highway. In 1932 the first ski tow was established in this vicinity, and skiers paid five cents to be hauled up the hill by a system of pulleys, ropes and tackle, powered by an automobile engine.

Continue on Rte. 117 for 5km/3mi, continuing through Prévost (*see box above)*. Turn left on Rte. 364 and continue for 2km/1.2mi.

Saint-Sauveur-des-Monts★

Nestled in the mountains, this charming and lively village boasts a variety of restaurants, discount fashion outlets and handicraft shops, cafés, bars and discos, most of which are located along the busy main street (*rue Principale*), near the church of Saint-Sauveur (1903). Saint-Sauveur is the oldest Laurentian resort, having welcomed visitors since 1930. The **Mont-Saint-Sauveur** ski center is one of the largest in the Laurentians, boasting more than 25 ski lifts within 3km/1.8mi of the community.

Pavillon 70★

From rue Principale, turn left on Ave. Saint-Denis and continue 1km/.6mi to Mt. Saint-Sauveur, at the foot of slope no. 70.

This ski lodge, a veritable wooden palace designed by Peter Rose of Montreal, was completed in 1977. A monumental façade topped by two massive chimneys characterizes the internationally acclaimed building, credited with introducing the post-Modern style to Quebec.

Return to Rte. 117.

Route 117 continues its course through the mountains. The Rouge River offers sports enthusiasts exciting whitewater rafting opportunities as it flows past several communities.

Sainte-Adèle★

9km/5.6mi.

Nestled deep in the Laurentians, this community occupies a lovely **site★** surrounding the small Lake Sainte-Adèle. In 1834 Augustin-Norbert Morin (1803–65), lawyer and politician, founded this village named for his wife, Adèle. Today the community is dominated by the vast and luxurious resort **Hôtel Le Chantecler** (1-888-916-1616; www.lechantecler.com). Popular with artists and writers, the village features numerous restaurants and charming country inns, and is home to the Chantecler Ski Resort. Nearby Morin Heights is the site of Ski Morin Heights, while Ski Mont-Gabriel is found near Saint-Sauveur. The Laurentian's small, family-oriented ski centers are famous for producing first-rate freestyle skiers, especially mogul and aerial specialists, including members of the Canadian national team as well as Olympic and world champions.

The Jackrabbit

The community of Prévost was for many years the home of Hermann Johannsen, better known as "Jackrabbit." This intrepid sportsman almost single-handedly introduced cross-country skiing to the Laurentians, laying out many trails by himself, including the famous Maple Leaf Trail that ran from Prévost to Mont Tremblant.

From the center of Sainte-Adèle, take Rte. 370 to the right. About 24km/15mi round-trip.

Sainte-Marguerite-du-Lac-Masson★

After 4km/2.5mi, the road crosses the Nord River and passes the Alpine Inn, an imposing log structure built in 1934 in the rustic style. Several lakes can be glimpsed before the road reaches Sainte-Marguerite-du-Lac-Masson, a quiet village on **Lake Masson**. A narrow road circles the lake, offering panoramas of the area. Many more ski centers can be seen, their ski trails cutting swathes of green down the mountainsides in summer. Route 117 passes through Val-Morin and Val-David, known for their summer theater and resort hotels.

Return to Sainte-Adèle and continue on Rte. 117 for 8km/11mi.

Sainte-Agathe-des-Monts★

Set on the shores of Lac des Sables (Sand Lake), amidst rolling mountains rising to 580m/1,902ft, this charming community is the main town of the Upper Laurentians region. Settlers founded Sainte-Agathe in 1849, but construction of the Montreal and Occidental railway in 1892 hastened the development of the area, helping the town become the region's earliest tourist center. A lively resort with numerous restaurants and inns, Sainte-Agathe is today home to **Le Patriote**, the best-known summer theater in the Laurentians (French-language plays only) for decades. The historic downtown area has been renovated and revitalized. Of all the numerous service towns in the tourism-oriented Laurentians Region, Sainte-Agathe-des-Monts is probably the one with the most pleasant environment of mountains, lakes, and forests. That is why the town has so many accommodations and restaurants relative to its size.

Over the next 21km/13mi, the road crisscrosses the former route of the famed "P'tit train du nord" (little train of the north), immortalized in a song by Félix Leclerc. This popular shuttle made the trip (in the years prior to the establishment of ski areas) between Montreal and the Laurentians throughout the winter, serving the region's agricultural communities. The service was eventually superseded by the automobile, and the tracks have been removed to be replaced by an amazing pedestrian pathway extending from Saint-Jérôme north to Mont-Laurier, (*see box below*).

To the south of Saint-Faustin, the **Mont Blanc** (945m/3,100ft) ski center is visible.

Lac des Sables★★ (Sand Lake)

Located at the foot of rue Principale, in the downtown area, Lagny Park provides excellent **views★** of this lake, whose sparkling waters emanate from natural springs. The lake reaches a depth of 25m/82ft and is shaped like a wiggly "H". It offers over 13km/8mi of public (plage Tessier) and private beaches. Among the famous (and infamous) people who have sojourned here are Jacqueline Kennedy Onassis, Queen Elizabeth II, and the Nazi war criminal Baron von Ribbentrop. The former residence of millionaire Lorne McGibbon was acquired by the Oblate fathers after the stock market crash of 1929, and the palatial mansion has been transformed into a hospital and rest home for their missionaries.

A **scenic cruise** enables visitors to discover this magnificent lake and the homes lining its shores (departs from dock at foot of rue Principale early–late

200km Trail Lures Outdoor Enthusiasts

Access – Rte. 15 and/or Rte. 117 from St-Jérôme or any of the 23 towns and villages along the former train bed. Open Dec–Apr for cross-country skiing and snowmobiling, and in summer for cycling and walking. The section between St Faustin-Lac-Carré and Mont-Tremblant is off-limits, in winter, to snowmobiles, pedestrians and dogs. $12 cross-country skiing, no charge for cycling. 450-224-7007 & 1-800-561-6673. www.laurentians.com. For more than 70 years the railway line P'tit Train du Nord brought nature lovers to the fine parks and resorts of the Laurentians. Today hikers, cyclists, skiers and snowmobilers cherish the "linear park" for its 200km/124.3mi of maintained pathways. Val-David and Mont Tremblant are the most popular village access points. Former train stations operate as service centers offering information, cafés, bicycle repair, restrooms, and showers. The hard-packed trail and gentle grade allow all levels of outdoor enthusiasts to enjoy the fields, forests, lakes, and rivers of the Laurentian wilderness. Day-trippers favor the St-Faustin–Lac Carré to Mont Tremblant section for a picnic lunch and swim at the municipal beach at the Old Mont Tremblant Village, while more ambitious visitors prefer week-long journeys with overnight stays at the quaint B&Bs located close to the path.

Jun, daily 10:30am, 11:30am, 1:30pm, 2:30pm and 3:30pm; additional departures late Jun–mid-Aug, 5pm and 7:30pm; mid-Aug–mid-Oct, 10:30am, 11:30am, and 1:30, 2:30, 3.30pm, departures at 5pm until Sept 1; round-trip 50min; commentary; $12; Les Croisières Alouette 819-326-3656; www.croisiere alouette.com).

30km/18.6mi on Rte. 117, continuing through St-Faustin-Lac Carré (*see panel on Le P'tit Train du Nord, opposite*).

A Literary Classic

A native of Sainte-Adèle, the writer and journalist Claude-Henri Grignon (1894–1976) published his famous novel *Un Homme et son péché* (published as *The Woman and the Miser* in English) in 1933. Set in Sainte-Adèle and centered on the miserly **Séraphin Poudrier**, the novel takes the reader back to the days when the so-called *Pays d'en Haut* (the highlands) were being settled. It won the Prix Anathase David in 1935 and was subsequently adapted for radio, television, and film. Grignon's masterpiece, written in the realist-naturalist style, remains a classic of Quebec literature.

Mont-Tremblant

Three widely separated towns and a parish, set in the valley of the Rivière du Diable (Devil's River), were combined in 2000 to form the city of Mont-Tremblant, which can be confusing for visitors. The former town of Saint-Jovite, just off Highway 117, composes most of the new city, while the scenic former town of Mont-Tremblant, on Mercier lake, lies some 10 km north. The famous resort of the same name is on Lake Tremblant, to the east of the old village. A municipal bus service links these far-flung locations, and signs direct motorists. Visitors will find restaurants and charming shops at all three sites; big box stores have been kept to the city outskirts, along Hwy 117.

From rue Saint-Jovite turn right on rue Limoges (Rte. 327).

The lovely Lac Ouimet (6km/3.7mi) is encircled by hills, with the long ridge of Mont-Tremblant visible to the north. Remains of the once-celebrated Gray Rocks Resort Hotel and ski center, founded in 1905 but now closed, are still visible along the shore. Where Lac Ouimet ends, chemin St. Bernard on the right leads to the Domaine St-Bernard, (www.domainesaintbernard.org, 819-425-3588), a popular center for cross-country skiing run by the Brothers of Christian Instruction, now owned by the municipality of Mont-Tremblant. The Velan Observatory near the Domaine welcome center offers star-gazing with commentary every Saturday at 8pm ($20). In winter, 45 kilometers of enchanting cross-country and snowshoe trails, both groomed and back-country, attract skiers of all levels (9am–4pm, skiing $18.50, snowshoeing $9), and Domaine trails connect with those of the Mont-Tremblant ski center. Fluffy chickadees will peck birdseed (available at the welcome center) from your hand, while deer wander near the shelters to observe the tourists. In summer, walkers can stroll the paths (late Jun–Oct 9am-5pm, $5), and the

Parc national du Mont-Tremblant

© Parc national du Mont-Tremblant / Tourism Laurentians / laurentians.com

Domaine also offers simple lodging, with kitchen access, in all seasons.

Continue northward on Rte. 327.

Old Mont-Tremblant Village

4km/2.5mi. Lake Mercier marks the entrance to the village. The road continues toward Lake Tremblant (3km/1.8mi) and the Mont-Tremblant ski center and year-round resort (www.tremblant.com).

Located on the shores of Lake Tremblant, the resorts, hotels, boutiques, and eateries of Mont-Tremblant delight visitors in all seasons with their beauty and wide range of activities. The village is renowned for its lively events and nightlife, as well as downhill and cross-country skiing, snowshoeing, golf, tennis, sailing, swimming, rock-climbing, hiking, and lively summertime festivals.

Lac Tremblant (Lake Tremblant)

A pleasant **cruise** (70min) sails the waters of Lake Tremblant (12km/7.5mi from Quai Fédéral; $18; Croisières Mont Tremblant; 819-425-1045; www.croisierestremblant.com). Near the boat dock, a tributary of the Diable River, known simply as Décharge-du-Lac, leaves the lake in a display of falls and whirlpools. Luxurious homes line the lake shores, while the imposing Mont-Tremblant looms to the east. At the beginning of the 20C, this was a logging area with no roads. The northern end of the lake is still inaccessible by car; residents reach their homes by boat in summer and snowmobile in winter. The lake is famous for its fish (landlocked salmon, trout, muskie) and its clean waters, and it has beaches and watersports. At the Mont-Tremblant ski station, the great ridge of the mountain dominates the resort community at its base. The tiny Roman Catholic church with a prominent red roof is a replica of the church built in Saint-Laurent, on the Île d'Orléans, in the early 18C.

Mont-Tremblant (968m/3,175ft) can be reached by chairlift. On clear days, the peak offers a magnificent **view★**.

From Lake Tremblant, follow the Chemin Duplessis (follow sign for Lac Supérieur) for 13km/8mi to the junction with the road from Saint-Faustin. The entrance to the park is 5km/3mi north of the junction.

Parc du Mont-Tremblant★

In the summer season when all roads in the park are open, exit at the Saint-Donat entrance and continue to Saint-Donat. Off season, visitors must return to the Lac Supérieur (Saint-Faustin) entrance.

The road follows the **Diable River★** from the Mont-Tremblant ski center to the Croches Falls.

Quebec's public parks system, called **SEPAQ** *(www.sepaq.com)*, is the envy of the world, and this 1500 sq km/900 sq mi park is the oldest and second-largest park in its staggering inventory of preserves. Six jumbo rivers carry the surging waters of over 200 lakes and streams, providing both nourishment and recreation to wild creatures and visiting humans. Over 200 species of birds (hummingbirds, eagles, and woodpeckers), as well as 40 species of mammals (fox, wolf, black bear, beaver, deer, etc) join throngs of visitors every month in a dreamy wild kingdom. Every activity possible in the wild is available here, including the "Via ferrata du Diable," a 500m climbing path built in the park. Accommodations on-site range from yurts to chalets to cabins, and reservations are recommended.

Chute du Diable★ (Devil's Falls)

8km/5mi from Lake Monroe. Park and follow the trail on foot for 800m/2 624ft.

The dark waters of Diable River drop steeply in a forceful fall and suddenly change course, leaving a mass of shattered rocks at the base of the falls.

10km/6.2mi after the waterfall, head east towards Saint-Donat and Chute-aux-Rats on Park Road no. 2 and continue over 24km/15mi.

Chute aux Rats★

The Pembina River plunges 18m/59ft over a layered cliff, and at the end of

Aerial view of Mont-Tremblant village

the Chute-aux-Rats hiking trail is one of the prettiest falls in the Lanaudière region. Picnic tables are located in the swimming area and a wooden stairway scales the side of the mountain, following the falls to the top.

Continue on Park Road no. 3 to the exit (5km/3mi). Take Rte. 329 for 10km/6.2mi.

Saint-Donat-de-Montcalm

The resort town of Saint-Donat lies in the Lanaudière region at an elevation of 472m/1,548ft and is surrounded by mountains. It is set on the shores of Lake Archambault, but stretches as far as Lake Ouareau to the east.

Continue on Rte. 329 Sud to Sainte-Agathe-des-Monts.

The road affords beautiful views of Lake Archambault.

ADDITIONAL SIGHTS

Saint-Eustache

This quiet residential and farming community is situated on the Mille Îles River as it leaves Lake Deux Montagnes and joins the Chêne River. Founded in 1768, it was named for the seigneur of Mille-Îles, Louis-Eustache Lambert-Dumont. In 1837, Saint-Eustache was the site of one of the most crushing defeats of the Patriots' Rebellion.

On December 14, 1837, 200 French-speaking "rebels" led by **Jean-Olivier Chénier** faced 1,200 British soldiers under the command of General Sir John Colborne. The ill-equipped rebels did not expect such a mighty British force and took shelter in the church, which was bombarded and set on fire. Seventy patriots, including Chénier, died before the rest surrendered. The survivors were imprisoned in Chénier's home, and Colborne burned the then village of Saint-Eustache during what was called "the bloody night" (*la nuit rouge*), and village women and children were thrown out of their homes to face the rigors of winter. The brutality of the repression and the carnage at Saint-Eustache are remembered with sadness.

Église Saint-Eustache★ (St. Eustache Church)

123 rue Saint-Louis. Visit by guided tour (45min; English or French) only, Jun 24–Labor Day, Tue–Fri 9:30am–4:30pm, Sun noon–4:30pm; rest of the year by appointment. Contribution requested. 450-974-5170.

With its imposing façade and two elegant steeples, the St. Eustache church was erected in 1780 and enlarged in 1831. Badly damaged in 1837 during the Patriots' battle against the British army, it was carefully rebuilt from the remains in 1841 and enlarged in 1906. Cannonball marks are still visible on the façade. The light and spacious interior contains an ornate barrel vault and is often used by the Montreal Symphony Orchestra for recording sessions because of its excellent acoustics. To the right is the presbytery; to the left is a former convent that now serves as the town hall. Behind the church, a pleasant park has fine views of the Mille Îles River.

Manoir Globensky (Globensky Manor)

235 rue Saint-Eustache.

A huge porticoed entrance dominates the façade of this lovely Victorian manor (1903). The second manor erected on this site, this grandiose structure belonged to Charles-Auguste-Maximilien Globensky, last seigneur of the Chêne River seigneury. After his death, two local mayors used it as a residence. The manor became the city hall in 1962 and today still houses municipal offices. Le Manoir Globensky also houses a permanent exhibit related to the Battle of Saint-Eustache in 1837.

Moulin Légaré (Légaré Mill)

236 rue Saint-Eustache, across from the manor. Open Jan–May 9am–noon and 1:30pm–5pm. Jun–mid-Oct, 10am–5pm. $5. 450-974-5170.

The only building to survive "the bloody night" of December 14, 1837, this seigneurial mill on the Chêne River was built in 1762 and has operated ever since. It is named for the Légaré family who ran it from 1908 through 1978. The original mechanism and equipment can be seen inside, and visitors can purchase wheat and buckwheat flour produced at the mill. From the bridge behind the structure, the turbine gate, the river and the towers of St. Eustache church are visible.

Rue Saint-Eustache

The city's main street is lined with several buildings of historical interest. The former Presbyterian Church (1910) at no. 271 now houses an art gallery that presents temporary exhibits. At no. 163, the gabled, redbrick Plessis-Bélair House has been converted into a restaurant. The building (1832) at no. 64, with its distinctive overhanging eaves, belonged to Hubert Globensky, and the store at no.40 is the former Paquin House (1889).

PARC NATIONAL D'OKA (OKA PARK)

14km/8.7mi by Rte. 148 and Rte. 640. Main entrance on Rte. 344, other entrance (closed in winter) at the end of Rte. 640. Open year-round, daily 8am–sunset. $8.50. 1-800-665-6527. www.sepaq.com/pq/oka.

Set beside Lake Deux Montagnes, this park covers 24sq km/9sq mi of a former seigneury belonging to the Sulpicians. Created in 1962, it was originally named for Paul Sauvé, Premier of Quebec (1959–60) and a representative for the constituency.

The park comprises a wide sandy beach and several trails that wind through the magnificent deciduous forest (located near the main entrance). The Oka Beach (plage d'Oka) is one of the few beaches in the Montreal area and is thus extremely popular in summer.

Abbaye cistercienne (Cistercian Abbey)

3km/1.8mi west of the intersection of Rte. 640 and Rte. 344. Parking lot after the main entrance, before the Calvary of Oka. 450-479-8361.

In 1881 the Sulpicians of Oka donated land to a group of Cistercian monks from the Bellefontaine abbey in France. The Cistercians erected a large monastery, la **Trappe d'Oka**, where, keeping a tradition of hospitality, the monks welcomed visitors who wished to participate in their life of retreat. Since 2009, the monks have moved on to a new contemporary building elsewhere (*see Abbaye Val-Notre-Dame, p217*), and a non-profit organization continues to operate the structure as a hotel and education centre. The site is famous for its Oka cheese.

Calvaire d'Oka★

On the slopes of Oka Mountain (150m/492ft) stands a series of simple whitewashed stone sculptures representing the Stations of the Cross and Calvary. The four oratories and three chapels were built between 1740 and 1744 by Hamon Le Guen, a Sulpician from Brittany, in an effort to evangelize the indigenous population. The mountainside provides a good **view** of the park and of Lake Deux-Montagnes. Locals frequent forested trails all year, enjoying walking, snowshoeing, or cross-country skiing.

Oka

The name of this community on the shores of Lake Deux-Montagnes comes from an Algonquian word for "pike," a tasty game fish once found in abundance in the lake. A mission was founded here in 1717 for Iroquois, Nipissing, and Algonquin peoples; the reserve still exists. The community gained international notoriety in the summer of 1990 during the outbreak of the "Oka crisis," a Native uprising regarding the territorial claims of Canada's First Nations.

SAINT-ANDRÉ-D'ARGENTUEIL – DISTRICT CARILLON

Located on the Ottawa River close to the treacherous Long-Sault rapids, the historic village of Carillon was named for Philippe Carrion de Fresnay, a French officer who ventured here to trade furs in 1671. In 1682 Carillon was incorporated into the Argenteuil seigneury granted to Charles-Joseph d'Ailleboust, and remained a trading post throughout the turbulent fur-trading times.

In the 19C Carillon became a military settlement protecting the canal system built to circumvent the rapids. More recently, Hydro-Québec built a power plant harnessing the rapids. In 1999, Carillon became a borough of the regional municipality of St-André-d'Argenteuil.

Musée régional d'Argenteuil (Argenteuil Regional Museum)

On Rte. 344: 44 Rte. du Long-Sault. Open summer (call to check dates) Wed–Sun 10am–5pm, closed Mon–Tue; early Sept–late Oct Sun only, 11 am–4pm. Rest of year, Tue–Fri by appointment only. $5. www.museeregionald argenteuil.ca 450-537-3861.

This classic stone structure was completed as a military barracks in 1837 and was used to protect the canal. During the Patriots' Rebellion (1837–38), it accommodated 100 British soldiers and officers. It was later converted into a hotel. Since 1938 it has housed a museum dedicated to local history. Exhibits are devoted to Dollard des Ormeaux and Sir John Abbott (1821–93), member of parliament for Argenteuil County and prime minister of Canada from 1892 to 1893. Many 18C and 19C musical instruments, clocks, and French and Canadian furniture are on display.

Centrale hydro-électrique de Carillon (Carillon Generating Station)

240 rue du Barrage, Saint-André-d'Argenteuil, Entrance off Rte. 344 (Rte. du Long-Sault), towards Parc de Carillon. Visit by free guided tour (1hr 15min) only, mid-May–Jun 23, Mon–Fri 9:30am, 11:15am, 1pm, 2:45pm; Jun 24– last Sun in Aug, Wed–Sun 9:30am, 11:15am, 1pm and 2:45pm. 800-365-5229. www.hydroquebec.com.

Built between 1959 and 1964 at the foot of the Long-Sault rapids, this power station is a run-of-the-river plant with an installed capacity of 654,500kw. Its 14 turbines harness the flow of the Ottawa River, and the plant and its spillway span the river. The guided tour of the plant includes a short film (*15min*) and a visit to the turbine chamber, the control room and the roof, from which the reservoir and can be seen.

Lieu historique national du Canada du Canal-de-Carillon (Carillon Canal National Historic Site of Canada)

Open daily sunrise to 11pm, locks open for boats mid-May–mid-June and mid-Sept–mid-Oct daily 9:30am-4pm. $2. 450-537-3534. www.parkscanada.gc.ca.

This 60m/197ft-long navigation **lock** replaced seven older ones. It provides the greatest single lift (nearly 20m/66ft) of any conventional lock in Canada. Navigation to Ottawa upstream from this lock is unimpeded.

The stone building of the **Maison du collecteur** (toll house) was built in 1843 for the toll collector, who levied the tolls on barges and other vessels. Beside it, parts of the former 19C canal and lock system still remain.

A Flawed Hero

Carillon's renown is linked to a much-disputed act of apparent bravery that took place there in May, 1660. Adam Dollard des Ormeaux (1635–60), who had been exiled from early Montreal for multiple crimes, was lying in wait with an armed gang near Carillon, either to save young Montreal from a band of marauding Iroquois, or, more likely, to ambush a group of hunters and steal their furs. To his great surprise, as the story goes, he and his gang instead waylaid a large Iroquois war party, and were all killed. Dollard was later reinvented as a hero who saved early Montreal and helped launch the fur trade, though the May Fête de Dollard has been renamed the Fête des Patriotes, in an apparent acknowledgement that Dollard was, at best, a rather flawed hero.

Parc Carillon (Carillon Park)

Entrance just upstream from the power plant.

Extending about 3km/1.8mi along the shores of the reservoir, this park provides picnic spots. Near the dam stands a **monument** to Dollard des Ormeaux and his cohorts (*see box, above*). Jacques Folch-Ribas fashioned the 18 granite monoliths (8m/26ft high) to commemorate the battle.

ADDRESSES

STAY

Côte Nord Tremblant – *141 chemin Tour du Lac, Lac Superior. 1-888-268-3667 (in Canada), 1-450-327-6130. www.cotenordtremblant.com.* These spacious rental chalets, featuring contemporary log-cabin designs, overlook Lake Superior. Two- to five-bedroom units are available, each surrounded by nearly an acre of land, complete with full kitchen, A/C, TV, telephone and Wi-Fi. The complex has access to lake and swimming pool, tennis, kayaks, and nearby Mont-Tremblant.

EAT

A La Tablée des Pionniers – *1357 rue St-Faustin, Saint-Faustin–Lac Carré. 819-688-2101. www.latableedespionniers.com. Open late Feb-early May only (during sugar season). Thu–Sat 10am–10pm, Sun 10am–6:30pm. Reservations required.* For an authentic Québécois experience, don't miss a meal at this one-of-a-kind "gastronomic sugar shack." A new restaurant, on the site of the former Cabane à sucre Millette, offers an updated version of the traditional sugaring-off meal. While still heavy on pork, pea soup, pudding and maple syrup, the menu has been refined so the pulled pork comes in a light pastry crust with mushrooms, and some salad greens can also be seen.

Cabane à sucre de la Montagne – *Station Mont-Tremblant, Chemin des Voyageurs 450-839-7138. www.cabaneasucretremblant.com.* Located in a rustic shop at the south base of the Mont-Tremblant ski hill, this shop offers traditional maple syrup products including candy, tire à l'érable (hot syrup hardened on snow), maple sugar and syrup gift products, all produced in the Laurentian area.

ACTIVITIES

Station Mont-Tremblant – *819-686-4848. www.tremblantactivites.com.* An activity centre where visitors can enjoy a covered pool with waterfalls, snowshoeing, dogsledding or Scandinavian Baths *(www.scandinave.com).*

Lanaudière

Located on the southern edge of the Canadian Shield, the Lanaudière region forms a corridor of fertile plains extending from the St. Lawrence in the south to Lake Taureau in the north, and from the Laurentians in the west to the Mauricie region in the east. One of the earliest areas to be settled by the French, the region (one of Quebec's 17 administrative regions) takes its name from Marie-Charlotte de Lanaudière, daughter of the seigneur de Lavaltrie and wife of Barthélemy Joliette, who built several mills in the area and financed the construction of the first railway in the mid-19C. The Lanaudière region provides a wealth of outdoor activities, from boating and hiking in summer to skiing and snowmobiling in winter. The international music festival of Lanaudière (*see Festivals & Events***), in Joliette, and the agricultural exhibition in Berthierville attract visitors from far and wide.**

- **Population:** 429,053.
- **Info:** 1-800-363-2788. www.lanaudiere.ca.
- **Location:** The Lanaudière region extends northwest from the St. Lawrence River, from Montreal east to Berthierville, and all the way west to the Laurentian mountains (Lanaudière comprises a large part of Mont Tremblant Park).
- **Don't Miss:** Sir Wilfrid Laurier National Historic Site.
- **Timing:** Avoid driving from Montreal to Lanaudière at peak traffic periods. Make time to visit Old Terrebonne while you're here.
- **Kids:** Arbraska, forest of adventures (www.arbraska.com).

 DRIVING TOUR

CIRCUIT FROM TERREBONNE

305km/190mi. Allow one day.

Terrebonne★

This attractive city lies on the north shore of the Mille Îles River, north of Montreal. Terrebonne's refurbished 18C and 19C old quarter, bounded by rues Saint-Louis and Saint-Pierre, is a delightful place to stroll, with its quaint stone and wooden buildings, many of which house restaurants, cafés, boutiques, and galleries.

Terrebonne has expanded considerably in recent years as a suburb of Montreal, and it is the main gateway to the Southern Lanaudière region. Terrebonne makes an excellent day trip from Montreal where you can relax, enjoy French Seigneurial architecture, and ride a bicycle for the day on a beautiful network of cycle paths inside and outside the city.

Situated on high ground above the river, **Rue Saint-Louis** is lined with attractive stone buildings topped by steeply pitched roofs. At no.901, note the former Masson Manor (1850), built in the Neoclassical style with a symmetrical façade and pediments. The former residence of Geneviève Sophie Raymond, the building now serves as a school. The church (Église Saint-Louis-de-France), erected in 1878, with its tall central steeple and two side towers, stands nearby.

La Maison Bèlisle (open Jun 24–Sept 1 Wed–Sun 1pm–8pm, Sept–late Feb and early Mar–Jun 23 Thu–Sun 1pm–5pm. Mid-Feb–early Mar (school break) Tue–Sun 1pm–5pm. $3 www.lamaison-belisle.com 450-471-0619) is a historic jewel at 844 rue Saint-François-Xavier. Built in 1759 (the year of the British conquest), la Maison Bélisle, classified as a historical monument, offers a glimpse into the cultural and agricultural past of the Lanaudière Region through an inter-

The History of Terrebonne

Terrebonne's story begins in 1673 when the seigneury was granted to Daulier des Landes, but settlement only began in the 18C. The community soon became known for its fertile soil, hence the name Terrebonne, meaning "good land." The first mills in the area were built by the abbot Louis Lepage, between 1718 and 1745, on one of the islands (Île des Moulins) in the Mille Îles River.

After the Conquest, Île des Moulins flourished under the Scottish merchants of the Northwest Company. Simon McTavish, one of the stockholders, acquired the Terrebonne seigneury in 1802. Within a few years, he had established an industrial and commercial center on the island, whose fame extended well beyond the region's borders. In 1815 the mills of Terrebonne were reputedly the finest and best equipped in all of Canada. Activity subsided during the 1820s as electricity gradually replaced hydraulic power, and Île des Moulins was reduced to serving the needs of farmers in the area. In 1832, Joseph Masson, a banker from Montreal, acquired the seigneury and its mills. While he was unable to restore the village's past glory, his widow, Geneviève Sophie Raymond, tried to address the various needs of the community and created a road network, the Terrebonne Turnpike, extending from Saint-Vincent-de-Paul to Mascouche. However, business continued to decline and by the end of the 19C all mills had shut down.

active historical exhibit on the ground floor and an art gallery on the second.

From Blvd des Seigneurs, turn right on Ave Moody, left on rue Saint-Louis and right on Blvd des Braves, which becomes rue St. Pierre. 866 rue St. Pierre.

Île des Moulins★ (Mill Island)

Îles des Moulins is a municipal park open year-round daily 7am–11pm. Activities and exhibitions take place, particularly during the summer; nominal fees are sometimes charged. ✕ ✆450-471-0619. www.ile-des-moulins.qc.ca.

The island features an impressive collection of 19C buildings restored by the Quebec government. These structures can best be viewed from rue des Braves, on the other side of Masson Pond, which was used as a reservoir.

Both types of mills that prevailed in Quebec in the 18C and 19C can be found here. The French Regime mills were often constructed on a causeway or bridge having supports high enough to permit the wheel to turn under them. By the late 18C, English technology had established mills on land, using diversion canals to augment the flow of water.

Crossing the causeway, the first building visible is the **flour mill** (*moulin à farine*), built in 1846 on the site of the seigneurial mill of 1721. Both this restored mill and the adjacent **sawmill** (1804) have been converted into the municipal library, an acclaimed example of adaptive building reuse. The pleasant and innovative interior displays remnants of the mills. Visitors can gaze out the large rear windows and observe the pond water trickling down the original wheel mechanism.

The next building, on the island itself, is the **seigneurial office** (*bureau seigneurial*), a stone structure built for the mill foreman's widow around 1850. It houses an **interpretation center** with an exhibit on the history of the site (same hours as Mill Island).

Beside it is the old **bakery** (*boulangerie*). Built in 1803, this massive building reflects traditional French architecture. The last building, the so-called **new mill** (*moulin neuf*) of 1850, has two floors and an attic and houses a cultural center. The rest of the island is a pleasantly landscaped park dotted with modern sculptures, benches, picnic sites, and an outdoor amphitheater. Bike paths meander throughout the park.

The Old Terrebonne sector is the home of **Théâtre du Vieux-Terrebonne** (known as **TVT**), a beautiful and well-appointed 656-seat venue hosting shows year-round. TVT programming accurately portrays the performance arts scene in Quebec, from classics to avant-garde, in performance, singing, humor, classical music, dance, jazz and world beats. TVT also presents a summer season of high-quality theater (in French).

Take Rte. 125 to Rte. 25 and exit onto Rte. 640. At Exit 22 Est take Rte. 138 Est.

Repentigny

Set on the banks of the St. Lawrence River at the confluence of the Prairies and Assomption rivers, this community of 76,237 inhabitants is named after Pierre Le Gardeur de Repentigny, who was granted the seigneury in 1647.

The strikingly modern **Église Notre-Dame-des-Champs★** (187 Blvd Iberville; turn left from rue Notre-Dame; open year-round prior to mass: Tue and Thu 8:30am, Sat 4:30pm, Sun 10am; www.notre-dame-des-champs.org. ✆450-654-5732) was conceived in 1963 by Roger d'Astous, a former student of Frank Lloyd Wright. The building's curved walls resemble a tent, enclosing a harmonious interior space lit from a row of windows that punctuate the upper portions of the walls. A modern clock tower stands beside the covered walkway leading to the church. **Église de la Purification** (445 rue Notre-Dame between rue Hôtel-de-Ville and rue Brien; open last week Jun–last week Aug, Wed–Sun 1pm–5pm, open on Labor Day, Canadian Thanksgiving and last weekend Sept; rest of the year by appointment only; ♿ ✆450-581-2484), with its twin towers, was built in 1723 during the French Regime.

Take Rte. 138 (Chemin du Roy) towards the northeast and continue 1km/0.6mi after the junction with Rte. 158.

The road hugs the St. Lawrence shore, affording numerous views of the broad and majestic river.

Chapelle des Cuthbert (Cuthbert Chapel)

46km/28.5mi. 461 rue de Biebville. Open Jun–Labor Day, daily 10am–6pm. ♿ P ✆450-836-7336. www.patrimoineberthier.org.

In 1765, Scottish-born James Cuthbert, aide-de-camp to General Wolfe, purchased the seigneury of Berthier. Cuthbert's wife, Catherine, is buried in this chapel, which he constructed in 1786 to perpetuate her memory. Dedicated to St. Andrew, the chapel served as the first Presbyterian place of worship for the area, and remained in use until 1856. It is the oldest Protestant chapel in Quebec.

From Mill Town to Modern Cultural Center

In 1828 the notary **Barthélemy Joliette**, a descendant of the famed explorer Louis Jolliet who mapped the Mississippi River with Jacques Marquette in 1673, built a mill on the banks of the Assomption River. Joliette and his wife, Marie-Charlotte de Lanaudière, were the town's first benefactors, providing land for the church and a college.

Joliette gained a reputation as a cultural center through the efforts of various religious orders, especially the Viatorian clerics. A member of this order, **Father Wilfrid Corbeil** (1893–1979), played a key role in developing the arts. Among his achievements were the creation of the Joliette Art Gallery, and his role in designing the rebuilt abbey of the Clercs de St-Viateur. The town's prestigious music festival was the brainchild of Father Fernand Lindsay.

Skaters on the Assomption River, Joliette

© Sime / Photononstop

Return to the junction and continue on Rte. 158 towards Joliette (westbound).

Joliette★

Set on the banks of the Assomption River, the industrial and commercial center of Joliette is the capital of the Lanaudière region. An important artistic and cultural center, it is also the seat of a Roman Catholic bishopric and home to several Catholic orders.

Musée d'art de Joliette★

145 rue du Père-Wilfrid-Corbeil. ♿ P. Open Tue–Sun noon–5pm. Closed holidays. $10 (6–12 years $6). 450-756-0311. www.museejoliette.org.

The museum, which opened in 1976, underwent a major renovation and was scheduled to reopen in mid-2015. Its constantly growing collection now contains nearly 9,000 works, making it one of the largest in Quebec. The permanent exhibition, Centuries of Images, introduces visitors to the fascinating work of artists such as Ozias Leduc, Suzor-Côté, Emily Carr, Alfred Pellan, Jean-Paul Riopelle, Guido Molinari, Henry Moore and Arman. Alongside its permanent displays, the MAJ offers temporary exhibition galleries focusing on contemporary art, as well as taking visitors on a journey of discovery through ancient and contemporary art bringing together Québécois, Canadian and international artists. The museum also organizes cultural and educational activities (screenings, lectures, talks, workshops, and guided visits).

Subterranean Water

Six sources of fresh river water come together here for treatment, thanks to Pierre "Pit" Laforest who, in 1883, discovered the subterranean sulfuric water that is still used today at the water treatment plant. Located near the art museum in Renaud Park, this unusual site is a curiosity for most visitors. Nearby you will see a formidable statue of Barthólémy Joliette, namesake of the town.

Cathédrale de Joliette

Open Mon–Thu 11:30am–3pm; Sat–Sun, during mass: Sat 4:30pm, Sun 10:30am, but hours may vary. 2 rue St. Charles Borromée. 450-753-7596.

Home to many beautiful works of art by famous local Quebec artist Ozias Leduc, this magnificent neo-Roman structure, constructed 1887-1892 and dedicated to Saint Charles Borromée, dazzles in a play of light and architectural splendor. Note the graceful interior sweep of columns supporting trancepts, and the unusual palette of colorful light reflected throughout. Immediately behind the cathedral is a wonderful skating site on the Assomption River, where you can ice skate for a remarkable 4.5km/2.7mi.

Maison Provinciale des Clercs de Saint-Viateur

132 rue Saint-Charles-Barromée Nord.

This heritage monastery of the novitiate of Saint Viateur stands next to the cathedral. The order arrived in Joliette in 1847 to teach at the Collège de Joliette, but the abbey they built was largely destroyed by fire in 1937, and a new stone building in a fanciful Norman Romanesque/ medieval Germanic style, designed by Wilfrid Corbeil, himself a clerc de Saint-Viateur, and architects René and Gérard Charbonneau, rose in its place.

The interior attracts attention for its wonderful windows, created by Henri Perdriau in 1912, which depict stories from the Old Testament. The antique clock, mounted high in this gracious space, is the finest in town. Equally appealing are the Stations of the Cross created by Georges Delfosse (1869–1939), the work by Antoine Plamondon of the 16C Italian Cardinal, Charles Barromée, and the stunning paintings by Ozias Leduc hanging over the transept in the nave, which relate impressions about the life of Christ and mysteries of the Holy Rosary. For religious enthusiasts, make a reservation at the quaint Chapel to see works decorating the space by Antoine Plamondon's descendant, Marius, especially The Way of the Cross sculpture.

Take rue Saint-Charles-Borromée (which beomes Rue de la Visitation) and continue north towards Rue Davignon for 2km/1.2mi.

Maison Antoine-Lacombe

895 rue de la Visitation, Saint-Charles-Borromée. Open Jun 24–Sept 1 Tue–Sun 10am–noon, and 1pm–5pm; Sept–mid-Dec and Feb–Jun Wed–Sun 1–5pm. Closed mid-Dec–Jan. Gardens open Apr–Oct dawn to sunset. 450-755-1113. www.maisonantoinelacombe.com.

This beautiful stone residence, built in 1847, was renovated in 1968. Today it is a magnet for art and culture in the region – a hub for art exhibitions, concerts, and conferences. The garden, in both French and English styles, is especially attractive.

From Saint-Charles-Borromée, continue north along rue de la Visitation (Rte. 343) and turn right on Rte. 348, which follows the Assomption River (through Sainte-Mélanie) until the junction with Rte. 131 (28km/17.4mi). Continue on Rte. 131 (26km/16mi). Turn right on Rte. 131 and continue for 4.5km/2.7mi.

Abbaye Val-Notre-Dame

250 chemin de la Montagne-Coupée. Church hours vary; store is open Mon–Sat 9am–5pm, and Sun 10am–5pm. P 450-960-2889. www.abbayevalnotredame.ca.

The construction of a new monastery is a rare enough event in Quebec for it to be noteworthy, especially when the monks opt to hold an architectural competition to choose the winning candidate. On March 1 2009, the 24 monks of the Cistercian abbey of Oka (see p210) took up residence in their brand-new home designed by the Québécois architect Pierre Thibault. While retaining the layout of a medieval abbey around its cloister, the building's environmentally friendly architecture boasts very contemporary clean lines, dominated by glass and wood. The design was selected from among 60, which are presented in a book on sale in the shop, alongside fruitcakes, sweets, and chocolates made by the monks, who continue their order's tradition of manual work. Only the church can be visited, along with the porterie (gatehouse). It is possible to stay in the Monastery guesthouse, but booking in advance is strongly recommended *(14 rooms)*. Three-day silent spiritual retreats, without preaching, are also offered.

Continue on Rte. 131 towards Sainte-Émélie-de-l'Énergie (29km/18mi). As the countryside becomes more mountainous, Route 131 enters the narrow **Noire River valley★**. The road criss-crosses the dark and shallow river, punctuated with splendid waterfalls and rapids.

Parc régional des Sept-Chutes★

20km/12.4mi from Sainte-Émélie-de-l'Énergie. In Parc régional des Sept-Chutes, 4031 chemin Brassard Sud (Rte. 131). Open May–Nov, daily 9am–5pm. $6. P 450-884-0484 & 1-800-264-5441. www.parcsregionaux.org.

Only one of the waterfalls, the "Bridal Veil" (Voile de la mariée), is accessible. Though spectacular during the spring thaw, the 60m/197ft-high cascade dries up in summer. Sturdy wooden steps lead to the top of the falls and continue to Lake Guy. From there, the trail meanders through birch trees and moss-covered rocks to hidden waterfalls and, a little farther, vast and peaceful Lake Rémi (*15min from Lake Guy*). Across the lake, an impressive cliff rises abruptly out of the water.

For a longer hike, return to Lake Guy and follow the Mont Brassard circuit, which leads to a lookout, at 150m/492ft, offering a wonderful **view★** of the U-shaped valley of the Noire River to the south. The trail continues through a lush forest of birch and pine trees. Before reaching the steep descent to the cascades, the Mont-Brassard belvedere offers an expansive **view** of Lake Rémi and the Laurentians to the west.

Continue on Rte. 131 Nord.

Saint-Zénon

This community, surrounded by mountains, dominates the valley of the Sauvage River. Near the church, a fine **view** extends to the north of the valley known as the Nymph's Corridor (*Coulée des nymphes*).

Saint-Michel-des-Saints

The village of Saint-Michel-des-Saints is situated beside the Matawin River, just upstream from the spot where its wild waters empty into the calm **Taureau Reservoir★**.

Founded by Father Léandre Brassard and two colleagues in 1862, the tiny village was at that time 80km/49.7mi north of any other inhabited place in Quebec. Monsignor Ignace Bourget named it in 1883. Today the lumber industry, tourism, water sports, hunting, and fishing support the local economy.

Réservoir Taureau★ (Lake Taureau)

Called Lac Toro by native Attikamek, this large reservoir has a circumference of nearly 700km/435mi. It was created in 1931 to control water flow in the Saint-Maurice River and supply the power station at Shawinigan. The dam creating the lake stands at the former location of the Taureau Rapids on the Matawin River. Lake Taureau has many sandy beaches, a huge resort, and is popular for watersports.

Route 131 continues to the Mastigouche Wildlife Reserve. Covering 1,574sq km/607.7sq mi, the reserve is home to a variety of fish and game, including brook trout. Hunting and fishing are the most popular activities.

Return to Saint-Michel-des-Saints and take Rte. 131 south to Sainte-Émélie-de-l'Énergie (47km/29.2mi), then Rte. 347 west towards Saint-Côme.

The ski center at **Val Saint-Côme** (*12km/7.4mi from intersection of Rtes. 347 and 343*), with more than 20 slopes, is one of the area's largest winter resorts.

Continue S on Rte. 343, then 337.

Rawdon★

Situated in the foothills of the Laurentian Mountains, this small community lies in the heart of a popular recreation area. The Rouge and Ouareau rivers flanking the center of town form spectacular waterfalls and cascades on their journey south to the St. Lawrence. Originally part of lands granted to Loyalists in 1799, Rawdon was first settled in the late 1810s by Irish immigrants, who were followed by Scots and French Canadians (mainly Acadians). In the course of the 20C, the town has become home to a sizable Eastern European population. To this day, Rawdon remains a multicultural community, as evidenced by its diverse mix of religious buildings, including a Russian Orthodox church (located at the junction of rue Woodland and 15e Ave). Also of particular interest is the small Anglican church (corner of rue Metcalfe and 3e Ave). The stone structure (1861), topped by a wooden belfry and bordered on one side by a small cemetery, is the town's most charming sight.

Centre d'interprétation multiethnique

3588 rue Metcalfe. Sat–Sun 1–4pm. www.cimrawdon.info. 450-834-3334.
The center for multi-ethnic interpretation holds performances and exhibitions showcasing the region's diversity.

Parc des Chutes Dorwin★ (Dorwin Falls Park)

Located in a park off Rte. 337 (which is also 1e Ave), just before reaching the center of Rawdon, coming from Montreal. Open May–Oct, daily 9am–7pm. $5. ($3), www.parcsregionaux.org. 450-834-2596.
The Ouareau River cascades over rocks, then plunges 30m/98ft into a small pool and branches off into a narrow, rocky gorge. Enjoy 2.5km/1.5mi of hiking trails.

According to a Native legend, the falls sprang forth when Nipissingue, a wicked sorcerer, pushed a beautiful maiden, Hiawitha, into a chasm. He was turned to stone by a clap of thunder, while she was transformed into a waterfall. Popular belief holds that the profile, carved into the rock at the edge of the falls, is that of the sorcerer (*best viewed from the observation deck midway down*).

The Rouge River also drops in a lovely waterfall, the Mason Falls (*on 3e Ave and Rue Maple*). *Access to the bottom of the falls is difficult.*

Parc des Cascades★ (Cascades Park)

6669 Blvd Pontbriand. From rue Queen, turn onto Rte. 341 toward Saint-Donat. Open mid-May–mid-Oct daily 9am–6pm. $6. 450-834-2596.
This magnificent cascade, tumbling down a broad staircase of rocks, is at the northern edge of Lake Pontbriand, on the Ouareau River. In summer, visitors can wade into the middle of the stream and enjoy the clear cool water. The paths leading through the pine forest (interpretation signs) and picnic areas make this site an enjoyable resting place. Fishing is permitted.

Saint-Lin-des-Laurentides

This small industrial and commercial town was the birthplace of Sir Wilfrid Laurier (1841–1919), lawyer, politician, and Prime Minister of Canada from 1896 through 1911.

Lieu historique national du Canada de Sir-Wilfrid-Laurier (Sir Wilfrid Laurier National Historic Site of Canada)

Corner of 12e Ave (Rte. 158) and Rte. 337. Visit by guided tour (1hr) only; late Jun–first week Sept, daily 10am–5pm. $4. 450-439-3702 & 1-888-773-8888. www.pc.gc.ca/laurier.
The interpretation center here details the former Prime Minister's life and the important role he played in Canadian politics. The simple brick house adjacent to the center is furnished to reflect life around 1850, when Laurier was a boy, and when Laurier's father was the mayor of Saint-Lin-des-Laurentides. The seventh Prime Minister of Canada, Wilfrid Laurier is a key figure in Canadian history. He was the first French-Canadian prime minister, and he encouraged immigration and the development of the west, and is considered the father of modern bilingual Canada.

Trois-Rivières★★

Capital of the Mauricie region, this industrial center is located on the north shore of the St. Lawrence River at the mouth of the Saint-Maurice River. Just before it enters the St. Lawrence, the Saint-Maurice River branches around two islands, thereby creating the three "rivers" for which the city is named. Major annual events in Trois-Rivières include an international poetry festival, an international festival of vocal arts, and sports-car racing at Le Grand Prix de Trois-Rivières (*see Festival & Events*).

- **Population:** 26,323.
- **Info:** 1457 rue Notre-Dame. 819-375-1122 & 1-800-313-1123. www.tourismetroisrivieres.com/ www.tourismemauricie.com.
- **Location:** Trois-Rivières is situated about halfway between Montreal (85km/53mi) and Quebec City (80km/50mi) on the north shore of the St. Lawrence. Both Rte. 40 (Center-Ville Exit) and Rte. 138 go through the city.
- **Don't Miss:** Strolling on the Harborfront Park—Trois-Rivières boasts the best urban access to the St. Lawrence River. The small streets of Old Trois-Rivières are also exceptional, and they are not commercialized.
- **Timing:** Between Montreal and Quebec City, Trois-Rivières is a pleasant stop. Accommodation is much cheaper here than in the larger cities.

A BIT OF HISTORY

First Settlers – In 1634, Samuel de Champlain sent Nicolas Goupil, Sieur de Laviolette (c.1604–60), here to establish a fur trading post. For his fort, Laviolette chose an elevated spot (known as the Platon) high above the St. Lawrence. Furs were transported on the Saint-Maurice River until 1737, when the King's Road (chemin du Roy) was inaugurated, connecting the settlement to the city of Quebec. During New France's heyday, Trois-Rivières was home to many great explorers, including Jean Nicolet and Nicolas Perrot. The joint explorations of **Pierre-Esprit Radisson** and **Médard Chouart, Sieur des Groseilliers**, led to the founding of the Hudson's Bay Company in 1670, and the renowned **Sieur de la Vérendrye** was the first European to reach the Rocky Mountains.

Pulp and Paper Capital – In the 1850s, logging companies began exploiting the vast forests of the Saint-Maurice River valley. Large lumber mills sprang up in Trois-Rivières, along with a port and, later, hydroelectric installations. When a process for making paper from wood pulp was developed, a thriving pulp and paper industry took root in the area. By the 1930s, Trois-Rivières was the world capital for the production of newsprint, a distinction the city holds to this day, as three large pulp mills currently operate in the city. The elegant **Pont Laviolette** across the St. Lawrence was inaugurated in 1967. It is the only bridge linking the river's banks between Montreal and Quebec. Suspended 46m/150ft above the river, it is 3km/1.8mi long. The **Université du Québec à Trois-Rivières** (UQTR) opened outside the downtown district in 1969.

WALKING TOUR

2.9km/1.8mi. *Circuit outlined in green on the town map opposite.*

A fire in 1908 destroyed or damaged hundreds of buildings, devastating the heart of the old city. The relatively few buildings that survived the disaster have been carefully restored.

Begin the walking tour at the Boucher de Niverville Manor.

Manoir Boucher de Niverville★

168 rue Bonaventure. Open Jun–Aug 10am–6pm; Sept–Oct and Apr–May noon–5pm; Nov–Mar by appointment only. No charge. 819-372-4531. www.manoirdeniverville.ca.

This whitewashed stone manor house with red shutters was constructed c.1729 by François Châtelain, on the foundations of a house begun in 1668. His son-in-law, Claude-Joseph Boucher, Sieur de Niverville, gave the manor its name when he inherited it in 1761. The residence is decorated with typical 18C Quebec furniture. Outside stands a **statue of Maurice Duplessis** (1890–1959), a native of the city. Premier of Quebec from 1936 through 1939 and from 1944 through 1959, Duplessis lived down the street *(240 rue Bonaventure)* and graduated from the Trois-Rivières Seminary.

Walk south on Rue Bonaventure.

Le Flambeau (Flaming Torch)

On Place Pierre Boucher. The monument is illuminated at night.

The striking obelisk in the center of the Pierre Boucher Square was erected to celebrate Trois-Rivières' 325th anniversary. Pierre Boucher, Sieur de Grosbois (1622–1717), was the governor of Trois-Rivières in 1654 when the settlement was attacked by the Iroquois. He later founded Boucherville.

Walk south to Rue des Ursulines and turn left.

Rue des Ursulines★

This charming street is lined with some of the oldest buildings in the city, most spared by the 1908 fire.

Manoir de Tonnancour★

864 rue des Ursulines. Open Tue–Fri 10am–noon and 1:30pm–5pm, Sat–Sun 1pm–5pm. Charge for guided tours and

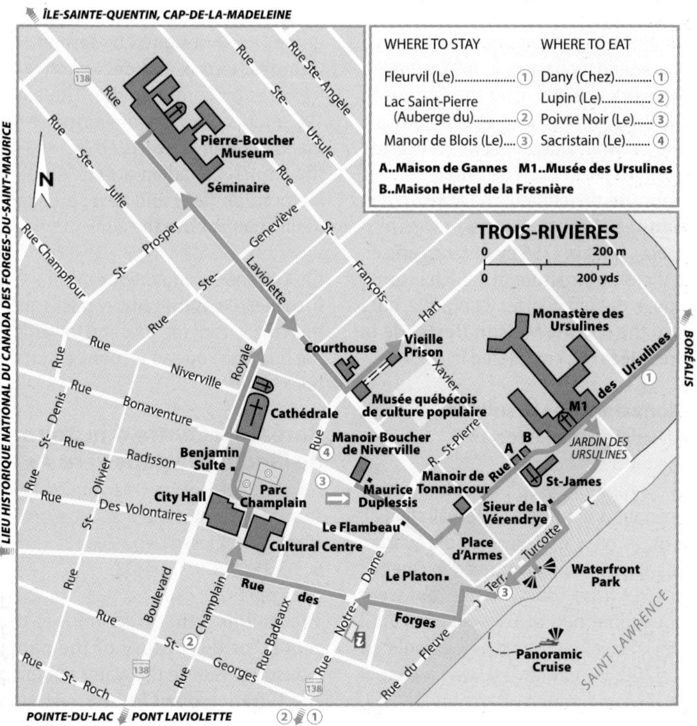

special activities. 819-374-2355. www.galeriedartduparc.qc.ca.
This three-story edifice was completed in 1725 by René Godefroy de Tonnancour, seigneur of Pointe-du-Lac, and rebuilt by Judge Pierre-Louis Deschenaux after a fire in 1795. The structure served as an officers' barracks, a presbytery and a school. It has been restored and now houses the **Galerie d'art du Parc**. Note the unusual style of the pitched roof, which reveals a Loyalist influence. The foundations and stone walls are original.
Opposite the manor house lies the **Place d'Armes**. Prior to 1800, the square served as a camping ground for Algonquin Indians who came to trade furs at the fort. Reserved for military use from 1751 through 1815, the square has been converted into a pleasant park.

St. James' Church

811 rue des Ursulines. Guided tours (1hr) available year-round by appointment only. 819-372-4614, ext. 1241.
The Récollets (reformed Franciscan monks) began construction here on a chapel and monastery in 1693, completing work in 1742. After the Conquest, the building was used as a court of law and a prison. The chapel was converted to an Anglican church in 1823.
Opposite the church, the **Maison des Gannes** (**A**) (*no. 834; private residence*), built in 1756 by a French officer, is the only structure of French inspiration in the old quarter. At no. 802, note also the historic **Maison Hertel de la Fresnière** (**B**), completed in 1829.

Monastère des Ursulines (Ursulines Monastery)★

784 rue des Ursulines.
This religious complex, replete with a gracious dome and a large wall sundial, is the jewel of Trois-Rivières' old quarter. The Ursuline Sisters arrived in Quebec in 1639 from Tours, France, but were not summoned to Trois-Rivières until 1697. Their first monastery, completed in 1700, was enlarged with a chapel in 1714 and rebuilt after a fire in 1752. A second fire struck in 1806, but the French Regime style of the buildings was maintained during reconstruction. Six subsequent additions were made between 1835 and 1960. The Ursuline Sisters operate a private girls' school, which today has an enrollment of some 1,200 students. The inscription on the sundial (1860) reads, in Latin, *Dies Sicut Umbra* (days flee like shadows).

Musée des Ursulines (M1)

Open Jun 24–Sept 1 daily 10am–5pm; Mar–Apr Wed–Sun 1pm–5pm, May–Jun and Sept–Oct Tue–Sun 10am–5pm, Nov–Feb by appointment only $5. 819-375-7922. www.musee-ursulines.qc.ca.
This museum includes ceramics, plates, books, etchings, furniture and pieces of art from the monastery, plus temporary exhibits throughout the year. A maquette (scale model) shows the monastery as it was in the 19C.

Chapel★

734 rue des Ursulines.
The chapel is topped by a beautiful dome (1897) designed by Joseph and Georges Héroux and decorated with frescoes by Luigi Capello. The early 19C altar is the work of François Normand. Paintings executed in 1840 by the French Canadian artists, Antoine Plamondon (*left*) and Joseph Légaré (*right*), hang above the altar.

Continue along the rue des Ursulines, cross the railway tracks and then the vacant lot, heading towards the building you can recognize by its brick tower.

Boréalis – Centre d'histoire de l'industrie papetière ★★

200 ave des Draveurs. Open Jun 24–Sept 10am–6pm; rest of the year, Tue–Sun 10am–5pm. Closed Dec 24–Jan 3. $13.25. 819-372-4633. www.borealis3r.ca.
The building that now houses the center for the history of the paper industry was once the water pumping and filtration plant for the vast pulp

factory that occupied the adjacent lot until 2006. The center is a remarkable example of the rehabilitation of an industrial building: against the backdrop of concrete, pipes and machines, visitors are introduced to the industry that earned Trois-Rivières its reputation as paper capital of the world. The exhibition uses models, photographs, videos, and objects to explore all aspects of the industry, from the technical side to its social effects (the workers' district, sports clubs, factory life), as well as the work of the lumberjacks and raftsmen. The emphasis is on people's stories, the most poignant of which are projected on the walls and pillars of the old underground cistern. The visit ends with a paper-making workshop.

Return to the Monastère des Ursulines, then go through the park opposite, the Jardin des Ursulines.

A **monument** at the eastern end of the Waterfront Park commemorates Pierre Gaultier de Varennes, **Sieur de la Vérendrye**.

Waterfront Park★

Once part of the estate of Mayor Joseph-Édouard Turcotte, this attractive terrace affords superb **views** of the river and of the south shore. In 1857 Turcotte gave the land to the city for use as a public park.

Walk along the waterfront to Le Platon.

Le Platon

In 1634 the Sieur de Laviolette built his fort on this plateau 35m/115ft above the river. The area's name is derived from the word plateau. A **bust** of Laviolette and a plaque were placed here in 1934 to celebrate the city's tricentennial.

River Cruise★

Departs from the Parc waterfront, 1515 rue du Fleuve. Open mid-Jun– early Sept. Round-trip 90min. Commentary. Reservations recommended. $30. 1515 rue du Fleuve. 819-375-3000 or 1-800-567-3737. www.croisieres.qc.ca.

This cruise offers an unequalled **view** of the port of Trois-Rivières and its pulp and paper mills. Visitors also get a good look at the impressive Laviolette Bridge.

Rue des Forges

Shops and restaurants with outside tables line this busy street, which combines the flavor of the old port with the energy of a bustling university town.

From rue des Forges between rue Hart and Blvd Royale, turn right between the city hall and the cultural center and climb stairs to Parc Champlain.

Parc Champlain

The modern, concrete structures of Trois-Rivières' **city hall** and **cultural center** (*hôtel de ville* and *centre culturel*) border this pleasant square dotted with fountains and trees. The center houses a theater, library, and art gallery. Built in 1967 to celebrate the centennial of

Canada's confederation, this ensemble has been acclaimed for its architectural design, and it was thoroughly renovated in 2006. In the square, a **monument** to Benjamin Sulte (1841–1923) commemorates the well-known French-Canadian historian.

Cathédrale de Trois-Rivièresa

364 rue Bonaventure, at the edge of Parc Champlain. Open year-round, hours vary. Inquire about mass times. ♿ P ☎819-374-2409.

The Gothic Revival-style Cathedral of the Assumption of the Virgin Mary, with its copper-clad steeple, was designed by Victor Bourgeau. The building was consecrated in 1858, but financial difficulties delayed the erection of the steeple until 1905. The interior is dominated by Guido Nincheri's richly colored **stained-glass windows**. Produced between 1935 and 1954, they depict the "Lorette Litanies" of the Virgin Mary. Beside the cathedral stands a statue of Louis-François Laflèche, Bishop of Trois-Rivières from 1870 to 1898.

▶ Walk along blvd. Royale. Turn left on rue Laviolette and continue 400m/437yd.

Séminaire de Trois-Rivières

858 rue Laviolette.

Founded in 1860, the St. Joseph Seminary was rebuilt after a fire in 1929. Embellished by columns and a statue of St. Joseph, the main entrance of the long, impressive limestone structure is surmounted by a large, squat copper dome. Untouched by the fire, the chapel (*behind the reception desk*) is open to visitors and displays the seminary's collection of religious objects, as well as artworks by Jordi Bonet (1932–79). Galleries on each side of the entrance hall make up the **Pierre Boucher Museum**, which presents exhibits of the region's historic, ethnographic and artistic heritage (Jun–Sept Mon–Fri 10am–noon, 1pm–5pm, Sat–Sun 11am–5pm; rest of year Tue and Sun 1:30pm–4:30pm; Wed, Fri and Sat 6:30pm–8:30pm; www.museepierreboucher.com P ☎819-376-4459). On view here are works by Antoine Plamondon, Roy-Audy, Berczy, Ozias Leduc, Suzor-Côté, Rodolphe Duguay, Gaston Petit, and Raymond Lasnier.

▶ Double back on rue Laviolette to rue Hart.

The old **courthouse** (palais de justice) stands at the corner of Rue Laviolette and Rue Hart. Designed by François Baillairgé and built in 1823, it was enlarged and restored in 1913.

▶ Continue on rue Hart.

Musée québécois de culture populaire★ (Quebec Museum of Folk Culture)

200 rue Laviolette, at the intersection with rue Hart. Open late Jun–Labor Day daily 10am–6pm; rest of the year, Tue–Sun 10am–5pm. Closed Jan 1–2 and Dec 24–31. $12. ✕♿ ☎819-372-0406. www.culturepop.qc.ca.

Opened in 1996, this large museum offers visitors an opportunity to immerse themselves in Quebec folk culture. Permanent and temporary exhibits display selections from an ethnography collection totaling more than 80,000 objects (tools, furniture, textiles, toys, etc.), illustrating provincial customs and mores, folk arts, traditional occupations, farming methods, and domestic life. The museum also features a permanent archeological collection of more than 20,000 artifacts of prehistoric First Nations and European cultures.

Vieille Prison★ (Old Prison)

200 rue Laviolette. Open Jun 24–Labor Day, daily 10am–6pm; Sept–mid-Oct and mid-Apr–June 23 Tue–Sun 10am–5pm; mid-Oct–mid Apr Fri–Sun 10am–5pm. Tours available; check for times. Closed Dec 24–Jan 2. $12 ($19 combined ticket with the Folk Culture Museum). ✕♿ ☎819-372-0406. www.culturepop.qc.ca.

Linked to the museum by a covered walkway. Designed by François Baillairgé and erected between 1816 and 1822, the imposing stone structure features some of the best surviving examples of Palladianism in Quebec. Note its massive size, three-story framework, severe portal, and wide pediment dominating the central façade, all characteristic of a style that marked the British presence throughout the Colonial Empire. The nine chimney stacks on the roof are evidence of a concern for the prisoners' comfort. The building stopped operating as a jail in 1986. Today it features an interpretation center, and 20 of its cells present different aspects of prison life, such as discipline, hygiene, and visitation.

ADDITIONAL SIGHT

Parc de l'Île-Sainte-Quentin

10 place de la Rosalie, Trois-Rivières. Access via bus route 2 (in summer) or by car toward Quebec City on Rte. 138. Jun 24–Sept 1 daily 9am–9pm rest of year 11am–4:30pm, Sat 9am–9pm, Sun 9am–4:30pm. www.ilestquentin.com. 819-373-8151. $4.50.

Residents of Trois-Rivières take advantage of this island's 46ha/114 acres all year round. A 750m/833yd interpretative walkway leads to the northeastern point of the island, through a silver maple grove and marshlands (high water in Apr–May) that are particularly popular with pike. Bird species inhabiting the trees include northern flickers, blue tits, and Baltimore orioles. The island is also covered by 4km/2.5mi of trails and a 3.5km/2mi cycle path. In wintertime, they become cross-country ski runs or skating areas. In summer, the beach, as well as the volleyball and pétanque courts and children's play areas, never fail to bring in the crowds.

EXCURSIONS

Moulin seigneurial de Pointe-du-Lac★

About 20km/12.4mi by Rte. 138, on the shores of Lake Saint-Pierre.

In 1721, René Godefroy de Tonnancour established a **seigneurial mill** here, on the banks of the Saint-Charles River. By 1788 the two-storey stone structure was Quebec's sixth most productive wheat mill, and ground grain until 1965, while the sawmill here operated until 1986. Restored in 1978 by the Quebec government, the *Moulin Seigneurial* has been converted into an art gallery and exhibition hall, presenting changing displays related to milling (open Jun and Sept 10am–5pm, Jul–Aug 10am–6pm. $3.50; P 819-377-1396; www.moulin-pointedulac.com). Nearby, the Église Notre-Dame-de-la-Visitation (1882) is recognizable by its small steeple.

Rebirth of an Island

The records state that on Oct 7, 1535, Jacques Cartier planted a cross on the Île St-Quentin, an island in the St. Lawrence River. The land was used for farming until the 1930s, before becoming a popular destination for outdoor leisure activities. The water quality deteriorated, however, due to bacteriological pollution linked to log transport on the Saint-Maurice River, to the point that bathing was banned in the early 1970s. From then on, the island was used as a refuse disposal site, until the Corporation du Développement du Parc de l'Île St-Quentin was set up in 1982 to clean up and refurbish the island.

Parc des Chutes Sainte-Ursule★ (Sainte-Ursule Falls Park)

11km/7mi by Rte. 348 and a small, well-marked road. Open May–mid-Oct, Mon–Fri 9am-5pm, Sat–Sun 9am-6pm $7. P 819-228-3555 and 1-855-665-3555. www.chutes-ste-ursule.com. Chalet rental year-round.

The Maskinongé River drops 70m/230ft at this point where the Canadian Shield abruptly meets the St. Lawrence Lowlands. In 1663 an earthquake changed the course of the river to cut through this rocky gorge of gneiss and pink granite. Trails follow the river as it tumbles through the gorge, leading to the site of a 19C paper mill; only its foundations remain. An observation tower offers views of the entire series of seven falls.

Saint-Paulin

Seigneurie Volant, Auberge Le Baluchon, 3550 chemin des Trembles. 819-268-2555 or 1-800-789-5968 (no charge). www.baluchon.com. P.

Visit the manor, the forge, the windmill, the chapel, and the sugar house that were built for the filming of the television series Marguerite Volant, a historical drama based on the adventures of the Seigneurie Volant estate in 18C New France. The complex offers various activities, including horseback riding, mountain biking and kayaking, or in winter, cross-country skiing and dogsledding, not to mention the opportunity to sample beers brewed according to traditional recipes, while the restaurant serves particularly refined cuisine. A perfect one-stop shop for a full day's entertainment.

DRIVING TOUR

TROIS-RIVIÈRES TO QUEBEC CITY

130km/81mi by Rte. 138 and Rte. 40/440, along the north side of the St. Lawrence River.

Leave the city by Rte. 138.

Cap-de-la-Madeleine

Cap-de-la-Madeleine is on the north shore of the St. Lawrence, east of the St. Maurice River. "Le Cap" is a borough of Trois-Rivières, but it has a distinct history and identity. Founded in 1635 by the Jesuit Father Jacques Buteux, who was later killed by the Iroquois, Cap-de-la-Madeleine is a renowned Marian pilgrimage site, and has been since the 19C when French-Canadians were among the most intensely Roman Catholic peoples in the world.

Although public pilgrimages to the church began as early as 1883, news of the second miracle (*see box)* brought worshippers flocking to Cap-de-la-Madeleine. Specially constructed steamship quays and railroad lines facilitated access to the shrine, and in the 1950s, a new basilica was built to receive growing numbers of pilgrims. Today, thousands of people make the pilgrimage annually. The Oblate fathers have administered the shrine since 1902.

The Miracles of Cap-de-la-Madeleine

In the mid-17C, a wooden chapel to Mary Magdalene was erected on this site by European settlers. A stone church did not appear until 1717, when a community was established here. Father Luc Désilets, who arrived in the mid-19C, renewed the ministry, and by 1878 a larger church was required to accommodate the growing congregation. Father Désilets planned to bring stones for the new church across the St. Lawrence over an ice bridge, but unusually mild weather left the river free of ice, prompting Father Désilets to vow to preserve the existing 18C church in exchange for a miracle that would allow the stone to be transported across the river. On March 16, 1879, the temperature dropped and ice appeared on the river, remaining just long enough for the parishioners to bring the stones across. After the last load had arrived, the now-famous "Bridge of Rosaries" (pont des Chapelets) promptly broke up.

Regarding the ice bridge as a miracle from Our Lady of the Rosary, Father Désilets kept his vow and preserved the old church, adorning the interior with a statue of the Virgin, donated by a parishioner. On the night of the consecration in June of 1888, the priest, along with Father Frédéric Jansoone and Pierre LaCroix, an afflicted pilgrim, witnessed a second miracle, when the eyes of the statue of the Virgin appeared to open in their presence.

Sanctuaire Notre-Dame-du-Cap★★

At 626 rue Notre-Dame, in the east of town. Follow the signs. Open daily 9am–8pm (6pm in winter). ♿ P. ☎819-374-2441. www.sanctuaire-ndc.ca.

This fine octagonal building, designed by the architect Adrien Dufresne, was begun in 1955 and inaugurated in 1964. The central tower stands 78m/260ft tall, and the façade is adorned with a 7m/23ft stone statue of the Virgin Mary. Belying its bulky appearance from the outside, the building reveals an elegant interior decorated in blue and gold—the colors of the Holy Virgin. It can seat more than 1,800 people under the vaulted ceiling, with no columns to obstruct the view of the main altar, which is built of Italian marble. The magnificent Casavant organ was built in Saint-Hyacinthe from 1963 through 1965 and boasts 75 stops and more than 5,500 pipes.

The interior of the basilica is renowned for its superb stained-glass windows by the Dutch Oblate father Jan Tillemans (1915–80), who created them between 1956 and 1964 following the medieval tradition. Each one consists of a rose window measuring almost 8m/26ft across and with five lancets.

Small sanctuary and grounds – Close to the basilica, you will find the old church dating from 1717, which has become a votive chapel. Along with the church of Saint-Pierre on the Île d'Orléans, this small building is one of the oldest churches in Quebec. The statue of the Virgin stands above a wooden altar decorated with paintwork and gilding.

A modern annex, added in 1973, incorporates some of the stones transported on the ice bridge in 1879 *(see box, opposite)*.

The small sanctuary is set in the grounds overlooking the river. In the southern section, the Stations of the Cross lead to models of Calvary and Christ's tomb in Jerusalem. Another section represents the mysteries of the Rosary, with 15 bronze statues imported from France (1906–10).

The little lake and the Pont des Chapelets commemorate the ice bridge.

▶ Continue on Rte. 138 for 24km/15mi.

Vieux presbytère de Batiscan★ (Old Presbytery of Batiscan)

On right, before entering the village. Open end-May–Jun and Sept, daily 10am–5pm, Jul–Aug 10 am-6pm. $3.50. ♿ P ☎418-362-2051. www.presbytere-batiscan.com.

The first presbytery on this site was erected by Jesuit priests in 1696. In 1816, hoping to obtain the appointment of a resident parish priest, the parishioners replaced the dilapidated structure with the present edifice (built of materials recovered from the original construction). The interior, typical of early 19C rural houses, is furnished with pieces from the collections of the Museum of Civilization in Quebec City.

▶ Continue into Batiscan (2km/1.2mi).

Batiscan's church (1866) stands overlooking the St. Lawrence River. The spires of the church in Saint-Pierre-les-Becquets are visible on the opposite shore. After leaving the village, the road crosses the Batiscan River.

Sainte-Anne-de-la-Pérade

10km/6.2mi from Batiscan.

This community on the Sainte-Anne River is famous for its ice fishing. In January and February, millions of Atlantic tomcods, known in Quebec as *poulamon, or petits poissons des chenaux,* leave the salt water of the Gulf of St. Lawrence and seek out fresh water to spawn. As the 20–30cm/8–12in fish arrive every year on the same spot at the mouth of the St. Anne River, an actual village of colorful shanties springs up on the frozen surface, inhabited by anglers from all over the province. The scene is particularly impressive at night. Fishing goes on 24 hours a day and requires no special skill. In the off-season, the huts are stacked on the riverbank, creating an unusual site.

Musée du Centre thématique sur le poulamon

8 rue Marcotte. Open Jun 24–Sept 1 daily 8:15am–7pm; rest of the year Mon–Fri 8:15am– 4:15pm. ℘418-325-2475. www.bounjourquebec.com.

This museum takes a light-hearted look at the many aspects of fishing for tomcods in Sainte-Anne-de-la-Pérade.

The community's large Gothic Revival church (1859) was inspired by Montreal's Notre-Dame Basilica. After the town of **Grondines**, the road follows the St. Lawrence River, providing views of Lotbinière and the ferry that crosses to the opposite bank. Quebec's first underwater transmission line passes through a tunnel under the St. Lawrence between Grondines and Lotbinière. The line is an important link in the 1,487km/924mi direct-current network between Radisson substation in James Bay, and the Sandy Pond substation in Massachusetts (USA).

Moulins de La Chevrotière (Chevrotière Mills)

20km/12.4mi; after 15km/9.3mi, turn left on rue de Chavigny. 105 rue de Chavigny, Deschambault. Open mid-Jun–Aug daily 9:30am–5:30pm; Sept Wed–Sun 9:30am–5:30pm, closed Mon and Tue. $4. P ℘418-286-6862.

These two stunning mills stand on a lovely site next to La Chevrotière River. The smaller of the two dates to 1767; the larger, surmounted by a dormered roof, was built in 1802. Inside, visitors will find temporary exhibits on such topics as sculpture, painting, antique tools, and others.

Deschambault★

Overlooking the river, the **Church of Saint-Joseph** (c.1835, Thomas Baillairgé), distinguished by its wide, lateral galleries, was inspired by Quebec City's Anglican cathedral. Between its twin steeples is a statue of St. Joseph, attributed to Louis Jobin (1845–1928). Inside, the choir is adorned with statues of exceptional quality by François and Thomas Baillairgé (open Jun 24–Aug, daily 10am–5pm; Sept Wed–Sun 10am–5pm, closed Mon–Tue. P ℘418-286-6891). In a pleasant park behind the church at 117 rue Saint-Joseph stands the former **presbytery**, built in 1815 (open Jun 24–Aug, daily 9:30am–5:30pm; Sept Wed–Sun 9:30am–5:30pm, closed Mon–Tue. $5 P ℘418-286-6891). Recently restored, the structure offers exhibits, and cultural activities in summer. The former **assembly hall** (1840) is now a café.

After Deschambault, a pleasant drive passes through Portneuf. At **Cap-Santé**, the village church features a lovely façade, modeled on that of Our Lady of Quebec Cathedral. Bordering the riverbank, the Vieux-Chemin extends from behind the church. Originally part of the Chemin du Roy, this charming street is lined with 18C homes of French inspiration.

Route 138 then crosses the Jacques-Cartier River and enters **Donnacona**, known for its large pulp mill. From here, the **view** encompasses the river and the countryside around Neuville.

Continue for 28km/17mi to Rte. 365.

Pont-Rouge

18km/11mi round-trip on Rte. 365.

This attractive community is located on the banks of the Jacques-Cartier River, which tumbles in a series of cascades on its descent to the St. Lawrence. Beside the bridge stands the four-storey **Moulin Marcoux** (Marcoux Mill), erected in 1870; restored in 1974, it houses an art gallery, a restaurant and a theater.

Return to Rte. 138 and continue for 3km/1.8mi.

Neuville

32km/19.8mi from Deschambault. Turn left on rue des Érables.

Originally called Pointe-aux-Trembles, the parish of Neuville supplied freestone, a high-quality type of limestone, to construction sites in Quebec City beginning in the late 17C. Numerous families of stonecutters and masons settled here to work in the local quarries.

Rue des Érables

The availability of both materials and skilled labor explains the exceptional concentration of stone houses in the village. Although only a single main floor is apparent at street level, the houses on rue des Érables were built to take advantage of the sloping ground, and actually comprise two or three storeys on the river, giving them a mill-like appearance. The Fiset house (*no. 679*) and the Pothier house (*no. 549*), both constructed around 1800, are fine illustrations of such architecture. The seigneurial manor (*no. 500*), erected in 1835, reflects Quebec's vernacular architecture.

Église Saint-François de Sales (Church of St. Francis de Sales)

714 rue des Érables. Open Jun 24–Sept 1 guided tours only 10am–5pm. 418-876-0000.

Neuville's church was erected in several stages: the choir dates from 1761, the nave from 1854 and the façade from 1915. In the sanctuary is a baldachin commissioned in 1695 by Msgr. de Saint-Vallier to ornament the chapel of his episcopal palace in Quebec City. In 1717 the bishop, then in retirement, offered the baldachin to the Neuville parish in exchange for wheat for the poorest citizens of the community. Four twisted columns encircle the tabernacle, sculpted by François Baillairgé around 1800. The church also contains some 20 paintings by **Antoine Plamondon** (1804–95), a native of Neuville.

The road leaves the banks of the St. Lawrence and heads inland as it approaches the industrial suburbs of Quebec City. Rte. 40 leads to **Cap Rouge** *(Exit 302)*, where a high trestle railway bridge (1906–12) spans the river of the same name. It was here that Jacques Cartier, under Sieur de Roberval's orders, attempted to establish a settlement in 1541.

Quebec City★★★

See QUEBEC CITY.

ADDRESSES

STAY

Le Fleurvil – *635 rue des Ursulines. 819-372-5195. www.fleurvil.qc.ca. 10 rooms.* This guesthouse near Ursulines monastery offers well-kept rooms with or without private bathrooms, a pleasant breakfast nook, river views from the back garden, and a pool for refreshing dips in the summer.

Le Manoir de Blois – *197 rue Bonaventure. 819-373-1090 or 1-800-397-5184 (no charge). www.manoirdeblois.com. 5 rooms, all with bathrooms.* The house is more than a hundred years old, having been spared by the fire of 1907, and offers comfortable, carefully presented rooms named after famous figures. Furniture consists of family heirlooms or second-hand finds, and everything has been carefully thought out to re-create a period atmosphere.

L'Auberge du Lac Saint-Pierre – *10911 rue Notre-Dame Ouest (Pointe-du-Lac sector). 819-377-5971 or 1-888-377-5971 (no charge). www.aubergelacst-pierre.com. 30 rooms. $15.* Located just out of town, L'Auberge offers an attractive location next to Saint-Pierre Lake, and comfortable rooms—some recently renovated—equipped with whirlpool baths. Ask for a view of the St. Lawrence River. Pool, tennis, sauna and spa services.

EAT

Chez Dany – *195 rue de La Sablière. Head towards Montreal for 6km/3.5mi on Route 138, then turn right into the Grande Allée. At the end, turn right into Chemin Ste-Marguerite, then after 1km/0.6mi, take the second exit on the left. 819-370-4769 or 1-800-407-4769 (no charge). www.cabanechezdany.com. Open year-round noon and evenings, but opening times vary. Call ahead.* The Néron brothers preside over this large sugar house, one in the kitchen and the other front of house, ensuring that no one goes without baked beans, grilled salt pork, meat pie, pickled beets, or maple syrup pancakes.

Le Sacristain – *300 rue Bonaventure. 819-694-1344. www.lesacristain.ca Mon–Fri 9am–4pm.* The plain decor and colored glass recall this café/restaurant's past as a Methodist chapel, and the sandwiches and crunchy salads are served with a smile. Everything is home-made, including the date cakes, which make a fine accompaniment to a good cup of coffee.

⊖⊜ **Le Lupin**– *376 rue Saint-Georges. ✆819-370-4740. www.lelupin.ca Tue–Fri 11am–2pm and 5pm–closing, Sat 5pm–closing. Closed Sun–Mon.* In a quaint little house set back from the bustle of the rue des Forges, this cozy restaurant offers a menu of traditional standards such as lamb's liver and sweetbreads, but cooked with care and creativity. Mussels are a specialty, and patrons can bring their own wine.

⊖⊜⊜ **Le Poivre Noir**– *1300 rue du Fleuve. ✆819-368-5772. www.poivrenoir.com Wed–Fri 11am–2pm and 5:30pm–closing, Tue and Sat–Sun 5:30pm–closing. Closed Mon.* In a large, sun-filled room with wide windows overlooking the St. Lawrence river, this popular establishment offers a menu that changes daily, emphasizing local produce, fish and game prepared with imagination and international flair.

TAKING A BREAK

Café Morgane – *100 rue des Forges. ✆819-691-4399. Mon–Fri 6am–11:30pm, Sat–Sun 6am–midnight.* A bustling Quebec-style Internet café offering a variety of Italian coffees, along with light fare and luscious desserts.

Nord Ouest Café – *1441 rue Notre-Dame Centre. ✆819-693-1151.* With its strategic location at the corner of the two main streets, visitors can watch all of Trois-Rivières go by from the terrace. A rustic pub-style venue with craft beers and Scotch whiskies.

SHOPPING

Carpe Diem – *30 rue des Forges. ✆819-378-3436. 10am–5pm (Thu–Fri 9pm).* This shop, run by the handcrafted soap company located in Bécancour, on the other side of the St. Lawrence River, stocks no fewer than 50 different varieties of natural soap. Customers can also make their own soap.

DRINKS

Le Temps d'une Pinte – *1465 rue Notre-Dame Centre. ✆819-694-4484. www.letempsdunepinte.ca Mon–Wed 7am–midnight, Thu–Fri 7am-1am, Sun 8am–midnight.* This new gastropub has maintained the menu offered by the popular coffee shop, Le Torréfacteur, that it replaced, and as before, a wide range of coffee and tea, as well as sandwiches, soup and pastries can be enjoyed, along with upscale pub fare and fine selection of craft beer.

Suite Soixante – *60 rue des Forges. ✆819-841-0090. www.suite60.net Tue–Wed and Sun 2pm–7pm, Thu–Fri 2pm–10pm, Sat 2pm–8pm.* An art gallery as well as a café-bar with a peaceful atmosphere, where patrons can drink coffee or wine surrounded by artworks.

EVENTS

"Danse Encore" Festival – *✆819-376-2769. www.festival-encore.com.* A week of dance performances held in June.

National biennial of contemporary sculpture – *Information from the Galerie d'Art du Parc ✆819-691-0829.* An exhibition of artistic work held on even years only, from mid-June to the end of summer.

FestiVoix – *✆819-372-4635. www.festivoix.com.* This nine-day celebration of singing and music takes place in late June and early July.

Festival international de la poésie – *✆819-379-9813. www.fiptr.com.* The international poetry festival, held in October each year, lasts around ten days, bringing together poets and poetry enthusiasts. Venues around town include classrooms, restaurants, concert halls, and the occasional bar.

Mauricie★

Since 2001, the Mauricie region has been known as the "Forestry Capital of Canada," a feature best appreciated by following the course of the Saint-Maurice River, which flows southward for 560km/348mi, from the Gouin Reservoir in the northern part of central Quebec to the St. Lawrence River. The Saint-Maurice River was named for Maurice Poulin de la Fontaine, who explored the waterway in 1668. Trois-Rivières is the major industrial center of the region.

- **Info:** 1-800-567-7603. www.tourismemauricie.com.
- **Location:** The valley of the Saint-Maurice River extends from Trois-Rivières north to La Tuque, along Rtes. 55 and 155.
- **Don't Miss:** Tranquil, clear waters plus night-time constellations at Normand Lake in Saint-Maurice Wildlife Reserve.
- **Timing:** Shop for supplies before visiting Saint-Maurice Wildlife Reserve, as you're only allowed out of the reserve for an hour before another charge is applied for re-entry.
- **Kids:** At the Forges-du-Saint-Maurice, kids can handle authentic artifacts and tools as well as compare dress worn in the 18C, when the forge was in its heyday.

A BIT OF HISTORY

The valley of the Saint-Maurice River has been an important industrial area since the 18C. Rich veins of iron ore were first mined here in 1730, and forestry has dominated the regional economy since 1850. In the late 19C, hydroelectric plants were established in Grand-Mère, Shawinigan and La Gabelle.

The energy they produced, together with the invention of floating booms (chains of logs enclosing free-floating logs), led entrepreneurs to establish pulp mills between 1890 and 1900. Chemical plants later opened in Grand-Mère and Shawinigan, and eventually, a major aluminum plant was built in Shawinigan.

DRIVING TOUR

FROM TROIS-RIVIÈRES TO LA TUQUE

170km/105.6mi.

Leave Trois-Rivières by Boulevard des Forges.

Forges-du-Saint-Maurice★★

10000 blvd des Forges. Open late Jun–first week Sept, daily 10am–5pm, last admission 4:30pm. $4. 819-378-5116. www.pc.gc.ca/forges.

The ironworks on the banks of the Saint-Maurice River operated for 150 years (1729–1883) and engendered Canada's first industrial community. By special warrant of King Louis XV, François Poulin de Francheville established the first blast furnace in 1730 as part of an initiative to exploit the natural resources of New France. At its productive zenith, the furnace was capable of reducing 19 tonnes of raw ore per day to four tonnes of liquid cast iron, and iron was smelted here until 1883. Today this national historic site commemorates the inception of Canada's massive iron and steel industry.

The Grande Maison (1737), which housed managers' offices, a store and living quarters, today serves as the park's reception center. Displays on the first floor explain the economic and social conditions in Canada during the early years of the forge's operation. Objects produced at the forge, which included guns and ammunition, cooking pots, wheel hubs, horseshoes

Seaplane on the Saint-Maurice River, Shawinigan

and cast-iron bedsteads, are on view in the basement. On the upper floor, a "sound and light" narration uses a scale model of the forge village as it appeared around 1845.

From the Grande Maison, a path leads to the vestiges of the **blast furnace**. The shape of the structures comprising the ironworks has been re-created by a three-dimensional metal structure. At the blast furnace (*haut fourneau*), an excellent interpretation center explains the smelting process in layman's terms; particularly interesting is reconstructed hydraulic machinery of the type used during the 18C. Other displays show the sources and types of ore, and a small, furnished cabin illustrates the life led by forge workers and their families during the late 18C.

A pleasant path leads down to the Saint-Maurice River; along the way, other vestiges of the industrial past are visible, including the **upper forge** (*forge haute*), the smoke stack of the **lower forge** (*forge basse*), and the **mill** (*moulin*). On the river's shore, a spring known as the **Devil's Fountain** (*Fontaine du Diable*) is a source of natural gas.

▶ Continue northward on Blvd. des Forges and take Rte. 55. After 10km/6mi, take a right toward chemin de la Gabelle and continue for 2km/1.2mi.

Barrage la Gabelle

The dam opened in 1922 and is the only crossing point over the St-Maurice River between Trois-Rivières and Shawinigan (alternating traffic). It is located in the heart of La Gabelle nature park, in what was once an area of active trading between indigenous people and settlers.

▶ Continue until the junction with Route 157, where you should turn left.

Shawinigan

23km/14.3mi (Exit 217 South).

This community was formerly referred to as "la ville de l'électricité" (the city of electricity) because it generated all the power needed to supply Montreal. The name Shawinigan is from the Algonquian word *ashawenikan,* meaning "portage on the crest."

In 1852 a water slide was built to transport logs around the various falls on the Saint-Maurice River. In 1899 the falls were harnessed for their hydroelectric power; this in turn led to the construction of pulp mills, chemical plants, and an aluminum smelter.

La Cité de l'énergie

1000 Ave. Melville. Open early-Jun–Sept, daily 10am–5pm (last admission 2pm, but partial visits of 90 min are offered for $12). $18. 819-536-8516 or 1-866-900-2483. www.citedelenergie.com.

Constructed next to Shawinigan Falls, the City of Energy shows the key role hydroelectric power played in the history of Quebec. A science center with interactive displays, an observation tower and two hydroelectric plants bring the industry to life.

Although the rocky beds of the **chutes de Shawinigan** (Shawinigan Falls) are scenic throughout the year, the falls are most impressive during spring run-off or after heavy rainfall.

Just after the powerful Shawinigan Falls there is a whirlpool called **Trou du Diable**, which is rumored to be bottomless. Legend says that anyone falling into the hole cannot be saved. There is also a very popular local micro-brewery pub of the same name in town. *See Addresses.*

Parc national de la Mauricie★★

Park open year-round. Visitor centers at the Saint-Jean-des-Piles and Saint-Mathieu entrances offer information, entrance permits and canoe rentals and interpretative displays; open Jun–early Sept, daily 9am–9:30pm; last two weeks of May and Sept 8 to mid-Oct daily 9am–4:30pm (Fri 9:30pm). $7.80. 1-888-773-8888 or 819-538-3232. www.pc.gc.ca/mauricie.

Established in 1970 with a view to preserving a representative slice of the Laurentian Mountains, Mauricie National Park comprises 536sq km/207sq mi in a transition area between the deciduous woods of the south and the boreal forest. Maples and conifers thickly cover rounded hills rising some 350m/1,148ft and interspersed with numerous rivers and lakes. For 5,000 years, the region's rich natural resources have attracted indigenous peoples, trappers, loggers, raftsmen, anglers and hunters. Before being designated a national park, it was one of the largest private hunting and fishing grounds in North America.

You can take a drive which meanders through the pink metamorphic rocks of the Canadian Shield. The road follows the long, finger-shaped **Lac Wapizagonke** over 16km/10mi, providing several viewpoints of cliffs and sandy beaches. The observation deck at Le Passage (30km/18.6mi) offers a superb view. The road leads to **Lac Édouard**, a narrow stretch of water surrounded by a natural beach, then descends to the eastern entrance of the park, offering pleasant views of the Saint-Maurice River.

Return to Rte. 55.

Grand-Mère

10km/6.2mi (Exit 223).

In 1890 a hydroelectric power station was built here and pulp mills soon followed. The town was named for a giant rock that protruded from the middle of the river, resembling the head of an old woman (*Grand-Mère* means "grand-

Parc national de la Mauricie

© desfa24 / Fotolia.com

Grandes-Piles

mother"). To make room for the Hydro-Québec dam in 1916, the rock (rocher de Grand-Mère) was relocated, piece by piece, to a tiny park in the center of town (corner of 5e Avenue and 1re Rue).

Leave Grand-Mère by the bridge over the Saint-Maurice River and take Rte. 155.

Grandes-Piles

17km/10.5mi.

Founded in 1885 as a transfer point for lumber boats, this community is perched on a cliff overlooking the river. The municipality was named for the pile-shaped rocks located in the waterfall south of the village.

Musée et village du Bûcheron★ (Lumberman's Museum and Village)

780 5e Ave. Grandes-Piles. Open mid-June–mid-Oct daily 9:30am–4:30pm. Guided tours at 10am, 11:30am, 1:30pm, 3pm. $10. 819-538-7895 or 1-877-338-7895. www.boite-a-bois.com.

Some 20 buildings and a collection of more than 5,000 objects re-create a typical Québécois logging village during the early 20C. The rough, axe-hewn timber structures evoke the rudimentary living conditions of the men who cut and transported wood as a way of life. In each of the buildings, objects and furnishings highlight the living conditions of loggers, fire watchmen and storage guards. Visitors can enjoy a snack in the restored cook's house and visit the sawmill, forge, lumbermen's quarters and stables.

Continue on Rte. 155.

Between Grandes-Piles and Saint-Roch-de-Mékinac, the drive affords lovely **views★** of the powerful Saint-Maurice River and the rocky cliffs on the opposite shore. In spring, osprey (*balbuzard*), large, fish-eating hawks, nest here, and visitors can often see them circling above the river.

Continue to Rivière-Matawin (38km/23.6mi).

Réserve faunique du Saint-Maurice (Saint-Maurice Wildlife Reserve)

Accessible only by bridge across the Saint-Maurice River (round-trip toll: $12/car, cash only). A welcome center (2km/1.2mi from Rivière-Matawin, at 3774 Rte. 155, Trois-Rives) provides maps and information for activities like camping, fishing, hunting, canoe-camping, nature study, dogsledding, and hiking. (For lodging, call 819-646-5687). Note: you can leave the reserve for a maximum of one hour, and not be charged a re-entry fee, if you leave your ticket at the gatehouse. Open mid-May–

early Sept, Mon–Fri 7:30am–9pm, Sat–Sun 9am–6pm; late Sept–Nov, Mon–Fri 9am–4:30pm, Sat–Sun 7:30am–9pm (hours may vary; call in advance). ✗♿ P ☎819-646-5687. www.sepaq.com. This vast wilderness of forests, lakes, and streams is a haven for anglers and canoeists. Numerous campgrounds are scattered around Lake Normand, which is famous for its clear waters and long, sandy beaches.

The 22km/13.6mi **Pioneers Circuit**, a canoeing and camping route, runs through the hills and woods of the reserve. Other sights include waterfalls, unusual rock formations, and a trail through the boreal forest.

Return to Rte. 155 in the direction of La Tuque (69km/42.8mi northwest).

La Tuque

A former fur trading post, La Tuque, like many other towns in this region, owes its existence to vast forested areas and a powerful waterfall. It boasts a pulp and paper mill and a hydroelectric plant (1909); its name derives from a hill shaped like the popular woollen hat known as a *tuque*. La Tuque is the birthplace of singer-composer **Félix Leclerc** (1914–88), who became the first Quebec songwriter to acquire international fame. His songs praise the beauty of the forests and rivers of Quebec, especially the St. Lawrence River.

ADDRESSES

STAY

Auberge Gouverneur Shawinigan – *1100 Promenade du Saint-Maurice. ☎819-537-6000. www.gouverneurshawinigan.com. 106 rooms.* On the well-developed bank of the Saint-Maurice River, which is also home to the town's liveliest bars and restaurants, this upscale hotel offers well-equipped, recently renovated rooms, as well as an attractive spa and an indoor pool.

Hôtel Sacacomie – *4000 chemin Yvon-Plante, St-Alexis-des-Monts.* ✗♿ P Spa *☎819-265-4444 or 1-888-265-4414. www.sacacomie.com. 109 rooms.* The famous, almost mythical Hôtel Sacacomie sits in the pristine Mastigouche wildlife reserve above a tranquil lake. Constructed of logs, and filled with comfortable wood-panelled rooms, this year-round resort offers a wealth of outdoor activities, including hiking, fishing and ice fishing, skating, snowmobiling, canoeing, mountain biking, cross-country skiing, and dogsledding.

EAT

Roulotte Beauparlant – *712 5e rue, Shawinigan. Mid-Mar–Oct Mon–Fri 9am–11pm, Fri–Sun 9am–midnight.* A fast-food caravan that has become a Shawinigan institution and dates back to 1939 in its first incarnation. Prime Minister Jean Chrétien never missed an opportunity to eat here, and the menu covers all the bases for lovers of French fries and poutine.

Le Trou du Diable – *412 Ave. Willow. ☎819-537-9151. www.troudu diable.com. Bar open Sun–Tue 3–11pm, Wed–Thu 3pm–1am. Kitchen open Tue–Sun 5–9pm.* This evening restaurant serves up a delicious range of regional dishes and original creations such as confit of rabbit shoulder or Quebec lamb burger. Live music or theater several times a week.

EVENTS

Cité de l'Energie – *1000 av Melville, Shawinigan, Cité de l'Énergie. ☎1-866-900-2483 (no charge). www.citedelenergie.com. Open Jun–Sept.* This complex offers open-air shows in an amphitheater with protection from the weather. Shows and schedules change every summer, so check the website.

Fête National du Québec – June 24, or St-Jean-Baptiste day, is celebrated across Quebec with parades, picnics, concerts, dances and bonfires in the evening. While you will find lively entertainment throughout the province, the celebrations at Parc de la Rivière at Grand-Mère have a special village charm.

East of Montreal

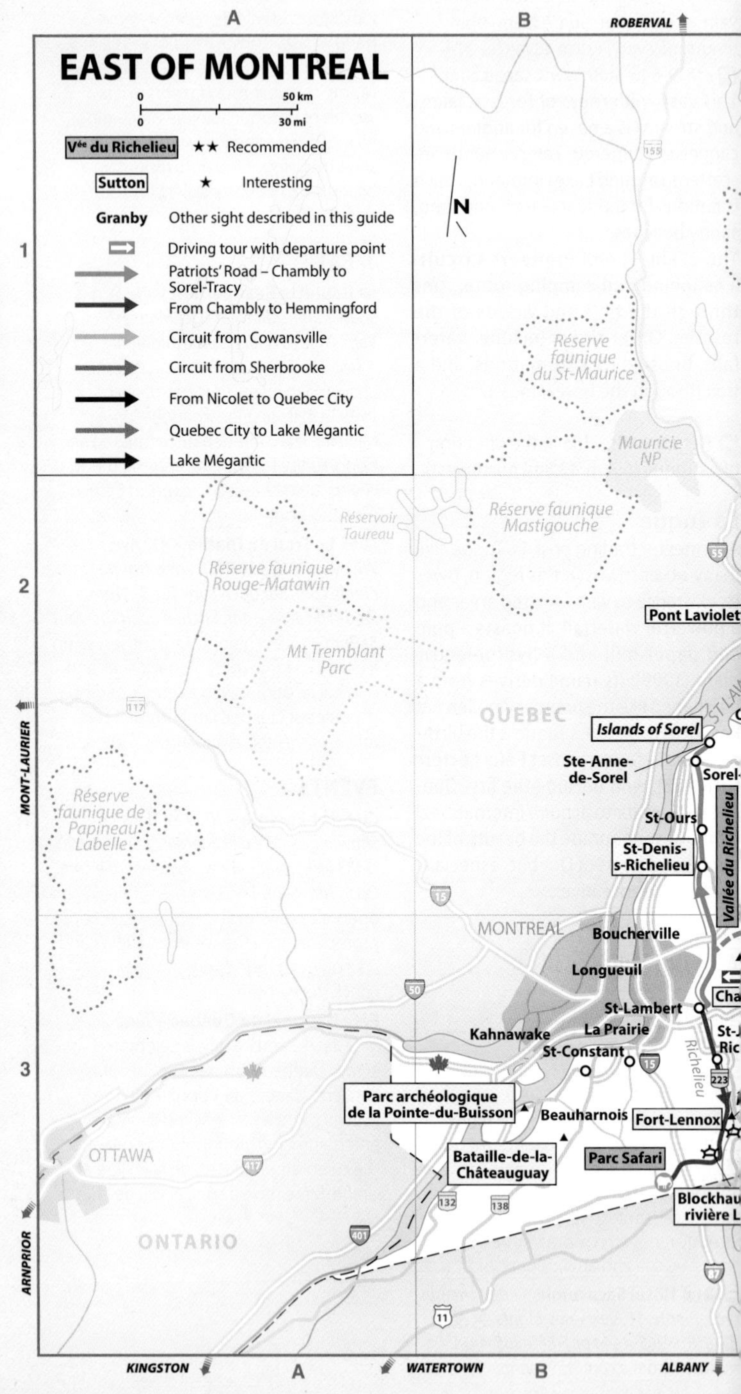

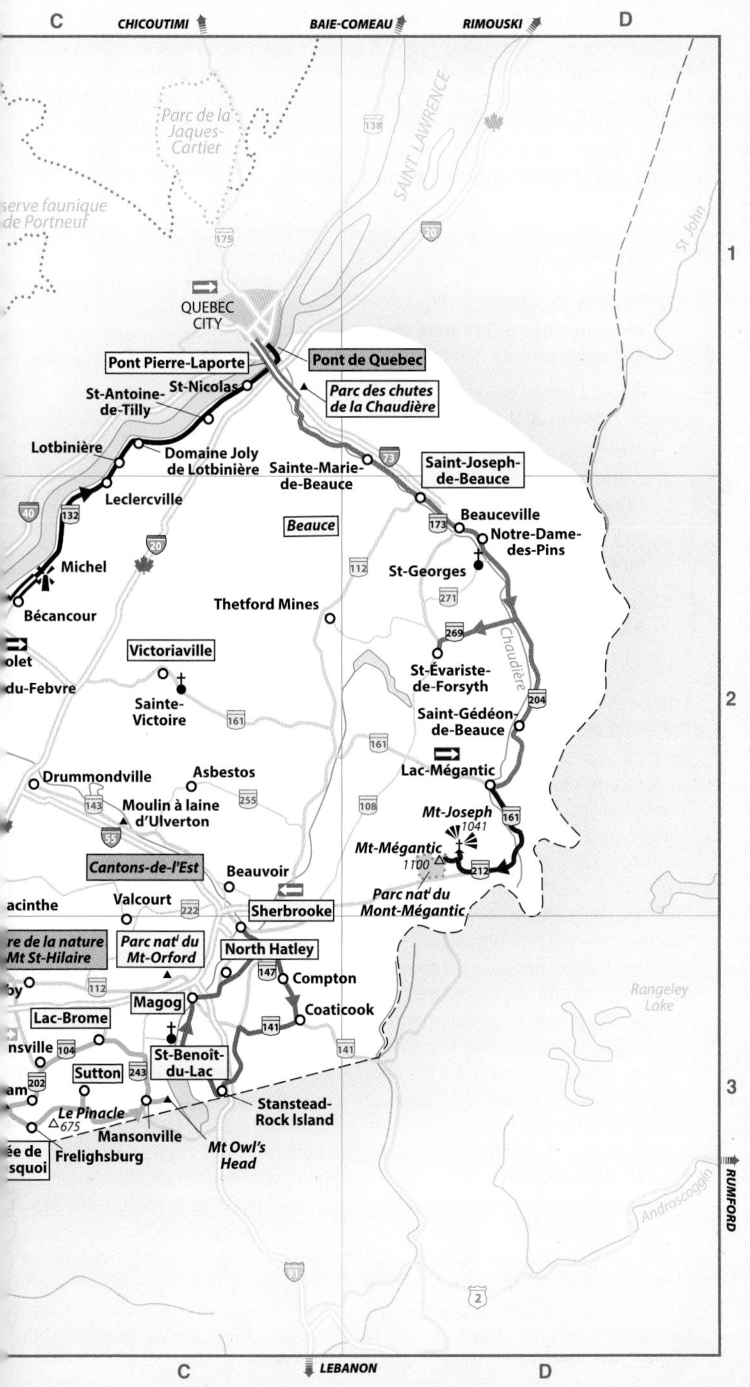

C
CHICOUTIMI
BAIE-COMEAU
RIMOUSKI
D
Parc de la Jaques-Cartier
serve faunique de Portneuf
SAINT LAWRENCE
St John
QUEBEC CITY
Pont Pierre-Laporte
Pont de Quebec
Parc des chutes de la Chaudière
St-Nicolas
St-Antoine-de-Tilly
Lotbinière
Domaine Joly de Lotbinière
Sainte-Marie-de-Beauce
Saint-Joseph-de-Beauce
Leclercville
Beauceville
Notre-Dame-des-Pins
Beauce
Michel
St-Georges
Bécancour
Thetford Mines
Victoriaville
olet
du-Febvre
Sainte-Victoire
St-Évariste-de-Forsyth
Chaudière
Saint-Gédéon-de-Beauce
Lac-Mégantic
Drummondville
Asbestos
Moulin à laine d'Ulverton
Mt-Joseph
1041
Mt-Mégantic
1100
Cantons-de-l'Est
Beauvoir
Parc nat[l] du Mont-Mégantic
acinthe
Valcourt
Sherbrooke
re de la nature Mt St-Hilaire
Parc nat[l] du Mt-Orford
North Hatley
Compton
by
Magog
Coaticook
Lac-Brome
Rangeley Lake
nsville
St-Benoît-du-Lac
Sutton
am
Le Pinacle
675
Mansonville
Stanstead-Rock Island
Mt Owl's Head
ée de squoi
Frelighsburg
Androscoggin
RUMFORD
LEBANON
1
2
3

East of Montreal

The phrase "East of Montreal" encompasses a mammoth geographical area that embraces the regions south of the St. Lawrence River, and extends from the south shore of Montreal to Quebec City, an immense territory that features a remarkable abundance of sights and attractions. From the south-shore communities of Longueuil, La Prairie, and Beauharnois, to the Richelieu Valley, Cantons-de-L'Est, and the Beauce region, "East of Montreal" offers a rich cornucopia of attractions and destinations.

Highlights

1. Take a guided tour at the **Site archéologique de la Pointe-du-Buisson** in Melocheville (p247)
2. Ride in a hot-air balloon in **St-Jean-sur-Richelieu Valley** (p256)

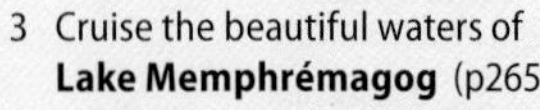

3. Cruise the beautiful waters of **Lake Memphrémagog** (p265)
4. Visit the **modern Cathedral** at Nicolet (p277)
5. Stargaze from Mont Mégantic's **ASTROlab** (p285)

The Best of Quebec

The land covering the mighty river's southern front is compelling for even the most experienced of travelers. The suburban communities of Longueuil and Saint-Lambert provide industrial homes for Montreal's robust global economy, and are within easy reach of beautiful nature reserves and idyllic lake landscapes—not least the Îles de Boucherville—and lush farmlands preserving the rich bread basket of the province. Quaint villages and towns are steeped in French traditions, while many are known for their artistic history including Mont-Saint-Hilaire (once home of Ozias Leduc and Paul-Émile Borduas) and Magog-Orford, known for the Centre d'arts Orford.

First Nations Culture

Kahnawake, a First Nations community south of Montreal, has associated itself with other local communities to provide centers in Mont-St. Hilaire (La Maison Amerindiénne) and Odanak (home of the first Native museum in Quebec). To fully appreciate this stunning area, a visitor should become acquainted with the roots and traditions of these Native communities in these centers. In July the Kahnawake reservation hosts the Pow Wow festival—a gathering of tribes from around the world that celebrates First Nations music, traditions, and food.

A Heritage-rich Landscape

The land itself, in addition to the many churches and heritage structures, speaks of a community-based society. Apple orchard tours in Hemmingford attract seasonal visitors to the southern part of the province, while hot-air ballooning attracts clients to the Vallée du Richelieu.

East of Montreal lies Cantons-de-l'Est—usually called Estrie— which also has much to offer. From the ski hills of Mont-Orford Mont-Sutton, and Owl's Head, to the lazy summer retreats of Brome Lake, Lake Memphrémagog, and Lake Mégantic; visitors have attractions to enjoy no matter what their tastes, as lavender fields give way to red barns filled with antiques while historic abbeys overlook graceful lake waters, and tour boats putter lazily offshore.

Local Products

Entrepreneurship is growing rapidly, and travelers benefit by having handmade products to buy and services to enjoy, as organic farmers and merchants, full-service spas, hotels, and guesthouses abound.

Souvenir-seekers can buy porcelain products in Saint-Jean-sur-Richelieu, while gourmets might enjoy the hand-crafted cheese and cider made at Saint-Benoît-du-Lac Abbey near Magog. Travelers in search of fresh fruit and vegetables—and some outdoor activity—can visit the farms near Lennoxville, which are open in season, to people who want to pick their own produce.

Longueuil

You will pass through this residential suburb of Montreal before reaching Mont-Saint-Hilaire or Chambly Fort. Shipping enthusiasts will want to visit Saint-Lambert Lock, which marks the entrance to the St. Lawrence Seaway, while families can relax in Îles-de-Boucherville national park.

- **Population:** 231,969.
- **Michelin Map:** p236–237: B3.
- **Info:** 205 Chemin de Chambly. ℘450-670-7293. www.tourisme-monteregie.qc.ca.
- **Location** Longueuil is 9.3km/5.7mi southeast of Montreal by the Jacques-Cartier Bridge. It can also be reached by Métro and, from mid-May to early October, by a water shuttle ($7 one-way) connecting Old Montreal to the Longueuil marina and bike path system *(℘514-281-8000; www.navettesmaritimes.com).*
- **Parking:** Metered and not always easy to find in Old Longueuil.
- **Timing:** Crossing the Jacques-Cartier bridge on weekends is easier.

A BIT OF HISTORY

Located on the south shore of the St. Lawrence, Longueuil was part of the seigneury granted to Charles Le Moyne in 1657. Between 1685 and 1690, Le Moyne built a massive stone fort that would serve as an outer defence to protect Montreal against the Iroquois and named it Longueuil after his birthplace in Normandy, France. The fort was demolished in 1810. Le Moyne fathered 12 sons, several of whom were famous in their own rights. He left his seigneury to his eldest son Charles, who was granted a patent of nobility by Louis XIV. Among his other sons were the explorer Pierre Le Moyne d'Iberville, who helped Pierre de Troyes defeat the English at James Bay in 1686 and became governor of the conquered trading posts. His son Jean-Baptiste Le Moyne de Bienville founded New Orleans in 1718.

Today Longueuil is an industrial suburb of Montreal and is home to manufacturing plants for aircraft parts, textiles, furniture, and toys.

SIGHTS

Cathédrale Saint-Antoine-de-Padoue (St. Anthony of Padua Cathedral)

55 rue Sainte-Élizabeth. Open year-round, daily 9am–5pm. Closed major holidays. ℘450-674-1549.

This imposing stone church (1885–87) with its single steeple and dome is actually a "co-cathedral" for the diocese of Saint-Jean–Longueuil along with the cathedral in Saint-Jean-Sur-Richelieu. It stands on the former site of Le Moyne's fort. The ornate interior has three naves, and features paintings by the noted artist Jean-Baptiste Roy Audy. From the end of the chemin de Chambly, the tower of Montreal's Olympic Stadium is visible.

Rue Saint-Charles Est (Old Longueuil)

A number of historic houses, most of them made of stone, line rue Saint-Charles Est, the core of Old Longueuil. The **Couvent de Longueuil** *(no. 70)* was originally built in 1769, and a convent wing was added in 1844. The **Maison Daniel-Poirier** *(no. 100)* dates from 1749.

The **Maison André-Lamarre** *(no. 255)*, built in 1740, is Longueuil's oldest home. The original pitched gable was replaced by a mansard roof in 1895. Today the house is the headquarters of the Société d'histoire de Longueuil (www.societedhistoirelongueuil.qc.ca ℘450-674-0349). Take time to enjoy the relaxed, sophisticated ambiance of Old Longueuil.

A Network of Paths

Behind the Maison André-Lamarre *(255 chemin de Chambly)*, four footbridges cross Route 132 and lead to a network of bike paths along the St. Lawrence. At the eastern end of this network, a ferry crosses to Charron Island and the Boucherville Islands Park. Crossing times change with the seasons. *$8.50 round-trip; Croisières Navark 514-871-8356; www.navark.ca.*

EXCURSIONS

Boucherville

12km/7.2mi N of Longueuil.

Boucherville is one of Quebec's oldest communities. In 1667, the seigneury featuring beautiful islands was granted to Pierre Boucher, governor of Trois-Rivières. Boucher and the first settlers arrived the following year. For almost three centuries Boucherville developed, first, as an agricultural community, and later as a resort town. The opening of the Louis-Hippolyte Lafontaine Tunnel under the St. Lawrence in 1967 transformed Boucherville into an industrial and residential suburb of Montreal, yet it has kept a historical core and beautiful parks.

Boucherville is the birthplace of Louis-Hippolyte Lafontaine (1807–64), Prime Minister of the United Canadas, 1842–43 and 1848–51.

Boulevard Marie-Victorin, the main thoroughfare, is lined with handsome 19C houses, several of which belonged to descendants of the city's founder. Note the mid-18C manor house at no. 470, built for François-Pierre Boucher de Boucherville, and the 19C brick structure at no. 486, built for Charles-Eugène Boucher, premier of Quebec from 1874–78 and 1891–92.

Louis-Hippolyte Lafontaine House

314 Blvd Marie-Victorin inside De La Broqerie Park facing the water, near exit 18 of Rte. 132. Open Jun 23–mid-Aug, Tue–Sun 10am–5pm; Jun 1–Jun 23 and Sept–early Oct, Fri–Sun 1pm–5pm. Closed holidays. (no charge) 450-449-8347.

Located in a park near the St. Lawrence, this dwelling belonged to the father-in-law of Louis-Hippolyte Lafontaine. Constructed in 1766 and rebuilt after the fire of 1843, the house was moved from Boucherville's historic center to its present site in 1964. The house is a fine example of New France home architecture. It is now a small Boucherville heritage museum.

Lafontaine lived here from 1813 through 1822, before undertaking his law studies in Montreal. The highlights of his career are displayed. Lafontaine is generally considered to be the main proponent of "responsible government," a term used to designate a government empowered by a locally elected assembly rather than the British Crown. This form of government was essential to ease the tensions between Canadians and their British rulers.

Église de la Sainte-Famille★

560 Blvd Marie-Victorin. Open year-round, daily 9am–4pm. 450-655-8311.

This church (1801) rises above a small square also occupied by a cultural center and a nursing home. It was designed by the parish priest, Father Pierre Conefroy, who supervised the construction. His efficient and cost-effective management of the project became codified as the "Conefroy plan specifications" (*plan-devis Conefroy*), which were thereafter adopted as a blueprint for the construction of churches throughout the province. Father Conefroy adopted the Latin cross floor plan to provide badly needed space for rural parish churches, which had experienced a population explosion in the late 18C. In recognition of his successful endeavor, Father Conefroy was named Vicar-General of the diocese and supervised all church construction in Quebec.

The original interior décor, commissioned from the studio of Louis-Amable

A 400-Year-Old Dream Comes True

St. Lawrence Seaway – The opening of the seaway in 1959 marked the realization of a 400-year-old dream. In the early 16C, Jacques Cartier's quest for the Northwest Passage to the Orient was thwarted by the tumultuous Lachine Rapids, located west of present-day Montreal. The rapids were but the first of a daunting series of natural obstacles that rendered the river unnavigable between Montreal and the Great Lakes. Sadly for Montreal though, the St. Lawrence Seaway, by allowing ships to go to Toronto, marked the start of a major economic shift towards the Ontario capital.

Conquering the river – Throughout the 300 years that followed Cartier's discoveries, Natives, soldiers, and settlers repeatedly attempted to conquer the shoals, rapids, and falls of the St. Lawrence River upstream from Montreal by constructing canals and locks around such insurmountable obstacles as the mighty Niagara Falls. The Industrial Revolution fueled an American interest in the creation of a seaway to facilitate the transport of goods between the US and major ports in Canada and Europe. Years of negotiation between the Canadian and American governments led to a joint project to construct, maintain and operate international locks and canals.

Finally, on April 25, 1959, the icebreaker *Iberville* began the first complete voyage through the St. Lawrence Seaway, which was officially inaugurated on June 26 of that same year, by Queen Elizabeth II, US president Dwight Eisenhower and Canadian prime minister John Diefenbaker.

The seaway is 3,800km/2,361mi long and has a minimum depth of 8m/26ft. Sixteen locks raise and lower vessels a total of 177m/580.7ft, the difference in altitude between Montreal (6m/19.7ft) and Lake Superior (183m/600ft). The massive seaway ships, known as **lakers**, measure up to 222m/728ft long and 23m/75.4ft wide. They transport ore (principally iron) from Quebec and Labrador to the steel mills of the Great Lakes region, and huge cargoes of grain from the American heartland to ports on the St. Lawrence River.

Quévillon, was destroyed in the fire of 1843. Renovated by Louis-Thomas Berlinguet, the architectural treatment is typical of the style of Thomas Baillairgé. The Louis XV paneling exemplifies Berlinguet's attention to detail and ornamentation. The main altar and side altars, designed by Quévillon, survived the fire of 1843. The massive Baroque **tabernacle** is a major work dating from the French Regime.

Across the street, a monument to Pierre Boucher commands a view of the Boucherville islands and East Montreal. The neighboring streets, especially rue de la Perrière and rue Saint-Charles, are lined with 19C houses.

Boucherville Islands National Park

Rte. 25 (Exit 1 on Charron Island), also small ferries (pedestrians, bicycles) from Montreal, Boucherville and Longueuil in summer 514-871-8356. Open Apr–Oct 8am–sunset; rest of year 8am–4:30pm. $10 (return fare includes admission to park). Bicycle, canoe, rowboat and kayak rentals mid-May–Oct, showshoe and crampon rental in winter. RV camping area (water and electricity) $36/night. 450-928-5088 & 1-800-665-6527. www.sepaq.com.

Five islands form this popular Quebec national park. From the information center on Sainte-Marguerite Island, a passenger ferry and footbridges provide access to the other islands.

Bike paths (27km/17mi), hiking trails (27km/17mi), and canoe circuits lace the islands, affording **views** of Montreal. Hundreds of deer roam freely, with no predators in sight.

Parc du Mont-Saint-Bruno

Near Saint-Bruno-de-Montarville, 18km/11mi E of Longueuil. Open 8am to sunset. P. $10. 450-653-7544, 1-800-665-6527. www.sepaq.com.

This national park was created in 1985 and covers most of Mont Saint-Bruno, the famous member of the Monteregian hill group, which stands 218m/726ft above the surrounding plain. With its five lakes, its apple trees and its 18C watermill, it forms a protected green oasis in the midst of the urban landscapes of the Montreal region. Outdoor fun ranges from picnics and walking to cross-country skiing.

From the car park, a pleasant footpath (1hr round trip) takes you past the site of the former Jesuit school of Mont-Saint-Gabriel and leads, through a grove of red oaks and a grove of maples, to two lakes: Lac du Moulin and Lac Seigneurial. On the shore of the former stands an old stone watermill dating from 1761, the only survivor of a number of mills that used to operate in the area. It now houses an interpretation centre. The apple trees beside the mill and along the shores of the lake are a reminder of the era of the Seigneurie de Montarville. Longer paths lead to Lac des Bouleaux (birch tree lake), Lac à la Tortue (turtle lake) and Lac Atocas (which takes its name from a First Nations word meaning cranberries).

Écluse de Saint-Lambert

© SuperStock / age fotostock

Saint-Lambert

5km/3mi S of Longueuil.

This residential suburb of Montreal on the south shore of the St. Lawrence was originally part of the seigneury of Longueuil. Because the land was so marshy, the district was commonly called Mouille-pied ("wet feet"). In 1857 the municipality adopted the name Saint-Lambert in honor of an associate of the Sieur de Maisonneuve, **Lambert Closse**. Today Saint-Lambert is the port of entry to the St. Lawrence Seaway.

Écluse de Saint-Lambert★ (Saint-Lambert Lock)

From Victoria Bridge, follow signs for Rte. 20 Sud and turn right immediately, following signs. Belvedere open year-round, 8:30am–8:30pm; reservations required 24hrs in advance to tour tower and a minimum of four persons required in the group. P 450-672-4110 ext. 2237. www.greatlakes-seaway.com.

This was the first lock in the St. Lawrence Seaway system. It raises and lowers vessels 4.6m/15ft, enabling them to bypass the treacherous rapids just upstream from the Montreal harbor. The lock works in conjunction with the **Victoria Bridge★**, an impressive structure built between 1854 and 1859 to carry the Grand Trunk Railway across the river. At the time, the 2,742m/8,996ft bridge was the longest in the world and a great engineering feat. Rebuilt in the late 19C and again in the 1950s, it now carries cars in addition to trains. From the lock's **observatory**, visitors can watch enormous lakers pass through the lock on their way upriver to the Great Lakes or down to Port-Cartier and Sept-Îles.

La Prairie

This residential suburb of Montreal stands on the south bank of the St. Lawrence River. As well as being close to Montreal, a further attraction of the little town is that it has managed to preserve some buildings that typify the urban architecture that developed in Canada under the French, and some wooden buildings of the sort that would have been found in the suburbs of Montreal in the early 19C. La Prairie also makes a good gateway for a visit to the Musée Ferroviaire Canadien (Canadian Railway Museum) in Saint-Constant or the Battle of the Châteauguay National Historic Site.

- **Michelin Map:** p236–237: B3
- **Info:** 1-866-469-0069 or www.tourisme-monteregie.qc.ca.
- **Location:** 11,000 sq km/ 6,600 sq mi in four sectors: South-Shore, Suroît, Richelieu River, and Monterégie East.
- **Kids:** Exporail, Parc Safari, Grandby Zoo, and Biophare.
- **Timing:** Though they are accessible all year, it is best to call venues in advance.

WALKING TOUR

LE VIEUX-LA PRAIRIE

The fires of 1846 and 1901 did not spare many of the old buildings in the historic district known as Le Vieux La Prairie. However, some interesting sandstone structures with a hint of early English classicism are still standing (120 chemin de Saint-Jean and 166 rue Saint-Georges). Two other buildings provide an example of the architectural style born in New France (115 and 150 chemin de Saint-Jean), while most of the other buildings in Le Vieux-La Prairie are wooden constructions of the sort you might have found in the suburbs of Montreal in the early 19C (234, 238, and 240 rue Saint-Ignace).

Église de la Nativité de la Sainte Vierge

155 chemin Saint-Jean. Open prior to mass, Sun 10:30am, Tue 9am, Fri 4:30pm, Sat 3:30pm. 450-659-1133.

The old village, which the locals call "le vieux-fort" (the old fort), is dominated by this church dating from 1841. With its monumental Neoclassical façade and bell tower, over the years it has become the symbol of La Prairie. Two rows of colonnades and the bell tower topped with a dome recall the far-off model of Montreal's old Catholic cathedral. The architecture inside, however, was inspired by the church of St. Martin-in-the-Fields in London and exhibits the symmetry and order of the Neoclassical style.

Musée du Vieux-Marché

249 rue Sainte-Marie. Open Jun–Sept, daily 10am–5pm, Oct–May Mon 1pm–5pm, Tue–Thu 10am–5pm. No charge. 450-659-1393. www.laprairie-shlm.com.

This classically styled brick building dates from 1863 and has been used as a market, a firehouse, and a police station. In its current incarnation, it is a historical museum and home of the History Society of La Prairie de la Magdeleine. Exhibitions chart the history of Le Vieux-La Prairie, while a documentation room gives researchers access to genealogical records, reference works, and archive documents.

EXCURSION

Saint-Constant

20km/12mi S of Montreal.

Located on the south shore of the St. Lawrence, this former farming community was thrust into industrialization in 1888 with the construction of the Canadian Pacific Railway bridge across the St. Lawrence. Today a residential suburb of Montreal, Saint-Constant is also the birthplace of **Gustave Lanctot** (1883–1975), historian, archivist, and author of numerous works on New France.

Exporail, le Musée Ferroviaire Canadien★ (Canadian Railway Museum)

110 rue Saint-Pierre (Rte. 132 to Rte 209), walking distance from the Saint-Constant suburban train station (www.amt.qc.ca). Open mid-May–Jun 23 daily 10am–5pm; Jun 24–Labor Day daily 10am–6pm; rest of Sept–Oct, Wed–Sun 10am–5pm; Nov–Apr, weekends 10am–5pm. $21. 450-632-2410. www.exporail.org.

Established and operated by the Canadian Railroad Historical Association, this large museum site composed of several buildings highlights the important role played by railroads in the development of Canada. In addition to some 6,000 artifacts, 185,000 archival documents and a restored train station, the museum preserves an exceptional collection of more than 130 locomotives and other railway vehicles (including 44 railway cars in the main building), many of which are in working order. Regular demonstrations on the operation of the trains allow visitors to recapture the past.

Among the steam locomotives is a replica of the tiny **Dorchester**, which pulled the first Canadian train in 1836. Built in England and transported to Saint-Jean-sur-Richelieu by barge, the engine had the power to pull just two cars, and had to be supplemented by horses at even slight inclines. Also on display is an exact replica of the **John Molson**, built in Scotland and shipped to Canada for use from 1850 through 1874 (*demonstrations in summer*). The **CNR 5702**, a locomotive built for passenger service, reached speeds of over 160kph/99mph in 1930. One of the largest locomotives ever constructed, the **CP 5935** hauled trains over the Rockies and the Selkirk Mountains in British Columbia in the 1950s. The **CP 7000**, Canadian Pacific's first electric locomotive with a diesel engine, was used from 1937 through 1964. Among non-Canadian vehicles is a French locomotive, the **SNCF 030-C-841** "Châteaubriand," dating from 1883, which retired after 83 years of service. A gift from British Rail, the **BR 60010** "Dominion of Canada" belonged to the class that established the world record for steam locomotives with a speed of 204kph (126.5mph) in 1938.

The museum also owns a large collection of old Montreal streetcars, one of which is used to give tours of the site. The star of the streetcar collection is "the Golden Streetcar," a gold-painted, touring, roofless car that brought Montrealers to large parks on weekends in the early 20C. Locals called it "le tramway observatoire."

Also visible are an enormous rotary snowplow used to clear the tracks during the long Canadian winters, as well as snowplowing locomotives.

Écluse de la Côte Sainte-Catherine (Côte Sainte-Catherine Lock)

About 6km/3.7mi from the Exporail museum. Drive north to Rte. 132 on Rue Saint-Pierre (Rte 209), turn left, then right on Rue Centrale and follow signs. Open daily Apr–Dec. 450-672-4110 (St. Lawrence Seaway).

This is the second lock on the St. Lawrence Seaway system. At this point, vessels are raised 9m/30ft, from the level of La Prairie Basin to that of Lake Saint-Louis, around the Lachine Rapids. The parking lot provides a good **view** of the vessels passing through the lock, and of the Montreal skyline in the distance.

Kahnawake

The reserve is 30km/18.5mi west of La Prairie, via Rte. 132, Rte. 15, Rte. 20, exit 63. www.kahnawake.com.

Kahnawake is situated on the southern shore of the St. Lawrence River, near Montreal. The word "Kahnawake" means "on the rapids" in the Mohawk language. In 1668 Jesuit missionaries founded the Saint-François-Xavier Mission in La Prairie, which intended to convert the local native population to Catholicism. In 1717 the mission was moved to

Mohawks with cultural dress and face painting, Kahnawake

© McPHOTO / R. Burch / age fotostock

its current site in Kahnawake. Known for their amazing lack of vertigo, the Mohawks of Kahnawake have gained renown throughout North America for their expertise in tall construction projects, including skyscrapers. They often work on sites in the major cities of Canada and the US.

Saint-François-Xavier Mission

Open May–Sept, daily 9am–4pm; rest of year Mon–Fri 9am–4pm, Sun after 10:45am mass–1pm. $5 for a guided tour, or $2 for self-guided tour booklet. 450-632-6030. www.kateritekakwitha.net.

Built by the Jesuit priest, Félix Martin, the church contains the tomb and relics of Kateri Tekakwitha, *Lily of the Mohawks*, who was beatified by John Paul II. Inside, the small **museum** features displays about a young woman and the Mohawk way of life.

Lieu historique national du Canada de la Bataille-de-la-Châteauguay★ (Battle of the Châteauguay National Historic Site)

On Rte. 138 between Howick and Ormstown, 24km/15mi S of Beauharnois. Open late Jun–Labor Day daily 10am–5pm. $4. 450-829-2003. www.pc.gc.ca.

The Châteauguay River valley, located south of Montreal, is a peaceful stretch of rural communities. However, for a short time during the War of 1812, it became the setting of an important battle, a turning point in the failed US attempt to invade Canada.

On October 26, 1813, 300 Canadian troops (French-Canadians and a few dozen Mohawk Indians from nearby Kahnawake) under the command of Lieutenant-Col. **Charles-Michel de Salaberry** (1778–1829) met an American

A Global Gathering of First Nations

Held one weekend in mid-Jul annually. $8. 450-632-8667. www.kahnawakepowwow.com. Across the Mercier Bridge off the Island of Montreal, the Kahnawake First Nations Reservation is the famous site of the yearly Pow Wow, a gathering of tribes from around the world to celebrate traditional values, culture, food, and games. Every year in July, thousands assemble to enjoy the dancers, drummers, storytellers and cooks, in a two-day festival of life. The highlight is the dancing competition, where experts and novices alike compete for top prizes in different categories. Transportation is available from the Métro Agrignon. There is a No-Drugs, No-Alcohol, and No-Firearms policy.

army of 2,000 soldiers led by Major-Gen. Wade Hampton. Salaberry managed to outwit the larger force by playing on the Americans' lack of familiarity with the territory, and succeeded in repelling the attack.

An interpretation center stands beside the Châteauguay River, adjacent to the battle site. A model shows the positions of US and Canadian forces, and illustrates the hardships of army life in the early 19C.

Marguerite-D'Youville Wildlife Refuge

480, Blvd D'Youville, Île Saint-Bernard, Châteauguay.

This refuge on the Saint-Bernard is also an easy excursion from the valley. *See MONTREAL AND SURROUNDINGS, p175.*

Beauharnois

28km/18mi N of historic Bataille-de-la-Châteauguay. Rejoin Rte. 138, then after Sainte-Catherine, turn right and take Rte. 205.

This industrial suburb of Montreal, part of the municipality of Beauharnois-Salaberry, was founded in 1819, and named for the Marquis de Beauharnois (1671–1749), 15th Governor of New France, who was granted a seigneury in this area. Today the small city is the site of a major power plant and a canal that diverts ships on the St. Lawrence Seaway around the rapids connecting Lakes Saint-François and Saint-Louis.

Construction of the power plant by the Beauharnois Light, Heat and Power Co. began in 1929, but was not completed until 1948. In 1953 and 1961, the canal was widened and the power station enlarged, making Beauharnois the largest hydroelectric plant in Canada at the time.

The current **Beauharnois Canal** was completed in 1932. Water is diverted from the original channel of the St. Lawrence into the canal by a system of dams and control works near Coteau-du-Lac. It is nearly 25km/16mi long by 1km/.6mi wide and 9m/29ft deep, and has two locks.

Centrale de Beauharnois★★ (Beauharnois Power Plant)

Visit by free guided tour (90min) mid-May–Labor Day, daily 9:30am, 11:15am, 1pm, 2:45pm. Visitors must present photo ID. 1-800-365-5229. www.hydroquebec.com.

This enormous hydropower plant is among the most productive in Quebec, with a generating capacity of 1,645,810 kilowatts. With a total length of 864m/2,834ft, it is also one of the longest in the world. Its run-of-the-river dam uses neither reservoir nor falls to control or speed the water flow. Instead, the station harnesses the powerful flow of the St. Lawrence River, notably the 24m/79ft drop between Lakes Saint-François and Saint-Louis. Water passes through the canal at a rate of 8 million liters/2.1 million gal per second. During the long winter, Quebec consumes all the power generated; for the remainder of the year, excess capacity is transmitted to Ontario and the US by 735,000-volt power lines.

In the interpretation center (located in Melocheville, across the canal), a permanent exhibit provides an excellent introduction to the site. On the tour, visitors will see the enormous **alternator hall** (864m/2,833ft long), where electric vehicles or tricycles are used by staff to check the turbines. Each of the 36 turbines weighs over 100 tons, is 4m/13ft high and 6m/20ft in diameter; their installed capacity, or optimal output, is 1,645,810 kilowatts. The tour also includes a visit to the **control room**, where computers monitor operations and regulate output. The rooftop of the plant affords a spectacular view of the intricate network of power lines extending in all directions. Montreal and the St. Lawrence are visible in the distance.

Beauharnois Locks – 2km/1.2mi west of the power plant by Rte. 132 Ouest. Parking area next to the lock. From this vantage point near the power plant, visitors can view the lower of the two Beauharnois locks. They enable vessels to bypass the power plant by raising them 12.5m/41ft. The upper lock, located 3.2km/2mi upstream, provides an additional 12.5m/41ft lift to the level of the Beauharnois Canal. The lock system is best viewed from the parking area.

Site archéologique de la Pointe-du-Buisson★

Melocheville, 5km/3mi west of lock by Rte. 132. Park and Musée québecois d'archéologie open mid-May–Labor Day Tue–Sun 10am–5pm; rest of Sept–mid-Oct, Tue–Sun 10am–5pm $11. 450-429-7857. www.pointedubuisson.com.

This pleasant, wooded peninsula protruding into the St. Lawrence is popular with anglers in search of sturgeon, brill, and eels in the rapids. Remains of human life nearly 7,000 years old have been found here, making it an important archeological site. In summer, visitors can watch archeologists in action. Two **interpretation centers** display the recovered artifacts and re-create the different eras of human activity at Pointe-du-Buisson. Paths lead through the park, providing good views of the rapids. Note the **Potsdam sandstone**, the oldest sedimentary rock in the Montreal area, exposed by river erosion.

Vallée du Richelieu★★

Montérégie region

The majestic Richelieu River constitutes a major link in the waterway flowing between Montreal and New York City. Approximately 130km/81mi long, the river flows from its source in New York State to join the St. Lawrence River at Sorel (now Sorel-Tracy).

- **Info:** Mont-Saint-Hilaire, 1080 chemin des Patriotes Nord (Rte. 133), Mont-Saint-Hilaire. 450-536-0359 & 1-888-736-0395. www.vallee-du-richelieu.ca/ www.regiongourmande.com.
- **Location:** Chambly is located approximately 30km/18.6mi east of Montreal by Rte. 10 (Exit 22) or Rte. 112. Itinerary 1 follows the Richelieu River on Rte. 133. Itinerary 2 follows Rte. 223, on the left bank (west side).
- **Don't Miss:** The view of the region, including Montreal, from the summit of Mt. Saint-Hilaire.
- **Kids:** The Safari Park towards Hemmingford is a real treat—a chance to see lions, tigers, and bears.
- **Timing:** Rte. 133 is slow, and Rte. 223 is very slow, so allow plenty of time to accommodate delays.

A BIT OF HISTORY

Samuel de Champlain discovered the waterway in 1609, and called it the Iroquois River. It was later named for Armand Jean du Plessis, Duke of Richelieu (1585–1642), better known as Cardinal Richelieu, Chief Minister of Louis XIII, who actively supported the development of New France.

Settlers moved into the valley in the early 18C to cultivate the fertile land of this region, which remains one of the richest agricultural areas in Quebec. Today a popular weekend retreat for Montrealers, the Richelieu Valley attracts thousands of travelers and tourists every weekend in the summer and autumn seasons.

Tour boats ply the waters regularly for a wonderful overview of the waterfront on both sides.

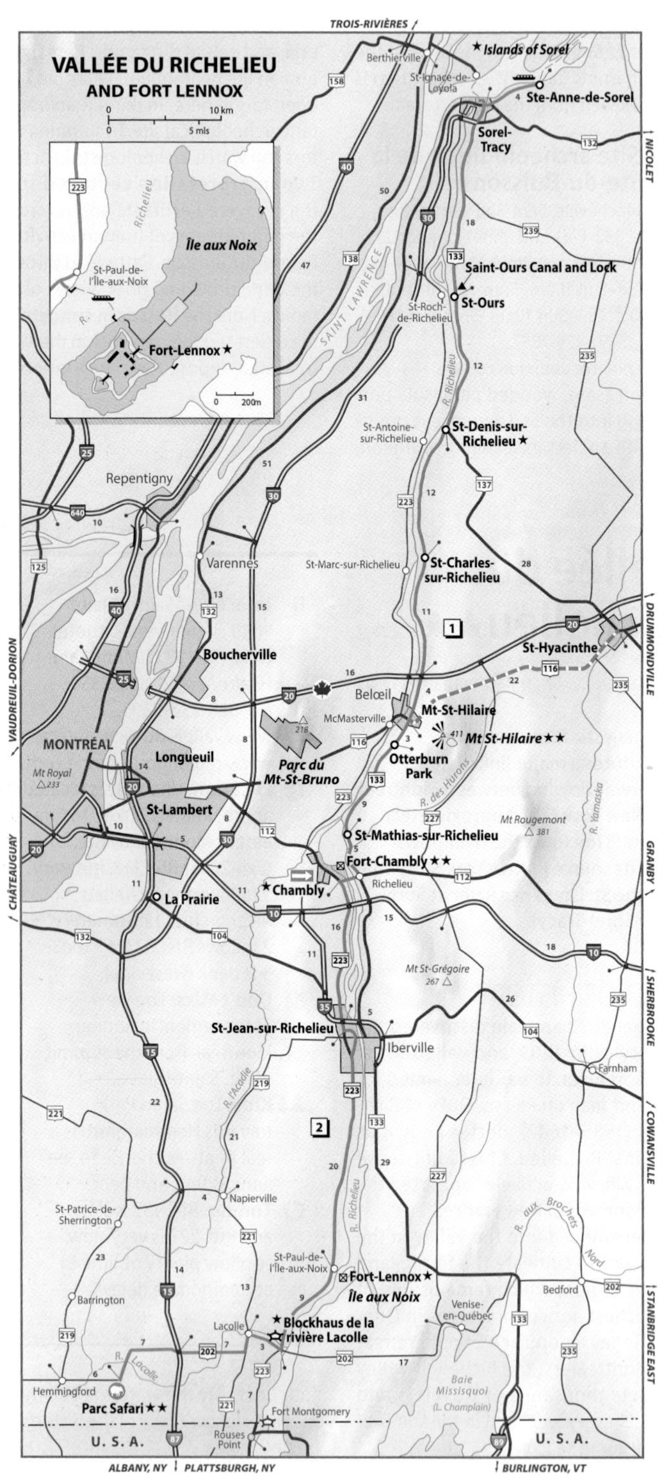
VALLÉE DU RICHELIEU
AND FORT LENNOX
Île aux Noix
St-Paul-de-l'Île-aux-Noix
Fort-Lennox ★
Islands of Sorel
Ste-Anne-de-Sorel
Sorel-Tracy
Saint-Ours Canal and Lock
St-Ours
St-Denis-sur-Richelieu ★
St-Charles-sur-Richelieu
St-Hyacinthe
Boucherville
Mt-St-Hilaire
Mt St-Hilaire ★★
Otterburn Park
Parc du Mt-St-Bruno
MONTRÉAL
Longueuil
St-Lambert
St-Mathias-sur-Richelieu
Fort-Chambly ★★
Chambly
La Prairie
St-Jean-sur-Richelieu
Iberville
Fort-Lennox ★
Île aux Noix
Blockhaus de la rivière Lacolle
Parc Safari ★★
U. S. A.
TROIS-RIVIÈRES
NICOLET
DRUMMONDVILLE
GRANBY
SHERBROOKE
COWANSVILLE
STANBRIDGE EAST
VAUDREUIL-DORION
CHÂTEAUGUAY
ALBANY, NY
PLATTSBURGH, NY
BURLINGTON, VT

Fort Chambly along the Richelieu River

© Jack_Art / iStockphoto.com

Valley of Forts

Owing to its strategic location, the Richelieu Valley was fortified early in the French Regime. Forts were built at Chambly, Saint-Jean-sur-Richelieu, Lennox (on Île aux Noix) and Lacolle. These fortifications were initially built to protect Montreal against attacks by Iroquois, and later by British troops (1759–60) and Americans (1775–76).

In the mid-19C the threat of invasion subsided, marking the beginning of a new era of trade. The objective was no longer to prevent access from the south but to facilitate transportation between Montreal and the US. An extensive canal system was built to achieve this goal.

DRIVING TOURS

PATRIOTS' ROAD—CHAMBLY TO SOREL-TRACY

78km/48.4mi via route 133.
Circuit traced in green on the map opposite.

Chambly★

A residential suburb of Montreal, the city of Chambly occupies a splendid natural site on the western shore of the Chambly Basin. Formed by the widening of the Richelieu River just below significant rapids, the basin is often

The Patriots' Rebellion (1837–38)

The Richelieu Valley played an important role in the conflict between the Patriots of Lower Canada and the British government. The constitutional struggles of the period, combined with a fierce sense of French Canadian nationalism, led Louis-Joseph Papineau and his supporters, the Patriots, to denounce the British regime and seek self-determination. As patriotic fervor increased, citizens loyal to the British government then in power formed armed militias to support the British army, and violent confrontations occurred in the Richelieu Valley and around Montreal. British troops under Colonels Charles Gore and Charles Wetherall faced the rebels at Saint-Denis-sur-Richelieu, defeated them at Saint-Charles-sur-Richelieu, and finally crushed them at Saint-Eustache.

Route 133, on the east side of the river, is called the **Patriots' Road** (chemin des Patriotes). The rifle, knitted hat, woven belt, and sometimes the pipe are symbols of the Patriots and can be seen in numerous illustrations depicting the event. The green, white and red **Canadian tricolor** was their principal flag.

dotted with sailboats. Fort Chambly is a rare example of large French military fortifications in North America.

Start at city hall at the corner of rue Bourgogne and rue de Salaberry.

The Charles-Michel de Salaberry **memorial**, erected in 1881 in front of Chambly's city hall, is one of the first historical bronzes created by the great sculptor, Louis-Philippe Hébert. Just north on rue Martel, in front of St. Joseph's Church (1784), stands the sculptor's last known work: a statue of Father Pierre-Marie Mignault, parish priest of St. Joseph's for 40 years.

Follow rue Bourgogne east to reach the Chambly Canal.

Lieu historique national du Canada du Canal-de-Chambly

Near the marina. Parking available across the bridge on rue Bourgogne. Open daily, sunrise–11pm; path maintained Apr 15–Nov 15. 450-658-4381 & 1-888-773-8888. www.pc.gc.ca/canalchambly.

Completed in 1843, this historic canal runs about 19km/11.8mi, from Saint-Jean-sur-Richelieu to the Chambly Basin, skirting numerous rapids in the Richelieu River. Its nine locks (eight of which are operated manually) raise passing vessels more than 24m/79ft. At the turn of the 19C, the canal was a busy commercial waterway used by more than 4,000 crafts annually. Today, although the canal has lost its economic importance, it is still used for boating and other recreational activities. Parks Canada owns the canal and manages, with the Friends of the Canal, an information office that displays photo exhibits. Some of the locks' original mechanisms still exist, and visitors can observe locksmen operating the cranks that open and close the sluice gates. A bicycle path follows the banks of the canal to Saint-Jean-sur-Richelieu.

Continue along rue Bourgogne to rue du Fort.

Lieu historique national du Canada du Fort-Chambly★★ (Fort Chambly National Historic Site of Canada)

2 rue de Richelieu, where the rapids reach the basin. Open late Jun–Labor Day daily 10am–6pm; mid-May–late June and Labor Day–mid-Oct Wed–Sun 10am–5pm. Last admission 45min before closing. $5.70. 450-658-1585. www.pc.gc.ca/fortchambly.

Chambly in History

A Montreal Fort – In 1665 Captain **Jacques de Chambly** was ordered to build a fort here to defend the route to Montreal against raids by the Iroquois. For services rendered to the colony, he was granted the seigneury in 1672. Today the town still bears his name. The river rapids were harnessed early in the 19C to activate seven mills including carding, sawing, and fulling mills. In 1843 the Chambly Canal was completed, facilitating navigation and trade between Canada and the US. Strings of barges pulled alongside the shore by horses were traditionally used to transport wood and other raw materials south to the New England states. During this period Chambly enjoyed great commercial prosperity. Today the city still attracts some light industry.

Artists and Heroes – Chambly's beautiful setting has long attracted artists. The Impressionist painter Maurice Cullen (1866–1934) lived here, as did his stepson Robert Pilot (1898–1967). Chambly is also the birthplace of Emma Lajeunesse (1847–1930). Better known by her stage name, Albani, Lajeunesse was an internationally acclaimed opera singer and one of the greatest sopranos of her generation. The city's most illustrious native son is Charles-Michel de Salaberry (1778–1829), hero of the Battle of the Châteauguay.

Reenactment at Fort Chambly

© Philippe Renault / hemis.fr

Located in a magnificent park where the river widens to form the Chambly Basin, this fort has been restored to its 18C appearance. Vestiges of the original stone structure, conceived by military engineer Josué Boisberthelot de Beaucours, can still be seen. Fort Chambly is the only remaining fortified complex in Quebec dating back to the French Regime. Erected between 1709 and 1711 during the Anglo-French wars, the stone fort replaced an earlier wooden structure erected by Jacques de Chambly in 1665, to defend the Richelieu rapids on the crucial trade route between Montreal and Albany, New York. The new fort was laid out in a square with bastions at each corner, and with the main entrance located on the western flank. Several buildings with dormer windows overlook the inner courtyard. A chapel topped by a mansard roof and small steeple faces the main entrance. Located inside the fort, an **interpretation center** features displays on the history of Fort Chambly and its occupants under the French Regime, and a description of the restoration project. Slide shows and dioramas re-create life at the fort and in the surrounding region.

Corps de Garde (Guard House)

On rue Richelieu near the fort.
Also accessible through the park.

After the Conquest, British officials established extensive military installations in Chambly. During the War of 1812, the fort was garrisoned with as many as 6,000 men and enlarged to accommodate the infantry, cavalry and artillery. Several expeditions launched against the Patriots in 1837–38 originated from Chambly. The fort and military camp were abandoned when the garrison departed in 1851.

The façade of the stone guardhouse (1814) features an imposing pediment supported by columns, exemplifying the Palladian style adopted by the military throughout the British colonies. The house contains displays on the period of occupation by the British garrison (1760–1851) and on the development of the city.

Église Saint-Stephen (St. Stephen's Church)

2000 rue Bourgogne. ☎450-658-5883
www.st-stephens-church-chambly.org

This fieldstone edifice, built in 1820 to serve as the garrison church, was modeled after the Catholic churches of the period. The liturgical furnishings and the sombre décor, however, distinguish the interior as a Protestant place of worship. The cemetery contains several interesting funeral monuments, among them one belonging to the Yule family, former seigneurs of Chambly.

▶ Continue along rue Richelieu to the junction with Rte. 112.

Rue Richelieu★

Several attractive houses line this street, a former portage route established along the rapids in 1665.

Near the guardhouse at no. 12 stands the **Maison Beattie**, a brick structure (1875) now privately owned. The first section of rue Richelieu, from the guardhouse to rue des Voltigeurs, passes through the former military domain. Buildings erected by the British army were transformed into residences at the end of the 19C. At no. 10 stands a former barracks (1814). The stone house at no 14 was once the commandant's residence.

From rue des Voltigeurs to rue Saint-Jacques, the second section of rue Richelieu crosses the former seigneurial domain, where several military officers settled in comfortable residences.

The **Manoir de Salaberry**, at no. 18, was constructed in 1814 for Charles-Michel de Salaberry, who lived here until his death in 1829. With its pediment and two-story portico, the residence is one of the finest examples of Palladian-inspired architecture in Quebec.

At no. 27 stands a monumental stone house built in 1816 for the merchant John Yule, brother of seigneur William Yule. The house at no. 26, built in 1920, was once the studio of the noted painter Maurice Cullen.

Rue Richelieu stretches alongside the **Parc des Rapides**, providing **views** of the tumultuous Chambly rapids and the Chambly dam. On this site stood the Willett wool factories and mills; powered by the river current, they were the source of Chambly's prosperity throughout the 19C.

Leave Chambly by Rte. 112, cross the Richelieu River in the village of Richelieu and take Rte. 133 north for 7.4km/4.6mi.

Saint-Mathias-sur-Richelieu

The first settlers came to Saint-Mathias in 1700, when it was still part of the seigneury of Chambly. Today, lovely homes and marinas border the Chambly Basin. The wayside cross on the right, where Rte. 133 straddles the Huron River, is one of several that still exist along the Richelieu River.

The interior décor of the **church of Saint-Mathias-sur-Richelieu** (1784) at 279 chemin des Patriotes, on the east side of Rte. 133, dates from the 1820s and is the work of René Beauvais (known as Saint-James) and Paul Rollin, two companions of Louis-Amable Quévillon, who executed the pulpit and the main altar in 1797 (visit by guided tour only: May–Oct, Mon, Wed, Fri 9am–noon; contribution requested, call to book a tour. 450-658-1671. www.paroissest-mathias.com).

Continue to Mont-St-Hilaire.

The municipality of **Otterburn Park** (*9km/5.6mi*) boasts several splendid mansions. Across the river stands the McMasterville industrial complex, where explosives have been manufactured since 1878.

13.5km/8.4mi northeast by Rte. 133.

Mont-Saint-Hilaire

Vallée du Richelieu tourist information: 255 Blvd Laurier, bureau 220, McMasterville. 450-464-4188 and 1-877-464-4188 (no charge). www.regiongourmande.com.

Home of the renowned painter **Ozias Leduc** (1864–1955) and birthplace of 20C artist **Paul-Émile Borduas**, Mont-Saint-Hilaire is a well-known artistic center.

Upon arriving in the community, notice the **Rouville-Campbell Manor** at 124 chemin des Patriotes on the banks of the Richelieu River. This Tudor-style manor house with its tall brick chimneys was built in the 1850s for Major Thomas Edmund Campbell, who took over the Hertel de Rouville seigneury after the Rebellion of 1837. The mansion was modeled after the Campbell ancestral home in Inverane, Scotland. Artist Jordi Bonet (1932–79) restored the manor in the 1970s; it now houses an inn and a fine restaurant.

The charming little stone **church of Saint-Hilaire-de-Richelieu** by the river was built in 1837 and decorated by Ozias Leduc in 1898 (260 chemin des Patriotes Nord. Open Mon–Fri 9am–noon, 1:30pm–4:30pm; Sun 1pm–5pm; contribution requested; 450-467-4434). On the opposite bank in the town of Belœil, the beautiful towers and turrets of the Église Saint-Mathieu-de-Belœil (St. Matthew of Belœil Church) are visible.

Musée d'Art de Mont-Saint-Hilaire

Rue du Centre-Civique. ♿ Open Mon–Fri 9am–5pm (Tue to 8:30pm), Sat–Sun 1–5pm. $5–8 depending on the exhibition. 450-536-3033. www.mbamsh.qc.ca.

The museum contains contemporary paintings and works by artists who lived in Mont-St-Hilaire, such as Ozias Leduc, Jordi Bonet, and Paul-Émile Borduas.

Maison des Cultures Amérindiennes

510 Montée des Trente. ♿. Mon–Fri 9am –5pm, Sat–Sun 1–5pm. $5. 450-464-2500. www.maisonamerindienne.com.

Devoted to raising awareness about the First Nations of Quebec, the center explores the Native traditions of maple, maize, and squashes, and in season, visitors can explore a First Nations kitchen garden and a garden of edible wild berries. There are also seasonal exhibits on maple (winter–spring), corn (summer) and squashes (fall), exhibitions of contemporary work by indigenous artists and an interpretation trail in the maple grove. In addition, the museum organizes tastings of dishes based on local Native produce.

Make a detour (10km/6.2mi round-trip) to get to the Mt. Saint-Hilaire Nature Centre. Turn right on Rte. 116 (signposted) and right again on Rue Fortier which becomes chemin Ozias-Leduc. After 3km/1.8mi, turn left on Chemin de la Montagne, and left again on Chemin des Moulins.

Centre de la nature du mont Saint-Hilaire★★ (Mt. Saint-Hilaire Nature Centre)

422 chemin des Moulins.
Open year-round, daily 8am–1hr before dusk, reception hours vary with the seasons. $6. ♿ 450-467-1755 (information on state of trails). www.centrenature.qc.ca

Rising abruptly above the Richelieu Valley, Mt. Saint-Hilaire (411m/1,348.4ft) is the most imposing of the eight Monteregian Hills. The lush forest covering about 11sq km/4sq mi of the mountain has remained practically intact since the arrival of Europeans in Canada. Apple orchards (*in bloom late May*) blanket the mountain's lower slopes, as the Richelieu Valley is one of Quebec's main apple-growing regions.

Mont-Saint-Hilaire is the former estate of Brigadier **Andrew Hamilton Gault** (1882–1958), founder of Princess Patricia's Canadian Light Infantry. He bequeathed his estate to McGill University in order to preserve its beauty and keep it from development. Today a 6sq km/2.3sq mi section of the park is open to the public, while a 5sq km/2sq mi tract is reserved for scientific research. Some 22km/13.6mi of **trails** criss-cross the mountain. From the main summit (known as Pain du Sucre, or "Sugarloaf"), visitors can enjoy sweeping **views★★** of the Richelieu River, the St. Lawrence valley, and the Olympic Tower in Montreal. Some trails lead to Lake Hertel where Gault erected his residence; it has since been converted into a conference center. A small rest area is available for hikers and cross-country skiers. Local legends abound here, so watch out for the three fairies believed to inhabit various caves.

Return to Route 133. Before you reach St-Charles-sur-Richelieu, there is a possible detour to visit Saint-Hyacinthe. Leave Mont-Saint-Hilaire, then turn right onto the 20 Eb.

Saint-Hyacinthe

The Saint-Hyacinthe region is the breadbasket of Quebec, renowned for the fertility of its land and the abundance of its harvests. The city was founded in the late 18C around the mills of the Yamaska River. A pleasant walk on rue Girouard takes you along the banks of the river from the Porte des Anciens-Maires to the town centre. You will pass some fine Victorian houses, particularly between rue Desaulniers and rue Després. Nearer to the center, the street is bordered by some remarkable public buildings, including the **Cathedrale de St-Hyacinthe-le-Confesseur (Cathedral of St. Hyacinthe the Confesser)**, which contains Ozias Leduc's painting of the Eternal Father, and the town hall overlooking Casimir-Dessaulles Park. Further south, along rue des Cascades, you will find shops and restaurants. And on the corner of rue Saint-Denis is the Marché-Centre, Quebec's oldest public market, which is still operating today.

Return to Rte. 133 and continue north for 16km/10mi.

Saint-Charles-sur-Richelieu

It was here that the Patriots were defeated on November 25, 1837, by Colonel Wetherall, two days after the first victory at Saint-Denis (*see below*). In the waterfront park, note the small bas-relief monument dedicated to the Patriots. On the river, the boat L'Escale features theatrical productions during the summer.

Saint-Denis-sur-Richelieu★

11.8km/7.3mi northeast on Rte. 133.

This prosperous agricultural community was the site of the Patriot victory over Colonel Gore, on November 23, 1837. In a pleasant square located in the center of the village, the Patriots' green, white and red tricolor flag flies above a wooden pedestal, beside a **monument** erected in their honor. The florid inscription written by René Lévesque reads (in translation): "They fought for the recognition of our people, for political liberty and for a democratic system of government." It was placed here in 1987, to commemorate the 150th anniversary of the failed Rebellion.

Nearby, the **church★** (Église de Saint-Denis-sur-Richelieu, 1796) is surmounted by large, twin copper towers, one of which contains the liberty bell used to call the Patriots to battle (visit by guided tour only (1hr); 636 chemin des Patriotes, Rte. 133; P 450-787-2020; www.eglisestdenis-surrichelieu.com). The first religious structure in Quebec to have been built with two storeys, it features a double row of windows on the exterior. It is considered to be a "quasi-cathedral" because a monumental look and size was achieved despite the difficulty of finding construction materials comparable with what was used in Europe. A modern façade has hidden the original structure since 1922. The interior décor of carved wood dates, for the most part, from the 1810s and is attributed to Louis-Amable Quévillon.

Maison Nationale des Patriotes★ (Patriots' National House)

610 chemin des Patriotes (Rte. 133). Open May 1–Sept 30, Tue–Sun 11am–6pm; Oct–Dec 1pm–5pm; Jan–Apr group reservations only. $8. P 450-787-3623. www.mndp.qc.ca.

Built in 1810 for Jean-Baptiste Mâsse, a blacksmith, innkeeper, and merchant, this stone house serves as an interpretation center on the Patriots' Rebellion of 1837–38. Displays and a slide show explain the background of the uprising and highlight the events that led the Patriots in their long fight for freedom and democracy. The battles of Saint-Denis, Saint-Charles, and Saint-Eustache are described. *Note: Displays and slide show in French only.*

Saint-Ours

11.8km/7.3mi northeast on Rte. 133.

In 1672, this seigneury was granted to Pierre de Saint-Ours. The river shoals impeded passing vessels until a dam and lock were completed in 1849. Erected in 1933, the present **Saint-Ours Canal and lock** (open mid-Jun–mid-Aug, daily 9am–6:30pm; mid-Aug–Labor Day, Mon–Fri 9am–4pm, Sat–Sun 9am–5pm; mid-May–mid-Jun and early Sept–mid-Oct, daily 8:30am–3:30pm $2.90; P $4/day; 450-785-2212; www.pc.gc.ca/stours) is 103m/338ft long by 14m/46ft wide, and allows boats to be raised 1.5m/5ft in five minutes. At the turn of the 20C, ships carried timber, hay and cereals to the US, and returned with coal, iron, copper, and building materials. Today a pleasant park surrounds the lively lock area.

Beyond the lock (3km/1.8mi), a ferry links Saint-Ours to Saint-Roch. Return to Saint-Ours.

Sorel-Tracy

Located at the confluence of the Richelieu and St. Lawrence rivers, this community was named for Pierre de Saurel, who received the seigneury in 1672. In 1781 Sir Frederick Haldimand, governor of Quebec, granted Sorel a municipal charter and renamed the town William-Henry (in honor of Prince William-Henry, the future King George IV). He also erected a garrison beside the Richelieu to counter the threat of an American invasion and ensure the security of the Loyalists established in the seigneury. Subsequently, the government acquired a large wooden house to lodge the commander of the garrison, General von Riedesel. It was in this house, remodeled several times and today known as the **Governor's House** (*90 chemin des Patriotes*), that the Riedesels, of German origin, introduced the Christmas tree to Canada.

Carré Royal★ (Royal Square)

Created in 1791 to serve as the parade ground of the military town, this pleasant green space is today a park. Numerous footpaths criss-cross it so that, by design, it resembles a British Flag from the air (*bound by rue du Roi, rue Charlotte, rue du Prince, and rue George*). Sorel-Tracy is the site of the oldest Anglican mission in Canada (1784). The present **Christ Church** (1842), designed in the Gothic Revival style by John Wells, architect of the Bank of Montreal head office in Montreal, stands facing the Royal Square on rue Prince. Between the square and the waterfront, a succession of bustling shops, restaurants, and cafés leads to the old market, a yellow brick building constructed in the 1940s. To the east (*rue Augusta*), a waterfront park with a raised gazebo offers panoramic **views** of the port, the confluence of the Richelieu and St. Lawrence rivers, and the small, lively marina.

Sainte-Anne-de-Sorel

3.7km/2.3mi east by Rte. 132, then right onto chemin Sainte-Anne.

The vault and walls of the nave of **Église Sainte-Anne** (St. Anne's Church, 1876) are adorned with 13 superb frescoes executed by the painter Suzor-Côté (Tours Jul–mid-Aug Sat–Sun; ℘450-743-7909).

Excursion to the Islands★

Maison du Marias, 3742 chemin du Chenal-du-Moine. To visit the winding channels around the Sorel Islands, embark on a 12-seat wooden excursion boat piloted by a guide. Open late May to Labor Day, Mon–Fri departures at 10am and 2pm; Sat–Sun departure at 10am. $37 for a two-hour tour. Reservations required. ℘450-742-5716 & 1-800-361-6420.

Starting at the Du Moine Canal, the boat passes a series of largely undeveloped islands, among them Île du Moine, Île de Grâce and Île d'Embarras. Several of the islands, laced with numerous intricate passageways, are accessible only by boat and are popular with birders, hunters, and anglers. Be sure to bring sun screen, insect repellant, hat, drinking water, and rain gear. Another summertime tour of the islands in a 12-passenger boat is offered by Randonée nature, which leaves from the Biophare (6 rue Saint-Pierre, corner of rue George; ℘1-877-780-5740; www.randoneenature.com, $36.50) on a three-hour tour. Reservations are recommended.

Good to know: *Gibelotte* is a specialty dish made with local fish and vegetables; try it at one of the restaurants on Île d'Embarras.

FROM CHAMBLY TO HEMMINGFORD

80km/50mi by Rte. 223. *Circuit traced in green on the map on p248.*

Leave Chambly by Rte. 223 south for 16km/10mi. The Chambly Canal is visible on the drive south (picnic areas border the canal).

Saint-Jean-sur-Richelieu

Birthplace of Félix-Gabriel Marchand, premier of Quebec from 1897 through 1900, Saint-Jean-sur-Richelieu is located on the west bank of the Upper Richelieu River, across from its twin city, Iberville. The history of the community can be traced to 1666, when a small wooden fort was constructed here, forming one of the links in the chain of fortifications established by the French along the Richelieu River during the French-Iroquois wars. After the American Revolution, many Loyalists, faithful to the English Crown, settled in the town, which was then known as Dorchester. It was an important port for commerce with the states surrounding Lake Champlain, namely New York and Vermont. Today the city is famous for its balloon festival, the **Festival de montgolfières de Saint-Jean-sur-Richelieu**, which takes place every August.

The 19C was a period of growth and prosperity for Saint-Jean-sur-Richelieu. In 1836, the Champlain and St. Lawrence Railroad Company built the first railway in Canada, connecting the town to La Prairie. The **Chambly Canal** was inaugurated seven years later. Benefiting from these two new transportation routes, Saint-Jean became a manufacturing center for dishes, teapots, jugs and other pieces of white ceramic. In 1840 Moses Farrar opened the first stoneware factory, and one of his relatives began manufacturing glazed white earthenware for hotels and restaurants. With the financial support of several bankers, Moses created the **Saint-John's Stone Chinaware Company** in 1873. Pieces from both this company and the **Farrar** factories are now collectors' items. The industry still exists, producing mainly structural porcelain and fixtures. Crane Canada is the only remaining industrial potter from that era.

A Mysterious Stranger

The Sorel Islands are forever imprinted on the Quebec imagination by the classic novel, *Le Survenant* (The Outlander), published in 1954, by Germaine Guèvremont. Made into popular serials on both radio and television, as well as a film (2005), it recounts the arrival of a stranger at the Chenal du Moine. He enchants the locals throughout the long winter with his exotic stories and remarkable skills but, as summer ends, he vanishes into the fog. Many locations in the region reference *Le Survenant.*

Musée du Haut-Richelieu (Upper Richelieu Museum)

182 rue Jacques-Cartier Nord, on the Market Square (Place du Marché). Open late Jun–Labor Day, Mon–Fri 11am–4:30pm, Sat 11am–5pm, Sun 1pm–5pm (rest of the year, same hours but closed Mon). $5. P 450-347-0649. www.museeduhaut-richelieu.com.

Housed in the former market building (1859), this museum presents interesting displays on the First Nations presence and the military history of the Upper Richelieu and the "Valley of Forts." It also features a unique collection of pottery and dishes signed "Saint-John's Stone Chinaware Company," notably several settings of the famous **Saint-John's Blue** dinner service, produced about 1890.

Continue along Place du Marché.

Adjoining the rear of the market building is the former **Fire Hall** (1877), topped by a small tower. On the other side of rue Longueuil, note the **St. John's United Church**, a dark brick structure dating from 1841. Attractive Victorian-style homes line the neighboring streets, and the Neoclassical **courthouse** (1850) anchors the corner of rue Saint-Charles and rue Longueuil.

Église anglicane St. James

Corner of rue Jacques-Cartier and rue Saint-Georges.

With its white tower and Neoclassical entryway, the structure (1816) resembles a New England church. Today it serves the Roman Catholic parish of St. Thomas More, as well as the Anglican community.

Cathédrale de Saint-Jean-l'Évangéliste

Rue Longueuil. Open year-round, ask for entry at the presbytery. Mon–Fri 8:30am–noon and 1pm–4:30pm. Open only for Masses on weekends: 11am Sun and 4pm Sat. 450-347-2328.

Originally built between 1828 and 1853, this church features a central copper tower and an elaborate interior. It was enlarged in 1866 by Victor Bourgeau, and became a cathedral when the diocese was created in 1933.

Musée du Fort Saint-Jean

15 rue Jacques-Cartier Nord. Undergoing renovation as of mid-2015, opening date unknown. 450-358-6500 (ext. 5769). www.museedufortsaintjean.ca.

Housed in the former Protestant Chapel (1850) located on the campus of the **Collège militaire royal de Saint-Jean**, this museum traces more than 325 years (1666–1995) of military history in this area. The collection of weapons, uniforms and other military artifacts is bolstered by an exhibit on the development of the fort. A first wooden structure, built by the French in 1666 as a defence against the Iroquois, was replaced by a second in 1748 to protect New France against British forces. In 1759, after the capture of Fort Lennox, Fort Saint-Jean was burned by its French defenders to avoid capture by the British. The structure was rebuilt by Guy Carleton in 1775 and captured by the Americans the same year, when the fort's small garrison surrendered after a 45-day siege. Having sustained severe fire damage, the fort was rebuilt after the Patriots' Rebellion of 1837–38. Visitors can tour the remains of the old ramparts on the nearby grounds.

Continue along route 223 for 20km/12.4mi towards St-Paul-de-l'Île-aux-Noix.

Île-aux-Noix

Access by ferry from Saint-Paul-de-l'Île-aux-Noix.

Situated near the US border, this 85ha/210-acre island in the Upper Richelieu was named Île-aux-Noix for the walnut trees (*noix* means "nut") that once flourished on it. As a reward for a brilliant career as a navy captain, Pierre Jacques Payan, Sieur de Noyan, was granted the island seigneury in 1733 by the Marquis de Beauharnois, governor of New France. The first inhabitant of the island was a soldier named Pierre Jourdanet; his rent was fixed at one bag of nuts annually!

Fort Lennox★

Open mid-May–mid-Jun, Mon–Fri 10am–5pm, mid-Jun–Labor Day, daily 10am–6pm; rest of Sept–mid-Oct, Fri–Sun 10am–5pm. $7.80 (ferry & visit to fort; last ferry to fort 75min before closing). 450-291-5700 & 1-888-773-8888. www.pc.gc.ca.

Fort Lennox was erected between 1819 and 1829 at about the same time as the Citadel in Quebec City. It was named for Charles Lennox (1764–1819), Duke of Richmond, governor-in-chief of British North America, who ordered its construction. The fort was completed just as an improved road system was established along the Richelieu River banks. The roads shifted the military threat from the water to the land, and the fort, no longer strategically positioned, was abandoned for nearly four years. The Trent Affair and the Fenian uprising in the 1860s brought new threats to the British, who re-garrisoned Fort Lennox until 1870. The bastion-type fortress is typical of 19C military architecture. The fort is surrounded by a wide moat, which forms a five-pointed star around a series of tall earthen ramparts. The corners are protected by bastions that open onto the inner yard. Visitors cross a footbridge and pass under a massive stone archway to enter the main courtyard, which is surrounded by a group of Neoclassical stone structures. The guard house (1823) and officers' quarters (1825–28) are arranged in a symmetrical pattern and are decorated with columns and arches. The fort complex includes two warehouses (1823), a powder magazine (1820) and 17 firing stations located under the ramparts. The fort occupies a pleasant **site★** overlooking the Richelieu River, and the island features several relaxing picnic areas.

Continue on the 233 for 9km/5.6mi.

Blockhaus de la rivière Lacolle★ (Lacolle River Blockhouse)

1 rue Principale, Île-aux-Noix. Open mid-May–Labor Day, daily 9am–5pm. Guided tours. 450-246-3227. www.ileauxnoix.com.

This two-level log structure was built in 1781 as part of the British defense system to repel American invasion. Located on the Lacolle River, a tributary of the Richelieu, it is the only defense of its kind remaining in Quebec. During the war of 1812, it withstood attack on three occasions, and bullet holes are still visible on the façade. Recently restored by the Quebec government, the interior houses displays on the military history of the blockhouse. Note the loopholes for muskets and the openings for cannons.

Continue on the 233 south towards Hemmingford, and take a right onto route 202.

Parc Safari★★

280 Rang Roxham, St-Bernard-de-Lacolle. Open late Jun–Aug daily 10am–7pm; shorter hours in spring, fall and winter. $45 (Jun–Aug); children (under 16yrs) $30. 450-247-2727. www.parcsafari.com.

Some 265 animals of 28 different species roam freely in large enclosures in this zoological park. Required to remain in their vehicles, visitors can follow the **Car Safari** (*4km/2.5mi*) along which they can take photographs, touch, and feed the animals. The **Aquapark** combines an amusement park and water slides in a zoo-like setting. On the **Olduval Footbridge**, visitors can observe macaques and chimpanzees and cross bridges to look down on lions, tigers, and bears. Animal shows at the theater (*Théâtre sous les Arbres*) and a circus in the stadium (*regular performances*) provide further entertainment; pony rides and a petting zoo complete the visit.

Cantons-de-l'Est★★

Eastern Townships Region

Contrary to their name, the Eastern Townships (usually called *Estrie* in French) occupy the southwest part of Quebec along the US border. The area was named in the 18C because of its location east of Montreal. The Townships, as they are generally called in English, are situated in a mountainous region of the Appalachian chain, which extends from Alabama to Newfoundland. In the Townships, tree-covered hills rising to nearly 1,000m/3,280ft are interspersed with deep valleys and lakes. The region is popular with Montrealers attracted by leisure activities, including watersports in the summertime and skiing during the winter.

- **Info:** 1-800-355-5755. www.easterntownships.org.
- **Location:** Cowansville is about 80km/50mi southeast of Montreal by Rtes. 10 and 139. Sherbrooke is 150km/93mi east of Montreal by Rtes. 10 and 112.
- **Don't Miss:** Historical museums in Missisquoi and Brome County; Coaticook Gorge Park; pretty Loyalist towns like North Hatley.
- **Timing:** If you allow a full day for each of the two tours described here, you'll have the time to enjoy the many scenic stops and the interesting museums along the way.
- **Kids:** The Coaticook Gorge park.

A BIT OF HISTORY

After the American Revolution (1776–83), the uninhabited land along the border to the southeast and southwest of Montreal was surveyed by the British authorities and plots were granted to Loyalists who had left the US after the war. These first settlers were mainly from New England, and the towns and villages they established reflect this heritage. After 1850, however, increasing numbers of French-speaking people moved into the region, and today its population is mostly francophone.

DRIVING TOURS

1 CIRCUIT FROM COWANSVILLE

159km/98.7mi.

See local map p236–237.

Cowansville

225 Place Municipale. 450-266-4058. www.ville.cowansville.qc.ca.

Located on the south arm of the South Yamaska River, Cowansville is today a small industrial center. This predominantly francophone community was founded by Loyalists in 1802, and named for its first postmaster, Peter Cowan. Numerous Victorian houses line rue Principale and rue Sud in the residential area. The Bromont ski center is located nearby.

Follow rue Sud (becomes Rte. 202 after crossing the Rte. 104 bypass) to Dunham.

Dunham

3738 rue Principale (Municipal Library). 450-295-2273. www.ville.dunham.qc.ca.

One of the first Loyalist settlements, Dunham was established in 1796 on land granted to Thomas Dunn, a British administrator. The village is known for its vineyards. Its charm is enhanced by three steepled churches (Roman Catholic, Anglican, and United) and several stone houses.

Continue west on Rte. 202 to Stanbridge East (10km/6.2mi).

The road between Dunham and Stanbridge East is often called the **Route des Vins** (Wine Route) because it crosses a region in Quebec where the climate is favorable to the cultivation of grapes. Elsewhere, the climate is too harsh.

Musée de Missisquoi★ (Missisquoi Museum)

2 rue River, in Stanbridge East. Open late May–mid-Oct, daily 10am–4:30pm. $10. P 450-248-3153. www.museemissisquoi.ca.

Three buildings make up the rural museum created by the Missisquoi Historical Society. The main edifice is a three-story brick **mill** built by Zébulon Cornell, a Vermont native, in 1832 to replace an earlier stone structure on the picturesque Brochets River (Pike River). The mill closed in 1963 and was converted into a museum. Rooms on the main floor re-create life in the 19C, and the displays on the upper floor illustrate various activities and handicrafts of the era. Visitors can see the original water wheel, still turning in the river current. To the east (*20 River St.*), **Hodge's General Store** is stocked with goods and provisions from the period, thus preserving its 19C charm.

The 12-sided **Walbridge Barn** (189 chemin Mystic, off Rte 235 about 7km away in St. Ignace de Stanbridge) displays traditional farm machinery.

Take Rte. 237 southeast to Frelighsburg.

Frelighsburg

1 pl. de l'Hôtel-de-Ville. 450-298-5630. www.village.frelighsburg.qc.ca.

A gristmill was established in 1794 on this enchanting site in the Brochets River valley, near Mt. Pinacle. A small community soon developed and was later named for Abram Frelighsburg, a physician who moved here from New York in 1800. Today Frelighsburg is best known for its apple orchards.

Turn left on rue Principale (Rte. 213). After 2km/1.2mi turn right on rue Selby, continue for 4km/2.5mi and turn right on rue Dymond (proceed cautiously on gravel roads), which becomes rue Jordan after 3km/1.8mi. Continue for 10km/6.2mi; turn left on Rte. 139 to Sutton and continue 2km/1.2mi.

The road passes to the north of **Le Pinacle** (675m/2,214ft), providing fine **views★** of the Sutton valley.

Sutton★

24-A rue Principale Sud. 450-538-8455 or 1-800-565-8455. www.infosutton.com.

Mt. Sutton (972m/3,188ft) towers over this lovely winter resort, especially popular with skiing enthusiasts. The first settlers arrived in 1795 and constructed a foundry in the valley. In 1871 a new railway opened the area to vacationers. Today numerous arts and crafts studios and shops enhance the town's charm.

Drive south on Rte. 139 for 2km/1.2mi, turn left on rue Brookfall and immediately right on chemin Scenic. After 11km/6.8mi, turn left on Rte. 105A and left again on Rte. 243 to Mansonville (24km/15mi).

The road offers several entrancing **views★** of the Sutton area, then follows the valley of the Missisquoi River. The Jay Mountains in Vermont are visible to the south.

Mansonville

37km/23mi.

This community in the Missisquoi River valley is named for its first settler, Robert Manson, who moved from Vermont in 1803 and built a gristmill and a sawmill.

The town has a New England-style village green and also claims one of the few remaining round barns in Quebec (*visible from Main St. across from the Church of St. Cajétan*). The circular structure was conceived by the Shakers, a religious sect of the Quakers; its purpose was to keep the devil from haunting any corner.

Mount Owl's Head

12km/7mi, through Vale Perkins.

This mountain (751m/2,463ft) was named for Chief Owl, an Abenaki Indian. According to legend, his profile could be seen on the mountain after his death. Today Owl's Head is a popular ski resort. The path leading to the top (*climb of about 1hr*) affords spectacular **views★★** of Lake Memphrémagog.

Return to Mansonville. Take Rte. 243 to South Bolton (13km/8mi).

Lac-Brome★ (Knowlton)

www.ville.lac-brome.qc.ca

Part of the municipality of Lac-Brome, the community of Knowlton has a pleasant setting on Lake Brome. Founded by New England settlers in the early 19C, the town was named for Paul Knowlton, who built the community gristmill and a general store in 1834. Many of the brick and stone buildings are housed by boutiques, art galleries and antique shops. Just to the south lies the community of Brome, home of the **Brome Agricultural Fair**, the largest annual agricultural event in the area.

Musée historique du comté de Brome★ (Brome County Museum)

130 rue Lakeside (Rte. 243). Open mid-May–mid-Oct, Mon–Sat 10am–4:30pm, Sun 11am–4:30pm. $5. 450-243-6782. www.bromemuseum.com

This museum comprises several period buildings. The old Knowlton "Academy" (1854) offers the chance to see a schoolroom of yesteryear.

The Martin Annex houses military exhibits including a **Fokker DVII**, a German World War I fighter plane acquired for the museum by Senator G. G. Foster, a Knowlton resident. In the courthouse (1854), a renovated reception room evokes the solemn atmosphere of a turn-of-the-19C court. A re-created general store occupies the Fire Hall (1904).

Return to Cowansville (20km/12mi) by Rte. 104.

2 CIRCUIT FROM SHERBROOKE

153km/95mi.

See local map pp262–263.

Sherbrooke★

See SHERBROOKE.

Leave Sherbrooke and take Rte. 143 to Lennoxville.

Lennoxville Region

British Loyalists founded Lennoxville in 1794, naming the town for Charles Lennox, Duke of Richmond, who became governor-in-chief of British North America in 1818. The town is located at the junction of the Massawippi and Saint-François rivers, a site formerly occupied by the Abenaki and later by French missionaries. Lennoxville is home to an agricultural research center.

Bishop's University

An educational and cultural center, this small yet prestigious English institution (1843) features medieval-style buildings. Nearby is **St. Mark's Chapel**, a Gothic Revival edifice adorned with luminous stained-glass windows and richly carved woodwork. The benches on each side face each other across the center aisle.

Uplands Cultural and Heritage Center – 9 rue Speid. Open end Jun–early Sept, Tue–Sun 10am–4:30pm; rest of the year, Wed–Sun 1pm–4:30pm. Closed Jan. No charge. 819-564-0409. www.uplands.ca. From its base in a fine Belle Époque house, the center sets out to promote and raise awareness of the cultural heritage of the Eastern Townships, with activities including English tea served in period costume on the veranda *($10, year-round Sat–Sun 1pm–4:30pm)*. It also holds temporary exhibitions of the work of local and regional artists, concerts and workshops.

The center is the starting point for a 2.2km/1.3mi circuit taking you past Lennoxville's most attractive houses.

Continue south on Rte. 143 for 3km/1.8mi, then turn left on Rte. 147 to Compton.

Compton

This quiet village was the birthplace of **Louis-Stephen Saint-Laurent** (1882–1973), 12th prime minister of Canada. The eldest of seven children born to a French-Canadian storekeeper and an Irish schoolteacher, Saint-Laurent studied law at Laval University. He went into private practice and soon gained recognition for his eloquence in both English and French. At the age of 60, after a long and successful career as a lawyer, Saint-Laurent decided to enter politics. He was asked by Prime Minister Mackenzie King to serve as his Quebec lieutenant during World War II, and succeeded Mr. King as head of the Liberal Party in 1948.

An ardent Canadian nationalist, "Uncle Louis," as he was fondly called, fought to establish a distinct Canadian identity during his years as prime minister (1948–57).

Lieu historique national du Canada Louis-S.-St-Laurent★(Louis S. St. Laurent National Historic Site of Canada)

On rue Principale (Rte. 147) in Compton. Open late Jun–late Sept, Wed–Sun and holidays 10am–5pm, last admission 30min before closing. $4. 819-835-5448 or 1-888-773-88888. www.pc.gc.ca/st-laurent.

The authentically re-created general store of J.B.M. Saint-Laurent, the prime minister's father, is stocked with replicas of the goods sold here at the turn of the 19C. During its heyday, the general store served as a place for locals to visit and exchange ideas; politics were a frequent topic of discussion. Visitors can use headphones to eavesdrop on simulated conversations around the pot-bellied stove. A **multimedia biography** (*20min*) presents the highlights of Saint-Laurent's

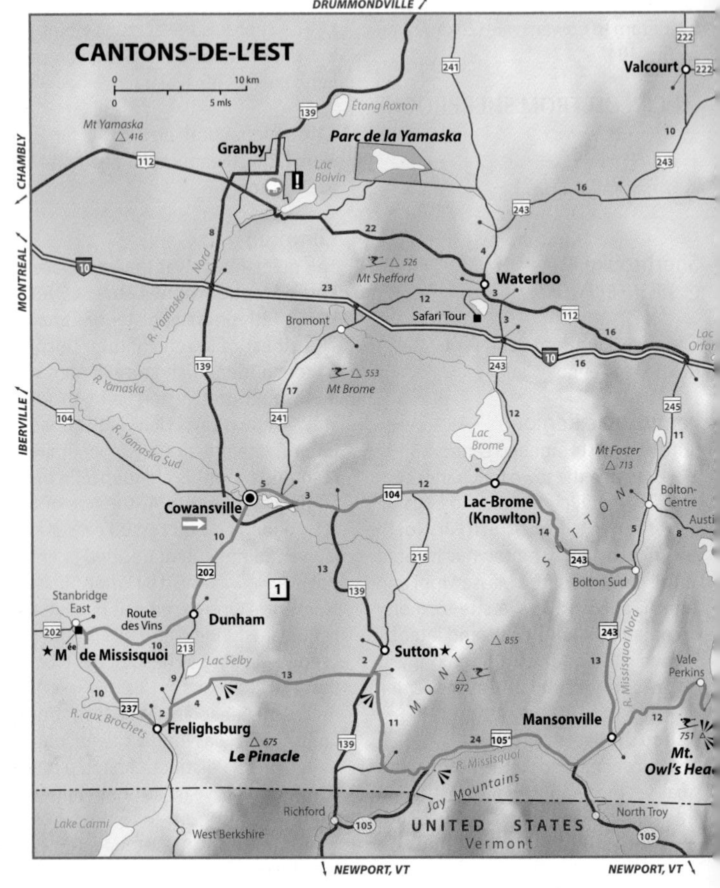

life and career. Also open to visitors is the simple clapboard house full of mementoes of the Saint-Laurent family, who lived in it until 1969.

Coaticook

137 rue Michaud. 1-866-665-6669. www.tourismecoaticook.qc.ca.

This town on the Coaticook River takes its name from the Abenaki word *koatikeku,* meaning "river of the land of pines." The first settler, Richard Baldwin, recognized the economic potential of harnessing the falls. Today Coaticook is a small industrial town and the center of a thriving dairy industry.

Parc de la Gorge de Coaticook★

Access from Rte. 147 at northern edge of town. Open mid-Jun–end Aug daily 8am–6pm; shorter hours in spring, fall and winter. $7.50 for hiking; prices vary for differnet activities. 819-849-2331. www.gorgedecoaticook.qc.ca.

The Coaticook River is enclosed by a narrow, rocky, 1km/.6mi gorge whose sides rise to 50m/165ft, then turns at a sharp angle and tumbles over several sets of falls. Skiing or hiking allows for beautiful discoveries along the several kilometers of scenic pathway. An impressive suspended footbridge (169m/554ft) affords a nice **view** of the gorge.

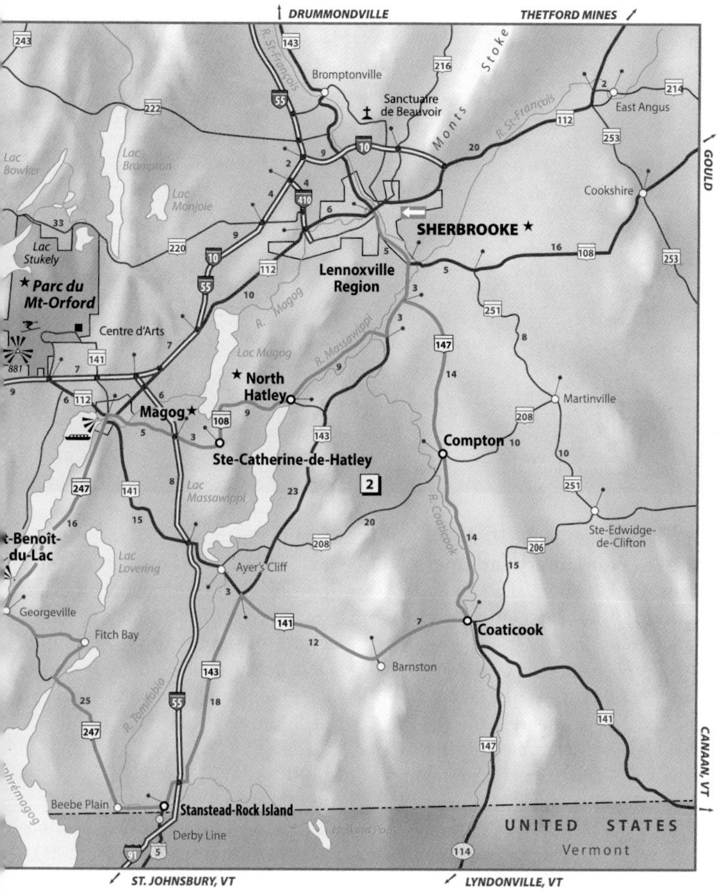

Musée Beaulne

96 rue de l'Union. From Rte. 141 (rue Main), turn left on rue Lovell at railway tracks, left again on rue Norton, then right on rue de l'Union. Open mid-May–mid-Sept, daily 10am–5pm; rest of the year, daily 1–4pm. Closed Dec 21–Jan 5. $7. 819-849-6560. www.museebeaulne.qc.ca.

Take a passage through time at this museum located in the refurbished **Château Norton★**, a magnificent mansion (1912) owned by **Arthur Osmond Norton** (1845–1919), proprietor of the most important manufacturer of railway jacks in the world at the turn of the 19C. Rooms, particularly the Victorian living room (adorned in fine oak panelling) and dining room, have been restored and decorated with period furniture.

From the town center, take Rte. 141 toward Magog for 19km/11.8mi and turn left on Rte. 143. Continue 18km/11mi, crossing over Rte. 55 to Rock Island.

Stanstead Rock Island

Located on a rocky island in the Tomifobia River, this town (three former villages in one: Stanstead Plain, Rock Island, and Beebe Plain) overlooks the picturesque river valley.

The Tomifobia River marks the Canadian-American border. Vehicles crossing the bridge must proceed through US Customs (on the right) before continuing into Vermont or returning to Canada.

Lake Memphrémagog

© Sebastien Larose / Tourisme Cantons-de-l'Est

Opéra et bibliothèque Haskell (Haskell Free Library and Opera House)

1 Church St. Heading south on Rte. 143, turn left onto Cordeau St. immediately after the bridge beyond Canadian Customs. Turn left and park on rue Church P. The entrance to the building is on the US side, but you do not have to clear US Customs to enter the Vermont library. Visit by guided tour only (30min): mid-May–mid-Oct, Tue–Fri 9am–5pm (Thu 6pm), Sat 9am–2pm. $5 donation. 819-876-2471; for Opera House box office ext. 205. www.haskellopera.org.

Martha Stewart Haskell funded the construction of this handsome building between 1901 and 1904. The half-stone, half-brick turreted building, erected in memory of Haskell's husband, sits squarely on the Canadian-American border; the line of demarcation is indicated on the floor. The ground floor serves as a public library for residents of both countries and the upper floor is occupied by a delightful theater. The players perform in Canada, while most of the audience sits in the US.

Take Rte. 247 through Beebe Plain and Georgeville to Magog.

The road veers eastward through the tiny community of Fitch Bay before heading northwest to Georgeville, a small, English-speaking community. Upon leaving Georgeville, there is a lovely view of the abbey of **Saint-Benoît-du-Lac★** *(see Additional Sights, below)* on the other side of Lake Memphrémagog, and of Mt. Orford in the distance.

Magog★

2911 Milletta (Exit 115 off Hwy 10). Open Jun 24–Labor Day daily 8:30–7pm; rest of year daily 9am–5pm. 819-843-2744 or 1-800-267-2744 (no charge). www.tourisme-memphremagog.com.

This community on the shores of beautiful Lake Memphrémagog was originally named Décharge du Lac (the "outlet"), because of its location at the source of the Magog River. In 1888 the town adopted the name Magog, a shortened version of the Abenaki word Memphrémagog, meaning "large expanse of water." The first settler was Loyalist Ralph Merry who arrived in 1799. Today Magog is a textile manufacturing center and a popular resort, spawned by its lakeside location and the proximity of Mt. Orford Park.

Parc de la Pointe-Merry★

Just south of rue Principale *(Rte. 112)*.

This pleasant green space affords splendid **views★** of the northern end of the lake, which stretches over 50km/31mi, crossing the border into Vermont. The wooded peaks of Mt. Orford and Owl's Head are visible from the lake.

Scenic Cruises★

Two cruise boats leave from the Quai MacPherson: Croisières Escapades Memphrémagog (819-843-7000 or 1-888-422-8328, www.escapades memphremagog.com) offers Sun brunch, lunch, afternoon and dinner cruises (a band plays Wed–Sat evenings) on a boat with a large indoor restaurant (176 person capacity) Jun–Oct; prices vary, the least expensive 2-hr afternoon cruise is $43.

Les Excursions l'Air du Lac (819-345-7450, www.lairdulac.com) offers 1-hr lake cruises on a pontoon boat May–Sept daily 1pm, 2:15, 3:30 and 5pm ($28), as well as a 2.5-hr tour that visits the St. Benoît-du-Lac Abbey daily 10am ($60.50 – reservations only). The boat can also be rented for fishing trips and the company arranges ice fishing in winter. The cruises carry passengers onto some of the prettiest sections of the lake.

Leave Magog on Rte. 108.

Sainte-Catherine-de-Hatley

8km/5mi.

Situated atop a hill in the center of town, the Sanctuaire Saint-Christophe (Sanctuary of St. Christopher) affords expansive **views** of Lake Magog and Mt. Orford.

Continue on Rte. 108.

North Hatley★

9km/5.6mi.

North Hatley (named for an English village near Cambridge) occupies a lovely **site** on the northern bank of Lake Massawippi where the river of the same name leaves the lake. A drive along the lakeshore provides glimpses of nice homes and inns.

Return to Sherbrooke via Rte. 143.

ADDITIONAL SIGHTS

Abbaye de Saint-Benoît-du-Lac★ (Saint-Benoît-du-Lac Abbey)

20km/12.4mi from Magog. Leave Magog on Rte. 112 Ouest; turn left after 5km/3mi. Open year-round, daily 5am–9pm. Reservations for visits (or accommodation) must be made by phone at times shown on the website to respect prayer schedules. 819-843-4080. www.st-benoit-du-lac.com. The monks' boutique sells the abbey's famous cheese as well as other products (open Jun–mid-Oct daily 9am–10:45am and 11:45am–6pm. Rest of the year closes 5pm; closed Sun).

The drive to Saint-Benoît-du-Lac, whose only inhabitants are the monks of the Benedictine abbey, offers scenic glimpses of Lake Memphrémagog. The abbey (1912) was founded by members of the Saint-Wandrille-de-Fontenelle abbey in Normandy, who were exiled to Belgium after being banned from France in the early 20C. The monks founded a novitiate on the site in 1924, and Saint-Benoît-du-Lac was elevated to the rank of abbey in 1952. The monastery complex, surmounted by an impressive bell tower, occupies a magnificent **site★★**, striking for its peace, serenity and sheer beauty. Most of the structures were designed in 1938 by French Benedictine monk, **Dom Paul Bellot** (1876–1944), who lies buried in the abbey cemetery. The buildings were completed and blessed on July 11, 1941. Montreal architect Dan S. Hanganu designed the abbey church, consecrated on December 4, 1994. Visitors can attend vespers in the oratory and listen to Gregorian chants at daily services. St. Benedict taught his monks to practise hospitality, so adults can stay at the abbey ($60 room & board) for a short visit or a retreat: men can remain on-site, while women stay at nearby Saint Scholastica's Villa. The monks produce cider, as well as two well-known cheeses, L'Ermite and Mont-Saint-Benoît, which are sold in a small shop on the premises.

St-Benoît-du-Lac-Abbey

Parc du Mont-Orford★ (Mt. Orford Park)

In Magog-Orford, 3321 chemin du Parc (Rte 141). Park open year-round, daily. Le Cerisier Visitors Center open mid-Jun–Aug Sun–Thu 8am–8pm, Fri–Sat to 10pm; shorter hours rest of year. $8.50. (mid-May–mid-Oct) (\$8/vehicle) 819-843-9855 & 1-800-665-6527. www.sepaq.com.

Parc du Mont-Orford, a Quebec national park, covers an area of 58sq km/23sq mi in the Appalachian Mountains of Quebec. Mt. Chauve (600m/1,968ft) towers to the northeast, while Mt. Orford (881m/2,890ft), a well-known ski center, dominates the southwest horizon.

Mont Orford (Mount Orford)

On Rte. 141, 1km/.6mi from western park entrance. Access by chairlift or on foot.

From the top of the chairlift, splendid **views★** extend over Lake Memphrémagog and the surrounding mountains. The summit (short walk around television tower) offers a **panorama★★** north to the St. Lawrence Valley, west to the Monteregian hills, south to Lake Memphrémagog and east to the Appalachian Mountains.

Lac Stukely (Lake Stukely)

Turn left off Rte. 141, 4km/2.5mi from western entrance, and follow secondary road for 6km/3.7mi.

This pretty lake is reached after a pleasant drive beside the Cerises (Cherry) River and Cerises Pond. Stukely Lake is bordered by sandy beaches and features several rocky islets.

Centre d'arts Orford (Orford Arts Centre)

3165 chemin du Parc. On Rte. 141, 1km/.6mi from eastern entrance or 1km/0.6mi from road leading to Lake Stukely. Open mid-Jun–mid-Aug, daily 8am–10pm. Main building open Mon–Fri 9am–4:30pm, no guided tours. 819-843-3981 & 1-800-567-6155. www.arts-orford.org.

The Orford Arts Centre, founded in 1951, enjoys a fine reputation for its courses in musical training. The 500-seat concert hall (salle Gilles-Lefevre), in the shape of an amphitheater, is located on a lovely wooded site. The Man and Music pavilion of Montreal's Expo '67 is a special part of the music school complex. It has a theater, several residences, and a reasonably priced auberge (inn), plus **outdoor sculptures** scattered among maple and birch woods. The celebrated center draws artists from around the world to its **Orford Arts Centre Summer Festival**, featuring classical and jazz music, in June and August annually (*see Festivals & Events*).

EXCURSIONS

Granby

Rte. 10 (also known as l'Autoroute de l'Estrie) southeast from Montreal to exit 68 or 74. 111 rue Denison. 450-372-7056 or 1-800-567-7273. www.tourismegranbyregion.com.

Settled by Loyalists in the early 19C, Granby was named for John Manners, Marquis of Granby, commander of British forces in North America in 1766. The rubber and tobacco factories that developed here on the banks of the Yamaska Nord River soon transformed the town into an industrial center. The wealth generated from this development is evidenced by the large and gracious Victorian houses along Rues Elgin, Dufferin, and Mountain. Palmer Cox (1840–1924), whose famous elf stories for children were inspired by Scottish folklore, is a native of Granby.

Jardin zoologique de Granby★ (Granby Zoo)

Entrance and parking at 1050 Blvd David-Bouchard (Rte. 139), admin. at 525 rue Saint-Hubert. Open late May–late Jun, daily 10am–5pm; late Jun–late Aug, 10am–7pm or 9pm; Sept–Oct Sat–Sun 10am–5pm; closed rest of year. $36.95; children (ages 12 and under) $23.95 (plus tax). 1-877-472-6299. www.zoodegranby.com.

This popular zoo features nearly 1,000 animals from all over the world. In addition to indigenous species and African mammals, the 62-year-old zoo boasts an aqua park, nocturnal animals' cave, camel rides, and Himalayan slide. Of particular interest is the new Japanese Macaques exhibit, opened in 2015. The heated wave pool is the largest of its kind in Quebec.

Centre d'interprétation de la nature du lac Boivin (Lake Boivin Nature Interpretation Center)

700 rue Drummond. Turn left on rue Drummond from rue Principale. Open year-round weekdays 8:30am–4:30pm, weekends 9am–5pm. $5. 450-375-3861. www.cinib.org

Set on the shores of Lac Boivin, this nature center offers visitors a choice of four short trails through the marshland surrounding the lake. From the observation towers, visitors can admire **views** of Mt. Brome and Mt. Shefford.

Parc de la Yamaska

6km/3.7mi northeast of Granby, via chemin Ostiguy, 1780 Chemin Roxton south, Roxton Pond. 8am–8pm. $8.50; parking $8. 800-665-6527 or 450-776-7182. www.sepaq.com.

This protected area preserves a representative sample of the natural region of the Appalachian lowlands. A central feature of the park is the vast expanse of the Réservoir Choinière, which provides an opportunity for canoeing, kayaking, and fishing.

Waterloo

19km/11.8mi east of Granby on Rte. 112.

The town was named Waterloo to commemorate Wellington's victory over Napoleon. A hill there resembles the one in the Belgian Waterloo.

ADDRESSES

STAY

Auberge Ripplecove – *700 Ripplecove, Ayer's Cliff, 17km/10.5mi southeast of Magog on Route 141. 819-838-4296 or 1-800-668-4296. www.ripplecove.com. 33 rooms. Packages that include meals, lodging and activities are available.* With its very British style, this guesthouse will please anyone who loves nature and tranquil comfort. It has a fine location in a green oasis with direct access to Lake Massawippi; activities on offer include fishing, tennis, bicycling, skiing, and more. Fish takes pride of place on the menu of Le Riverain , the hotel restaurant, alongside game and meat dishes. The Arborescence Spa offers massages, exfoliation and facials.

Manoir Hovey – *575 chemin Hovey, North Hatley. 819-842-2421. www.manoirhovey.com. 37 rooms. . Evening meal included, along with some activities.* With its peaceful, refined atmosphere in the English style and its wonderful location beside Lake Massawippi, this former summer residence built by the Atkinson family in 1898 is undeniably charming. A member of the Relais & Châteaux chain, the hotel maintains both tradition and modern comfort. The restaurant, Le Hatley, owes its reputation to chefs Roland Ménard and Francis Wolf, while the pub in the old stables boasts an open fire, comfortable chairs and antique decorations such as a birch canoe, tomahawks, and an ice saw.

SHOPPING

A bit of Advice – Some farms, particularly to the south of Lennoxville, are open to the public for pick-your-own fruit and vegetables, so in season, visitors can come and pick their produce direct from the field.

Ferme Groleau – *225 chemin Cochrane, leave Compton on the 147, towards Coaticook, turn left onto the 208, and after 700m/770yd, turn right and continue for around 3km/1.8mi. 819-835-9373. www.fermegroleau.com.* A dairy farm with 60 cows, a quarter of which are Canadienne breed cattle, and a similar number of goats. Their milk is used to make delicious cheeses on the farm, including a washed rind cheese known as Le Vent d'Est, cottage cheese, and Canadien, made of half cow's and half sheep's milk. The cheeses, along with fresh milk and four kinds of butter, are sold on site.

Bleu Lavande – *891 chemin Narrow (Route 247, Stanstead (Fitch Bay), 4km/2.5mi south of Fitch Bay on the 247. 1-888-876-5851 (no charge). www.bleulavande.ca. May–Oct daily 10am–5pm; weekdays only for the rest of the year.* More than 210,000 lavender plants stretch as far as the eye can see across the 22ha/55 acres of this century-old farm. Visits are available Jun to Sept *(departing every 15 minutes; 10am–5pm; $8)*. Flowers appear in June, and are harvested and distilled in August, but you will find the resulting products year round in the shop, including the "Être" skincare range, soap, air fresheners, essential oils, a recipe book, and more.

Sherbrooke★

Eastern Townships region

- **Population:** 150,751.
- **Michelin Map:** p236–237: C2-3.
- **Info:** 20 rue Don-Bosco Sud. 819-820-2020 & 1-800-355-5755. www.easterntownships.org.
- **Location:** Sherbrooke is 150km/93mi east of Montreal by Rte. 10 and Rte. 112.
- **Parking:** Generally easy to find, metered in the downtown core.
- **Don't Miss:** Cathédrale Saint-Michel.
- **Timing:** From Sherbrooke, you can easily go to either Montreal, Quebec City, or Vermont (USA).
- **Kids:** There are two beaches and a water-ski school on Lac des Nations.

Located on the steep slopes of a valley, at the confluence of the Saint-François and Magog rivers, Sherbrooke was originally called "the great fork" by Abenaki Indians. It is now Quebec's sixth-largest city. Originally anglophone, the population is now overwhelmingly francophone. Today Sherbrooke serves the mining and agricultural concerns of the region.
Mt. Bellevue, across the Magog River, is a popular local ski center.

A BIT OF HISTORY

The first settlers arrived from Vermont about 1800. Soon thereafter, Gilbert Hyatt built a flour mill, and the community became known as Hyatt's Mills. In 1818 the name Sherbrooke was adopted in honor of the governor-in-chief of British North America, Sir John Coape Sherbrooke (1764–1830). During the 19C, mills sprang up on the banks of the Magog River, soon followed by the textile mills. The advent of the railway accelerated economic growth, and the Université de Sherbrooke, opened in 1954, enhanced the city's position as an important urban center.

WALKING TOUR

TOWN CENTER

From the War Memorial, go east down the hill to rue Wellington, turn left and continue for two blocks.

Chapelle des Fondateurs (Founders' Chapel)

Behind main altar to the left.

Added in 1980, this chapel features a mural of enamelled copper by Patricio Rivera, portraying the five founders of the Canadian Catholic Church: Marie de l'Incarnation, Marguerite d'Youville, Monsignor de Laval, Kateri Tekakwitha, and Marguerite Bourgeoys.

Musée des Beaux-Arts de Sherbrooke (Sherbrooke Museum of Fine Arts)

241 rue Dufferin. Open Jun 24–Labor Day Tue–Sun 10am–5pm; rest of the year, Tue–Sun noon–5pm. $10. 819-821-2115. www.mbas.qc.ca.

Housed in a historic structure in downtown Sherbrooke, this museum presents an interesting collection of Quebec art, focusing on the Eastern Townships. Note in particular works by Robert Whale (1805–87), Suzor-Côté (1869–1937), and Wayne Seese (1918–80). A collection of paintings in the naïve style includes pieces by Arthur Villeneuve, and by such international artists as Dragan Mihailovic and Jean-Marie Godefroy.

The museum also organizes temporary exhibits of works by local artists and offers various educational activities.

Hôtel de Ville (City Hall)

145 rue Wellington. Closed to the public.

Completed in 1906 as a courthouse, this imposing edifice exemplifies the Second Empire style. The architect, Elzéar Charest, reused the plans he had submitted to the 1890 city hall competition in Quebec City. Dominating lovely Strathcona Park, the structure has housed the city hall since 1988.

Musée de la Nature et des Sciences

225 rue Frontenac. Open Jun 24–Labor Day daily 10am–5pm; rest of the year, Wed–Sun 10am–5pm. $13, children (ages 4–17) $9. 819-564-3200 or 1-877-434-3200. www.naturesciences.qc.ca.

The museum displays around 65,000 objects and specimens relating to the natural sciences, in both permanent and temporary exhibitions.

Musée des Beaux-Arts de Sherbrooke

© Tourisme Cantons-de-l'Est

Cathédrale Saint-Michel and Mt. Bellevue

Aimed primarily at children, the exhibitions use modern interactive techniques, and are changed every few years. The current group, scheduled until 2020, includes an explanation of changes in the Earth's surface over the ages, featuring displays that visitors can manipulate; an exhibition of archeological discoveries made about First Nations, including recent finds; and an exploration of animal habits within an electronic jungle of displays that children can scamper around in.

Basilique-Cathédrale Saint-Michel★ (St. Michael's Basilica-Cathedral)

Rue de la Cathédrale, at the corner of rue Marquette. Open year-round Mon–Tue and Thu–Fri 7am–9am (during mass), Wed 7am–4pm, Sat 9am–6pm. Sun open for mass at 10am and 5pm. ♿ P ✆819-821-1919 .

This imposing Gothic Revival structure stands on a hill known as the Marquette Plateau, in the center of Sherbrooke. Consecrated in 1958, the cathedral was built by Louis-Napoléon Audet, who also designed the basilica at Sainte-Anne-de-Beaupré. In the façade's principal stained-glass window hangs a 3m/9.8ft-high aluminium crucifix, by the Montreal artist Cassini. Inside, ceilings over 20m/65.6ft high enclose a light and spacious interior. The large stained-glass windows, by Raphaël Lardeur and Gérard Brassard, portray biblical scenes. To the left of the altar is a striking oak statue of the Virgin Mary by the 20C artist Sylvia Daoust.

Monument aux morts (War Memorial)

Rue King Ouest between rue Gordon and rue Brooks.

This imposing sculpture by George W. Hills stands in the center of rue King. It was erected in 1926 to commemorate the Sherbrooke residents who gave their lives in World War I. From this vantage point the **view** encompasses the city and the Saint-François River. There are also superb French formal gardens.

The Invention of the Snowmobile

As a boy in Valcourt, Joseph-Armand Bombardier (1907–64) dreamed of creating a vehicle that would travel on snow. He trained as a mechanic and worked in a garage next to his father's farm, inventing in his spare time. In 1937 he received his first patent, for a sprocket wheel/track system, which paved the way for vehicles guided by skis. In 1959, Bombardier introduced the Ski-Doo, which transformed life in the north, and gave birth to a new mode of transport and a new sport. Today J.-A. Bombardier Industries makes and sells snowmobiles, Sea-Do's and all-terrain vehicles all over the world. It also manufactures locomotives, passenger aircraft, and many other transportation-related items.

EXCURSIONS

Rocher Mena'Sen (Mena'Sen Rock)

1.5km/1mi north of town. From rue King Est, turn left on Rue Bowen, then bear left onto Blvd. Saint-François Nord.

An illuminated cross stands on this islet in the Saint-François River, replacing a lone pine tree (*mena'sen* in Abenaki) that was destroyed in a storm in 1913. According to Abenaki folklore, the tree commemorated the Abenaki victory over the Iroquois. Another legend tells of two young Native lovers who, having escaped capture in Massachusetts, stopped here on their way to Odanak. The girl died at this spot and her boyfriend planted the tree in her memory.

Sanctuaire du Sacré-Cœur de Beauvoir (Shrine of the Sacred Heart of Beauvoir)

8km/4mi north of town by Blvd Saint-François Nord and chemin Beauvoir. Open May–Nov, daily 10am–7pm; rest of the year, daily 10am–5pm. (summer) 819-569-2535. www.sanctuairedebeauvoir.qc.ca.

In 1915 Abbé Joseph-Arthur Laporte placed a statue of Christ at this spot, 360m/1,181ft above the Saint-François River. A simple stone chapel was constructed in 1920. Today many pilgrims find their way here seeking peace and tranquility, and to enjoy the **panorama★** of the Sherbrooke area.

In the woods behind the chapel and the newer church (1945) is the Gospel Walk, consisting of eight **sculptures★** representing the life of Christ.

Valcourt

42km/26mi W via the 222.

A tiny agricultural community until the 1930s, Valcourt has become famous for the snowmobile, the brainchild of one of its residents (*see box above*), and is now the site of a world-class industry.

Musée J.-Armand Bombardier★

1001 Ave J.-A. Bombardier.

Take rue St-Joseph. Turn right onto the Blvd. du Parc, then right to Ave. J.-A.-Bombardier. Follow blue road signs for the museum. The museum is scheduled to re-open in spring 2016 after renovations. 450-532-5300. www.museebombardier.com.

This museum is a fascinating tribute to Valcourt's favorite son. The **J.-Armand Bombardier** Exhibit and the **Bombardier Garage** trace the inventor's life and re-create the atmosphere in which he worked during his early career.

The **International Snowmobile Exhibit** illustrates the machine's assembly and its use throughout the world from 1959 through the present.

Centre culturel Yvonne L. Bombardier

1002 Ave. J.-A.-Bombardier. Exhibit center open Tue–Sun 10am–5pm (Wed and Fri open until 8pm. Also open Mon 10am–5pm late May–Labor Day. 450-532-3033. www.centreculturelbombardier.com.

The Yvonne L. Bombardier cultural centre is supported by the J. Armand-Bombardier foundation. It contains a library and a visual arts exhibition center.

ADDRESSES

STAY

Marquis de Montcalm – *797 rue Général-de-Montcalm. ℘819-823-7773. www.marquisdemontcalm.com. 5 rooms. Breakfast included.* This period house on the edges of the Vieux-Nord neighborhood has been fully restored and offers plush rooms with Parisian names (d'Orsay, Place des Vosges, Jardin du Luxembourg, etc), and each with a private bath. The three-course breakfast is made up of a series of beautifully presented dishes.

EAT

Café Bla-Bla – *2 rue Wellington Sud. ℘819-565-1366. www.cafeblabla.ca. Sun–Wed 11am–10pm, Thu–Sat 11am–midnight.* For more than 30 years, people have been coming to this café to drink a beer or coffee, eat a bagel or enjoy the daily menu (soup and a main dish), or a hamburger, pizza, or pasta. In the evenings, after the last meals have been served (9–10pm), nachos and snacks from the "Pique Assiette" menu are available for folks who want something to nibble with drinks.

Le Bouchon – *107 rue Frontenac. ℘819-566-0876. lebouchon.ca. Mon–Fri 11:30am–2:30pm, 5:30pm–9pm. Closed Sat lunch, Sun and Dec 23–Jan 7.* A touch of designer chic and a friendly atmosphere in which to enjoy fresh takes on classic dishes. A sophisticated bistro menu (table d'hôte) is served at lunch, while the evening menu offers inventions such as a trio of tartares (beef, duck, tuna) and foie gras with bread pudding and cranberries. The wine selection is ample, and you can order by the glass. Good value for money.

TAKING A BREAK

Brûlerie Faro – *180 rue Wellington Nord. ℘819-820-1223. www.bruleriesdecafe.com. Mon–Fri 7:30am–11pm, Sat 8am–11pm, Sun 9am–11pm.* Where Sherbrooke's students hang out. The atmosphere is studious, especially in the second room with its exposed brick walls and leather seats, while the mezzanine has computers and free web access for customers. This Quebec chain, which roasts its own coffee, runs cafés in four other cities, and sells its products in-store and on-line.

SHOPPING

Marché de la Gare – *719 Place de la Gare ℘819-821-1919. www. marchedelagare.com. Mon–Wed and Sat–Sun 9am–6pm; Thu–Fri 9am–8pm.* A former train station converted into a covered market with five permanent businesses: a café offering Italian ice cream and sherbet as well as light meals and a terrace, a greengrocer, a cheesemonger (see below), a butcher and sausage specialist, and a shop selling an array of nuts. In winter, the enclosed train station becomes a Christmas market.

Fromagerie de la Gare – *710 rue de la Gare. ℘819-566-4273. www.fromageriedelagare.com.* This stall at the Marché de la Gare offers no fewer than 130 Québécois cheeses. Depending on the season, you might find raw sheep's milk cheeses such as Étoile Bleue or Tomme du Kamouraska, and raw cow's milk cheeses such as 14 Arpents, Saguenay, or Gré des Champs from St-Jean-sur-Richelieu.

EVENTS

La fête du lac des Nations – *Parc Jacques-Cartier, 220 rue Marchant ℘819-569-5888. www.fetedulacdesnations.com. Tue–Thu 4pm–midnight, Fri–Sun noon to midnight. $14.* Held over six days in mid-July on the shores of the Lac des Nations (Magog River), this annual festival features some 30 shows and concerts, children's activities and fireworks.

Centre culturel de l'Université de Sherbrooke – *2500 Blvd de l'Université. ℘819- 820-1000. www.centrecultureludes.ca.* The concert hall (Salle Maurice-O'Bready) offers a range of popular and classical music concerts, plus films and theater, while the gallery displays contemporary art.

Drummondville

Centre-du-Québec region

Drummondville was founded by British authorities after the War of 1812 as a military outpost on the Saint-François River. Frederick George Heriot, a Scottish officer, established a settlement here in 1815, naming it for the British governor Sir Gordon Drummond. At Heriot's death in 1843, the community was well established, operating several riverside mills, factories, and stores. The nearby falls were later harnessed for hydroelectricity. Today Drummondville is an important industrial center, producing textiles and other manufactured goods. Every July, the Mondial des cultures de Drummondville is celebrated throughout the city.

- **Population:** 68,091.
- **Michelin Map:** p236–237: C2.
- **Info:** 1350 Rue Michaud. 819-477-5529 & 1-877-235-9569. www.tourisme-drummond.com.
- **Location:** Drummondville is 110km/68mi northeast of Montreal by Rte. 20 (Exit 177). It is a logical stop between Montreal and Quebec City.
- **Don't Miss:** The historic Village Québécois d'Antan.
- **Timing:** Allow 3–4 hours to tour the Village Québécois d'Antan in Drummondville. Drive to the Ulverton Woolen Mills and return via Asbestos.
- **Kids:** Horse and buggy rides at the Ulverton Woolen Mill.

SIGHTS

Village Québécois d'Antan★ (Québécois Village of Old)

1425 rue Montplaisir, Rte. 20 (Exit 181). Open Jun–early Sept; hours vary. $30. 819-478-1441 & 1-877-710-0267. www.villagequebecois.com.

Knowledge of French is essential for understanding the guides, signs, and brochures. English-speaking visitors are advised to tour the village with someone who can act as an interpreter. Tours in English (large groups only) can be arranged in advance.

This village re-creates life in the region between 1810 and 1930. Some 70 authentic period buildings have been brought from their original sites to this wooded terrain near the Saint-François River. Each dwelling, shop, and barn is "inhabited" by a guide in period costume who welcomes visitors and explains the lifestyle of the former occupants. The structures exemplify a broad variety of architectural styles, from the log cabins of the first settlers through the maison québécoise with its cantilevered roof, to the mansard-roofed dwellings introduced by the Loyalists after the American Revolution. Note in particular the village **church**, a reconstruction of Drummondville's Church of St. Frederick (1822); the stained-glass windows (1950) by Guido Nincheri were created for the Chapel of Mont-Saint-Antoine in Montreal, and brought to the village in 1984. The neighboring presbytery (1833) is an excellent example of the *maison québécoise*. The Townships school (1892) is divided into two rooms, one for boys and one for girls. Visitors can tour the homes of the apothecary, the shoemaker and the notary, as well as the forge, the carding and sawmills, and the farm (1895) with its stables for horses and oxen.

A covered bridge (1868) from Stanbridge spans a small stream. In the operator's home (1910), early telephones and an 1876 switchboard are exhibited. Visitors can buy bread as it was made the 1870s, eat meals typical of the period, and have their photographs taken in period costumes.

Domaine Trent

Parc des Voltigeurs, Rte. 20 (exit 181). Open Jun 24–Labor Day, Wed–Sun 11am –5:30pm. No charge. ✕ P ℘819-477-1360. www.tourisme-drummond.com.

When the former British naval officer George Norris Trent decided to retire to Canada, he had this stone manor house built beside the Saint-François River in 1838. The house was extended in 1848, and his descendants lived there until 1963. Today, it contains a culinary museum dedicated to Quebec's rich gastronomic tradition.

EXCURSIONS

Moulin à laine d'Ulverton (Ulverton Woolen Mills)

About 30km/18.6mi south by Rte. 143; turn right at Ulverton. 21 chemin Porter. Also accessible from Rte. 55 (Halte du Moulin exit). Open mid-Jun–Labor Day daily 10am–5pm; early Jun and mid-Sept–mid-Oct, Fri–Sun 10am–5pm. $15. ✕ P ℘819-826-3157. www.moulin.ca.

The large shingled structure of this former carding mill rises above the Ulverton River, a tributary of the Saint-François River. Built by William Dunkerley in 1849, it changed hands several times. The mill fell into decay after 1949 but was renovated in the early 1980s. The operation of early 20C carding and spinning machines is demonstrated inside the mill.

Asbestos mine

60km/37mi southeast by Rtes. 143, 116 and 255; 170km/105.6mi east of Montreal by Rtes. 20, 55 and 116; 60km/37mi north of Sherbrooke by Rtes. 143 and 249.

Asbestos grew and prospered around the gigantic, crater-like open-pit Jeffrey asbestos mine, the second largest in the world. The Jeffrey mine has been closed since 2011, as has Quebec's other asbestos mine, at Thetford Mines. The mine pit, still an impressive site, is 335m/1,099ft deep, and about 2km/1.2mi across. Visitors can observe the pit from a lookout.

Victoriaville★ (Arthabaska)

Centre-du-Québec region

Incorporated with the city of Victoriaville, the former town of Arthabaska lies on the shore of the Nicolet River, at the foot of Mt. Saint-Michel. It is the capital of the Bois-Francs (hardwood) region, so-named because of the predominance of maple trees in the area. The town's name is derived from the Native word *ayabaskaw,* meaning "place of bulrushes and reeds."

- **Population:** 41,316.
- **Michelin Map:** p236–237: C2.
- **Info:** 122 rue Aqueduc. ℘819-758-0597.
- **Location:** Victoriaville is located 164km/101mi northeast of Montreal by Rtes. 20 and 161.
- **Parking:** Metered downtown parking is generally easy to find.
- **Don't Miss:** Maison Laurier.

A BIT OF HISTORY

In 1834 the arrival of the first French-speaking settler, Charles Beauchesne, heralded the influx of French-Canadians into the southern part of the province, then primarily inhabited by English-speaking Loyalists.

Maple products quickly became the backbone of the local economy and remain so today, although forestry and dairy cattle are also important. After the opening of the railway in 1861, nearby Victoriaville replaced Arthabaska as a major industrial center, although Arthabaska retained its plethora of cultural opportunities and historical sites. The town was home to many notable Quebecers, including Prime Minister Wilfrid Laurier and the renowned painter-sculptor Marc-Aurèle de Foy Suzor-Côté.

Victoriaville, nicknamed "Victo," also gets called "Capitale des Bois-Francs" and is noted for its high-quality wood products. There are plenty of cycle paths in Victoriaville, including one going all the way up to Mont Arthabaska. The town also holds the International New Music Festival every May, www.fimav.qc.ca.

SIGHTS

Musée Laurier★ (Laurier Museum)

16 rue Laurier Ouest. The street intersects Blvd Bois-Francs Sud just south of the town center. Open Jul–Aug Mon–Fri 10am–5pm, Sat–Sun 1–5pm; rest of the year Tue–Fri 10am–noon and 1–5pm, Sat–Sun 1–5pm. Closed mid-Dec–mid-Mar. $7 (entrance to both buildings). 819-357-8655. www.museelaurier.com.

This National Historic Site commemorating Arthabaska's beloved native son occupies two separate buildings. The **Sir Wilfrid Laurier House** (*16 rue Laurier Ouest*), an attractive residence built for Laurier in 1876, features overhanging eaves, decorative brackets, quoins, and bay windows. Laurier lived here until his death in 1919, although he spent most of his time in Ottawa after becoming prime minister in 1896.

The first floor rooms re-create the era during which Laurier lived here with his wife, Zoé Lafontaine. The bedroom, dining room (boasting a Tiffany lamp) and living room, all appointed in the style of the day, are open to visitors. In the living room is an 1885 Kranick and Bach piano given to Lady Laurier by her husband. Laurier's political career and anecdotes about the couple's life in their home are presented in displays throughout the house. Laurier's study is located in the second floor.

Erected in 1910 in the Second Empire style, the **Musée de l'Hôtel des Postes** (*949 Blvd Bois-Francs Sud, 819-357-2185*) mounts temporary exhibits of ethnology, history, and art. Visitors can admire a charming re-creation of a typical post office from 1910–1920, while outside the museum is a bust of Sir Wilfrid Laurier by Alfred Laliberté.

Église Saint-Christophe d'Arthabaska (St. Christopher's Church)

40 rue Laurier Ouest. Mon–Thu 8:30am–4pm; if the church is closed, contact the presbytery to visit. 819-357-2376.

Restored in 1997, this charming stone church (1873, J. F. Peachy) in the Romanesque style has a remarkable **interior**. The ceiling is decorated with 76 frescoes and paintings, the work of an artist from Saint-Hyacinthe, Joseph Thomas Rousseau, aided by Suzor-Côté. The statue of

Sir Wilfrid Laurier, Supporter of Canadian Unity

Lawyer, journalist, and politician, Wilfrid Laurier (1841–1919) became the first French-Canadian prime minister of Canada (1896–1911) and a legend in his own time. Renowned for his liberalist views, he headed the Canadian Liberal Party from 1887 to 1919, and espoused Canadian unity and the country's emancipation from Great Britain. He also promoted the settlement of the Canadian West by supporting the construction of the Grand Trunk Railway and the creation of the provinces of Alberta and Saskatchewan. Although he was born in the small town of Saint-Lin (now also known as Saint-Lin-Laurentides), 45km/28mi north of Montreal, Laurier spent most of his life in Arthabaska.

Musée de l'Hôtel des Postes

St. Christopher, on top of the altar, was sculpted by students of Louis-Philippe Hébert. Note the Baroque-style scrolls, paintings and friezes, as well as 43 stained-glass windows by the **Hobbs Company**.

Mont Arthabaska

From rue Laurier, take Blvd Bois-Francs Sud 1.5km/1mi. Turn left on rue Mont-Saint-Michel.

A small park with benches and picnic tables affords a lovely **view★** of Victoriaville and the Nicolet River valley. Among the prominent landmarks are the tower of Arthabaska College, operated by the Sacred Heart Brothers, and the steeples of the churches of St. Christopher and St. Victoria. An iron cross, towering 24m/79ft high, was erected on the summit in 1928.

EXCURSIONS

Moulin La Pierre★ (La Pierre Mill)

6km/3.7mi. On chemin Laurier (no. 99) between Victoriaville and the village of Norbertville. Open Jul–Aug. Visit by guided tour for groups of 20 only (1hr) in French only. Call for reservations. $4. 819-369-9639. www.moulinlapierre.ca

Straddling the Gosselin River, this is one of the few remaining operating water mills in Quebec. It was built on this site by Jean Goulet in 1845. Visitors can observe the milling process, purchase the high-quality organic flour produced here from a variety of grains. Boutique open Tue–Wed 8:30am–noon, 1–5pm; Thu–Fri 8:30am–6pm. Bread made on-site sold Thu–Fri after 1pm.

Église Sainte-Victoire (Church of St. Victoria)

99 rue Notre-Dame Ouest, about 5km/3mi by Rte. 161. Open year-round, Mon–Fri 8am–11:30am, Sat–Sun 9am–5pm. 819-752-2112.

This Neoclassical-style church was completed in 1897; its main steeple measures 60m/197ft tall. The ornate **interior** features elaborate woodwork in the apse, a vault richly decorated with wood sculpture, and imposing lateral galleries. The stained-glass windows were produced in Montreal in 1928.

Nicolet

Centre-du-Québec region

Set on the banks of the Nicolet River, 3km/1.8mi from its junction with the St. Lawrence, this community is named for one of Samuel de Champlain's companions, Jean Nicolet (1598–1642). Settlement began in 1756, when Acadian refugees arrived and established their farms, transforming Nicolet into an agricultural center. A diocese was inaugurated in 1877, and the city is now home to several religious orders. Nicolet is also the site of the Quebec Police Academy. In 1955 a landslide pushed much of the old city into the Nicolet River.

- **Population:** 7,827.
- **Michelin Map:** p236–237: C2.
- **Info:** 20 Rue Notre-Dame. 819-293-6960 and 1-888-816-4007. www.ville.nicolet.qc.ca.
- **Location:** Nicolet is 170km/105mi northeast of Montreal by Rte. 40, Rte. 55 (Laviolette Bridge) and Rte. 132. It is 25km/15.5mi southwest of Trois-Rivières.
- **Don't Miss:** Spring migration of snow geese at **Centre d'Interprétation de Baie-du-Febvre**. Traditional native meal at the Abenaki museum.
- **Timing:** Rodolphe Duguay House invites artists to set up their easels in the garden every Sat (Jun–Sept) from 10am–5pm; incorporate this into your visit.

SIGHTS

Cathédrale Saint-Jean-Baptiste★★ (Cathedral of St. John the Baptist)

671 Blvd Louis-Fréchette. To visit, contact the presbytery Mon–Thu 9am–noon, 1pm–4pm. Normally, a side door is left open for visitors. 819-293-5492.

Distinguished by its detached campanile, this impressive cathedral (1961, Gérard Malouin) resembles a ship's sails. Built of reinforced concrete, it replaced the previous cathedral, which was demolished after a landslide in 1955. The Cassavant organ, which features pipes made by Cavaillé-Coll workshops in France, survived and was integrated into the present cathedral.

Interior

A magnificent **stained-glass window** (50m/164ft wide by 21m/69ft high), the work of Jean-Paul Charland, adorns the façade; surrounding a figure of St. John the Baptist (patron saint of Nicolet), the abstract design bursts into hundreds of colorful prisms as the morning sun shines through. The white oak and hickory nave seats 1,200 people. The Stations of the Cross are engraved on its stucco walls, beneath portraits of Nicolet's former bishops. The stained-glass window in the apse, by Brother Eric de Taizé, is a stunning representation of the risen Christ.

Ancien collège-séminaire (Old College Seminary)

350 rue d'Youville.

Religious authorities established the college-seminary in 1803 to encourage young men from urban areas to join the priesthood. The building, designed by Father Jérôme Demers and Thomas Baillairgé, was constructed in 1828; a fire destroyed half of the structure in 1973. The building is now occupied by the Quebec Police Academy.

Musée des religions du monde (Museum of the Religions of the World)

900 Blvd Louis-Fréchette, just off rue Notre-Dame in the center of Nicolet. Open mid-May–Dec daily 10am–5pm; rest of year Tue–Fri 10am–4:30pm, Sat–Sun 1–5pm. $12. 819-293-6148. www.museedesreligions.qc.ca.

Dedicated to the study and preservation of religious heritage, this museum reopened in 1991 in a new, contemporary structure topped by a glass pyramid. On the first floor, exhibits present various world religions (Buddhism, Christianity, Hinduism, Islam, and Judaism) using objects from the permanent collection. In recent years, a special effort has been made by the museum to provide a religious context to major events that shape the world in an era of globalization (mass migration, terrorism, etc.). Temporary thematic exhibits invite reflection on such topics as human spirituality. On the lower level, the Nicolet Seminary Archives are available for research purposes.
The museum's collection consists of more than 120,000 works of art, including Canada's most comprehensive collection of sacred images.

Maison Rodolphe-Duguay (Rodolphe-Duguay House)

195 Rang Saint-Alexis. 1km/0.6mi by Rte. 132 over the Pierre-Roy Bridge; turn left on Rang Saint-Alexis. Open late May–Oct, Tue–Sun 10am–5pm; rest of year by appointment only. $5. P 819-293-4103. www.rodolpheduguay.com.

The birthplace and home of artist Rodolphe Duguay (1891–1973) stands on a pleasant site overlooking the Nicolet River. The adjacent studio was added by the artist himself following his return in 1927 from a long sojourn in Paris. In his lifetime, Duguay was best known for his wood engravings, and was a follower of Suzor-Côté. Temporary exhibits present his life and works, and allow a glimpse into the environment in which he worked. There are many special activities including poetry readings in the summer, and Halloween events.

EXCURSIONS

Baie-du-Febvre

13km/8mi by Rte. 132.

Nestled along Lac Saint-Pierre lies this small village that serves as the welcome spot for the return of Quebec's snow geese each April. Surrounding fields flooded by the winter's melted snow become shallow lakes that serve as the perfect place for waterfowl that stop for a rest during their annual return home. To get better acquainted with the most important snow goose migration layover in Quebec, visit the **Centre d'Interprétation de Baie-du-Febvre** (420 Rte. Marie-Victorin; open Apr–early May (for goose migration) Wed–Sun 10am–4pm; Jun 25–early Sept Mon–Thur 10am–4pm. $2; 450-783-6996; www.baie-du-febvre.net). This center also showcases some of the best animal art by Quebec artists.

Odanak Indian Reserve

25km/15.5mi by Rte. 132. Turn left in Pierreville following signs.

Located on the banks of the Saint-François River, this Abenaki reservation (population 424), known as Arsigontekw, was settled in 1700 by members of the Sokoki and Abenaki communities. The small **church**, the fifth on this site, was entirely decorated by the native population. Note the wooden frieze along the walls, and the statues, especially the one of Kateri Tekakwitha. Don't miss the opportunity to taste traditional foods, such as sagamite and bannock.

Musée des Abénakis (Abenaki Museum)

In former convent beside church, 108 Waban-Aki, Odanak. Open May–Sept daily 10am–5pm; rest of year Mon–Fri 10am–5pm, Sat–Sun 11 am–5pm. $8.50. P 450-568-2600. www.museedesabenakis.ca.

Temporary and permanent exhibits offer glimpses of the traditional lifestyle of the Abenakis, Odanak history, and the foundation of the Catholic mission. Works by native artists are displayed on a rotating basis. The permanent exhibition, Wôbanaki (people of the rising sun), takes visitors into the spiritual and cultural core of these First Nations residents. Workshops are organized where, for a nominal fee, visitors can learn how to make traditional ornaments.

DRIVING TOUR

FROM NICOLET TO QUEBEC CITY

142km/89mi via Rte. 132, along the south of the St. Lawrence River.
See regional map p237.

Starting in Nicolet continue east on Rte 132 passing under Rte. 55 which leads back to Laviolette Bridge and Trois-Rivières.

Pont Laviolette★

The elegant bridge across the St. Lawrence was inaugurated in 1967. It is the only bridge linking the river's banks between Montreal and Quebec. Suspended 46m/150ft above the river, it is 3km/1.8mi long.

Reach Bécancour via Rte. 30.

Bécancour

32km/19.2mi.

Bécancour was created in 1965 through the amalgamation of 11 villages and parishes. The name is now principally associated with the industrial park, the site of a huge aluminum smelter and other installations associated with the metallurgical industry.

Moulin Michel

675 Blvd Bécancour, from Leclercville, on the right. Open mid-Jun–Labor Day, daily 10am–5pm; Labor Day–mid-Oct Sat–Sun 10am–5pm. Restaurant open 11am–2pm when mill is open. Guided tours $5. 819-298-2882 & 1-866-998-2882. www.moulinmichel.qc.ca.

This mill was restored in 1992. During the summer, visitors can taste bread baked on site. A short trail leads up the adjacent hillside to a lookout point offering a fine view.

Leclercville

First settled by Acadians, this village overlooks the confluence of the Chêne and St. Lawrence rivers. The brick church, dedicated to St. Emmélie, was built in 1863.

The road continues through Deschaillons and Saint-Pierre-les-Becquets, affording expansive views of the St. Lawrence. On the right (7km/4.3mi from Leclercville), a plaque marks the huge 272kg/600lb boulder allegedly placed here by Modeste Maillot (1763–1834), the legendary "Canadian Giant," who stood 2.25m/7'4" tall. Maillot was born in Saint-Pierre-les-Becquets and died in Deschaillons.

West of Leclercville, the valley widens and gives way to plains. Farther on, the road passes through a region both agricultural and industrial, marked by the massive complex of Gentilly 2, Quebec's only nuclear power station.

Lotbinière

Set in pastoral farming country, the village of Lotbinière offers views of Deschambault across the river.

Église Saint-Louis (St. Louis Church)

Open on request at the presbytery (next to church) Mon–Fri 9am–5pm. 418-796-2044.

The façade of this lovely white church (1818) overlooks a square bordered to the north by the former convent. The splendid interior was decorated by Thomas Baillairgé in 1845. The retable—shaped like a triumphant arch over the sanctuary—is surmounted by two Neoclassical statues, *Faith* and *Hope*, both crafted by Baillairgé.

Maison Chavigny de la Chevrotière (Chavigny de la Chevrotière House)

7640 rue Marie-Victorin.

This monumental structure was erected in 1817 for Ambroise Chavigny, a notary from Chevrotière. Its roof is evocative of the style of the French Regime.

Domaine Joly de Lotbinière (Joly de Lotbinière Estate)

7015 Rte de Pointe Platon, Sainte-Croix. Drive east on Rte.132 for 8km/4.8mi and veer left onto Route de Pointe-Platon and follow signs; site will be on your left. Open mid-May–late Sept, daily

Le Pont de Québec

10am–5pm. Interpretive Center open late May–mid-Jun and Labor Day–late Sept Sat–Sun 10am–noon, 1–5pm; mid-Jun–Labor Day daily 10am–noon, 1–5pm. $16. 418-926-2462. www.domainejoly.com.

This charming white clapboard structure surrounded by wide verandas adorned with a maple-leaf frieze was built in 1840 by Julie-Christine Chartier de Lotbinière and her husband, Pierre Gustave Joly, as a summer residence. It was also used by their son, Henri-Gustave Joly de Lotbinière (1829–1908), premier of Quebec (1878–79), Minister of Revenue in Wilfrid Laurier's cabinet (1896–1900) and Lieutenant-Governor of British Columbia (1900–06).

The mansion has been converted into an interpretation center, featuring displays on the history of the Lotbinière seigneury and the local natural environment. The beautiful grounds and lush, colorful gardens lend themselves to pleasant walks and picnics with views of the river.

Continue on Rte. 132 for 26km/16mi. Turn left on Chemin de Tilly.

Saint-Antoine-de-Tilly

A small road descends from the church (1788) to the St. Lawrence. From here, the view extends across the river to Neuville. The Manoir de Tilly, an old seigneurial manor built during the early 19C, has been converted into a country inn. The road continues through Sainte-Croix with views of Donnacona and the church at Cap-Santé, on the opposite shore.

Saint-Nicolas

Follow Rte. 132 for 15km/9mi to Rue de l'Entente, turn left to arrive opposite the water tower. Open year-round Mon–Fri 9am–noon, 1.30–4.30pm; 418-831-9622.

Topped by a bell tower shaped like a sail, this intriguing church was erected in 1693. The center altar is surrounded by pews and resembles, both visually and symbolically, a ship's helm. Natural light filters into the church at the edges of the dropped ceiling, reflecting on the marble and wood interior. The balcony provides fine views of the river and the two bridges leading to Quebec City.

Follow Rte. 132 for 3.2km/1.9mi. to Quebec City Bridge (Rte. 175) and cross the St. Lawrence River into Quebec City.

Le Pont de Québec★★ (Quebec City Bridge)

This remarkable structure, brightly lit at night, has a steel span extending 549m/1,801ft between its two main pylons; it was the world's longest cantilever-type bridge of its day. Construction proved to be a nightmare for the railroad company in charge: the bridge collapsed while under construction in 1907, and in 1916 the center span fell into the river as it was being installed. Inaugurated in 1917 as a railway bridge, the Quebec City Bridge has been open to vehicular traffic since 1929. Just next to it is the Pont Pierre-Laportea, opened in 1970. Measuring 668m/2,191ft, it is Canada's longest suspension bridge.

ADDRESSES

STAY

La Maison Normand – *3894 chemin de Tilly, Saint-Antoine-de-Tilly. 418-886-1314. www.gitescanada.com/8002.html. 5 rooms; breakfast included. Both shared and private baths.* The former general store on the church square, now a charming Québécois house with five stylish and tastefully furnished rooms.

EAT

Chez Le Gardeur– *3884 chemin de Tilly, Saint-Antoine-de-Tilly. 418-413-3303. Tue–Sun 5pm–10pm, open for lunch in summer 10am–2pm, closed Monday.* The new owners of this restaurant set in a pretty house have changed the menu to feature Mediterranean cuisine, but the atmosphere remains relaxed and the fare refined.

Beauce★

Chaudière-Appalaches–Cantons-de-l'Est regions

The name Beauce refers to the area drained by the Chaudière River as it flows from Lake Mégantic into the St. Lawrence River, just north of the American border. Like its French namesake, a region to the southwest of Paris, "la Beauce" is a vast, flat area of fertile farmlands. The region becomes more mountainous farther south. Throughout this region, visitors will see the greatest concentration of maple groves in Quebec. A popular tradition rich in folklore and special events has developed around the theme of the maple tree and is reflected in regional folk art. During the sugaring-off season in spring, people gather in sugar shacks to sample maple taffy *(tire d'érable)* and take part in the festivities known as sugaring-off parties *(parties de sucre)*. Cascading over numerous falls interspersed with more tranquil areas, the Chaudière River is navigable in only a few places, and its frequent floods often make newspaper headlines. Despite the construction of a dam at Saint-Georges-de-Beauce, the Chaudière may still inundate the villages along its banks in the spring.

- **Michelin Map:** p236–237: CD1-2
- **Info:** 13055 Blvd Lacroix, Saint-Georges. 418-227-4642 & 1-877- 923-2823. www.destinationbeauce.com.
- **Location:** Maine's Rte. 201 becomes Rte. 173 at the border and travels northwest toward Quebec City through valleys and forests along the Chaudière River.
- **Don't Miss:** The colorful maple forests in the fall and sugar shacks in the early spring.
- **Timing:** Most of Beauce's attractions are along the Rte. 173 corridor.
- **Kids:** The long covered bridge near Notre-Dame-des-Pins.

A BIT OF HISTORY

President Kennedy Road (Rte. du Président Kennedy) – In 1775, twelve years after New France was ceded to England in the Treaty of Paris, an American expeditionary force of 1,100 men led by Col. Benedict Arnold traveled along the Kennebec River to the state of Maine, and from there marched northward along the Chaudière River in an attempt to capture Quebec City. The 13 American colonies engaged in the fight against British rule hoped to persuade the Canadians to join their cause. A great many soldiers died during the arduous northern trek; the survivors were defeated by troops under the command of Guy Carleton.

Every year some 600,000 Americans en route to Quebec follow this road (Rte. 173), now named for former US president John F. Kennedy.

The Gold Rush of 1846 – In the 19C the Beauce region was the El Dorado of Canada. In 1846 a gold nugget the size of a pigeon's egg was discovered on a tributary of the Chaudière, and prospectors poured in to sift the sands of the stream between Notre-Dame-des-Pins and Saint-Simon-les-Mines. By the beginning of the 20C, $1 million worth of gold ore had been extracted. Vestiges of the mining heyday are still visible today.

DRIVING TOUR

QUEBEC CITY TO LAC-MÉGANTIC

221km/137mi.

See regional map p237.

Leave Quebec City by Rte. 73 south and cross the Pierre-Laporte Bridge continuing south; 1km/0.6mi after the bridge, turn off at Exit 130. Follow the signs to Parc des Chutes de la Rivière Chaudière.

Parc des Chutes-de-la-Chaudière★ (Chaudière River Falls Park)

In Charny. Open early May–Oct, daily 8am–9pm. Tourisme Lévis. 418-838-6026. www.tourismelevis.com.

Just before it joins the St. Lawrence, the Chaudière River drops over a cliff in spectacular falls, 35m/115ft high and 121m/397ft wide. The Abenaki Indians named these falls asticou, meaning "boiler," because of the kettle-shaped basin at the foot of the cascades. The name chaudière, the French word for "boiler," was subsequently given to the entire river.

Steps descend to a suspension bridge hung across the river. From here, visitors can enjoy exceptional views of the falls, magnificent during the spring run-off.

Parc des Chutes-de-la-Chaudière

Return to Rte. 73 and at Exit 123 take Rte. 175 south. At Saint-Lambert, cross the Chaudière River and take Rte. 171 south. At Scott (34km/21mi), the road crosses the river again and becomes Rte. 173 south.

Sainte-Marie-de-Beauce

9km/5.6mi from Scott.

One of the oldest communities in the region, Sainte-Marie was part of the seigneury given to **Thomas-Jacques Taschereau** in 1736. Taschereau was a member of an influential family which included Elzéar-Alexandre Taschereau (1820–98), the first Canadian to be made a cardinal in the Roman Catholic Church, and Louis-Alexandre Taschereau (1867–1952), premier of Quebec from 1920 to 1936. Sainte-Marie was also the birthplace of **Marius Barbeau** (1883–1969), writer, ethnomusicologist, and founder of the Quebec folklore archives at Laval University, in Quebec City.

Today Sainte-Marie's economy thrives on the baked-goods industry. In 1923 Arcade Vachon and his wife, Rose-Anne Giroux, purchased a bakery in Sainte-Marie and began making the "petits gâteaux Vachon" (snack cakes) that are now famous throughout the province.

Église Sainte-Marie (St. Mary's Church)

60 rue Notre-Dame. Open Mon and Fri–Sat 8am–8pm, Sun 8am–11am. Visits can be arranged outside these hours by calling presbytery. 418-387-3233.

The church (1856, Charles Baillairgé) is one of the first Gothic Revival structures built for the Catholic Church in Quebec. The exterior is English in inspiration while the interior is modeled after the work of Viollet-le-Duc. A rare harmony is achieved in its overall effect, and the interior can be compared to Montreal's Notre-Dame Basilica, designed by Victor Bourgeau.

After 10km/6.2mi, the road passes through **Vallée-Jonction**. Located at a railway junction, this small community overlooks the Chaudière River. Rte. 112 to **Thetford Mines** crosses the river at this point.

Turn off Rte. 173 and enter Saint-Joseph-de-Beauce.

Saint-Joseph-de-Beauce★

9km/5.6mi from Vallée-Jonction.

Set in the valley of the Chaudière River, this former seigneury was conceded to Joseph Fleury de la Gorgendière, a wealthy Quebec merchant, in 1737.

Town center

Intersection of rue Sainte-Christine and Ave. du Palais.

Designed by F.-X. Berlinguet, **Église Saint-Joseph** (St. Joseph's Church) features a narrow façade surmounted by a tall steeple. Its interior was completed in 1876 by J.F. Peachy. Facing the church, a large brick **presbytery** (1892, G.-É. Tanguay) evokes the design of small 16C French châteaux.

The former **convent** (1889, J.F. Peachy) and **orphanage** (1908) are in the Second Empire style. Behind the church stands the **Lambert School** (1911, Lorenzo Auger), an edifice enlarged in 1947 and again in 1995.

The institutional ensemble is completed by the **courthouse-prison**, a Neoclassical structure erected between 1857 and 1862. To the rear, a post-Modern addition blends harmoniously with the original structure.

Continue on Ave. du Palais which rejoins Rte. 173 south of the town center.

Beauceville

15km/9.3mi.

Built on the steep slopes of the Chaudière River valley, this community was the birthplace of the poet **William Chapman** (1850–1917), emulator and rival of Louis Fréchette.

Across the river stands the **Église Saint-François d'Assise** (Church of St. Francis of Assisi); of note in its interior are the main altar and angel statues (open during services only).

Parc des Rapides du Diable (Devil's Rapids Park)

3km/1.8mi south of town.

The park is strewn with paths leading to the Chaudière River and the "devil's rapids" that tumble over the rocky riverbed. The foundations of a mill, used to extract gold from quartz rock during the gold rush, are still visible.

Turn off Rte. 173 and head toward Notre-Dame-des-Pins.

Notre-Dame-des-Pins

8km/5mi from Beauceville.

In the mid-19C gold prospectors gathered here before embarking on their journey along the Gilbert River to Saint-Simon-les-Mines.

Covered bridge

Turn right on 1re Ave., just before the modern bridge.

The 154.5m/507ft covered bridge across the Chaudière River is the longest in the province. First built in 1927, it was carried away by ice during the winter of 1928. Rebuilt in 1929 with three central piers, the bridge remained in use until 1969 when it was closed to vehicular traffic *(picnic area near bridge)*.

Continue south; turn off Rte. 173 at Saint-Georges exit.

Saint-Georges

9km/5.6mi.

The industrial capital of the Beauce region was originally named Sartigan, meaning "changing river," by the indigenous Abenaki villagers. In 1807 a German settler by the name of **George Pozer** bought the land and gave the town its present name. Saint-Georges experienced some growth after the American invasion of 1775, but its greatest economic expansion followed the opening of the Kennebec Route to New England in 1830. In 1967 the Sartigan dam was erected to control the capricious flow of the Chaudière River.

Église Saint-Georges★ (St. George's Church)

On 1re Ave. in Saint-Georges-Ouest, across the river. Open early Jun–late Aug Mon–Fri 10am–noon and 1–4pm, Sun 1–4pm; Sat and rest of the year by appointment with the presbytery. P 418-228-2558.

This beautiful church (1902, David Ouellet), with its monumental cut stone façade, dominates the west bank of the Chaudière. Three spires, one 75m/246ft tall, rise above the edifice. The present church replaces a previous stone building (1862) and an earlier wood structure (1831). Before the entrance stands a copy of Louis Jobin's masterpiece, *St. George Slaying the Dragon*. The original (1912), an enormous wooden sculpture sheathed in bronze and gilded, is displayed nearby at the Centre culturel Marie-Fitzbach on the second floor. The ornate **interior** of this three-story church features tiered balconies embellished with painted and gilded woodwork. The altar is surmounted by a broad canopy with St. George at its summit.

An optional excursion is a short drive west to Saint-Évariste-de-Forsyth.

Saint-Évariste-de-Forsyth

44km/27mi by Rtes. 173, 204, 269 and 108.

Perched on a hill, this community affords lovely views of the surrounding countryside.

Return to Rte. 204.

Saint-Gédéon-de-Beauce

38km/24mi.

The countryside opens onto Lake Mégantic, source of the Chaudière River and the surrounding mountains.

Lac-Mégantic

5490 rue de la Gare. Open from early Jun–mid-Oct daily 9am–6pm; mid-Oct–May 9am–noon, 1pm–4:30pm. 819-583-5555 and 1-800-363-5515. www.tourisme-megantic.com.

This municipality (population 5,949) is located on the northern shores of Lake Mégantic, where it empties into the Chaudière River. It was founded in 1885 by Scottish settlers who left their

architectural signature in the numerous redbrick buildings along the main street. A pleasant park beside the lake (*behind the courthouse*) provides good views of the mountains, notably the peak of Mt. Mégantic to the west.
The **Église Sainte-Agnès** (Church of St. Agnes, at 4872 rue Laval) houses a lovely **stained-glass window**, depicting the Jesse Tree, created in 1849 for the Church of the Immaculate Conception, located in London's Mayfair district (UK) (open year-round, 9:30am–noon, 1:30–4.30pm; P 819-583-0370).

Lac-Mégantic

This lovely lake covers 26sq km/10sq mi and reaches depths of 75m/246ft. Located near the US border, its southern end is surrounded by the Blanches Mountains. From Lake Mégantic, the Chaudière River flows northward across the southern part of the province to join the St. Lawrence near Quebec City. The park was declared a dark-sky reserve in 2007, and is kept free of artificial light pollution for astronomical reasons.

EXCURSION TO MONT-MÉGANTIC

59km/36.6mi.

Leave Lac-Mégantic by Rte. 161.

The road rises above the lake, overlooking the Blanches Mountains to the south. At Woburn (27km/16.7mi), turn right on Rte. 212 and continue for 18km/11mi. The road reaches **Notre-Dame-des-Bois**, the village with the highest altitude (549m/1,801ft) in the province.

In Notre-Dame-des-Bois, turn right following signs to ASTROlab and Parc National du Mont-Mégantic Park.

Mont-Mégantic

At the base of Mont-Mégantic's peak (1,100m/3,608ft) find the **ASTROlab**, an astronomy activity center open in the day and in the evening, which houses a high-definition multimedia room. There are two observatories on the summit which you can visit during guided day or evening tours. Mont-Mégantic's telescope is the largest in eastern North America, measuring 1.6m/5.2ft in diameter and weighing approximately 26 tons. A second, public telescope is of professional caliber (61cm/24in). Popular night-time astronomy evenings allow visitors to observe stars and constellations through it (when visibility permits). Reservations are required for tours of the summit, but not to visit the ASTROlab at the mountain's base. Call or check website to select from many different tours available from mid-May–early Nov, reservations required; $21 (plus $8.50 park fee. Children (under 18) free. 819-888-2941; www.sepaq.com.

Return 3km/1.8mi and turn left, following a rough road that climbs steeply for 1km/.6mi up Mont Joseph.

Mont Joseph

Father Corriveault of Notre-Dame-des-Bois constructed the small sanctuary here in 1883 after the village inhabitants were miraculously saved from devastating tornadoes after praying to St. Joseph. The summit affords a stunning **view★★** of the surrounding mountainous region.

Mont-Mégantic ASTROlab

©Nadine Mitchell/Dreamstime.com

Discovering Quebec City

Hôtel du Parlement, Quebec City

© Jean-Guy Lavoie / Quebec City Tourism

Quebec City

Ancien bureau de poste (Louis S. St-Laurent Building) overlooking Place Royale

© Yves Tessier, Tessima / Québec City Tourism

Quebec City and Surroundings

International revelers converged for the 400th Anniversary of Quebec City in 2008, celebrating Quebec's historic place in developing the country, and the continent. Then and now, visitors to the city discover an broad range of contemporary attractions in a clean, safe and upbeat locale. The vibrant areas beyond the heritage walls are rich in local joie de vivre, breathtaking geography, and memorable sights. Quebec City has truly arrived on the global stage, and tourism entrepreneurs, as well as residents, are welcoming guests with open arms and typically warm French–Canadian passion.

Highlights

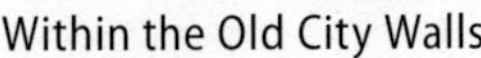

1. Visiting the civic, military, and religious heart of **Old Quebec** (p298)
2. The City's most prominent landmark, **Château Frontenac** (p307)
3. The **Cartier-Brébeuf National Historic Site of Canada** (p331)
4. Huron nation heritage and housing at **Wendake** (p335)
5. **Île d'Orléans**, island of spirits and maple syrup (p336)

Within the Old City Walls

Nouvelle France is very much alive in this small sample of modern Quebec: fieldstone buildings with steeply pitched roofs, and narrow, winding streets. The battlefield of the Plains of Abraham recalls what's still known as *La Defaite* (The Defeat) by French Canadians. Indeed, Quebec City embodies a resolve to preserve, protect, and develop the largest French-speaking society in the Western Hemisphere.

Sophisticated Quebec City also claims many fine hotels and restaurants, and many winter pleasures. Come in winter to experience the city against a carpet of snow, in spring or summer when flowers bloom alongside stone ramparts, or in fall when the countryside glows in glorious shades of red and gold.

The UNESCO-designated World Heritage Site of the Old City also continues to grow in popularity as a travel destination.

Quintessential Quebec City sights include Château Frontenac, La Citadelle, Musée de la Civilization, Musée de la Allée, Cap Diamant, Hôtel du Parlement, Place Royale, Rue du Petit-Champlain, Parc des Champs-de-Batailles (Battlefields Park), Vieux-Port .... The list goes on. Try to see as many churches and religious sites as possible while walking the city. Religious highlights include Basilique-Cathèdrale Notre-Dame-Québec, Èglise Notre-Dame des Victoires, Monastère des Ursulines, and Seminaire de Québec.

Little-Known Treasures

Beyond the Old Town lies another series of delights that most tourists miss. All too often, the areas surrounding the city

Country landscape on Île d'Orléans

Château Frontenac

© Luc-Antoine Couturier / Québec City Tourism

are lumped into itineraries that leave little time to explore the host of intriguing towns and villages. Cross the Pont de l'**Île d'Orleans** to discover the gracious countryside of farmlands and tiny communities dedicated to traditions of handmade crafts and home-grown fruits and vegetables. Time seems to stand still when visiting these artisan shops, cozy cafés, or farms where owners tend to their land and livestock. Stay overnight and wake to the freshest breakfast possible, while the ripple of the passing river and the fresh island air sooth the spirit.

Meanwhile, the borough of Sainte-Foy-Sillery, southwest of the city, attracts legions of visitors to the **Quebec Aquarium**, now part of the provincial park system called SEPAQ. Near the Quebec Bridge, this child-friendly site boasts more than 10,000 specimens of marine life, reptiles, and sea mammals.

While in the area, visit the Bois-de-Coulonge Park, a fine example of the original seigneury domains and a peaceful place to enjoy the summer gardens or the winter arboretum.

Head northwest up Rte. 73 outside the city to the **Hôtel de Glace**, on the former grounds of the Jardins zoologique du Québec. Happy to have a permanent home ten minutes from the city, this frozen attraction is only open in the coldest winter months.

Nearby, in the same sector, is the evocative aboriginal town of Wendat. The **Huron-Wendat Onhoüa Chetek8e** Traditional Site welcomes visitors with an eco-friendly hotel, conference center, and museum on their Saint Charles River domain. No visit to the province is complete without witnessing how the original residents lived, their relationship with nature, and the inspiring ways in which they communicate through storytelling, drumming, and crafts.

Embrace the outdoors in any season in **Parc de la Jacques-Cartier**, where a heavenly weave of rivers, mountains, lakes, and trails intersect. Also managed by SEPAQ, this stellar wildlife preserve is worth a trip for anyone who loves the outdoors.

Glacial valleys are cut through by rivers up to 500m/3,000ft deep in places, while the river ranges from calm to turbulent. Eleven winter trails cover 79km/49mi of zigzagging routes, through some of the finest topography on the continent.

Winter Collaborations

People here are proud of their survival instincts, especially during the long winter months. The annual **Carnival** in February celebrates the season within the city walls. Other fine winter destinations include the hills and trails of Mont Sainte-Anne ***(42km/26mi)***,and Stoneham Tourist Station ***(32km/20mi)***, and the new train service to the Massif peaks in Charlevoix.

Quebec City and Surroundings

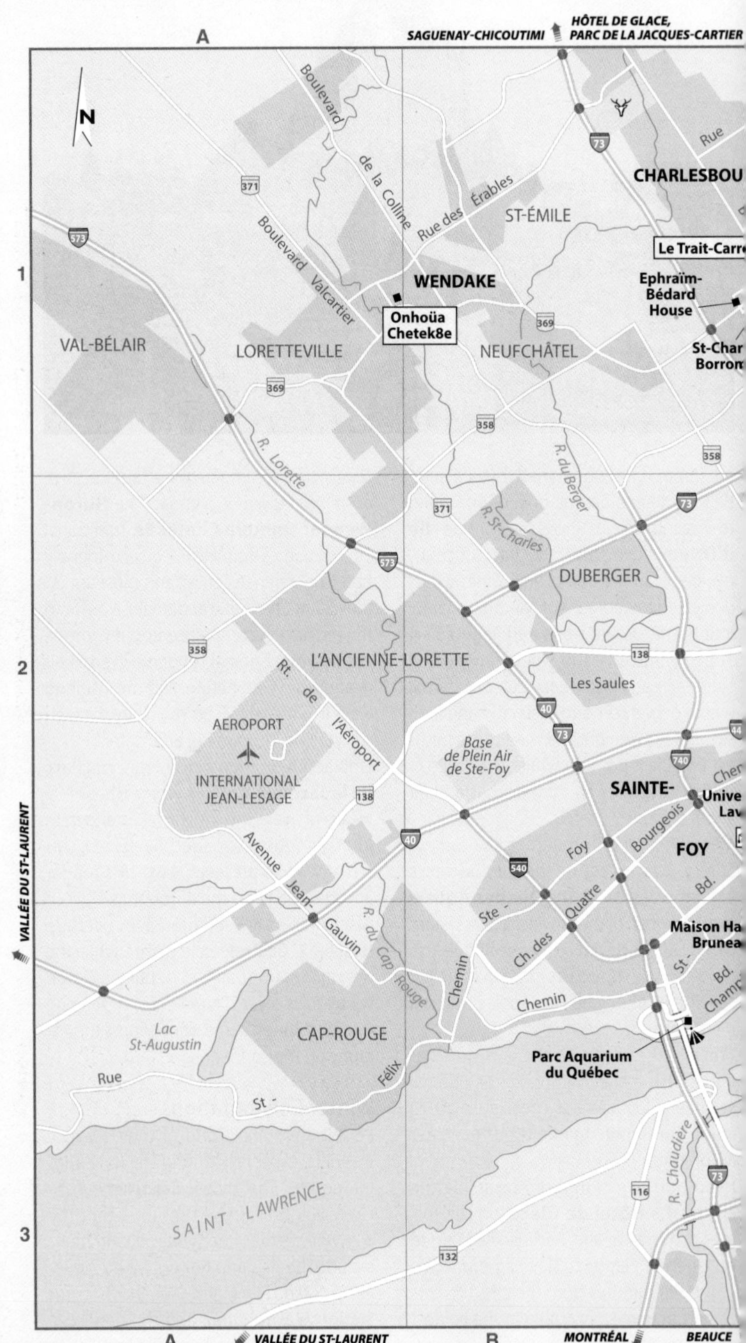

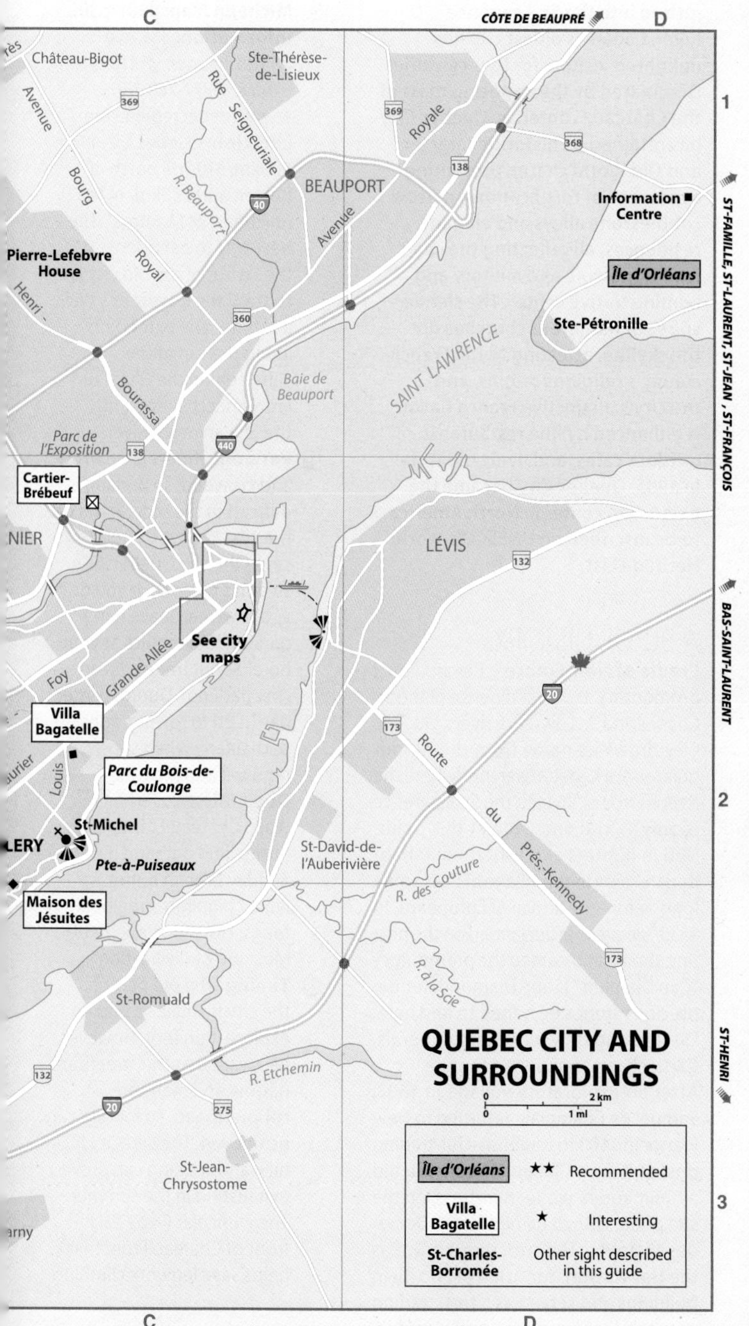

QUEBEC CITY AND SURROUNDINGS
CÔTE DE BEAUPRÉ
ST-FAMILLE, ST-LAURENT, ST-JEAN , ST-FRANÇOIS
BAS-SAINT-LAURENT
ST-HENRI
Château-Bigot
Ste-Thérèse-de-Lisieux
Rue Seigneuriale
Avenue Royale
BEAUPORT
R. Beauport
Avenue Bourg-Royal
Henri-Bourassa
Pierre-Lefebvre House
Information Centre
Île d'Orléans
Ste-Pétronille
SAINT LAWRENCE
Baie de Beauport
Parc de l'Exposition
Cartier-Brébeuf
LÉVIS
See city maps
Grande Allée
Foy
Villa Bagatelle
Parc du Bois-de-Coulonge
Louis
St-Michel
Pte-à-Puiseaux
Maison des Jésuites
Route du Prés.-Kennedy
St-David-de-l'Auberivière
R. des Couture
R. à la Scie
St-Romuald
R. Etchemin
St-Jean-Chrysostome
Recommended
Interesting
St-Charles-Borromée
Other sight described in this guide
2 km
1 ml

Quebec City★★★

Built atop a rocky promontory jutting into the St. Lawrence River, Canada's oldest city has delighted visitors for four centuries. Dominated by the imposing mass of the Château Frontenac, Quebec City has retained its historic character and Old World charm, presenting a mélange of fortifications, narrow cobblestone alleys and elegant residences, all reflecting the city's traditional role as a military and administrative center. The slender spires of numerous churches dot the skyline, attesting to the French colony's religious origins, and the city's distinctive French flavor is enhanced by fine restaurants, outdoor cafes, and lively nightlife. In 1985, Quebec City became the first urban center in North America to be inscribed on UNESCO's World Heritage List.

- **Population:** 516,622 (metropolitan area 765,706).
- **Michelin Map:** p301, p309.
- **Information:** 835 Ave Wilfrid-Laurier. ℘418-641-6290 & 1-877-783-1608. www.quebecregion.com.
- **Location:** Quebec City is 500km/310.7mi north of Boston and 230km/143mi northeast of Montreal. The best way to get a sense of the layout of the old city is to stroll the Governor's Walk, a promenade extending along the top of the cliffs behind the Château Frontenac, overlooking the St. Lawrence River.
- **Parking:** Streets are narrow and crowded, so parking is difficult in the older parts of the city. You won't need a car in the Old Quebec City, so don't hire one. If you drive your own car, leave it in a parking lot (enquire at your hotel about free/reduced-cost parking). During winter, pay heed to towing signs, particularly when snow removal is in process.
- **Don't Miss:** Governor's Walk; Château Frontenac (inside and out) and its Sunday brunch buffet, which highlights regional foods; Hôtel du Parlement; Museum of Civilization.
- **Timing:** The old part of the city is small, so plan to explore it on foot. However, be aware that the streets are narrow and many are cobblestoned, so footing can be uneven. The Old City is hilly and walking can prove exhausting in the summer. The Funicular (*$2.25*, in front of Château Frontenac) helps save legwork climbing

A BIT OF HISTORY

Cradle of New France – Perched on a promontory at the confluence of the St. Charles and St. Lawrence rivers, Quebec City draws its name from the Algonquian word Kebec, meaning "where the river narrows." In fact, the St. Lawrence is only 1km/0.6mi wide at this point. Native hunters and fishermen inhabited the area in the village of Stadacona long before the arrival of Europeans. In 1535, Jacques Cartier landed on the pristine shores and named the promontory "Cap Diamant" (Cape Diamond) for the precious stones he hoped to find here. Discovering only worthless minerals, Cartier soon abandoned the site.

After an exploratory voyage in 1603, Samuel de Champlain returned to New France in 1608 to establish a fur-trading post at Kebec. Champlain constructed a rudimentary wooden fortress, on the site of the church named Notre-Dame-des-Victoires. The structure, known as the **Habitation**, consisted of two main buildings and served as a fort, trading post and living quarters, and a garden.

up the cliff, to and from the Basse-Ville (Lower Town).

Kids: In winter, don't miss the old-fashioned toboggan run (*$2*) swooshing down beside the Château Frontenac onto the Governor's Walk (fun for adults, too). Visit the Quebec Aquarium.

A second, larger U-shaped fortress was built on the same site in 1624. Champlain also established a fortification on the Cape Diamond heights and named it Château Saint-Louis.

In the 17C, the first settlers arrived in Quebec. Primarily craftsmen and merchants attracted to the profitable fur trade, they erected houses in the Lower Town, which became the center of commercial activity. Seeking protection offered by the fortifications, the colonial government and numerous religious institutions settled in the Upper Town. Reluctant to divide up land plots in the Upper Town, the institutions effectively halted development on Cape Diamond for more than a century. The Lower Town remained the main residential and commercial center until the mid-19C.

Strategic Location – Quebec City's location enhanced its development as the political, administrative, and military center of New France. Towering 98m/321.5ft above sea level, the Cape Diamond promontory provided the colony with a strategic military location, thereby earning the sobriquet "Gibraltar of America." From this naturally fortified area, the French repelled successive attacks by the Iroquois and by the British. In 1629 the settlement was captured by British conquerors, the **Kirke Brothers**, and retaken by the French in 1632. In 1690, it was besieged unsuccessfully by the British **Admiral Phips**. Hostility between the small French colony and Britain escalated during the 18C, culminating in the Battle of the Plains of Abraham that precipitated the Conquest of 1759. Following the Treaty of Paris in 1763, Quebec City, the former capital of the French colony, assumed a new role as capital of the British dominion.

Economic Growth – Situated on the north shore of the St. Lawrence, the town quickly assumed a dominant position as port of entry and exit for ocean-bound vessels carrying goods, travelers and immigrants to North America.

Old Quebec City at night in winter

© Jean-François Bergeron, Enviro Foto / Québec City Tourism

PRACTICAL INFORMATION

TELEPHONE AREA CODE: 418

GETTING THERE

By Air – Jean-Lesage International Airport: 16km/10.2mi (*approximately 20min*) from downtown; no public transport is available. A taxi costs $34.25 plus tip. Airport information: ☎418-640-3300 or www.aeroportdequebec.com. Air Canada ☎1-888-247-2262; Westjet ☎1-877-956-6982; Delta Airlines ☎1-800-325-1999; Porter Airlines ☎1-888-619-8622; United Airlines ☎1-800-538-2929; Continental Airlines ☎1-800-231-0856; US Airways ☎1-800-428-4322; Air Transat ☎1-866-391-6654.

By Train – Gare du Palais: 450 rue de la Gare-du-Palais; Gare de Sainte-Foy: 3255 chemin de la Gare. Information: ☎1-888-842-7245 or www.viarail.ca.

By Bus – Gare du Palais Terminal: 320 rue Abraham-Martin ☎418-525-3000; Sainte-Foy Terminal: 3001 chemin des Quatre-Bourgeois. Information: ☎418-650-0087. Orléans Express Coach Lines: ☎1-888-999-3977.

GETTING AROUND

PUBLIC TRANSPORTATION

A local bus service is provided by Réseau de transport de la Capitale (RTC) (*☎418-627-2511; www.rtcquebec.ca*). Regular buses operate from 5:30am–1am. Tickets may be purchased in local tobacco shops and newsstands (*$2.55*) or on board the bus ($3.25 *exact change required*). Day passes are also available (*$7.50/day*).

A bus terminal is located in the heart of Old Quebec at Place d'Youville. Several city buses also leave from the Train & Bus Station (Gare du Palais).

Cars – Rental car companies: Avis (at Hilton Hotel) ☎418-523-1075; Budget (in Old Quebec) ☎418-692-3660; Enterprise (at Delta Hotel) ☎418-523-6661; Hertz (in Old Quebec) ☎418-694-1224; Hertz (at the airport) ☎418-871-1571; or Discount cars and motorhome rentals at ☎418-522-3598 *(www.discountquebec.com)*. Streets are narrow and can be congested in the Old Town, Upper and Lower; it is easiest and most pleasant to visit these areas on foot. Visitors may wish to park in one of the city's designated parking areas.

Taxis – Taxis Coop Québec ☎418-525-5191; Taxis Québec ☎418-525-8123; Taxis Coop Sainte-Foy Sillery ☎418-653-7777.

GENERAL INFORMATION

Province of Quebec Tourism – Centre Infotouriste: 12 rue Sainte-Anne (across from Château Frontenac); open late Jun–Labor Day, daily 8:30am–8:30pm, rest of the year, daily 8:30am–5pm. *☎418-641-6290 and 1-877-783-1608; www.quebecregion.com)*.

Accommodation – *For specific listings of hotels, see Addresses.* Quebec City Tourism (*above*) can provide specific information about hotels, Bed & Breakfasts, chalets and campgrounds.

Local Press – in English: *The Chronicle-Telegraph* (*weekly*). French: *Le Journal de Québec, Le Soleil.*

Post Office – Open Mon–Fri 8am–7:30pm, Sat 9:30am–5pm. Upper Town Post Office (*near Château Frontenac*): 5 rue du Fort ☎418-694-6102.

CURRENCY EXCHANGE OFFICES

Caisse populaire Desjardins (Old Quebec) – 19 rue des Jardins ☎418-522-6806.

Montreal Currency Exchange – 12 rue Sainte-Anne ☎418-694-1014.

Montreal Currency Exchange – 46 rue du Petit-Champlain ☎418-694-0011.

Transchange International – 46 rue Saint Louis☎418-692-3586.

USEFUL NUMBERS

Police–Ambulance–Fire (emergency calls only) ☎911

Sûreté du Québec (Provincial Police) (toll-free) ☎310-4141 or *4141 (cell) or 418-623-6262

Directory Assistance ☎411

Alcoholics Anonymous: 8am–midnight ☎418-529-0015

Health Info daily, 24hrs, answering service provided by registered nurses ☎811

Brunet Drugstore, 57 rue Dalhousie (in the Old Port) ☎418-694-1262

Tourisme Québec 1-877-266-5687
Canadian Automobile Association (CAA/AAA) *(member services)* 1-800-686-9243 *(emergency road services 24hrs/day)* 1-800-222-4357
Road conditions 511
Weather (24hrs/day) 418-648-7766 or www.meteo.ec.gc.ca.
Entertainment – For current entertainment schedules, consult the free tourist publications *Québec Scope and Voilà Québec,* and the weekly cultural newspaper *Voir* (French), or review the arts and entertainment section of the newspapers (weekend editions). Tickets for major events may be purchased at the venue or through **Billetech** 418-643-8131.

Sports – Ice Hockey: Remparts de Québec (Canadian Hockey League), season Sept–Mar at the Colisée Pepsi: 250 Blvd Wilfrid-Hamel; 418-525-1212; www.remparts.qc.ca. **Baseball:** Capitales de Québec (Can-Am Baseball League) at Stade Municipal: 418-521-2255; www.capitalesdequebec.com. **Horse Racing:** Hippodrôme Trois Rivieres, 819-374-6734.

Shopping and Dining – The following streets lend themselves to strolling, window-shopping, and dining: Saint-Jean, Saint-Louis, Saint-Paul and Sainte-Anne, Petit-Champlain quarter, Côte de la Fabrique, Grande-Allée, 3rd Avenue, Cartier and Maguire.

Quebec City's religious institutions – An online map available from the Corporation du patrimoine et du tourisme religieux de Québec shows locations of religious sites. 418-694-0665; www.patrimoine-religieux.com.

During the 18C and 19C, the Old Port became the transit point for trade of raw materials needed by Britain. The loading of fur, cereal, and wood cargoes destined for foreign shores, the unloading of goods imported from France, the Antilles, England, and Scotland, and a major shipbuilding industry all contributed to the feverish activity along the shores of the St. Lawrence.

Expansion of the lumber trade with Britain, after Napoleon's embargo in the early 19C, enabled Quebec City to maintain a competitive position with Montreal until the mid-19C. Then the trade in raw timber, superseded by lumber, declined, and Quebec City gradually lost its position as center of production and trade in New France.

Competition from railroad companies located on the south shore of the St. Lawrence increased, and the impact of technological development in ocean-going vessels, enabling them to bypass the city and sail to Montreal, contributed to the city's decline. In addition, the section of the St. Lawrence between the two cities was dredged, allowing larger ships passage. A decrease in demand for wooden ships hastened the demise of the large shipbuilding industry.

To remedy the situation, Quebec City tried to attract various railroad companies, and built the Quebec City bridge to establish a rail link between the northern and southern shores, but to no avail. After 1850, Montreal became a center of trade, finance and industry, engendering a westward shift of population and economy. Quebec City experienced a short period of expansion with the footwear industry in the 1920s, but most jobs today are related to public administration, defense, and the service sector.

Population – Prior to the Conquest, the town's population was made up of French settlers. The influx of British and Irish immigrants in the early 19C led to an increase in the anglophone population, which numbered 41 percent in 1851, and reached 51 percent by 1861. Following Quebec City's economic decline, the population shift westward decreased the number of anglophones to 31.5 percent in 1871, and 10 percent in 1921. In 2011, anglophones accounted for just 1.45 percent of Quebec City's residents, thereby affirming the city's distinct francophone character.

Quebec City Today – Throughout the centuries, Quebec City has retained its role as a capital city and a bastion of French culture. The colonial French city is much more in evidence here than in Montreal. In the last three decades, the growth of the provincial government has given the city a new boost, and a bustling metropolis has developed outside the old walls. In contrast to the modern cities of North America, Quebec City has retained a cachet deeply reminiscent of Old World capitals.
The city's main event is its famous winter **Carnival**. Held in February, this festival attracts thousands of visitors. For 17 joyous days, Quebec City bustles with festivities that include a great parade, the construction of a magnificent ice palace, an ice sculpture contest, and canoe races over the partially frozen St. Lawrence. The activities are overseen by an enormous snowman, nicknamed Bonhomme Carnaval.

WALKING TOUR

1 BASSE-VILLE★★★ (Lower Town)

2.2km/1.4mi. Traced in green on the local map on p278–279.

From Dufferin Terrace, take the steep Frontenac stairway to the Lower Town. Follow Côte de la Montagne down the hill to the Casse-Cou stairway on the right descending to rue du Petit-Champlain. A funicular (cable car) also connects Dufferin Terrace (in front of Château Frontenac) to the Lower Town (in service year-round, daily 7:30am–11:30pm; $2.25; ☎418-692-1132; www.funiculaire-quebec.com).

Maison Louis-Jolliet (Louis-Jolliet House)

16 rue du Petit-Champlain.
Completed in 1683 according to plans by the French stonecutter and architect, Claude Baillif, this two-story stone structure was owned by Louis Jolliet, who discovered the Mississippi River along with Father Jacques Marquette in 1673. Since 1879 the house served as

A Brief History of Lower Town

The Lower Town began in the early 17C as a fur-trading post, established by Champlain on the area around his "Habitation." In 1636, the year following Champlain's death, the first city plans were drawn up. Between 1650 and 1662, more than 35 parcels of land were conceded to merchants who began building shops and residences around the Habitation and its adjoining square, then called the Market Place (*place du marché*). Limited space in the Lower Town inspired the residents to fill in parts of the shore northeast of the square and erect wharves along present-day rue Saint-Pierre.

In August 1682 a fire devastated the Lower Town. As a result of this disaster, building standards, such as the use of stone rather than wood, were imposed on new constructions, giving rise to the simple stone box construction visible throughout the quarter today.

As commerce, shipbuilding and port activities grew in the 19C, the area occupied by the Lower Town doubled in size. Port activity declined after 1860, severing the economic lifeline of the Lower Town and resulting in deterioration of the buildings over the next century. In 1967 the Quebec Government passed legislation to support restoration of Place Royale. The archeological and restoration work began in 1970 and continues today. The Lower Town's commercial vocation still marks the area, as evidenced in the market squares, wharves, and warehouses.

Rue du Petit-Champlain

© Gregory B. Gallagher / Michelin

the lower station for the funicular linking the Upper and Lower towns.

Rue du Petit-Champlain★

Extending along the foot of the cliff, this cobblestone pedestrian alley was developed in the 1680s. First known as rue De Meulles, the street was renamed rue du Petit-Champlain (Little Champlain Street) when the larger Blvd Champlain, situated parallel to it along the river, was created during the 19C. The early wooden dwellings along the street were inhabited by craftsmen and laborers until the 19C, when Irish immigrants who found work associated with the port moved into the district. Much of the neighborhood fell into decay in the early 20C as a result of the economic decline of the port. Recent restoration work carried out by a joint public and private effort has transformed the street into a festive district enlivened by restaurants, boutiques and art galleries. It is deemed the "oldest commercial district in North America."

▶ At the end of rue du Petit-Champlain, turn left onto Blvd Champlain (off map).

Maison Chevalier★ (Chevalier House)

Corner of rue du Marché-Champlain and Blvd Champlain, on Place Royale. Open Jul 12–Labor Day daily 10am–5pm. www.mcq.org. ✆418-646-3167 & 1-866-710-8031.

This three-story stone building occupies the site of the **Cul-de-Sac,** a natural port discovered by Champlain in 1603. The King's shipyards, originally established at the mouth of the St. Charles River, were moved here in 1745, but the basin was filled in during the mid-18C in an effort to enlarge the area of Lower Town.

The imposing structure is composed of three separate buildings. The west wing was built in 1752 for the wealthy merchant and shipowner, Jean-Baptiste Chevalier. The construction was so solid that the walls and foundation withstood bombardment by the British in 1759. However, the house was destroyed by fire and rebuilt in 1762.

Acquired by the Quebec Government in 1956 to serve as part of the Museum of Civilization, the Chevalier House underwent extensive interior renovations, and now features exhibits on traditional Quebec architecture and furniture.

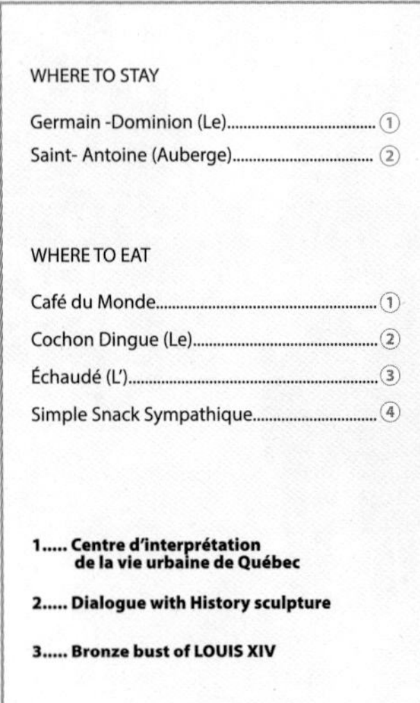

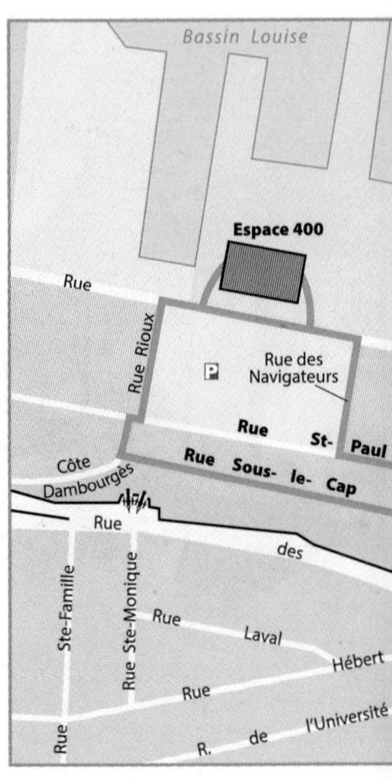

Continue to the corner of rue du Marché-Champlain and Blvd. Champlain to enjoy the superb **view★** of the imposing Château Frontenac, looming over the Lower Town.

▶ Return to the Maison Chevalier; turn right on rue Notre-Dame and right on rue Sous-le-Fort.

Batterie Royale (Royal Battery)

Rampart at the end of rue Sous-le-Fort and rue Saint-Pierre.

Constructed in 1691 at the request of Louis XIV, King of France, this thick, four-sided earthen rampart formed part of the fortifications designed to strengthen Quebec City's defenses against the British. Situated at the edge of the river, the battery suffered from the elements and was frequently in need of repair. Destroyed during the Conquest, the defense was not rebuilt. Instead, the British erected two warehouses and a wharf on the site. The royal battery was gradually buried and forgotten until two centuries later, when archeologists excavating the area unearthed it in 1972.

Today this historic rampart has been reconstructed, and replicas of 18C cannons are positioned in 10 of the 11 embrasures; the eleventh was left empty, because any gun set at such an angle, if ever it was fired, would have destroyed buildings along Rue Saint-Pierre. During the summer, visitors can see demonstrations of cannon operations during the French Regime.

▶ Turn right on rue Saint-Pierre.

Centre d'interprétation de la vie urbaine de Québec (Quebec City urban interpretation Centre)

20 rue St-Pierre. ☎418 692 4800. www.civuquebec.ca. 5$; children (age 12 and under) free.

An interactive center (**1**) about the history of Quebec, conceived for the 25th anniversary of Quebec city's inscription on the UNESCO World Heritage list. The impressive Augmented Reality exhibition puts visitors in the 3D world of the old city (there's also a demonstration on their website). They run GéoRallyes, which are fun tours of the city using GPS ($8, $4 for children, GPS rental $10, $20 for the family).

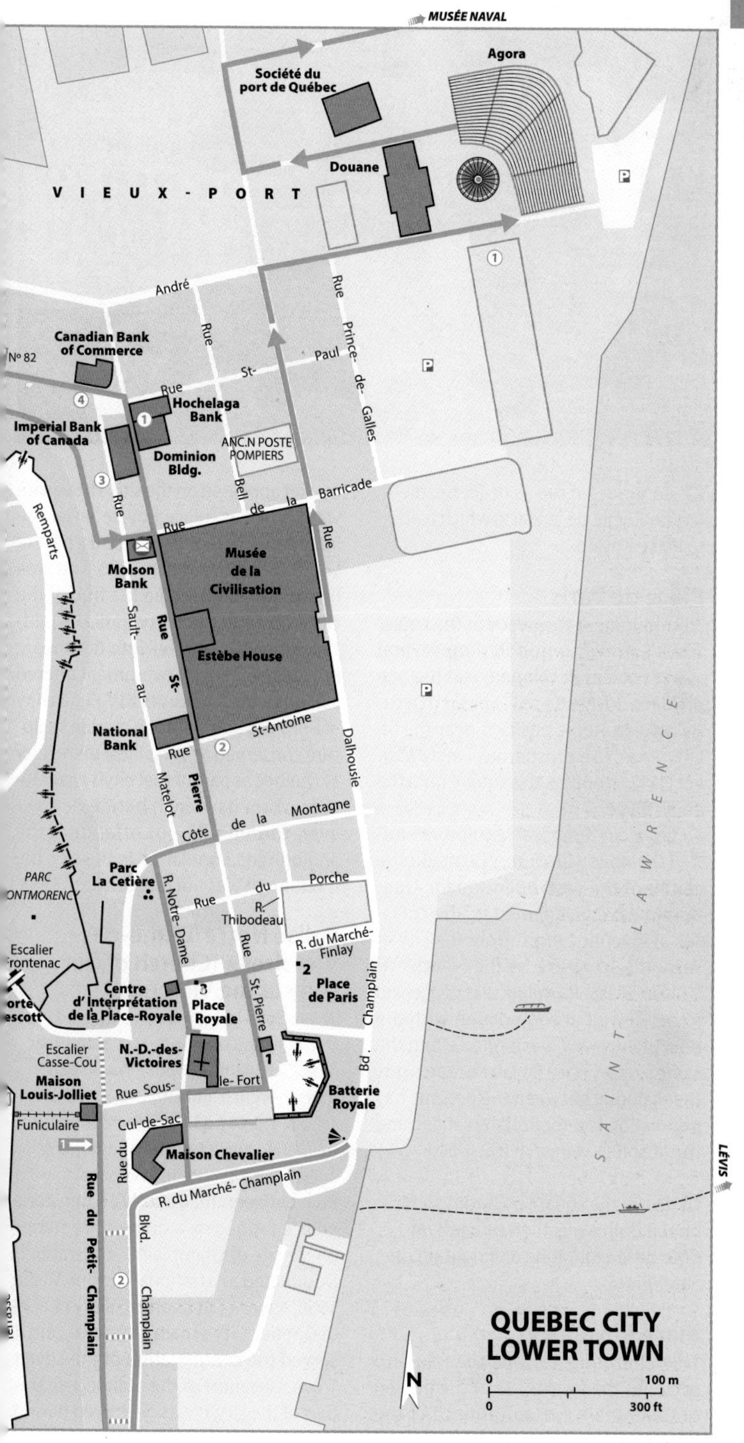
MUSÉE NAVAL
Agora
Société du port de Québec
Douane
VIEUX-PORT
André
Rue St-Paul
Rue Prince-de-Galles
Canadian Bank of Commerce
Nº 82
Hochelaga Bank
Imperial Bank of Canada
Dominion Bldg.
ANC.N POSTE POMPIERS
Rue de la Barricade
Rue Bell
Remparts
Molson Bank
Musée de la Civilisation
Estèbe House
Rue Sault-au-Matelot
Rue St-Pierre
National Bank
Rue St-Antoine
Dalhousie
Côte de la Montagne
Parc La Cetière
PARC MONTMORENCY
R. Notre-Dame
Rue du Porche
R. Thibodeau
R. du Marché-Finlay
Escalier Frontenac
Centre d'Interprétation de la Place-Royale
Place Royale
Place de Paris
Rue St-Pierre
Bd. Champlain
Escalier Casse-Cou
N.-D.-des-Victoires
Maison Louis-Jolliet
Rue Sous-le-Fort
Batterie Royale
Funiculaire
Cul-de-Sac
Maison Chevalier
Rue du
R. du Marché-Champlain
Rue du Petit-Champlain
Blvd. Champlain
SAINT LAURENCE
LÉVIS
QUEBEC CITY LOWER TOWN
N
0 100 m
0 300 ft

Batterie Royale
© Luc-Antoine Couturier / Quebec City Tourism

Continue on rue Saint-Pierre, then left on Ruelle de la Place, which leads to Place Royale.

Place de Paris

To supplement the needs of the Lower Town's growing population, several market places developed near the one on Place Royale (see opposite). Occupying a strategic position near the St. Lawrence, the prosperous Finlay Market (1817) stood on this square until the early 1950s.

Today, a contemporary sculpture entitled *Dialogue with History* (**2**) marks the center of the vast, open square. Quebecers have nicknamed it "the colossus of Quebec." A gift from the city of Paris, the sculpture, by the French artist Jean-Pierre Raynaud, was conceived to be viewed in conjunction with the bust of Louis XIV, positioned along the same axis on Place Royale; it represents the dialogue between the present-day population (symbolized by a mass) and the absolute monarch (the bust).

Leave the square by turning left on rue Dalhousie, then turn left on Côte de la Montagne and right on rue Saint-Pierre.

Place Royale★★

This charming cobblestone square occupies the former site of the garden of Champlain's "Habitation." As the town developed around the fortress, a market appeared on the site. The square was known as "place Royale" after the Intendant Champigny erected a bust of Louis XIV on the site in 1686. The area flourished and became the hub of the city's economic activity until the mid-19C, when the port fell into decline.

In 1928 the French Government offered a **bronze bust of Louis XIV** (**3**) (a copy of Bernini's original 1665 marble sculpture conserved at Versailles) to the City of Quebec as part of that city's program to reaffirm its French heritage. However, through fear of offending the anglophone population in the city, the monument was not erected until 1948.

Église Notre-Dame-des-Victoires★ (Church of Our Lady of the Victories)

32 rue Sous-le-Fort. Open May–mid-Oct, daily 9:30am–5pm; rest of the year, Mon–Sat 10am–7:30pm. Guided tours in French and English. 418-692-1650 & 418-692-2533, www.notredamedequebec.org/fetes-du-350e/horaire/eglise-notre-dame-des-victoires.

Built between 1688 and 1723, this stone edifice topped by a single spire stands on the site of Champlain's "Habitation." Designated as a National Historic Site in 1988, it was built as an auxiliary chapel of Quebec City's main cathedral, and it served the congregation of the Lower Town. Like most of the buildings in this part of the city, it was destroyed during the Conquest and rebuilt soon after.

The church was named in thanksgiving for two successful occasions on which Quebec City resisted the sieges of the British. Frescoes adorning the choir recall these victories: One in 1690, during which Admiral Phips' fleet was defeated by the troops of the Count de Frontenac, and the other in 1711, when most of Admiral Walker's fleet was shipwrecked during a storm. The model ship suspended in the nave represents the *Brézé,* a 17C vessel that carried French troops to Quebec. To the left of the reliquary in the left side chapel hangs a painting of St. Genevieve (1865) by Théophile Hamel. Located above the high altar, the magnificent **retable** (1878, David Ouellet) represents the fortified city.

Leave Place Royale by rue Notre-Dame.

Centre d'Interprétation de la Place-Royale

27 rue Notre-Dame. Open end Jun–early Sept, daily 9:30am–5pm; rest of the year, Tue–Sun 10am–5pm. Closed Dec 25. $7; children (age 16 and under) $2. 418-646-3167 or 1-866-710-8031 (no charge). www.mcq.org.

The interpretation center occupies two historic houses, one of which dates from 1682 and was the home of the merchant François Hazeur. Inside, there are three floors of exhibits examining the arrival and development of French and francophone civilization, through the history of the site. In the basement, in a fine vaulted limestone cellar dating from 1684, you will find numerous period costumes along with interpretative panels giving an insight into life in Place Royale in 1800. The upper floors deal with the subject of trade and the history of the area, starting with its Amerindian inhabitants.

Continue along rue Notre-Dame.

Parc La Cetière

Archeological excavations undertaken here in 1972 revealed the remains of foundations from structures dating back to 1685. Destroyed during the Conquest, the five stone houses of the block were rebuilt on the same foundations. However, a fire in 1948 and another in 1957 levelled the area. In the scant ruins exposed in the park, it is possible to distinguish an internal partition wall of one dwelling and the chimney base of another.

Take rue du Porche and turn right on rue Thibaudeau.

Rue Saint-Pierre★

During the 19C, this busy thoroughfare developed as Quebec's principal financial district. Numerous banks and insurance companies established their headquarters near or along this street.

Place-Royale

© Juliane Martini / Michelin

Among the noteworthy commercial buildings that have been preserved are the **National Bank** *(no. 71)*, built by J. F. Peachy in 1862; the former **Molson Bank** (*no. 105*), now occupied by the local post office; and **Imperial Bank of Canada** (*nos. 113–115*), which dates from 1913. Between rues Saint-Antoine and Saint-Jacques, note the low porte-cochère of the **Estèbe House**, part of the Museum of Civilization. The former **Hochelaga Bank** (*no. 132*) stands next to the **Dominion Building** (*no. 126*), Quebec City's first skyscraper. Dominating the corner of rues Saint-Paul and Saint-Pierre, the **Canadian Bank of Commerce** *(139 rue Saint-Pierre)* exemplifies the Beaux-Arts style in vogue at the turn of the 20C.

Continue along rue Saint-Paul.

Rue Saint-Paul★

Built directly on the wharves of the St. Charles River in 1816, this portion of rue Saint-Paul was widened in 1906. At that time, every building was demolished and replaced, with the exception of the old Renaud warehouse (*no. 82*), which had been built in a slightly recessed spot in 1875. Most of the houses on the south side of the street date back to 1850 and have been converted into antique shops, art galleries, and restaurants.

Turn right on rue des Navigateurs.

Espace 400

Bassin Louise.

This gleaming building was erected for the city's 400th anniversary in 2008 and played a key role in the celebrations, with attractions including the "Passengers" exhibition, which explored the history of Quebec's settlement with images, music, and personal stories. The building now hosts temporary exhibitions *(information from the tourist office)*.

Return to rue Saint-Paul by rue Rioux.

Rue Sous-le-Cap

Situated at the foot of the Cap Diamant rock, this narrow alley provided the only link between the Place Royale area and the smaller Faubourg Saint-Nicolas, located to the north, until the 19C. Before the development of rue Saint-Paul, the houses that now face that artery were turned toward rue Sous-le-Cap. Because the cramped design of the buildings made it impossible to build staircases inside the houses, outside sheds were constructed and connected to the main houses by footbridges spanning the street. These bridges are maintained by the owners.

Musée de la civilisation★★ (Museum of Civilization)

Main entrance on 85 rue Dalhousie. Open Jun 24–Labor Day, daily 9am–7pm; rest of the year, Tue–Sun 10am–5pm. $10. 418-643-2158. www.mcq.org.

Occupying the entire block between rues Saint-Antoine and de la Barricade, the award-winning structure by the prominent architect, **Moshe Safdie**—acclaimed for his Habitat '67 complex in Montreal and for the National Gallery of Canada in Ottawa—opened in the fall of 1988. Topped by a copper roof pierced by stylized dormers, the edifice consists of two sleek, angular masses of limestone accentuated by a glass campanile. Between the buildings, a monumental staircase leads to a terrace overlooking the **Estèbe House** (Maison Estèbe), a 1752 stone structure preserved and integrated into the museum as a reminder of the bond between past and present. Inside the spacious entrance hall note *La Débâcle*, a massive sculpture representing ice breaking up in spring, by the Montreal artist Astri Reusch.

The museum's stated purpose is to present life and culture in an open and objective manner in order to encourage visitors to examine their own traditions and values with respect to other cultures and civilizations. The museum's collection comprises some 250,000 objects and documents in several divisions (costumes and textiles, arts, ethnology). In addition to permanent exhibits illustrating such themes as thought, language, natural resources, the human body and society, the museum organizes four to six temporary exhibits throughout the year.

Le Temps des Québécois (People of Quebec, then and now)
Inspired by the impact of the past on Quebec's society today, this insightful permanent exhibition provides an opportunity for citizens to become reacquainted with their roots and for visitors from outside Quebec to understand the culture of the province. The objects presented evoke, with some nostalgia, the lives of the French since their arrival here four centuries ago and their struggles to build a new life in an unknown land. It presents an overview of the events that have shaped Quebec and that helped create what is now a unique society and identity in North America.

C'est Notre Histoire: Premières Nations et Inuit du XXIe siècle (This is Our Story: First Nations and Inuit in the 21C)
Following a recent fire, this permanent exhibition, which documents the history and culture of the First Nations and Inuit people who inhabit Quebec, was set to re-open in late summer 2015. The museum has collaborated with 11 First Nations of Quebec to create a powerful exhibit on what it means to be a Native today. Large screen projections interweave between Aboriginal contemporary art including over 400 objects from decorative baskets to rare clothing. The permanent exhibition is also divided into five themes such as "Who We Are Today," and "What Are Our Dreams For the Future?"

▶ Continue on rue Dalhousie.

Vieux-Port★ (Old Port)

Access at the corner of rues Dalhousie and Saint-André.

Covering an area of 33ha/81.5 acres, the port installations are located around the Pointe-à-Carcy where the St. Charles River joins the St. Lawrence. From the settlement of the colony until the mid-19C, the port played a major role in the development of Canada. Imported goods, exported furs and timber, and thousands of immigrants passed through this harbor. Activity declined in the second half of the 19C, and the port fell into disrepair. In the mid-1980s, a revitalization project financed by the federal government changed the face of the old port with the creation of the **Agora★** complex, which includes

Vieux-Port

© Luc-Antoine Couturier / Québec City Tourism

an open-air amphitheater, and a wide boardwalk along the river. A marina for several hundred pleasure boats complements the former maritime hub.

Édifice de la Douane (Customs House)

2 rue Saint-André.

Overlooking the St. Lawrence, the majestic Neoclassical structure (1856–60) was designed by the English architect, William Thomas. Cut stone masks and masonry dressing ornament the first floor windows. Fire ravaged the interior of the Customs House in 1864, and again in 1909, destroying the upper level and the dome. The door knocker on the main entrance originally hung on the first English Customs House established in Canada in 1793 in Quebec City. The building was completely restored between 1979 and 1981 and is still occupied by the administrative offices of the Customs Service. Today it is known as one of Quebec's most beautiful buildings and is part of the city's identity.

Société du port de Québec (Quebec Port Authority)

150 rue Dalhousie. ✆418-648-3640. www.portquebec.ca.

Designed by local architect Thomas R. Peacock, the building (1914) stands on the site where, in 1909, a fire destroyed a grain elevator and also damaged the Customs House.

Musée Naval

170 rue Dalhousie. ✆418-694-5387. www.mnq-nmq.org. Ask for information about opening times. No charge.

This little naval museum facing the St. Lawrence River regularly hosts exhibitions on the river's history and subjects like submarines and the vessels that were torpedoed in the waters around the Gaspé peninsula between 1942 and 1944.

2 HAUTE-VILLE★★★ (Upper Town)

2km/1.2mi. Route marked in green on the local map on p308–309.

Begin the tour at Place d'Armes.

Place d'Armes★★

Located outside the confines of the Fort Saint-Louis, the square (1620) originally served as grounds for drill exercises and parades. With the building of the citadel in the early 1900s, Place d'Armes lost its military function and became a public park. Today, this fine green square is bordered by prestigious buildings. At its center is the **Monument de la Foi** (**1**) (Monument of Faith), a Gothic Revival sculpture (1916, David Ouellet) standing atop a fountain; it commemo-

Château Frontenac

A "Barren Rock" Becomes the Heart of Old Quebec

Originally described as an "inhospitable rock, permanently unfit for habitation," the massive Cap Diamant (so named because it has the shape of a rough diamond) was the site of Champlain's strategic Fort Saint-Louis (1620), built in the center of a staked enclosure. Enlarged in 1629 and renamed **Château Saint-Louis**, the modest wood structure was replaced by a single-story building in 1692. At the request of the Count of Frontenac, it became the official residence of the governor of the colony. Rebuilt after sustaining severe damage during the Conquest, the edifice was razed by fire in 1834.

The Upper Town was not developed until a group of wealthy merchants, the Company of One Hundred Associates *(Compagnie des Cent-Associés)*, decided to increase settlement in the colony. The land belonging to a handful of seigneurs was redistributed, and the parcels owned by religious institutions were reduced. The first efforts to urbanize the Upper Town were initiated under Governor Montmagny's administration (1636–48). Though constrained by the hilly topography of the site, as well as the presence of vast lands belonging to institutions, Montmagny planned to erect a large, fortified city. The first houses appeared toward the end of the 17C, near the Place d'Armes and along rue Saint-Louis. However, the Ursuline, Augustine and Jesuit orders long refused to divide up their land plots, and the military opposed the construction of buildings near fortifications, thus halting any rapid development of the town. By the late 18C, the buildings still reflected the administrative and religious presence in the district.

During the 19C, a new and very elegant residential neighborhood evolved along rues Saint-Louis, Sainte-Ursule and d'Auteuil, and avenues Sainte-Geneviève and Saint-Denis, to be surpassed only in 1880, by the Grande Allée, sometimes known as the "Champs Élysées" of Quebec City. Today, the Upper Town forms the heart of Old Quebec (Vieux-Québec), and still functions as the city's administrative center.

rates the third centennial of the arrival of the Récollet missionaries in Quebec. The bas-reliefs represent the arrival, in 1615, of Father Dolbeau, the city's first priest, as well as the missionary work of the Récollets and the first Mass celebrated by that order.

Château Frontenac★★

Quebec City's most prominent landmark, the Fairmont Château Frontenac Hotel, is inextricably linked with the image of the old city. Named for Louis de Buade, Comte de Frontenac, governor of New France (1672–82, 1689–98), the hotel stands on the site of the Château Haldimand, also known as the "Vieux Château." Built in 1786 for Governor Frederick Haldimand, it faced the Château Saint-Louis, which housed the administrative services and reception rooms of the colonial government. In 1880, as part of the numerous beautification projects planned by Lord Dufferin, the idea of building a luxury hotel on the site finally took root.

Bruce Price (1843–1903), who was selected by the Canadian Pacific Railway to design the hotel, found inspiration in the château-style architecture that was very much in favor in the city. The American architect adapted an initial design by Eugène-Étienne Taché. He chose a horseshoe plan and selected copper roofing that contrasted with the brick walls adorned with cut stone. The French château style thus acquired a distinctly Canadian flavor which, up until the 1940s, became the trademark of railway companies and of Canada, a nation whose existence is closely linked to the development of railways from east to west.

Upon its opening in 1893 following completion of the Riverview wing, the hotel was an instant success. The Citadel wing (1899) and the Mont-Carmel

wing (1908), bordering the Governor's Garden, were added according to Price's plans. The Rue Saint-Louis wing was annexed a few years later. Between 1920 and 1924, an imposing tower was constructed, reinforcing the hotel's monumental appearance. With the recent addition of the beautifully integrated Claude Pratt wing (1993), the hotel boasts more than 600 rooms. The hotel's architects adorned the monument with coats of arms and emblems. The coat of arms of the Comte de Frontenac (rooster claws) can be seen above the porte cochère leading to rue Saint-Louis. Above the arch overlooking the courtyard is a stone engraved with the Maltese Cross; it is dated 1647 and was taken from Governor Montmagny's Château Saint-Louis. The interior was rebuilt after a fire in 1926. The entrance and reception halls, the Salon Verchères and the Champlain dining room are eloquent examples of the careful attention brought to the design of this jewel of Canadian architecture.

The prominence of Château Frontenac in the city's landscape can best be appreciated from high atop the citadel, from the Marie-Guyart Building observatory, or from the Lévis terrace.

Continue along rue Saint-Louis.

Ancien Palais de Justice★ (Old Courthouse)

12 rue Saint-Louis.

Now housing the Ministry of Finance, this Second Empire-style building (1887) was erected on the site of the former Récollet convent and church, both destroyed by fire during the late 18C. The façades were fashioned after 16C Loire Valley châteaux. On each side of the main entrance, note the coats of arms of Jacques Cartier and Samuel de Champlain. The capitals, adorned with fleurs de lis, add a French flair to the imposing edifice.

Maison Maillou★ (Maillou House)

17 rue Saint-Louis.

Located next to Château Frontenac, this large stone structure now houses the Quebec Chamber of Commerce. Built c.1736 by the architect Jean Maillou (1668–1753) as his personal residence, the single-story dwelling was heightened in 1767 and enlarged on its western side in 1799. During the early 19C, the house was occupied by the British army. The metal exterior shutters on

WHERE TO STAY

- Acadia (Hôtel) ..... (1)
- Belley (Hôtel) ..... (2)
- Château Bonne-Entente ..... (3)
- Fairmont Le Château Frontenac ..... (4)
- Manoir d'Auteuil ..... (5)
- Québec (Auberge internationale de) ..... (6)
- Saint-Louis (Auberge) ..... (7)
- Vieux-Québec (Hôtel du) ..... (8)

WHERE TO EAT

- Aux Anciens Canadiens ..... (1)
- Billig (Le) ..... (2)
- Bossus 620 (Les) ..... (3)
- Café Krieghoff ..... (4)
- Café-restaurant du Musée ..... (5)
- Ciel ..... (6)
- Continental (Le) ..... (7)
- Graffiti (Le) ..... (8)
- Hobbit Bistro ..... (9)
- Petit Coin Latin (Le) ..... (10)
- Portofino ..... (11)
- Pub Saint-Alexandre ..... (12)
- Saint-Amour (Le) ..... (13)
- Yu-Zu ..... (14)
- 47e Parallèle ..... (15)

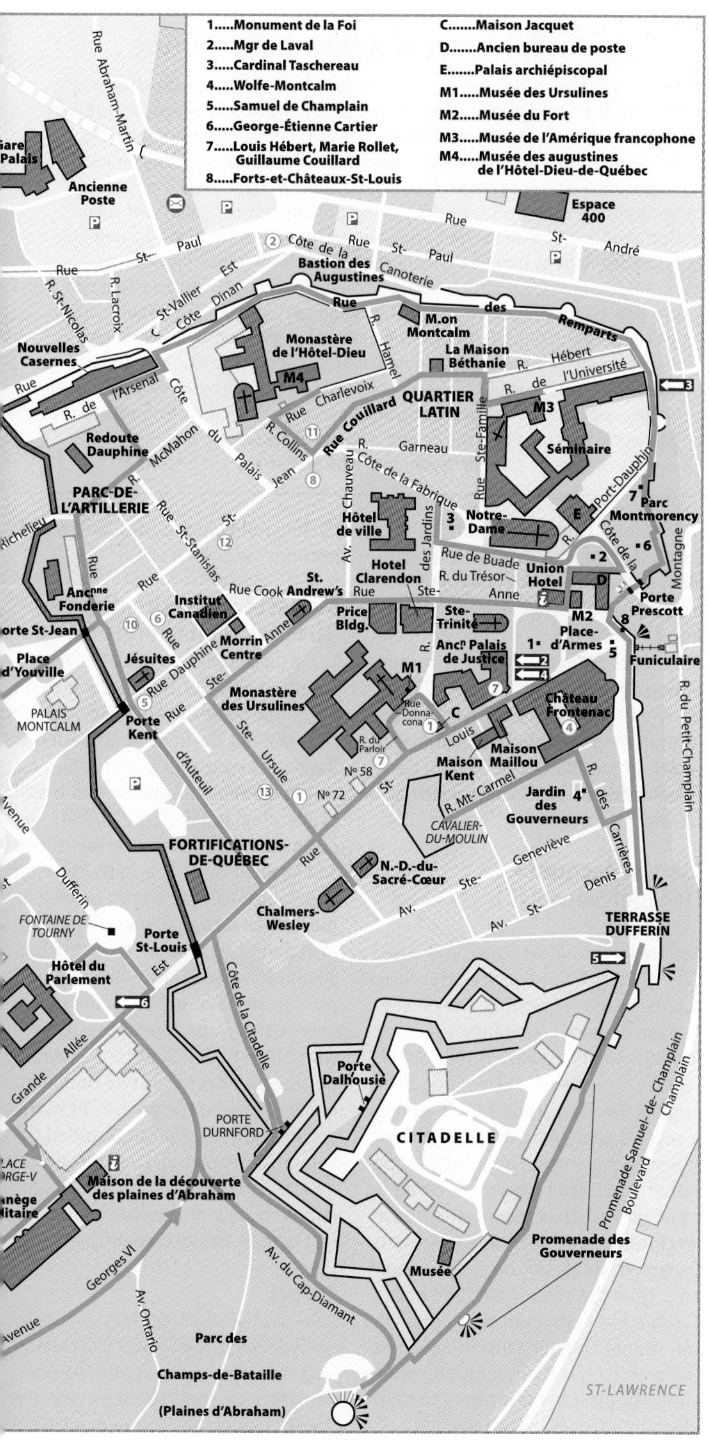
1.....Monument de la Foi
2.....Mgr de Laval
3.....Cardinal Taschereau
4.....Wolfe-Montcalm
5.....Samuel de Champlain
6.....George-Étienne Cartier
7.....Louis Hébert, Marie Rollet, Guillaume Couillard
8.....Forts-et-Châteaux-St-Louis
C.......Maison Jacquet
D.......Ancien bureau de poste
E.......Palais archiépiscopal
M1.....Musée des Ursulines
M2.....Musée du Fort
M3.....Musée de l'Amérique francophone
M4.....Musée des augustines de l'Hôtel-Dieu-de-Québec
Rue Abraham-Martin
Ancienne Poste
Espace 400
Rue St-Paul
Rue St-André
Côte de la Canoterie
Bastion des Augustines
Rue des Remparts
R. St-Nicolas
R. Lacroix
Côte Dinan
Rue St-Vallier Est
Nouvelles Casernes
Monastère de l'Hôtel-Dieu
M4
M.on Montcalm
La Maison Béthanie
R. Hamel
R. Hébert
R. de l'Université
QUARTIER LATIN
M3
Séminaire
Rue de l'Arsenal
Redoute Dauphine
McMahon
Côte du Palais
Rue Charlevoix
R. Collins
Rue Couillard
R. Garneau
Rue Ste-Famille
Côte de la Fabrique
Port-Dauphin
PARC-DE-L'ARTILLERIE
Richelieu
Rue St-Stanislas
Jean
Av. Chauveau
Hôtel de ville
R. des Jardins
Notre-Dame
Parc Montmorency
Côte de la Montagne
Rue de Buade
R. du Trésor
Union Hotel
Hotel Clarendon
St. Andrew's
Rue Cook
Rue Ste-Anne
Anc.ne Fonderie
Institut Canadien
Morrin Centre
Price Bldg.
Ste-Trinité
M2
Place-d'Armes
Porte Prescott
Funiculaire
Porte St-Jean
Place d'Youville
Jésuites
Rue Dauphine
Anc.n Palais de Justice
M1
Rue Donnacona
R. du Parloir
Château Frontenac
Monastère des Ursulines
Rue Louis
Maison Kent
Maison Maillou
PALAIS MONTCALM
Porte Kent
Rue d'Auteuil
Rue Ste-Ursule
No 58
No 72
R. Mt-Carmel
Jardin des Gouverneurs
R. des Carrières
R. du Petit-Champlain
CAVALIER-DU-MOULIN
Avenue Dufferin
FORTIFICATIONS-DE-QUÉBEC
Rue St-Louis
N.-D.-du-Sacré-Cœur
Av. Ste-Geneviève
Av. St-Denis
Chalmers-Wesley
TERRASSE DUFFERIN
FONTAINE DE TOURNY
Porte St-Louis
Hôtel du Parlement
Grande Allée Est
Côte de la Citadelle
Porte Dalhousie
PORTE DURNFORD
CITADELLE
Promenade Samuel-de-Champlain
Boulevard Champlain
Maison de la découverte des plaines d'Abraham
Avenue Georges VI
Av. Ontario
Av. du Cap-Diamant
Musée
Promenade des Gouverneurs
Parc des Champs-de-Bataille
(Plaines d'Abraham)
ST-LAWRENCE

An Epicenter of Anglophone Culture

The Morrin Centre (*44 Chaussée des Écossais in the Old City; open mid-May–Sept 5; guided tours daily 1pm–6pm, (in French and English), rest of year group tours by appointment. $8.75 418-694-9147; www.morrin.org)* fosters English-speaking culture in Quebec City, shares it with the French-speaking population and tourists, and encourages cultural exchanges in French and English. The center offers a range of activities including library services (open year-round Tue and Thu noon–8pm, Wed, Fri, Sun noon–4pm, and Sat 10am–5pm, guided tours, readings by prominent authors, discussions on stimulating topics, writing workshops, poetry classes, and more. Tours begin with a descent into the dark prison cells of the Quebec City Common Gaol (1813–68). There you will understand the daily lives of criminals and political prisoners who were incarcerated (and sometimes hanged) in this building. The tour also explores the anglo-Protestant life of Morrin College (1868–c.1900) by visiting the former College Hall, classroom for classics, and science lab. The role of learned societies in the 19C is examined in the beautiful library of the Literary and Historical Society of Quebec. Complete your tour with English tea and biscuits.

the windows date from this period. Carefully restored in 1964, the Maillou house constitutes a fine traditional urban ensemble typical of the 1800s. At no. 25, the offices of the Consulate General of France occupy the former **Maison Kent** (Kent House). Dating back to the 18C, this large white structure adorned with bright blue trim was rebuilt in the 1830s. The Duke of Kent, father of Queen Victoria, is said to have resided here from 1792 through 1794.

Maison Jacquet★ (Jacquet House) (C)

34 rue Saint-Louis.

Reputedly the oldest house in Quebec City, this small one-story structure, topped by a steep red roof, was erected on land acquired by François Jacquet from the Ursuline Nuns in 1674. Architect François de la Jouë enlarged the original dwelling around 1690, adding a second story. The addition to the side was constructed in 1820. Philippe Aubert de Gaspé lived in the house from 1815 to 1824, giving the house its current name, Maison des Anciens Canadiens (home of the early Canadians), from the title of his 1863 novel. Today a fine restaurant specializing in traditional Quebec cuisine occupies the premises. It is arguably the most authentic place in the province to sample traditional Québécois food.

Turn right onto rue des Jardins and left onto rue Donnacona.

Monastère des Ursulines★ (Ursuline Monastery)

12 rue Donnacona. 418-694-0694.

Founded in 1639 by Madame de la Peltrie and Marie Guyart (mère Marie de l'Incarnation), the Ursuline Monastery is the oldest educational institution for young women in America and is still in operation today. Begun in 1641, the complex was devastated by fire in 1650 and again in 1686. The Saint-Augustin and Sainte-Famille wings, as well as the kitchen area that links them, were built during a period of reconstruction lasting from 1685 through 1715, and provide the basic outline for the square inner courtyard. The Sainte-Famille wing's steeply pitched roof exemplifies the architectural style dominant under the French Regime. In 1836, the architect Thomas Baillairgé added the Sainte-Angèle wing. Despite several new constructions during the 20C, the imposing gray complex has retained its vast garden and an orchard.

Chapel

12 rue Donnacona. Open May–Nov daily 10am–11:30am, 1pm–4:30pm (closed Sun –Mon 9am–1pm). free. 418-694-0694.

Replacing an early 18C structure, the current chapel (1902) is designed in the

eclectic style characteristic of religious architecture in Quebec at the turn of the 19C. The stair-turret visible at the back of the church is reminiscent of château-style architecture. It was added in 1889 and survived the demolition of the former chapel.

The interior is composed of two sections: The "exterior chapel," where sat the lay faithful; and the "interior chapel" used by the cloistered nuns. The stunning interior **decoration★★** was taken from the 18C chapel and beautifully preserved, including the pulpit and sounding board surmounted by a trumpeting angel; the side retable dedicated to the Sacred Heart; and the main retable, a fine example of wood carving executed in the Louis XIV style, in the shape of a triumphal arch. These ornaments, as well as the high altar, were created between 1726 and 1736 under the supervision of the famed Quebec sculptor Pierre-Noël Levasseur. The sculptures are embellished with fine gilding applied by the Ursuline nuns, who maintained a gilding workshop for over two centuries to supply the needs of their order. The sculpted decor found in this chapel is truly unique: Figures of St. Augustine (*left niche*), St. Ursula (*right niche*) and St. Joseph (*upper niche*) represent the epitome of the art of woodcarving in Quebec. The vast nuns' choir, with its stalls and galleries, is surmounted by a wooden vault adorned with cupolas. Most of the paintings decorating the chapel were acquired in Paris around 1820 by Abbot Louis-Phillipe Desjardins (1753–1833), formerly the chaplain for the Ursulines. On the right side of the nave hangs *The Parable of the Ten Virgins* by Pietro Da Cortona. On the reverse side of the façade, note the painting by Philippe de Champaigne, *Jesus in the home of Simon the Pharisian.* The nuns' choir features an anonymous work painted in France around 1670, entitled *France bringing Faith to the Hurons of New-France.*

Located on the north side, a commemorative chapel houses the tomb of Marie de l'Incarnation (d. 1672), who was beatified in 1980.

Musée des Ursulines★★ (Ursuline Museum) (M1)

12 rue Donnacona. Open May–Sept, Tue–Sun 10am–5pm, rest of the year, Tue–Sun 1–5pm. ⊕$8. ☏418-694-0694. www.museedesursulines.com.

Since 1979, this remarkable museum has occupied the former site of the small house belonging to the order's benefactor, Madame de la Peltrie. Representing the occupations and talents of the Ursuline nuns, the collection includes works of art, archival documents, decorative arts, indigenous art, and other materials tracing the heritage of the community from 1639 (the Ursulines' arrival in Quebec) through to 1759 (the British Conquest).

The historical introduction offered in the first room on the museum's main floor immerses the visitor in that period's social and religious context. The second room, containing cabinets and various personal items, re-creates the living quarters of Madame de la Peltrie. Handicrafts on view here illustrate the social and educational influences that the Ursuline sisters had on the young French girls of the time, and the cultural exchanges that occurred between the nuns and the First Nations (Marie de l'Incarnation completed the first Iroquois and Algonquian dictionaries).

On the second floor, a room dedicated to monastic life offers a glance at the organization and architecture of the first monastery—an Ursuline's cell, chapel, refectory—through such items as furniture, religious costumes and kitchen utensils. On the same floor, the last room features gilding and glorious **embroideries**, two art forms for which the Ursuline nuns were renowned. Religious art in the collection include altar frontals and ecclesiastic vestments from the 17C and 18C, delicately embroidered with gold and silver threads.

▶ Return to rue Saint Louis by rue du Parloir and turn right.

Across from no. 58, on rue du Corps-de-Garde, a cannonball is exposed in the roots of a tree. The wall of the Cavalier-

du-Moulin park rises in the background. At no. 72, a plaque attests that General Montgomery's remains were brought here after the failed attack on Quebec City by Americans in 1775–76.

Turn left on rue Sainte-Ursule.

Église Unie Saint-Pierre (Chalmers-Wesley United Church)

78 rue Sainte-Ursule. Open late Jun–late Aug, daily 9am–8pm for guided tours in English and French (on Sunday, English Mass at 11:15am and French Mass at 9:15am). 418-692-0431.

Two Protestant congregations, one francophone, the other anglophone, share this Gothic Revival structure (1853, J. Wells). Staggered buttresses flank the slender steeple. Inside, note the superb stained-glass windows dating from 1909, and the elaborate woodwork adorning the apse and the pews. The early 19C organ was restored in 1985, and concerts are presented on Sundays at 6pm during summer.

Across the street stands the **Sanctuaire de Notre-Dame-du-Sacré-Cœur** (*no.71*), built by F. X. Berlinguet in 1910. The sanctuary is a replica of the Gothic chapel dedicated to Our Lady of the Sacred Heart at Issoudun, in France.

Backtrack on rue Sainte-Ursule past rue Saint-Louis.

On the northwest corner of rues Saint-Louis and Sainte-Ursule stood the first city hall of Quebec City, founded in 1833. When the present City Hall opened in 1896, combining under one roof the administrative and judicial offices for the city, row houses were erected by David Ouellet along rue Sainte-Ursule (*nos. 60–68*), lending the street a picturesque appearance.

Continue to the intersection with rue Sainte-Anne, turn right and continue to the intersection with rue Cook.

St. Andrew's Presbyterian Church

106 rue Sainte-Anne. Open Jul–Aug Mon–Fri 10am–4pm. A bilingual guide shows visitors around the church. English Mass Sun 11am. 418-694-1347. www.standrewsquebec.ca

Built in 1810 for Presbyterian Scots in Quebec City, the church was enlarged in 1823. Its steeple recalls the one found on the Holy Trinity Anglican Cathedral (*opposite*). Initially, the congregation consisted almost entirely of the Fraser Highlanders, a battalion in General Wolfe's army of 1759.

Continue along rue Sainte-Anne.

Price Building★

65 rue Sainte-Anne.

Quebec City's first skyscraper rises conspicuously over the Upper Town. Designed by Montreal architects, Ross and MacDonald, it was built in 1930 to house the head office of Price Brothers, famed for introducing the pulp and paper industry to the Saguenay region. The 16-story building stands on a narrow piece of land some 24m/78ft wide. Its profile resembles a ziggurat, a pyramid with a series of upward steps. Like numerous other North American corporations at that time, Price Brothers selected the Art Deco style, integrating embellishments that reflected its Canadian origin (pinecones, squirrels, aboriginals) and its business activities (lumber and paper). In order that the building blend in with the old city, the company opted for a pavilion roof with copper covering.

In the entrance hall, bas-reliefs and copper doors (entrance and elevator) combine to produce a fine Art Deco ensemble. The building has housed municipal offices since 1984.

Hotel Clarendon

57 rue Sainte-Anne.

In 1858, Charles Baillairgé erected two houses here for a printer named Desbarats. The property was converted into a hotel in 1875. The following year, an Art Deco entrance pavilion was annexed.

In the entrance hall, two large bronze *torchères* (tall light stands) provide rare examples of the Art Nouveau influence in Quebec.

La Cathédrale de la Sainte-Trinity★ (The Anglican Cathedral of the Holy Trinity)

31 rue des Jardins. Open mid-May–mid-Oct, Mon–Sat 10am–5pm; rest of year and Sun 12:30pm–5pm. English choral Eucharist Sun 11am and French Mass Sun 9:30am. English Mass Thu at noon. ♿ ☎418-692-2193. www.cathedral.ca

Designed in 1799 by the army engineers Major Robe and Captain Hall, this edifice was the first Anglican (Episcopal) cathedral to be built outside the British Isles. Completed in 1804, the building is modeled on the Church of St. Martin-in-the-Fields, in London (England), designed by the architect James Gibbs. Erected on part of a property formerly owned by the Récollet Order, the cathedral features a simple floor plan. The central nave, side aisles, and lateral galleries dotted with a double row of windows contribute to the church's innovative design. The façade is turned away from Place d'Armes so that the chancel faces east, in the time-honored Christian tradition. The church steeple, which contains an eight-bell peal, is actually a meter or so higher than that of the Our Lady of Quebec Basilica. The pitch of the roof had to be raised approximately 3m/10ft in 1816, since its low grade proved too weak to sustain massive snowfall. As a result, the pediment appears somewhat heavier and the great height of the massive church tower seems slightly diminished. A Celtic cross fashioned in AD 542 marks the church entrance.

Interior

The wooden vault spanning the nave simulates stucco coffers. The Ionic columns and pilasters were sculpted by the Montrealer, Louis-Amable Quévillon, who was nearly excommunicated for having participated in the interior decoration of a non-Catholic church. King George III provided the funding for the cathedral, and sent English oak from the Royal Forests of Windsor for the pews. On the left side of the tribune is a royal pew reserved for the British monarch, head of the Church of England, or his/her representative. To the right of the altar, the bishop's chair was carved out of wood from an elm tree that had flourished in the churchyard for some two hundred years. The cathedral treasure, which includes silverware donated by George III, is exhibited on special occasions.

To the right of the cathedral stand a large Neoclassical rectory (1841) and a church hall (1890). In summer, artists gather in the courtyard.

▶ Return to rue Sainte-Anne.

In the quaint pedestrian street of **rue du Trésor**, artists exhibit sketches and engravings depicting typical scenes of the city.

Ancien Hôtel Union (Former Union Hotel)

Facing the Place d'Armes, the large structure (1805–12) exemplifies Palladian-style architecture, characterized by a simple plan, a massive shape, sash windows, and a low-pitched roof. It is now the information centre.

Musée du Fort★ (Fort Museum) (M2)

10 rue Sainte-Anne. Open Feb–Mar & Nov Thu–Sun 11am–4pm; Apr–Oct daily 10am–5pm. $8. ☎418-692-2175. www.museedufort.com.

Erected in 1840, this square white building topped by a gray roof was modified in 1898, giving it a whimsical appearance. An excellently narrated sound-and-light presentation, (*30min*) cast upon a large-scale model of Quebec during the 18C traces the city's military and civil history from its foundation in 1608 until the American invasion of 1775–76. The maquette (model) provides a unique perspective of the city's topography.

▶ Turn left on rue du Fort and continue to rue Buade.

Ancien bureau de poste (Old Post Office) (D)

Entrance on 5 rue du Fort. Open Mon–Fri 8am–7:30pm, Sat 9:30am–5pm. ♿ ☎418-694-6102.

Constructed as the city's main post office in 1873, this edifice presents an imposing façade adorned with Beaux-Arts embellishments. Faced with decorated cut stone, it was enlarged to more than twice its original size in 1914. Above the entrance, a carved bas-relief advertises the Chien d'Or (The Golden Dog), an inn that occupied the site until 1837. The building was renamed the Louis S. St-Laurent Building in honor of the former Canadian Prime Minister and continues to operate as a working post office. Inside, the Canadian Parks Service presents exhibits on the development of historical and natural sites in Canada.

Monsignor de Laval Monument (2)

In front of the old post office stands a monument to Monsignor François de Montmorency-Laval (1623–1708), first bishop of Quebec. It was erected in 1908, as part of the celebrations marking the bicentennial of his death. Installation of the monument, designed by sculptor Louis-Philippe Hébert, necessitated the demolition of an entire block of eight houses, thus creating an imposing public square.

Rue Buade ends at the **Charles-Baillairgé Stairway** (1893), named in honor of the architect who, after an illustrious career designing buildings, devoted his talents to civil engineering. This cast-iron stairway is one of several Baillairgé designed for the city.

▶ Descend the stairs and continue up Côte de la Montagne.

From the foot of the stairs, note the monumental false front of the old post office dominating the Lower Town.

Palais archiépiscopal (Archbishop's Palace) (E)

2 rue Port-Dauphin.

This Neoclassical structure (1847) replaced the first archbishop's residence, erected in the late 17C in Montmorency Park. As part of Lord Dufferin's beautification projects in the late 19C, a false front was erected toward the Côte de la Montagne, making the building visible from the St. Lawrence River. The original façade of the large edifice dominates the main courtyard, leading to the old seminary.

▶ Return to rue Buade.

Facing the Beaux-Arts style presbytery (*16 rue Buade at the corner of rue du Fort*), a plaque draws attention to the foundations of a funeral chapel thought to contain the tomb of Samuel de Champlain. There are at least ten theories regarding the possible location of Champlain's tomb.

Basilique-cathédrale Notre-Dame-de-Québec★ (Basilica-Cathedral of Our Lady of Quebec)

20 rue de la Baude. Open May–mid-Oct, daily 7am–8:30pm; rest of the year, daily 7am–4pm. Guided tours (French and English) plus many events year-round: Check calendar on website. ♿ ☎418-694-0665. www.notredamedequebec.org/en/.

Declared a historical monument in 1966, the basilica is the most European of Quebec's churches. Its complex architectural history has yielded an impressive structure that bears witness to the contributions of three generations of Quebec's renowned family of architects.

Early construction

In 1674, following a papal order creating the Diocese of Quebec, the original structure here (1650) was consecrated as a cathedral. Under the direction of François de Laval, who had been appointed Bishop of New France, the building was enlarged and renovated. In 1743, Gaspard Chaussegros de Léry, the royal engineer, enlarged the apse, raised the nave and added to it a clerestory and side aisles by opening arches

into the walls of the old nave, leaving thick pillars in place. A new façade was built overlooking the market square, now known as Place de l'Hôtel de Ville. Completed in 1749, the structure was destroyed during the Conquest of 1759.

A Baillairgé Masterpiece

Reconstruction of the church took place between 1768 and 1771 and was modeled on Chaussegros de Léry's work. Jean Baillairgé (1726–1805), the first in the renowned Baillairgé family of joiners, painters, sculptors, and architects, rebuilt the south belfry with its two openwork drums surmounted by domes. In 1787, after studying at the Royal Academy of Painting and Sculpture in Paris, his son, François Baillairgé (1759–1830), undertook the task of decorating the interior. He designed the plans for the magnificent baldachin, executed by André Vermare.

François' son, Thomas Baillairgé (1791–1859), continued his father's work and, in 1843, designed the monumental Neoclassical façade whose construction was interrupted two years later when the base of the first of two projected towers showed signs of weakness. Charles Baillairgé (1826–1906), whose father was a cousin of Thomas, designed the plans in 1857 for the brass-plated cast-iron gate that encloses the porch, which enabled him to declare that the building of the monument was indeed a family effort. The church was consecrated as a basilica in 1874 to emphasize its history and status as one of Canada's most important churches.

After the structure was destroyed by fire on Dec 22, 1922, the authorities decided to restore it to its original appearance in order to retain the familiar image of "Monsignor de Laval's church." The current monument was built between 1923 and 1925 from old plans and photographs.

Interior

Re-created after the fire in 1922, the interior evokes the principal features of the 18C cathedral despite the use of concrete, steel, and plaster. Immediately upon entering, the eye is drawn to the light and delicately sweeping baldachin executed by André Vermare. The luminous stained-glass windows of the upper level are French in origin and represent saints, evangelists, and archangels. Those of the lower level are German and American and recall important events in the life of the Virgin Mary. The cathedral crypt (*guided tour only, available mid-Jun–Sept Tue – Fri 1pm–6pm; Sat 10:30am–5pm; Sun 1pm–5pm; $5, inquire at the reception desk*) houses the sepulchres of Quebec's bishops and of some of the governors of New France. The lamp in the chapel on the right near the entrance to the crypt was a gift from Louis XIV. The Casavant organ of 5,239 pipes is flanked by statues of shepherds, one reading (symbolizing inspiration), and the other playing an instrument (symbolizing improvisation). In 1993, the remains of Monsignor de Laval were interred in a small commemorative chapel (*right side aisle*); a small display to the right of the choir presents his life and works.

Place de l'Hôtel de Ville

This large open square, designed in conjunction with the cathedral in 1650, became the principal marketplace of the Upper Town in the 18C. Its commercial vocation ended in the late 1880s with the construction of City Hall. Placed in its center, the 1923 **Cardinal Taschereau monument** (**3**) by André Vermare is dedicated to the first Canadian cardinal. The bas-reliefs represent the institution of the Forty Hour Prayer in the diocese (*facing the cathedral*), the career of the Superior of the Quebec Seminary (*facing rue des Jardins*) and the Cardinal aiding Irish victims of the typhoid epidemic at Grosse-Île, in 1848 (*facing rue Buade*).

Hôtel de Ville de Québec (Quebec City Hall)

2 rue des Jardins.

The majestic structure stands on land formerly belonging to the Jesuit Order, who erected a college and church on this site in the very center of Old Que-

bec, in 1666. The college was demolished in 1877, to be replaced by the City Hall, built in 1896 according to plans by Georges-Émile Tanguay. Stylistically, Tanguay's building presents a curious blend of the Second Empire and French Château styles, embellished with Richardsonian Romanesque detailing.

3 QUARTIER LATIN★

See map pp308–309.

Located north of the basilica, Quebec City's **Quartier Latin★** (Latin Quarter) is the oldest residential district in the Upper Town. Formerly belonging to the Quebec Seminary, the land was divided up during the late 17C, while the parceling of other vast properties, belonging to the Ursulines, Jesuits, and Augustinian nuns did not commence until a century later. The narrow streets criss-crossing the quarter are remnants of the passageways that once connected these large holdings. Between 1820 and 1830, the craftsmen who initially populated the district gave way to a French-speaking bourgeoisie, eager to reside in the vicinity of the seminary and its clergy. After World War II, influences from the Parisian existentialist movement gave rise to a bohemian student life in Old Quebec at the same time that Laval University was expanding into the district, occupying dozens of old houses. Although still inhabited by a few longtime residents and families, the neighborhood today caters mainly to students.

Séminaire de Québec★★ (Quebec Seminary)

This influential institution was founded in 1663 by Monsignor de Laval to train and recruit priests destined to work in the newly created parishes of New France. In 1852 the seminary was formally granted a university (Université Laval), Canada's first francophone higher education institution. In 1950 Laval University moved to a new campus in Sainte-Foy but the university's school of architecture remained here, and today occupies several of the structures in the complex.

Vieux-Séminaire (Old Seminary)

Entrance at 1 Côte de la Fabrique (Welcome Pavilion). Guided tours of the seminary available in summer (includes admission to the Museum of French America). ♿ P ($8/day) 418-646-1217.

The old seminary comprises three sections arranged around an inner court, as is typical of French monastic architecture in the 16C and 17C. The visitor enters by a porte cochère framed by a portal designed by François Baillairgé and bearing the Seminary's coat of arms. Traditional building crafts were employed in the construction of the

Séminaire de Québec above Rue Saint-Paul

three wings, creating a stylistically homogeneous ensemble.

The **Procure Wing** was built between 1678 and 1681 to house the Grand Séminaire; its walls and vaults survived fires in 1701, 1705, and 1865. After the last fire, the building was raised by one stone story. The sundial on the façade bears the inscription *Nos jours passent comme une ombre* ("Our days pass like a shadow"). Within this wing is the marvelous **Monsignor Olivier Briand Chapel**★, noteworthy for the fine wood paneling adorning its walls. Executed by the master sculptor Pierre Émond in 1785, the décor exemplifies two distinct styles—Louis XIII and Louis XV. Émond also designed the olive branches framing the engraving of the *Marriage of the Virgin* that dominates the altar piece.

To the right, the **Parloirs Wing** or former Petit Séminaire dates from 1823, as does the **Congregation Wing**, where the porte cochère is located. The **Congregational Chapel** here, a low-ceilinged shrine devoted to the Virgin Mary, is divided into three naves, separated by two rows of Ionic columns. The main altar, flanked by two similar columns, is surmounted by a gilded **statue**★ of the Virgin, one of the few known wood carvings crafted by the hand of the architect, Thomas Baillairgé.

Musée de l'Amérique Francophone (Museum of French America) (M3)

Main entrance at 2 Côte de la Fabrique (Welcome Pavilion). Open Tue–Sun 10am–5pm. Closed Dec 25. $8. 418-692-2843 or 1-866-710-8031. www.mcq.org.

Operated since 1995 as part of the Museum of Civilization, the collections of the Museum of French America encompass objects and works of art reflecting France's rich historic, cultural and social heritage in North America. The museum's holdings include an extensive archive of historical documents; some 195,000 rare books and journals; European paintings from the 15C–19C and Canadian paintings from the 18C–20C; gold and silver ware for religious and domestic use; and extensive collections of textiles, furniture, scientific instruments, stamps and coins, birds and insects as well as botanical, zoological and geological specimens.

The collections are housed in three buildings, of which **Welcome Pavilion** serves as the museum's reception and information center and temporary exhibition space. The second building occupies the seminary's former outer chapel. Erected between 1888 and 1900 according to plans by J. F. Peachy, the chapel features an interior modeled after the 19C Trinity Church in Paris. The Quebec version, made of galvanized steel painted in trompe-l'oeil, provided better protection against fire. In addition to beautiful pieces of silverware by François Ranvoyzé, Guillaume Loir, Laurent Amiot and others, the chapel contains one of the most important collections of **relics**★ outside St. Peter's in Rome. The 16 gilded reliquary busts of the Apostles were carved by Louis Jobin. The columns around the chapel are adorned with representations of the Seven Sacraments, and each lamp symbolizes a gift of the Holy Spirit.

The third structure, the **Jérôme Demers Pavilion**, houses two permanent exhibits. The first, dedicated to the French experience in North America, presents the seven major francophone communities on the continent: Quebec, Acadia, Louisiana, French Ontario, Métis, and French-American communities in the West and in New England. The second exhibit incorporates the highlights of the seminary's impressive collections to underscore the institution's religious, cultural, and educational mission. Temporary exhibits here invite discovery of Quebec by its provincial arts, crafts, folklore, and history.

Leave the museum by rue de l'Université and turn right on rue Sainte-Famille. Take rue Couillard on the left.

Charming **rue Couillard** received its name in the 18C, in honor of the sailor, Guillaume Couillard (1591–1663), son-

in-law and heir of the lands of Louis Hébert. Its sinuous path leads past the former Hospice de la Miséricorde (*no. 14*), built between 1878 and 1880 for the Sisters of the Good Shepherd.

Maison Béthanie

14 rue Couillard, between rue Ferland and rue Saint-Flavien. ♿ ✆418-694-0243.

This remarkable Gothic Revival structure, with its brick walls pierced by ogive windows, serves as the main building of the **Maison Béthanie★** (1878, David Ouellet). Until its closing in 2014 it served as the Good Shepherd Museum, which chronicled the history of the Good Shepherd community, a lay order founded in 1850 by Marie Fitzbach (later known as Marie-du-Sacré-Cœur). The collection has been relocated to Sainte-Foy. The former house of the Mercy Hospice, a caring institution founded and operated by the Sœurs du Bon-Pasteur (Sisters of the Good Shepherd) was a refuge and halfway house for young women.

▶ Turn right on rue Collins and continue to rue Charlevoix.

Monastère de l'Hôtel-Dieu de Québec (Augustine Monastery)

32 rue Charlevoix.

The founding sisters of the Augustinian Hospitallers of Quebec, Marie Guenet de Saint-Ignace, Marie Forestier de Saint-Bonaventure and Anne Le Cointre de Saint-Bernard, took up residence in 1640 in a makeshift hospital located next to the Jesuit mission, in Sillery. In 1644, upon completion of the monastery, the nuns moved to this site in the old city. The first hospital erected by the nuns was made of wood. In 1695, François de la Jouë enlarged the structure by annexing a stone building; the two structures now form part of the convent and can be clearly seen from the garden. The hospital underwent several expansions during the 19C and 20C, reaching its current capacity in 1960.

Musée des Augustines de l'Hôtel-Dieu de Québec★ (Augustine Museum) (M4)

Open year-round except major holidays. Guided tours in French and English. ⊕$10. ♿ ✆418-692-2492. www.augustines.ca/en.

A complete restoration of this historic property was completed in the summer of 2015, unveiling a new contemporary museum with state-of-the-art displays. The location also offers an array of services, among them a hotel, archive center, health and wellness center, restaurant, and boutique. Opened in 1958, the museum presents a collection of objects and artworks tracing the Augustinian nuns' history and heritage in New France over four centuries. It includes one of the foremost collections of New France-era paintings in Quebec, including portraits of Louis XIV and the Intendant Jean Talon, as well as of the order's benefactors, the Duchesse d'Aiguillon and Cardinal Richelieu; various pieces of furniture, including Louis XIII chairs from the Château Saint-Louis; and a fine collection of surgical implements. From the museum, it is possible to descend to the cellar, where the nuns took shelter during the Conquest (when more than 40,000 cannonballs fell upon Quebec).

The relics of the Blessed Catherine-de-Saint-Augustin, a nun who arrived in Quebec in 1648 and was beatified in 1989, are among the 1,000 artifacts on display.

Church★

Same hours as museum.

To counteract the proliferation of non-Catholic community chapels that appeared in Quebec City with the influx of Irish Protestant immigrants in the early 19C, the Church of Quebec encouraged the nuns to erect a large Catholic church. Designed by Pierre Émond in 1800, under the supervision of Father Jean-Louis Desjardins, the structure features polygonal chapels and an apse, connected to the convent. The Neoclassical façade (1835) boasts a beautifully sculpted Ionic portal created by Thomas

Baillairgé. The small belfry was placed over the façade in 1931.
The sculpted, gilded wood **interior décor** was crafted by Thomas Baillairgé, between 1829 and 1832. Highlights include the high-altar **tabernacle**, a veritable small-scale model of St. Peter's in Rome; the retable, in the shape of a triumphal arch; and the basket-handle wooden vault. The painting above the altar, *The Descent from the Cross*, executed by Antoine Plamondon in 1840, was inspired by Rubens' famous masterpiece which now hangs in the Antwerp Cathedral in Belgium. The church features a collection of paintings confiscated from churches in Paris during the Revolution and sent to Quebec in 1817. One of these, *The Vision of Sainte-Thérèse d'Avila,* now hangs in the Notre-Dame-de-Toutes-Grâces chapel.

4 FORTIFICATIONS★★

See map pp308–309.

In the 17C, Quebec City played a key role in the defense of northeastern French America. As a consequence of the city's strategic location, several fortification projects were undertaken over the years. However, the construction of batteries, redoubts, and cavaliers in both the Lower and Upper towns ceased following the signing of the Utrecht Treaty of 1713, which temporarily suspended hostilities between the European factions. During the peace that followed, peripheral forts were the most common means of defense.
The fortification of Quebec City resumed in 1745 in reaction to the capture of Louisbourg, on the island of Cape Breton in present-day Nova Scotia. French military engineer Gaspard Chaussegros de Léry initiated the new fortification project, which was completed by the British after the Conquest of 1759. The British erected a temporary citadel in 1783, then added four circular Martello towers (1805–12), and finally built a new, permanent citadel between 1820 and 1832. The fortifications were faced with red sandstone from a Cap-Rouge quarry.

Following the departure of the British garrison in 1871, local military authorities approved the demolition of certain city gates in order to facilitate passage between the Lower and Upper towns and the Saint-Jean and Saint-Louis suburbs. Influenced by the historical romantic movement then popular in Europe, **Lord Dufferin**, governor-general of Canada from 1872 through 1878, insisted on the preservation of Quebec's fortifications. In 1875, he submitted a plan for the beautification of Quebec City, which included refurbishing the fortified enceinte (enclosure), rebuilding the gates to the city and demolishing all the advanced military works that formed a 60m/200ft-wide strip along the ramparts, in order fully to expose the complex in the manner of medieval fortifications.
As a result of Lord Dufferin's initiative, visitors can now stroll along the fortification walkways and enjoy panoramic views of the city and surrounding areas.

From Place d'Armes, follow rue Saint-Louis to Côte de la Citadelle, turn left and follow the street to its end. Enter through Porte Durnford (Durnford Gate).

La Citadelle★★

Visit by guided tour (1hr) only, Apr 10am–4pm; May–Oct 10am–6pm; Nov–Apr 10am–4pm; bilingual tours daily. $16. 418-694-2815. www.lacitadelle.qc.ca.
Though the Citadel was built at a time of peace and never used for defensive purposes, its conception dates back to the founding of the city. In 1615, Samuel de Champlain proposed that a citadel be erected on the Cap Diamant heights in order to control access to the hinterlands by way of the St. Lawrence River. Engineer Chaussegros de Léry submitted a similar project in 1716 and, in 1720, he drew the plans of a citadel much like the one that was built a century later, under the supervision of Lieutenant-Colonel Elias Walker Durnford.
The star-shaped plan of the present citadel (1820–52) is typical of Vauban

fortifications. Sébastien le Prestre, **marquis de Vauban** (1633–1707), military engineer and marshal of France under Louis XIV, perfected French military architecture by developing advanced works (or outworks) that protected entrances and ramparts from enemy fire. So sophisticated was the Vauban system that the British used it until the beginning of the 19C.

Surrounding the citadel were sloping earthworks known as glacis, which forced the enemy to expose itself to cannon fire from the garrison. Enemy fire, on the other hand, could not reach the stone walls unless it was exceptionally precise. The enclosure is formed of bastions linked together by curtains (straight walls). The bastions were shaped so as to protect the ditches by means of cannon fire, while the tenailles (isolated bastions located in the ditches) protected the curtains and entrances to the citadel.

The Neoclassical **Porte Dalhousie** (Dalhousie Gate, 1830) is the main entrance to the citadel and the site of the changing of the guard ceremony (Jun 24–Labor Day, daily 1pm; 35min) and the retreat (Jul–Aug, Sat 6pm; 30min). Paired columns adorn the main façade, creating a monumental effect intended to evoke military might and rigor.

Some areas of the Citadel are off-limits, as it is still a military base for the Royal 22nd Regiment. Guided tours begin at the powder magazine (1831), which was renovated as a chapel in 1927. The tour then leads to one of the *tenailles*, which formerly housed a prison and today serves as an annex to the Museum of the Royal 22nd Regiment. On view here are many types of arms, military decorations, uniforms, and World War I artifacts. From the King's Bastion, visitors can take in a superb **view★★** of the Château Frontenac and the Upper Town. The tour then leads past the Cap-Diamant redoubt (1693); the residence of the governor-general, partly destroyed by fire in 1976 and subsequently rebuilt; and the hospital (1849), which today functions as an administrative building. Occupying the old powder magazine (1750), the **Museum of the Royal 22nd Regiment** contains a collection of military objects from the 17C to the present, including uniformed mannequins posing as soldiers from the various regiments of New France, and several dioramas illustrating the major battles of the 18C. The tour also leads to the Prince of Wales bastion, the highest natural point in the city, from which a sweeping **view** extends over the St. Lawrence River and the Plains of Abraham.

▶ Leave the citadel by Porte Durnford and take the path to the left, which ascends to the fortifications; continue toward the St. Lawrence River.

Terrasse Dufferin

Promenade des Gouverneurs

© M. Sanchez / Michelin

The path leading to the Governor's Walk runs alongside the citadel's outer wall and the National Battlefields Park. One of the Martello towers is visible in the distance.

Promenade des Gouverneurs★★ (Governor's Walk)

Closed in winter.

Rising over the park, a belvedere affording magnificent **views★★** of the St. Lawrence and the Quebec region marks the beginning of this spectacular walk. Precariously suspended between the heavens and the dark waters of the St. Lawrence along the steep cliff, the boardwalk leads from the belvedere to Dufferin Terrace. The **panorama★** extends northeast to Île d'Orléans, Mt. Sainte-Anne and the Laurentians.

5 THE RAMPARTS★★

2km/1.2mi. Map p308–309.

Begin the tour at Dufferin Terrace.

Terrasse Dufferin★★★ (Dufferin Terrace)

Stretching 671m/2,200ft above the majestic river, this popular vantage point offers breathtaking **views★★** of the Lower Town, St. Lawrence River and surrounding region. The terrace, a large wooden boardwalk, is an extension of Lord Dufferin's beautification project. It was built to provide a view of the river at a time when the Lower Town was overrun by commercial buildings and warehouses.

The section of the terrace that faces Château Frontenac lies over the remains of the colonial governor's residence, the **Château Saint-Louis**, destroyed by fire in 1834. Governor Durham had a terrace built over the site. It bore his name until the present terrace was built.

Dufferin Terrace rapidly became a focal point of city life. It acquired electric lighting in 1885 and, shortly thereafter, ice slides were set up. The terrace's kiosks and public benches introduced Quebecers to urban fixtures akin to those found on Parisian boulevards and created a lively, bustling atmosphere. Don't miss the spectacular tobaggan rides here during winter.

Jardin des Gouverneurs (Governor's Garden)

This small park beside the Château Frontenac was created in the mid-17C for the enjoyment of the governor-general of New France. The **Wolfe-Montcalm Monument** (**4**) (1827) is a joint memorial to the two enemies who died in combat and, as was observed at the time, whose meeting resulted in the

creation of the Canadian nation. The shape of the monument symbolizes death: Note the cenotaph forming the base of the structure and, particularly, the dignified obelisk. The inscription reads in translation from Latin: "Valor gave them a common death, history a common fame, posterity a common monument."

To the right of the garden, follow rue du Mont-Carmel to the Cavalier-du-Moulin park. Continue to the end of Dufferin Terrace.

Erected in 1898, the **Samuel de Champlain Monument** (**5**), by Paul Chevré, honors the "father of New France." Nearby stands a monument made of bronze, granite and glass that commemorates the inscription of Quebec's historic district on UNESCO's World Heritage List, in December 1985. A **funicular** links Dufferin Terrace to the Lower Town.

Saint Louis forts and châteaux – National historic site of Canada (8)

Open end May–mid-Oct daily 10am–6pm. $4. 418-648-7016. www.pc.gc.ca.

Beneath the boardwalk of the Terrasse Dufferin, a visit to this archeological site will reveal the remains of the former residence of the governors of Quebec. You can discover the cellars, the ice house, the kitchen, and the access ramp used to bring supplies into the building. The architectural details reveal the successive French and British influences that shaped the building until it was destroyed by a fire on a January night in 1834.

Take the Frontenac staircase and cross the Prescott gate to Montmorency Park.

Inaugurated on July 3, 1983 to commemorate the 375th anniversary of the founding of Quebec City, the **Porte Prescott** (Prescott Gate) is a reconstruction of a previous gate that was erected on the same spot in 1797, and demolished in 1871.

Parc Montmorency (Montmorency Park)

It is here, at the summit of Côte de la Montagne, that the intendant of New France, Jean Talon, had a house built in 1667. At the end of the 17C, Msgr. de Saint-Vallier, second bishop of Quebec, purchased the house and constructed a vast episcopal palace (1691–96).

The Legislative Assembly of Lower Canada occupied the building from 1792 onwards. Reconstructed in the early 19C, the structure housed the Parliament of the Union Government, which held sessions intermittently in Quebec City, Kingston, Montreal and Toronto. It was later destroyed by fire.

The park features a **monument** (**6**) to the memory of **George-Étienne Cartier**, and another (**7**) to **Louis Hébert**, **Marie Rollet** and **Guillaume Couillard**. Created by sculptor Alfred Laliberté (1918), the latter commemorates the tricentennial of the arrival of the first settlers in New France (their names are inscribed on the back of the monument).

The park provides a good view of the Quebec Seminary, in particular the five-story building currently housing Laval University's School of Architecture. From this vantage point, the visitor can appreciate the elegant **lantern** placed atop the central dome, which has become a familiar landmark in Old Quebec.

Rue des Remparts★

Until approximately 1875, this street was a mere path that ran alongside the ramparts, connecting bastions and batteries. Located across from the seminary buildings, the Sault-au-Matelot and Clergé batteries, erected in 1711, protected the Quebec harbor. Today black cannons overlooking the Lower Town permit the visitor to recapture the atmosphere of the old fortified city.

Continue along rue des Remparts to rue Sainte-Famille.

Located at the foot of Rue Sainte-Famille until 1871, the Hope gate closed off access to the Upper Town. Branching off Rue des Remparts, the sinuous Côte de la Canoterie has linked the Upper and Lower towns since 1634; it used to lead to a tiny cove, known as l'Anse à la Canoterie, that served as a merchandise landing and a shipyard for the construction of small crafts.

Maison Montcalm (Montcalm House)

45–49 rue des Remparts.

Situated in a slightly recessed spot, this majestic residence contains three separate structures. The middle part, built in 1725, was soon flanked by two similar buildings. The house is named for Louis-Joseph de Saint-Véran, **marquis de Montcalm**, who lived on the first floor of the center section from December 1758 through June 1759. In 1810, the middle structure was raised one story; the two neighboring houses followed suit in 1830. Across the Montcalm House, the Montcalm Bastion, a small, tranquil square, offers lovely views of rue des Remparts and the fortifications.

Bastion des Augustines (Augustine Bastion)

Across from Augustine Monastery, 75 rue des Remparts.

Facing the Saint-Charles River, the northern section of the fortifications was long neglected because the cliff provided an adequate natural defense. After the American invasion of 1775–76, it was decided to complete this section of the walls surrounding the Upper Town. Completed in 1811, the masonry wall was so high that peering through the gun embrasures proved the only way to look out over the countryside.

The Palace Gate, demolished in 1871, once stood before the Augustine Monastery. In the Monastery garden, adjacent to the entrance portal, note the former powder magazine, built in 1820 to supply the northern cannon batteries.

A few blocks past the Augustine Bastion, the **Gare du Palais** (Palais Station) and the **Old Post Office** are visible to the right. Constructed of local granite, stone and brick, both buildings reflect the architectural style imposed throughout Canada by the Canadian Pacific Railway on its buildings following the construction of the Château Frontenac in 1893. *A 20min detour to the train station is recommended for those wishing to visit the refurbished interior.* Restored to their former splendor, the original porcelain tiles and steel arches adorn a surprisingly modern and functional entrance hall.

▶ Cross Côte du Palais and take rue de l'Arsenal leading to the back entrance of the Artillery Park.
If renovations are in progress and the back entrance is closed, proceed along Côte du Palais and turn right on to rue Saint-Jean, then right on rue D'Auteuil.

Lieu historique national du Canada du Parc-de-l'Artillerie★ (Artillery Park National Historic Site of Canada)

The main entrance at 2 rue d'Auteuil is located near the St. John Gate.
Access to the Artillery Park (Arsenal Foundry, Dauphine Redoubt and Officers' Quarters) mid-May–mid-Oct daily 10am–5pm; Apr–mid-May by reservation only. $3.90. ♿ ☎418-648-7016. www.pc.gc.ca/artillery.

This vast site, which includes barracks, a redoubt, and an old foundry, commemorates three centuries of military, social, and industrial life in Quebec City. Originally a residential district, the area now occupied by the Artillery Park was transformed by the construction of army barracks in 1749. After the Conquest, soldiers of the Royal Artillery Regiment took up residence here and erected several additional buildings over the years. The area's industrial vocation began in 1879, when the Canadian government acquired the site to convert it into a cartridge factory, later named the Dominion Arsenal. The industrial complex was abandoned in 1964, and in 1972 the Canadian Parks

Service began a program of renovations. Today the site features several noteworthy buildings.

Ancienne Fonderie **(Old Foundry)**

The large windows and skylights of this 1903 foundry recall its original function. Today the building houses a reception and interpretation center for the Artillery Park complex. Focal point of the exhibit, the **scale model★★** of Quebec City presents a stunning picture of the city as it appeared at the beginning of the 19C. Created between 1806 and 1808 by military engineers, the model reproduces topographical features and public buildings with great precision. On the lower level, visitors can see the ruins of a powder magazine and its protective wall (1808), and objects recovered during archeological digs at the site.

Dauphine Redoubt

Construction of the impressive white edifice began in 1712 but was interrupted in 1713, following the signing of the Treaty of Utrecht. Remains of the bastioned stone wall along the structure can still be seen today. Completed in 1748 by Chaussegros de Léry, the redoubt was converted into barracks. After the Conquest, the British army built an additional story over part of the structure and also added massive buttresses to contain the masonry and prevent the vaults from collapsing. The informative exhibits combine costumes, paintings, and artifacts to offer insight into a soldier's life during the 18C and 19C.

Nouvelles Casernes **(Barracks)**

Chaussegros de Léry designed this 160m/525ft-long stone structure in 1750 as a succession of row houses, an unusual concept at the time. The barracks contained armories, stockrooms, a guard room, and six prison cells. The building was partially rebuilt during the late 19C.

▶ Exit at the St. John Gate.

Porte Saint-Jean (St. John Gate)

As of 1867, a larger gate replaced the one designed in the 18C. To facilitate traffic flow between the various parts of the city, this gate was demolished in 1897. The current structure was built in 1936. It is the most famous of the numerous gates giving access to Old Quebec City.

Place d'Youville

Located on the site of the former Montcalm market, this lively square has been a cultural and entertainment center for residents of Quebec City since 1900. Note the Montcalm Palace (*Palais Montcalm*), erected in 1930; the sober architecture and lack of ornamentation testify to the magnitude of the economic crisis that marked that era. Adjacent stands the Capitole Theater (Théâtre du Capitole); its rounded façade is typical of the Beaux-Arts style popular during the early 20C.

▶ Return through the St. John Gate and turn right on rue d'Auteuil.

Porte Kent (Kent Gate)

Named in honor of the Duchess of Kent, this opening in the western rampart was created in 1879.

Chapelle des Jésuites (Jesuit Chapel)

20 rue Dauphine, at the junction of rue d'Auteuil. Open year-round Mon–Fri 11:30am–1:30pm. Closed major holidays. ☏418-694-0601. www.patrimoine-religieux.com.

This chapel has been dedicated to Canadian martyrs since 1925. The small structure (1820) stands on land formerly belonging to the Jesuit College. The building was enlarged in 1857 and a new façade added in 1930. The gilded wooden statues of the Virgin and St. Joseph were sculpted by Pierre-Noël Levasseur. Médard Bourgault, of Saint-Jean-Port-Joli, carved the Stations of the Cross.

Ice skating at Place d'Youville

© Claudel Huot / Québec City Tourism

Lieu historique national du Canada des Fortifications-de-Québec (Fortifications of Québec National Historic Site of Canada)

2 rue d'Auteuil, near the St. Louis Gate. Open mid-May–mid-Oct daily 10am–5pm; rest of year by reservation. $3.90. 418-648-7016. www.pc.gc.ca/fortifications.

Contained within the surrounding wall, the **interpretation center** presents the history of Quebec via the evolution of its defense systems and organizes guided tours ( ) of the imposing wall surrounding the city. Near the center, to the right of the St. Louis Gate, lies the **poudrière** (powder magazine), built in 1810 on the Esplanade, a vast field used for military exercises during the 18C.

Porte Saint-Louis (St. Louis Gate)

The St. Louis gate—like its counterparts, the Kent, St. John and Prescott gates—no longer controls access to the city. Instead, it provides a bridge for visitors using the fortifications walkway to tour the old city. Replete with towers, turrets, battlements, and machicolations, the gate was designed in 1878 by Irish architect W.H. Lynn, a collaborator of Lord Dufferin. The St. Louis gate influenced the development of a Château-style architecture in Quebec City.

6 GRANDE ALLÉE★

5km/3mi

See map pp308–309.

Begin the walking tour at the Parliament Building.

Departing from the St. Louis gate and extending southward of Old Quebec, the Grande Allée is the city's Champs-Élysées. Lined with an abundance of restaurants, bars, outdoor cafés, boutiques and offices, Quebec City's premier thoroughfare provides an elegant setting for the city's nightlife.

Hôtel du Parlement★★ (Parliament Building)

1045 rue des Parlementaires. Guided tour (French, English, 30min) only, late Jun–Labor Day, Mon–Fri 9am–4:15pm, weekends 10am–4:15pm; rest of the year Mon–Fri 9am–4:15pm. 418-643-7239 & 1-866-337-8837. www.assnat.qc.ca. Photo ID required for security purposes.

Overlooking the old city, this majestic edifice is the finest example of Second Empire architecture in Quebec City. In

1875 the deputy minister of the Department of Crown Lands, **Eugène-Étienne Taché** (1836–1912), was mandated by the provincial government to draw up the plans of a building to house the parliament and various government ministries. Originally designed to occupy the former site of the Jesuit college in Old Quebec (now City Hall), the project was transferred to the Cricket Field, in the Faubourg Saint-Louis, after the devastating fire of 1876.

The Parliament building forms a quadrangle surrounding an inner courtyard. The imposing **façade** presents a historic tableau featuring bronze figures that commemorate the great names of Quebec history. Some of these sculptures were created by Louis-Philippe Hébert. His *Nigog Fisherman* is encased in a niche before the main entrance; above the niche stands his work entitled *The Amerindian Family*, which was displayed during the 1889 Universal Exhibit in Paris. In front of the façade is a diagram identifying the various bronze figures and their creators.

The entrance hall bears the national emblems of various countries, a reminder that, at the time of construction, Quebec was chiefly comprised of immigrants from France, England, Ireland, and Scotland. A staircase leads to **Le Parlementaire**, a sumptuous dining room not to be missed for its traditional dishes and fresh local fare like tourtière, maple eggs, and wild caribou terrine (open to the public Mon and Wed–Fri 7am–3pm, Tue 5pm–8pm, reservations recommended ℘418-643-6640), and decorated in the Beaux-Arts style (1917). The restaurant entrance is a stained-glass passageway, flooded with light, that evokes an Atlantic seascape.

Parliamentary Chambers

On the first floor, an antechamber leads to both parliamentary chambers through finely chiseled doors.

Quebec's bicameral parliamentary system, as established by the Constitution Act of 1867, required two distinct halls: The Chamber of the National Assembly and the Chamber of the Legislative Council. Quebec's National Assembly (elected) now sits in the Chamber of the National Assembly. The Chamber of the Legislative Council, similar in size and decor, was used by the Legislative Council (appointed) until the council was abolished in 1968. Since then, it has hosted meetings of parliamentary

Bronze historical figures, Hôtel du Parlement

From Country Road to Modern Thoroughfare

Grande Allée developed along the east-west axis that separated the land plots allotted to a few major property holders on the Quebec plateau in the early 17C. Originally a country road, it acquired a sudden popularity in the late 18C when it was transformed into a resort district by the British. In just a few years, magnificent villas appeared along the south side of Grande Allée, and the Faubourg Saint-Louis began taking shape. Adding to the shift of business activity to Montreal and the move of the Canadian Parliament to Ottawa, the departure of the British garrison in 1871 hastened the decline of Quebec City. Inspired by the new city of Edinburgh, which developed alongside the original medieval town, the municipal engineer Charles Baillairgé suggested that Grande Allée be transformed into one of Quebec City's main arteries.

A major fire destroyed the Faubourg Saint-Louis on July 1, 1876, clearing much of the area and prompting the decision to erect the Parliament Building on this site. Following construction of the imposing edifice in 1886, the boulevard was designed as a corridor for official processions, linking the Parliament Building to Bois-de-Coulonge Park, the official residence of the lieutenant-governor.

The first residents of the remodeled Grande Allée (1886–90) were the political elite of the city, who built opulent villas in the Second Empire style. Between 1890 and 1900, the upper portion of the boulevard was further developed with the arrival of a new bourgeoisie reaping the benefits of the Lower Town's industrialization. The heyday of Grande Allée continued well after World War I, and came to an end with the opening of the Quebec City Bridge to car travel in 1929, which gradually transformed the elegant residential district into a busy thoroughfare.

committees and official receptions. Following the British parliamentary system, the majority party, which forms the government, sits face to face with the "loyal opposition" made up of one or several parties.
Ministers and the principal members of the opposition are separated by a space, which in former times was said to equal "the length of two swords."
Above the throne of the National Assembly Speaker hangs a painting by Charles Huot (*The Debate on Languages,* 1910–13) representing the January 21, 1793 sitting of the Legislative Assembly of Lower Canada, during which the historic linguistic debate that granted official status to the French language took place.

Gardens

Several commemorative monuments to Quebec premiers and other notable Québécois are strewn throughout the gardens ("les pelouses") of the Parliament Building.

On the north side, monuments to **Robert Bourassa**, premier of Quebec 1970–76 and 1985–94, father of Quebec's hydropower; **René Lévesque** (1976–85), the sovereignist premier; and premier **Jean Lesage** (1960–66), leader of the *Quiet Revolution*. There is also an *inukshuk*, a monument of stacked stones, paying tribute to the Inuit peoples of Northern Quebec.
On the south side of the gardens, there are monuments to nationalist premier **Maurice Duplessis** (1936–39 and 1944–59); and to premier **Honoré Mercier** (1887–91), a champion of Quebec's autonomy.
On Grande-Allée, near Porte Saint-Louis (St. Louis Gate), stand monuments to **François-Xavier Garneau**, Quebec's first national historian in the 19C; **Louis-Joseph Papineau**, chairman of the Assembly Chamber of Lower Canada (1816–38); and progressive premier **Adélard Godbout** (1936 and 1939–44).

Continue south on Grande Allée.

Aerial view of the Plains of Abraham

Manège militaire (City Armoury)

Behind Place George-V.

Built between 1884 and 1887 by Eugène-Étienne Taché, the Château-style building once served as a provincial exhibit pavilion and a military exercise hall. At the turn of the 20C, an annex was added to the eastern wing and more recently, it housed a military regiment and museums.

The Manège Militaire suffered a catastrophic fire the night of April 4, 2008, though 90 percent of the historic artifacts were saved. Only the brick-wall façade and two towers remained standing after the blaze that devoured the old wood structure, but a $104 million restoration project has been approved, and is targeted for completion by 2017.

Turn right on rue de la Chevrotière.

Maison de la découverte des plaines d'Abraham★ (Discovery Pavilion of the Plains of Abraham)

835 Wilfrid-Laurier Avenue. Open Jul–Labor Day daily 9:30am–5:30pm; rest of year daily 9:30am–5pm. $15.

2009 marked the 250th anniversary of the Battle of the Plains of Abraham; the site is now covered by a park (*see p330*), but this centre helps visitors discover traces of the battle and understand its importance. Tickets include a bus tour, a visit to Martello Tower 1 and the 1½ hour **Odyssey★** multimedia show. The show is presented in a journalistic style, with contributions from the key figures, interviews, and presentations of the forces on the field and the events of the battle. You are then given an overview of the plain's 250 years of history.

Continue along rue Wilfred-Laurier. Turn right into rue Bertholet, then right again into rue St-Amable, then left into rue de la Chevrotière.

Observatoire de la Capitale (Édifice Marie-Guyart)

Entrance at 1037 rue de la Chevrotière. Open Jun 24–mid-Oct, daily 10am–5pm; rest of the year, Tue–Sun 10am–5pm. $10.45. 418-643-3117 & 1-888-497-4322. www.observatoirecapitale.org.

The observatory occupying the 31st floor (221m/685ft up) of this administrative building provides a splendid **view★★** of Old Quebec, the citadel and fortifications, the St. Lawrence River as well as the surrounding areas. Édifice Marie-Guyart is the tallest building in Quebec City.

Return to Grande Allée and turn right (off map).

Église Saint-Cœur-de-Marie (Church of the Sacred Heart of Mary)

At the corner of rue Scott and Grande Allée (No. 530).

Erected in 1920, the brick edifice was built for the Eudists, also known as the Congregation of Jesus and Mary, founded in the 17C. The quaint steeple distinctly contrasts with the otherwise modern structure.

Joseph-Aristide-Tardif Building

500 Grande Allée Est.

The headquarters of this insurance company occupy a structure (1962) that embodies the functionalist tendency of modern architecture in Quebec City. Towards the rear, a new façade of mirrored glass overlooks the Park of French America (Parc de l'Amérique française).

Take Ave. Taché on the left to view the Martello tower no. 2.

Return to Grande Allée.

Maison Stewart (Stewart House)

82 Grande Allée Ouest, northeast corner of Ave. Cartier. www.historicplaces.ca/en/rep-reg/place-lieu.aspx?id=7871

Surrounded by a small park, this 1849 cottage features large French windows adorning the façade. Topped by a central chimney stack, the overhanging roof covers the lateral galleries.

At no. 95 stands the **Ladies' Protestant Home**, an elegant example of the Renaissance Revival style exemplified here by the massive cornice and lantern. To the right of the structure, facing the Avenue Cartier, the **Krieghoff House** (closed to the public) was named for the painter Cornelius Krieghoff (1815–72) who lived here intermittently in 1859 and 1860. Built in 1850, this "rustic cottage" is in fact a country house for city dwellers; the style derives from Quebec vernacular architecture.

Turn left on Ave. Wolfe-Montcalm and follow signs to the Quebec Museum of Fine Arts (Musée national des beaux-arts du Québec, off map).

The avenue runs alongside a military parade ground used by the British army after they abandoned Place d'Armes in 1823. For years, major events such as the historic parades marking Quebec City's 300th anniversary took place on the site. Facing the museum, the **Wolfe monument** marks the spot where the victor of the Battle of the Plains of Abraham, General James Wolfe, died on September 13, 1759.

Musée national des beaux-arts du Québec★★ (Quebec Museum of Fine Arts)

Entrance is located between the two main buildings, on ground level. Open Jun–early Sept daily 10am–6pm (Wed 9pm); rest of the year Tue–Sun 10am–5pm (Wed 9pm). $18. ($2.50 for first hour, $1 subsequent hours). 418-644-6460 and 1-866-220-2150. www.mnba.qc.ca.

Situated on the site of the Parc des Champs-de-Bataille (Battlefields Park), this remarkable museum complex provides a comprehensive overview of Quebec art from the 18C to the present. The greatest visual artists of Quebec are represented, Jean-Paul Riopelle and Jean-Paul Lemieux in particular. Temporary and permanent exhibits, drawn from a collection of over 23,000 works of art, including those of the former Brousseau Museum of Inuit Art, are organized throughout three buildings.

Main Hall

Situated between the two other structures, the Main Hall is the main entrance to the museum. The modern structure, capped by skylights, houses the reception area, an auditorium and other amenities.

Gérard Morisset Pavilion

The monumental façade of this structure (named for a former museum director) reflects the Beaux-Arts style that was adopted for many of Quebec's government buildings. The granite-clad building features an imposing central staircase leading to an Ionic portico. The sculpted stone pediment evokes the Province's economic history and the history of two groups: The First Nations (*left side*) and the discoverers and missionaries (*right side*). Aluminum-plated bas-reliefs representing various events in the history of Canada and traditional agricultural scenes adorn the structure's lateral wings. Pieces from the permanent collection are on view here, including ancient, modern, and contemporary art; the works offer a sweeping view of the development of Quebec art.

Baillairgé Pavilion

Erected according to plans by Charles Baillairgé, this monumental Renaissance Revival-style structure (1871) housed, until 1967, the old "plains prison." An entire cell block has been preserved as an exhibit of prison life during the last century. One gallery here features one of the most important paintings in the history of Canada: The renowned *Assemblée des six comtés* (*Assembly of Six Counties*). A masterpiece of Charles Alexander Smith, this impressive canvas illustrates one of the key moments of the insurrections of 1837–38: In the foreground, Louis-Joseph Papineau, leader of the Patriots, addresses an attentive crowd.

In the tower of this structure (*4th floor*), note the curious statue of a diver sculptured in the late 1960s by David Moore.

The Brousseau collection of Inuit Art★★

3rd floor.

The museum acquired the 2,635 works of Inuit art making up the Brousseau collection in 2005, including 2,017 sculptures from all the regions of northern Canada. About 300 works are on display in the gallery at one time, on a rotational basis, and through these pieces, produced between the 1940s and the 2000s, visitors are immersed into Inuit culture, with its profound links to the natural environment. The artists worked with reindeer horn, whale bone, and narwhal ivory, but most of all with stone, such as serpentinite, with its marbled effects, soapstone and gneiss.

On the same floor, you will find a gallery containing around twenty works by Alfred Pellan (1906–88), an artist dubbed the "champion of free expression" and known for the colorful, almost fairy-tale world he created. His work included set and costume designs for the theater, including a series of masks for Shakespeare's *Twelfth Night*.

▶ Upon exiting from the museum, turn left on Ave. Georges-VI and continue to Grey Terrace.

This observatory was named in honor of A.H. Grey, governor-general of Canada from 1904 through 1911, during which time the park was constructed.

▶ Doubling back, take Ave. Ontario through National Battlefields Park.

Parc des Champs-de-Bataille★ (Battlefields Park)

The park is open daily year-round at no charge. The **Plains of Abraham Museum★** presents a multi-media history of the battles. Open Jul–Labor Day daily 9:30am–5pm. ♿ P ($15) ✆418-648-4071; www.ccbn-nbc.gc.ca. Continuing straight ahead, the Ave. du Cap-aux-Diamants leads to the Governor's Walk (promenade des Gouverneurs) belvedere.

Created in 1908, on the tricentennial of the founding of the city, this national park stretches over 108ha/266 acres along a cliff on the south side of the Quebec City plateau. Overlooking the St. Lawrence River, the site commemorates the battles fought between the British and French armies during the Conquest.

The park, completed in 1954, was landscaped by Frederick G. Todd, a student of Frederick Law Olmsted, renowned designer of New York City's Central Park and Montreal's Mt. Royal Park. Inspired by English country gardens, the rambling park introduces a green space into the cityscape, providing a natural-looking environment that contrasts with the structured, rational layout of classical gardens.

The Battle of the Plains of Abraham

A large section of the park occupies the former plains of Abraham, so named after Abraham Martin, a wealthy farmer living on the Quebec City heights in the 17C. On this site, the French and British armies fought the battle that eventually sealed the fate of the French colony. On September 13, 1759, some 5,000 British troops under the command of General Wolfe scaled the steep cliff and launched an attack on the city. Without waiting for reinforcements, the French general Montcalm urged his ill-prepared army against the British lines, who in turn crushed the attempt in less than 15 minutes. Both generals were mortally wounded during the short but decisive event. Five days later, Quebec had been completely occupied and the French troops, under the command of François-Gaston de Lévis (1719–87), retreated to Montreal for the winter. The following April, Lévis and the French army returned to battle the British at Sainte-Foy (a monument located in Braves Park north of Chemin Sainte-Foy commemorates the event). Though the French were victorious, their hopes were dashed the following month when a ship arrived bearing British reinforcements, sealing the fate of New France. The territory was officially turned over to the British by the Treaty of Paris in 1763.

Fearing that Americans would initiate another invasion following a failed attempt by Bostonians in 1775–76, and still awaiting London's decision regarding the construction of a citadel, the British military erected four **Martello towers** between 1808 and 1812 as an advanced defensive line. Three towers remain, two in the park and one on rue Lavigueur (Faubourg Saint-Jean-Baptiste). Named for the Corsican point where they originated, Martello towers are circular defensive outposts, topped by a platform mounted with cannons. The section of the wall built to resist the enemy is very thick, while the section facing the garrison is thinner; thus, if the tower were to be overtaken by the enemy, it could be easily destroyed by the besieged troops.

EXCURSIONS

Cartier-Brébeuf National Historic Site of Canada★

3km/1.8mi from St. John Gate, by Côte d'Abraham, rue de la Couronne, Drouin Bridge and 1re Ave. Turn left on rue de l'Éspinay. Open Apr 6–Jun 23 Mon–Fri 9am–noon; Jun 24–end Aug daily 9am–noon and 1pm–4pm. $4.90. 418-648-4038. www.pc.gc.ca/brebeuf.

Located on the northern shore of the Lairet Basin, this site commemorates Jacques Cartier, who wintered on this spot in 1535–36, and Jean de Brébeuf, a Jesuit missionary. The interpretation center features insightful displays, which recall Cartier's second voyage to New France and his meetings with the Iroquois, as well as the Jesuits' first mission, established in 1626.

SAINTE-FOY-SILLERY

From Old Quebec, follow rue Grande-Allée west. The combined district begins just after du Boisé-de-Sillery, and the street name changes to Blvd Laurier at that point. i 3300 Ave. des Hôtels, Sainte-Foix. 418-641-6290 or 1-877-783-1608. www.regiondequebec.com.

Located on the banks of the St. Lawrence barely 1km/0.6mi from Quebec, the community of Sillery was named after the French nobleman, Noël Brulart de Sillery. The settlement traces its origins to the Jesuit mission founded in 1637 to convert First Nations. However, ravaging epidemic diseases and alcoholism led to the abandonment of the settlement in the 1680s. After

the Conquest, Jesuits rented the territory to several wealthy merchants. The expanding lumber and shipbuilding industry prompted an economic surge during the mid-19C, as Sillery's coves and bays were used for unloading, squaring off, warehousing and exporting timber. Several of the sumptuous mansions erected during this prosperous era were later acquired by various religious organizations. After World War II, Sillery quickly developed as a residential suburb of Quebec City. Today, the town presents a subtle mix of old-world charm and bustling city activities.
Past Battlefields Park, Grande Allée becomes chemin Saint-Louis. A wooded median divides the boulevard, which is lined with prestigious office buildings.

Parc du Bois-de-Coulonge★ (Bois-de-Coulonge Park)

1215 Grande Allée Ouest, in the borough of Sainte-Foy-Sillery. Open daily year-round. Guided tours (French only) Fri–Sun hourly from noon–3pm. $5 ♿ P ($1/hr weekdays, weekends free). ✆418-528-0773 & 1-800-442-0773.
This pleasantly landscaped park constitutes a small part of the old Coulonge seigneury granted to Louis d'Ailleboust, Sieur de Coulonge, in 1649. During the Conquest, the British temporarily occupied the site. In 1780 the domain was subdivided, and one of the first country homes on this land was erected 10 years later. Built in the Palladian style, the villa was renamed **Spencer Wood** in honor of British prime minister Lord Spencer, in 1811, and would become the residence of Lord Elgin, governor-general of the United Canadas, in 1852. It was rebuilt in 1860 after a fire. Following Confederation, it became the property of the provincial government and served as the residence of the lieutenant-governor.
Renamed Bois-de-Coulonge in 1947, the vice-regal residence was destroyed by fire in 1966. Since then, Bois-de-Coulonge Park has been open to the public. The **guardian's house**, a small Château-style construction covered with decorative cedar shingles (1891), serves as the park's visitor center. Various old buildings, gardens, and a belvedere overlooking the river also await park visitors.

Villa Bagatelle★

1563 chemin Saint-Louis, in the borough of Sainte-Foy-Sillery. Open Jun–Sept Tue–Sun 11am–5pm; Apr–May and Oct–Dec, Wed–Sun 1–5pm; Jan–Mar, weekends only 1–5pm. ♿ ✆418-654-0259.
Villa Bagatelle was built in 1927 after a fire the previous year. The villa closely resembles a small Gothic Revival cottage erected in 1848 in the park. The house, surrounded by an English garden, is the Sillery Interpretation Center, housing an exhibit and documentation center, and mounts temporary thematic exhibits.

▶ Continue along chemin Saint-Louis.

The road passes by the St. Michael Anglican church, with its squat steeple and large buttresses.

▶ Turn left on Côte de l'Église.

Église Saint-Michel (St. Michael Church)

1600 rue Persico, in Sillery. Open year-round Mon–Sat 9am–5pm; Sun 10am–noon. Guided tours (French and English) from late Jun–Labor Day. Closed Sat from Nov–May. ♿ P ✆418-527-3390.
The Gothic Revival church dates from 1854. Five paintings from the Desjardins collection are preserved in the interior: *Emmaüs' Disciples, Death of St. Francis of Assisi, St. Francis of Assisi Receiving the Stigmata, the Annunciation* and *The Adoration of the Magi*.
Outside, on a terrace below the church, the lookout at **Pointe-à-Puiseaux** affords a superb **view★** of Quebec City, Sillery's coves, the Quebec City and Pierre-Laporte bridges and the south shore.

Return to chemin Saint-Louis.

Maison Hamel-Bruneau (Hamel-Bruneau House)

2608 chemin Saint-Louis, in Sainte-Foy. Open approx Apr–Aug Tue–Sun 11am–5pm, Sept–Dec 1–5pm.

This little cottage, a synthesis between the ornate English cottage and the Quebec vernacular style, was built as a country home in 1858. It houses temporary exhibits and offers free cultural activities during summer.

Turn left on Ave. du Parc.

Parc Aquarium du Québec (Quebec Aquarium)

1675 Ave. des Hôtels. Open daily Jun–Aug 10am–5pm; Sept–May 10am–4pm. Closed Dec 25–1 Jan. $18, children (age 3-17) $9. 418-659-5264 & 1-866-659-5264. www.sepaq.com/aquarium.

Established in 1959 on a site overlooking the St. Lawrence River, the aquarium houses more than 1,700 specimens of exotic fish, reptiles and sea mammals as well as specimens representing the ecosystems of the St. Lawrence. Of special interest are the outdoor seal pools. Upon leaving the aquarium, stop at the little lookout in the parking lot to enjoy a magnificent **view★** of the St. Lawrence River, and the Ponts (bridges) de Québec City and Pierre-Laporte.

Descend toward the St. Lawrence, take Blvd Champlain and continue to Côte de Gignac. Turn left, then right onto chemin du Foulon.

Maison des Jésuites★ (Jesuit House)

2320 chemin du Foulon. Open Jun–Sept, Tue–Sun 11am–5pm; Apr–May and Oct–Dec, Wed–Sun 1–5pm; Feb–Mar, Sun 1–5pm. 418-654-0259. www.museocapitale.qc.ca.

The current early 18C stone house was erected on the site of the St. Joseph mission (the first Jesuit mission in North America), established by Jesuits in 1637 in order to convert the Montagnais, Algonquins and Atikamekw to a sedentary lifestyle. So as to protect themselves from attacks by Iroquois, the Jesuits and First Nations lived in an enclosure surrounded by stakes, which was later replaced by a stone fort. Facing the house, vestiges of the fort and the Saint-Michel chapel have been unearthed. The British writer, Frances Moore Brookes, lived in this two-story edifice in 1763. In 1769, she published *The History of Emily Montague,* which takes place in this house. By 1929, the Jesuit House was classified as one of the earliest historical monuments in Quebec. It now houses a small museum of exhibits focusing on the history of indigenous peoples, as well as archeology of the site and local history. In the gardens, note the re-created native camp, which highlights the site's importance as a meeting place between missionaries and indigenous peoples during the era of New France.

Along chemin du Foulon, note the old wooden houses, formerly inhabited by shipyard employees.

Université Laval (Laval University)

In Sainte-Foy, 7km/4.3mi from St. Louis Gate by Grande Allée, chemin Saint-Louis and Blvd Laurier (Rte. 175).

Founded in 1852 by the Quebec Seminary, Laval University began building a campus (*cité universitaire)* in the western suburb of Quebec City in 1949. The north-south axis opens onto a view of the Laurentian Mountains, while the east-west draws attention to the Grand Seminary and the Faculty of Medicine. The university underwent considerable expansion in the 1960s; today its 13 departments, nine specialty schools and several research centers accommodate more than 40,000 students.

The **Louis-Jacques Casault Pavilion** (formerly the Grand Seminary) was built in 1958. Inside, the Gothic-style university chapel was redesigned to house the Quebec national archives. Facing the Casault Pavilion are two new buildings, erected in 1990: The **Laurentienne**

Pavilion and the award-winning, post-Modern **Alexandre-de-Sève Pavilion**. With its Classic composition, inner courtyard and façades articulated by sunshields of white concrete, the **Charles-de-Koninck Pavilion** (1964) is today considered the main building of the university complex. The **Comtois Pavilion** (1966) also reflects the desire to achieve a Classical appearance through the use of prefabricated modules. With its inner courtyard and pillared structure, it is one of the most interesting buildings in the Quebec City region.

A squat building marked by horizontal lines, the impressive sports complex known as "le PEPS" (Pavillon de l'Éducation Physique et des Sports, 1971) stretches out over terraced grounds covering large underground parking areas. Facilities include an Olympic-size pool, an indoor stadium, skating rinks and several sporting areas.

CHARLESBOURG

Take Rte. 73 Nord to Exit 150 (80e Rue Ouest).

Le Trait-Carré★

Departure point for walking tour of the Trait-Carré: Moulin des Jésuites at 7960 Blvd Henri-Bourassa, reachable by city Métrobus 801 (open mid-Jun–Sept, daily 10am–5:30pm; early Sept–mid-Jun Sat & Sun 10am–5pm; 418-624-7720; www.moulindesjesuites.org).

The heart of old Charlesbourg, commonly referred to as the Trait-Carré historical district, comprises a square lot located in the midst of a star-shaped land division plan. Dating back to 1660, it is the only such design in New France. Throughout Quebec, land concessions traditionally took the form of long, narrow strips of land known as rangs, which prevented large population concentrations.

The Trait-Carré design was devised in Charlesbourg by Jesuit priests and the intendant Jean Talon, who wanted all homes located near the main square, to improve their defensibility in case of attack.

Today the center of Trait-Carré is bordered by four streets. In the middle is the institutional center of old Charlesbourg, which includes a church, a municipal library housed in the old Saint Charles College (1903), and the Bon-Pasteur Convent, built in 1883.

Église Saint-Charles-Borromée (St. Charles Borromeo Church)

Visit by guided tour only (by appointment). 418-623-1847.

With its two steeples and high façade dominated by a large pediment, this edifice (1827–30) exemplifies the influence of English Palladianism on the religious architecture of Quebec.

The focal point of the interior is the imposing triumphal arch adorning the flat apse. Salvaged from an earlier church erected on this site, two statues (1742) by Pierre-Noël Levasseur stand in lateral niches. Also worth noting are works by François Ranvoyzé, Louis Jobin, Charles Vézina and Paul Lambert.

At the southeast corner of the Trait-Carré stands the **Ephraïm Bédard House,** a typical rural dwelling from the early 19C (7655 chemin Samuel; open Tue, Thu 1:30–4pm; otherwise by appointment 418-624-7745; www.societe-historique-charlesbourg.org).

The **Pierre-Lefebvre House**, a representative 19C wood structure, has been converted into the Trait-Carré Gallery of Visual Arts (7985 Trait-Carré Est; open mid-Jun–mid-Aug Wed–Sun 11am–6pm; mid-Sept–mid-May Fri 7–9pm, weekends 1–5pm; 418-623-1877), www.trait-carre.org. Other historic structures in the quarter have also been converted into cultural centers, among them the Magella-Paradis House (1833), which boasts a distinctive roofline.

Hôtel de Glace★ (Ice Hotel)

530 rue de la Faune. Open Jan–Mar daily 10:30am–4:30pm. $18, children (age 6–12) $9. 418-623-2888 or 1-877-505-0423. www.hoteldeglace-canada.com.

The only hotel of its kind in North America and a fine example of ephemeral architecture. The metal molds are put in place in December and snow machines are used to apply a coating of snow that becomes harder than ice. The walls created using this process are up to 1.2m/4ft thick at their base. Once the molds are removed, artists take over to sculpt luxury suites within the walls. Blocks of pure, translucent ice are used for the colonnades, light fittings and "furniture." The result has a fairy-tale charm, with 44 rooms and suites, a chapel and a bar, all extending over a floor area of more 3,000sq m/33,000sq ft. Each year, more than 15,000 tons of snow and 500 tons of ice are used in the amazing feat of artistry that gives shape to this incredible hotel.

WENDAKE

Take Rte. 73 Nord to Exit 154. Turn left on rue de la Faune (which becomes rue des Érables and rue de la Rivière). Then turn right on rue Max Gros-Louis.

Expelled from the Great Lakes region by the Iroquois, and beset by epidemics and famine, the Hurons sought the protection of the French in the mid-17C. Accompanied by Father Chaumonot, a Jesuit missionary, they settled in the Upper Town (near Fort Saint-Louis), and moved on to Île d'Orléans in 1651. In 1668, they emigrated to Sainte-Foy, on the present site of Laval University, and then to Ancienne-Lorette, in 1673. From there they moved one last time to Jeune-Lorette, or Wendake, in 1697. Today a stroll through the streets of the **Huron Village** (Village-des-Hurons) reveals the uniqueness of this place. The buildings on the reserve were erected on communal land in the local First Nations tradition, without individual land allotments or European cadastral boundaries. The community is located near the Saint Charles (or Kabir-Kouba) River, whose waterfalls have inspired many artists.

Site traditionnel huron-wendat Onhoüa Chetek8e★ (Huron-Wendat Onhoüa Chetek8e Traditional Site)

575 rue Stanislas-Kosca, Village-des-Hurons (Wendake). Visit by guided tour (45min) only, May–mid-Oct daily 9am–5pm; rest of the year 10am–4pm. $13.50. 418-842-4308. www.huron-wendat.qc.ca.

"Koey Koey ataro..." (Welcome, friend...) Thus begins a visit to this re-created traditional Native village, which offers a fascinating introduction to the

Hôtel de Glace

© D. Reeve / Michelin

history, heritage, and customs of the First Nations, and of the Huron Nation in particular. Visitors step inside a longhouse (multi-family dwelling), and view a smokehouse and a traditional sauna, a small structure in which steam is produced by pouring boiling water onto heated stones. From May to October, experience the animation of Huron legends and traditional dance.

Notre-Dame-de-Lorette chapel

Corner of rues Chef-Maurice-Bastien and Chef-Nicholas-Vincent. Open May–Oct Mon–Fri 9am–5pm, weekends 10am–5pm. ✗♿🅿 ✆418-847-3569. www.wendake.ca.

The church, a National Architectural and Historic Site designated by the Minister of Canadian Heritage, occupies the site of the Jesuit Mission of 1697. The present structure (1865) was erected on the site of an earlier church (1730) that was destroyed by a fire in 1862. The very simple décor includes a high altar tabernacle believed to have been made in 1722 by Pierre-Noël Levasseur. Above the altar, a simple sculpture represents the Santa Casa of Loretto, in Italy, supported by two angels. The chapel treasure, which includes religious furnishings left behind by the Jesuit missionaries, is exhibited in the sacristy.

ÎLE D'ORLÉANS★★

▶ 10km/6.2mi northeast of Quebec City via Routes 440 or 138. ℹ **A tourist information center** (✆418-828-9411; 866-941-9411; www.tourisme.iledorleans.com/en/) is at the intersection of the bridge road (côte du Pont) and Rte. 368 (it will be on your right when you arrive on the island).

Wedged in the St. Lawrence, within view of Quebec City, this almond-shaped island covers an area of 192sq km/74sq mi. It boasts a varied landscape of maple groves in the north and on the central plateau, oak forests in the southwest, marshes in the center and sand along the water's edge. Although joined to the mainland by bridge in 1935, the Île d'Orléans still retains the pastoral tranquility that inspired the 19C artist Horatio Walker and the *chansonnier* (singer) Félix Leclerc.

Route 368 runs along the island's 67km/41.6mi circumference, passing through six communities. Driving along the road, visitors will discover splendid scenery and magnificent **views★★** of the Beaupré Coast and the Bas-Saint-Laurent shoreline. The itinerary along

Île-d'Orléans

From 'Bewitched' to Bacchus to Île d'Orléans

Long before the arrival of Europeans, the indigenous population called the island Minigo, meaning "bewitched" in Algonquian, because they considered it to be a land of spirits. When Jacques Cartier came ashore in 1535, the abundance of vines growing on the island prompted him to dub the site the Isle of Bacchus. The following year the name was changed to Île d'Orléans in honor of the son of King François I, the Duke of Orléans. Under the French Regime, the seigneury was laid out in strips of land (rangs) perpendicular to the St. Lawrence, providing optimal access to the waterfront. Today, vast expanses of farmland produce strawberries, raspberries, apples, asparagus, and potatoes. The island is also known for its maple syrup.

Many islanders trace their ancestry back to French colonists who arrived here more than three centuries ago, at a time when the island was more populous than the capital city. In fact, in 1667, the Île d'Orléans claimed a population of 529 while the residents of Quebec City numbered only 448.

the southern coast, from Sainte-Pétronille to Saint-François, is particularly picturesque. The return trip along the northern side of the island offers scenic views of the Montmorency Falls and Mont Sainte-Anne.

Sainte-Pétronille

5km/3mi from junction of bridge road.
Located on the site of the island's first settlement, this community was conceded in 1649. Hurons sought refuge here in the 1650s after warring with the Iroquois.

The small chapel dating from that period has since disappeared. In 1855 a wharf was constructed to load island produce, and a steamship ferry service linked Sainte-Pétronille to Quebec City. This connection led to the development of tourism in the late 19C, and many affluent families erected Victorian-style villas here as summer homes. A three-hole golf course built in 1866 is one of the oldest in North America.

The village was known as L'Anse-au-Fort, then as Bout de l'Île (tip of the island) and Village de Beaulieu before acquiring its present name in 1870.

Église de Sainte-Pétronille (Church of Sainte-Pétronille)

Turn left on chemin de l'Église, then right before the cul-de-sac facing the golf course. Opening times vary. 418-828-2656.

This religious complex includes a convent (1875), a presbytery and a church (1871) designed by J.F. Peachy. The interior was decorated by David Ouellet.

Continue along chemin de l'Église, which runs into the chemin du Bout-de-l'Île. A walkway borders the shoreline. Turn left, then right on rue du Quai.

La Goéliche

22 chemin du Quai. www.goeliche.ca.
Known as the Château Bel Air when it was constructed in 1880, and then as Manoir de l'Anse, this inviting Victorian hotel and restaurant offers a perfect perch overlooking the St. Lawrence, as well as delicious cuisine and a tradition of hospitality.

Return to Rte. 368 and continue to Saint-Laurent for 11km/6.8mi.

Saint-Laurent-de-l'Île-d'Orléans★

Traditionally the maritime centre of the Île d'Orléans, Saint-Laurent enjoyed a thriving shipbuilding industry in the mid-19C when some 20 family-owned shipyards produced flat-bottom boats, called *chaloupes*. Famous for their clean lines and sturdy construction, these boats remained the primary means of transportation for the islanders until a bridge joined the island to the main-

land in 1935. The village still claims the island's only marina, which can accommodate up to 130 boats.
Situated 2km/1.2mi before the town limit of Saint-Laurent, the **Gendreau House** (*no. 2385 chemin Royal*), with its steep roof and unusual double row of dormer windows, was erected in 1720. For at least eight generations, it was inhabited by members of the Gendreau family. Next to the marina in the heart of the village, the **Église Saint-Laurent** (St. Lawrence Church, 1860) is topped by a tall, well-proportioned steeple. In the old section of the village, a small processional chapel stands beside the courthouse. Upon leaving town, note the early 18C flour mill, the **Moulin Gosselin** (*left side of road*), which now houses a fine restaurant.

Saint-Jean-de-l'Île-d'Orléans★

11km/6.8mi.
Founded in 1679 by Monsignor de Laval, this community was home to the island's pilots and navigators. Between 1850 and 1950, the village experienced a period of intense economic growth with the arrival of numerous Charlevoix pilots, who brought with them opportunities for maritime and industrial development. The maritime cemetery commemorates the lives of these seamen, many of whom perished in the course of difficult voyages on the tumultuous waters of the St. Lawrence. Today, the village's residents still pursue the maritime and agricultural activities of their ancestors. Their homes, decorated with nautical adornments, are clustered on the hillsides and along the St. Lawrence shoreline.

Manoir Mauvide-Genest★ (Mauvide-Genest Manor)

Guided tours (45 min) $9 (self-guided $6), mid-May–mid-Oct Wed–Sun 10am–5pm. 418-829-2630. www.manoirmauvidegenest.com.
The original house was constructed in 1734 for Jean Mauvide, surgeon to the king and a successful French merchant, and his wife, Marie-Anne Genest, of the Saint-Jean region. By the mid-18C, the wealth accumulated by Mr. Mauvide through his business ventures in the Antilles enabled him to enlarge the rural dwelling into a veritable manor. In 1752, Mr. Mauvide bought half of the Île d'Orléans seigneury. A few years later, when his business failed, he sold the seigneury to his son-in-law. In 1926, Judge J.-Camille Pouliot purchased the manor and undertook its restoration. It is now considered the finest extant example of rural architecture from the French Regime. The manor contains a museum exhibiting furnishings and objects collected by Judge Pouliot.

Saint-François-de-l'Île d'Orléans

11km/6.8mi.
Formerly the seigneury of François Berthelot, the parish was founded in 1679. The community encompasses the eastern extremity of the island as well as the tiny Madame and Ruaux islands. The St. Lawrence changes from fresh to salt water 20km/12.4mi beyond this point. Agriculture, mainly potato crops, is the primary means of revenue for the villagers. Ravaged by fire in 1988, the **Église Saint-François** (Church of St. Francis, 1736) was reconstructed on its original foundations in 1992. On the southern side of the church, note the **presbytery** (1867), in the Quebec vernacular style, with a large balcony.
A processional chapel marks the town limit. Just outside the village, a lookout tower affords **views**★★ of both banks of the St. Lawrence.

Sainte-Famille

Monsignor de Laval founded this parish, the oldest on the island, in 1661, and had the first church erected here in 1669. Among the most interesting buildings in the village is the 17C fieldstone farmhouse of Norman inspiration, today occupied by a restaurant specializing in traditional French-Canadian cuisine. A horse and buggy picks up diners from the parking lot on the main road to the house.

Église Sainte-Famille★★ (Holy Family Church)

Opening times vary; call for times. ♿ P ✆418-828-2656.

This tri-steepled edifice is considered the most important church dating from the French Regime. Built between 1743 and 1748, the church was modified in 1807 with the addition of two lateral bell towers. In the Neoclassical **interior** (1921, Thomas Baillairgé), the nave slopes toward the altar and baldachin. The sculpted vault (1812) by Louis-Bazile David, a student of Quévillon, represents a starry sky. Dating from 1749, the tabernacle of the main altar is the work of the Levasseur family, while the tabernacles of the lateral altars are attributed to Pierre Florent, brother of François. Hanging to the right of the nave is a painting of the Holy Family attributed to Brother Luc, a Récollet painter who visited New France about 1670.

Saint-Pierre-de-l'Île-d'Orléans

The parish of Saint-Pierre is distinguished by its two churches. When the parishioners decided to build a new church in 1955, the government acquired the old church, erected between 1715 and 1719, to protect it from demolition.

Old Church★

Opening times vary; telephone for details. ♿ P ✆418-828-9824.

Damaged during the Conquest, the church was restored and then enlarged in 1775 when the parish priest became auxiliary bishop of Quebec City. The church was again remodeled in the 1830s by Thomas Baillairgé.

The interior contains three altars executed by Pierre Émond in 1795 and a sanctuary lamp carved in wood. Note also the box pews, introduced to Quebec by Protestant groups, and, at the front and back of the church, the woodstoves with sheetmetal pipes that heated the nave.

PARC DE LA JACQUES-CARTIER★

▶ 40km/24.8mi N of Quebec City via Rte 175. Open mid-Dec–mid-Mar and mid-May–Oct, daily. Call for hours. $8 adults; 17 and under free △ ✕ P ✆418-848-3169. www.sepaq.com.

Located in the highlands of the Laurentian Mountains, Jacques-Cartier Park covers an area of 670sq km/259sq mi. The coniferous boreal forest extending from Quebec across to Alaska reaches its southernmost point here, on the rolling mountaintops of the massif, which ends in an abrupt 600m/1,968ft drop to the Jacques-Cartier River. Here, the coniferous forest gives way to deciduous vegetation. Extensive logging of the plateau disrupted the fragile environmental equilibrium, causing the disappearance of caribou and salmon, two species well adapted to the cold climate of the region. The park was created in 1981 in an effort to better monitor logging operations and preserve the area's magnificent natural heritage.

Centre d'accueil et d'interprétation (Welcome and Interpretation Center)

▶ Turn left off Rte. 175 from Quebec City at la Vallée secteur entrance. Continue 10km/6.2mi into the park. Maps of the park and activity information are available at the welcome center (closed during winter).

A permanent exhibit on the Laurentian Massif and an audiovisual presentation on the geographical formations found in the area provide explanations of the geological forces that shaped the park's spectacular landscapes. The road into the park begins to the left of the interpretation center and follows the Jacques-Cartier River behind the center. After crossing the river, the road surface changes from asphalt to gravel. The trail known as **Sentier des Loups** (*10km/6.2mi round-trip*) offers splendid **views**★★ of the entire Jacques-Cartier River valley.

Trips down the Jacques-Cartier River

Book boats from the rental center located at kilometer 10 on the Route de la Vallée. ℘1-800-665-6527. www.sepaq.com.

The 177km/110mi Jacques-Cartier is the only river in Quebec that belongs to the Canadian Heritage Rivers System. Within the park, it offers a navigable stretch of 26km/16mi, with cliff walls towering nearly 500m/1,660ft above a ribbon of calm water interspersed with short stretches of rapids. You can choose from a range of different options, from canoes to recreational kayaks, mini rafts, inflatable canoes, or inner tubes, with routes for beginners as well as experienced boaters.

Long-distance backcountry skiing

Because it receives more than 6m/20ft of snow per year, the park provides excellent conditions for cross-country skiing, snowshoeing, or snow walking, and it is an ideal spot for long-distance skiing enthusiasts.

ADDRESSES

STAY

⊜ Auberge internationale de Québec – *19 rue Sainte-Ursule. ♿ ℘418-694-0755 or 1-866-694-0950. www.hostellingquebec.com. 277 beds.* ☕$32. Located within the walls of the Old City, this large, historic hostel is a member of Hostelling International. Open year-round, it offers **dorm-style rooms** accommodating two to eight people, as well as private rooms with or without en-suite bathroom. The **private rooms** provide the best value for money in the walled city. **Family rooms** (for up to five people) with a bathroom are available. Both a cafeteria and kitchen are available on site for hostelers. Common rooms allow for rest and conversations.

⊜⊜ Hôtel Acadia – *43 rue Sainte-Ursule. ℘418-694-0280 or 1-800-463-0280. www.hotelacadia.com.* 🅿. *40 rooms.* ☕. *from $82.* The building dates from 1822, but the comfort of the English, Romantic, or French-style rooms is a match for anything a modern hotel can offer, with air conditioning, TV, WiFi, etc. The twists and turns of its corridors, meanwhile, as well as the exposed brick or stonework in some of the rooms, give it a charm all of its own.

⊜⊜ Hôtel Belley – *249 rue Saint-Paul, place du Marché du Vieux-Port.* ♿ 🅿 *℘418-692-1694 or 1-888-692-1694. www.hotelbelley.com. 8 rooms. Restaurant⊜.* Old World charm in the form of brick walls and exposed beams, coupled with a great location in the Old Port, make for a comfortable and reasonably priced stay here that is ideal for families or budget-conscious couples.

⊜⊜ Manoir d'Auteuil – *49 rue d'Auteuil. ℘418-694-1173. www.manoirdauteuil.com.* 🅿 *27 rooms.* ☕. A venerable hotel opposite the ramparts and their open spaces, in one of the city center's nicest streets. The rooms are small but cozy and impeccable, in 19C manor-house style.

⊜⊜ Auberge Saint-Louis – *48 rue Saint-Louis. ℘418-692-2424 or 1-888-692-4105 (no charge). www.aubergestlouis.ca. 27 rooms.* ☕. A three-storey hotel occupying two houses built in 1830. The rooms have been renovated in a contemporary, functional style in shades of gray and black. Ideally situated a stone's throw from the Château Frontenac, in the heart of Old Quebec.

⊜⊜⊜⊜ Auberge Saint-Antoine – *8 rue Saint-Antoine.* ♿ 🅿 *℘418-692-2211 or 1-888-692-2211. www.saint-antoine.com. 95 rooms.* A renovated 1822 warehouse and an adjoining 1720s English merchant's house are located on one of the city's major archeological sites. Artifacts from the digs are displayed in the hotel, offering a unique way to learn more about daily life in 17C–19C Quebec. Several rooms and suites—many with the original stone walls and hand-hewn beams—offer stunning views of the St. Lawrence River or the city's fortifications. Member of the *Relais & Châteaux.* Dining onsite is a treat at upscale Panache inside a renovated marine warehouse.

$$$$ **Château Bonne-Entente** – *3400 chemin Sainte-Foy, near Rte 540.* ♿ P Spa *☎418-653-5221 or 1-800-463-4390. www.chateaubonneentente.com. 160 rooms.* Occupying a landscaped, wooded site convenient to both Old Quebec and the airport, the Château Bonne Entente offers the charms of a country inn while supplying the amenities of a 5-star hotel. Pamper yourself with massages, an outdoor heated whirlpool and other spa services at the Amerispa. Guest rooms boast distinctive décor; family suites feature bunk beds and toys for the kids.

$$$$ **Fairmont Le Château Frontenac** – *1 rue des Carrières.* ♿ P *☎418-692-3861 or 1-800-441-1414. www.fairmont.com/frontenac-quebec. 611 rooms. Restaurant$$$$.* Built in 1892, the regal copper-roofed Château Frontenac towers above Old Quebec as the most enduring symbol of the city. Over the years, this grande dame has hosted the likes of Queen Elizabeth and Sir Winston Churchill. The bustling lobby, lined with elaborate wood paneling, reflects the opulence of those bygone days. A $70 million refurbishment has transformed much of the interior, adding sleek modern room décor in soft tones, and a brighter lobby. Well-appointed rooms vary in size (some are relatively small), shape and view. The hotel's restaurant, **Le Champlain**, serves French/Québécois dishes that celebrate produce from the *terroir* (region), while the hotel bar provides great views of the river.

$$$$ **Hôtel du Vieux-Québec** – *1190 rue St-Jean.* ♿ P *☎418-692-1850 or 1-800-361-7787. www.hvq.com. 46 rooms*☕. A good bet for families and student groups, this carefully restored century-old brick hotel in the Latin Quarter, which finished a $2 million renovation in 2014, offers attractive rooms with sofas, private baths and mini-refrigerators; some even have kitchenettes. During Jul–Aug rates include continental breakfast and a one-hour orientation on Quebec's culture. One of the best continental dining options in town onsite.

$$$$ **Le Germain-Dominion** – *126 rue Saint-Pierre. ☎418-692-2224 or 888-833-5253. www.hoteldominion.com.* ♿ P. *60 rooms.* Located in a nine-story commercial building constructed in 1912 for Dominion Fish and Fruit, Ltd., this Québécois-owned boutique hotel sits in the heart of the Old Port district. Stained glass and ironwork highlight the exquisitely decorated lobby and reading room. Natural light floods the spacious, high-ceilinged guest rooms through tall windows, and goose-down duvets and pillows wrap guests in comfort. Rate includes a refined continental breakfast.

EAT

$ **Le Billig** – *481 rue Saint-Jean. ☎418-524-8341. Mon–Fri 11am–10pm, Sat–Sun 10am–10pm.* The decor in bright colors and red brick creates a warm atmosphere at this crêperie. The owner hails from Pontivy in Brittany and makes savory buckwheat pancakes in the pure Breton tradition. Don't miss the *cancalaise* (scallops, leeks, and hollandaise sauce), a dish best enjoyed with Quebec cider.

$ **Les Bossus 620** – *620 rue St-Joseph Est. ☎418-522-5501. www.lesbossus.com. Open Mon–Wed 9am–10pm, Thu–Sat 9am–11pm, Sun 11am–10pm.* A contemporary-style bistro with large black and white tiles on the floor, designer banquettes and a long counter lit by globe-shaped lamps. The cuisine is traditional, however, with a menu featuring soups and dishes such as *confit de canard*, horse burger, French fries and crème brûlée.

$ **Hobbit Bistro** – *700 rue Saint-Jean. ☎418-647-2677. www.hobbitbistro.com. Open Mon–Fri 8am–10pm, Sat–Sun 9am –10pm. Closed 1 Jan.* A neighborhood restaurant par excellence: service with a smile, a convivial atmosphere and good food, with *wood* and stone featuring strongly in the decor. Some customers come for specialties from the grill, others just for a sandwich. Wines by the glass. Good value for money.

$ **Café Krieghoff** – *1089 Ave. Cartier. ☎418-522-3711. www.cafekrieghoff.qc.ca. Mon–Fri 7am–10pm, Sat 8am–11pm, Sun 8am–9pm.* This café serves light meals and excellent breakfasts, attracting a varied clientele to its small, simply decorated dining rooms. There are also comfortable, reasonably priced rooms onsite at Petit Hôtel, and walking to the best sights from here is both informative and within reach during any season.

⊖ **Café-restaurant du Musée du Québec** – *In National Battlefields Park. ℘418-644-6780. www.mnba.qc.ca.* Located within the Quebec Museum of Fine Arts, this restaurant offers imaginative regional French fare, carefully prepared and served with flair. Natural light floods the vast dining room, where immense windows offer a superb view of the Plains of Abraham. In summer, take a table on the terrace to admire the surrounding countryside.

⊖ **Le Petit Coin Latin** – *8 1/2 rue Sainte-Ursule. ℘418-692-0700. Open daily 7:30am–10pm.* Steps away from rue Saint-Jean, Le Petit Coin is the perfect spot to enjoy breakfast, a light meal or a peaceful cup of coffee; the staff keep a selection of periodicals on hand for guests to read at their leisure.

⊖ **Pub Saint-Alexandre** – *1087 rue Saint-Jean. ℘418-694-0015. www.pubstalexandre.com.* Even the most formidable thirst doesn't stand a chance at an English pub with live music where an amazing selection of 200 imported beers complements the menu of pasta, salads, sausages, and steak-and-fries.

⊖⊖ **47e Parallèle** – *333 rue St-Amable. ℘418 692 4747. www.le47.com. 11:30am–2pm, 5pm–10pm. Closed weekend lunch.* Opposite the Grand Théâtre, this exciting restaurant offers a great menu with worldwide influences. The regularly changing menu offers the likes of venison, local fish cooked in exotic styles and dishes inspired by cuisines that combine sweet and sour.

⊖⊖ **Café du Monde** – *84 rue Dalhousie (Old Port). ♿ ℘418-692-4455. www.lecafedumonde.com.* Find delicious staples like ***steak-frites*** (steak and French fries), ***magret de canard*** (breast of duck) and ***moules*** (mussels) in this popular waterfront Parisian-style bistro. In addition to the tasty food, a cozy atmosphere and gregarious waiters in white aprons make for a pleasant dining experience in a large and lively dining room.

⊖⊖ **Le Cochon Dingue** – *46 Blvd Champlain. ℘418-692-2013. www.cochondingue.com.* One of Old Quebec's most inviting eateries sports a terrace and an attractive façade of stone pierced by large windows (1911). Friendly service and a relaxed ambiance enhance the savory bistro food, especially steak-and-fries (the house specialty), mussels and desserts. Breakfast is plentiful and delicious.

⊖⊖ **Le Graffiti** – *1191 Ave. Cartier. ℘418-529-4949 www.restaurantgraffiti.com.* Features high-quality Italian and French cuisine accompanied by an excellent wine list. A glass-brick wall enhances the warm, welcoming interior.

⊖⊖ **Portofino** – *54 rue Couillard.* **P** *℘418-692-8888 and 1-866-692-8882. www.portofino.qc.ca.* This lively trattoria is located in a home from 1760. You can choose from 24 varieties of home-made pasta and 15 different wood-fired pizzas, complemented by a good Italian wine from an extensive list, or you could sample specialties such as veal scallopini or rack of Quebec lamb. Throw in the noise level of a good time and the flags of popular Italian soccer teams, and even the most reticent in your party will soon be singing "Amore."

⊖⊖ **Simple Snack Sympathique** – *71 rue Saint-Paul (Old Port). Mon–Fri 11:30am–10:30pm, Sat–Sun 5pm–10:30pm. ℘418-692-1991 www.restaurantsss.com.* This popular neighborhood restaurant, known to the locals as SSS, offers two atmospheres in one: the lounge in front has high tables and trendy music, while the back section is subdued, with a crackling fireplace and diners enjoying a contemporary seasonal menu featuring the chef's spin on poutine using pulled pork, and other local plates. One of the few restaurants in the area that stays open late.

⊖⊖⊖ **Aux Anciens Canadiens** – *34 rue Saint-Louis. ℘418-692-1627. www.auxancienscanadiens.qc.ca.* Charmingly situated in a historic white house with red trim (1675), this oldest restaurant in the city specializes in local cuisine, offering a delicious introduction to traditional fine dining à la Québécoise. The menu lists classics—

pea soup, ***tourtière*** (meat pie)—and newer favorites such as ***feuilleté de saumon*** (salmon in puff pastry). For dessert, try maple-syrup pie, or sugar tarts with cream.

⊖⊜⊜ **Le Continental** – *26 rue Saint-Louis.* ♿ ✆*418-694-9995.* ***www.restaurantcontinental.com.*** The oldest gourmet restaurant in the city, located in an 1845 mansion, this local favorite near Château Frontenac serves up classic specialties such as rack of lamb and duckling ***à l'orange*** as well as seafood and steak. Professional service prevails in the dining room, where dark blue walls and wood paneling impart a simple elegance.

⊖⊜⊜ **Ciel** – *1225 pl. Montcalm, in Le Concorde Hôtel.* ✆*418-640-5802.* ***www.cielbistrobar.com. Open Mon–Fri 11:30am–10pm, Sat–Sun 9am–10pm.*** This restaurant offers dining with great views of the city. Quebec City's only revolving restaurant, it serves continental cuisine prepared with regional ingredients and affords views of the St. Lawrence, Old Quebec City, Île d'Orléans, Lévis and the Charlevoix Coast. The aerial view is particularly spectacular in winter. In summer, watch the sun set to live piano music (***Tue–Sun evenings***), enjoy a nightcap or discover the popular Sunday brunch ***(10am–3pm).***

⊖⊜⊜ **L'Échaudé** – *73 rue Sault-au-Matelot.* ✆*418-692-1299.* ***www.echaude.com.*** This restaurant serves a tempting variety of beautifully prepared and presented meat, fish and poultry dishes as well as salads. The service is attentive, even when there's a crowd.

⊖⊜⊜ **Le Saint-Amour** – *48 rue Sainte-Ursule.* ✆*418-694-0667.* ***www.saint-amour.com.*** Dine in casual elegance here in the tile-floored Winter Garden, the Saint-Amour's cheery atrium. ***Foie gras de canard du Québec*** (Quebec duck foie gras), ***saisie de caribou des Inuits aux baies de genièvre*** (Inuit caribou steak with juniper berries) and ***crème brûlée à la mure*** (blackberry crème brûlée) typify the traditional cuisine crafted with a nouvelle twist by chef Jean-Luc Boulay. Treat yourself to the nine-course ***menu découverte,*** where each dish finds its perfect match from the wide-ranging international wine list. Service is professional and friendly.

⊖⊜⊜ **Yu-Zu** – *438 rue du Parvis.* ✆*418-521-7253.* ***www.yuzu.ca. Open 11am–8pm.*** The stylish feel of this sushi bar is visible in the contemporary décor in shades of black, light wood and leather. On the table, the likes of tempura, maki sushi, nigiri sushi, sashimi or veal tataki are all presented in a similarly minimalist style. To experience this sophisticated place for yourself, you could try a lunchtime visit for "yuzu direct" with imperial rolls and maki sushi ($9.50) or General Tao chicken ($11.95).

TAKING A BREAK

Le Buffet de l'Antiquaire – *95 rue Saint-Paul.* ✆*418-692-2661,* ***www.buffetdelantiquaire.com.*** Busiest at mealtimes, but you can also stop by at other times for a substantial snack in the company of the antique dealers who come to chew the fat and discuss their latest finds.

SHOPPING

Good to know – The Petit-Champlain neighborhood (www.quartierpetitchamplain.com) boasts all sorts of stores, many specializing in regional fine arts and crafts.

Writing home? Try **L'Oiseau du Paradis** *(80 rue du Petit-Champlain;* ✆*418-692-2679)*, where the selection of fine, handmade papers includes cards, tablets and other writing materials, as well as lamps and masks.

Colorful silk scarves and ties are displayed in all their shimmering glory at **La Soierie Huo** (*see below*), where you'll also find scarves of wool and chiffon. The following areas are also particularly good for a wander: rue Saint-Jean, rue Saint-Louis, rue Saint-Paul (antiques), rue Sainte-Anne and rue Cartier, Côte de la Fabrique, Grande Allée and 3e Avenue.

Le Forgeron d'Or – *23 1/2 rue du Petit-Champlain* ✆*581-981-4445.* ***www.leforgerondor.com.*** Since 1989 this Quebecois jewelry designer—who specializes in Canadian diamonds—has created unusual, original gold and silver pieces, now on display in this recently opened boutique.

A Night at Le Capitole

972 rue Saint-Jean. Information and reservations ℘418-694-4444. Just steps away from the St. John Gate, this century-old building houses one of Quebec's most prestigious live-performance theaters. With a seating capacity of 1,300, the sumptuous interior lends itself to large-scale productions as well as more intimate concerts. Before or after the show (or for breakfast), stop at Il Teatro (*in the Capitole building; ℘418-694-4444; www.lecapitole.com*), a charming eatery serving fine Italian cuisine in a modern, welcoming setting. In summer the terrace offers a wonderful view of rue Saint-Jean.

Marché du Vieux-Port – *160 Quai Saint-André. ℘418-692-2517. www.marchevieuxport.com. Open Mon–Fri 9am–6pm, Sat–Sun 9am–5pm.* With goodies such as flowers, honey, maple products, cider, fruit and vegetables from the Île d'Orléans, charcuterie and meat on offer, your shopping basket will soon fill up on a trip around this market hall in the Old Port. A few restaurants have also moved in, so you can satisfy any hunger pangs while you shop.

La Soierie Huo – *91 rue du Petit-Champlain. ℘418-692-5920. www.soieriehuo.com. Jun–Sept daily 9:30am–8pm; rest of the year 9:30am–5pm.* Dominique Huo and Hugues Beaulieu opened their bright and colorful silk shop nearly 20 years ago. They are sometimes to be found painting on silk amidst the scarves ($35), ties ($65), hair slides ($15) and clip-on earrings ($20) that are made and sold on site.

La Dentellière – *56 Blvd Champlain. ℘418-692-2807. www.quartierpetitchamplain.com/La-dentelliere. Open Jun–Sept daily 9am–9pm; rest of year Sun–Wed 9:30am–5:30pm (closes 9pm Thu–Fri; Sat 5pm).* From the window to the back of the shop, nothing but lace: doilies, underwear, sheets, tablecloths, and more, all in beautiful shades of white.

Erico – *634 rue Saint Jean, ℘418-524-2122, www.ericochocolatier.com. Open Mon–Wed 10:30am–6pm; Thu and Fri 10:30am–9pm; Sat 10:30am–6pm; Sun 11am–6pm.* The deep aroma of chocolate gives away this local establishment. Since 1988, this chocolatier has created a huge range of handmade artisanal chocolate, all made on the premises. Visitors can learn the history of chocolate at the store's museum and enjoy sculptures carved from solid chocolate.

Maison Jean-Alfred Moisan – *699 rue Saint-Jean. ℘418-522-0685. www.jamoisan.com. Mon–Sat 8:30am–9pm; Sun 10am–7pm.* Since 1871, this local institution has been supplying the Faubourg Saint-Jean neighborhood with fresh fruit and vegetables, bread, charcuterie, and cheeses from France, Italy and Quebec. Also worth a look for its period shelving and counters with prominent displays of confectionery imported from Europe.

ÎLE D'ORLÉANS

Good to know – The island is famous for its strawberries, and from late June to early July, the roads are lined with stalls selling fresh fruit as well as strawberry jams or tarts fresh from the oven. Some growers also operate a pick-your-own system. If you're there at the right time, don't miss out, as the season only lasts a few weeks each year.

Au Goût d'Autrefois – *4311 chemin Royal, Sainte-Famille. ℘418-829-9888. www.augoutdautrefois.qc.ca.* Goose is another specialty of the Île d'Orléans, in all its forms.

DRINKS

Le Sainte-Angèle – *26 rue Ste-Angèle. ℘418-692-2171.* From the outside, only the green door distinguishes this tiny, friendly little place, giving it the feel of a conspirators' hang-out. The bar serves excellent cocktails and well-chosen beers, and is famous for its jazz concerts on Thursday and Friday evenings.

La Barberie – *310 rue Saint-Roch. ℘418-5224373. www.labarberie.com.* On the eastern edge of the trendy Saint-Roch neighborhood, you can choose from ten different beers produced by this microbrewery (including one organic choice), as well as others brewed in the region, which are offered on a rotational basis. Nice terrace.

Taverne Belley – *249 rue Saint-Paul. ℘418-692-4595.* This bar opened in the 1930s, and it offers a fine selection of beers in a setting reminiscent of the Quebec City of old. From the terrace, you can look out over the street and the old port, and it's not unusual to see customers playing a game of pétanque on a strip of ground nearby.

GOING OUT

Good to know – To get an idea of what's on, take a look at free tourist publications like Québec Scope, Voilà Québec and Voir, or the Arts and Entertainment sections of the newspapers (weekend editions). Tickets for cultural events are on sale at the following outlets: **Billetech** – *℘418-643-8131.* Department stores (two in Quebec City, one in Sainte-Foy). Major credit cards accepted.

Le Cercle – *226 1/2 and 228 rue Saint-Joseph. ℘418-948-8648, www.le-cercle.ca.* This hip evening venue has stylish décor with exposed brick walls, an industrial feel, and a crowd that is up to speed on the latest trends. Share tapas with friends and enjoy a fine choice of wines.

Le Sacrilège – *447 rue Saint-Jean. ℘418-649-1985. www.lesacrilege.com. Noon–3am. DJ Fri–Sat nights.* Perhaps the most convivial of the city's bars, and a good place to meet for a chat over a micro-brew. The music, the bare brick walls and the contemporary art add to the appeal. The shady little terrace to the rear is also a major bonus in summer.

Maurice – *575 Grande Allée. ℘418-647-2000. www.mauricenightclub.com. Thu–Sat 9pm–3am.* Beneath the tower of the Hôtel Concorde, you will find one of the city's best-known nightclubs, with two floors playing hip hop, dance, R&B, and electro, and with a strong lounge theme to the decor.

SPORTS EVENTS

Ice hockey – *Quebec Remparts (AHM de Sainte-Foy), Pepsi Coliseum, 250 blvd Wilfrid-Hamel. ℘418-525-1212 . www.remparts.qc.ca. Season: Sept–Mar.*

Baseball – *Quebec Capitales, Stade Municipal, 100 Rue du Cardinal-Maurice-Roy. ℘418-521-2255. www.capitalesdequebec.com.*

Horse racing – *Hippodrome Trois Rivieres. ℘819-374-6734.*

ACTIVITIES

Station Touristique Duchesnay – *40km/25mi NW of Quebec City (from the St. Lawrence River) on Autoroute 40 (towards Montreal), exit 295 then Route 367 to Ste-Catherine-de-la-Jacques-Cartier. ℘418-875-2711 or 1-866-683-2711. www.sepaq.com/duchesnay.* This center on the shore of Lac St-Joseph offers a variety of open-air activities: walking, cycling, accrobranche (tree climbing adventure course) and windsurfing in summer; ice skating, snowmobiling, cross-country skiing, and ice fishing in winter, plus Scandinavian spa and an ice hotel.

EVENTS

Carnaval de Québec– *Feb 1–17 ℘418-626-3716. www.carnaval.qc.ca.* Also known as "bonhomme," Quebec City's carnival is a fantastic celebration. Making the most of the wintry season, the festival includes dog sled races, ice skating, arctic spas, snow baths (only for the very brave) and snow slides. There are also night parades with marching bands and colorful floats. The carnival follows the New France tradition of Quebecers having a rowdy celebration before the beginning of Lent, keeping them positive in the face of the winter's hardships. The first large winter carnival in Quebec City took place in 1894, and since then it has grown into an enormous tourist draw with new activities and competitions emerging every year, but be aware that airlines and hotels raise prices during the event.

Salon international du livre de Québec (Quebec international book fair) – *℘418-692-0010. www.silq.ca.* Mid-Apr.

Festival d'été de Québec (Quebec summer festival) – *℘418-529-5200. www.infofestival.com.* First two weeks of July.

Les fêtes de la Nouvelle-France (New France Festival) – *℘418-694-3311. www.nouvellefrance.qc.ca .* First two weeks of August.

Northwest of Quebec City

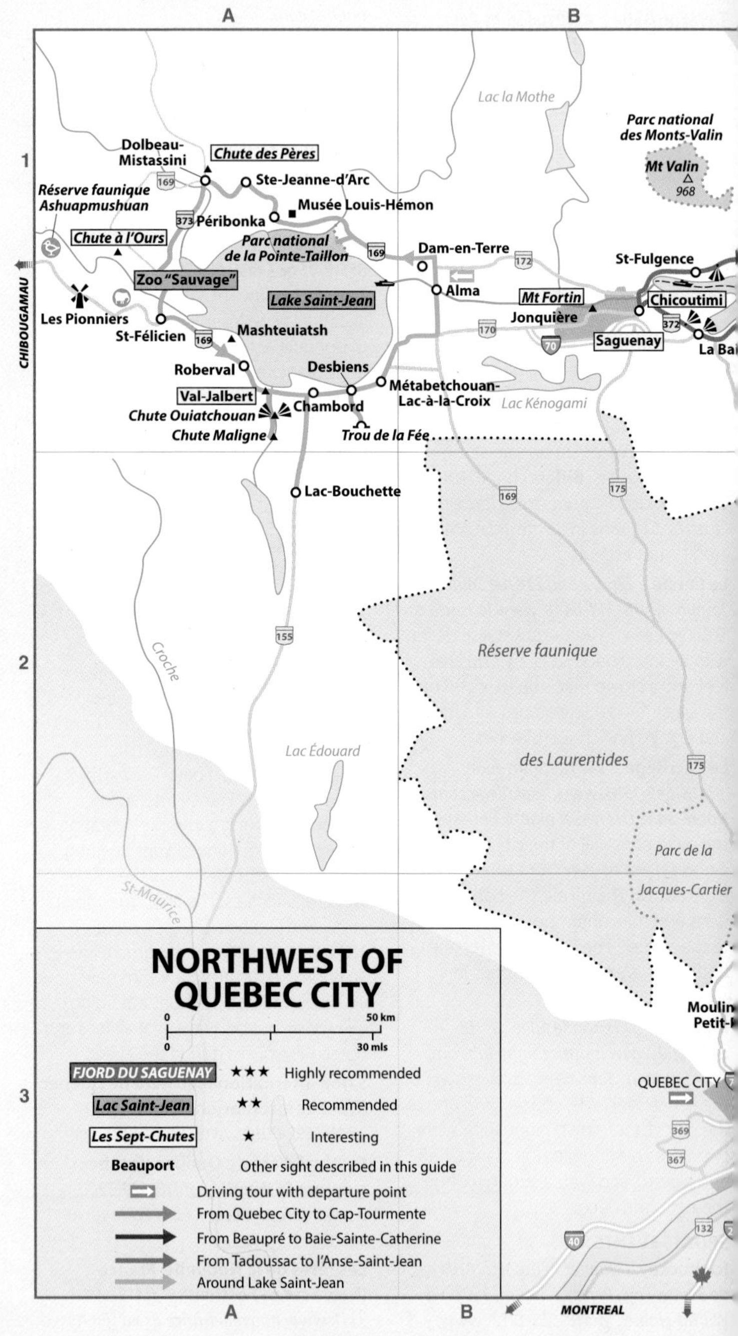

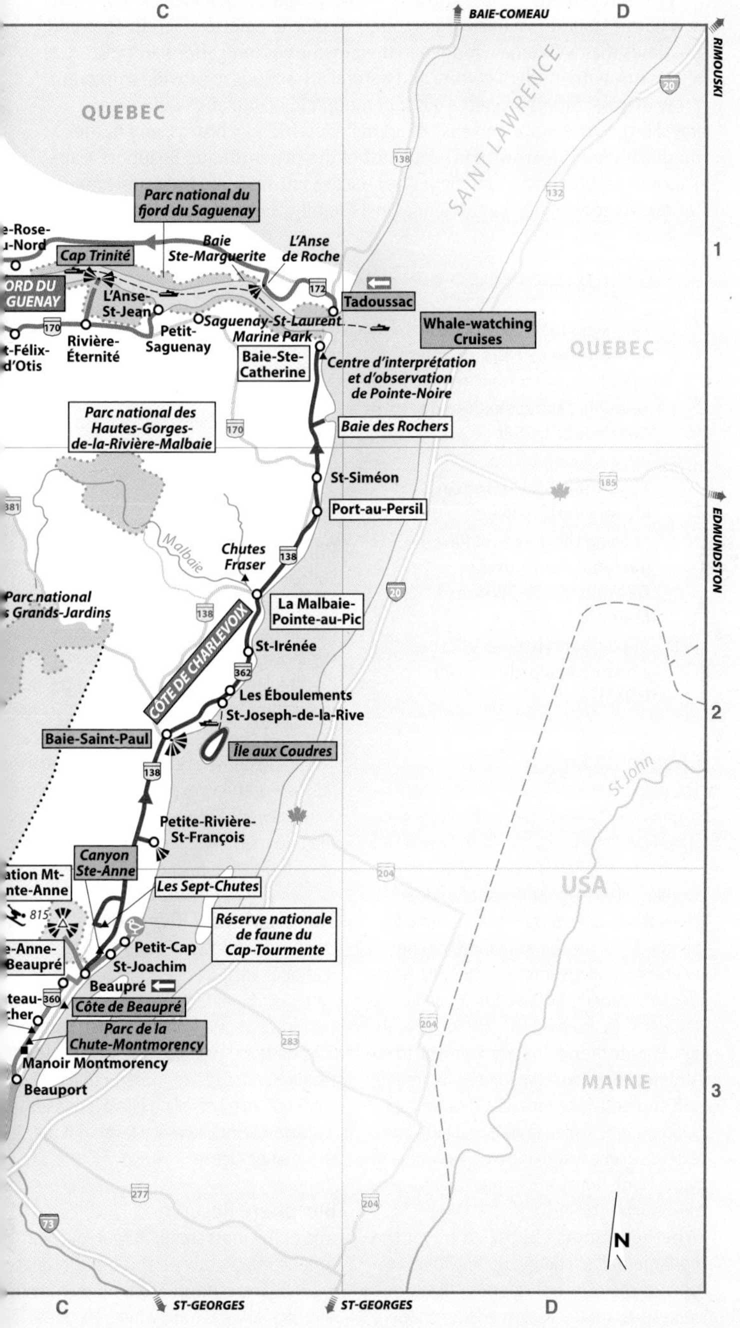

C
BAIE-COMEAU
D
RIMOUSKI
QUEBEC
SAINT LAWRENCE
Parc national du fjord du Saguenay
Baie Ste-Marguerite
L'Anse de Roche
Cap Trinité
Tadoussac
L'Anse-St-Jean
Saguenay-St-Laurent Marine Park
Whale-watching Cruises
Rivière-Éternité
Petit-Saguenay
Baie-Ste-Catherine
Centre d'interprétation et d'observation de Pointe-Noire
QUEBEC
Parc national des Hautes-Gorges-de-la-Rivière-Malbaie
Baie des Rochers
St-Siméon
Port-au-Persil
EDMUNDSTON
Malbaie
Chutes Fraser
La Malbaie-Pointe-au-Pic
Parc national des Grands-Jardins
CÔTE DE CHARLEVOIX
St-Irénée
Les Éboulements
St-Joseph-de-la-Rive
Baie-Saint-Paul
Île aux Coudres
St John
Petite-Rivière-St-François
Canyon Ste-Anne
Les Sept-Chutes
USA
Réserve nationale de faune du Cap-Tourmente
Petit-Cap
St-Joachim
Beaupré
Côte de Beaupré
Parc de la Chute-Montmorency
Manoir Montmorency
Beauport
MAINE
N
ST-GEORGES
ST-GEORGES
1
2
3

Northwest of Quebec City

No matter where travelers go after leaving Quebec City, they cannot fail to have a good time. Each region offers a colorful palette of landscapes and pastimes that will remain lodged in their memories long afterward. Historical sights mix with modern culture and natural attractions to provide a dizzying array of possibilities: from the vigor of mountain hiking and whitewater kayaking, to the grace and ease of art galleries, friendly bistros, and home-made cuisine. These districts northwest of the city, including Beauport, Cap-Tourmente, Charlevoix, and Saguenay–Lake Saint-Jean, are irresistible magnets for guests seeking new experiences in a friendly, fun, and historic area.

Highlights

1. The "sugarloaf" cone of ice at **Montmorency Falls** in winter (p352)
2. The sights along the **Côte de Charlevoix** (p358)
3. Whales and fjords at **Saguenay–St. Lawrence Marine Park** (p365)
4. Cruising the gorges of **Parc national des Hautes-Georges-de-la-Rivière-Malbaie** (p366)
5. **Val-Jalbert Historic Village**, a restored pulp ghost town (p385)

Chemin du Roy

The magic beyond Quebec City starts on the chemin du Roy (also called La Route de Nouvelle-France or The King's Highway) in Old Town, where visitors pass through the former working-class neighborhood of Saint-Roch, cross the Charles River into Cité-Limoilou, and begin to see the increasing number of heritage buildings, former seigneurial mansions, riverfront estates, windmills, churches, and other treasures of this historic territory just outside the urban zone. From the town of **Beauport** (1634) the road becomes Rte. 138 and begins to meander around captivating seigneurial mansions and farms, and extends all the way to the oldest pilgrimage site in North America, Basilique Sainte-Anne-de-Beaupré (1658).

Whether visitors choose to travel the heritage trail of chemin du Roy for examples of historic architecture, like stone mansions, root cellars, roadside chapels, and churches, or the quicker highway option that takes them to the pilgrimage shrine of Sainte-Anne-de-Beaupré and nearby Cyclorama; either way, it does not take long to realize the city has been left far behind. The fantastic **Le Massif de Charlevoix** (*see p350*) is reachable from here. With a focus on sustainable tourism this popular ski resort has an emphasis on renewable energy, and blends in beautifully with its surroundings.

Parc de la chute Montmorency

Follow the Saint Lawrence River heading east just outside the city, and you will view the captivating sight of Montmorency Falls, reminding visitors of what's in store in this pristine land of lakes, rivers, forests, and mountains. There is excitement in the power of the mist shroud, and one can only imagine what it must have been like for the European explorers sailing up the Saint Lawrence River near Île d'Orléans , as the river narrowed, and a new continent unfolded before their eyes.

The Charlevoix Riverside

Once beyond Mont Sainte-Anne's recreational area, travelers are well into the Canadian Shield topography, containing the oldest geology on the planet. Entering the Charlevoix near Baie Saint-Paul, a spectacular landscape of more than 6,000 sq km/3,600 sq mi of rolling hills overlooks the widening Saint Lawrence River as it meets the Atlantic Ocean.

Biosphere Reserve

One of the most stunning routes in North America takes drivers through undulating rolls and climbs, surprising them with exceptional vistas everywhere. This area is a UNESCO Heritage World Biosphere Reserve

Baie-Saint-Paul, Charlevoix

(1985), and visitors will want to see Parc national des Hautes-Gorges-de-la-Rivière-Malbaie, for its sheer rock faces and incredible diversity of flora and fauna, including caribou, foxes, eagles, and wolves.

Mountains and Marine Park

The Parc National des Grands-Jardins attracts hikers to its 100km/60mi trail called La Traversée de Charlevoix, which ends at Mont Grand Fonds, and the Saguenay-Saint-Lawrence Marine Park, a whale-watching mecca with 15 species of sea mammals attracted to the fjord water, which mixes the fresh water of the Great Lakes with the salt water of the ocean. The river winds through a majestic fjord with breathtaking rocky walls that have a special fascination. To the north extends a vast wilderness of forests and lakes that is brimming with adventure.

Many of the 277,000 residents of the Saguenay–Lake St.-Jean region live in riverside towns that feature vibrant local culture.

The Landscape that Inspired a Circus

Quaintness is the hallmark of places like Baie Saint-Paul, Sainte-Îrenée, Port-au-Persil, La Baie, Rivière Éternité, Alma and Saint-Félicien. Colored rooftops, B&Bs, cafés, farmers' markets, and unique craft shops are there to discover, savor and remember. Local artisans make more than 400 cheeses, traditional dishes like *soup aux gourgannes* (large bean soup), *cipaille* (six-layer meat pie), *poutine* (French fries and cheese curds with gravy), and maple sugar pie.

Whether it's enjoying art, nature, history, or gastronomy, venturing outside the city is an experience for solo travelers, groups of friends, or families. Make sure enough time is allocated. This, after all, is the landscape that inspired Cirque du Soleil, and after a visit to this enchanting region, it is easy to see why.

Skier at Le Massif de Charlevoix

LE MASSIF DE CHARLEVOIX

Le Massif (one hour from Quebec City) has an awe-inspiring view of the mighty Saint Lawrence River. Known primarily as a ski resort created by Daniel Gauthier, one of the founders of the Cirque du Soleil, it has the largest vertical drop east of the Rockies (770m/2,526ft).

The annual snowfall can reach 6.5m/21ft, which attracts legions of downhill skiers, snowboarders and cross-country fans, many of whom board a light rail transit from Quebec City along the Charlevoix coast. Visitors can also overnight in a contemporary hotel called **Hôtel La Férme** (the farm) which offers 145 rooms designed in five pavilions to reflect the original farm that once stood on this site.

Combined with a lively town square, spa, and conference center for 500, the site also features a fresh produce market. After a day's exertion on the slopes, head to Massif's **Summit Cafeteria**, a haven of casual dining on top of the mountain, featuring the robust flavors of Chef Guy Bessone's local produce combined with European influences. Braised lamb shank, roasted charcuterie, fish, meat and game are among the many reasons to visit. Le Massif, with its 53 trails and 6 lifts and enviable annual snowfall, is open to all skiers and sightseers alike.

1350 rue Principale, Petite-Rivière-Saint-François. www.lemassif.com. 418-632-5876 or toll-free 1-877-536-2774.

Côte de Beaupré★★

The Beaupré Coast is a narrow stretch of land nestled between the Canadian Shield and the St. Lawrence River, east of Quebec City. It extends from Montmorency Falls to the river estuary of Cap-Tourmente. The name of the region supposedly derives from an exclamation made by Jacques Cartier who, noting the meadowland alongside the river, said ***"Quel beau pré!"*** **(What a fine meadow!). The Beaupré Coast, dotted with villages established during the French Regime, is known for the popular shrine at Sainte-Anne-de-Beaupré, and the resort area of Mont Sainte-Anne.**

- **Michelin Map:** p346–347: C3
- **Info:** 1-877-783-1608. www.cotedebeaupre.com. www.quebecregion.com.
- **Location:** The Beaupré Coast is accessible from Quebec City by Rte. 440, which becomes Rte. 40 and then Rte. 138. If time allows, visitors are advised to take the much more interesting Rte. 360 (Ave. Royale) from Beauport.
- **Parking:** Ave. Royale is often narrow and street parking is limited: use designated lots near attractions.
- **Don't Miss:** Montmorency Falls; the drive along Avenue Royale; Cap-Tourmente National Wildlife Reserve; skiing at Mont-Sainte-Anne.
- **Timing:** Although not a long drive, a full day on the Beaupré Coast is a day well spent. To visit both Montmorency Falls and Cap-Tourmente, plan to use the faster Rte. 360 one way and the scenic Ave. Royale the other.
- **Kids:** Family packages (*$31–42*) provide access to the Montmorency Falls Park for a full day, and include parking and unlimited use of the cable car.

A BIT OF HISTORY

The seigneury of Beaupré was among the largest in New France, stretching from the Montmorency River to Baie-Saint-Paul. Champlain established his first farm here in 1626, which was destroyed by the notorious adventurers, the Kirke Brothers, in 1629. Settlers began working this fertile land in the 1630s and founded the first rural parishes in New France. Beaupré's seigneur from 1668 through 1680 was François de Laval, the first Bishop of Quebec City. Monsignor de Laval was responsible for planning the King's Highway (chemin du Roy), which ran from Quebec City to Saint-Joachim and is known today as the Avenue Royale. After de Laval's death, the seigneury remained in the hands of the Quebec Seminary until the end of the seigneurial regime in 1854.

DRIVING TOUR

FROM QUEBEC CITY TO CAP-TOURMENTE

48km/30mi.
See regional map, p347.

From Quebec City, take Rte. 440 east to Exit 24, then Ave. d'Estimauville to Rte. 360 (also called Ave. Royale as far as Beaupré); turn right and continue 3km/1.8mi.

Beauport

This community, the oldest settlement on the Beaupré Coast, is now a suburb of Quebec City. The first settlers arrived in 1634 and named the village for a medieval abbey on the north coast of Brittany.

Bourg du Fargy★

In the heart of Beauport stands an impressive group of buildings known as the Bourg du Fargy. The **Maison Bellanger-Girardin** (*600 Ave. Royale, ℘418-641-6471*) is typical of the residential architecture found throughout the Beaupré Coast. Its elongated form is the result of two distinct construction stages (1722 and 1735); its steep roof is characteristic of the heavy beam framework popular in the late 17C. Restored in 1983, the house is now used to display the work of local artists. Also situated in this neighborhood are a number of attractive Victorian houses.

Note the **Beauport Convent** (1866, F.-X. Berlinguet) with its mansard roof topped by a large statue of the Virgin Mary. The **Église Notre-Dame-de-la-Nativité** (Church of Our Lady of the Nativity), originally designed by Charles Baillairgé, was built in 1849. Twice destroyed by fire, the church was subsequently rebuilt within the same walls. Only its two towering spires were not replaced after the fire of 1916. The stone **presbytery** (1903) stands nearby. The road continues along an escarpment overlooking the Île d'Orleans.

Parc de la Chute-Montmorency★★ (Montmorency Falls Park)

5km/3mi. Open year-round, Jun–late Aug 8:30am–7:30pm, early Sept–late Oct 9am–6pm, early Nov–late Apr 10am–4pm, May–Jun 9am–6pm. ♿ P ($8.75/car). ℘418-663-3330. www.sepaq.com/ct/pcm/en.

Good to know: The "cove" area at the Parc de la Chute-Montmorency is illuminated after nightfall, highlighting the spectacular waterfall, the surrounding cliffs, and the Manoir Montmorency.

Before emptying into the St. Lawrence, the Montmorency River cascades over a cliff in a spectacular falls 83m/272ft high (30m/98ft higher than Niagara Falls). Named by Samuel de Champlain for Charles, Duc de Montmorency, who was Viceroy of New France from 1620 through 1625, the falls have long been a major attraction. In winter, the spray creates a great cone of ice known as a sugarloaf, which sometimes exceeds 30m/98ft in height. Before the last ice age, the Montmorency Falls emptied directly into the St. Lawrence River. They are now about 450m/1,476ft away from the river and mark the edge of the Canadian Shield.

Parc de la Chute-Montmorency

With its enormous energy potential and its excellent location near the St. Lawrence, the site proved ideal for a powerful commercial empire that grew up here during the 19C. In 1811 a sawmill was established at the foot of the falls, an enterprise that by mid-century had become the most important of its kind in British North America. Under the direction of Peter Patterson and subsequently his son-in-law George Benson Hall, the company grew and diversified, but did not survive an economic crisis that eventually weakened the demand for lumber. In 1884 a **power plant** was established here, the first in the world to transmit hydroelectric power over long distances *(11.7km/7mi)*. A second power plant began service in 1895, and in 1905 a cotton mill was built at the foot of the cliff. Only a few traces remain today of these two centuries of early industrial activity.

Manoir Montmorency (Montmorency Manor)

This elegant house with terraces overlooking the Montmorency Falls has changed hands several times and undergone numerous modifications over the years. It was built in 1780 as a vacation home for Frederick Haldimand, governor-general of British North America. From 1791 through 1794, it was inhabited by Edward, Duke of Kent. Peter Patterson and his descendants also made their home here. At the turn of the 19C it was renovated as a popular luxury hotel known as "Kent House." Destroyed by fire in May 1993, the structure was rebuilt along its original architectural lines. Today Montmorency Manor houses a gourmet restaurant and reception rooms in addition to a **visitor center★** (open Jun–Sept daily 8:30am–8pm; reduced hours the rest of the year. ✕♿🅿 ✆418-663-3330) presenting the area's history. Don't miss their famous Sunday Brunch (open 10am–3pm; $29.95).

Upper Lookout

From the Montmorency Manor, a footpath traces the flank of the cliff leading to a bridge above the falls. From here, a spectacular **view★★** reveals the furious waters tumbling over the cliff. The silhouette of the **Île d'Orléans** *(see ÎLE D'ORLÉANS)* is visible in the distance. The footpath continues on the other side to a smaller bridge over a side crevice; from here you can see the sites of the power plant and the former cotton mill, with the towers of Quebec City and the Château Frontenac looming in the distance. Farther along, note the traces of a redoubt built here in 1759 by the British general James Wolfe during his siege of Quebec. Helped by their Native American allies, the French militia overtook this redoubt using combat techniques developed by the indigenous population.

Lower Lookout

A panoramic stairway dotted with numerous lookout points leads to the bottom of the falls, allowing superb, close-up **views** of the powerful waters (waterproof gear is advised to protect from the spray). Over time, the falls have carved out a large cauldron at their base, creating an immense, powerful whirlpool. The force of these turbulent waters (an average 35,000 liters/9,248gal per second) was harnessed in 1885 to activate sawmills and provide electricity for Quebec City. A dramatic **cable car transports** visitors to the upper level over the falls (open late Apr–late Oct daily 8:30am; rest of the year call for hours; $11.83 one-way, $13.95 round-trip; ✆418-663-3330).

Return to Rte. 360.

Observe the high-tension power lines strung on large pylons, which carry electricity from the Manic-5 power station to Montreal, across the St. Lawrence. Past this point the road takes on a more rural character.

Moulin du Petit-Pré (Mill)

9km/5.6mi from Montmorency Manor.
7007 Ave. Royale, Château-Richer.

This large three-story stone mill, located just beyond the Petit-Pré River, was built in 1695 by the Quebec Seminary to supplement its income and to supply the needs of Quebec City merchants; it was the first "industrial" mill in New France. The mill was destroyed during the Conquest and rebuilt in 1764, and it remained in operation until 1955. The historic site encountered heavy water damage in the summer of 2013 and has remained closed. There are hopes that the mill might re-open in the future. The **Beaupré Coast Interpretation Center** (open mid-May–mid-Oct daily 9am–5pm; rest of the year Mon–Fri 9am–4pm; $6; 418-824-3677) housed in the mill loft, provides information on the geology, history, and socio-economic development of the region. Displays include photographs, documents, sketches, games, and videos.

Château-Richer

First settled in 1640, this community was named for a priory in France. The **Église La-Visitation-de-Notre-Dame** (Church of the Visitation of Our Lady, 1866) dominates the village from high on the cliff above the river. From the church, **views** of the coast reach as far as Cap-Tourmente. A quarry carved out of the cliff is visible to the north of the town. In the 18C and 19C, limestone from Château-Richer was used in the construction of many buildings in Quebec City. Regular in form and light gray in color, the stone from this quarry replaced the darker limestone of Beauport by the early 19C.

On Ave. Royale, large bread ovens stand next to some of the older homes; the ovens were often built separately from the houses because of the danger of fire. One is still in use, and visitors can enjoy its fresh-baked bread.

Rte. 360 gradually descends to river level as it approaches Sainte-Anne.

Sainte-Anne-de-Beaupré★

Situated on the north shore of the St. Lawrence overlooking Île d'Orléans, Sainte-Anne-de-Québec is named for the patron saint of Quebec. Its shrine, administered by the Redemptorist fathers, is a major Catholic pilgrimage center, visited by over one-and-a-half-million people every year. Sainte-Anne is a logical stop between Quebec City and the Charlevoix Region.

The Shrine★★

Basilica

Open throughout year: information desk open year-round, daily 8am–10pm. Church open daily from 7am until the end of the last Mass of the day—check website. www.ssadb.qc.ca. Bilingual guided tours Jun–early Sept, Mon–Sat 1pm $2. 418-827-3781. www.ssadb.qc.ca.

This enormous, twin-spired medieval-style basilica was designed by the architects Maxime Roisin and Louis-Napoléon Audet. Built in the shape of a Latin cross, with a steel frame and a veneer of white granite, it is 98m/321.5ft long, 60m/196.8ft wide at the transept, and 90m/295ft high. Between the two spires stands a large gilded statue of St. Anne, saved from a fire that destroyed the previous church.

Interior

Inside, the visitor is struck by the immense size of the basilica. The interior is divided into five naves separated by huge columns. Each column is topped by a carved capital, the work of Émile Brunet and Maurice Lord.

The interior is lit by 240 **stained-glass windows**, created by the French artist Auguste Laboret who was assisted by the master glassmaker Pierre Chaudière. Note especially the windows of the transepts and the rose window above the organ. The barrel vault above the main nave is decorated with glimmering **mosaics** portraying the life of St. Anne. Also the work of Auguste Laboret, aided by Jean Gaudin, they combine cream and brown coloring highlighted by red and gold. A particularly beautiful mosaic of the Holy Family is located above the main altar. An ambulatory surrounds the sanctuary with 10 radiating chapels.

On a marble pedestal in the left wing of the transept stands a statue of St.

The Origins of the Healing Basilica

According to legend, 17C French sailors caught in a storm on the river landed safely on the banks here after praying to Ste. Anne, the mother of the Virgin Mary. In thanks for their rescue, in 1658 they laid the foundations for a small wooden chapel in her honor. During construction, one of the workmen, Louis Guimont, was miraculously cured of lumbago. His was the first of many healings and, as a result, Sainte-Anne soon became a place of pilgrimage. Throngs of devotees, many seeking healing, came on foot, by canoe, and later by steamboat and car. The original wooden chapel was replaced by a sturdier structure in 1661, followed by a stone church in 1676. But so numerous were the pilgrims and parishioners that by the 19C a larger building was required. Completed in 1876, the immense and imposing new structure was in turn destroyed by fire in 1922 and replaced by the present basilica, which was dedicated in 1934.

Anne cradling the infant Mary in her arms. The chapel behind it contains a relic of St. Anne. Opposite, in the right wing of the transept, note the wooden sculpture (c.1920) of the Holy Family by Louis Jobin.

Chapelle Commémorative (Memorial Chapel) – Open mid-Apr–mid-Oct daily 8am–7:30pm. Built in 1878 on the site of the 1676 parish church, the structure incorporates elements of the original chapel, notably the steeple and its two cupolas.

Chapelle du Saint Escalier (Chapel of the Scala Santa) – Erected in 1891 next to the Memorial Chapel, this sanctuary contains a replica of the **Scala Santa** (Holy Stairs), which Christ climbed before being sentenced to death by Pontius Pilate. The original staircase was taken to Rome about AD 325 by St. Helena, mother of Emperor Constantine. Many pilgrims mount the steps on their knees. On the hillside behind the Chapel of the Scala Santa are life-size representations of the Stations of the Cross. They were cast in bronze by French craftsmen between 1913 and 1946.

Musée de Sainte Anne (Sainte Anne Museum)

9803 Blvd Sainte-Anne, near the basilica. Open early May–mid-Oct, daily 9am–5pm www.sanctuairesainteanne.org/index.php?lang=en&Itemid=211. $2. ℘418-827-3782 ext.2700.
Opened in 1997, this museum of religious art presents the life of St. Anne and the development of the community, as well as the history of the shrine.

Cyclorama de Jérusalem★ (Cyclorama of Jerusalem)

8 rue du Sanctuaire, beside the basilica. Open May–Oct daily 9am–6pm. $10. ℘418-827-3101. www.cyclorama.com.
The large edifice houses an enormous, impressively realistic painting (measuring 1,540sq m/16,576sq ft) showing Jerusalem on the day of the Crucifixion. Painted in Munich (1878–82) by the French panoramist Paul Philippoteaux and five assistants, and installed at Sainte-Anne-de-Beaupré in 1895, it is 14m/46ft high by 110m/361ft in circumference. It remains the largest panoramic painting of its kind in the world.

Atelier Paré – Economuseum of Woodcarving

9269 Ave. Royale, Sainte-Anne-de-Beaupré. Open mid-May–mid-Oct daily 9am–5:30pm; rest of the year Wed–Sun 1pm–4pm. Donations are welcome. ℘418-827-3992. www.atelierpare.com.
Quebec has been a fertile ground for legends and woodcarving, and they come together at this museum/workshop (this type of establishment is called an economuseum in Quebec). In front of visitors, artists carve and bend (fiberglass is also used) the pieces that will be exposed in the economuseum's garden and the gift shop. Atelier Paré is a family business.

Edison Phonograph Museum

9812 Ave. Royale. Open daily 10am–noon, 1pm–6pm; call in advance. Guided tours in English and French (by appointment). $5. 418-827-5957. www.phono.org/beaupre.html.

Jean-Paul Agnard has been a passionate phonograph collector since 1970. His museum showcases some 250 phonographs and accessories. The collection is equally divided between American and European phonographs (British, French, German and Swiss). Edison's 19C hand-driven talking dolls are unforgettable.

Beaupré

Located on the Sainte-Anne-du-Nord River, just before it joins the St. Lawrence, Beaupré was part of the town of Sainte-Anne-de-Beaupré until 1927. Now it is a separate community, dominated by its pulp mill.

Rte. 360 towards Mont-Ste-Anne.

Station Mont-Sainte-Anne★

Park open daily during winter ski season Nov–late Apr, and in summer season late May–mid-Oct. Camping 7km/4mi east in St. Ferréol-les-Neiges ($35 fee for no-service site to $54 for full-service site). Camping: 418-827-5281, toll free 1-800-463-1568, in season 418-826-2323. Ski park: 418-827-4561 and 1-888-827-4579. www.mont-sainte-anne.com.

Created in 1969 as a sports center for the city of Quebec, this park covers the broad slopes of Mt. Sainte-Anne as well as part of the Jean-Larose River valley. An internationally known downhill skiing center that has hosted several World Cup races, the ski park boasts abundant snowfall, especially on the north side of the mountain. Ski areas include more than 200km/124mi of cross-country trails and over 50 downhill runs (vertical drop: 625m/2,060ft). At night the trails are lit over a long distance, creating a magical effect.

Panorama★★

Access to the summit (15min) by gondola late Jun–mid-Oct daily 10am–4:30pm. Round-trip 30min. $17.56. Ski hours Nov–Apr, Mon–Fri 9am–10pm, Sat–Sun 8:30am–10pm. $68/day or $43/half-day (call for ski packages 1-888-386-2754); mountain bike packages and rentals available.

The summit of Mont Sainte-Anne affords an outstanding view of the mighty St. Lawrence River. To the south, the Beaupré Coast, punctuated by the twin spires of Sainte-Anne-de-Beaupré's Basilica, is visible, as well as Île d'Orléans and Quebec City. To the east of Île d'Orléans, the St. Lawrence

Mountain biking, Mont-Sainte-Anne

reaches a width of 10km/6.2mi and separates two distinct landscapes: The Laurentian Shield (Beaupré Coast) and the Appalachians, on the south shore. The Laurentian Mountains rise on the horizon to the north.

Chutes Jean-Larose (Jean-Larose Falls)

From ski center, walk eastward about 700m/2,296ft to a charted path.

Before joining the Sainte-Anne River, the Jean-Larose River drops about 68m/223ft in a steep, narrow canyon, creating a series of falls, one of which is 33m/108.2ft high. The rock has been carved away by the water, and the falls, hidden in the trees, are very picturesque. The path descends steeply (*397 steps*), providing several good viewpoints.

Return to Beaupré (4km/2.5mi) and take Ave. Royale to Saint-Joachim. Turn right onto rue de l'Église.

Saint-Joachim

Located north of Quebec City, near the St. Lawrence, the present village of Saint-Joachim was founded soon after the Conquest. On their way to the capital, the British fleet burned the villages along the St. Lawrence shore. Wiser for the experience, the inhabitants of Saint-Joachim established their new community farther inland. Today the peaceful village is known for its lovely church.

Église Saint-Joachim★★ (St. Joachim Church)

Open mid-May–mid-Oct daily 9am–5pm. ♿ P ✆418-827-4020.

Designated an Historical Site in 1959, the structure is dedicated to the father of the Virgin Mary. A small church (1779) replaced an earlier sanctuary built in 1685 and destroyed by the British during the Conquest. It is one of the oldest churches in Quebec. The façade, designed by David Ouellet in 1895, blocks the view of the more traditional structure, best seen from the cemetery. The church is reputed for its **interior**, fashioned from 1815–1825 by **François Baillairgé** and his son, **Thomas**, acting here as both architects and sculptors. Highlights include the the sumptuous **main altar**, the **chandeliers**, the **choir,** and the **Presbytery**.

Petit-Cap

Just before the Cape Tourmente National Wildlife Reserve.

Petit-Cap is the site of the Seminary, a unique and monumental group of 18C buildings. The main edifice, Château Bellevue, overlooks the St. Lawrence. It dates back to 1779 and was enlarged in the original style in 1875. Adjacent to it are the late 18C chapel and the caretaker's house.

Réserve nationale de faune du Cap-Tourmente★ (Cape Tourmente National Wildlife Reserve)

4km/2.5mi. Open Apr–early Oct daily 8:30am–5pm; early Jan–Mar 8:30am–4pm. $6. ✕ ♿ P ✆418-827-4591. www.ec.gc.ca/ap-pa/default.asp?lang=En&n=0533BC0A-1.

Cap-Tourmente was named for the stormy winds that sweep through the St. Lawrence River valley, east of Île d'Orléans. The wildlife reserve is a haven for more than 290 species of birds. In April, May and October, thousands of Snow Geese arrive on this massif during their spring and winter migrations, and thousands of visitors come to see them. The bulrushes that proliferate on the marshy edges of the St. Lawrence provide the sustenance required for the enormous distance the geese must travel between their winter home on the coast of Virginia and their summer nesting grounds north of the Arctic circle, on Baffin Island.

Displays can be seen in the **interpretation center**, 1.5km/1mi from the entrance (open May–Oct daily 9am–4:45pm; Apr and Nov weekends only).

At the entrance to the reserve stands **La Petite-Ferme**, built on the spot where Samuel de Champlain established, in 1626, the first farm of New France.

Côte de Charlevoix★★★

Charlevoix region

The Charlevoix Coast, a rugged landscape marked by mountains sweeping down into the mighty St. Lawrence River, is one of Canada's most beautiful regions. In this area, the river becomes an arm of the sea and is called "la mer" (the sea), while its wide banks are referred to as "la côte" (the coast), suggesting that this large body of saltwater is no longer a river. The pristine coast provides good views of the river, and on clear days the opposite shore can be seen. Designated a UNESCO World Biosphere Reserve in 1989, the region is also a mecca for art and nature lovers attracted by the natural beauty, maritime past, and old-time resort tradition. The Cirque du Soleil founders were street performers here when they created their popular circus concept.

- **Michelin Map**: p346–347: C1-3.
- **Info:** 1-800-667-2276. www.tourisme-charlevoix.com.
- **Location:** Charlevoix is accessible by Rtes. 40 and 138, northeast of Quebec City. Rte. 138 traverses the region, which starts at the border of Cap-Tourmente, about 40km/25mi from Quebec City. Rte. 362 also connects Baie-Saint-Paul to La Malbaie–Pointe-au-Pic.
- **Don't Miss:** Scenic Rte. 362; Baie-Saint-Paul and its art galleries; the understated yet moving Musée maritime de Charlevoix.
- **Timing:** Stop at the information center on Rte. 138 just before entering Baie-Saint-Paul for a superb view of the region and to get current details about local events. Visit Baie-Saint-Paul, then follow Rte. 362 along the coast. If you have the time, take the ferry from Saint-Joseph-de-la-Rive to explore Îsle-aux-Coudres before continuing along the coast to Malbaie.
- **Kids:** Activities at the spectacular Canyon Sainte-Anne, and whale-watching near the Saguenay Fjord.

A BIT OF HISTORY

The first settlers moved into the Charlevoix region toward the end of the 17C. They were predominantly loggers and navigators, since the coast did not lend itself to agriculture. Some remote communities remained inaccessible by road until the mid-20C. Charlevoix is named for Pierre-François-Xavier de Charlevoix (1682–1761), a Jesuit historian who wrote the noted *History and General Description of New France* (*Histoire et description générale de la Nouvelle- France*).

Charlevoix Schooners – Until the late 1960s, small schooners, called *goélettes*, sailed the St. Lawrence carrying provisions and wood destined for the Charlevoix Coast, the Côte-Nord, Bas-Saint-Laurent and the Gaspésie. More than 300 of these vessels, known locally as voitures d'eau (literally "water cars"), were built in Charlevoix. The small vessels were originally equipped with sails, and later with motors. Today their hulls lie abandoned along the shore. Visitors stopping along the clifftop roads of this region can often hear the rumbling of powerful motors from freighters passing in the distance on the St. Lawrence River. These freighters gradually replaced the traditional schooners.

A Choice Resort – As early as the 1760s, visitors flocked to Charlevoix, attracted by the beauty of its landscapes. After

River or Mountains? Visitors Have a Choice

Two themed routes run through the Charlevoix region, starting from Baie-Saint-Paul. The Route du Fleuve *(www.routedufleuve.ca)* follows the north bank of the St. Lawrence River for the stretch of around 60km/37mi between Baie-Saint-Paul and La Malbaie, sometimes looking down on the river from on high and sometimes coming down to water level. The Route des Montagnes *(www.routedesmontagnes.com)*, meanwhile, explores the mountainous backcountry, from Saint-Urbain to Saint-Aimé-des-Lacs and beyond to the national parks of Grands-Jardins and Hautes-Gorges-de-la-Rivière-Malbaie.

the Conquest, two Scottish officers, Capt. John Nairn and Lieutenant Malcolm Fraser, received the former seigneury of La Malbaie–Pointe-Au-Pic from military governor Gen. James Murray (1721–94), and named it Murray Bay. In the mid-19C, Charlevoix became a popular resort area. City dwellers began refurbishing traditional residences and later built elegant summer homes. Canada Steamship Lines brought wealthy tourists to the region aboard their luxurious cruise ships, and built the enormous Manoir Richelieu Hotel in 1899. Rebuilt in 1929 after a fire, the hotel is the sole survivor among the grand hostelries of the period. The great white boats *(bateaux blancs)* discontinued their visits in the 1960s, when the opening of the Côte-Nord road marked the end of an era. Today numerous inns welcome tourists.

Artists' Haunt – Charlevoix has long attracted and inspired painters, poets and writers. Its villages and panoramas are immortalized in the works of such well-known Canadian artists as Clarence Gagnon, Marc-Aurèle Fortin, René Richard, Jean-Paul Lemieux, and A.Y. Jackson. Baie-Saint-Paul, especially, is known as a gathering place for artists, as are Port-au-Persil and Les Éboulements. Among the writers and poets who have lived here are Laure Conan and Gabrielle Roy.

DRIVING TOUR

FROM BEAUPRÉ TO BAIE-SAINTE-CATHERINE

220km/136mi.

Leave Beaupré on Rte. 138. After 4km/2.5mi, turn left, following signs.

Canyon Sainte-Anne

© Canyon Sainte-Anne

Canyon Sainte-Anne★★

Open Jun 24–Labor Day daily 9am–6pm; May–Jun 23 and early Sept–Oct, daily 9am–4pm. $13. 206 Rte. 138 Est. 418-827-4057. www.canyonsa.qc.ca. Leashed dogs allowed.

This splendid wilderness gives visitors a chance to observe the sedimentary rock marking the beginning of the St. Lawrence Plain, next to the granitic gneiss that forms the Canadian Shield. At this point, the Sainte-Anne-du-Nord River drops in a steep and narrow waterfall, plunging 74m/243ft into a mass of foam and whirlpools. Interpretative panels dot the paths leading through the woods to the river and falls; three footbridges span the river, allowing excellent views. A third footpath leads to the bottom of the canyon.

Rejoin Rte. 138; after 15km/9.3mi turn left on Rte. 360 for Saint-Ferréol-les-Neiges. Continue for 10km/6.2mi, following signs.

Les Sept-Chutes (Seven Falls)

Drive past Les Sept-Chutes where the Sainte-Anne-du-Nord River cascades over seven separate falls. A dam and generating station were built between 1912 and 1916, and it remained in operation until 1984. Operations resumed in 1999 and a park was later established in this spot, but closed in 2014.

Return to Rte. 138. After 30km/18.6mi turn right to Petite-Rivière-Saint-François and continue for 10km/6.2mi.

Petite-Rivière-Saint-François

The road descends steeply through the forest to a small community located on the St. Lawrence, at the base of an impressive cliff.

In the village, turn left after the church.

The pier affords a **view★** of the Charlevoix mountains plunging into the St. Lawrence along the rock-strewn shores. The Massif de Charlevoix *(see p350)* can be accessed from Pente-Rivière-Saint-François.

Return to Rte. 138 and continue to Baie-Saint-Paul.

There are wonderful **views★★** on the descent to Baie-Saint-Paul.

Baie-Saint-Paul★★

Baie-Saint-Paul occupies a spectacular site at the confluence of the Gouffre and St. Lawrence rivers. The community long remained the only settlement between Saint-Joachim and Tadoussac. Surrounded by rolling green hills, Baie-Saint-Paul has inspired many artists and today boasts dozens of art galleries, an exposition hall and an art center, and charming accommodation set in traditional Québécois houses. During the 1970s, the town was the hub of acrobats, clowns and jugglers who later founded the Cirque du Soleil, a brand that has become famous worldwide.

August brings the annual Canada Young Painters Symposium to the Baie-Saint-Paul Arena, as artists produce large-scale works of art while the public looks on.

Arriving in Baie-Saint-Paul from the south on Rte. 138, enjoy a **view★★** of the St. Lawrence valley and river.

Stroll the village's narrow streets and admire the old houses of picturesque Rue Saint-Jean-Baptiste. Note in particular Nos. 143–145. Wander down Saint-Joseph Street to shop at art and antique boutiques, then go to the wharf and perhaps take a cruise or sea-kayaking trip.

Carrefour culturel Paul-Médéric (Paul Médéric Cultural Center)

4 rue Ambroise-Fafard. Open year-round except major holidays. Hours vary; call ahead. $4. 418-435-2540.

This art gallery (1967, Jacques Deblois), built as a commemorative monument to the Canadian Confederation, displays the works of Charlevoix artists. In the weaving and tapestry studios, craftspeople create works using traditional and modern techniques.

Musée d'art contemporain de Baie-Saint-Paul

23 rue Ambroise-Fafard. Open 11am–5pm low season and 10am–5pm during high season (approx. Jun 24–Labor Day). $10. 418-435-3681. www.macbsp.com.

Designed by architect Pierre Thibault, the center plays host to traveling exhibits from around the world. Seen from the wharf on Rue Sainte-Anne, Îsle-aux-Coudres seems to block the entrance to the bay.

Habitat 07

212 rue Sainte-Anne. Open daily 10am–6pm. $5. 418-435-5514. www.habitat07.org.

A demonstration house standing in an isolated field facing the river, where visitors can discover the workings of a home built using environmentally friendly techniques. The house also produces some of its own energy and recycles its own waste water. The subject is explored in detail in the guided tours.

Leaving the city by Rte. 362 Est, pause where an overlook provides another **view★★** of Baie-Saint-Paul, the St. Lawrence and the south shore. Nearby, on the right, the chemin Vieux Quai reaches the shore and provides a closer view of Îsle-aux-Coudres.

Leave Baie-Saint-Paul by Rte. 362. Rte. 362, and later Rte. 138 from La Malbaie–Pointe-au-Pic, provide views of the St. Lawrence. As the road leaves Baie-Saint-Paul, a rest stop overlooks the Gouffre valley and the Îsle-aux-Coudres.

Les Éboulements

This community, perched on the mountain's edge 300m/948ft above the St. Lawrence, takes its name from the series of landslides (**éboulements**) that followed a violent earthquake in 1663, propelling half the mountainside into the river. In 1710 the seigneury was granted to Pierre Tremblay who settled here and built a mill.

Moulin seigneurial des Éboulements (Old Stone Mill)

Just before the junction with the road to Saint-Joseph-de-la-Rive. Access road to the right, before the Du Moulin River. Open late Jun–early Sept daily 9am–5pm. $3. 418-635-2239 or Canadian Heritage in Quebec at 514-393-1417. www.hcq-chq.org/the-seigneurial-mill-of-les-eboulements.

This stone flour mill (Laterrière Mill) was built in 1790 for Seigneur Jean-François Tremblay atop a waterfall on what then became "Rivière du Moulin." The mill still operates with its original equipment. Visitors watch the grain being ground into flour. The former seigneurial manor of the Sales-Laterrière family stands nearby. With its mill and other outbuildings, the manor illustrates life under the seigneurial regime, which was abolished in 1854.

Turn off Rte. 362 to the right toward Saint-Joseph-de-la-Rive and follow a very steep descent to the St. Lawrence.

Saint-Joseph-de-la-Rive

Sandwiched between the St. Lawrence and the mountains, the community offers fine views of Îsle-aux-Coudres and the river. It was one of the main shipbuilding centers for the traditional Charlevoix schooners, many of which lie scattered along the village shore. The ferry to Îsle-aux-Coudres leaves from this town.

Take time to tour the schooners at the **Musée maritime de Charlevoix** (305 rue de l'Église; open mid-May–late Oct daily 9am–5pm, rest of the year by reservation. $7 418-635-1131; www.museemaritime.com/en/) for a taste of Charlevoix's maritime past. At the **Papeterie Saint-Gilles** (304 rue Félix-Antoine-Savard; open year-round, summer daily 9am–5pm, call ahead for rest of the year; 418-635-2430, www.papeteriesaintgilles.com; $5), an old paper workshop founded by priest and writer Félix-Antoine Savard, guides explain how 17C paper was made. This was the first member (1992) of the distinguished home-grown Economuseum network *(www.economusees.com)*, now comprising more than 30 artisanal sites throughout Quebec.

Île-aux-Coudres★★

M.V. Joseph-Savard ferry service (free): Depart from Saint-Joseph-de-la-Rive Apr–Oct daily 6:30am–11:30pm every hour; during high season every 30 minutes; rest of the year daily 7:30am–11:30pm (Jan–Feb 11pm) every 2hrs. Société des traversiers du Québec. ♿ ✆1-877-787-7483. www.traversiers.gouv.qc.ca.

Today Île-aux-Coudres is linked to the mainland year-round by ferry. Before this link was established, however, crossing the icy St. Lawrence in the winter required special skills acquired over many years of practice. The crossing was achieved by a combination of canoeing through the unfrozen waters and getting out of the canoe to pull it over the ice floes. This ability to navigate the icy waters is demonstrated each February during a dangerous, spectacular, and quite famous canoe race at the **Quebec Winter Carnival** (*see Festivals & Events*). It is one of the highlights of the Winter Carnival.

Visitors can **tour** the island by car or bicycle (*c.26km/16mi*). Beached schooners, remnants of a past age, can be seen in several places. The site of Pointe du Bout d'en Bas, at the northern edge of the island, provides a picturesque **view**★ of the lush green landscape of the village of Les Éboulements.

Musée Les Voitures d'Eau★ (Schooner Museum)

1933 chemin des Coudriers in Îsle-aux-Coudres village, and part of the Hotel-Motel Las Voitures d'Eau. www.hotelmotelvoituresdeau.com. Open year-round. $5. P ✆418-438-2208.

Devoted to the schooners known as voitures d'eau, literally "water cars," this maritime museum presents displays and photographs of a mode of transportation which, until roads were developed in the 1960s, was a way of life for the islanders. The schooner *Mont-Saint-Louis,* built in 1939 and in service for 35 years, can be boarded.

Église Saint-Louis (Church of St. Louis)

In Île-aux-Coudres. Open year-round daily 9am–8pm. ♿ P ✆418-438-2442.

Built in 1885, this church boasts a charming interior décor and an altar sculpted by Louis Jobin. The statues of St. Louis and St. Flavien were carved by François Baillairgé between 1804 and 1810. The care with which the clothing and the anatomy of the statues were executed reflects the great talent of this eminent artist. Note the two **processional chapels** (*about 200m/656ft before and after the church*), built by volunteers in 1837.

Les moulins de l'Îsle-aux-Coudres★ (Îsle-aux-Coudres Mills)

In Île-aux-Coudres. Open Jun 24–mid-May daily 10am–5:30pm; shorter hours rest of the year. $8.59. P ✆418-438-2184. www.lesmoulinsdelisleauxcoudres.com.

A stone windmill (1836) stands next to a water mill (1825) on this site beside the Rouge River. The two mills, built by Thomas and Alexis Tremblay respec-

Îsle-aux-Coudres mill

tively, operated until 1948. Restored by the Quebec government, they provide a rare opportunity to compare the two different mechanisms. An **interpretation center** in the former miller's house explains their history. Visitors can also buy wheat flour ground by millstones. Farm equipment dating from the turn of the 19C is on display outside the mills. Member of the Economuseum Network *(www.economusees.com).*

Return to Saint-Joseph-de-la-Rive and Rte. 362 to Les Éboulements and continue toward Saint-Irénée.

Along this stretch, the St. Lawrence can often be seen. Take the unpaved Cap-aux-Oies road for 1km/0.6mi and stop at the bottom of the steep hill for a **panorama** of the cape and the south shore of the St. Lawrence. As it sweeps down to river level, Rte. 62 again reveals spectacular **views**.

Saint-Irénée

15km/9.3mi from Les Éboulements.

Saint-Irénée was the birthplace of lawyer and poet **Adolphe-Basile Routhier** (1839–1920), who wrote the French lyrics to the Canadian national anthem. Rodolphe Forget (1861–1919), who built the railway that follows the north shore of the St. Lawrence, had a summer home here. Known as **Le Domaine Forget** (www.domaineforget.com), this estate is set in a picturesque area overlooking the river. Today it is devoted to the performing arts, and concerts are held throughout the summer. The road passes through or nearby La Malbaie–Pointe-au-Pic and Cap-à-l'Aigle. Small protestant churches can be seen along the way.

La Malbaie-Pointe-au-Pic★

Samuel Champlain dubbed this place *malle baye* (bad bay) in 1608, when he anchored his ships here only to discover, the following day, that they had run aground. After the Conquest, the land surrounding the bay was granted to two Scots, Malcolm Fraser and John Nairn. They called it **Murray Bay** in honor of General James Murray, chief administrator of the colony, and welcomed many visitors to the area. The most famous of the hotels that gradually replaced the hospitality of the local seigneurs is the Fairmont **Richelieu Manor** *(Manoir Richelieu; access by Rte. 362 and chemin des Falaises)*, a vast, picturesque, Château-style edifice overlooking the St. Lawrence. Hollywood stars and politicians have come to play here since the Roaring Twenties, including Jean Harlow, Charlie Chaplin, and US President William Taft. Near the hotel, which was rebuilt in 1929 after a fire, stands a second building (1930) housing the **Charlevoix Casino**. The golf course has one of the most challenging hill courses in North America, and a spectacular view of the Saint Lawrence River to match.

Vacation Villas

Most of the villas and summer residences on the two hillsides surrounding La Malbaie were built between 1880 and 1945. The influence of the "Shingle" style of architecture popular along the Atlantic Coast of the US can be seen in the cedar-shingled dwellings. Vacationers visiting the region for hunting and fishing came to appreciate the rustic character of the sober interiors and simple furnishings that local architect Jean-Charles Warren (1868–1929) designed. Warren erected about 60 of these grand villas, initiating a "Laurentian" style that integrated buildings into their surroundings by using local materials and positioning the structure to take full advantage of the magnificent scenery.

Musée de Charlevoix (Charlevoix Museum)

10 chemin du Havre. Open daily Jun–mid-Oct 9am–5pm, mid-Oct–May Mon–Fri 10am–5pm, Sat–Sun 1pm–5pm. $7. ℘418-665-4411. www.museedecharlevoix.qc.ca.

Paintings, sculptures, and textiles in the permanent collection provide an understanding of local Charlevoix art, heritage, and history. The museum also presents changing exhibits on various

Champlain and Baie-Sainte-Catherine

In 1609 Samuel de Champlain met the Montagnais chief, Sagamo, at the southern point of the bay. Their meeting led to an alliance against the Iroquois, which was to have serious consequences for New France. The first settlers arrived in Baie-Sainte-Catherine in 1820, and for many years they logged trees to produce timber for the European market.

themes. The rotunda affords an impressive view of the surroundings.

Chutes Fraser (Fraser Falls)

In Rivière-Malbaie, about 3km/1.8mi. After the bridge over the Malbaie River, turn left and take chemin de la Vallée for 1.5km/1mi, then turn right following signs for the campground. Open mid-May–mid-Oct daily 8am–10pm. $30. ℘418-665-2151. www.campingchutesfraser.com.

These falls on the Comporté River drop about 30m/98.4ft, forming a lace-like pattern across the rocky ledges. In spring, or after a heavy rainfall, the Fraser Falls can be particularly dramatic given the sheer volume of water that cascades through here.

Rejoin Rte. 138.

The road leads up the mountainside to Saint-Fidèle, providing a view of the Îles de Kamouraska (a Quebec nature reserve), and then descends to river level.

6km/3.7mi after Saint-Fidèle, turn right for Port-au-Persil.

Port-au-Persil★

30km/18.6mi from La Malbaie–Pointe-au-Pic.

This cove on the St. Lawrence has long been a favorite with artists. Beside the old quay, a tiny Anglican church and a waterfall add a picturesque element.

Saint-Siméon

494 rue Saint-Laurent. ℘418-665-4454 or 1-800-667-2276. www.saintsimeon.ca.

This town is the location of the large ferry (*65min*) that crosses the St. Lawrence to Rivière-du-Loup. Ferry service on the N.M. Trans-Saint-Laurent (capacity 100 cars, 399 passengers): depart from Saint-Siméon daily year-round, one to five

Port-au-Persil

Saguenay–St. Lawrence Marine Park

Since 1998, the Saguenay-St. Lawrence Marine Park *(www.parcmarin.qc.ca)* has provided a protected environment for species and ecosystems at the meeting point of the St. Lawrence Estuary and the Saguenay Fjord. The marine park is divided into five sectors, each offering a different environment:

Estuary sector: Pointe-Noire interpretation center in Baie-Sainte-Catherine *(see below).*

North fjord sector: the center d'interprétation des battures et de réhabilitation des oiseaux (salt marsh and bird rehabilitation center) in Saint-Fulgence, and the Beluga interpretation centre in Baie-Sainte-Marguerite *(see Fjord du Saguenay).*

South fjord sector: fjord interpretation center in Baie-Éternité, within the Saguenay park *(see Fjord du Saguenay).*

Whale sector: Archéo-Topo (archeology and topography) interpretation center, Cap-de-Bon-Désir interpretation and observation center in Les Bergeronnes; marine mammal interpretation center in Tadoussac *(see Côte-Nord).*

Navigators sector: Île aux Basques, Parc de l'aventure basque en Amérique (an interpretation center examining Basque history and culture in the Americas), Île du Pot-l'Eau-de-Vie and Île aux Lièvres.

crossings a day depending on the time of year. $45 (vehicle), $19 (passenger). 418-638-2856 and 418-638-5530. www.traverserdl.com. This crossing is spectacular and takes about 65 minutes. In winter, the ship bumps into ice floes on the river.

Baie des Rochers★

An unpaved road (*about 3km/1.8mi*) leads to this deserted bay, dominated by an old wharf. A small island close by is reachable at low tide.

Return to Rte. 138.

The St. Lawrence comes into view again near Baie-Sainte-Catherine.

Baie-Sainte-Catherine★

621 Rte. 138. 418-665-4454 or 1-800-667-2276. www.tourisme-charlevoix.com.

This community is set on a low plateau bordering a bay at the mouth of the Saguenay River, on the north shore of the St. Lawrence. Today whale watching is the major attraction in Baie-Sainte-Catherine as well as in Tadoussac *(see CÔTE-NORD)*, across the fjord.

Whale-watching cruises★★

Depart from the municipal wharf May–Oct daily 9:30am, 12:45pm and 4pm. Round-trip 3hrs. Commentary. Reservations required. $70. Croisières AML. 418-237-4021 and 1-866-856-6668. www.croisieresaml.com.

Cruises offer the opportunity to view whales up close and discover the marine environment of the St. Lawrence via underwater cameras. The marine mammals of the St. Lawrence river include killer whale, humpback whale, northern Atlantic right whale, minke whale, pilot whale, blue whale, beluga whale, Atlantic white-sided dolphin, harbor porpoise, and gray seals.

Centre d'interprétation et d'observation de Pointe-Noire

On Rte. 138, just before the descent to the Saguenay. Open mid-Jun–Labor Day, daily 9am–6pm; Sept–early Oct Fri–Sun 9am–5pm. $6. 418-237-4383. www.pc.gc.ca/eng/amnc-nmca/qc/saguenay/index.aspx.

Situated on a cape overlooking the mouth of the Saguenay River, the Pointe-Noire observation center affords

Parc national des Hautes-Gorges-de-la-rivière-Malbaie

a fine **panorama** of the St. Lawrence estuary and the cliffs embracing the Saguenay Fjord. The interpretation center (part of the Saguenay-St. Lawrence Marine Park) introduces visitors to this unique natural environment, where salt and fresh water meet.

EXCURSIONS

Parc national des Grands-Jardins

56km/34.7mi NE from Baie-Saint-Paul. Open late May–early Oct for camping, cycling and canoeing; year-round for hiking; self-registration kiosks at trail entrances or when visitor centers are closed. $8.50; children (age 17 and younger) free. 1-800-665-6527. www.sepaq.com/pq/grj/.

Just over an hour's drive from Quebec City, and reflective of the province's northern regions, lies Grands-Jardins (literally "great gardens"), a Quebec provincial park (though, like many provincial parks in Quebec, it is called a national park). Clear blue lakes surrounded by forests of black spruce and a ground cover of lichen (cladonie), on which caribou feed in winter, are typical of the taiga found in subarctic climates. The park was created in 1981 to preserve the caribou's habitat. As many as 4,000 caribou roamed the land at the beginning of the century, but by the 1920s they were extinct as a result of over-hunting. Between 1969 and 1972 some 80 caribou were reintroduced to the area; today the population has increased to between 100 and 125 caribou. The park is recognized as core to the Charlevoix World Biosphere Reserve designated by UNESCO.

Secteur du Mont du lac des Cygnes

1.5km/1mi from Thomas-Fortin Center.

A 2.7km/1.7mi hiking trail leads to a viewpoint where visitors can admire a striking **panorama**★★ of the St. Lawrence River and the Charlevoix valley, with its scattered lakes and villages. On the climb to the summit (980m/3,214ft), hikers encounter three distinct types of vegetation. Mountain vegetation is characterized by forests of silver birch, poplar and pine. In the subalpine environment, taiga dominates, while tundra prevails in the alpine region.

Château-Beaumont Interpretation Center

Open May–mid-Oct daily 9am–8pm. 418-439-1227.

A new artists studio and gallery has replaced the former interpretation center. Next door, the new Athabasca Center, which opened in 2015, showcases a new exhibit of the park and its unique natural environment. The center also serves as the point of departure for various nature activities and excursions.

Parc national des Hautes-Gorges-de-la-Rivière-Malbaie★

Take Rte. 138 and turn left toward Saint-Aimé-des-Lacs. Continue 35km/21.7mi. Park open year-round. Visitor Center open late May–mid-Oct daily

7am–9pm. 800-665-6527 or 418-439-1227. www.sepaq.com/pq/hgo. The mountains in this spectacular park rise more than 1,000m/3,280ft, dominating the high gorges of the Malbaie River and the valley of the Martres River. A **cruise** leads to the steep-sided gorges of the Malbaie River (departs from the wharf at the end of the dirt road mid-Jun–mid-Oct, 11am, 1pm, 2:45pm; Jun 24–Labor Day additional 4:30pm and 6:30pm cruises; round-trip 1hr 30min; commentary, reservations required. $35; children (age 17 and under) free; 418-439-1227; www.sepaq.com).

ADDRESSES

STAY

Les Colibris – *80 rue Sainte-Anne, Baie-Saint-Paul. 418-240-2222. www. charlevoix.net/lescolibris. 5 rms.* With its charming hospitality, this large place has the feel of an old-fashioned family guesthouse. It is set slightly apart from the bustle of the town centre, in a street leading to the bay, and offers very well-kept rooms decorated in a rustic but refined style.

L'Estampilles – *24 chemin Cap-aux-Corbeaux, Baie-Saint-Paul. 418-435-2533. www.lestampilles.com. 11 rooms. Restaurant*. A large, modern house in the local style standing on the high ground around Baie-Saint-Paul. Impeccable rooms in a refined rural style. Gastronomic restaurant.

EAT

Mouton Noir – *43 rue Sainte-Anne, Baie-Saint-Paul. 418-240-3030. www. moutonnoirresto.com. End Jun–mid-Oct 11am–10pm; rest of the year Wed–Sun 5–10pm.* Without doubt one of best restaurants in Charlevoix. The carefully prepared food, based on local produce, revisits the classics (salmon tartare, gaspacho), while adding sweet and sour or fusion elements and a touch of creative flair.

Chez Bouquet – *39 rue Saint-Jean-Baptiste, Baie-Saint-Paul. 418-240-3444. www.lamuse.com. Open daily 7am–2pm; summer until 4pm.* This "eco-bistro" aims to look after the environment (using local produce) as well as the health of its customers with its refined, balanced cuisine highlighting ingredients like veal, duck and locally sourced emu meat. Brunch served on weekends.

La Bohème – *955 rue Richelieu, La Malbaie. 418-202-0544. www. grillade laboheme.com. Open May–Oct 11am–midnight; rest of the year open from 4pm.* A strong western flavor marks the atmosphere at this specialist grill serving high-quality meat (beef and emu from Charlevoix) and fish from the river. Music every evening in summer.

DRINKS

Le Saint-Pub – *2 rue Racine, Baie-Saint-Paul. 418 240 2332. www.saint-pub.com. Open daily 11:30am–midnight (Fri–Sat 1am).* In the main center, this pub has a reputation throughout Quebec for great beer: Vache Folle and Dominus Vobiscus are the most popular options.

ACTIVITIES

Walking – *www.traverseedecharlevoix. qc.ca.* The 105km/64mi Traversee de Charlevoix is one of the finest long-distance walking paths in North America. The circuit forms a corridor between the Grands-Jardins and national parks. Six chalets and six shelters are located along the trail.

Charlevoix Lightrail Transit – *418-240-4124 ext. 4052, 844-737-3282. www.reseaucharlevoix.com. $75.* This train between Quebec City and Baie Ste Paul is a temporary rail service until the popular Train du Massif de Charlevoix resumes in the future. The 125km/78mi journey along the St. Lawrence River passes idyllic towns like La Malbaie and offers fine views of the river.

EVENT

Symposium international d'art contemporain – *Baie-St-Paul. www.symposium-baiesaintpaul.com. Aug.* Organized by the Museum of Contemporary art in Baie-St-Paul, this gives young artists a platform to exhibit their work.

Monts-Valin

HIGHLIGHTS OF THE SAGUENAY-LAC-SAINT-JEAN REGION

Mashteuiatsh Amerindian Museum

1787 rue Amishk, Mashteuiatsh, Lac-Saint-Jean. www.museeilnu.ca. ☏418-275-4842 or 1-888-875-4842.

Located on the south coast of Lac-Saint-Jean between Roberval and Saint-Prime, this fascinating museum preserves the First Nation Ilnu legacy of over one thousand years with a permanent exhibition, while a new Ilnu Cultural Interpretation Site on the shores of Pekuakami River introduces a comprehensive variety of experiential options for visitors. *www. kuei.ca.*

Pourvoirie Cap au Leste

Rte. 172 (km 88) in Ste-Rode-du-Nord. ☏418-675-2000 or 1-866-675-2007 (free). www.capauleste.com.

A new restaurant and meeting facility enhance this unique log accommodation. Stay in a tepee or hotel room and explore the surroundings, with spectacular views of the Saguenay Fjord. The log-style chalet pavilions that are perched on the cliffs above the fjord are a firm favorite with many guests.

Parc national des Monts-Valin

☏418-674-1200. www.sepaq.com/pq/mva/.

Located north of St. Fulgence on the north side of the fjord, this mountain park features a dominating mountain 984m/2,700ft in elevation. Hikers can enjoy a new long-distance hiking trail along the summits: the "Sentier des pics" is a 20km/12mi hike. Luggage transportation is available and well-equipped overnight refuges are provided on route. Hikers can pick 10 varieties of wild blueberries along the way. The views, of course, are spectacular.

Fjord du Saguenay★★★

Saguenay-Lac-Saint-Jean region

The 155km/96mi Saguenay River is the only river draining Lake Saint-Jean. In the upper section, between Alma and Jonquière, the once roaring torrent, which drops about 90m/295ft, has been harnessed and has spawned one of the most industrialized areas in Canada. At Saint-Fulgence, the river flows into the majestic Saguenay fjord that extends to Tadoussac, and empties into the St. Lawrence.
The deep channel through which the Saguenay flows below Saint-Fulgence was gouged in Precambrian rock by glaciers during the last ice age. As the ice receded, the sea swept into the valley, and tidewaters still reach upriver as far as Chicoutimi, 16km/10mi from Saint-Fulgence. The channel is 1,500m/4,920ft wide in places and has an average depth of 240m/787ft, while rocky cliffs plunge into the dark waters from heights of up to 457m/1,500ft. The Saguenay is the southernmost fjord in the northern hemisphere.

- **Michelin Map:** p346–347: BC2.
- **Info:** www.saguenaylacsaintjean.net; www.sepaq.com/pq/sag.
- **Location:** The fjord is accessible from Quebec City either by Rte. 175 north to Chicoutimi (about 200km/124mi) or by Rte. 138 northeast to Tadoussac (220km/136mi). Rte. 172 runs along the north shore of the fjord; Rte. 170 follows the south shore.
- **Don't Miss:** The drive down the Éternité River valley to the interpretation center on the shore of the fjord.
- **Timing:** Although roads circumnavigate the fjord, panoramic views are rare. The best way to see it is by taking a cruise from Chicoutimi, Baie Éternité or Tadoussac. Hikers can enjoy spectacular views of the fjord from trails at Baie Éternité and L'Anse-St-Jean.

A BIT OF HISTORY

For more than 4,000 years the Saguenay has been the *chemin qui cours,* or water route, for the First Nations who

View from Sacré Coeur

© Charles-David Robitaille / Tourisme Saguenay - Lac-Saint-Jean

Sacré Coeur

Another stop along Rte. 172 that offers an impressive view of the fjord is Sacré-Coeur. Visit the wharf at Anse-de-Roche, engage in some aquatic activities or rent a kayak. At Rivière Éternité enjoy the 175 Nativity scenes from around the world at the Exposition Internationale de Crèches at the Église de Rivière-Éternité, 418, rue Principale (*418-272-2807, www.villagedecreches.com)*. In winter, each home in the village has its own Nativity scene.

paddled upstream to reach their hunting grounds. Upon landing here in 1534, Jacques Cartier first heard of the vast riches of the **Royaume du Saguenay** (Kingdom of the Saguenay). Colonization began in 1838 when William Price created *Société des vingt et un:* 21 hard-working men who left Charlevoix to start new lives in complete wilderness. The area's industrial riches proved illusive until the beginning of the 20C, when the river was harnessed for hydroelectricity, giving the local economy an important boost. The Upper Saguenay (Haut-Saguenay) has since been extensively industrialized, and hydroelectric power plants, pulp mills and aluminum smelters dot its shores. In contrast, the undeveloped Lower Saguenay (Bas-Saguenay) is lined with long stretches of uninhabited land. The Saguenay's stark and untamed beauty has attracted visitors for years. Most choose to take a scenic river cruise, but the fjord can also be enjoyed by exploring the villages nestled along its shores. A spectacular natural park has been created to preserve part of the shoreline (*difficult access*). The recent popularity of sea kayaking has allowed soft adventure seekers to enjoy fully the beauty of the fjord.

DRIVING TOUR

FROM TADOUSSAC TO L'ANSE-SAINT-JEAN

250km/155mi.

There are several ways to visit this region—by boat, kayak or car. Because no bridges cross the fjord, begin on the north shore at Tadoussac, cross the Saguenay River at Chicoutimi, then explore the southern shore.

Tadoussac★★

See CÔTE-NORD.

Take Rte. 138 north for 6km/4mi, then turn left on Rte. 172 and continue for 11km/6.8mi to Sacré-Cœur. Take another left and continue for 8km/5mi.

L'Anse de Roche (Rock Bay)

25km/15.5mi. Turn left in Sacré-Cœur.

This tiny cove offers a splendid **view★** of the fjord and the massive power lines that span it, carrying electricity from the Manicouagan region to Montreal and the rest of southern Quebec.

Return to Rte. 172.

Baie-Sainte-Marguerite

This is a good place to watch the beluga whales of the St. Lawrence River. These white whales sometimes stay for several hours, moving around on the surface, and can be watched from the river bank. At the look-out point (Anse à la Barge), guides specializing in natural history reveal the secrets of the beluga's lifestyle and explain the importance of protecting its habitat.

Centre d'interprétation Le Béluga (beluga interpretation center)

1121 Rte. 172 Nord. Open end May–end Jun, Sat–Sun 9am–4pm; end Jun–mid-Jul 9am–6pm; mid-Jul–Sept 9am–9pm; Sept–mid-Oct 9am–4pm. $8.50.

An interactive exhibition explaining the whales' habitat and the relationship between humans and the belugas of the St. Lawrence that has developed over the centuries.

After 69km/43mi, turn left, following the signs.

Sainte-Rose-du-Nord

69km/43mi. Turn left at sign.

Founded in 1838, this charming village is nestled in a cove between two rocky escarpments. A stroll down to the wharf reveals an exceptional **site★★**, while a walk to the scenic lookout provides a great view of the village and fjord. The small **nature museum** contains a collection of nature's oddities, including wood twisted and polished into fantastic shapes, and wild mushrooms (open daily mid-May–mid-Sept, 8:45am–8:30pm; mid-Sept–mid-May until 6:30pm. $7; P 418-675-2348; www.museedelanature.com). On its descent towards **Saint-Fulgence** (28km/17.4mi), Rte. 172 affords a magnificent **panorama★** of the fjord's western end. **Mt. Valin** (968m/3,175ft) lies about 20km/12.4mi to the north of the town. Weather patterns are difficult to predict in southern Quebec's ski resorts, but Mt. Valin is a reliable source of beauty and recreation in winter.

Travel for 28km/17mi on Rte. 172.

Saint-Fulgence

The descent into Saint-Fulgence offers a splendid **view★** over the western end of the fjord.

Centre des Battures et de Réhabilitation des Oiseaux (Centre for tidal flats and bird rehabilitation – CIBRO)

100 chemin Cap-des-Roches. Open end Jun–early Sept 8:30am–6pm; May–end Jun and Sept–Nov 9am–4pm. $8. 418-674-2425. www.cibro.ca.

The rocky walls of the fjord give way to wide expanses of marshland at Saint-Fulgence, where a spit of land extends more than 650m along the coast. The centre explains these unusual phenomena and introduces you to the area's abundant plant life and the 265 bird species that visit the tidal flats. In May, the "journée de la Bernache" provides an opportunity to watch more than 10,000 black geese (bernaches) and ducks feeding on the wetlands.

Parc national des Monts-Valin (Monts-Valin national park)

28km/17.5mi N of St-Fulgence via the chemin du Lac-Léon. Visitors' Center at 360 Rang Saint-Louis, $8.50. 418-674-1200 or 1-800-665-6527. www.sepaq.com.

The park was created to protect the Massif du Mont Valin (968m) from intensive forestry, and is now a paradise for fishing and canoe-camping enthusiasts. In winter, the exceptional snowfall makes the area prime territory for cross-country skiing, as well as short- and long-distance snowshoeing.

Follow Rtes. 172 and 175 south to Chicoutimi, crossing the Saguenay.

Chicoutimi★

16km/10mi from Saint-Fulgence.

See SAGUENAY.

La Baie

19km/11.8mi by Rte. 372.

See SAGUENAY.

Follow Rte. 170.

Saint Felix d'Otis

Site de la Nouvelle-France. 370 Vieux-chemin. Open Jun–Aug, Tue–Sun 9:15am–4pm. Guided tours in French leave every 30min, and last 1hr 30min. Equestrian show at 11am lasts 1hr. $16. Ask for information about ticket packages (show–tour–meal or cruise–tour). 418-544-8027 or 1-888-666-8027. www.sitenouvellefrance.com

This former film set will immerse you in the history of the French settlement of Quebec. You will discover the lifestyle of the indigenous people and the first settlers through attractions including a small Huron village, a Montagnais camp (the Montagnais were Indian allies of the French) and an old French farmstead with outbuildings. The area was occupied by First Nations for 5,000 years: they regularly set up camps here, and the archaeological remains found here are among the most important in the province.

Follow Rte. 170 to Rivière-Éternité (43km/26.7mi). Turn left at sign.

Rivière-Èternité

This village is one of the gateways to the Saguenay national park, and provides access to part of the Saguenay-St. Lawrence Marine Park.

A superb footpath *(25km/15.5mi)* links Rivière-Éternité to L'Anse-Saint-Jean *(accommodation is available at campsites and in shelters).*

Parc national du Fjord du Saguenay★★

Open mid-May–mid-Oct daily 8am–8pm; only the Baie Éternité sector is open the rest of the year from 8:30am–4pm. $8.50. Sightseeing cruises start at $55 418-272-1556 or 1-800-665-6527. www.sepaq.com/pq/sag.

Created in 1983 to protect the banks of the fjord, the park offers hiking, kayaking, and cross-country skiing. The park covers roughly 300sq km/116sq mi and extends about 100km/62mi from La Baie to Tadoussac. Popular areas within the park include Sainte-Marguerite Bay, Tadoussac Dunes, and Éternité Bay. The latter is one of the prettiest coves on the fjord, dominated by the large twin cliffs, Cape Trinité and Cape Éternité.

The capes are best appreciated by taking a scenic **mini-cruise** (departs from Riviere Éternité late May–late Sept, daily 11:45am; round-trip 1.5hr; commentary; $60; Les Croisiéres du Fjord 418-543-7630 or 1-800-363-7248, www.croisieres-dufjord.com). A footpath beside the bay also affords attractive views.

An **interpretation center** located at the end of the Éternité River valley features exhibits tracing the origins of the fjord (open early Jun–Aug 24, daily 9am–6pm; rest of Aug–Sept daily 9am–4pm; 418-272-1509).

Cap Trinité★★.

So named because of its three ledges, this cape rises 518m/1,700ft over the fjord. It is renowned for the impressive statue of the Virgin Mary that stands

Cruises on the Fjord du Saguenay

Croisières du Fjord *(418-543-7630 or 1-800-363-7248; www.croisièresdufjord.com)* organizes excursions on the Saguenay Fjord from May to October. This is a fine way to see its geological features, dizzying cliffs and magnificent waterfalls, and to discover the exceptional natural phenomena of this glacial valley, in particular the rocky promontories of Cap Trinité and Cap Éternité and their colonies of common seals. Cruises depart from several different points:

Tadoussac: *see CÔTE-NORD.*

Sainte-Rose-du-Nord: Crossing with 2hr excursion to L'Anse-Saint-Jean and return *(Jun and Oct, departing 11:15am, return 4pm)* and excursion to Cap-Trinité *(Jul–Aug, departs 10:10am and 1pm)*, $68.

La Baie: *see SAGUENAY.*

Rivière Éternité: 1hr 30min excursion to Sainte-Rose-du-Nord *(Jun and Sept, departing 11am and 1:30pm)* and Cap-Trinité *(Jul–Aug, departs 9:30am and 2pm)*, $55.

L'Anse-Saint-Jean: Service to Rivière-Éternité and Sainte-Rose-du-Nord takes 2hr 30min *(Jun–Oct; additional departures Jul–Aug)*, $56.

on the first ledge about 180m/590ft above the black waters of the Saguenay. Known as **Our Lady of the Saguenay**, the statue was created in 1881 by Louis Jobin at the request of a businessman, Charles-Napoléon Robitaille, who had vowed to honor the Virgin after his life was spared on two occasions.

A steep path leads from the interpretation center to the statue (*about 7km/4.3mi round-trip, allow 4hrs*) and provides dramatic **panoramas★★**. This path requires good fitness but is not technically difficult. If you have time for only one hiking excursion in the Saguenay Fjord region, this is one you should do.

Return to Rte. 170 (11km/6.8mi).

L'Anse-Saint-Jean

23km/14.3mi. Turn left at sign.

This tiny community at the mouth of the Saint-Jean River was founded in 1828. A good **view★** of the fjord can be enjoyed from the marina and the wharf. Note also the **Faubourg Bridge** (1929), a 37m/121ft-long covered bridge that spans the Saint-Jean River.

Cross the bridge, continue for 5km/3mi and turn right.

Located on the only cape accessible by car, the lookout at Tabatière Bay (Anse de Tabatière) affords a superb **view**.

Return to Rte. 170 and head towards Petit-Saguenay.

Petit-Saguenay

The Sentier Les Caps trail follows the Saguenay River from Baie-Éternité via L'Anse-St-Jean and stops on the quay of this little village, with its spectacular view of the fjord.

ADDRESSES

STAY

Cap au Leste – *follow Rte. 172 W for 9km/5.5mi after leaving Sainte-Rose-du-Nord and follow the signs on the left for 7km/4.3mi, 5551 chemin du Cap au Leste. 418-675-2000. www.capauleste.com. Closed Nov, Apr, and May.* P *39 rooms. $13.* A veritable eagle's nest surrounded by nature with the fjord below. The nice, perfectly equipped rooms are divided among several chalets. If your heart is set on a Canadian cabin, look no further.

La Fjordelaise – *370 rue Saint-Jean-Baptiste, Anse-Saint-Jean. 418-372-2560. www.fjordelaise.com.* P *9 rooms.* A charming wooden house with a veranda that has operated as a hotel for more than a century. Simple, friendly hospitality with small, well-kept rooms. The best are the three rooms with a view of the fjord.

EAT

L'Islet – *354 rue Saint-Jean-Baptiste, Anse-Saint-Jean. 418-272-9944. www.restaurantlislet.com. Lunchtimes and evenings.* A highly recommended place with a vantage point over the waters of the fjord. The home-smoked trout is a must, but you should not overlook the other delicious specialties, such as venison sausage and seafood.

TAKING A BREAK

Les 3 G – *100 rue Du Quai, Sainte-Rose-du-Nord. 418-675-2380.* Stopping for an ice cream at Les 3 G is an obligatory ritual for two reasons: because of their famous soft ice with maple butter, and because you get to eat it on the jetty looking out at the immensity of the fjord.

Bistro de l'Anse – *319 rue Saint-Jean-Baptiste, Anse-Saint-Jean. 418-272-4222. www.bistrodelanse.com. Open mid-May–mid-Oct.* This bistro in a 150-year-old house is a cultural magnet in these parts. Along with local beers and tasty snacks, you can tuck into their home-made pâtés, and, in the evenings, venison hamburgers ($20).

Saguenay★

A city, a fjord: the tourist slogan for Saguenay sums up the main attraction of this new city formed in 2002. Its territory includes Chicoutimi, Jonquière, and La Baie, and the city stretches from Lake Kénogami to the Saguenay and from the Rivière aux Sables to the Baie des Ha! Ha! It stands at the center of two major tourist destinations—Lac Saint-Jean and the Fjord du Saguenay—so anyone who wants to enjoy the unforgettable panoramas offered by the Saguenay River should definitely visit.

- **Info:** 295 rue Racine Est. ☏418-698-3167 & 1-800-463-6565. www.saguenaylacsaintjean.ca/en.
- **Location:** Chicoutimi is 200km/124mi northwest of Quebec City on scenic Rte. 175.
- **Don't Miss:** Cruise the Saguenay Fjord on La Marjolaine.
- **Timing:** The Croisières du Fjord will take 6–7hrs *(10am–5:30pm)*.
- **Kids:** Parc Mille Lieux (Park of a Thousand Places).

SIGHTS

CHICOUTIMI★

Chicoutimi is the economic, cultural, and administrative center of the Saguenay region as well as its episcopal seat. The University of Quebec maintains a campus here.

Chicoutimi was the site of a major fur-trading post as early as 1676, but it was not founded as a community until 1842, when Métis trader Peter McLeod built a sawmill at the foot of waterfalls on the Du Moulin River. This event marked the beginning of the area's important forestry industry. Chicoutimi draws its name from the Montagnais word *eshkotimiou,* meaning "to the edge of deep waters."

From Chicoutimi the visitor can behold a fine **view**★ of the rounded cliffs flanking the Saguenay River on its descent toward the St. Lawrence. The Saguenay can be crossed by car on the Dubuc

Chicoutimi

Bridge (*pont Dubuc*), or on foot or by bicycle via the Sainte-Anne footbridge. Every February, Chicoutimi celebrates its **Carnaval-Souvenir**, during which the inhabitants dress in furs and period costume, and re-create the winter activities of a bygone era.

Croix de Sainte-Anne★ (St. Anne's Cross)

On north side of the Saguenay, 3km/1.8mi from the Dubuc Bridge. Turn left on rue Saint-Albert, right on rue Roussel, and left on rue de la Croix.

Located high above the Saguenay, the terrace offers a wonderful **view** of Chicoutimi and the area. The current 18m/59ft-high cross (1922) is the third to stand on this site. The first was erected in 1863 to guide the ferries sailing up the river and prevent accidents. The second (1872) was erected in gratitude for the protection accorded the city during the Great Fire of 1870, which devastated much of the land around Lake Saint-Jean and the Saguenay River. Below this viewpoint one can see the façade of Église Sainte-Anne (St. Anne's Church, 1901).

The Jacques Cartier lookout (*intersection of rue Jacques Cartier Est and Blvd Talbot*) and the Beauregard lookout (*east of the Jacques Cartier lookout, near the statue of Our Lady of the Saguenay*) also afford excellent views of the Saguenay.

La pulperie de Chicoutimi, Centre d'Interprétation★

300 rue Dubuc. Open Jun 24–early Sept, daily 9am–6pm; Jan–Jun Wed–Sun 10am–4pm. $14.50. ♿ P ☎418-698-3100 and 1-877-998-3100. www.pulperie.com.

This former pulp and paper mill, standing on a picturesque **site★★** at the mouth of the Chicoutimi River, was one of the most important industrial complexes in Quebec. The mill was founded in 1896 by the Chicoutimi Pulp and Paper Co., Canada's largest producer of pulp by 1910. In 1920 the company employed over 2,000 people in its four mills and mechanical workshop. The mill closed after the Crash of 1929.

Near the entrance at the top of the gorge stands Building 1921. This enormous former workshop of pink granite today serves as an **interpretation center**.

Farther down, along the river, stand the remains of two paper mills, dating from 1898 and 1912. Part of the enormous conduit that brought water down to power the mills still exists. Steps lead up the river to a hill that overlooks the entire mill. The water tower is still functioning. Architect René P. LeMay (1870–1915) designed several of these buildings using local stone instead of the brick traditionally used in industrial buildings. The choice of stone as a building material contributes to the charm of the site.

Maison Arthur-Villeneuve (Arthur Villeneuve House)

In Building 1921.

Beginning in 1994 local efforts to highlight the region's heritage resulted in the relocation to this site of the home of painter Arthur Villeneuve, formerly located at 669 rue Taché Ouest. Villeneuve (1905–90) worked for many years as a barber while painting in his spare time. A deeply religious man, he gave up his shop in 1957 and dedicated the rest of his life to painting after hearing a sermon on the use of one's talents. The fame of this local folk painter has spread far beyond his simple home. Villeneuve decorated his house with colorful (and sometimes terrifying) murals.

Cathédrale Saint-François-Xavier (Cathedral of St. Francis Xavier)

Rue Racine at rue Bégin. Open year-round daily 8am–11:30am and 1:30pm–4pm. ☎418-549-3212.

The twin square towers flanking the stone façade of the cathedral (1915) overlook the city of Chicoutimi. The cathedral was rebuilt after a fire in 1919. Inside, note the sculpture of Christ by Médard Bourgault, the pulpit and Bishop's throne by Lauréat Vallières and the organ manufactured by the Casavant Brothers of Saint-Hyacinthe.

Parc Mille Lieux (Park of a Thousand Places)

200 rue Pinet, on the north side of the Saguenay River. Go north of Rte. 172 on rue Saint-Gerard and north on rue Pinet. Open Jun 26-Labor Day daily 9am–7pm; mid-Sept–end Oct Mon–Fri 9am–4pm, Sat–Sun 9am–7pm. $5.75; children (age 9 and older) $10, (ages 2-8) $12.75. 418-545-6925. www.parcmillelieux.com.

This family theme park opened in the summer of 2015, and is designed for children 2-8 years old, who can climb on a mountain, mine for coal, race around a track, board a train, puzzle through a maze, and encounter a pirate.

JONQUIÈRE

This major industrial center located south of the Saguenay River was formed in 1975 by the merger of three municipalities: Jonquière, Arvida (named for its founder, philanthropist Arthur Vining Davis) and Kénogami. Then, in 2002, a new city—Ville de Saguenay—was formed by the merger of the cities of Chicoutimi, Jonquière, La Baie, and Laterrière, and some adjacent townships. The original town of Jonquière was founded in 1847 by Marguerite Belley and her sons, who moved here from the Charlevoix region. They named the new community after the Marquis of Jonquière, governor of New France from 1749 through 1752. Two major industrial concerns were established in the early 20C: the Price Paper Co. at Kénogami in 1912, and the Alcan aluminum smelter at Arvida in 1926. Until the 2004 closure of many of the Arvida facilities, it was the largest producer of aluminum in the western world.

Centrale hydro-électrique de Shipshaw

1471 Rte. du Pont. 418-699-1547. Open Jun–Aug Mon–Fri 1:30pm–4:30pm. Guided tour (1hr). Closed Jun 24. Booking required.

The dam at the Shipshaw hydroelectric power plant dates back to 1941, and the power station is a fine example of industrial Art Deco architecture.

Église Notre-Dame-de-Fatima★ (Church of Our Lady of Fatima)

3635 rue Notre-Dame. Access from Blvd du Royaume at the corner of rue de Montfort. Open year-round daily 9am–5pm. 418-542-5678.

Known as the "teepee," this modern church (1962) rises more than 25m/82ft above the surrounding area. It is shaped like a white concrete pyramid, split vertically. Two stained-glass windows by Guy Barbeau lend a striking luminosity to the interior; the windows rise the full height of the building, joining the two halves of the pyramid.

Mont Jacob

Access from rue Saint-Dominique by rue du Vieux-Pont.

Mont Jacob dominates the western part of Jonquière and affords a superb **view** of the region. At its summit, the **Centre national d'exposition** (open Jul–Aug daily 10am–6pm; rest of the year, Mon–Fri 9am–5pm, Sat–Sun noon–5pm. 418-546-2177) serves as the setting for cultural activities and events celebrating the city's history, art and architecture.

Mont Fortin★

Access from Blvd du Saguenay by rue Desjardins.

The summit is accessible by car when the gate is open. The view from this mountain, the site of a ski center in winter, encompasses a fine **panorama** of the entire area. The aluminum bridge and Shipshaw dam can be seen in one direction, while Kénogami and Jonquière, indicated by the spire of the Church of Our Lady of Fatima, are visible in the other.

LA BAIE (SAGUENAY)

The industrial borough of La Baie occupies a magnificent **site★** in a bay on the Saguenay Fjord, which is more commonly known as the **Baie des Ha! Ha!** In 1838, settlers belonging to the Société des Vingt-et-Un arrived in the area. The purpose of this association was to begin settlement of the Saguenay–Lac-Saint-Jean region. The three municipalities that they founded on the shore of the bay—Bagotville, Port-Alfred, and Grande-Baie—merged in 1976 to form the town of La Baie.

The town became a center for wood processing, and still boasts a large paper mill, but its importance derives mainly from its port facilities, with their majestic industrial buildings standing in the centre of the town. Huge cargo ships from the Caribbean and South America bring bauxite to supply La Baie's aluminium plants, as well as those at Jonquière.

Summer months offer the chance to catch a performance of the historical stage show **La Nouvelle Fabuleuse ou les Aventures d'un Flo** *(www.fabuleuse.com)* , in which the story of the hero Florian (Flo) evokes the history of the region from 1603 to the present day.

Scenic route

Just before Rte. 372 plunges down towards the Rivière-à-Mars in the Baie des Ha! Ha!, you can enjoy a wonderful **view★★** of the bay. On a clear day the panorama extends to a distance of 48km/30mi. A little further on, Rte. 372 joins Rte. 170, which follows the shore of the bay for a dozen kilometers, offering exquisite views.

Parc Mars

Where Rte. 170 (rue Bagot) meets Rte. 372 (Blvd Saint-Jean-Baptiste), take rue Bagot, then turn left into rue Mars.

This waterside park has been set up for cyclists and pedestrians and offer a fine **panorama★** of the bay and the surrounding hills, as well as a vantage point to watch the imposing ships that ply the river. About 200,000 tons of wood and paper, and more than three million tons of bauxite pass through the port each year.

Musée du Fjord

3346 Blvd de la Grande-Baie Sud (Route 170). ♿ P. End Jun–Sept 9am–6pm; rest of the year Tue–Fri 9am–4:30pm, Sat–Sun 1–5pm. $15; children (age 5 and under) free. ☎418-697-5077 or 1-866-697-507. www.museedufjord.com.

The Fjord Museum was partially destroyed in the flood of 1996, but has gained a new lease of life in an elegant modern complex. The exhibitions range from the scientific (the formation of the fjord, the aquatic flora and fauna, and the Baie des Ha! Ha!) to the historical (on the Saguenay region) and the artistic. The star attraction is the Fjord Aquarium, with its specimens of the creatures that inhabit the depths of the Saguenay. The museum also offers excursions in which visitors are transformed into scientists and set off accompanied by a guide in search of the organisms that inhabit the shores of the Baie des Ha! Ha! Back at the museum, they analyse their specimens under the microscope.

Baie des Ha! Ha!

Some think this unusual name comes from the Rue des Ha! Ha!, a dead-end street in 17C Paris, while others believe that the name derives from the exclamations of the first explorers when they realized that the river they were exploring was actually a bay. The joke, apparently, was on them.

Pyramide des Ha! Ha!

Parc des Ha! Ha!, rue Monseigneur-Dufour. ☎418-698-3167 or 1-800-463-6565; $3.

The Pyramide des Ha! Ha! in the Parc des Ha! Ha! should not be missed. The aluminum pyramid stands 21m tall and measures 24m at its base. It was designed by the artist Jean-Jules Soucy and is covered in 3,000 triangular red and white "give way" signs.

The French term for "give way" is "cédez le passage", and this sets up a play on words as "cédéz" shares the same pronunciation as "s'aider" (to help each other), so the work is a reminder of the spirit that helped people to cope with the disastrous floods that hit the region in 1996.

Scenic Cruise, Rivière-Éternité, Fjord du Saguenay

La passe migratoire à saumons de la Rivière-à-Mars

3232 chemin St-Louis. Open mid-Jun–end Aug 8am–8pm; end Aug–mid-Sept 8am–5pm. $3.25. 418-697-5093. www.peche.riviereamars.com.

A fish ladder has been installed in the center of town on a section of the Rivière-à-Mars to help migrating salmon swim upriver. The observation windows set beneath the surface of the water allow visitors to observe the salmon in their natural habitat.

Scenic Cruises to le Fjord du Saguenay★★

Departures from Tadoussac. Depart from dock at bottom of 49 rue La Lafontaine Jul–Sept daily 9:30am and 10am. Duration 5hrs. Bilingual commentary. Return to Chicoutimi by bus. Starting at $64. Croisières du Fjord 418-543-7630 or 1-800-363-7248. www.croisieresdufjord.com.

Cruises on the majestic Saguenay Fjord are among the most spectacular and popular excursions in Quebec. The boats sail the river to the lovely village of Sainte-Rose-du-Nord; stop below the rocky promontory known as the Tableau (150m/492ft high); pass by Saint-Basile-du-Tableau, one of the smallest villages in Quebec; and enter Eternity Bay (Baie Éternité), dominated by the towering peaks of Cape Eternity and Cape Trinity. The highlight of the cruise is the dramatic arrival at the foot of **Cap Trinité**. Set in this wild and rocky setting is a gigantic statue of the Virgin. The three ledges for which the cape was named are clearly visible from the boat; rock climbers can sometimes be seen on the cliffs. On the return trip, the views of Ha! Ha! Bay and Chicoutimi itself are equally pleasant.

ADDRESSES

Good to know – The tourist office offers three booklets with comprehensive itineraries introducing you to the historical heritage of Chicoutimi, La Baie, and Jonquière.

STAY

Auberge le Parasol – *1287 Blvd du Saguenay Est, Arr. Chicoutimi. 418-543-7771. www.aubergeleparasol.com.* P. *80 rooms.* This well-kept motel has a 1960s feel to it, and from its location on a hill, you have the city at your feet. From the restaurant terrace, visitors can enjoy wonderful views of Chicoutimi and the Saguenay River at sunset.

Hôtel Chicoutimi – *460 rue Racine Est. 418-549-7111 or 1-800-463-7930. www.hotelchicoutimi.qc.ca.* P. *85 rooms.* This historic hotel in the heart of Chicoutimi overlooks the bustle of the main street. All rooms have been carefully renovated in a rustic-chic style, and those on the higher floors have a good view of the river.

EAT

La Vieille Garde – *461 rue Racine Est, Arr. Chicoutimi. 418-602-1225. http://www.lavieillegarde.com/index.php/en/. Open Tue–Sat.* A wine bar with an impressive choice of quality bottles, as well as a restaurant with a designer look is popular with Chicoutimi's in-crowd. In the kitchen, the cream of the region's chefs use local ingredients to create French-inspired dishes with a hint of Québécois influence.

⊖⊖ **La Cuisine** – *387 rue Racine Est. ℘418-698-2822. www.restaurantlacuisine.ca. Open Mon–Fri lunchtime and evening; Sat and Sun evening.* An excellent restaurant serving French-inspired food, but with the odd foray into more exotic territory. The place is famous for its fish tartare on Fridays, which is prepared with a different fish every week.

TAKING A BREAK

Café Cambio – *405 Racine Est, Arr. Chicoutimi. ℘418-549-7830. www.cafecambio.ca. Open daily 8am–11pm.* A visit to this organic café is not to be missed. Home-roast coffee and great snacks, such as bagels, muffins, and salads, as well as delicious hamburgers including four different vege-burgers.

DRINKS

La Voie Maltée – *2509 rue Saint-Dominique, Arr. Jonquière. ℘418-542-4373. www.lavoiemaltee.com. Open 11:30am–3am (weekends from noon).* Welcome to the world of beer: This micro-brewery creates more than a dozen brews, with evocative names like La Polissonne (little scamp), La Graincheuse (the grouch) and La Rabat-Joie (spoil sport). All that remains is to find the one that suits you.

Lake Saint-Jean★★

Saguenay–Lac Saint-Jean region

Located north of Quebec City, at the southern tip of the Saguenay region, Lake Saint-Jean fills a shallow glacial basin 98m/321ft above sea level. The modern body of water, covering an area of 1,350sq km/521sq mi, is a small remnant of the original lake that was created by melting glaciers more than 10,000 years ago. Nowhere deeper than 63m/207ft, it has an average depth of 20m/66ft. The lake is fed by a number of rivers, including the Péribonka, Mistassini and Ashuapmushuan, but empties into only one: the Saguenay. The Lake Saint-Jean area resembles a crater with walls sloping downward toward the lake, creating spectacular rapids and falls.

- **Info:** ℘1-877-253-8387. www.saguenaylacsaintjean.net.
- **Location:** Lake Saint-Jean is 180km/112mi north of Quebec City by Rte. 169 or Rte. 175 (via Chicoutimi), from Trois-Rivières by Rte. 155 and from Chicoutimi by Rte. 170.
- **Don't Miss:** Saint-Félicien Zoo and Val-Jalbert Historic Village.
- **Timing:** Allow several hours more if you intend to explore the northwest section of Lake Saint-Jean, where fewer attractions are.
- **Kids:** Dam-en-Terre Recreation Area at Alma has many kid-friendly activities plus a heated wading pool.

A BIT OF HISTORY

Unlike its neighboring industrial regions, the Saguenay and the Mauricie, the Lake Saint-Jean area supports agriculture; however, farming has only been practiced here since the Great Fire of 1870, which cleared much of the surrounding forest and opened broad tracts of land. First called Piékouagami ("flat lake") by the Montagnais, the lake was renamed for **Jean Dequen**, the first Frenchman to visit its shores in 1647. The fur trade between the Natives and the French, initially established at Tadoussac, soon moved into the region. In 1676 a trading post was built on the shores of the lake at the mouth of the Métabetchouane River, a site that later became the village of Desbiens.

The area remained unsettled until the mid-19C, when sawmills and pulp mills were built. The 20C was marked by the harnessing of the rivers for hydroelectricity and the building of an aluminum smelter at Alma. Despite industrialization, the shoreline communities also thrive on agriculture and tourism.

Today Lake Saint-Jean is known for the **granite** found near its shores, notably at Saint-Gédéon, near Alma. Many of the large churches of the region are built of this stone, which has a pinkish hue. The lake is famous for its abundance of landlocked salmon, known in Quebec as **ouananiche**, a favorite catch for sports fishermen. Gourgane (a large bean) is among the region's predominant crops, and wild **blueberries**, or bleuets, grow so plentifully on the north shore of the lake that inhabitants are often referred to as "Bleuets." These small, wild blueberries are truly delicious and are a folksy symbol of Quebec.

DRIVING TOUR

AROUND LAKE SAINT-JEAN

220km/132mi circuit from Alma by Rte. 169. See regional map, p346.

Alma

1682 Ave. du Pont Nord.
418-668-3611 or 1-877-668-3611.
www.tourismealma.com.

Just east of Lake Saint-Jean at the mouth of the Saguenay River lies the regional capital of Alma. Founded in 1864, the city was named in commemoration of that year's Anglo-French victory over the Russian army at the Alma River in the Crimea.

Experience the history of the region from the last ice age though industrialization at **L'Odyssée des Bâtisseurs** (1671 Ave. du Pont Nord; open mid-Jun–mid-Aug daily 9am–5:30pm; late Aug–Sept daily 9am–4:30pm; rest of year call for hours. $15 P 418-668-2606 or 1-866-668-2606, www.odysseedesbatisseurs.com).

This historical theme park reviews carefully and completely the fascinating story of the Lake Saint-Jean Region. The "Odyssey of the Builders" presents a wide range of hands-on, recreational and learning activities featuring the region's culture and nature. From logging to hydropower plants and the ensuing massive industrialization, l'Odyssée des Bâtisseurs will allow you to grasp how this remote area became one of the most vibrant, dynamic, and interesting areas of Quebec. If you enjoy learning about history and industry, allow yourself at least three hours to fully appreciate l'Odyssée des Bâtisseurs.

Complexe touristique Dam-en-Terre

8km/5mi. Exit the city center by Ave. du Pont, heading north, and turn left on Blvd des Pins; turn right on chemin de la Dam-en-Terre and right again on chemin de la Marina. Dam-en-Terre is at 1385 chemin de la Marina.

The dam, built between the islands of Alma and Maligne in the early 1950s, was designed to harness the river and raise the level of the lake, thus increasing its hydroelectric potential. Established on the bay in 1979, the **Dam-en-Terre Recreation Area** (open late May–mid-Sept daily 8am–9pm; rest of the year Mon–Fri 8am–4pm. P $31 418-668-3016 or 1-888-289-3016; www.damenterre.qc.ca) includes a campground, beach, wading pool, picnic shelters, cottages for rent, restaurant and theater, hiking trails, and a marina. Visitors can also rent canoes, pedal-boats and bicycles, and during summer there is theater, a cruise, and dinner—all can be purchased singly, or through a variety of packaged combinations. A **scenic cruise** is a good way to visit the Alcan plant, the Isle-Maligne hydroelectric dam and the numerous villages of Lac Saint-Jean (departs Jul–Sept Tue–Sun at 2pm; round-trip 2hrs; commentary; reservations required; $35; ♿ ✆418-668-3016 & 1-888-289-3016; www.damenterre.qc.ca).

▶ Take Rte. 169 for 25km/15.5mi to Saint-Henri-de-Taillon and continue 6km/3.7mi to Pointe-Taillon Park (follow signs).

Parc national de la Pointe-Taillon (Pointe-Taillon Park)

31km/19mi. Located at 835 Rang 3 Ouest, Saint-Henri-de-Taillon. Opening times vary according to the sector of the park and the weather. South (Taillon) sector May–Oct; north (Sainte-Monique) Sector and Véloroute des Bleuets park gatehouse Jun–Oct. $8.50. ⛺ ✕ ♿ P ✆418-347-5371 or 1-800-665-6527. www.sepaq.com/pq/pta/. Interpretation center open mid-Jun–mid-Aug daily 8am–9pm; end May–mid-Jun & early Sept–mid-Oct, 9am–5pm; mid-Aug–Labor Day 8am–8pm.
Located at the mouth of the Péribonka River along the north bank of Lake Saint-Jean, the Pointe-Taillon peninsula was formed by post-glacial alluvial deposits. It stretches for nearly 20km/12.4mi and covers 92sq km/35sq mi. Mainly a land of marshes, swamps and peat bogs, it is also covered with a forest of black spruce and birch. On the shore of the lake, the forest gives way to a fine sandy beach that attracts migrating ducks and geese in the fall. The park has several hiking trails and a 32km/20mi bike (rentals available) path, as well as canoeing, kayaking, pedal-boating, and sailboarding. Pointe-Taillon is the largest and arguably the best beach on Lake Saint-Jean. It is one of very few public beaches in Quebec where night camping is allowed. When you hike, watch for beavers, turtles, and other wildlife.

▶ Return to Rte. 169 and continue to Péribonka.

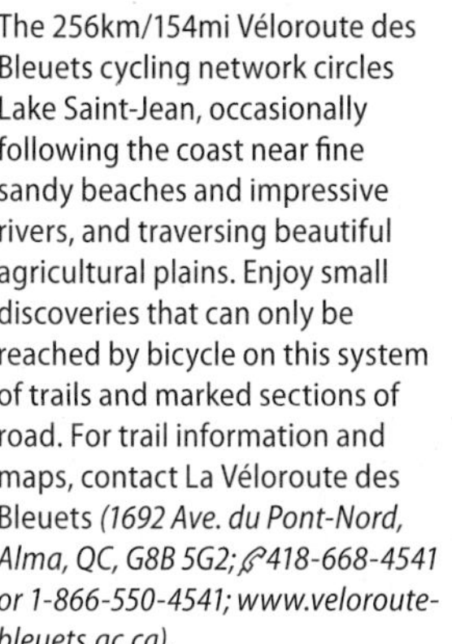

256km of Cycling

The 256km/154mi Véloroute des Bleuets cycling network circles Lake Saint-Jean, occasionally following the coast near fine sandy beaches and impressive rivers, and traversing beautiful agricultural plains. Enjoy small discoveries that can only be reached by bicycle on this system of trails and marked sections of road. For trail information and maps, contact La Véloroute des Bleuets *(1692 Ave. du Pont-Nord, Alma, QC, G8B 5G2; ✆418-668-4541 or 1-866-550-4541; www.veloroute-bleuets.qc.ca).*

After Sainte-Monique, Rte. 169 crosses the Péribonka River and, 4km/2mi farther along, reaches a charming **viewpoint** and picnic area.

Péribonka

This pretty community located on the banks of the Péribonka River, just above its outlet into Lake Saint-Jean, has subsisted on forestry and farming since its foundation in 1887. The mighty Péribonka River, which means "river dug in the sand" in Montagnais, exceeds 460km/285mi in length, making it the largest tributary of Lake Saint-Jean. Today its rushing waters are harnessed by two reservoirs and three power stations.
The French author Louis Hémon (1880–1913) spent a few months in Péribonka in 1912, a visit that inspired the creation of his posthumously published and best-known French-Canadian novel, Maria Chapdelaine (published in 1916), a love story of bygone days. The novel is a reflection on the hardships endured by men and women in the region in the early 20C. The community is also the departure point for the famous Lake Saint-Jean **International Swim Marathon**, which takes place during the last week of July.

Musée Louis-Hémon – Complexe touristique Maria-Chapdeleine

200 Rte. Maria-Chapdelaine 5km/3mi east of Péribonka on Rte. 169 (700 Rte. 169). Open mid-Jun–Labor Day daily 9am–5pm; rest of the year Tue–Fri 9am–4pm. Guided tours in French and English, interpretative signs in French only $7. ℘418-374-2177. www.museelh.ca.

Focusing on the life and work of French writer Louis Hémon as well as literature in general, this vast museum complex has a collection of some 1,400 works of art, documents, and ethnological artifacts from the world of letters. Also open to the public are the house of Samuel Bédard, where young Louis Hémon stayed and worked as a farm hand in 1912, and a contemporary pavilion (1986) built of quartz. Exhibits here trace the author's life from his birth in Brittany to his tragic death when he was hit by a train in Chapleau (Northern Ontario).

Scenes from *Maria Chapdelaine* (*see above*) are re-created in the museum and the film made from the novel can be seen.

Continue on Rte. 169 to road junction (13km/8mi). Turn right and continue 1km/.6mi.

Sainte-Jeanne-d'Arc

This village is located at the confluence of the Little Péribonka and the Noire rivers. Erected next to a waterfall on the Little Péribonka in 1907, the **old mill** operated until 1974. Visitors can observe the original milling mechanisms and carding machine (open mid-Jun–late Aug daily 9:30am–5pm. $5; ℘418-276-3166). At one time, the river was harnessed to run a sawmill, shingle mill and flour mill, in addition to the carding mill.

Return to Rte. 169.

Dolbeau-Mistassini

Now a shared municipality with Mistassini, Dolbeau was founded in 1927, with the establishment of the Domtar pulp and paper mill. Named for the Récollet missionary Jean Dolbeau, who arrived in Tadoussac in 1615, the town is famous for its **Festival des dix jours western de Dolbeau** (*see Festivals & Events*) held in July. Mistassini, meaning "large rock" in Cree, stands on the Mistassibi River beside a lovely waterfall, known as **Chute des Pères★** (Pères Falls), named for the Trappist monks of Oka who came here in 1892. The twin towers of the original monastery are visible from a spot near the confluence of the Mistassini and Mistassibi rivers. In 1980 the Trappists moved north to Saint-Eugène, but their chocolate and other products are still on sale at the factory near the old monastery. Mistassini is known as Quebec's blueberry capital.

Saint-Félicien

1209 Blvd Sacré-Coeur. ℘418-679-9888 or 1-877-525-9888. www.ville.stfelicien.qc.ca.

Saint-Félicien is located on the western shore of Lake Saint-Jean, at the confluence of the Mistassini, Ticouapé and Ashuapmushuan rivers, which rush over falls and rapids for 266km/156mi before emptying into the lake. Soaring above Blvd Sacré-Cœur in the centre of town are the twin steeples of Saint-Félicien's large pink-granite church, erected in 1914. Across the street, Sacré-Cœur Park overlooks the Ashuapmushuan River. The town is best known for its zoo, created in 1960 by local citizens.

Zoo sauvage de Saint-Félicien★★

Centre de conservation de la biodiversité boréale – 6km/3.7mi via Blvd du Jardin (Rte. 167). Open Jun–Aug 9am–6pm (8pm from mid-Jul–mid-Aug), May and Sept–Oct 9am–5pm. $37.50; children age 6–14 $25.66; age 3–5 $15.66. ℘418-679-0543 or 1-800-667-5687. www.zoosauvage.org.

With a pretty location on an island in the Rivière aux Saumons, a tributary of the Ashuapmushuan River, this zoological park provides a wonderful

Zoo sauvage de Saint-Félicien

© Charles-David Robitaille / Zoo sauvage de Saint-Félicien / Tourisme Saguenay – Lac-Saint-Jean

introduction to Canadian wildlife, with over 75 species in total. Caribou, elk, black bears, wolves, bison, and other animals are free to roam in the 324 hectares of the **Nature Trail★★** park, whereas visitors travel in vehicles protected by cages. The site also immerses visitors in the region's history, thanks to its historic buildings, including a pioneer house dating from 1875, a trading post, a Montagnais camp and a 1930s lumberjack camp.

Chute à l'Ours★ (Bear Falls)

After the Saint-Félicien bridge, turn left off Rte. 169 toward Dolbeau onto the road bordering Rte. Saint-Eusèbe Nord and continue 15km/9.3mi. Follow signs for campground located in Normandin. Open late May–late Sept daily 8am–11pm. $25. ✕ P ✆418-274-3411. www.chutealours.com.

A footpath leads alongside these Ashuapmushuan River rapids, which extend over a distance of more than 1,500m/4,920ft. The falls were named by the early explorers, whose progress they hindered. Among these was Jesuit father Charles Albanel, the first Frenchman to reach the shores of James Bay, in 1672.

Moulin des Pionniers★ (Pioneers' Mill)

4201 rue des Peupliers in La Doré, 20km/12mi from Saint-Félicien by Rte. 167. Open mid-Jun–mid-Sept daily 9am–6pm (last guided tour at 4pm). $18. ✕ ♿ P ✆418-256-8242. www.moulindespionniers.com.

Built in 1889 by Belarmain Audet, this wooden mill served to grind wheat, drive the blacksmith's forge, saw wood and cut shingles until 1977. The original mechanism is still in perfect working order, and is quite impressive as it slices large pieces of lumber into thin construction wood. The site of the mill, on the Salmon River, is also the largest spawning ground for the landlocked salmon (*ouananiche*), which return to

Saint-Félicien History

Founded in 1865, Saint-Félicien thrived on agriculture and lumber before becoming the gateway to the rich mining area of Chibougamau, to the northwest, in the 1950s. A large paper mill was established here in 1978, and a steam power plant in 1997.

On May 19, 1870, a disaster known as the Great Fire started in Saint-Félicien and eventually ravaged the southern shores of the lake and the forests as far as La Baie. Entire communities were destroyed, and the process of recovery was long and arduous.

their place of birth each year (*Jul–Oct*) to reproduce.

The pioneer's house (1904), a two-story log cabin, stands next to the mill. The oldest house in the town of La Doré, it was moved to this site in 1977 and is furnished with period pieces. Hiking trails provide fine **views** of the Salmon River; those interested in fishing can try their luck at one of the fishing ponds located along the river's banks.

Réserve faunique Ashuapmushuan

South entrance is 33km/20.5mi (north entrance is 178km/110.6mi) northwest of Saint-Félicien on Rte. 167, toward Chibougamau (which is 232km/144mi from Saint-Félicien). Open mid-May–Oct, daily 7am–9pm. $8.50. 418-256-3806. www.sepaq.com/rf/ash.

This 4,487sq km/1,732sq mi wildlife reserve is a hunting and fishing paradise, and one of the region's largest spawning grounds for the landlocked salmon (ouananiche). Its name in Montagnais means "place where one stalks moose." Dedicated to the preservation and promotion of wildlife, the reserve is governed by strict laws intended to protect both animals and visitors to the park. A stop at the welcome center to obtain all necessary information and permits is highly recommended. Simply driving through the reserve requires no special permit.

The **Ashuapmushuan River** marks the territory of the Wildlife Reserve, which includes over 1,200 bodies of water. The river is 266km/165mi long and is one of the largest tributaries of Lake Saint-Jean. At one time, it served as a route for communication and trade between the Cree and the Montagnais. Also known as the doorway to Quebec's northern regions, it formed part of the route to James Bay. Fur trading became the principal activity with the arrival of the first Europeans. Several trading posts established along the shores and at the mouth of the river remained in use until the turn of the century.

Return to Saint-Félicien.

Rte. 169 passes through Saint-Prime, a village renowned for its cheddar cheese and other dairy products. Saint-Prime's *Perron* cheese is sold across Canada and is exported to England.

Mashteuiatsh

1516 rue Ouaiatchouan. 418-275-7200 and 1-888-222-7922. www.kuei.ca.

This strip of land jutting into Lake Saint-Jean is the site of a reserve created in 1856 for the local indigenous population, mainly Montagnais Indians (also called Innu). Visitors can browse through the shops of the Pointe-Bleue village, featuring Native handicrafts, and walk along the lake. Fur hats and coats here cost 50 percent less than they would in Montreal. A First Nations celebration called *Jeux autochtones inter-bandes* (Indigenous Games) is held in July.

Mashteuiatsh Amerindian Museum

1787 rue Amishk. Open mid-May–mid-Oct daily 9am–6pm, mid-Oct–mid-May, Mon–Fri 9am–noon and 1–4pm. $12. 418-275-4842, 1-888-875-4842; www.museeilnu.ca.

This intriguing museum introduces visitors to the history and culture of the **Pekuakamiulnuatsh** (Montagnais Indians from the Lake Saint-Jean region), including their traditional lifestyle, customs, language and role in today's society. A small shop offers handicrafts created in the village of Mashteuiatsh.

Roberval

Located on the southwestern shore of Lake Saint-Jean, this city is named for Jean-François de La Rocque, Sieur de Roberval, appointed first-lieutenant of Canada by King François I. It was under Roberval's orders that Jacques Cartier led an ill-fated expedition to colonize the St. Lawrence region in 1541 (Cartier's third voyage to the region). Today Roberval is an important service center for the area and the finish point of the **International Swim Marathon** (Traversée internationale du lac Saint-Jean, *see Festivals & Events*).

Église Notre-Dame-de-Roberval★ (Our Lady of Roberval Church)

484 Blvd Saint-Joseph at the corner of Ave. Lizotte, across from the hospital. Open year-round Sat 9:30am–8pm, Sun 8am–noon. ♿ P ✆418-275-0272.
Built in 1967, this church resembles a large copper tent topped by a white steeple. The interior is shaped like a pyramid rising above the central altar. The brightly colored stained-glass windows were fashioned by Guy Bruneau.

Roberval History

Founded in 1855, Roberval was the site of the prestigious Beemer Hotel at the end of the 19C, owned by the American lumber magnate Horace Jansen Beemer, who also operated two steamships on the lake. The magnificent mansion was destroyed by fire in 1908.

Rte. 169 hugs the lake for the entire distance between Roberval and Chambord, revealing a fine **panorama**.

Val-Jalbert★

Visits on foot or by tram. Open late-Jun–early Aug 9am–6pm, late May–mid-Jun and mid-Aug–Oct daily 10am–5pm. $26.95. ⚠ ✕ ♿ P ✆418-275-3132 or 1-888-675-3132. www.valjalbert.com.
Occupying a dramatic **site★** near the impressive falls of the Ouiatchouan River, this ghost town conjures up dreams of turn-of-the-20C industrial life. Over $20 million has been invested to upgrade this community, established originally as a company town around a pulp mill built by Damase Jalbert (1804–1904) in 1901. After his death, the mill was taken over and expanded by Alfred Dubuc. At the height of production in 1910, it produced up to 50 tons of pulp a day, and in 1915 the town became a municipality. By 1926, the population had grown to a peak of 950 inhabitants.
Trouble began in 1926: due to a sudden lack of demand, the price of pulp dropped, and increased competition led the mill to close the following year. The population gradually drifted away, and the village fell into ruin. A program of renovation begun in 1970 saved Val-Jalbert from obscurity. Today a veritable open-air museum, this heritage site offers a variety of activities.

Convent

The former convent-school of the Sisters of Our Lady of Good Counsel (1915) serves as an **interpretation center** for the historic village. A slide show (*15min*) and a model of the site recount the history of Val-Jalbert. The nuns' quarters and chapel on the second floor can be visited. Across the street stand the remains of the St. George's Church and its presbytery, overrun with vegetation.

Rue Saint-Georges

Along the village's main artery lies the former **general store** (*tourist accommodations are available on the second floor*). Destroyed by a fire in 1918, the structure was rebuilt soon after, to house the village's general store. Today a small boutique on the ground floor displays and sells a variety of objects from a bygone era. Behind the general store in the old butcher's stall, are an herbarium, and a craft store.

Residential Sector

The residential sector, now deserted, is situated on a plateau bounded by rues Sainte-Anne, Saint-Joseph, Dubuc, Tremblay, and Labrecque. At its peak, the village numbered about 80 employee residences (one is open to the public, on rue Saint-Georges, near the post office). When they were built between 1909 and 1920, these houses were considered state-of-the-art, equipped with central heating, electricity, running water and even telephones. The houses belonged to the company, and were rented to employees for about $10 a month (employees' salaries averaged around $27 a month).

Vieux Moulin (Old Mill)

Standing at the base of the Ouiatchouan falls, this mill produced pulp that was

Val-Jalbert

carried south by train. The remains of the rail line are visible.
The mill now houses an exhibit hall. A model explains the operation of the mill, and a film (*20min*) describes the process of transforming wood pulp into paper. The old mill machinery is on display.

The falls are both within easy walking distance of the village on Route de Val Jal-Jalbert.

Chute Ouiatchouan (Ouiatchouan Falls)

These extremely high (72m/236ft) falls were once the sole source of power for the pulp mill and the community. A steep but sturdy stairway (*400 steps*) leads to the top of the falls; visitors can also make the ascent by cable car (*$3*). From this spot, there is a magnificent **view★★** encompassing Lake Saint-Jean and the surrounding countryside. Downstream, the Ouiatchouan River is striking as it carves out a gorge in the rock.

Chute Maligne (Maligne Falls)

4.4km/3mi, allow 1hr 30min for round-trip. Trail begins in campground on west side of river. Note: Steep descent to falls.

A pleasant wooded trail climbs up the Ouiatchouan River valley to a point where the river plunges over a second set of falls. A lock and sawmill were once located here to prepare and cut the wood before it was floated down to the mill.

Return to Val-Jalbert.

A 2km/1.2mi drive along Route 169 leads to a fine **viewpoint★** of the lake.

Chambord

Established in 1857, this community grew in importance after the arrival of the railway from Quebec City in 1888. It is named after Henry V, count of Chambord, the last of the Bourbon royal line.

Take Rte. 155.

Lac-Bouchette

This small community, nestled between La Tuque and Lake Saint-Jean, was founded in 1890. It is named in honor of Joseph Bouchette, an engineer and land surveyor who mapped this area in 1820.

Pilgrimage destination – L'Hermitage Saint-Antoine at Lac-Bouchette is most famous for its shrine founded in 1907 by the abbot **Elzéar Delamarre** (1854–1925), Superior of the Chicoutimi Seminary. Father Delamarre spent his summers in the region, eventually building a summer retreat and a chapel near Lake Bouchette. In 1916 he discovered a natural grotto resembling the Massabielle grotto at Lourdes, France. Before his death, many pilgrims had made the trek to the grotto. Today this former summer retreat is owned by the Capuchin Brothers, and is visited by more than 200,000 faithful every year.

Ermitage Saint-Antoine★ (St. Anthony's Hermitage)

2km/1.2mi west of Rte. 155 across Lakes Ouiatchouan and Bouchette. Open year-round daily 8am–11pm. 418-348-6344. www.st-antoine.org.

The red-brick monastery of the Capuchin Brothers, built in 1924, dominates the site.

First chapel – The first chapel built by Father Delamarre in 1907 was dedicated to St. Anthony of Padua. After discovering a grotto similar to the one in Lourdes, Delamarre expanded the chapel and dedicated it to Our Lady of Lourdes. This later chapel has a Gothic Revival interior, embellished with arches and fan vaulting. The earlier chapel, now a side aisle, contains the tomb of Father Delamarre. The walls of the modest chapel are decorated with a group of 23 **paintings★** representing the life and miracles of St. Anthony, executed between 1908 and 1920 by Charles Huot (1855–1930).

Marian chapel – Built in 1950, this chapel resembles a grotto. The stained-glass windows (1971) were designed by Guy Bruneau. The large one at the back represents Bernadette Soubirous kneeling before Our Lady of Lourdes.

Steps lead from the Marian Chapel to the grotto discovered by Father Delamarre in 1916. Nearby stand an open-air chapel overlooking the lake, and a copy of the Holy Steps of Rome; a path leads up the hillside to the 14 Stations of the Cross, sculpted in stone.

Desbiens

Father Jean Dequen first saw Lake Saint-Jean from this spot in 1647. He established a Jesuit mission five years later, followed by a fur-trading post in 1676. The community is named for Louis Desbiens, who founded the first pulp and paper mill in 1896.

A wooden wharf just below the small Jean-Dequen Park is a good spot to observe fishermen and the lake.

Centre d'histoire et d'archéologie de la Métabetchouane

243 rue Hébert, right after the bridge that spans the mouth of the Métabetchouane. Open late Jun–Labor Day daily 9am–5pm. $9. 418-346-5341, www.chamans.com.

This interpretation center traces the colonial history of Lake Saint-Jean and re-creates living conditions at a 19C fur-trading post. It also features displays on First Nations and the prehistory of the region. The powder magazine at the entrance marks the exact spot of the original trading post, set on the banks of the Métabetchouane River. Note also the memorial honoring Jean de Quen.

Take 7e Ave. across from city hall (925 rue Hébert) in Desbiens. Fairy Cavern is 6km/3.7mi S.

Trou de la fée (Fairy Cavern)

Open mid-Jun–mid-Aug daily 9am–7pm; late Aug–Oct daily 10am–6pm. $15. 418-346-1242. www.cavernetroudelafee.ca.

Perched 68.5m/225ft above the Métabetchouane River, on the edge of an abrupt cliff, the cavern offers a spectacular **view** of the river. Deserters hiding in the cave during World War II claimed to have been saved by the fairy (fée) of the cavern. The 38m/125ft half-hour guided descent into the 10,000-year-old grotto is impressive, but extremely steep (sturdy shoes required; helmets provided).

Return to Rte. 170.

Métabetchouan-Lac-á-la-Croix

5km/3mi from Desbiens.

This village, founded in 1861, is the site of a well-known summer music camp, Camp Musical du Lac-Saint-Jean (Sunday evening concerts, www.campmusical-slsj.qc.ca). The camp provides a superb **view** of the lake.

Follow the Rte. 170 round to Alma.

Northeast of Quebec City

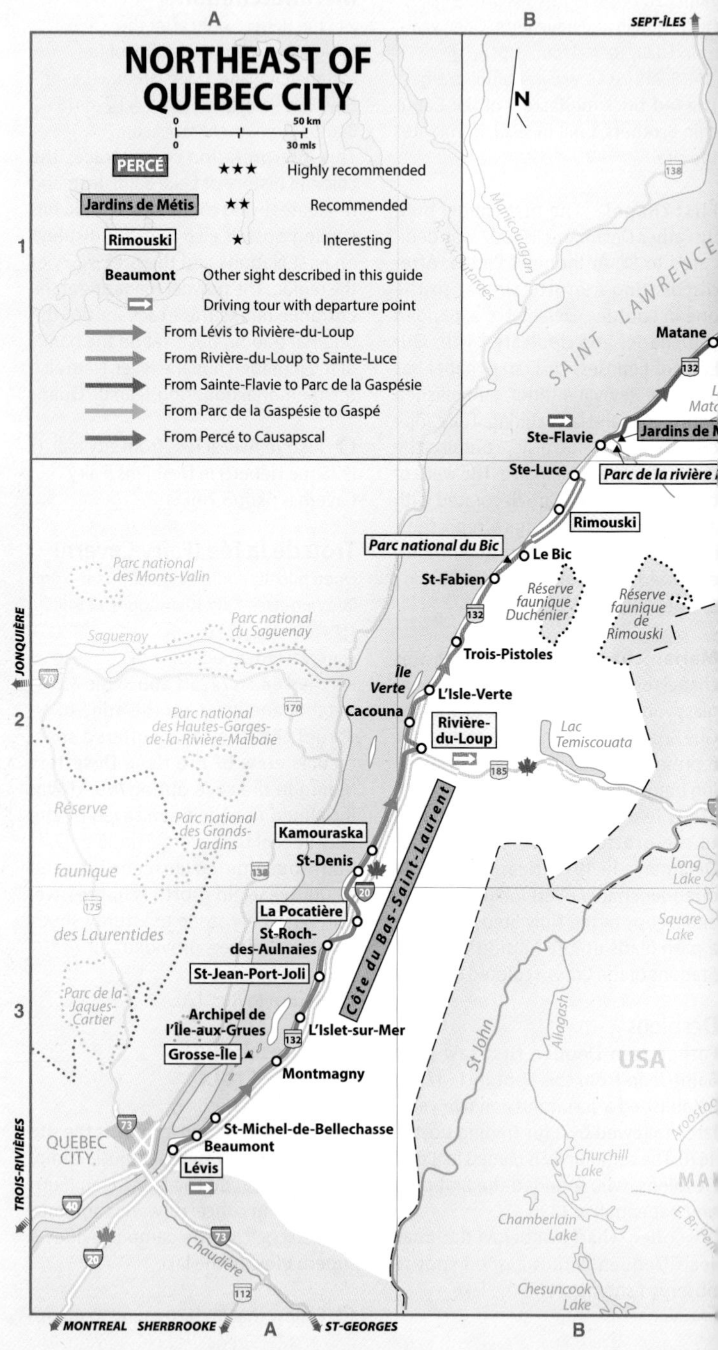

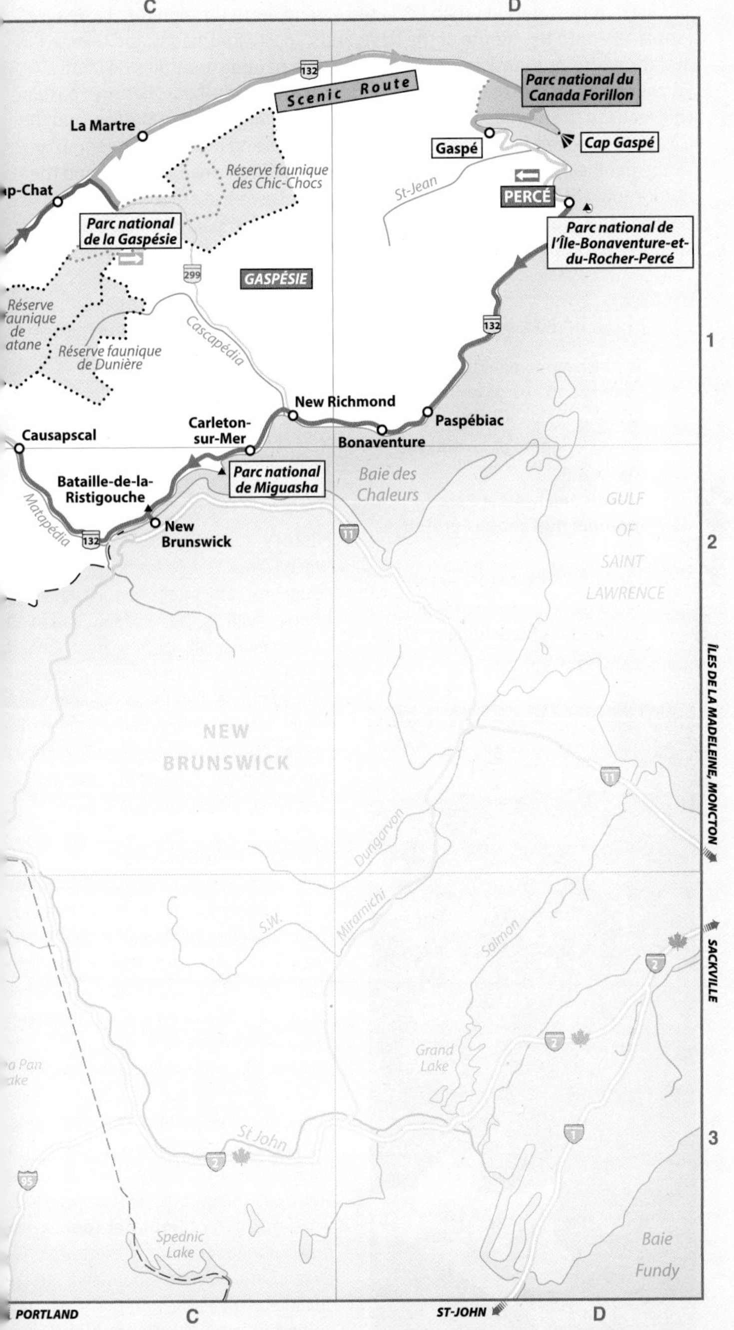
C
D
Scenic Route
132
Parc national du Canada Forillon
Cap Gaspé
Gaspé
La Martre
Réserve faunique des Chic-Chocs
St-Jean
PERCÉ
Parc national de l'Île-Bonaventure-et-du-Rocher-Percé
Parc national de la Gaspésie
299
GASPÉSIE
Réserve faunique de Dunière
Cascapédia
New Richmond
Paspébiac
Bonaventure
Carleton-sur-Mer
Causapscal
Parc national de Miguasha
Bataille-de-la-Ristigouche
Matapédia
New Brunswick
Baie des Chaleurs
GULF OF SAINT LAWRENCE
11
NEW BRUNSWICK
ÎLES DE LA MADELEINE, MONCTON
Dungarvon
S.W.
Miramichi
Salmon
SACKVILLE
Grand Lake
St John
Spednic Lake
95
Baie Fundy
PORTLAND
ST-JOHN
1
2
3

Northeast of Quebec City

Northeast of Quebec City usually means the south side of the Saint Lawrence River: routes start in urban Lévis and extend north through the "La Beauce" farmlands, onto the "Route of the Navigators," past Montmagny and Grosse-Île, and through Kamouraska and St-Jean-Port-Joli, pausing at Jardins de Métis. Further north, across the estuary boundary at Rivière-du-Loup, lies the coastline that leads to the marine port of Rimouski, the shrimp stands in Matane, and the Gaspé Peninsula, a landscape of rugged coastlines and impressive geography. At the peninsula's tip are the magical Parc national du Canada Forillon and the harbor town of Gaspé; and across the Gulf of St. Lawrence are the red sand beaches and grottos of the Magdalen Islands. No other part of Canada offers such a rich combination of history, tradition, local culture, and natural beauty.

Highlights

1. The Irish monument to immigration—**Grosse-Île** (p396)
2. Flower kingdom of **Jardins de Métis** (p408)
3. Beavers and bears at **Parc national du Canada Forillon** (p411)
4. The famous **Percé** rock (p414)
5. Red rocks and snowy owls of the **Îles de la Madeleine** (p421)

Îles de la Madeleine

© Egmont Strigl / age fotostock

Essence of the Province

Few areas typify the essence of Quebec like these three pristine districts: Chaudière-Appalaches, Bas-St.-Laurent, and Gaspésie. These lands provide a remarkable combination of rich historical remnants, a lively cultural renaissance, and captivating geography.

History

When French Europeans first staked their seigneurial settlements here, First Nations people, such as the Mi'kmaq, had lived here for more than 10,000 years. It remains a lush land ideally suited to a more sedentary lifestyle than the extreme regions, where nomadic tribes lived seasonally. By the early half of the 18C, the new residents had established a culture of entrepreneurship, family values, and outdoor fun.

Chaudière-Appalaches

While Île d'Orléans supplies a steady flow of fresh produce to the hotels and restaurants of Quebec City, the rolling farms and forests of this area defined by the Chaudière River and the Appalachian Mountains (what locals call "La Beauce") are considered the bread basket of the city.

Take Rte. 73 south and follow your instincts; take any exit to discover New England-style farms, inventive artisans, and welcoming merchants offering fresh produce and enjoyable activities everywhere you turn. Stop by the tourism office in St. Georges and, while in town, try a **Gourmet Tour** (www.bonjourquebec.com/qc-en/attractions-directory/route/arrets-gourmands-de-la-chaudiere-appalaches_258962426.html), visiting the best of local producers, who

Gaspésie landscape

© R. Haidinger / Anzenberger / Photononstop

provide plenty of regional flavor through the use of locally sourced ingredients.

Bas-Saint-Laurent

This zone has abundant coastal life and water access, with three ferry services crossing the mammoth Saint Lawrence River. The region extends south to the borders with New Brunswick and the State of Maine, and is studded with numerous rivers, reserves, and interesting sites. Take your pick of either the Route of the Navigators along the coast, or the Frontier Route inland. In either direction, travelers will enjoy numerous options.

To sample some Maritime flavor, try Bas-St.-Laurent. Packed with curious place names, like Brandy Pot Islands (Îles du Pot-à-l'Eau-de-Vie), Three Pistols (Trois Pistoles) and Shrill Scream (Croche-de-Criard), unmistakable character and rich historical traditions are the hallmarks of this region.

Gaspésie

The Gaspé Peninsula, a striking continuation of the Appalachian mountain range sculpted by wind and sea, is home to one of Canada's best-known landmarks, the Percé Rock, and is the stage for one of North America's most legendary scenic drives, the Gaspésie Tour.

The huge peninsula is rich in natural beauty and alive with local color. Its coastal treasures include Sainte-Flavie on La Côte, Sainte-Anne-des-Monts in La Haute-Gaspésie, La Pointe, home of the namesake town, Baie-des-Chaleurs, and the famous inland fishing waters of La Vallée. The First Nations people welcomed Viking explorers to this peninsula a millennium ago, followed by Basque fishermen, and finally French and English Europeans seeking passage to the Far East and the riches of the fur trade.

Modern Times

Through various wars, conflicts, and hard times, the Gaspé coast remains largely intact; a pristine geography rich in wildlife and natural resources, and with just enough human infrastructure to make traveling idyllic. Modern telecoms have arrived, and with them a surge of work-at-home sons and daughters determined to nurture their homeland and honor their roots in the modern age.

Rivers, Mountains, Ocean

Few places on the planet bring together a compelling set of natural assets like the Gaspésie does. From the maritime wonders of Bic National Park, to the natural delights of the Chic-Choc Mountains, Percé Rock, and beyond, visitors will surely notice nature's influence on the geology and geography of this rewarding landscape.

Northeast of Quebec City

CHIC-CHOCS MOUNTAIN LODGE

Far from the dizzying crush and hectic lifestyle of urban centers, Quebec's park system, SEPAQ, offers retreats for body, mind and spirit, including sights inside the **Reserve faunique de Matane** (part of the Parc national de la Gaspésie, *see p410*). Set at an altitude of over 615m/2,000 ft deep in the Appalachian's Chic-Choc Mountains, this log structure overlooks a remarkable paradise of outdoor pleasures.

Guests are picked up in the coastal community of Cap Chat, from where an all-terrain minibus or SnowCat climbs slowly up the incline from sea level to the heights of the peninsula. Gourmet cuisine is served by Chef Alain Laflamme from Montreal. Travelers experience mountain solitude between two peaks, Mont Collins and Mont Matawees, both higher than 1,000m/3,000 ft. Other gorgeous mountains are also close, like Mont Coleman, Mont Nicol-Albert, and many more. Don't miss a visit to Chutes Hélène, a dream-like waterfall more than 50m/164ft high.

Located in a unique weather zone, visitors will have pristine forest surroundings to enjoy unmatched snow conditions in winter (8m/26ft average annual snowfall), while hikers, walkers, and mountain cyclists have seemingly endless territory and topography to challenge appetites for back-country wheel-spinning. Over 60sq km/36 sq mi of mountain trails, valleys, and rivers make up the backyard environs, so there is plenty of room for everyone. Afterwards, enjoy the lodge's on-site spa, have a glass of wine or a local microbrew, and trade stories with other guests. There are 18 rooms; no TV, radio, or telephones. Free equipment during stay.

1-800-665-3091. www.sepaq.com/ct/amc.

Bas-Saint-Laurent★★

Chaudière-Appalaches–
Bas-Saint-Laurent

The regions of Chaudière-Appalaches and Bas-Saint-Laurent, located on the south shore of the St. Lawrence River between Quebec City and the Gaspé Peninsula, are characterized by fertile plains and plateaus, with the Appalachian Mountains looming to the south. The peaceful rural landscapes along the shore are divided into long, narrow strips of farmland, laid out perpendicular to the river in the manner of the old seigneurial 'rang' system. To the north, the Laurentian Mountains make a steep plunge into the St. Lawrence River, creating a landscape of rare natural beauty.

- **Population:** 200,292.
- **Michelin Map:** pp388–389: AB2-3.
- **Info:** Tourisme Bas-Saint-Laurent, 148 rue Fraser, 2nd Floor, Rivière-du-Loup. ℘418-867-1272 & 1-800-563-5268. www.bassaintlaurent.ca.
- **Location:** Chaudières-Appalaches is across the bridge from Quebec City. It spreads east to just before La Pocatière, where Bas-Saint-Laurent begins, and extends all the way to Gaspésie.
- **Don't Miss:** Grosse-Île; the Aulnaies Seigneurie in Saint-Roch-des-Aulnaies; Parc national du Bic in Cap-à-l'Orignal; and the the Musée de la mer et lieu historique national du Canada du phare de Pointe-au-Père in Rimouski.
- **Timing:** You can make a circuit following the shoreline of the St. Lawrence River to return to Quebec City by crossing on the ferry at Rivière-du-Loup. The routes described here follow the more interesting secondary roads, but if you need to go faster, use the four-lane Rte. 20 (to just beyond Rivière-du-Loup). The sun sets spectacularly on the St. Lawrence River, so plan a rest or meal stop along the river every day at dusk.
- **Kids:** Parc du Bic is a good place to camp, with many outdoor activities such as hiking and birdwatching.

 DRIVING TOURS

1 FROM LÉVIS TO RIVIÈRE-DU-LOUP

187km/116mi.

Lévis★

996 rue de la Concorde. ℘418-838-6026. www.tourismelevis.com.

The city of Lévis lies on the southern shore of the St. Lawrence, opposite Quebec City. A ferry links the two cities, transporting travelers from Quebec City towards the Gaspé Peninsula and the Lévis Forts National Historic Site, and providing a different view of Quebec City.

Terrasse de Lévis (Lévis Terrace)

From Rte. 132, take rue Côte-du-Passage, bear left on rue Desjardins, and turn left on rue William-Tremblay.

Built during the Depression, this terrace was inaugurated in 1939 by George VI and his daughter, the future Queen Elizabeth II. Located high above the river, it offers an excellent **view★★** of the older areas of Lévis and Quebec City, with the Citadel, Château Frontenac, and port. The view extends to Mont Sainte-Anne in the east, and as far as the Quebec City Bridge in the west.

Bombardment Site Is Now a Business Center

In 1759 British General James Wolfe built a redoubt on these rocky cliffs, from which he planned to bombard the capital of New France. Initially called Aubigny, the community was renamed in 1861 for François-Gaston, Duc de Lévis, who defeated the British at Sainte-Foy in 1760.

During the 19C, Lévis became a center for timber exports to England. In 1828 the Davie Shipbuilding Co., from the neighboring town of Lauzon, established the first shipbuilding center in Canada here. With the arrival of the railway in 1861, Lévis became a major business center, completing its swords-to-plowshares transition. Today the city is noted for its port and wood-related industries, and as the birthplace and headquarters of the Desjardins cooperative savings and loan company (Caisse populaire Desjardins).

Carré Déziel

In the heart of old Lévis, Déziel Square is surrounded by several interesting buildings, including the imposing **Église Notre-Dame-de-la-Victoire** (Church of Our Lady of Victory), erected in 1851. At the center of the square stands a **monument** to Joseph-David Déziel sculpted by Louis-Philippe Hébert. Déziel (1806–82) was the first parish priest and the head of the Lévis College, which he founded in 1851. Today he is considered to be the founder of Lévis.

Maison Alphonse-Desjardins★ (Alphonse-Desjardins House)

6 Ave. du Mont-Marie at corner of rue Guenette. Visit by guided tour (45min) only, year-round Mon–Fri 10am–noon, 1pm–4:30pm; Sat–Sun noon–5pm. Extended hours in summer. ♿ P ℘418-835-2090. www.desjardins.com.

Built between 1882 and 1884 in the Gothic Revival style, this small, white clapboard house was the home of Alphonse and Dorimène Desjardins for more than 40 years. The house was restored in 1982 by the Mouvement Desjardins as a tribute to its founder. Displays of artifacts describe Desjardins' life and the beginning of the cooperative movement. Desjardins' office and other rooms have been refurbished to reflect the period (1906) when the *Caisse Populaire de Lévis* had its head office in the house.

North America's First Savings and Loan

Alphonse Desjardins – On December 6, 1900, Alphonse Desjardins (1854–1920), a journalist and stenographer in the House of Commons, founded the first cooperative savings and loan company (Caisse populaire) in North America. This people's bank, based on a European concept and adapted to local conditions, sought to bring economic independence to French Canadians, thus slowing their exodus to the US. With his wife, Dorimène, Desjardins ran the first "caisse pop" from his home in Lévis and went on to open 184 branches throughout the province. Towards the end of his life, requests for federation with the Caisse populaire Desjardins were coming in from French Canadians living in other provinces, and from French Canadians who had formed "Little Canadas" in large New England cities like Manchester (New Hampshire). Although Desjardins laid the basic groundwork, the Caisse populaire centrale was not created until 1932, some 12 years after his death. Today the Desjardins Cooperative Movement (Mouvement Desjardins), with headquarters in Lévis, includes more than 1,300 caisses populaires and more than 5 million members. It is the largest financial institution in Quebec, and it is similarly active in English Canada.

Lieu historique national du Canada des Forts-de-Lévis★ (Lévis Forts National Historic Site of Canada)

2km/1.2mi by Rte. 132 Est and chemin du Gouvernement. Open mid-May–late Aug daily 10am–5pm. $3.90. ♿ P ✆418-835-5182 or 1-888-773-8888. www.pc.gc.ca/levis.

Fort No. 1 (1865–72) stands opposite Quebec City, atop Pointe Lévy, the highest point on the south shore. It is the sole vestige of three such forts built to protect the city from possible American attack during the American Civil War, and from the **Fenian Raids**. The Fenians were members of a secret, New York-based Irish society fighting to liberate Ireland from British domination and occupy British North America, or the Dominion of Canada. The fort was never completely garrisoned, and was nearly abandoned after the Treaty of Washington in 1871.

Shaped like an irregular pentagon, the fort is composed of a series of massive earthen ramparts with a tall embankment protecting the casemates, ditches and vaulted tunnels leading to the caponiers (stone and brick structures armed with small cannons). Its design marks the transition between two styles of fortification: the classical system, which involved enclosing protected areas with contiguous walls; and the mid-19C system of erecting a series of detached forts. Overlooking the river, the fort offers splendid **views★** of the Montmorency Falls Park and Île d'Orléans. Outside Lévis, Rte. 132 runs alongside the St. Lawrence, affording views of Quebec City and of the Montmorency Falls on the north shore.

Ferry for Quebec City★

Société des traversiers du Québec 7483. ♿ Departs from quai de Lévis year round every half hour Mon–Fri 6:30am–5:30pm, Sat–Sun 8:30am–7:30pm. For additional departures, check online. Crossing takes 10min. $3.35/pedestrian, $8/car. ✆1-877-787-7483 (Canada/US) or 418-643-2019. www.traversiers.com.

The ferry has been in service since 1812 and is by far the most picturesque way to reach Quebec City, offering an exceptional view of the city and its port.

▶ After 13km/8mi, turn left to Beaumont.

Beaumont

Built between 1726 and 1733, the **church** of Beaumont is one of the oldest in Quebec (after St. Peter's Church on Île d'Orléans and the votive chapel at Cap-de-la-Madeleine). It was here that the commander of the British troops, General Wolfe, posted a proclamation of British supremacy in 1759. When the villagers removed the proclamation, Wolfe's soldiers attempted to destroy the church by burning it, but the structure survived. The church was enlarged by extending the façade and adding a chapel on the north side, as well as a sacristy. Its simple nave ends in a circular apse. The church interior boasts a magnificent carved wood **décor** fashioned by Étienne Bercier, a craftsman from the Montreal studio of Louis-Amable Quévillon. Crafted between 1809 and 1811, the choir is graced with Louis XV-style paneling and a coffered vault. The finely sculpted tabernacle of the main altar dates from the 18C. Above it hangs a painting by Antoine Plamondon, *The Death of St. Étienne.*

▶ Continue through the village to rejoin Rte. 132.

Moulin de Beaumont (Beaumont Mill)

7km/4.3mi beyond the village of Beaumont, turn left. 2 Rte. du Fleuve (Rte. 132). Open Jun 24–mid-Oct daily 10am–4:30pm; mid-May–Jun 23 and Sept–Oct Sat–Sun 10am–4:30pm. $8. ✕ ♿ P ✆418-833-1867.

This four-story mill overlooking the Maillou Falls (chute-à-Maillou) was built in 1821 to card wool for the seigneury. In 1850 it became a grain mill and, later, a sawmill. The mill, restored to operating condition, was reopened in 1967, and local residents furnished the third floor and attic with early French-Canadian pieces. On the premises, visitors

can purchase bread made with freshly ground flour.
Behind the mill, a panoramic stairway leads to the base of the cliff, on the shores of the St. Lawrence, where the foundations of the Péan Mill can be seen. This mid-18C mill operated for 144 years until 1888. Occasional archeological excavations have been under way on this site since 1984.

Return to Rte. 132, continue for 4km/2.5mi and turn left.

Saint-Michel-de-Bellechasse

Located in the center of the village, the **church** dates from 1858. The **presbytery** (1739), built in the typical Quebec style, is adorned with shutters carved with a fleur-de-lis on the top and a maple leaf on the bottom. In 1759 it was shelled by the British and later renovated.

Return to Rte. 132.

This agricultural region is dotted with many houses with brightly colored trim. The road follows the water's edge, offering good views of the St. Lawrence and the islands that make up the Île-aux-Grues Archipelago.

Montmagny

45 Ave. du Quai. 1-800-463-5643. www.cotedusud.ca. 31km/19mi northeast of Saint-Michel.

After passing the bridge, turn left at the manor.

This charming town features several noteworthy sights. At the **Musée de l'Accordéon** (Accordion Museum), housed in the historic Manoir Couillard-Dupuis (around 1800), you can see accordions being made, and learn the history of the bellowed instrument (301 Blvd Taché Est; open Jun 24–Labor Day daily 10am–4pm; rest of the year Mon–Fri 10am–4pm; $8 418-248-7927; www.accordeon.montmagny.com). At the **Centre éducatif des Migrations**, interactive exhibits on white geese and a multimedia presentation on the Grosse Île quarantine complex are on view (53 Avenue du Bassin Nord; open Jun 23–Oct 22 daily 10am–5pm; $6; 418-248-4565). At the Snow Goose Festival held in October, you can sample the many ways that locals serve up their feathered friends.

Archipel de l'Île-aux-Grues (Île-aux-Grues Archipelago)

Guided excursion to the Archipelago departs from Berthier-sur-Mer late May–mid-Oct daily 9:45am; afternoon outings late Jun–Aug. Round-trip 6hrs. Commentary. Reservations required. $40. Croisières Lachance 418-259-2140 or 1-866-856-6668. www.croisieresaml.com .

Of the 21 islands comprising the archipelago, Grosse Île, Île-aux-Grues, and Île-aux-Oies are the most important. **Île-aux-Grues**, the only permanently inhabited island, is 10km/6.2mi long, and is accessible by air (Air Montmagny, depart from Montmagny daily on demand, reservations required. $20 one-way. 418-248-3545; www.airmontmagny.com) or ferry (depart from Montmagny Apr–Dec daily; one-way 25min; free, call ahead for schedule; 418-248-2379; www.traversiers.gouv.qc.ca).

European settlement of Île-aux-Grues dates from 1679. Today this tranquil haven draws lovers of nature and peace and quiet. Snow geese flock here during the spring and fall. On the southeast tip of the island, outside the village of Saint-Antoine, stands an elegant manor house overlooking the St. Lawrence.

Lieu historique national du Canada de la Grosse Île et le Mémorial des Irlandais★ (Grosse Île and the Irish Memorial National Historic Site of Canada)

Open mid-Jun–Aug daily; May–late Jun and Sept–mid-Oct Wed–Sun. 418-234-8841 or 1-888-773-8888. www.parkscanada.gc.ca. Ferries to Grosse Île depart from Berthier-sur-Mer; tours 6hrs. Commentary. Reservations required. Visit & ferry $60.

The ever-increasing number of European immigrants to Canada prompted the government to establish, in 1832, a quarantine station on Grosse Île to protect the country from the infectious diseases (especially cholera) that were then ravaging Europe. In the first year of operation some 50,000 immigrants first set foot on Canadian soil here. In 1847, tens of thousands of Irish fleeing famine, English oppression and typhus arrived, and more than 5,000 perished on Grosse Île before ever reaching Quebec City.

The island was divided into three zones. The western part of the island was known as the Hotel Sector. Healthy immigrants were lodged in hotels according to the class of passage they took on the ship coming from Europe. The Village Sector in the middle part of the island housed the employees of the quarantine station and their families. To the east, the Hospital Sector included 21 structures, of which one is still standing. The quarantine station on Grosse Île closed in 1937, after operating for more than a century. The facility was then taken over by Canadian and US military authorities as a research station for biological and chemical warfare. It later became a research center for animal diseases and an animal quarantine station. In 1990 it became a national historic site.

A veritable Ellis Island (see *The Green Guide New York City*) of Canada, Grosse Île offers the visitor a touching rendezvous with the past. On the island, a guided walk in the Hotel Sector includes a visit to the third-class hotel, the cemetery, the Bay of Cholera, and the **monument** erected in 1909 in memory of the Irish immigrants buried on the island. Visitors continue aboard a tourist trolley to the Village Sector, to view the chapels for employees and their families. The tour ends at the Hospital Sector.

L'Islet-sur-Mer

23km/14mi.

Built along the banks of the St. Lawrence, L'Islet-sur-Mer originally consisted of two seigneuries conceded to the Couillard and Bélanger families in 1677. Since the 18C, the community has thrived on maritime activity. Through the years, the village's native sons have taken to the sea as captains, pilots, sailors, or fishermen.

Église Notre-Dame de Bonsecours★ (Church of Our Lady of Perpetual Help)

Open Jun 24–Labor Day daily 9am–4pm. 418-247-5103.

The fieldstone church was built in 1768 and enlarged in 1884, when the façade was refurbished and twin steeples added. The statues in the niches of the façade, representing St. John the Baptist on the left and St. Francis of Assisi on the right, are the work of Amable Charron, who also designed the cornices of the interior. The main altar was fashioned by François Baillairgé and the tabernacle by Noël Levasseur. Six paintings by Antoine Plamondon grace the walls. The Stations of the Cross were carved in 1945 by Médard Bourgault, a native of Saint-Jean-Port-Joli.

Musée Maritime du Québec (Maritime Museum of Quebec)

200m/656ft beyond church, 55 chemin des Pionniers Est. Open mid-Oct–mid-May Mon–Fri 10am–4pm upon reservation, May–mid-Jun and Labor Day–mid-Oct daily 10am–5pm. Late Jun–Labor Day daily 10am–6pm. $12. 418-247-5001. www.mmq.qc.ca.

Dedicated to the memory of Capt. Joseph-Elzéar Bernier (1852–1934), a native of L'Islet-sur-Mer who was a navigator and a pioneer of Arctic exploration, the museum focuses on the maritime history of the St. Lawrence River. The collection includes elaborate models of different ships, in addition to numerous objects recovered from the 1914 wreck of the *Empress of Ireland*. Behind the museum, visitors can board the *Ernest Lapointe*, an icebreaker built in 1940 for the fleet of the Canadian Coast Guard, and the *Bras d'Or 400* (*Arm of Gold*), a hydrofoil used by the Canadian Navy between 1968 and 1972. Another permanent exhibition is "la chalouperie." A chaloupe is a rowing boat, and various models of every era show slices of maritime life in Quebec. The permanent exhibition gets rearranged, updated and upgraded from time to time. Spectacular temporary exhibitions portray specific aspects of life on the sea and significant achievements in sailing, fishing and dealing with the challenges of living by and from the sea.

Saint-Jean-Port-Joli★

3km/8mi. 20 Ave. de Gaspé Ouest (Rte. 132). 418-598-3747 or 1-800-278-3555. www.guidesaintjeanportjoli.com

Known as the craft and woodcarving capital of Quebec, the small town of Saint-Jean-Port-Joli boasts the largest concentration of artisans in the province. Numerous craft shops, specializing primarily in woodcarvings, line Rte. 132. Philippe Aubert de Gaspé (1786–1871) moved to this community in 1824 from Quebec City, intending to write Les Anciens Canadiens (The Canadians of Old), the novel that ultimately brought him great fame. Saint-Jean-Port-Joli is also the birthplace of a celebrated family of woodcarvers, the Bourgault brothers: Médard (1897–1967), André (1898–1958) and Jean-Julien (1910–96). The town holds a Sea Shanty festival, a Winter festival and an International Sculpture festival.

Site Philippe-Aubert-de-Gaspé

5km/3mi west of town center on Rte. 132.

On this site stood the manor house where Philippe Aubert de Gaspé wrote *Les Anciens Canadiens*, published in 1863. Fire destroyed the house in 1909, leaving only the bakery (1764), among the oldest remaining in Quebec. Visitors can see the foundations of the manor, and a cellar that predates 1759.

Musée de la Mémoire Vivante (Museum of Living Memory)

710 Ave. De Gaspé Ouest. Open Jun 24–Labor Day daily 9am–6pm; May–Jun and Sept–Oct daily 10am–5pm; rest of year Mon–Fri 10am–5pm. $8. 418-358-0518. www.memoirevivante.org.

On the site of the old seigneurial estate, the manor house of **Philippe Aubert de Gaspé** has been rebuilt as it would have appeared in the 19C. Inside, it houses a museum dedicated to personal stories, local history, and the writer de Gaspé. It also exhibits archeological finds from the site.

Musée des Anciens Canadiens (Historical Museum)

3km/1.8mi west of town center on Rte. 132, at 332 Ave. de Gaspé Ouest. Open May–Jun 23 daily 9am–5:30pm; Jun 24–Sept daily 8:30am–9pm; mid-Sept–Oct daily 8:30am–6pm; $7.50. 418-598-3392 or 1-866-598-3392.

The local history is illustrated by woodcarvings crafted by Saint-Jean-Port-Joli's finest artists, including the Bourgault brothers. A video (*15min*) presents the art of sculpture in wood, stone and ice; sculpture demonstrations are held here during the summer.

The museum is considered to be one of the best wood-carving museums in North America. Famous wood sculptors have some of their best pieces on display here. The 250-item collection includes life-size replicas of Harry Potter, the Beatles, former Quebec Premier René Lévesque, former Canadian Prime Minister Pierre Elliott Trudeau, legendary Quebec singer Félix Leclerc and Montreal Canadiens hockey legend Jean Béliveau.

Église Saint-Jean-Baptiste★ (Church of St. John the Baptist)

In the town center, 3km/1.8mi beyond the Musée des Anciens Canadiens. Open early May–mid-Jun daily 9am–5pm; late Jun–Labor Day daily 8:30am–9pm; mid-Sept–Nov 1 daily 9am–6pm. 418-598-3023, www.eglise-saint-jean-port-joli.com.

The slender spires and curved roof contribute to the charm of this edifice (1779). The ornate **interior** features works by Médard and Jean-Julien Bourgault. The main altar tabernacle (1740), attributed to Pierre-Noël Levasseur, stands in the sanctuary, decorated between 1794 and 1798 by Jean Baillairgé and his son, Florent. The barrel vault is composed of small coffers embellished with 4,300 carved flowers to simulate the heavens. The seigneurial pew has been preserved in honor of Philippe Aubert de Gaspé, last seigneur of Saint-Jean-Port-Joli, who is buried in the crypt of the church. In 1987, seventeen local woodcarvers pooled their skills to create a magnificent **Nativity scene★** (crèche de Noël). Although each linden figurine was carved by a different artist, the overall effect is remarkably harmonious.

Saint-Roch-des-Aulnaies

14km/8.7mi.
www.saintrochdesaulnaies.ca

Located on the south shore of the St. Lawrence, this peaceful community takes its name from the alder trees (aulnes) lining the Férée River. Granted to Nicholas Juchereau de Saint-Denis in 1656, the Aulnaies seigneury is among the oldest in the region. However, the land remained unsettled until the late 17C, owing to Iroquois hostilities. In 1837, the seigneury was sold to Amable Dionne (1781–1852), a wealthy merchant and mayor of Kamouraska for more than 30 years, who erected the magnificent manor house for his son, Pascal-Amable.

Completed in 1849, the Gothic Revival **Église Saint-Roch-des-Aulnaies** (3km/1.8mi east of the village entrance on Rte. 132; open mid-Jul–mid-Aug daily 10am–5pm; ♿ P ✆418-354-2552) displays several paintings by Joseph Légaré (1795–1855). The carved choir and altar were designed by François Baillairgé. Situated 400m/1,312ft beyond the church, the small fieldstone **processional chapel** was erected in 1792 (open Jun 24–Labor Day daily 10am–5pm).

Set on a promontory overlooking the junction of two rivers, the **Aulnaies Seigneurie** (3km/1.8mi east of the church on Rte. 132; turn right, go up the hill to the parking area and information booth; open early Jun–Labor Day daily 9:30am–6pm; rest of Sept–mid-Oct Sat–Sun 10am–5pm. $14. ✕ P ✆418-354-2800 or 1-877-354-2800; www.laseigneuriedesaulnaies.qc.ca), a Victorian-era wooden house flanked by two octagonal towers, was completed in 1853, according to a design by the noted architect Charles Baillairgé. Guides dressed in late-19C costumes conduct tours through the house and describe the life of the period. Outside, visitors can enjoy walks through the manicured gardens and the wooded park as well as visit the adjacent 1842 **gristmill** (moulin banal).

La Pocatière★

10km/6.2mi.

This pioneering center of Canadian agricultural education has maintained its educational tradition and is now the base for important research in various areas, with a particular emphasis on food production. The industrial sector is also represented by a plant belonging to Bombardier, a company that is globally famous for its snowmobiles, aircraft, and rail carriages.

Musée François-Pilote★

In building at rear of Collège Sainte-Anne. P Open mid-May–mid Oct daily 10am–5pm; mid-Oct–early Jan Thu–Sun 10am–5pm; rest of year by appointment. $8. ✆418-856-3145. www.museefrancoispilote.ca.

This museum of Québécois ethnology looks at rural life in the early 20C and is named for the founder of the first Permanent Agricultural School in Canada (1859), Abbot François Pilote. The activities of lumberjacks, joiners, blacksmiths, ropemakers, and weavers are represented by their tools, while farmers are represented by a collection of plowing equipment. The reconstruction of a "sugar house" introduces you to the traditional techniques for making maple syrup, and there is an interesting section devoted to the means of transport used at the time, including sleighs and horse-drawn carriages, as well as an exhibition on shipping along the coast from the mid-18C to the mid-19C, with scale models of boats and various navigation instruments. An exhibition presents the development of agriculture from the time of Champlain (first half of the 17C) up to the present day. A sitting room, dining room, and bedroom re-create the comfortable existence of a middle-class family in the 1920s, and seven rooms give an insight into the lives of farmers in Quebec in the late 18C and early 19C. The theme is completed with re-creations of a rural school and general store, as well as the workplaces of the country doctor, dentist, cobbler, barber, and notary. Finally, the history of agricultural education in Quebec is presented through various disciplines such as livestock and poultry farming, botany, zoology, chemistry, physics, astronomy and fisheries.

Rivière-Ouelle

10km/6.2mi.

Originally known as Rivière-Houel in commemoration of one of Samuel de Champlain's officers, the territory was conceded by the Intendant Jean Talon to Jean-Baptiste François Deschamps de Boishébert, who became the Sieur-de la Bouteillerie, in 1672.

The Route des Navigateurs (www.bassaintlaurent.ca), an itinerary taking in sites representing the area's maritime heritage, stretches from here to Sainte-Luce. The sites are marked with a blue sign emblazoned with a ship's wheel.

Saint-Denis

11km/6.8mi.

Maison des Chapais

2 Rte. 132 Est. Visit by 45min guided tour only, late May–mid Oct daily 10am–5pm. $6. P ♿ 418-498-2353. www.maisonchapais.com.

Located in the center of the village this building dates back to 1834. Built by Jean-Charles Chapais, one of Canada's Fathers of Confederation, the house remained in the Chapais family until 1968.

In 1866 the porch and spiral staircases were added, and the present interior furnishings were bought. The living-room furniture dates from the early 19C, while the dining room and bedroom are appointed in the Second Empire style.

The road passes across a wide flood plain, affording expansive views of the Laurentian Mountains across the St. Lawrence. Perpendicular to the shoreline, eel traps extend into the river.

Kamouraska★

69 Ave. Morel. 418-492-1325. www.tourismekamouraska.com. 10km/6.2mi.

The seigneury of Kamouraska (which means "where rushes grow by the water's edge" in the Algonquian language) was granted to Olivier Morel de la Durantaye in 1674 by Louis de Buade, Comte de Frontenac, governor of New France. The first settlers arrived the following year and by the 18C Kamouraska was one of the largest communities in the Bas-Saint-Laurent (Lower St. Lawrence) region. In the 19C grain, potato, and dairy farming became the town's principal economic activity, supplemented more recently by tourism.

The term "**Kamouraska roof**" refers to the curved overhanging eaves, a local architectural feature of many of the houses throughout the region. The design, which first appeared on several public buildings (including the church at Saint-Jean-Port-Joli), seems to add height to the first floor, which otherwise appears crushed by the heavy roof.

Musée régional de Kamouraska (Kamouraska Regional Museum)

69 Ave. Morel (Place de l'Église). Behind the church in the town center. Open mid-May–Jun 23 Mon–Fri 9am–5pm; Jun 24–Aug daily 9am–5pm; Sept–mid-Dec Tue–Fri 9am–5pm, Sat–Sun

Kamouraska

© A. Marsh / age fotostock

1:30pm–4:30pm; rest of year by reservation. $7; $15 for a guided walking tour. 418-492-9783. www.museekamouraska.com.
The building containing the museum was built as a convent in 1851. Devoted to the cultural history of the Kamouraska region, the museum displays household items and furniture typical of the homes and lifestyles of the early European settlers. Farm implements and craftsmen's tools illustrate the working conditions of the community's forefathers. A mock-up of a general store, with a large collection of fishing gear, models and other seafaring gear, explores the crucial role that the St. Lawrence played in the lives of local residents. The museum also houses an altar carved in 1737 by François-Noël Levasseur for Kamouraska's second church (1727), and the genealogy of the region is explored as well.

Berceau de Kamouraska (Old Kamouraska)

3km/1.8mi east of town center, Rte. 132.
The former heart of the village, now known as the "Kamouraska Cradle," was the site of the first two churches in the community (1709 and 1727), and it contains a cemetery where 1,300 pioneers are buried. A simple open-air chapel commemorates the spot.

Société d'écologie de la batture du Kamouraska (SEBKA)

9km/5.6mi east of Old Kamouraska, 3km/1.8mi west of Saint-André; located near the rest area on Rte. 132. Open Jun 24–Labor Day daily 8am–9pm; mid-May–Jun 23 and rest of Sept–mid-Oct daily 10am–6pm. $3. 418-493-9984. www.sebka.ca.
The interpretation center in this park, given the name of the organization that manages it, is designed to stimulate interest in and respect for the saltmarsh and river ecosystems. Experienced guides lead organized activities related to ecological themes, including plant and animal life in the marsh, beluga whales, peregrine falcons and other birds.
A trail (6km/3.7mi) leads to the salt marsh (*batture* in French), and on to a rocky promontory equipped with scenic balconies and birdwatching stations.

Rivière-du-Loup★

189 Blvd de l'Hôtel-de-Ville. 418-862-1981 or 1-888-825-1981. www.tourismeriviereduloup.ca.
Situated in the heart of the Bas-Saint-Laurent region between Quebec City and the Gaspé Peninsula, Rivière-du-Loup commands a geographical position favorable to both commerce and tourism. A ferry links the industrial city

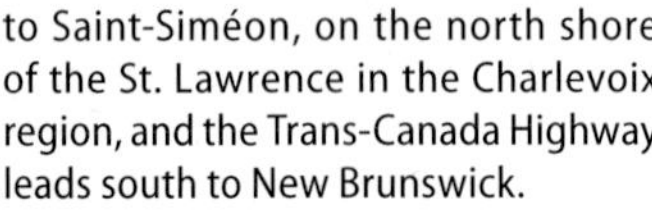

to Saint-Siméon, on the north shore of the St. Lawrence in the Charlevoix region, and the Trans-Canada Highway leads south to New Brunswick.

Hôtel de Ville (Town Hall)

At the corner of rue Lafontaine and Blvd Hôtel-de-Ville.

Completed in 1917, the city hall occupies the former site of the market building, destroyed by fire in 1910. An unusual architectural element is the main clock tower, typical of city halls found in the English-speaking provinces.

After leaving City Hall, turn right on rue Lafontaine. Cross rue Lafontaine to rue de la Cour.

Located at the corner of rue Lafontaine and rue de la Cour, the limestone and brick **Courthouse** was designed by David Ouellet in 1881. It has undergone three major renovations. The **Old Post Office** (1889), a stately dark brick building on rue Iberville (*turn right from rue Lafontaine*), exemplifies Anglo-Saxon institutional architecture. It is now a community center.

Continue on rue Iberville. Turn right on rue du Domaine, continue to rue du Rocher and turn right.

Bibliothèque municipale (Municipal Library)

The Second Empire stone structure was built in 1886 by David Ouellet. For nearly a century, it served as the convent of the Good Shepherd Sisters. After the religious community left in 1978, it was renovated and converted into a library (1983).

At the corner by the Parc Blais, turn left into rue Lafontaine, then return to the town hall.

Musée du Bas-Saint-Laurent (Bas-Saint-Laurent Museum)

300 rue Saint-Pierre. Open mid-Jun–mid-Oct daily 9am–5pm; rest of the year Wed–Sun 1–5pm. Closed Jan 1 & Dec 25. $5. 418-862-7547. www.mbsl.qc.ca.

Cultural heritage, contemporary art and technology are smartly incorporated into the museum's various exhibits. Works by local artists are also shown.

Chutes de la rivière du Loup★ (Loup River Falls)

Take rue Lafontaine north to rue Frontenac and turn right. The falls are three blocks away.

The Loup River drops 90m/295ft before joining the St. Lawrence, in a series of eight waterfalls within a distance of 1,500m/4,920ft. Here, the falls are 33m/108ft high. Steps lead to a lookout providing an expansive view of the town and river. The **illuminated cross** on a cliff overlooking the river is also visible from this point.

Île aux Lièvres and other islands

La Société Duvetnor (200 rue Hayward; various packages $25–$43.50; 418-867-1660; www.duvetnor.com; www.pharedupot.com) These packages take visitors to see the double-crested cormorants, great blue herons and black guillemots that live on the nature reserve made up of several islands off the shore (the Pèlerin islands, Île du Pot-de-l'Eau-de-Vie and Île aux Lièvres). Activities include marine excursions and camping.

Saint-Siméon

Traverse Rivière-du-Loup/Saint-Siméon. Runs Apr–early Jan. One way approx. 1hr, return without disembarking 3hrs. Round trip, pedestrians $24; children (age 6 and under) free. 418-862-5094. www.traverserdl.com.

A ferry connects Rivière-du-Loup with this former lumberjack community. The stretch of water between the two can only be described as an expanse of sea, as the St. Lawrence is about 20km/12mi wide at this point. The crossing is a good way to admire the beauty of the river from up close.

How the Wolf River Got its Name

There are many theories on the origin of the name Rivière-du-Loup (literally "river of the wolf"). According to one, a French ship named *Le Loup* may have spent the winter there around 1660, while local legend maintains that Champlain encountered a Native tribe called the Mahigans, or wolves, in this area. A third possibility is that the name commemorates the seals, or *loups-marins (lit. "sea wolves"),* that were commonly seen at the mouth of the river, and finally, there is the rather obvious idea that the river was a popular habitat for the packs of wolves that once lived there.

The seigneury of Rivière-du-Loup was granted to Charles Aubert de la Chesnaye, ancestor of writer Philippe-Aubert de Gaspé, in 1673. Together with his companion, Sieur Charles Bazire, he became one of the wealthiest traders in New France, profiting from the furs and fish found in the region.

The two partners had so little interest in settling the territory that from 1683 through 1765, the population grew from four to a mere 68. The colony began to expand significantly in 1802, when the seigneury was bought by Alexander Fraser, whose involvement in the lumber trade with England brought prosperity to Rivière-du-Loup. In 1860, the arrival of a railway linking the city with Windsor (in the Eastern Townships) to the south provided another important boost to the economy. In 1887 the Témiscouata Railway in turn connected the city to New Brunswick. The prosperity of the late 19C and early 20C is reflected in the opulent homes and public buildings of this period.

FROM RIVIÈRE-DU-LOUP TO SAINTE-LUCE

130km/80mi route beginning in Rivière-du-Loup. Exit town via Rte. 132.

Cacouna

10km/6.2mi from Rivière-du-Loup.

The seigneury here was conceded to Daulier Duparc in 1673, but the first colonists began settlement around 1750. First Nations named it Kakouna, meaning "land of the porcupine." In the mid-19C, Cacouna became a popular summer resort, and large hotels and luxurious vacation homes were constructed. Today, only the sumptuous Victorian houses along the water's edge recall the town's heyday.

Église Saint-Georges (St. George Church)

Turn right off Rte. 132 onto rue de l'Église and continue for 2 blocks. Open during mass only. ♿ P ✆418-862-4338.

The fieldstone church (1848) was partially rebuilt in 1896. The interior crafted by F.-X. Berlinguet (1858) is richly decorated with carved and gilded detailing; the crystal chandeliers and Italian paintings date from the late 19C. The organ dating from 1888 is one of the few remaining works of Eusèbe Brodeur, a predecessor of the Casavant Brothers of Saint-Hyacinthe. Nearby, the Neoclassical **presbytery** was built between 1835 and 1841.

L'Isle-Verte

With its coastline of headlands and coves, the waters around L'Isle-Verte village are home to a rich population of aquatic wildlife, allowing the locals to make a living from herring and eel fishing.

Réserve nationale de faune de la Baie-de-L'Isle-Verte (Baie-de-L'Isle-Verte National Wildlife Area)

371 Rte 132. Guided tour (2hrs) mid-Jun–mid-Sept daily. ✆418-898-2757 or 1-800-668-6767. www.ec.gc.ca.

This reserve contains one of the largest cordgrass marshes in Quebec. With its scattering of small natural pools known as marelles, the saltmarsh is one of the main North American breeding grounds of the American black duck. It is also an important stopping point for many other species of migratory birds. More than 260 species have been identified, 60 of which nest at the reserve.

The reserve is accessed via observation and interpretation trails. Maison Girard, to the east of the village of L'Isle-Verte, contains an interpretation center devoted to the site.

Île Verte

Ferry: La Richardière. 30min crossing $8. 418-898-2843. www.traverseileverte.quebec. **Taxi boat:** Caprice des marées or Jacques Fraser I. 15min crossing $8. 418-898-2199. www.entre-deuxmarres.com. Tourism: www.ileverte-tourism.com.

Facing the village of L'Isle-Verte is the island from which it takes its name. Île Verte is an enchanting destination, and is the only island in the Bas-Saint-Laurent that is inhabited all year round. Jacques Cartier landed here in 1535 and is said to have hit upon the name "green island" after seeing its carpet of vegetation. Other attractions to discover in this exceptional landscape include the lighthouse, the École Michaud, a former school now housing an interpretation center focused on island life, and the Musée du Squelette (Animal Skeleton Museum).

Return by ferry or boat to L'Isle-Verte.

Trois-Pistoles

400 rue Jean-Rioux. 418-851-4949. 36km/22mi. www.tourismelesbasques.com

The town derives its name from an old monetary unit used throughout Europe until the late-19C. According to local legend, a small vessel was shipwrecked on the coast of Île aux Basques in the early 17C. One of the sailors holding a silver mug lost it in the river and exclaimed: *"Voilà trois pistoles de perdues!"* (There go three pistoles). The seigneury here was granted to Denis de Vitré in 1687, but the region was frequented much earlier by Basque fishermen whose presence is confirmed by the remains of ovens on the **Île aux Basques**, located 4km/2.5mi offshore.

Parc de l'aventure basque en Amérique (PABA)

66 rue du Parc. Open daily 10am–6pm, Thu and Fri until 9pm. $7.50. 418-851-1556 & 1-877-851-1556. www.aventurebasque.ca.

An interpretation center presents the history and culture of the Basque fishermen who came to hunt whales on the St. Lawrence River in the 16C. The center's exterior resembles a native Basque village, and features Canada's only Basque pelota court, while the terrace also has a convivial café.

Église Notre-Dame-des-Neiges (Church of Our Lady of the Snow)

From the center of town, turn right onto rue Jean-Rioux. Open mid-Jun–Labor Day daily 9am–4.30pm; last Fri of Sept and two following days 9am–4:30pm; rest of year by reservation. $4 (guided tour). 418-851-1391. www.eglisetrois-pistols.com.

This monumental structure was built in the 1880s according to plans drawn up by David Ouellet. The bell towers and the angular lines of the four façades set this church apart. The ornate interior is the work of Canon Georges Bouillon, a proponent of the Romano-Byzantine style. Note the abundance of gilding, and the wooden Corinthian columns painted to resemble marble.

Traversier Trois-Pistoles

Les Escoumins, Compagnie de navigation des Basques, 11 rue du Parc. Open mid-May–Oct, 2 to 3 departures per day. Same-day return trip, pedestrians $25.40. 418-851-4676 or 1-877-851-4677. www.traversiercnb.ca.

This ferry links Trois-Pistoles to Les Escoumins on the north bank of the St. Lawrence River.

After 29km/18mi turn right for Saint-Fabien, continue for 2km/1.2mi.

Saint-Fabien

33 Rte. 132 Ouest. 418-869-3333. www.parcdubic.com.

Built in 1888, the **Adolphe Gagnon Octagonal Barn** (open mid-Jun–end

Aug Tue–Sun 9am–4:30pm. $7. 418-869-2088. www.grangeoctogonale.com), located at the center of the village, is the only one of its kind in the Bas-Saint-Laurent region. Blending into the landscape, the almost-round construction, conceived by American theorist Orson Squire Fowler, was designed to reduce wind resistance, eliminate wasted space, facilitate the storage of fodder, and keep the devil away: according to popular belief, the octagonal form made it impossible for demons to take refuge in the corners of the structure.

Parc national du Bic★

Main entrance at Cap-à-l'Orignal, 6km/3.7mi from center of Saint-Fabien. Open daily year-round. $8.50. 418-736-5035 or 1-800-665-6577. www.sepaq.com/pq/bic/en. Nature programs at the interpretation center (open Jun–mid-Oct daily 9am–5pm. 418-736-5035).

This 33sq km/13sq mi provincial conservation park was created in 1984 to preserve the plants and wildlife along the southern shoreline of the St. Lawrence River. The park boasts a variety of flora including both deciduous and boreal forests. Gray and harbor seals are occasionally spotted on the rocky coast in Orignal Bay.

Le Bic

15km/9.3mi from Saint-Fabien. 418-869-3333. www.parcdubic.com.

This small town is renowned for its spectacular **setting**★★ on the shores of the St. Lawrence. According to local folklore, when the world was created, the angel responsible for distributing mountains had a surplus at the end of the day while passing over Bic. To lighten his load, he emptied the remaining mountains on this spot.

Rimouski★

50 rue St-Germain Ouest. 418-723-2322 and 1-800-746-6875. www.tourisme-rimouski.org.

Built along the banks of the St. Lawrence, this industrial city has developed in a semicircular pattern around the mouth of the Rimouski River. Once a vast forest, the surrounding region long served as hunting grounds for the Mi'kmaq Indians. Granted as a seigneury in 1688, the territory was acquired in 1694 by the French merchant René Lepage, who settled here two years later. Rimouski is a Mi'kmaq term meaning "land of the moose."

The local economy, based on agriculture and seasonal fishing, experienced rapid growth during the early 20C, when the Price Brothers Company established sawmills and forestry operations. The city was rebuilt after the great fire of 1950 and is now considered the principal metropolis of eastern Quebec.

Musée régional de Rimouski (Rimouski Regional Museum)

35 rue Saint-Germain Ouest. Open mid-Jun–Labor Day daily 9:30am–6pm; rest of the year, Wed–Sun noon–5pm (Thu 8pm). $6. 418-724-2272. www.museerimouski.qc.ca.

The stone building that has housed the museum since the early 1970s was built in 1824 and served as the parish church until 1862. It was then used as a seminary, a convent, and a primary school. Dedicated to contemporary art, the museum mainly presents temporary exhibits.

Maison Lamontagne★ (Lamontagne House)

3km/1.8mi east of the center of town on Rte. 132; turn right onto Blvd du Rivage at Rimouski-Est. Follow signs. Open Jun 24–Labor Day daily 9am–6pm; day after Labor Day–mid-Oct Thu–Sun 9am–6pm; rest of the year upon reservation. $4. 418-722-4038. www.maisonlamontagne.com.

This large house was built in two phases: The longer section, of masonry half-timbering, dates from the second half of the 18C, while the full timbering section was completed around 1810. The structure is one of the few remaining examples of masonry half-timbering in North America; French settlers soon discovered that the stones between the timbering conducted cold and heat into the interior, making this type of construction unsuitable for the harsh Canadian climate. Occupied until 1959, the house was restored in 1981. Displays of building materials, artisan craftsmanship, construction techniques, and architectural styles, along with a virtual exhibition entitled *De pierre, de bois, de brique (Stone, Wood, and Brick)*, provide an overview of Quebec history.

Canyon des Portes de l'Enfer

1280 chemin Duchénier, via Route 232. Open mid-May–early Jul, and mid-Aug–mid-Oct daily 9am–5pm; early Jul–late Aug daily 8:30am–6:30pm. $11. 418-735-6063. www.canyonportesenfer.qc.ca.

The Portes de l'Enfer canyon begins with the Grand-Saut waterfall and extends nearly 5km/3mi, with its cliffs towering almost 90m/300ft above the Rimouski River. You can climb down to the river on the 300-step staircase leading to the Portes de l'Enfer (gates of hell), cross Quebec's highest footbridge, navigate the wood-built Maze of Hell, and explore a geocaching circuit.

Île Saint-Barnabé

This island just opposite the centre of Rimouski, 3km/1.8mi out into the river, was probably named by Samuel de Champlain when he sailed by in the early 17C on June 11, the feast of St Barnabas (Saint-Barnabé in French). The island used to be inhabited by a hermit by the name of Toussaint Cartier, whose story is shrouded in mystery, and now serves as a refuge for 72 species of bird. You can also watch the gray seals, go hiking (20km/12.4mi of trails) and stay the night (mid-Jun–early Sept 418-723-2280 or 1-800-746-6875. www.ilestbarnabe.com).

Pointe-au-Père Lighthouse

© Bruno Perousse / age fotostock

Musée de la mer et lieu historique national du Canada du phare de Pointe-au-Père★ (Maritime Museum and Pointe-au-Père Lighthouse National Historic Site of Canada)

1000 rue du Phare, Pointe-au-Père, 10km/6.2mi from Rimouski. Turn left off Rte. 132 onto rue Père-Nouvel, then right to the museum. Open early Jun–early Oct daily 9am–6pm. $22.75. 418-724-6214. www.pc.gc.ca/pointeauperelighthouse or www.shmp.qc.ca.

The first floor of the keeper's house is dedicated to the Empress of Ireland, nicknamed the "Titanic of the St. Lawrence," which sank close to shore on May 29, 1914, claiming 1,012 lives. Because of the start of World War I shortly thereafter, and the immigrant status of most of the passengers, the disaster was largely forgotten for half a century. Since the mid-1960s, hundreds of diving expeditions have recovered numerous objects from the wreck. Many of these artifacts are on display in the museum. A multimedia exhibition re-creates the sinking of the *Empress of Ireland*. In the adjacent **lighthouse** (1909), the second tallest in Canada, exhibits trace the daily life of a lighthouse keeper at the beginning of the 20C. Climb the 128 steps to the top for a good **view★** of the coastline. The lives of submariners can also be explored with a self-guided tour of the Canadian submarine *Onondaga*, in service from 1967 to 2000.

Réserve faunique de Rimouski

The information center for the Rimouski wildlife reserve is located 1km/0.6mi S of the junction of Rte. 232 and 234, 21km/13mi from the Rimouski turn-off on Rte. 20 (Sainte-Blandine exit). Open mid-May–mid-Nov daily. ✆418-735-2226 or 1-800-665-6527. www.sepaq.com. The reserve is renowned for the richness and diversity of its wildlife habitats. There are numerous sites set up for watching moose, white-tailed deer, and beaver, while opportunities for bird-watching are plentiful, especially at Lac Rimouski and Grand Lac Kedgwick. Many activities are offered here—fishing, canoe-camping, kayaking, hunting for moose, deer or black bear—while gourmets and children alike will be delighted by the opportunity to pick wild fruit.

Ferry to Forestville

CNM Évolution. Departs mid-May–mid-Sept, multiple crossings daily. Crossing lasts 55min. Same-day return trip, pedestrian $27, car $46. ✆418-125-2725 and 1-800-973-2725. www.traversier.com. Credit card required for booking (no reservations for pedestrians). Arrive 45min before departure (vehicles). Connects Rimouski to Forestville, on the north bank of the St. Lawrence River.

After 14km/8.7mi, at the junction with Rte. 298, turn left toward Sainte-Luce and continue for 4km/2.5mi.

Sainte-Luce

Cottages line the shore in this pleasant summer resort town, which occupies a pretty site on the St. Lawrence.

ADDRESSES

STAY

$$-$$$ Hôtel Rimouski & Convention Centre – *225 Blvd René-Lepage Est, SPA-Indoor Pool and waterslide, Rimouski. ✆418-725-5000 & 1-800-463-0755. www.hotelrimouski.com. 185 rooms, including 52 suites.* Rimouski's biggest and best hotel, with a great view of the river. Breakfast buffet $11.95.

$$-$$$ Auberge de la Pointe – *10 Blvd Cartier. SPA-Indoor Pool, convention center and live theater, Rivière-du-Loup. P ✆418-862-3514 or 1-800-463-1222. www.aubergedelapointe.com. 117 rooms, including 69 with a view of the St. Lawrence River and a private balcony. Restaurant$$-$$$.* The Auberge de la Pointe is a true resort located on a cliff high above the riverside. On site, you can swim, relax in the eight-seat whirlpool, enjoy the spa, or be treated at the award-winning restaurant. Close by, you can depart for whale-watching cruises and island tours. Breakfast $23.

EAT

La Cage aux Sports – *130 Ave. Belzile, Rimouski. ✆418-723-7433.* Quebec's original chain of sports bars and restaurants, La Cage aux Sports serves hearty, traditional Canadian food, roast chicken, grilled meats and barbecue pork ribs. Portions are enormous, just like the multiple TV screens connected to sports around the world.

ACTIVITIES

MARITIME

Kamouraska Zodiac Adventure – *Kamouraska municipal quay, ✆418-863-3131, www.zodiacaventure.com.* Tour the St. Lawrence shoreline and the Kamouraska islands in a 10-person zodiac, observing the marine mammals and bird colonies. The trained guide at the helm provides commentary on the flora, fauna, local history, and much else. There are two outings per day, mid-May to mid-Oct, each lasting 90 minutes.

BIRDWATCHING

Société Duvetnor Ltée – *200 rue Hayward, ✆418-867-1660, reservations by phone only starting Apr 1. www.duvetnor.com.* This society provides you with the opportunity to spot double-crested cormorants, great blue herons, and even black guillemots on a nature reserve composed of several islands—Les Pèlerins, Les Îles du Pot-de-l'Eau-de-vie, and l'Île-aux-Lièvres. Accommodation, cruises, and tours organized on your behalf from June to September. Rich wildlife and a secluded environment guarantee a visit accompanied only by the sounds of nature.

Gaspésie★★★

Gaspésie region

The Gaspé Peninsula, commonly known as "la Gaspésie" in French, is bounded by New Brunswick and the Baie des Chaleurs to the south, the Gulf of St. Lawrence to the east, and the St. Lawrence River to the north. Tiny fishing villages nestled in coves dot the wild, rocky and sea-battered northern coast of the peninsula, culminating in the breathtaking beauty of Forillon and Percé. In the Chaleur Bay area to the south, agriculture, fisheries and forestry form the backbone of economic activity, but the scenic wonders of both coasts have made tourism the region's principal source of revenue, and windmills now generate an increasing amount of electricity. The spectacular scenery is complemented by the charm of the peninsula's simple lifestyle. Except for a few towns and villages, the interior of the peninsula is a dense wilderness of mountains and forests.

- **Info:** 1-800-463-0323. www.tourisme-gaspesie.com.
- **Location:** From Quebec City, Matane is 355km/213mi. Rte. 132 follows the coast around the peninsula, and Rte. 299 crosses the Chic-choc Mountains.
- **Don't Miss:** Windmills at Cap-Chat, Forillon Park, Percé Rock, Bonaventure Island. Be sure to spend some time at the Jardins de Métis.
- **Timing:** Allow a day for each of the sections proposed below to take you around the Gaspé peninsula.
- **Kids:** Watch fish swim through the salmon ladder in Matane.

DRIVING TOURS

FROM SAINTE-FLAVIE TO PARC NATIONAL DE LA GASPÉSIE

167km/104mi on Rte. 132.

Sainte-Flavie

This agricultural village and resort town—renowned for its spectacular sunsets—is the gateway to the Gaspé Peninsula.

Centre d'art Marcel Gagnon

564 Rte. de la Mer. Open May–late Sept daily 7:30am–10pm. 418-775-2829 or 1-866-775-2829. www.centredart.net.

The main attraction at this small arts center is *The Great Gathering (Le grand rassemblement)*, contemporary artist Marcel Gagnon's composite sculpture of more than 100 figures emerging from the St. Lawrence River. A permanent exhibit of the artist's paintings and smaller sculptures occupies the interior, and visitors can witness Gagnon himself at work in his studio.

Jardins de Métis★★ (Reford Gardens)

9km/5.6mi. 200 Rte. 132, Grand-Métis. Open Jun and Sept daily 8:30am–6pm; Jul–Aug daily 8:30am–8pm. $18; children (age 13 and under) free. 418-775-2222. www.refordgardens.com.

In 1886 Lord Mount Stephen (1829–1921), president and founder of the Canadian Pacific Railway Company, purchased this tract of land at the confluence of the Mitis and Saint Lawrence rivers from the Seigneur of Grand-Métis, Archibald Ferguson. The land was to be Stephen's salmon fishing retreat, but he spent very little time at Grand-Métis, and in 1918 he gave the land to his niece, Elsie Stephen Reford. From 1926 through 1959, Mrs. Reford gradually transformed the estate into magnificent gardens. More than 3,000 varieties of flowers and ornamental plants, including many rare species, flourish in numerous distinct gardens that rank among the prettiest in the world.

Entrance Garden

This floral display shows off the brilliant colors of annual blooms from early June through late September. Perennials such as peonies, lupins, and daylilies bloom earlier in the season. Peeking among the spruce trees bordering this colorful array of flowers are forget-me-nots and horsetails, while begonias flower near the rock garden from mid-summer until fall.

Alpine Garden

On a slope beside a meandering stream lies a small alpine garden of saxifrage, spiraea, phlox, and alpine pinks. In the center bed is the rare **Bock willow**, a small shrub of Chinese origin introduced by Mrs. Reford. Nine types of ferns, including the ostrich fern, the Canadian maidenhair fern and the interrupted fern, can be found here.

Azalea Walk

The spectacular floral display of azaleas in early summer is followed by the blooming of roses, which continues until the first frost. A favorable microclimate and careful maintenance (soil enrichment, acidity testing, winter protection) account for the beauty of this garden, which also includes red Japanese maples.

Blue Poppy Glade

The pride of the gardens is the **blue poppy** (*meconopsis betonicifolia*). The floral emblem of the gardens, the blue poppy is native to the alpine prairies of the Himalayas and was introduced by Mrs. Reford, who painstakingly adapted it to her gardens. This rare and beautiful flower blooms from mid-June through mid-July.

Allée royale (The Long Walk)

A tribute to the English garden, this walkway, lined with annuals, perennials and shrubs, is designed so that at least one species is in flower throughout the season. From the end of July until mid-August, blooming delphiniums attract a multitude of ruby-throated hummingbirds.

Villa Estevan (Estevan Lodge)

To the left of the Long Walk, the sumptuous Victorian residence—named Estevan Lodge by Mrs. Reford—overlooks the gardens. Built by her uncle in 1887 as a fishing retreat, the house was enlarged as a summer home for the Refords in 1927. The first floor of the villa now houses a restaurant. A café is located in the adjacent coach house, and a garden shop and gift shop are in the visitor pavilion.

In the **museum**, located on the upper floors, visitors can see the Refords' sitting room overlooking the bay, their apartments, the darkroom, and the

Jardins de Métis

©Jean-Pierre Huard / ATRG

attic. On the other side of the attic, furnished rooms re-create several aspects of daily life on the estate.
At the end of the well-maintained lawn leading from the villa to Mitis Bay, a low wall constructed along the waterside promontory is bordered by poplars and conifers that protect the gardens from harsh winter winds.

Jardin des pommetiers (Crabapple Garden)

A stroll along the woods leads to this garden's beautiful flower beds, arranged in patterns of sweeping curves accented by crab-apple trees and patches of lawn and ground cover.

Jardin des primevères (Primula Glade)

The conifer with drooping branches at the entrance is a **False Sawara cypress** imported from Japan by Mrs. Reford. In spring, different varieties of primrose burst into bloom.

Sous-bois (Woodland Walk)

This section of the estate is a wooded area containing shrubs and other plants native to Quebec.

Parc de la rivière Mitis★ (Mitis River Park)

900 Rte. de la Mer. Open mid-Jun–early Sept daily 9am–5pm. $5. 418-775-2969.
In this park, an eco-tourism site, the trails are lined with displays on nature and its preservation. Magnificent landscapes of the St. Lawrence and Mitis rivers make the visit as enjoyable as it is informative.
Nature exhibits in the reception center help visitors appreciate and understand the vast and complex ecosystem around them.

Matane

55km/34m. 968 Ave. du Phare Ouest. 418-562-1065 and 1-877-762-8263 (no charge). www.tourismematane.com.
The community of Matane is renowned for its salmon fishing and shrimp production. In the town center, behind the city hall, a 44m/144ft **fish ladder★** (*passe migratoire*) built on the **Mathieu-d'Amours Dam** enables salmon to travel upstream (visitors can view the salmon passing by through porthole windows; open mid-Jun–Labor Day daily 7:30am–9:30pm; call for hours to end-Sept. $3. 418-562-7006).

Continue on Route 132.

Cap-Chat

To see the wind turbine, turn right 3km/1.8mi west of Cap-Chat bridge.
Towering above the landscape at 110m/361ft, the vertical-axis **wind turbine★**, named Éole, is the largest of its kind in the world (visit by 1hr guided tour only, late Jun–late Sept daily 9:30am–5:30pm; $10; 418-786-5719; www.eolecapchat.com). A rotor with two curved blades turns wind power into electricity. Éole, a joint project of the National Research Council and Hydro-Québec, has been in full automatic operation since 1988. Guides describe the turbine mechanism and discuss low-impact energy sources.

Cap-Chat Rock

From Rte. 132, turn left 2km/1.2mi west of village. Follow gravel road for 0.5km/0.3mi.
The village drew its name from this rock thought to resemble a sitting cat (chat). Nearby, a lighthouse dating from 1871 serves as the starting point for several nature trails.

Parc national de la Gaspésie★ (Gaspésie Park)

33km/20.5mi. After 16km/10mi, take Rte. 299 from Sainte-Anne-des-Monts. Open daily year-round. $8.50. 418-763-7494 or 1-800-665-6527. www.sepaq.com.
Three sectors of the park are devoted to recreational activities. In the **Mont-Albert Sector**, a hike ( ) to the mountaintop (1,151m/3,775ft) reveals a 13sq km/8sq mi plateau strewn with vegetation characteristic of the northern tundra. In the **Lake Cascapédia Sector**, the ridges of the Chic-Chocs

massif offer spectacular **views★★** of the Appalachians and the St. Lawrence Valley to the north, and the Sainte-Anne River valley to the east. Mt. Jacques-Cartier (1,268m/4,159ft) is found in the **Galène Sector**. Its windy dome, home to caribou and arctic-alpine flora, affords an expansive **view★★** of the McGerrigle Mountains.

Centre de découverte et de services (Discovery and Services Center)

Open mid-May–mid-Oct daily 8am–8pm; call to confirm other times. Hiking and camping equipment rental and sales. ℘1-800-665-6527.
A permanent exhibit provides an introduction to the fascinating landscapes found in the park and to the plants (arctic-alpine) and animals, especially caribou, that thrive on its mountaintops. During the summer, naturalists answer questions at the summit of Mt. Jacques-Cartier and Mt. Albert. In the evening, lectures, slide shows, plays, and films on themes related to the park are presented at the center.

FROM PARC NATIONAL DE LA GASPÉSIE TO GASPÉ

259km/161mi starting from Gaspésie Park.

See regional map, p388–389.

Return to Sainte-Anne-des-Monts and continue on Rte. 132 to La Martre.

La Martre

From this little village perched atop a promontory, the **view** encompasses the surrounding capes and the ocean. The top of the red octagonal lighthouse (*phare*) provides a spectacular **view**. The adjoining **Musée des phares** has exhibits dating from the 18C (by guided tour only, early Jun–late Sept daily 9am–5pm; $5. ℘418-288-5698).

Scenic Route from La Martre to Rivière-au-Renard★★

Rte. 132 hugs the coastline, up and over rocky cliffs, affording splendid views of hills, valleys, picturesque fishing villages and the ocean. In the region of **Mont-Saint-Pierre**, shale cliffs rim the bay, and just east of **Sainte-Madeleine-de-la-Rivière-Madeleine**, the lighthouse and surrounding buildings grace the lush, green hills. From the hilltop, before arriving at **Grande-Vallée**, the view of the village and its bay is remarkable. In the town center stands a covered bridge dating from 1923. Past the fishing village of **Rivière-au-Renard**, at the northern tip of Forillon National Park, expansive views sweep across fields to the Gulf of St. Lawrence.

International Garden Festival

International and provincial garden designers create avant-garde, experimental designs in landscape architecture and the visual arts at the Reford Gardens. Dates change, but are generally in late June to late September. See www.refordgardens.com for more information. ℘418-775-2222.

Cap-des-Rosiers

21km/13mi from Rivière-au-Renard.
This village, named for the abundance of wild roses Jacques Cartier found when he arrived here in the 16C, has witnessed numerous shipwrecks off its rocky coast. The **lighthouse** (*37m/121ft*) is the tallest in Canada (visit by 45min guided tour only: late Jun–late Sept daily 8am–6pm; $2 site entry, $5 tour. ℘418-892-5767).

Parc national du Canada Forillon★★

Open year-round, daily. $7.80 ($5.65 Labor Day–Jun 25). www.pc.gc.ca/eng/pn-np/qc/forillon/index.aspx.
Created in 1970, Forillon National Park of Canada is located on the eastern tip of the Gaspé Peninsula, where the Gulf of St. Lawrence meets the Bay of Gaspé. The majestic, remarkably diverse landscape (245sq km/95sq mi), created largely by erosion, includes limestone

The Lighthouse Loop

The "Route des Phares" connects the eleven lighthouses that watch over the coast of the Gaspé Peninsula, some dating back to the late 19C. The suggested route takes you in turn to the lighthouses of Matane, Cap-Chat, La Martre, Cap Madeleine, Pointe-à-la-Renommée, Cap-des-Rosiers, Cap Gaspé, Cap-d'Espoir, Pointe Bonaventure, Pointe Duthie, and Carleton. These highlights of Quebec's heritage have gained a new lease on life recently, being converted into museums, visitor attractions, and even a hotel. The lighthouses of Pointe-de-Mitis, Cap Blanc, and Port-Daniel-Ouest are not accessible to the public. *www.routedesphares.qc.ca.*

cliffs towering over the sea; mountainous forests of spruce, fir, poplar and cedar; wildflower meadows; and pebbly beaches tucked away in coves. Visitors can see black bears, beavers, fox, moose, and porcupines; seagulls, cormorants, kittiwakes, and guillemots; and seals and sometimes whales. Five whale species frequent the Bay of Gaspé— Blue, Fin, Humpback, Minke, and Pilot whales—along with White-sided Dolphins and Harbor Porpoises.

Interpretation Centre

Near Cap-des-Rosiers in the northern sector (Secteur nord) of the park. Open late May–late Jun and early Sept–mid-Oct daily 10am–4pm; late Jun–early Sept daily 9am–5pm. ♿ ☎418-368-5505 & 1-888-773-8888.

An informative exhibit describes the history of fishing in the region and the interaction between land and sea. **Aquariums** (👪) house many examples of marine life. Visitors can also see films about the flora, fauna and geology of the park. Pleasure cruises depart from a harbor near the center. Experienced sea kayakers can rent kayaks in the park and paddle on their own. Non-experienced kayakers can join a guided tour where, nature willing, they might see whales, dolphins or porpoises.

Cap Bon Ami

3km/1.8mi south of the interpretation center by a secondary road.

From the picnic lookout and along the walkway leading to the beach, **views★★** of the sea and the limestone cliffs of Cap Bon Ami are magnificent.

▶ Return to Rte. 132, and follow signs leading to the southern sector

Parc national du Canada Forillon

of the park. At the junction with the secondary road, turn left.

Grande-Grave★

16.5km/10mi from the interpretation center.

A thriving fishing community from the 19C to the mid-20C, this small village was inhabited by settlers from the Channel Islands of Jersey and Guernsey. Today several buildings have been restored to reflect the style of the 1920s. The first floor of the **Hyman & Sons General Store** is stocked with goods that would have been found in a general store at that time. On the second floor, an exhibit describes the activities of fishermen and their families throughout the year. The Blanchette House is the residential component of the Grande-Grave historic site.

From Grande-Grave you can attend organised whale-watching trips (Jun–mid-Oct daily outings for 2.5hours; $70, children (age 4–15) $40; 418-892-5500 or 1-866-617-5500; www.baleines-forillon.com).

Nearby, in **Anse-Blanchette**, stands the brightly painted house that belonged to Xavier Blanchette in the early 20C. The interior and outbuildings, including the *chafauds*, or racks for drying fish, re-create the life of a local fisherman.

Continue on secondary road to Anse-Saint-Georges and Anse-aux-Amérindiens.

Cap Gaspé★

8km/5mi round-trip on foot from Anse-aux-Amérindiens.

This pleasant walk through newly forested lands that were cleared at the turn of the 19C to build homes for fishermen offers **views**★ of the Bay of Gaspé and Île Bonaventure, an island famous for its bird reserve where countless shore birds can be seen.

Return to Rte. 132.

On the way back to Rte. 132, among other sites worth a visit are a Protestant church, an amphitheater, a campground, and a recreational and tourist center.

Grande-Vallée on the Gaspésie coast

© Gregory B. Gallagher / Michelin

Continue on Rte. 132 for 11.5km/7mi, in the direction of Gaspé.

Fort-Péninsule

The battery that was built here during World War II, combined with the naval base at Sandy Beach on the southern shore of Gaspé Bay, and other facilities, were all part of the Canadian government's efforts to stop German submarines from entering the St. Lawrence River. Locals still talk about the day that German submariners supposedly landed and walked though town, then got back in their sub and left.

Continue on Rte. 132 for 12.5km/7.7mi, in the direction of Gaspé.

Penouille

Penouille is a name of Basque origin meaning "peninsula," and the fine sandy beach here is ideal for swimming. The sandy coast and taiga ecosystem at this peninsula contrast with the looming limestone headlands and boreal forest of the rest of the park.

Gaspé★

On July 24, 1534, the Breton explorer Jacques Cartier set foot on this site and took possession of the land in the name of François I, King of France. Located on a hillside where the York River empties into the Bay of Gaspé, the town is now the administrative and commercial center of the peninsula. The name Gaspé is derived from the Mi'kmaq word gespec, meaning "land's end."

Musée de la Gaspésie★ (Museum of the Gaspé Peninsula)

80 Blvd de Gaspé (Rte. 132). Open Jun–Oct daily 9am–5pm, Nov–May Wed–Fri 10am–5pm, Sat–Sun 1pm–5pm. $10.50. 418-368-1534. www.museedelagaspesie.ca.

This regional museum is dedicated to the preservation of Gaspésian culture and ethnological heritage, and it highlights historical events and regional geography. Set on Jacques-Cartier Point, the museum offers fine **views★** of the Bay of Gaspé and the Forillon Peninsula.

Jacques-Cartier Monument

In the park next to the museum, six cast-iron steles form a monument (1984) commemorating the discovery of Canada and the first encounter between Cartier and the native population. The dolmen-shaped steles, adorned with bas-reliefs illustrating Cartier's arrival in the New World on one side and excerpts of texts written by Cartier and Father Le Clercq on the other, are the work of Jean-Julien and Gil Bourgault-Legros of Saint-Jean-Port-Joli.

From the museum, turn left onto Blvd de Gaspé in the direction of the town center. At the traffic light, turn right onto rue Adams, continue for two blocks and turn left onto rue Jacques-Cartier; the cathedral is on the left.

Activities

More than 40km/24.8mi of trails are maintained for hiking, and visitors can enjoy swimming, scuba diving, fishing, biking, and horseback riding. Campgrounds are located in the Forillon National Park at Des-Rosiers, Cap Bon Ami and Petit-Gaspé, and there are numerous picnic areas.

Cathédrale du Christ-Roi★ (Christ the King Cathedral)

Open year-round, daily 8:30am–4pm. 418-368-5541.

The cathedral's unusual lines and cedar exterior blend in with the environment. In the strikingly simple interior, sunlight filters past massive beams creating a warm glow on the wooden sheathing. A stained-glass window and a bronze portray a triumphant Christ. The fresco, donated by France in 1934, illustrates Cartier's arrival in the New World. Beside the cathedral stands the **Croix de Gaspé** (Cross of Gaspé), also known as the **Jacques-Cartier Cross**. The 9.6m/31.5ft cross was carved from a single block of granite from a quarry near Quebec City. It was unveiled during the 1934 celebrations.

FROM PERCÉ TO CAUSAPSCAL

337km/209.4mi starting at Percé, 76km/47mi from Gaspé.

See regional map, p389.

Percé★★★

142 Rte. 132 Ouest. 418-782-5448. www.perce.info.

Named for the massive rock that pierces (*percé*) the sea, standing just offshore, this village occupies a magnificent **site** that inspires artists and poets and attracts visitors from all over the world to the Gaspé peninsula. One of Jacques Cartier's landing points in 1534, the area was also frequented by European fishermen in the 16C and 17C. A mission was founded here in 1673, but was destroyed by the British in 1690, to be re-established only after the Conquest. A tiny, isolated fishing village until the advent of tourism in the early 20C, Percé now boasts some of the peninsula's finest restaurants and tourist facilities.

L'Anse à Beaufils Historic General Store

32 rue à Bonfils, in the L'Anse-à-Beaufils sector of Percé. Open mid-Jun–early Sept daily 10am–5pm; limited off-season schedule. Guided tours in English or French at 10am, 11am, 2pm, and 3:30pm. $6. 418-782-2225 (off season 418-782-5286).

The general store was a key institution in early Canada. With the Catholic church and the primary school, the general store completed the trilogy of village essentials in Quebec. And these stores were particularly essential in remote areas like Gaspésie.

This rare, authentically preserved general store features superb antique oak wainscoting. The daily life of the "Gaspésiens" is displayed through objects, tools and wares. Guides in period costumes tell stories and anecdotes inspired by the lives of Gaspésie pioneers.

Musée Le Chafaud

142 rue Principale, Percé. Open Jun 24–Sept 21 daily 10am–8pm. Guided tours in English or French at 11am, 2pm, 3:30pm, and 5pm. $5. 418-782-5100. www.musee-chafaud.com.

This charming site exists to promote the undeniable beauty of Percé through a continuously changing repertoire of visual arts. From cartographers and sailors, to students and artists inspired by Percé, the walls of this museum reflect impressions of the place in art. Refurbished heritage building (1845).

Parc national de l'Île-Bonaventure-et-du-Rocher-Percé★ (Bonaventure Island and Percé Rock National Park)

Open daily late May-early Oct. $8.50. 418-782-2240 or 1-800-665-6527. www.sepaq.com.

In summer Île Bonaventure is home to some 70,000 **gannets** that nest in the ledges and crevices of the 90m/1,259ft cliffs on the east side of the island. This sanctuary is the largest colony of gannets in North America. Other seabirds found here are kittiwakes, murres, puffins, razorbills, guillemots, cormorants, and gulls.

The **boat trip** to Île Bonaventure takes visitors past Percé Rock and then around the island (Les Bateliers de Percé Inc; 162 Rte. 132; 418-782-2974 or 1-877-782-2974. www.lesbataliersdeperce.com. P. 1hr 15min trip departs from quai de Percé from mid-May–mid-Oct 9am–5pm; commentary on board; $30; $20 direct to island). In summer, passengers can disembark on the island to take a closer look at the birds and walk along the nature trails.

Percé Rock – Once attached to the mainland, this mammoth rock wall is 438m/1,437ft long and 88m/289ft high. The limestone block was formed at the bottom of the sea millions of years ago, and contains innumerable fossils. At one time, it may have had up to four holes forming as many archways. One such archway crumbled in 1845, leaving a detached slab called the Obelisk. Today, only a 30m/98.4ft arch remains. The sculptured limestone is best viewed from rue du **Mont-Joli**. The rock is connected to Mont-Joli by a sandbar, exposed at low tide. *Check tide tables at the tourist office. The stairway to the beach and sandbar is accessible from the rue du Mont-Joli parking lot.*

The Coast★★★

The coast along Rte. 132 offers spectacular **views★★**. Just before entering Percé, a belvedere provides a good view of Aurore Peak (Pic de l'Aurore). Farther along the road, a path leads up to **Cape Barré**, which affords a commanding view of the cliffs known as **Trois Sœurs** (Three Sisters) to the west, and Percé Rock, Anse du Nord, Île Bonaventure and the village, to the east. Leaving Percé, the promontory at **Côte Surprise** offers yet another superb view of Percé Rock, the village and the island.

From Rte. 132, take Ave. de l'Église. Behind the church, a gravel road leads to Mt. Sainte-Anne. A steep but easy trail leads to the summit.

Mont Sainte-Anne

Allow 2hrs round-trip.

Rising 320m/1,050ft above Percé, the flat-topped mountain features extraordinary red rock formations that drop off on three sides. Lookouts stationed along the way to the summit provide increasingly expansive **views★★★** of Percé Rock, the bay, the village, and the surrounding area. A statue of St. Anne crowns the mountain summit.

La Grotte (Grotto)

On the return trip from Mt. Sainte-Anne, turn left at Chemin de la Grotte, and continue for 1km/.6mi.

In this scenic grotto, a waterfall cascades into a small pool surrounded by moss and ferns.

La Grande Crevasse★ (Great Crevice)

From the village, take Rte. des Failles up to the Auberge Gargantua (3km/1.8mi). The trail (1hr 30min round-trip) starts behind the inn; caution is advised as there is no guardrail.

Passing alongside the west cliff of Mt. Sainte-Anne, the trail offers glimpses of the peaks of the Chic-Choc Mountains to the west and the Bay of Gaspé to the north. The Great Crevice (*also visible from Rte. des Failles*) is a deep fissure in the red conglomerate rock which is a part of Mont Blanc, located northwest of Mont Sainte-Anne.

Take Rte. 132 through Grande-Rivière, Chandler and Port-Daniel to Paspébiac.

Paspébiac

109km/67.7mi.

In 1767 Charles Robin, from the Island of Jersey, chose this location to establish the headquarters of his cod fishing empire, the Charles Robin Company (CRC).

Site historique du Banc-de-Pêche-de-Paspébiac (Banc-de-Pêche-de-Paspébiac Historic Site)

Turn left off Rte. 132 onto Rte. du Banc and continue to the waterfront. Open mid-Jun–Sept daily 9am–5pm. $11 . 418-752-6229.

To ensure the success of his exports of dried, salted cod (known as "Gaspé Cure") to Europe, Charles Robin created an entire town, complete with a naval yard, blacksmiths, carpenters, and a company store.

Eleven buildings erected by the CRC around 1783 were restored after a fire in 1964. Visitors can tour the buildings and view live demonstrations of traditional activities like net-mending and barge-building.

West of Paspébiac extends the pleasant coastal region of the **Chaleur Bay**. This scenic body of water, which also washes the northern shores of New Brunswick, was discovered by Jacques Cartier in 1534. The area's moderate climate (*chaleur* means warmth) attracts visitors who like watersports.

Bonaventure

22km/13.6mi. 127 Ave. Louisbourg. Tourism office open early Jun–early Oct. 418-534-4014. www.tourismebonaventure.com.

The village, which takes its name from a ship that sailed into the Chaleur Bay in 1591, is well known for its salmon river, and it has a nice beach as well. Bonaventure exudes a colorful Acadian ambiance and spirit.

Musée acadien du Québec (Quebec Acadian Museum)

In the center of Bonaventure, east of the church on Rte. 132. Jun 24–Oct 13 daily 9am–6pm; shorter hours in fall and winter. $10. 418-534-4000. www.museeacadien.com.

The museum exhibits antiques and old photographs, and an audiovisual presentation recalling the Acadian contribution to Quebec culture.

New Richmond

35km/21.7mi.

A Loyalist stronghold, the town boasts several charming residential areas that still retain a late-19C Anglo-Saxon flavor.

Parc national de Miguasha

© François Rivard / ATRG

Village Gaspésien de l'héritage Britannique (Gaspesian British Heritage Village)

351 Blvd Perron Ouest. Open late Jun–late Sept Mon–Fri 10am–5pm. $8. ℘418-392-4487. www.gaspesianvillage.org.

Relive the bicentennial history of descendants from the British Isles in the Gaspé Peninsula. The 21 buildings in this reconstructed village came from the communities surrounding Chaleur Bay. The **Harvey House** exemplifies the Colonial Revival style popular in the US at the end of the 19C.

Other dwellings dating from the late 17C through the early 20C reveal architectural styles typical of their respective periods. The visit ends at the lighthouse overlooking Cascapédia Bay.

Carleton-sur-Mer

28km/17.4mi.

Founded by Acadians in 1756, the village was originally called Tracadièche, derived from the Native word *tracadigash* meaning "place of many herons." In the late 18C, Loyalists renamed the settlement in honor of Governor General Guy Carleton, later known as Lord Dorchester.

Nestled between mountains and the sea, Carleton's scenic location has contributed to its great success as a seaside resort.

Sentiers de l'Éperlan

These trails follow the course of a stream, the Éperlan, negotiating waterfalls and revealing mountain landscapes before ending up behind Mont Saint-Joseph.

Mont Saint-Joseph

Follow rue de la Montagne from the town center for around 6km/3.7mi.

From the 555m/1,800ft summit of Mont Saint-Joseph, the **view★★** takes in the Baie des Chaleurs, from Bonaventure to the Miguasha Peninsula, and extends to the New Brunswick coast to the south. A little stone sanctuary, the Oratoire Notre-Dame (1935), contains delicate mosaics and fine stained-glass windows (; open mid-Jun–Sept 9am–7pm; Sept–Oct, 9am–5pm; ℘418-364-3723).

After 18km/11mi, turn left, then continue for another 6km/3.7mi.

Parc national de Miguasha

Open early May–early Jun and most of Oct Mon–Fri 8:30am–noon and 1pm–4:30pm; early Jun–early Oct daily 9am–5pm. $8.50 park entry, $10 museum entry. ℘418-794-2475 & 1-800-665-6527. www.sepaq.com/pq/mig/en.

Miguasha is a Quebec provincial conservation park, where visitors are introduced to the fascinating world of fossils through exhibits and on-site observation of the cliff in the company of researchers and park personnel. In 1999 the park was designated a UNESCO World Heritage Site. *See panel on p418 for geological information about the park.*

Musée d'histoire naturelle (Natural History Museum)

Fossils on display represent ferns, invertebrates and many kinds of fish from the Upper Devonian Period. Among

The Famous Fossils of Miguasha

On the north shore of the Restigouche River, near Chaleur Bay, lies an escarpment containing fossils embedded in sedimentary rock since the Upper Devonian Period (370 million years ago). The site of Miguasha was once a tropical lagoon fed by several rivers and surrounded by lush plant life. The shifting of sands and deposit of sediments gradually buried aquatic and plant life layer by layer. Over millions of years, the sediments became rock, and the embedded life forms were preserved as fossils.

Two geological formations are visible at Miguasha: the Fleurant conglomerate, consisting mainly of sandstone (at the base); and the grayish Escuminac formation (at the top). The latter consists mostly of silt, sandstone, and argillaceous schist, and is only 8km/5mi long by 1km/0.6mi wide.

The storehouse of paleontological information contained in this cliff was discovered in 1842, although scientific study here did not begin until 1880. Soon afterwards, the site gained popularity with European geologists, who collected and removed many of the fossils. In the 1970s, as part of a move to protect the fossil deposits from unauthorized removal, the provincial government purchased portions of the cliff.

the outstanding finds of the Miguashan fossils is *Eusthenopteron foordi,* which resembles the earliest known amphibian, *Ichthyostega*. Fossils found in Greenland indicate that this amphibian may have lived some 20 million years after the Miguashan fish.

Amphitheater

Offers showings of "Dive Into the Origins," the first 2D/3D interactive immersion experience in North America. This collaboration between computer graphics designers and paleontologists brings ancient seas back to life.

Laboratory

Guides explain methods of disengaging fossils from the host rock. With the use of microscopes, visitors can examine fossil samples. A short walk down to the cliff offers a first-hand look at the sedimentary strata. Guides help visitors to locate fossils. A 3.5km/2.2mi interpretive trail surrounds the site. *Note: it is illegal to remove fossils from the park.*

Lieu historique national de la Bataille-de-la-Ristigouche (Battle of the Restigouche National Historic Site)

In Pointe-à-la-Croix. Open mid-Jun–Aug daily 9am–5pm. $3.90. 418-788-5676 or or 1-888-773-8888. www.pc.gc.ca/ristigouche.

France's last naval attempt to save its North American colony from British control was thwarted in the estuary of the Restigouche River in July 1760. Two merchant ships, protected by a frigate, were to deliver troops and ammunition to Quebec City, capital of New France. Upon reaching the Gulf of St. Lawrence, the French learned that five British warships had arrived ahead of them. To avoid battle, French commander La Giraudais moved his fleet to the head of Chaleur Bay, on the Restigouche River estuary, hoping that the larger British ships would be unable to enter shallower waters. Acadians and Mi'kmaq Indians helped the French set up batteries to block the river channel. After days of battle, the British finally forced the French to scuttle or abandon their ships.

Interpretation center

In the reception area, the giant anchor and part of the hull recovered from the frigate *Le Machault* are on display. An animated film (*15min*) recounts the battle. In the exhibit halls, scenes depict life on board, using many objects recovered from the wreckage, including personal items such as belt buckles, pipes, tobacco boxes, candle snuffers and clothing, as well as tools used to repair wood on board and tighten masts. Recovered contents of the holds include fabric, clothing for troops, and trade goods ranging from nails to combs. Earthenware, Chinese porcelain and other luxury merchandise are also on display.

Detour to New Brunswick

An interprovincial bridge links Restigouche with Campbellton, New Brunswick. Rte. 11 leads to the Acadian Historic Village (Village historique acadien, www.villagehistoriqueacadien.com) located 10km/6.2mi west of Caraquet, and to the Aquarium and Marine Centre at Shippagan. (aquariumnb.ca). For descriptions, consult The Green Guide Canada. Continue on Rte. 132 through Matapédia Valley through quaint villages, rolling forests, impressive hills, and the ever-present Matapédia River, famous for its salmon fishing.

Return to Route 132 and continue to Causapscal.

Causapscal

75km/46.6mi.

Located at the confluence of the Causapscal and Matapédia rivers, this town of 2,454 is a departure point for salmon-fishing expeditions. At the **Site historique Matamajaw** (53 rue Saint-Jacques Sud; open mid-Jun–early Sept Tue–Sun 9:30am–4:30pm. $7; 418-756-5999, www.sitehistoriquematamajaw.com), visitors can relive the lifestyles of High Society fishing enthusiasts at the Matamajaw Salmon Club, and in a specially designed channel, observe Atlantic salmon in their natural habitat.

ADDRESSES

STAY

Auberge Restaurant Chez Mamie – *195 Rte. Principale, Sainte-Madeleine-de-la-Rivière-Madeleine. 418-393-2212 or 1-866-393-2212 (toll-free).* For a proper introduction to Gaspésie's bounty of the sea, there is no better place than the former home of writer/doctor Jacques Ferron. This beachfront Victorian inn exudes the atmosphere of the region.

Centre d'Art Marcel Gagnon – *564 Rte. de la Mer, Sainte-Flavie. 418-775-2829. www.centredart.net. Closed early Oct–late Apr. 10 rooms.* Simple and clean describe the comfortable rooms on the upper floor of the art center. Free breakfast is served in view of Marcel Gagnon's composite sculpture, ***Le grand rassemblement***.

Hotel/Motel Fleur de Lys – *248 Rte. 132 Ouest, Percé. 418-782-5380 and 1-800-399-5380. www.fleurdelysperce.com. 34 rooms.* Families will be happy to settle here with a heated pool, a playground and a fire ring. Enjoy a breathtaking view of the Percé Rock from the hotel, and you can go around town with the hotel's own shuttle service. Direct access to the boardwalk leading to the wharf.

Manoir de Percé – *212 Rte 132 Ouest, Percé. 418-782-2022 or 1-800-463-0858. www.manoirdeperce.com. 40 rooms, including 30 with air-conditioning.* In the heart of Percé, facing the Rock and Bonaventure Island. Comfortable hotel-motel style accommodation. It serves nicely prepared, traditional Gaspésian cooking, including smoked salmon prepared by the owners.

Gîte du Mont-Albert – *Rte. du Parc, Sainte-Anne-des-Monts. 866-727-2427. www.sepaq.com. 48 hotel rooms, 12 lodge rooms, 2 lodge suites, 18 cabins.* This delightful establishment in Gaspésie Park offers well-kept rooms, comfortable accommodation and efficient service, making it a perfect place for a family holiday.

Auberge au Fil des Saisons – *232 Rte. 132 Ouest, Percé. 418-680-2325. www.aubergeperce.com. 6 rooms of differing sizes and configurations.* Outstanding value in this Victorian house facing the Gulf. Cozy rooms decorated smartly with pastel colors.

Auberge au Pirate 1775 – *169 Rte 132 Ouest, Percé. Dinner only. 418-782-5055, 5 rooms in this large B&B. Restaurant* . Wonderfully comfortable rooms, gregarious proprietors, and beautiful views of Percé

FLY FISHING

© R. Corbel / Michelin

Pull on your boots, pick up some fishing tackle and take to Quebec's pristine waters for a first-rate fly-fishing experience. Fly fishing requires proper equipment and casting technique, but it can become an enjoyable activity and even a passion. Fishing with artificial flies dates as far back as AD 1, when they were used to simulate insects too delicate to use as natural bait.

Select your flies, rod, reel, and fly line based on the fishing conditions. Make sure the reel has a reliable drag and carries plenty of extra line if your destination includes one of Quebec's famous Atlantic salmon rivers. Required gear includes boots or waders, a vest, hat, insect repellent, warm clothing, rain gear, and polarized sunglasses. Serious anglers study the characteristics of rivers and streams, understand effects of weather and tides, and know how these variables relate to fly fishing and fish behavior in different seasons. Local sporting goods stores can outfit you with the appropriate gear and provide information about fishing permits.

For additional information, contact Quebec's Ministère des Forêts, de la Faune et des Parcs: 1-866-248-6936 (an English message follows the French message) or www.mffp.gouv.qc.ca.

Rock await you at this Pirate's Inn, tucked into an 18C home. The acclaimed **dining room** pleases visitors with specialties such as *brandade de morue et sa compote de tomates fraîches* (puree of salt cod with fresh tomato compote), and *le trio du golfe en beurre blanc au vinaigre de framboises* (salmon, scallops and grilled shrimp in raspberry vinegar beurre blanc).

GETTING - THERE

BY TRAIN – The Gaspé Peninsula is the most interesting remote area in Quebec that is reachable by train. There are VIA Rail stations in Mont-Joli, Matapédia, Carleton, Percé, and Gaspé. The *Chaleur* train leaves Montreal Wed, Fri and Sun at the end of the afternoon and arrives in Gaspésie the next morning. There is a panorama car (featuring a glass dome) and a bar-lounge car. Sleeper cabins are available.

VIA Rail Canada: *1-888-842-7245, www.viarail.ca.*

Hôtel La Normandie – *221 Rte 132 Ouest, Percé. 418-782-2112 or 1-800-463-0820. www.normandieperce.com. 45 rooms. Restaurant.* A waterfront hotel in the most traditional sense, the Normandie offers tastefully decorated rooms, most with views of Percé Rock. An impressive wine list accompanies the table d'hôte menu.

EAT

La Maison du Pêcheur – *155 Place du Quai, Perché. 418-782-5331.* The Fisherman's House serves breakfast, lunch and dinner. For dinner, choose from delectable bistro classics or Québécois seafood specialties like lobster flavored with maple syrup (the restaurant has its own lobster farm) or the wood-fired pizzas such as La Spéciale du Pêcheur, made with tomato sauce, shrimp, scallops and lobster. Features a large dining room and a terrace that is very welcome in the summer.

Îles de la Madeleine★★

Magdalen Islands

This isolated and windswept outpost of Quebec lies in the middle of the Gulf of St. Lawrence, closer to Cape Breton (Nova Scotia) and Prince Edward Island than to the Gaspé Peninsula. Of the eight islands and numerous islets that make up the archipelago, six are linked by a series of sandy isthmuses, forming a hook-shaped mass about 72km/44.7mi long, stretching southwest to northeast. The islands offer a wealth of outdoor activities for the visitor, ranging from sightseeing to swimming and hiking.

- **Population:** 13,062.
- **Michelin Map:** p423.
- **Info:** 128 chemin Principal. ✆418-986-2245, 1-877-624-4437. www.tourismeilesdelamadeleine.com.
- **Location:** The Îles de la Madeleine are 920km/571.6mi northeast of Montreal and 250km/155.3mi southeast of Gaspé in the Gulf of St. Lawrence. Regular ferries run from Prince Edward Island 100km/62mi to the south, and a cruise ship designed to hold vehicles connects the islands to Gaspé and the St. Lawrence River through to Montreal.
- **Don't Miss:** The rock formations at the headlands of the beach near Cape Trou; the Maritime Museum on Havre Aubert Island; the view from Entry Island.
- **Timing:** Rent a car near the port at Cap-aux-Meules and you can drive the full length of the archipelago. As you drive south to Havre Aubert Island, stop along the long beach and watch the kite-surfers. The road northwest to the eastern islands travels along another long sand dune, but continue to the Grand Échouerie Beach where you'll find the water surprisingly pleasant for swimming in the summer. Before you leave, be sure to take the ferry across to Entry Island, and hike up the easy trail.
- **Kids:** Grand Échouerie Beach, and the Aquarium of the Islands in La Grave on Havre Aubert Island.

A BIT OF HISTORY

Discovery – During the 15C, the Magdalen Islands were a frequent stopping point for Basque and Breton fishermen in search of fish, seals, walruses, and whales. The archipelago was officially discovered in 1534 by Jacques Cartier during the first of his three expeditions in the Gulf of St. Lawrence. Cartier landed first at Rocher aux Oiseaux (Bird Rock), then at Île Brion, due north of the islands, which he described in the ship's log as "the best land we have yet seen. A single acre of this soil is worth more than all of Newfoundland. We found it full of beautiful trees, prairies, fields of wild wheat, and flowering pea plants as varied and as lovely as anything I have seen in Brittany, and appearing to have been planted with much labor."

In the decades following Cartier's discovery, the islands were inhabited sporadically by Mi'kmaq Indians and by French explorers and fur traders. The archipelago is thought to have been named for Madeleine Fontaine, wife of **François Doublet**, the nobleman who colonized the territory in the name of the French Crown in 1663.

The Acadian Deportation – The archipelago was not permanently inhabited

VISITOR INFORMATION

GETTING THERE

The Tourism Association (Tourisme Îles-de-la-Madeleine) information office *(128 chemin Principal, at the corner of chemin Débarcadère, Cap-aux-Meules, adjoining the ferry parking; ☏418-986-2245; www.tourismeilesdelamadeleine.com)* provides literature and information about guided tours of the islands, scenic cruises, outdoor activities, restaurants and accommodations.

Several private operators offer tours of the island (by van or boat) varying in length from several hours to a full day. To watch seals and view the cliff formations, scenic cruises are highly recommended. For close-up views of the cliffs and wildlife, hike along one of the trails around the islands (for information, contact **La Salicorne Auberge-Escapades** on Grande Entrée Island *(☏418-985-28336 and 1-888-537-4537; www.salicorne.ca)*.

TIME

The Magdalen Islands are on Atlantic time, which is one hour ahead of Eastern time (rest of Quebec).

ACCESS

BY AIR - Daily service between Montreal, Quebec City, Gaspé and Havre aux Maisons Island on Air Canada Express with connections for all Air Canada and Star Alliance destinations (*☏1-888-247-2262; www.aircanada.com*); and service between St-Hubert (Montreal), Quebec City, Bonaventure (Gaspésie), Bathurst (New Brunswick) and Havre aux Maisons Island on local airline Pascan Aviation Inc. (*☏450-433-0500 and 1-888-313-8777; www.pascan.com*).

BY CAR/BOAT - From Montreal, take Rte. 20 to Rivière-du-Loup, then Rte. 185 to Edmundston, New Brunswick (NB), and Rte. 2 to Moncton (NB). From there, take Rte. 15, then Rte. 16 to Cape Tormentine (NB), and cross the toll bridge (10min) linking New Brunswick to Prince Edward Island (PEI). From Borden, take Rte. 1 to Charlottetown (PEI), then Rte. 2 to Souris (PEI) for the ferry to Cap-aux-Meules. Ferry from Souris–Cap-aux-Meules (5hrs) runs daily Jul–Sept 7, with reduced operations the rest of the year. One-way $50/person high season, $32.75 low season, additional $94.50 for a vehicle. Reservations required, especially in summer. ✕ ♿ P CTMA Traversier Ltd. Cap-aux-Meules *☏1-888-986-3278. www.ctma.ca.*

The cruise ship *Vacancier* departs weekly Jun–Sept from Montreal to Cap-aux-Meules (2 days; one-way double occupancy $618–793, meals included; live nightly entertainment, reservations required).

For schedules, contact CTMA in Cap-aux-Meules (*☏418-986-3278*) or in Montreal (*☏514-937-7656*).

GETTING AROUND

COACHES

Les Sillons *(☏418-986-4621; www.autobuslessillons.com)* departs every Thu evening, early Jun–early Sept, from Quebec locations. Package includes bus travel from Quebec City ($1319 return low season) or Rivière-du-Loup ($1289), plus the bus crossing to the islands.

EXCURSIONS

Several companies offer excursions of varying lengths (by bus, helicopter, or boat). Panoramic cruises, for example, allow you to admire the archipelago's rock formations or to observe the seal colonies.

There are also opportunities for walking, with numerous trails criss-crossing the islands, providing interpretation and opportunities to observe the natural environment. Information from the Îles de la Madeleine tourist office.

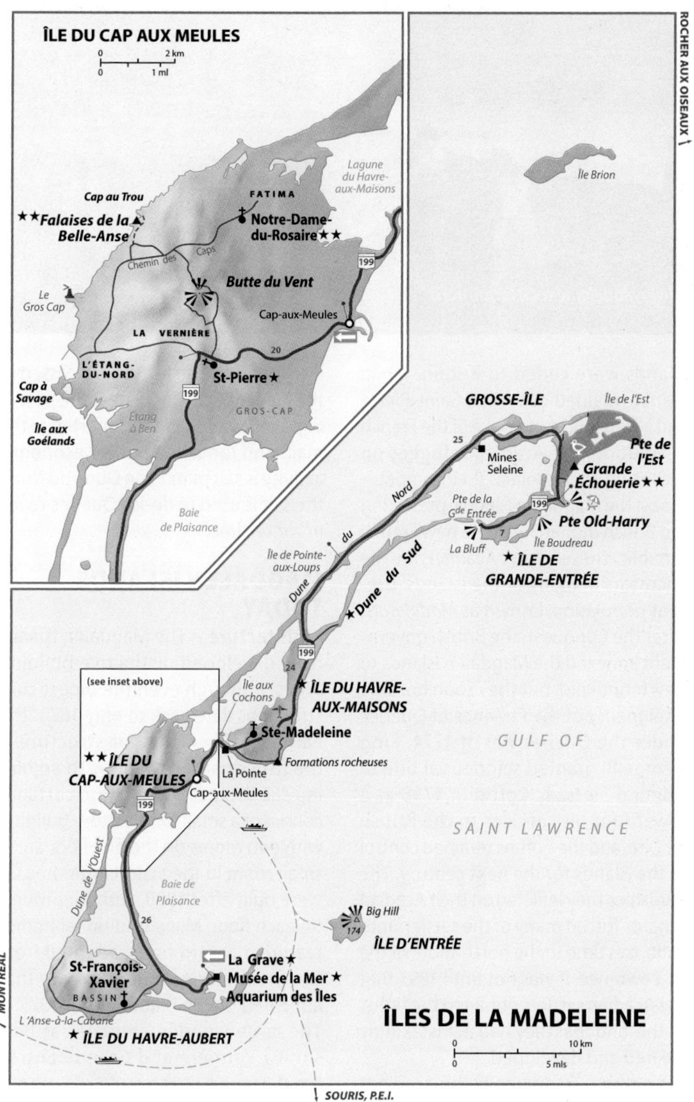

until after 1755, when it became a refuge for French colonists who had settled in Acadia (now the west coast of Nova Scotia). An area of territorial dispute between Britain and France from 1604 through 1710, Acadia was ceded to Britain in 1713 under the Treaty of Utrecht, which ended the War of the Spanish Succession in Europe.

When the Acadian settlers refused to swear an oath of unconditional allegiance to Great Britain, the governor of Nova Scotia, Charles Lawrence, issued a **Deportation Order** (August 1755), which forcibly expelled the Acadians to the American colonies. Several hundred escaped, fleeing to the Magdalen Islands and France's other remaining colonies, the islands of Saint-Pierre and Miquelon, off the southern coast of Newfoundland (*consult The Green Guide Canada*).

In accordance with the terms of the Treaty of Paris (1763), the Magdalen

Îles de la Madeleine rock formations

©Gregory B. Gallagher/Michelin

Islands were ceded to Britain, while France retained control of Saint-Pierre and Miquelon. In the wake of the French Revolution, the Acadian refugees on these two islands joined their compatriots on the Magdalen Islands, preferring the British monarchy to the new French republic. These former Acadians are the ancestors of many of the islands' present population, known as *Madelinots*. After the Conquest, the British government annexed the Magdalen Islands to Newfoundland, but they soon became a seigneury of the Province of Quebec under the Quebec Act of 1774. King George III granted seigneurial title to Admiral Sir Isaac Coffin in 1798 as a reward for his services to the British Empire, and the Coffins retained control of the islands for the next century. The hardships they inflicted on their Acadian tenants forced many of the settlers into exile, this time to the north shore of the St. Lawrence. It was not until 1895 that the Acadian settlers obtained the rights to the land that they had painstakingly cleared and developed.

Economy – Traditionally the Acadians were skilled fishermen and farmers. Fishing and agriculture were supplemented by logging in the 19C, which accounts for the bare hills found on the islands of Entrée and Havre aux Maisons. Today, fishing and tourism are the chief economic activities. The islands, actually the visible part of a vast undersea plateau, are surrounded by shoals which are a natural breeding ground for lobster, snow crab, scallops, and other shellfish. Cod, haddock, flounder, mackerel, and ocean perch are also found. These fish are processed at the Madelipêche plant near the port at Cap-aux-Meules and transported to the mainland for sale. Another economic activity is salt mining on Dune du Nord; the salt is used to de-ice Quebec roads in wintertime.

MAGDALEN ISLANDS TODAY

Architecture – The Magdalen Islands have developed distinctive building types, although even the oldest constructions date back to only 1850. The earliest known type of structure is the fisherman's cottage with adjoining subsistence farm. These cottages consist of a small, single-story building with two rooms on the first floor and a small room in the attic. Larger houses were built after 1900, with four rooms on each floor. Many traditional homes feature mansard roofs, adopted from the presbyteries and convents that appeared on the islands about 1875.

The large wooden churches at Bassin, La Vernière and Grande Entrée are designed in the style of Catholic churches in the Maritime Provinces (such as Church Point), while numerous Protestant churches bear witness to an active anglophone community. In the 1960s several new parishes were created on the islands, resulting in an unusually large number of contemporary religious churches in this part of Quebec.

Landscape – The Magdalen Islands' most striking features are the **rock formations** cut into the land by the pounding sea. In places, the red sandstone cliffs have been sculpted into arches, tunnels, caves, and defiant promontories topped by emerald-green grass. Expansive white beaches stretch away to meet the blue sea, creating a multicolored seascape that is both savage and serene.

Vegetation – Tall trees on the island are rare: Those that escaped the 19C lumbermen's axes have been twisted into unique, tortured shapes by the winds. Wildflowers abound in spring and summer. The **pitcher plant**, a carnivorous plant found in peat bogs, captures insects by drowning them in fluid secreted in its pitcher-shaped leaves. In freshwater marshes, the **multicolored iris** grows in colonies that are sometimes quite dense. Erosion is controlled by **dune hay** (*ammophile*), with its expansive root system, and moss, covering the dunes.

Wildlife – The archipelago's location in the middle of the Gulf of St. Lawrence makes it an ideal resting spot for migratory birds. Many species nest here year-round, including the Atlantic Puffin, the northern gannet and the endangered piping plover. The rare snowy owl (Quebec's bird emblem) is indigenous to the islands. Gray, common, and Greenland seals can also be found on many deserted beaches and islets.

DRIVING TOURS

ÎLE DU CAP-AUX-MEULES★★ (CAP AUX MEULES ISLAND)

The largest of the islands, this is the archipelago's commercial and administrative center. Its three separate municipal districts (Cap-aux-Meules, Fatima and Étang-du-Nord) are connected by scenic drives through the forested hills and along the coast.

The island was named for the millstones, or *meules,* quarried from the cape overlooking the port.

The quaint **port** at Cap-aux-Meules is the archipelago's lively gateway. Evenings are a good time for a stroll to observe a variety of boats and trawlers, some drydocked for repairs, others being readied for the next day's fishing.

Take Rte. 199 (chemin Principal) west to La Vernière. In La Vernière, Rte. 199 intersects with Chemin de l'Église.

Butte-du-Vent (Vent Hillock)

The chemin de l'Église leads up into the hills toward the Butte du Vent (*turn left on chemin Cormier and immediately right on chemin des Arsène; caution is advised on the unpaved roads; four-wheel-drive vehicle strongly recommended*). This is the highest point on the island, affording extensive **views★★** of the entire archipelago and Plaisance Bay.

Return to chemin de l'Église, turn left on chemin des Huet, then right on chemin des Caps to the municipality of Fatima.

Église Notre-Dame-du-Rosaire★★ (Church of Our Lady of the Rosary)

709 chemin des Caps, in Fatima. Open year-round daily 8am–5pm. 418-986-2685.

A lovely example of contemporary religious architecture, the church celebrates the archipelago's maritime way of life. From the outside the building resembles a scallop shell; the interior abounds in nautical symbolism, including porthole windows, an altar and pulpit evoking a breakwater, and recessed Stations of the Cross scattered across the wall in a wave pattern. The church's design, by Jean-Claude Leclerc, is reminiscent of the Ronchamps chapel in eastern France by the renowned 20C architect Le Corbusier.

Return south on chemin des Caps. Turn right on chemin de la Belle-Anse and drive to the coast.

Formations rocheuses★★ (Rock formations)

Visitors can walk northward along the coast from chemin de la Belle-Anse to **Cap au Trou** (Cape Trou) to see some of the most dramatic formations on the archipelago. Here the sea has bitten savagely into the red sandstone, leaving deep fissures and jutting promontories. In places where the arches have collapsed, only solitary columns of stone withstand the force of the sea. (*Note: the cliffs can be unstable; avoid the edges and use caution when walking in this area*).

Continue south on chemin de la Belle-Anse; turn right on chemin des Caps, then right on chemin de l'Étang-du-Nord.

Other impressive rock formations can be found along the coast near Étang-du-Nord, where a small, lively port provides a haven for numerous fishing trawlers. A stroll along rugged **Cap à Savage** (Cape Savage) is highlighted by good views of Cap aux Meules' western coast and of tiny **Île aux Goélands** (Goélands Island), named for the large gulls (*goélands* in French) that flock there.

Return to Cap-aux-Meules.

ÎLE DU HAVRE-AUBERT★ (HAVRE AUBERT ISLAND)

The gently rolling hills of the southernmost island in the archipelago are the setting for some of the prettiest examples of local domestic architecture. The community of Havre-Aubert is the center of the island's cultural life.

La Grave★

Northeast of Havre-Aubert.

This historic site takes its name from the words "la grave" from the word grève, meaning pebbly or sandy shore, in reference to the meeting place where merchants came to buy the fishermen's salted and dried products. Here, some 15 gray-shingled buildings line the road that skirts a small bay and leads out to Cape Grindley. This historic site includes stores, an ironworks, two **chafauds** (sheds where cod was dried and prepared) and several warehouses. Abandoned by the fishing industry, the buildings now house artisans' boutiques, where craftspeople create and sell objects made from local materials such as sand, alabaster, and sealskin.

Aquarium des Îles (Aquarium of the Islands)

Open daily mid-Jul–mid-Aug 10am–6pm; end Jun–mid-Jul and mid-Aug–Sept 10am–5pm. $8, children (ages 6-17) $5. 418-937-2277. www.aquariumdesiles.com.

Tanks of fish native to the archipelago surround a large, open pool where visitors can handle the fish. On the upper floors, a gallery features displays which explain and demonstrate the methods of fish preservation and processing (drying, smoking, and canning) that enable Madelinot fishermen to export their catches.

Musée de la Mer★ (Museum of the Sea)

Cape Gridley, Havre-Aubert, adjacent to La Grave. Open late Jun–late Sept Mon–Fri 9am–6pm, Sat–Sun 10am–6pm; rest of the year Mon–Fri 9am–5pm. $8. 418-937-5711. www.tourismeilesdelamadeleine.com/musee.

Here, displays of boats, navigational instruments and diverse artifacts acquaint visitors with the maritime history and culture of the Magdalen Islands. The exhibit also covers fishing methods and presents the story of the "ponchon," a mail barrel that was the only means of communication during February of 1910, when a severed telegraph cable resulted in the archipelago's complete isolation from the mainland.

From La Grave, return to the center of the island via Rte. 199, bearing left at Chemin du Bassin.

The scenic drive through the community of Bassin and along Anse-à-la-Cabane winds past colorful houses typical of the islands. Many structures feature mansard-style roofs; others have verandas and balconies, with finely crafted posts and railings and intricately carved corbels.

Église Saint-Francois-Xavier (St. Francis-Xavier Church)

In Bassin. Open year-round daily 8am–5pm. ♿ P ✆418-937-5580.
This large wooden church was built in 1939, in the Romanesque Revival style. The presbytery (1876), topped by multiple mansard roofs, is the best example of Second Empire architecture on the islands.

ÎLE DU HAVRE-AUX-MAISONS★ (HAVRE AUX MAISONS ISLAND)

One of the prettiest islands in the archipelago, Havre aux Maisons has retained its rural charm, with its scattered houses, winding roads, farmland and **baraques**—small buildings with sliding roofs designed to shelter hay. Several scenic drives skirt the coastline, affording charming views.

At Havre aux Maisons Island, turn left at chemin du Cap-Rouge, and again at chemin des Cyrs for views of Petite Bay, Cochons Island and La Pointe.

At **La Pointe**, small wharves buzz with activity. Lobster is sold live or cooked, and visitors can watch clams being cleaned and prepared.

Return to Rte. 199 and continue to chemin Central.

Église de Sainte-Madeleine (Saint Magdalen Church)

25 chemin Central. Open year-round daily 8:30am–5pm. ♿ ✆418-969-2212.
Built in 1969, the structure features great upward curves that unite the church and the presbytery around a central entrance. The nave, lit by a windowed wall, is in the form of an amphitheater. Its low ceiling confers a sense of intimacy to the vast space.

Return to Rte. 199 and turn left on chemin de la Pointe-Basse.

The drive to the harbor at Pointe-Basse, along the chemin du Quai (on the right), passes by a complex of abandoned fumoirs, large wooden smokehouses filled with rods on which the fish were hung during the smoking process.

Return to chemin de la Pointe-Basse.

The road offers views of this island's **rock formations**, which are concentrated around Anse-à-Firmin and Cape Alright. At **Dune du Sud★**, visitors will find a superb, wide beach and relatively calm currents.

Continue on chemin de la Pointe-Basse, which runs along the coast and becomes chemin des Échoueries before turning around and heading back to Rte. 199.

ADDITIONAL SIGHTS

EASTERN ISLANDS

The easternmost islands of the archipelago are connected to the others by **Dune du Nord**, a narrow ridge. North of the dune is a government-operated **salt mine** (mines Seleines), which produces salt used to de-ice Quebec's roads in winter.

Municipality of Grosse-Île

The smallest of the contiguous islands is inhabited mainly by English-speaking descendants of Scottish tenant farmers who arrived in the late 18C, having been forced off the lands they tended in their native Scotland, as a result of the development of sheep-rearing. It is here that the traditional lifestyle based on fishing and agriculture has changed the least. Grosse-Île (population 490) is governed by a municipal administration distinct from the rest of the Îles de la Madeleine municipality.

East Point National Wildlife Reserve

Open Jun 24–Aug. Information on the reserve: the Canadian Wildlife Service ✆1-800-668-6767.

Magdalen Islands glass blower

©Gregory B. Gallagher/Michelin

MAGDALEN ISLANDS ARTS AND CRAFTS

The Magdalen Islands are home to a number of artists' studios and craft workshops open to the public. Island artists and artisans use local materials such as wood, sand, shells, stones, and even algae to fashion a variety of items for sale. Here's a selection of studios and galleries:

Île du Cap-aux-Meules Boutique d'Art Tendance – *715 chemin Principal à, Cap-aux-Meules. ℘418-986-5111. www.art-tendance.ca.* Alabaster stone, sand, glass and wood objects; paintings accented with algae; greeting cards incorporating sand; shell brooches; and stained-glass works.

Galerie-boutique Le Flâneur – *1944 chemin de l'Étang-du-Nord. ℘418-986-6526.* Art gallery with restaurant and tea room. Watercolors and other paintings, as well as crafted dolls. A delicious home-made selection of teas and desserts.

Île du Havre-Aubert Galerie d'Art La Baraque – *489 chemin du Bassin, Bassin, Havre-Aubert. ℘418-937-5678.* Objects crafted from local alabaster stone; sculptures; watercolors and other paintings; and decorative sweaters.

La Banquise du Golfe – *998 chemin de la Grave, La Grave, Havre-Aubert. ℘418-937-5209.* Hand-knit clothing designed in Canada; watercolors and acrylic paintings; pottery made by Magdalen Islanders; and solid-brass objects.

Boutique Émerance – *949 chemin de La Grave, La Grave, Havre-Aubert. ℘418-937-9058.* Locally crafted jewelry: One-of-a-kind creations and wearables fashioned from precious metals.

Les Artisans du sable – *907 chemin de La Grave, La Grave, Havre-Aubert. ℘418-937-2917.* www.artisandusable.com. This remarkable boutique is a member of the Economusee Network, and features sand-made sculptures, big and small, in the sandy universe that is the Magdalens. You can watch the sculptures being made. During the annual sandcastle festival, most people congregate here.

Île du Havre-aux-Maisons Verrerie La Méduse – *638 Rte. 199, Havre-aux-Maisons. ℘418-969-4681. www.meduse.qc.ca.* Blown-glass objects and small sculptures. Artists may be seen at work in this glass-art studio.

Bordered to the southeast by a vast beach, this 1,440ha/3,557-acre area offers an excellent introduction to the world of sand dunes: their wildlife (seals, migratory birds), flora (dune hay) and glorious topography (beaches, marshes).

Plage de la Grande-Échouerie★★ (Grand Échouerie Beach)

This seemingly endless expanse of sand that stretches out and around the easternmost point of the wildlife reserve is considered the archipelago's loveliest beach. The term *échouerie* refers to the rocky ledges where walruses bask in the sun.

Île de la Grande-Entrée★

Lobster fishing formed the basis for settlement of this small stretch of land, which was colonized in 1870.

Pointe Old-Harry (Old Harry Point)

Grand Échouerie Beach leads to this point, now a small harbor protected by a typical Madelinot jetty made of dolosse, or anchor-shaped cement blocks. Walrus hunting, which began in the 17C, brought the first European settlers to the islands. The walruses were slaughtered and processed at Old Harry. Rte. 199 runs the length of the island, ending at the small fishing port of Grande Entrée, where docks and fishing boats are painted in bright colors.

Coastal hiking trails

These trails afford some of the archipelago's most impressive **views★★★** of jagged cliffs and jutting promontories, tidal pools and vast beaches, twisted trees, and colorful wildflowers. From the parking lot at the end of chemin des Pealey, hikers in search of vast panoramas can explore La Bluff and Boudreau Island, for vistas extending as far as Pointe-de-l'Est (East Point).

ÎLE D'ENTRÉE (ENTRY ISLAND)

Société des traversiers de Québec Ferry from Cap-aux-Meules harbor May–Dec, Mon–Sat 7:30am and 3pm crossings. Reservations recommended in summer. $31. 418 986-3278 or contact the Tourism Association office: 418-986-2245 or 1-877-624-4437. www.traversiers.com.

The only inhabited island that remains detached from the others, this outpost is home to around 200 English-speaking residents. Its smooth, treeless hills are laced with trails from which hikers can view fascinating rock formations and wildlife, especially the cormorant. From Big Hill, the highest peak in the islands (174m/571ft), the **view** embraces the entire archipelago.

ADDRESSES

STAY

Inns, hotels, motels, and B&Bs are concentrated on the islands of Cap aux Meules, Havre aux Maisons, and Havre Aubert. In addition, many residents offer B&B accommodation, as well as rooms, cottages, and houses for rent. It is advisable to reserve lodging well in advance for a stay during the peak tourism months of July and August. Contact the Tourism Association.

Domaine du Vieux-Couvent – *292 Rte. 199, Havre aux Maisons. 418-969-2233. www.domaineduvieuxcouvent.com.* The owners of this refurbished heritage convent welcome guests like old friends and take a sincere interest in every aspect of your happiness while touring their idyllic islands. Inspired gourmet cuisine in Le Réfectoire, plus goose-down comforters, contemporary decor in ten bedrooms, a friendly pub, and a central location. Ask about the You & Me package.

EAT

Eating is one of the highlights of the Magdalen Islands. Lobster is very affordable in season (early May to early July), while snow crab, scallops, and delicious local fish are cooked as regional specialties like *pot-en-pot,* or as ingredients in French classics like *bouillabaisse*.

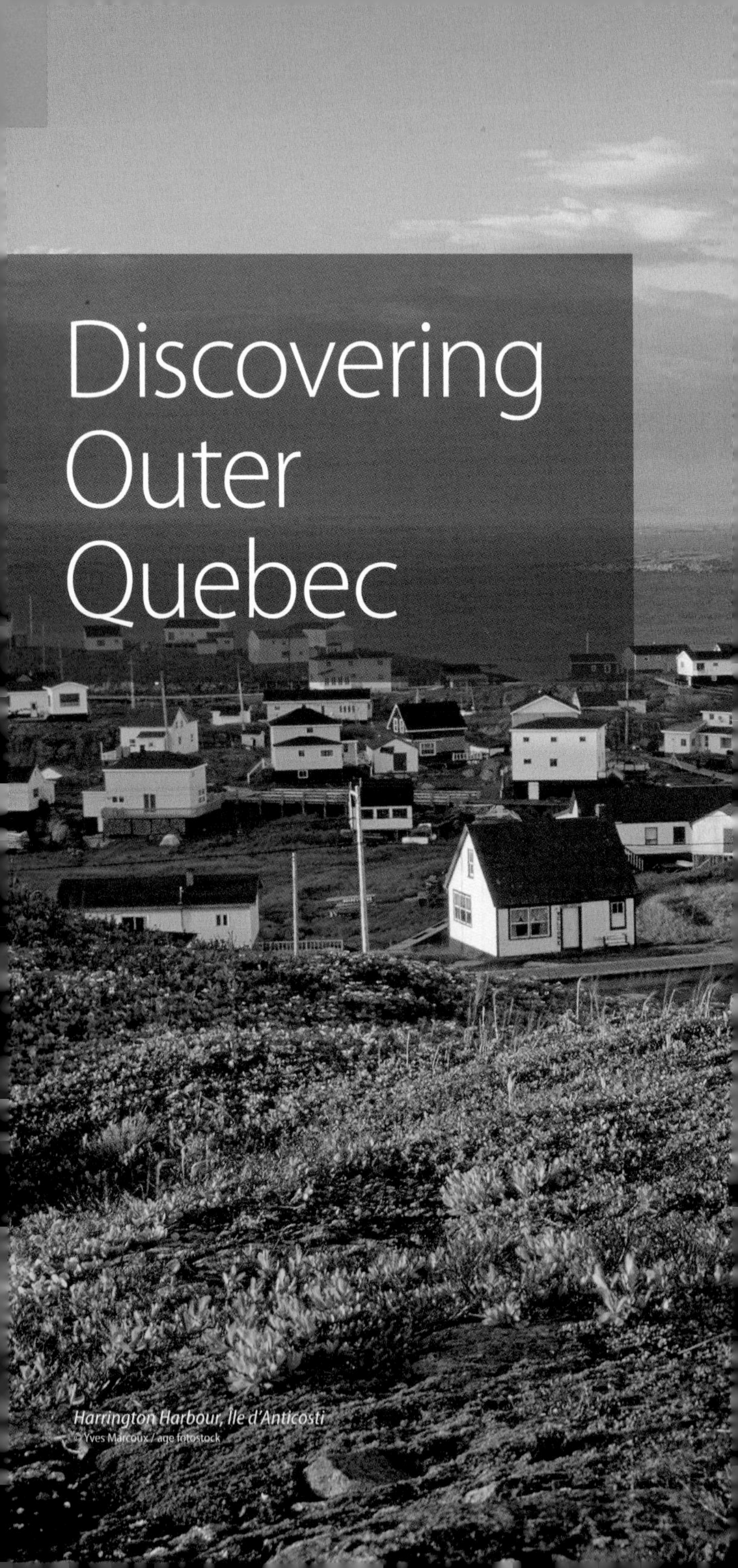

Discovering Outer Quebec

Harrington Harbour, Île d'Anticosti

© Yves Marcoux / age fotostock

Outer Quebec

Caniapiscau sunset

© Gregory B. Gallagher/Michelin

Côte-Nord

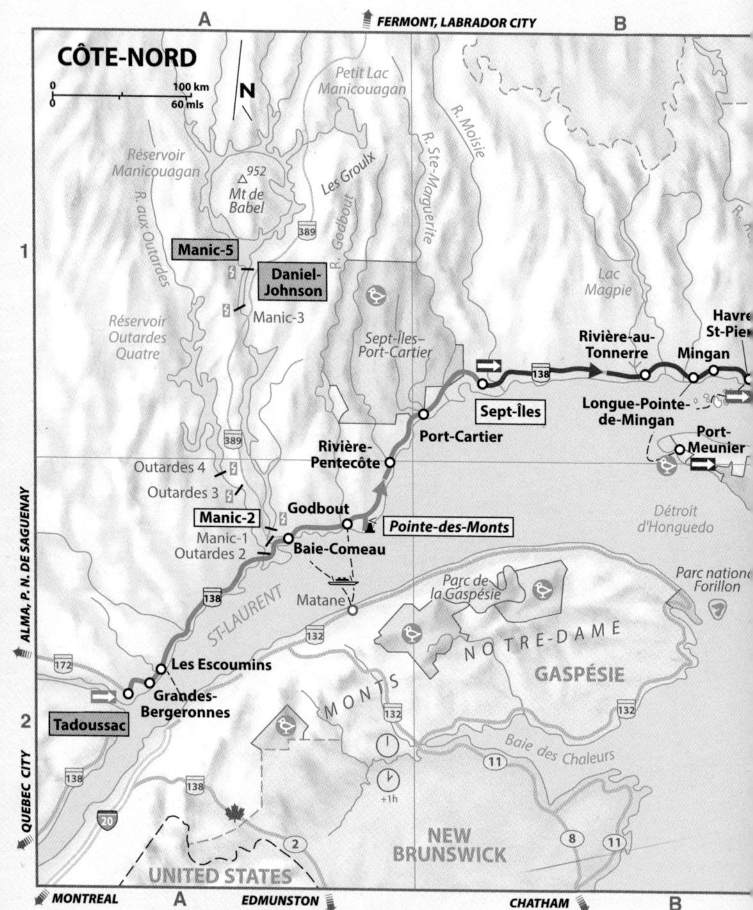

CÔTE-NORD
FERMONT, LABRADOR CITY
ALMA, P. N. DE SAGUENAY
QUEBEC CITY
MONTREAL
EDMUNSTON
CHATHAM
Réservoir Manicouagan
Mt de Babel
Petit Lac Manicouagan
Les Groulx
R. Godbout
R. Ste-Marguerite
R. Moisie
R. aux Outardes
Manic-5
Daniel-Johnson
Manic-3
Réservoir Outardes Quatre
Sept-Îles–Port-Cartier
Lac Magpie
Rivière-au-Tonnerre
Mingan
Longue-Pointe-de-Mingan
Sept-Îles
Port-Cartier
Rivière-Pentecôte
Port-Meunier
Outardes 4
Outardes 3
Manic-2
Godbout
Pointe-des-Monts
Manic-1
Outardes 2
Baie-Comeau
Détroit d'Honguedo
Matane
ST-LAURENT
Parc de la Gaspésie
NOTRE-DAME
GASPÉSIE
MONTS
Les Escoumins
Grandes-Bergeronnes
Tadoussac
Baie des Chaleurs
NEW BRUNSWICK
UNITED STATES

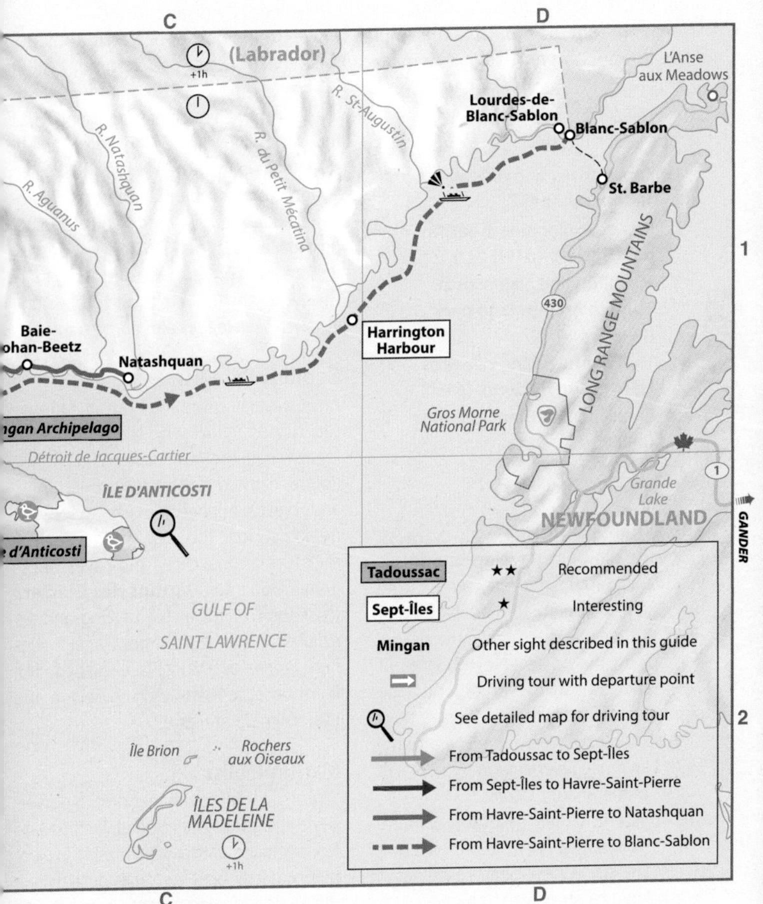

C
D
(Labrador)
+1h
L'Anse aux Meadows
R. St-Augustin
Lourdes-de-Blanc-Sablon
Blanc-Sablon
R. Natashquan
R. du Petit Mécatina
R. Aguanus
St. Barbe
1
LONG RANGE MOUNTAINS
430
Baie-Johan-Beetz
Harrington Harbour
Natashquan
Gros Morne National Park
Mingan Archipelago
Détroit de Jacques-Cartier
ÎLE D'ANTICOSTI
Grande Lake
NEWFOUNDLAND
GANDER
Île d'Anticosti
Tadoussac
★★ Recommended
Sept-Îles
★ Interesting
GULF OF SAINT LAWRENCE
Mingan
Other sight described in this guide
Driving tour with departure point
See detailed map for driving tour
2
Île Brion
Rochers aux Oiseaux
From Tadoussac to Sept-Îles
From Sept-Îles to Havre-Saint-Pierre
ÎLES DE LA MADELEINE
From Havre-Saint-Pierre to Natashquan
From Havre-Saint-Pierre to Blanc-Sablon
C
D

Côte-Nord

One of the few relatively untouched areas in North America left to explore combines long road expanses playing hide-and-seek with the Gulf of Saint Lawrence, stunning primeval geological outcroppings, and a rich cultural backdrop filled with former Basque fishing villages, First Nations communities, and enough Québécois characters to fill a memoir. Most travelers shy away from this distant region for its sheer scale, as one needs to set aside a generous amount of time; but those seeking serendipity will not be disappointed. Stretching from the mouth of the Saguenay River to the border of Newfoundland and Labrador, this north shore domain can be the experience of a lifetime.

Highlights

1. Knolls, coves, and cliffs at **Tadoussac** (p437)
2. Ice Age exploration at **Jardin des Glaciers** (p441)
3. Monoliths and mammals at **Mingan Archipelago park** (p448)
4. The colorful fishing village of **Harrington Harbour** (p450)
5. Excavations at **Blanc-Sablon** (p450)

The Whale Route

From the moment travelers and locals venture aboard the free ferry service from Baie-Sainte-Catherine to Tadoussac along Rte. 138, there is excitement in the air.

Perhaps it's the presence of 13 different whale species jostling with other marine mammals for food in the biodiverse waters of the Saguenay River as it mixes with the Saint Lawrence River stream and the salt waters of the Atlantic Ocean.

The mysterious energy one feels here could be because visitors are entering one of the last undeveloped coastlines in North America, stretching from Tadoussac to Blanc-Sablon—some 1,250km/775mi—simply known as "The Whale Route."

Most Beautiful Bay Club

A small pair of hills gives Tadoussac its aboriginal name, meaning "place of lobsters." A member of the international Most Beautiful Bays of the World Club and the epicenter of the Saguenay-Saint-Lawrence Marine Park, this welcoming village is the oldest French settlement in the Americas.

Long before European explorers arrived here, Tadoussac was already a busy trading post for Basque fishermen. Today, the focus is more upon preservation and study than conquest, with academics and professionals often seen in the cafés and restaurants.

Geology Paradise

After traversing the road out of Tadoussac, those familiar with the region stop for a swim in the warm waters of Longue-Pointe, halfway between Les Escoumins and Forestville. It becomes easy to see why geologists love this area, with its ancient rock formations, cliffs, and caves beckoning. Don't miss **Jardins des Glaciers** (*see p441*). Birdwatching, hiking, and sea excursions are the most popular activities from Pointe-des-Monts (see the beautiful lighthouse) to Sept-Îles Archipelago and into Havre-Saint-Pierre.

Maritime Bliss

Visitors marvel at the maritime biodiversity throughout the Mingan Archipelago (connected to Anticosti Island), and explore other coastal places like Natashquan (where the roads end), Harrington Harbour (home of great wooden walkways), Mutton Bay, and Blanc-Sablon, Quebec's easternmost town. At these points, the area feels like another continent.

Côte-Nord★

Manicouagan-Duplessis

The Côte-Nord, or North Shore, extends from the mouth of the Saguenay River north to the Labrador border. The Upper North Shore, the southernmost region, stretches from Tadoussac to Sept-Îles, and the Middle North Shore from Sept-Îles to Havre-Saint-Pierre. The Lower North Shore, so named because it is the closest to the ocean, encompasses the area between Havre-Saint-Pierre and Blanc-Sablon. In this vast expanse of taiga, the majority of towns and villages can be reached only by plane or boat.

- **Population:** 94, 909.
- **Michelin Map:** pp434–435.
- **Info:** 197 Rue des Pionniers, Tadoussac. ☏418-235-4744, 1-888-463-5319. www.tourismemanicouagan.com.
- **Location:** Rte. 138 traverses the Côte-Nord from Tadoussac to Natashquan. Most of the Lower North Shore is accessible only by boat or plane.
- **Don't Miss:** Manic-5 dam, Mingan National Park islands.
- **Timing:** From Tadoussac, Natashquan is 800km/500mi on Rte. 138. Unless you continue with your vehicle on board the M/V *Nordik Express* to Labrador and Newfoundland, you will need to retrace your route to return. From Baie-Comeau take a day trip (6hr there and back) along the Manicouagan River to the Manic-5 Daniel Johnson Dam. From Baie-Comeau, allow 3.5 hours to drive to Sept-Îles. Plan to spend a day at the Mingan Archipelago (about a 2.5hrs' drive farther east).

A BIT OF HISTORY

The Inuit and Montagnais have inhabited the area for thousands of years, and the Montagnais, living in seven reserves scattered along the coast, still form a major part of the population. In the late 15C, Basque fishermen came to this region to hunt whales. Fishing remained the primary industry until the 1920s, when pulp mill companies began exploiting the forest resources, thus creating an important forestry industry. In the 1950s, the discovery of rich mineral deposits, primarily iron ore, prompted another surge of economic growth, as did the harnessing of the Manicouagan and Outardes rivers for hydroelectricity in the early 1960s. The Manicouagan River basin was classified as a UNESCO Biosphere Reserve in 2007.

DRIVING TOURS

TADOUSSAC TO SEPT-ÎLES

450km/279mi by Rte. 138.

Tadoussac★★

Maison du tourisme. 197 rue des Pionniers. ☏418-235-4744 or 1-866-235-4744. www.tadoussac.com.

Situated at the mouth of the Saguenay River, Tadoussac occupies a beautiful **site★★** on the cliffs and sand dunes lining the north shore of the St. Lawrence. Its name is derived from the Montagnais word tatoushak, meaning "knolls," a reference to the pair of small hills west of the community. A boardwalk extends alongside the St. Lawrence linking the old chapel and the Chauvin trading post, just beneath the Hôtel Tadoussac, a long, red-roofed structure dating from 1941. Paths circle Pointe de l'Islet, which borders the bay, providing fine views of the landscape; others cross the knolls to a small cove (Anse-à-l'eau), where the ferry from Baie-Sainte-Catherine docks. The extremely lively town attracts a growing number of visitors, who come to observe the whales that visit the plankton-rich waters at the mouth of the Saguenay a few months each year.

Tadoussac

© Robert Chiasson / age fotostock

Petite Chapelle de Tadoussac (Indian Chapel)

On Rue du Bord-de-l'Eau. Open mid-Jun–early Sept daily 9am–8pm; early Sept–early Oct 9am–6pm. $3. 418-235-1415.

The small chapel, the oldest wooden church in North America, was built in 1747 by the Jesuit missionary, Claude-Godefroy Cocquart. The chapel houses a fine collection of religious objects.

Chauvin Trading Post

157 Rue du Bord-de-l'Eau. Open early Jun–mid-Oct daily 10am–7pm; early–mid-Jun and rest of Sept–mid-Oct daily 10am–6pm. $4. 418-235-4657.

This log structure with its steeply pitched roof is a reconstruction of Pierre Chauvin's fur trading post of 1600. Inside, old photographs as well as archeological and historical displays explain the fur trade between the Montagnais Indians and the French. The collection focuses on the Côte-Nord region.

Maison des dunes (House of the Sand Dunes)

4km/2.5mi east on Rue des Pionniers to 750 chemin Moulin Baude.

Located in a stone house (1915), an **interpretation center** (open mid-Jun–mid-Sept daily 10am–5pm; 418-232-6249) provides insight into the formation of the lovely marine terraces of fine sand lining the Saint Lawrence. Sparrows. Birds of prey are visible here from August to October.

Parc National du fjord du Saguenay (secteur de la baie de Tadoussac)★★

Access via Maison des Dunes (*see above*). Open year-round daily. $8.50, children 17 years and younger, free. 418-272-1556 or 1-800-665-6527. www.sepaq.com.

The Saguenay Park was set up in 1983 to create a protected area around the banks of the fjord. It extends over some 300sq km/186sq mi along a stretch of around 100km/62mi from La Baie (*see SAGUENAY*) to Tadoussac. The park offers many recreational opportunities.

Crossing the Fjord★★

Croisières du Fjord. Departs from quai de la marina. $55. 418-543-7630 and 1-800-363-7248. www.croisieresdufjord.com.

History of Tadoussac

Tadoussac was a meeting place for trade well before the arrival of Jacques Cartier on these shores, in 1535. In 1600, Pierre Chauvin built Canada's first fur trading post on this spot, and later the Jesuits established a mission. Tadoussac became a port of call for all vessels crossing the Atlantic. In 1628 the village was captured by the Kirke brothers, British adventurers, but it later returned to French hands and remained a trading center until 1839, when the first permanent residents arrived and erected a sawmill. With the advent of the steamship, the community developed as a choice resort in the mid-19C.

The Route of the Whales

Humpback whale tail

© Sebastien Cote / iStockphoto.com

Every June, Atlantic Ocean whales swim up the St. Lawrence River to the mouth of the Saguenay River. Here, the salty St. Lawrence and the fresh waters of the Saguenay combine to create a rich ecosystem for a multitude of flora and fauna. Krill and caplin, drawn by the plankton flourishing in these waters, attract whales, which consume several tonnes of the small sea creatures daily.

Fifteen species of whales have been sighted here, the most common being the **fin**, **pilot**, **harbor**, and **minke**. There is also a significant population of **belugas**. Occasionally, **humpback** whales are sighted, and lucky tourists may glimpse the huge **blue whale**, which is known to reach a length of 25m/82ft (blue whales in the southern hemisphere can grow to 30m/98.4ft), making it the largest mammal on earth. Seven individual blue whales regularly visit these waters.

Along the Route des Baleines (whale route), which stretches 900km/560mi from Baie-Sainte-Catherine (*see CÔTE-NORD*), on the opposite bank of the Saguenay, to the far east of Duplessis, there are several sites where you can watch the whales from the coast or in a boat. These are mainly in Tadoussac, but also at Les Escoumins, at the Pointe-des-Monts lighthouse, Sept-Îles, and Longue-Pointe-de-Mingan.

To fully appreciate the deep and wide Saguenay fjord—an ancient glacial valley flanked by precipitous cliffs—visitors are advised to take a boat trip.

Hikes

The Baie-de-Tadoussac section offers several short walking trails, including the Sentier de la Pointe de l'Islet, which goes to the end of the headland that encloses the bay. The path leads to a site for land observation of marine mammals (walk starts from the end of the federal wharf at quai fédéral de Tadoussac, 30min). Another footpath is the sentier de la Colline-de-l'Anse-à-l'Eau (starts from parking area for the park, Rte. 138 at the exit from the ferry, 45min).

Marine Mammal Interpretation Center

108 Rue de la Cale Sèche, near the pier. Open daily mid-May–early Jun noon–5pm; mid-Jun 9am–6pm; late Jun–late Sept 9am–8pm; end of Sept–mid-Oct 11am–6pm. $10.50. 418-235-4701. http://baleinesendirect.org.

This interpretation center (CIMM) presents interesting displays, videos, and slide shows on the marine life of this area, in particular whales, seals, and cormorants.

Whale-watching Tours★★

Depart from the Tadoussac marina May–Nov, at least three departures daily. Round-trip 3hrs. English and French commentary. Reservations required; $69, children $33 or $169 family (2 adults and 2 children). Croisières AML. 1-866-856-6668. www.croisieresaml.com.

At Tadoussac, the St. Lawrence is more than 10km/6.2mi wide. The boats head for the center, where the whales surface to breathe and dive to search for food. It is a magnificent experience to see these colossal creatures.

The entrance to the Saguenay fjord is marked by a lighthouse that stands 15m/49ft high and is visible for nearly 50km/31mi.

Ferry for Baie Sainte-Catherine

Société des traversiers du Québec. ♿ Departing from the wharf (quai de l'Anse-au-Portage). One way 10min. Free. 1- 877-787-7483. www.traversiers.gouv.qc.ca.

The ferry operates all year round and is the only means of crossing the mouth of the Saguenay for vehicles traveling on Route 138. The journey is guaranteed to impress, with the deep Saguenay Fjord to your right and the majestic waters of the St. Lawrence River to the left. In addition, whales or other marine mammals can sometimes be spotted during the short crossing.

26km/16mi from Tadoussac on Route 138, through Petites-Bergeronnes.

Grandes-Bergeronnes

Named Bergeronnettes (wagtails) by Samuel de Champlain in 1603, after he spotted a flock of these yellow, long-tailed birds, the region had already been frequented by Basque fishermen and Montagnais long before. The first European settlers arrived in 1844 and erected a flour mill in Petites-Bergeronnes and a sawmill in Grandes-Bergeronnes.

Today **whale watching** is the main attraction. Favorable ecological conditions in the area produce an abundance of plankton, which in turn attracts blue whales and belugas to these waters. It is possible to observe them at sea or from the shore at Cap-de-Bon-Désir.

Archeo-Topo Interpretation Center

498 Rue de la Mer, Les Bergeronnes (15 minutes northeast on Rte. 138 from Tadoussac). Open daily mid-May–Jun, and Sept–mid-Oct 9am–5pm; Jul–Aug daily 8am–8pm. $6. 418-232-6286. www.archeotopo.com.

Archeological exhibits here focus on the excavations carried out in the Grandes-Bergeronnes region, which have uncovered traces of human occupation dating back 5,500 years.

Cap-de-Bon-Désir Nature Interpretation and Observation Center

6km/3.7mi east of Grandes-Bergeronnes at 13 chemin du Cap-de-Bon-Désir. Les Bergeronnes. Open mid-Jun–early Sept daily 9am–6pm; rest of Sept–early Oct Wed–Sun 9am–5pm. $7.80. 418-232-6751.

Part of the Parc marin du Saguenay–Saint-Laurent (Saguenay–Saint-Lawrence Marine Park), the lighthouse center provides various activities and information to introduce visitors to regional history and the underwater environment of the estuary. Whales and other marine mammals are often visible from the observation tower *(binoculars available for rent)*.

Les Escoumins

13km/8mi.

Basque fishermen established this small community in the late 15C, naming it Esquemin. Now known as Les Escoumins, the charming town offers ideal spots for whale watching and is noteworthy for its fishing and scuba diving. When crossing over the Escoumins River, visitors can see an unusual construction to the left: a **salmon ladder** designed to help the salmon as they swim upstream to spawn in the waters where they were born.

Baie-Comeau

19 avenue Marquette . 418-296-4931 and 1-888-589-6497. www.ville.baie-comeau.qc.ca. 160km/99mi.

Named for Napoléon-Alexandre Comeau, a trapper, geologist and naturalist from Côte-Nord, the city of 48,789 inhabitants traces its industrial beginnings to Col. Robert McCormick and his establishment of the Quebec North Shore Paper Co. in 1936.

Constructed of multicolored granite stones and reminiscent of the works of the 20C French modernist, Auguste Perret, **Cathédrale Saint-Jean-Eudes** (open during Masses only, Wed, Fri–Sat 7.15pm, Sun 10am; ♿ P 418-589-2370) overlooks the mouth of the Manicouagan River. Situated in the Marquette sector to the east, **Amélie Quarter** boasts fine homes built in the 1930s. On Rue Cabot stands **Le Manoir Hotel**, rebuilt in the French Colonial style. **Église Sainte-Amélie** (37 Ave. Marquette; open Mon–Fri 9am–11:45am and 1pm–6pm; ♿ 🅿 ✆418-296-5578) is dedicated to the memory of Amélie McCormick, wife of the town's founder and benefactor. The **frescoes★** adorning the interior are the work of Italian artist Guido Nincheri and were restored in 1996.

Jardin des Glaciers

3 rue Denonville, 12km/7.5mi E of Baie-Comeau on Rte. 138. Open daily Jun–mid-Aug 8am–7pm; late Aug–early Sept 8am–6pm; mid-Sept–early Oct 9am–5pm. $15. ✆1-877-296-0182. www.jardindesglaciers.com.

An interpretation center exploring this section of the banks of the St. Lawrence, which was shaped over 10,000 years ago by the last glacial period. The center tackles the connections between man and the environment with an emphasis on education and raising awareness of ecological issues. Activities focus on three areas: the display zone (multimedia presentations, film screenings); the nature zone (excursions, guided visits to sites of scientific interest, excavation activities); and the adrenalin zone (hiking, extreme sports, wild camping).

EXCURSION

Manic-Outardes Complex

430km/267mi round-trip from Baie-Comeau on Route 389.

Today the combined capacity of Manic's seven power plants is 7,300 megawatts (1 megawatt = 1,000,000 watts). A network of 735,000-volt power lines (the first of this type used for commercial purposes) transports electricity from the plants to major cities. The three power plants comprising the **Outardes Complex** (closed to the public) are fed by a 652sq km/252sq mi reservoir established 93km/58mi upstream from the confluence of the Outardes and St. Lawrence rivers. Most of the dams and dikes of the Outardes complex are earth-and-rockfill constructions made of material found near the sites.

Begun in 1959, the mammoth undertaking of harnessing the energy of the Manicouagan and Outardes rivers took 20 years to complete. The project led to the development of new technologies that surpassed any previous engineering feats and established several world records. The completion of the seven power plants involved the mobilization of thousands of men and women and the transportation of tons of material into the vast forest wilderness of the Manicouagan region.

Beneath the site chosen for the construction of the main dam at Manic-3, permeable alluvial deposits threatened to allow water seepage into the projected structure. To prevent such seepage, engineers sank a double concrete wall 131m/429.8ft into the earth's surface, creating the world's largest waterproof shield.

Manic-2★

Visit by guided tour (1hr30min) only, 24 Jun–end Aug, daily 9.30am, 11.30am, 1.30pm and 3.30pm; rest of the year by appointment (7 days in advance) only. (Visitors 18 years and older must show official photo ID before entering facility). 🅿 ✆1-866-526-2642. www.hydroquebec.com.

Guides describe the Manic-Outardes dams and explain how electricity is produced and transmitted to consumers. Scale models complement the talk. Operating since the mid-1960s, Manic-2 was the first power plant of the Manic-Outardes Complex to produce electricity. The giant concrete wall is 94m/308.4ft high and 692m/2,270ft long and is one of the largest hollow-joint gravity dams in the world. Because of its tremendous weight, a gravity dam can withstand the enormous pressure exerted by the water trapped in its reservoir. The power plant, located at the base of the dam, has a head of 70m/229.6ft. The facility's turbine-alternators can generate up to 1,145 megawatts.

MANICOUAGAN-UAPISHKA WORLD RESERVE

Jardin des Glaciers

Baie-Comeau is the base-camp for this massive UNESCO-designated site encompassing over 55,000 sq km/21,000 sq mi. The prestigious status is a difficult journey for any proposed territory in the world. After studying an area extensively, and after designation is finally approved, the UN organization continues to demand sustainable involvement and standards from businesses, aboriginal groups, and residents.

Extending from the coast north through the Manicouagan Region to the Naskapi tribal area of Caniapiscau (Shefferville) and the mining town of Fermont, at the border with Newfoundland and Labrador, access to this pristine wilderness domain is via the Quebec-Labrador route 389-500. The unique Tshiuetin railway from Sept-Îles passes through some spectacular panoramas, especially near the Moisie River.

This is one of the largest such reserves in the world, and strangely can thank the impact of a huge meteor eons ago, creating a round lake and Île Réne-Levasseur at the center. In addition, the preserve contains Jardins des Glaciers, Mont Groulx *(1,100 m/3,600 ft)*, enormous hydroelectric facilities at Manic-5 and **Daniel-Johnson** Dam, and the Saint Lawrence Shipwreck Center at Baie-Trinité east of the old trading port of Godbout.

Réserve mondiale de la biosphère Manicouagan-Uapishka: www.rmbmu.com.

Manic-5★★

21km/13mi from Baie-Comeau by the 389. Guided tours (2hrs) 24 Jun–late Aug daily 9.30am, 11.30am, 1.30pm, and 3.30pm. No charge. 866-526-2642. www.hydroquebec.com/visitez.

Measuring 214m/702ft in height and 1,314m/4,307ft in length, the spectacular **Daniel Johnson Dam★★** is the largest arch-and-buttress dam in the world. The dam was completed in 1968 after seven years of construction, and is named for the former prime minister of Quebec, Daniel Johnson, who died on the site of the complex on the morning of its inauguration. The dam regulates the water supply to all the power stations of the Manicouagan complex.

With the construction of the dam, two semicircular lakes—the Manicouagan and the Mouchalagane—were united into an immense ring of water encircling an island. The diameter of the reservoir is 65km/40.3mi. A study of the reservoir led geophysicists to theorize that the natural depression of the lakes may have been created by a meteorite that crashed to earth some 200 million years ago. The depression is comparable with a moon crater, and rock found at the site is similar to samples of moon rock brought back to earth by astronauts. The Manic-5 power plant is located approximately 1km/0.6mi downstream from the dam. Its head is 150m/492ft high, and its turbines are capable of producing 1,596 megawatts. Guides present an overview of the dam. Then visitors board a bus that takes them to the base of the massive arches and across the top of the dam overlooking the countryside and the Manicouagan River.

Manic-5 PA

This underground power plant began production in 1989 with four generator sets. The initials "PA" stand for *puissance additionnelle* (additional power) because this new facility provides supplementary power to Manic-5 during peak periods. Its installed capacity is 1,064 megawatts.

Return to Baie-Comeau via Rte. 389.

Godbout

115 r. Pascal-Comeau. 418-568-7462 (during season). 54km/33.5mi northeast of Baie-Comeau.

The village occupies a beautiful **site★** in the bay between Pointe-des-Monts Cape and the mouth of the Godbout River. The village and the river were named for the pilot and navigator, Nicolas Godbout, who settled on Île d'Orléans in 1670. A ferry connects the village to Matane, on the south shore.

Musée Amérindien et Inuit de Godbout (Amerindian and Inuit Museum)

Facing the port, 2km/1.2mi south of Rte. 138. Open late Jun–late Sept daily 9am–10pm. $5. 1381 Chemin Pascal-Comeau. 418-568-7306.

Directors Cècile and Claude Grenier have created a warm and intimate museum exhibiting a fine collection of Inuit art and sculptures, mostly from the Northwest Territories. Splendid photographs of Arctic animals by Fred Bruemmer are hung throughout the museum. An authentic Algonquin bark canoe is suspended in the pottery workshop.

Continue on Rte. 138 for 29km/18mi, turn right on Route du Vieux Phare and continue for 12km/7.4mi.

Phare de Pointe-des-Monts★ (Pointe-des-Monts Lighthouse)

Open mid-Jun–mid-Sept daily 9am–5pm. $12. . Access by a narrow, winding road off Rte. 138. www.pharepointe-de-monts.com. 418-939-2400 or 1-866-369-4083 (off season).

Built in 1830, the 28m/91.8ft lighthouse stands at the point where the St. Lawrence River widens into a gulf. For 150 years the lighthouse served as a home for the lightkeepers and their families. Today the interior houses a small museum that re-creates the lives and duties of the various keepers; also on display are items salvaged from area shipwrecks. Activities organized here include trout and salmon fishing, deep-sea fishing, scuba diving, whale- and seal-watching, and excursions to observe and photograph local fauna, including black bears, ospreys, and gannets. A small inn and several vacation cottages are located on the site.

Return to Rte. 138.

Between Pointe-aux-Anglais and Rivière-Pentecôte, the road passes beside beautiful sandy beaches.

Rivière-Pentecôte

79km/49mi from Godbout.

The village and nearby river were named in the 16C by Jacques Cartier, when he stayed here on Whitsunday (*Pentecôte*). Rivière-Pentecôte was the birthplace of the North Shore's first newspaper, *L'Écho du Labrador,* founded in 1903 by Joseph Laizé, a Eudist missionary. From the tourist information center overlooking the village, the **view★** of the church and the tiny oratory of St. Anne, perched on a cape, is quite picturesque.

Port-Cartier

35km/21.7mi.

Owing to its deep-water port, this industrial and commercial town has become a major center for trans-shipping minerals and cereals in Canada. The town lies on the banks of the Rochers and Dominique rivers, at the point where they empty into the St. Lawrence. The two islands situated at the mouth of the rivers are devoted to recreational use, including swimming, camping and sport fishing (the region is known for its salmon). Located on Île Patterson is the Taiga, a botanical garden of native plants. On Île McCormick, a café-theatre called **Graffiti** (www.legraffiti.ca) exhibits works of local artists, and stages theatrical and musical performances.

Sept-Îles★

1401 Blvd Laure Ouest.
418-962-1238 and 1-888-880-1238.
www.tourismeseptiles.ca.

This dynamic city occupies a superb **site★★** in a large, almost circular bay on the north shore of the Gulf of St. Lawrence. Protected by the islands at its mouth, the bay remains navigable during all seasons, allowing for industrial activity throughout the year. The Baie des Sept-Îles allows for majestic scenery and fantastic sunsets. Today Sept-Îles is the administrative center of the Côte-Nord, and one of the largest municipalities in Quebec, covering 2180sq km/842sq mi. A lot of this area consists of forest, lakes, and rivers.

The earliest known mention of the region of Sept-Îles, or "Seven Islands," dates back to 1535, when Jacques Cartier noted several round islands blocking the entrance to the large bay. In earlier times, Montagnais Indians hunted caribou here. In the 15C, Basque, French, and Spanish fishermen came to the area in search of seals and whales from which they extracted oil much in demand in Europe.

In 1651 Father Jean Dequen arrived on these shores and founded the mission of Ange-Gardien. Several years later, the King of France agreed to the establishment of a series of trading posts, to be rented to French merchants. After the Conquest of New France, the King's posts were entrusted to a number of British merchants. The most influential of these, the Hudson's Bay Company, monopolized fishing, hunting, and fur-trading rights until 1859, after which the region was opened to settlement. In the early 20C, the paper industry became the principal economic activity, with the construction of a hydroelectric dam and pulp mill at Clarke City, today part of Sept-Îles. The paper mill shut down in 1967, but by the second half of the 20C, the transportation of coal and iron ore had boosted the community's economy. The city's natural deep-water port enables ocean-bound ships to trans-ship coal here. The Iron Ore Company of Canada (IOC) owns several wharves in the north-eastern sector of the bay, and Wabush Mines Company operates ore-handling facilities in the Pointe-Noire sector.

Parc du Vieux-Quai (Old Wharf Park)

A boardwalk lines the magnificent bay of Sept-Îles. Seafood enthusiasts can sample shrimp or enjoy a crab sandwich, while enjoying a leisurely stroll along the wharf. The shelters along the boardwalk display crafts by local artisans.

Maison de transmission de la culture innue, Shaputuan

290 Blvd des Montagnais. Open Mon–Fri 8am–4.30pm, Sat–Sun 1pm–4pm. $7. 418-962-4000.

Shaputuan means "the large meeting tent," and this museum devoted to the culture of the Innu people sets out to provide a place for people to come together, for events and activities and for the conservation of the Innu culture. The permanent exhibition illustrates their traditional life cycle and their relationship with time, the land, and life.

Musée régional de la Côte-Nord (North Shore Regional Museum)

500 Blvd Laure. Open late Jun–Labor Day daily 9am–5pm; rest of the year Tue–Fri 10am–5pm (Wed until 8pm), Sat–Sun 1pm–5pm. Closed Dec 23–Jan 6. $7. 418-968-2070. www.mrcn.qc.ca.

The museum of art and history was created by the local artist André Michel, as a reminder of the "eternal youth of this ancient land, its roots and the diverse origins of the great men and women who have lived here." The permanent exhibit "A Never-Ending Shore" describes the 1,100km/682mi of shoreline and forests of black spruce, and the successive waves of population growth that resulted from the exploitation of the area's natural resources.

The museum is housed within **Le Vieux-Poste** (Old Trading Post). Reconstructed according to its 18C-layout uncovered during archeological excavations, this group of buildings surrounded by a palisade occupies a historically significant site. Montagnais Indians and European settlers first traded here three centuries ago, and the site was visited by Jacques Cartier, Louis Jolliet and merchants of the Hudson Bay Company. The site re-creates the atmosphere of a trading post of years past; other exhibits offer an intriguing introduction to the Montagnais-Innu culture.

Another way to get in touch with the Montagnais-Innu culture is to listen to CKAU (90.1 and 104.5FM; www.ckau.com), Maniutenam/Sept-Îles' **aboriginal-run community radio station**. You will hear the Innu, French, and English languages during programming and understand the unique complexities of indigenous life in Quebec.

Parc Régional de l'Archipel des Sept Îles★ (Sept-Îles Regional Park) Virée des îles en bateau (Boat Tour of the Islands)

Cruises depart from Old Wharf ticket counter in front of the marina mid-May–mid-Oct daily 8am–5.15pm (several departures a day). Round-trip 3hrs. French and English commentary. Reservations suggested 24hrs ahead, but required in low season. $60 (from ticket counter in front of the marina). ℘418-968-2173 (in summer season); www.lescroisieresducapitaine.com, or contact Tourisme Sept-Îles ℘418-962-1238; www.tourismeseptiles.ca.

Scenic **cruises** by ferry, riverboat, and raft offer an introduction to the region, its history, and the natural beauty of the Sept-Îles archipelago. The lighthouse at the entrance to the bay rises on **Île du Corossol** (Corossol Island), a bird sanctuary with many species, including gulls, terns, and puffins.

Île Grande Basque

Ferry to island departs from Old Wharf ticket counter in front of the marina, Jun–Sept daily 9am–6.30pm. One-way 10–20min. Reservations suggested. www.lescroisieresducaptiaine.com. $25, rustic camping permitted on the island $10/night. Tourisme Sept-Îles ℘418-962-1238. www.tourismeseptiles.ca.

Located closest to the city, La Grande Basque is the only island that has been developed for hiking, picnicking, and camping. Numerous trails meander through grandiose and varied landscapes: huge rocky ridges, immense cliffs, and a peat bog. Beautiful sandy beaches line the western shore. Islands also reachable by sea kayak (with guided tour or rental kayak).

Schefferville (Kawawachikamach)

The mining town of Schefferville abuts the provincial boundary between Quebec and Labrador (province of Newfoundland-and-Labrador). It lies on the northern fringe of the boreal forest, just south of the tundra, on the watershed of the Atlantic and Hudson Strait/Hudson Bay drainage basins. Originally planned for a large population, Schefferville boasts a modern infrastructure. The iron ore mining went on from 1954 to 1982. An extensive road system links the mining sites, their equipment still in place, and leads to a fascinating variety of lakes and mountain ridges.

During its heyday, close to 8,000 people lived in this frontier town; a gigantic statue known as the Iron Man recalls the town's former prosperity. Today almost a ghost town, Schefferville is mainly a service center for the Native population; mining continues at a much slower pace. It has also become a departure point for excursions to the Great North of Quebec. Outfitters sell mainly all-inclusive packages (flights, lodgings, meals, fishing/hunting equipment, guides, etc.).

For more than 40 years, Montreal's McGill University has operated a **Subarctic Research Station** near the airport. The station hosts students and researchers year-round.

Matimekosh

Just north of Schefferville, on foot or by car by municipal road.

Montagnais Indians from the village of Lac-John created this village in 1960 on the shore of Lake John. The village later became a Native reserve. The Montagnais, Algonquian-speaking Indians with French as their second language, operate an active crafts center.

Kawawachikamach

14.7km/9.1mi northeast of Schefferville. www.naskapi.ca. Unpaved road.

Set amidst small lakes in the hilly region of the Canadian Shield, Kawawachikamach was built between 1981 and 1984. It is settled by **Naskapi Indians.**

Related to the Cree and Montagnais (Innu) Indians, the Naskapis are a nomadic people. They originated from the interior of the Ungava region, and followed the migratory route of the caribou. As their traditional hunting activities disappeared, Naskapis settled at the Fort Chimo trading post, now called Kuujjuaq. In 1956, they left Fort Chimo for Schefferville, in the hope of improving their living standards.

When the **Northeastern Quebec Agreement** was signed in 1978, the Naskapis surrendered aboriginal title to their land for financial compensation, land rights and new hunting, fishing, and trapping rights. They decided to build their village on the shores of Matemace Lake, leaving behind the reserve of Matimekosh, which they had shared with the Montagnais. This new village was designed to be specifically adapted to the local subarctic climate, one of the harshest in Canada.

SEPT-ÎLES TO HAVRE-SAINT-PIERRE

Circuit of 222km/138mi by Rte. 138, indicated on the map.

Rivière-au-Tonnerre

Rte. 138 (Rivière Manitou). 418-538-2732. 123km/76.4mi from Sept-Îles.

This pleasant fishing village takes its name from the thunderous rush of nearby waterfalls. Dominating the town center is the **Église Saint-Hippolyte** (Church of St. Hippolyte; open 24 Jun–early Sept daily 8am–5pm; 418-465-2842). Construction of the church began in 1905, according to plans designed by the parish priest. More than 300 church members each gave three months of work and two cords of wood per winter for its completion (one cord equals about 3.5cu m/13.7cu ft). The numerous carvings on the vault were done by a parishioner using only a penknife.

Longue-Pointe-de-Mingan

53km/33mi.

Set on a narrow strip of land jutting out into the Gulf of St. Lawrence, Longue-Pointe is considered the gateway to the Mingan Archipelago. An American military base was established here during World War II. Visitors can catch glimpses of the islands of the archipelago from the Rue du Bord-de-la-Mer.

Centre d'accueil et d'interprétation de Longue-Pointe-de-Mingan

625 Rue du Centre; open mid-Jun–Sept daily 8.30am–6pm; $5.80; 418-949-2126.

This is a research and interpretation center providing information on the various activities organized by the Mingan Archipelago National Park Reserve, including educational programs and tourist excursions. Presented here are the natural history of the region and marine mammals of the Gulf of St. Lawrence. Visitors can also make arrangements for **whale-watching cruises** (depart from Longue-Pointe-de-Mingan mid-Jun–mid-Oct daily at 7.30am; round-trip 6–8hrs; commentary; reservations required; $125; Station de recherche des Îles Mingan; 418-949-2845; www.rorqual.com).

Mingan

10km/6.2mi.

Of Basque origin, the name of this Montagnais reserve, created in 1963, means "strip of land." A trading post and fishing village during the French Regime, Mingan boasts a productive fishing ports along the coast. The Montagnais operate a fish packing plant and marketing company known as Les Crustacés de Mingan. At the village entrance, on Rte. 138, the **Musée montagnais** (Montagnais Museum) exhibits tools, household items, and photos illustrating the heritage of the Montagnais (open May–Oct daily 9am–6pm; rest of the year Mon–Fri 8am–4pm; $8.86; P ℘418-949-2234).

Montagnais Church★

15 Rue Nashipetimit. Open year-round daily 8am–7pm. ℘418-949-2272.

Located near the cultural center, the church was built in 1918 by Jack Maloney, the legendary Jack "Monoloy" of Gilles Vigneault's song, *Les bouleaux de la rivière Mingan* (The Silver Birches of the Mingan River). In 1972 the church was remodeled in the Montagnais style: The pulpit is decorated with caribou antlers; the Stations of the Cross are painted on skins stretched across frames of birch branches; the baptismal font is hollowed out of a maple trunk; and the tabernacle is in the form of a wigwam.

Havre-Saint-Pierre

1010 promenade des Anciens. ℘418-538-2512. 36km/22mi.

This industrial town was first settled in 1857 by Acadian fishermen from the Magdalen Islands. The town's economy was based on marine resources until 1948, when the mining company, QIT-Fer et Titane (Quebec Iron and Titanium),

Geographical Notes

The most visited section of Sept-Îles Regional Park includes the majority of the limestone islands and the monoliths of the archipelago, between Île aux Perroquets (opposite Longue-Pointe-de-Mingan) and Île Ste-Geneviève. The second section, the eastern side, includes the granite islands, islets and rocks to the east of Île Ste-Geneviève up to the mouth of the Aganus River near Aguanish. The islands include: Île aux Perroquets, Île Nue de Mingan, Grande Île, Île Quarry, Île de Niapiskau, Île du Fantôme, Île du Havre, Petite Île au Marteau, Île de la Fausse Passe, Île à la Chasse.

Monoliths – These spectacular rock formations were wrought by the elements over millennia. Because all the monoliths are approximately the same height (from 5m/16.4ft to 10m/32.8ft), it is believed they were once part of the same rock. The monoliths are nicknamed "flower pots" *(pots de fleurs)* in reference to the vegetation sprouting from their tops. Over the years, the residents of the area have come to recognize familiar shapes in the forms created by nature, and have given the monoliths whimsical names such as "Bonne Femme" (Matron) and "Tête d'Indien" (Indian Head).

Flora – The icy Labrador Current, distinctive soil deposits, high humidity and a powerful sea all contribute to the islands' unique bioclimate. Approximately half the land on the islands is covered with coniferous forest, but exceptional ecological conditions have fostered a diverse collection of plants, including ferns, orchids, mosses, and lichens, some of which are normally found only in Arctic or Alpine climates. Some 40 plants growing on the islands are extremely rare. The most notable is the Mingan thistle *(chardon)*, not known to be found anywhere else in eastern Canada; it was discovered in 1924 by Brother Marie Victorin, the founder of Montreal's Botanical Gardens.

Fauna – Of the many sea birds living in the archipelago, probably the most endearing one to residents and visitors alike is the cute Atlantic puffin *(macareux)*, whose red, yellow and blue beak and bright orange feet have earned it the nickname "sea parrot" *(perroquet de mer)*. Other birds to look for are the common eider, the black guillemot, and the common and Arctic tern. Three species of seal are found in the waters around the islands: The gray seal, the harp seal, and the harbor seal. The fin whale can sometimes be spotted.

Monoliths in the Mingan Archipelago National Park Reserve

© Yves Marcoux / age fotostock

began exploiting the world's largest known ilmenite deposits (naturally occurring iron and titanium oxides), discovered around Lakes Tio and Allard, 43km/26.7mi north of town.

Centre d'accueil et d'interprétation de la réserve du Parc national de de l'Archipel-de-Mingan

1010 Promenade des Anciens. Open mid-Jun–early Sept daily 8.30am–8pm; Jun–mid Jun and mid-Aug–mid-Sept 8.30am–noon, 1pm–5pm. ♿ P ✆418-538-3285, 1-888-773-8888 or 418-538-3331 (off season). www.pc.gc.ca.

The center displays photographs of flora and fauna found in the Mingan Archipelago and provides information on organized activities on the islands.

▶ Continue to Rue de la Berge and turn right.

Maison de la culture Roland-Jomphe

957 Rue de la Berge. Open mid-Jun–mid-Sept daily 9am–9pm. $2. ♿ ✆418-538-2450.

The interior of the former Clarke Trading Co. store (1926–63) has been refurbished to appear as it would have been in the 1940s. Displays recall the cultural heritage of the village and its economic evolution. The center also presents films and lectures on regional themes.

Réserve du parc naturel de l'Archipel de Mingan★★

Park open mid-Jun–late Aug (few services, including access to the islands, are available before or after that time period). $5.80. ⛺(mid-May–mid-Oct). www.pc.gc.ca/mingan.

The Mingan Archipelago is made up of approximately 40 islands lying in the Gulf of St. Lawrence, north of Anticosti Island. The string of islands measures 95km/59mi in length. The Mingan Archipelago National Park Reserve of Canada, created in 1984, extends from Longue-Pointe to Baie-Johan-Beetz, on the Côte-Nord.

The sedimentary rocks of the Mingan Archipelago were formed by the accumulation of limestone deposits at the edge of the Canadian Shield some 500 million years ago. The weight of glaciers, constant freezing and thawing, and relentless pounding of the sea caused fissures to form. Over time these eroded, slowly creating the string of islands and their characteristic monoliths.

Sea Cruises★

To fully appreciate the natural wonders of the Mingan Archipelago, visitors should tour the islands by boat. Cruises departing from Havre-Saint-Pierre specialize in geological interpretation; visitors disembark on Niapiskau Island to look at the monoliths (depart Havre-Saint-Pierre marina, mid-Jun–Labor Day daily 11:45am, 3.45pm; round-trip 4hrs; French commentary; reservations suggested; $75; ♿ P La Croisiere Jomphe Inc.; ✆418-538-3202, or 1-866-538-2865; www.smboreale.com).

Cruises leaving from Mingan offer views of the "flower pots," and concentrate on sighting marine life and sea birds (depart from the Parks Canada wharf mid-Jun–mid-Sept daily 10am and noon; round-trip 1hr30min; commentary by naturalists (mainly in French); reservations required; $25; ♿ P Société Duvetnor. ✆418-867-1660, or 1-877-867-1660; www.pharedupot.com).

The Mingan Islands Cetacean Study Research Station in Longue-Pointe-de-Mingan (✆418-949-2845; www.rorqual.com) schedules some combined **whale-watching and scientific research expeditions** that leave from the same Havre-Saint-Pierre dock.

Nature Information Centers

Parks Canada operates two information centers in the Mingan Archipelago National Park Reserve: one at Longue-Pointe-de-Mingan and the other at Havre-Saint-Pierre. Open from early June through early September, the centers organize workshops on plants, wildlife, geology, and geomorphology, as well as films, lectures and special exhibits on island-related themes. Visitors interested in organized interpretation programs, wilderness camping, scuba diving, and kayaking in the reserve must register at one of the centers.

Guided **walking tours** (3hrs) allow you to explore Grosse-Île-au-Marteau. Evening walks at Petite-Île-au-Marteau are truly special. The guides conduct the tours in French, but tours in English are available on request.

Natashquan marks the end of Rte. 138. The Lower North Shore is not linked to the rest of Quebec by road beyond that point. A boat trip from Havre-Saint-Pierre to Blanc-Sablon is described below. However, Baie Johan Beetz is not accessible by commercial vessels. Visitors may choose to drive to Natashquan and begin the boat trip there (details below).

HAVRE-SAINT-PIERRE TO BLANC-SABLON

Route via boat and car.

See map for route.

The Basse Côte-Nord (Lower North Shore) marks the eastern extremity of Quebec. The area is bordered by Labrador to the north; the island of Newfoundland lies to the southeast. Many villages along the Lower North Shore are former trading and fishing posts that date back to the French Regime. Yet of the 16 communities established within the 358km/222.4mi expanse between Kegasha and Blanc-Sablon, 12 are predominantly English-speaking (inhabited by descendants of fishermen from Newfoundland and the English Channel Island of Jersey), three are French-speaking and one is Montagnais.

Relais Nordik, Inc. operates a weekly **boat trip★** between Havre-Saint-Pierre and Blanc-Sablon aboard the *Nordik Express*. It is possible to purchase a ticket for passage only, but the plan including cabin and meals is recommended. The boat stops in most of the coastal villages and at Anticosti Island (departs Havre-Saint-Pierre mid-Apr–mid-Jan Wed 6:45pm, arrives at Blanc-Sablon Fri 8am; round-trip including cabin and meals $1,407/person for superior cabins; reservations required 30 days in advance for passage and vehicle transport for Anticosti, 4 months in advance for passengers/vehicles going east of Natashquan; P Relais Nordik, Inc. 418-723-8787, 1-800-463-0680; www.relaisnordik.com). Alternatively, as described below, you could choose to drive to Natashquan and pick up the *Bella* from Relais Nordik from there.

Baie-Johan-Beetz

Accessible by Rte. 138, not by boat trip.

This village bears the name of Johan Beetz, a Belgian aristocrat who emigrated to Canada in 1897. He first established a trade in luxury furs. Later on, he became a successful breeder of fur-bearing animals and attained international recognition for his breeding methods and scientific publications. His **house** (1899) is set on a rocky promontory overlooking the bay (open Jun–Aug; $5; P 418-365-5021; www.baiejohanbeetz.com; call ahead). An accomplished artist, Beetz decorated several doors and walls of his home with paintings of flowers and animals.

Natashquan

Rte. 138 or via the boat trip.

An atmosphere of calm and tranquility permeates this fishing village, birthplace of the noted poet and singer, Gilles Vigneault. Natashquan was colonized by Acadians from the Magdalen Islands in 1855. On a sandy point jutting out into the St. Lawrence, weathered fishing sheds (*galets*) are remnants of a bygone era. The name Natashquan signifies in Montagnais "the place where they hunt bear." Since 1952 the nearby village of Pointe-Parent has been a Montagnais community.

Rte. 138 ends at Natashquan. Passage from Natashquan to Blanc-Sablon is possible aboard the Bella from Relais Nordik (departs from Natashquan Apr–mid-Jan Wed 3pm; round-trip including cabin and meals $1,108/person, 3 nights, all meals; reservations required for passage and vehicle transport 60 days in advance; Relais Nordik, Inc.; 418-723-8787 or 1-800-463-0680; www.relaisnordik.com).

Harrington Harbour★

10hrs 45min from Natashquan.

It is better to disembark on the return journey to Natashquan, as the ferry calls at 5pm and not midnight.

Brightly painted houses welcome the Nordik Express in Harrington Harbour. The charming fishing village is on a small island; its port makes it one of the most accessible villages on the journey to Blanc-Sablon. Wide wooden sidewalks and bridges connect the rocky terraces dotted with picturesque houses and shops. The large grey building dominating the village was the first hospital of the region and is now a home for the elderly. Nearby, the **craft shop** offers a fine selection of handmade sweaters, parkas and hooked rugs, as well as Montagnais moccasins, and mittens.

In the afternoon of the second day, passengers aboard the Nordik Express can enjoy spectacular **views★** as the ship meanders by rocky islands speckled with lichens and moss, and skirts towering cliffs on which conifers form patterns of deep green.

Blanc-Sablon

21hrs 45min from Harrington Harbour.

Blanc-Sablon is situated 1.5km/1mi from the Quebec-Labrador border. The area around the Blanc-Sablon River is the site of key archeological digs, revealing a settlement dating back 7,200 years.

Ferry to St. Barbe, Newfoundland

Departs mid-Apr–mid-Jan (subject to change due to weather and ice conditions). One-way 1hr 30min. Reservations advisable mid-Jun–Oct. $8.25/person; $25.03/passenger and car. M/V Apollo operated by Labrador Marine. 1-866-535-2567 and 709-535-0810 (outside toll-free area). www.labradormarine.com.

Ferry crossings connect Blanc-Sablon to Sainte-Barbe, Newfoundland, located 139km/86mi south of l'Anse-aux-Meadows (*consult The Green Guide Canada*), site of the oldest known European settlement in North America. Iron work and other artifacts excavated from the site are Norse in origin and were dated back to approximately AD 1000.

Excursion to Loudes-de-Blanc-Sablon 5km/3mi from Blanc Sablon via Boulevard Docteur Camille Marcoux.

Lourdes-de-Blanc-Sablon

Just west of Blanc-Sablon, the largest village of the region boasts an airport and a hospital. In the Notre-Dame-de-Lourdes church, **Musée Scheffer** (Scheffer Museum; call ahead for open hours; 418-461-2000) is dedicated to Monsignor Scheffer (1903–66), first Bishop of Labrador from 1946 until his death.

ADDRESSES

STAY

Hôtel-Motel du Havre – *970 Blvd de l'Escale, Havre-Sainte-Pierre. 418-538-2800, 1-888-797-2800. www.hotelduhavre.ca. 69 rooms and 1 suite. Open year-round.* . Prices include a continental breakfast. Havre-Saint-Pierre's largest hotel is a reliable, clean, comfortable option. The staff are warm and helpful. Despite being near Rte. 138, it is far enough away from it to be quiet.

Hôtel Tadoussac – *165 r. du Bord-de-l'Eau, Tadoussac. 418-235-4421 or 800-561-0718. www.hoteltadoussac.com.* Spa. *Open May–Oct. 149 rms. Restaurant*. The Hôtel Tadoussac's red roof was made famous by the film *The Hotel New Hampshire*, and guests will feel they have traveled back in time to a different era. The lawns extend almost down to the water's edge, and most of the simply decorated rooms have river views.

EAT

Café Bohème – *239 r. des Pionniers, Tadoussac. 418-235-1180. www. lecafeboheme.com. Late Apr–late Oct daily 7am–11pm.* This pretty restaurant is all decked out in wood, with a terrace outside for dining in warm weather. The wood-smoked specialties such as the assiette du fumoir (platter of smoked fish and seafood) are what customers return for, but salads and salmon bagels, as well as traditional and tasty panini, cuisses de canard confit, and thin-crust pizzas draw in the regulars too.

La Promenade – *1197 Promenade-des-Anciens, Havre-Saint-Pierre. 418-538-2637.* This Promenade-des-Anciens is no Promenade-des-Anglais, but rather a pristine beach. La Promenade is a casual restaurant where proper seafood is taken seriously. It is an excellent place to enjoy the local fruits de mer. Reasonable prices for the seafood, and a non-seafood menu that is very affordable.

Île d'Anticosti★★

Duplessis

A true ecotourism destination, this island stretches more than 222km/138mi in length and 56km/35mi at its widest point. Pastoral Anticosti Island lies in the estuary of the St. Lawrence River, south of the Mingan Archipelago (Côte-Nord) and northeast of Forillon National Park (Gaspé Peninsula). Mantled with lush coniferous forests and criss-crossed by more than a hundred rivers teeming with Atlantic salmon and trout, Anticosti is a favorite for deer hunters. French industrialist Henri Menier, who purchased the island in 1895, created a private hunters' paradise upon it. Today, some 166,000 white-tailed deer are everywhere—on the streets and even on people's front lawns. Outside Port-Menier, the only village of the island, the 7,943sq km/3,067sq mi of Anticosti were divided into outfitting establishments and a national park. The island is not only a pleasant vacation spot for nature lovers, who can admire a rich variety of birds and wildflowers in a pastoral setting, but also a great place for a coastal tour by sea kayak. Limestone formations are laden with fossils, some of which date from the early Paleozoic era (420 to 500 million years ago).

- **Population:** 281.
- **Michelin Map:** p452–453.
- **Info:** 36 chemin des Forestiers, Port-Menier. 1-888-463-0808, 418-962-0808. www. tourismecote-nord.com.
- **Location:** There are two means of getting to Anticosti Island. **By air:** from Montreal, Quebec City, Mont-Joli or Havre-Saint-Pierre to Port-Menier, contact SÉPAQ Anticosti *1-800-463-0863. www.sepaq.com/antocosti.* **By boat:** Relais Nordik, a passenger and supply ship *1-800-463-0680*, departures from Rimouski 418-723-8787, Sept-Îles 418 968-4707, Havre-Saint-Pierre. 418 538-3533. www.relaisnordik.com.
- **Don't Miss:** Vauréal Falls and Canyon; while driving, *do* miss the many deer!
- **Timing:** When you arrive in Port-Menier, get a schedule of current activities: Hiking and sea kayaking are available seasonally. Rent a mountain bicycle or car for day trips. Learn about all the excursions available on Anticosti Island while you are there and select the most appropriate according to the weather.

A BIT OF HISTORY

Archeological excavations on the island trace the presence of humans here back 3,500 years. The name Anticosti may derive from the Indian word *notiskuan,* meaning "the place where bear are hunted," or it could have originated with Basque or Spanish fishermen who called it anti costa, or "before the coast."

Jacques Cartier mentioned the island after his first voyage to New France in 1534, but settlement occurred there only after 1680 when Anticosti was granted to Louis Jolliet in recognition of his discovery of Illinois and his expedition to Hudson Bay. The initial settlement was destroyed by Admiral Phipps' fleet in 1690. Anticosti was passed down to Jolliet's three children, and in 1763 it was annexed to Newfoundland, which had become a colony of the British Crown according to the terms of the Treaty of Utrecht (1713) (*see Introduction: History*).

During the next century, the island changed owners several times. In 1872 an English enterprise known as the Anticosti Island Company (or Forsyth Company) made an unsuccessful attempt to colonize the island, as did its successor, the Stockwell Company, and others.

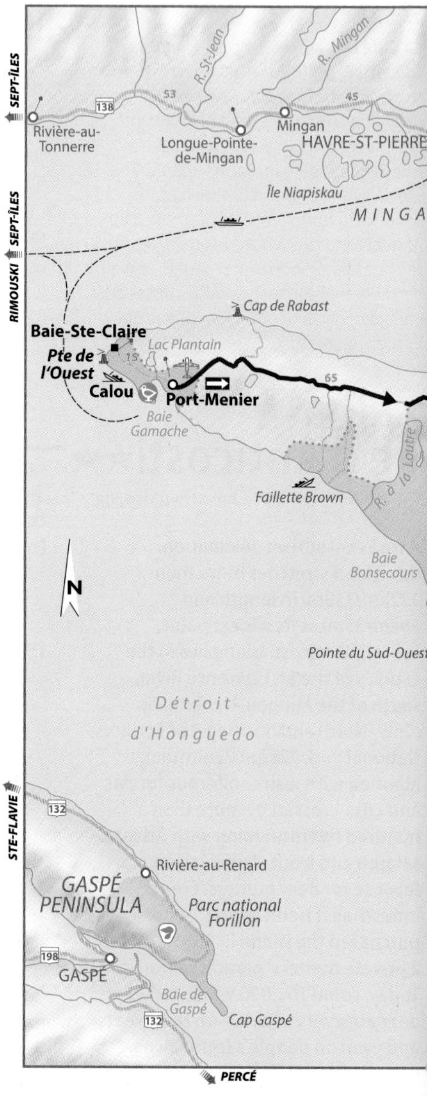

The Menier Era: 1895–1926 – French industrialist and heir to a fortune from the chocolate industry, **Henri Menier** set out in the late 19C to find a piece of land that would serve both as an investment property and as a hunting and fishing retreat for himself and his friends. On December 16, 1895, Menier purchased Anticosti Island for $125,000.

To ensure his comfort on visits to Anticosti and entertain his guests, Menier constructed a hunting lodge overlooking the bay between Port-Menier and Baie-Sainte-Claire. The sumptuous mansion, known as the "château" by locals, was of Norwegian and Norman inspiration. Upon Henri Menier's death in 1913, Anticosti was inherited by his brother Gaston Menier who, although appreciative of the island's beauty, was somewhat intolerant of his brother's extravagances. In 1917,

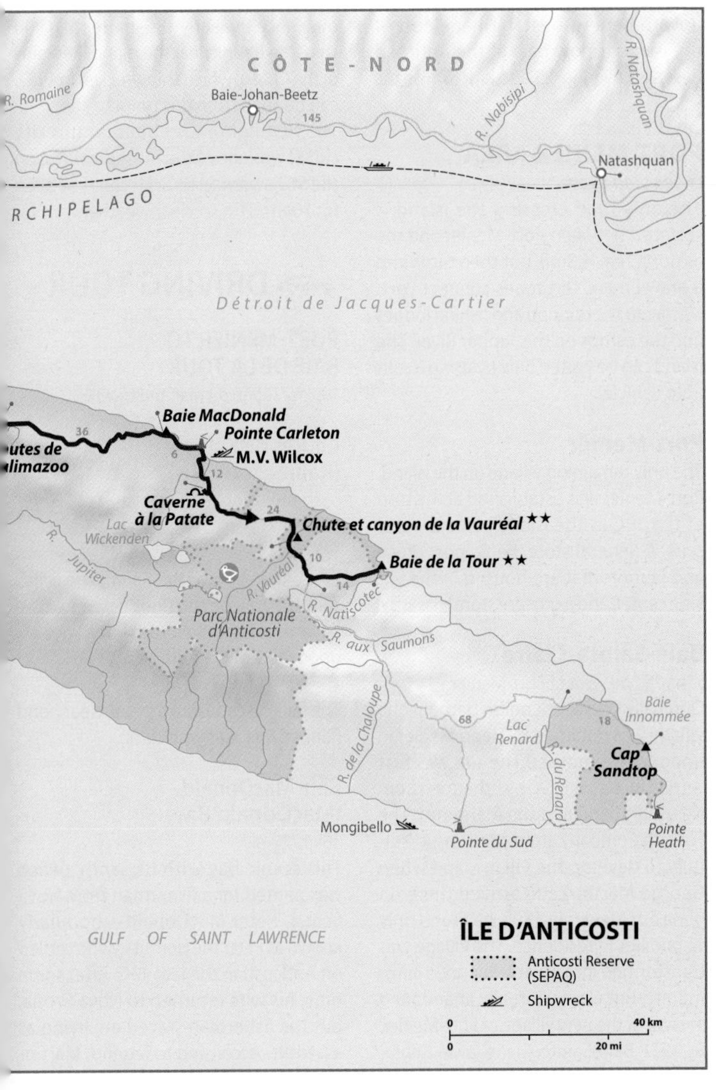

due to economic problems in France that weakened the powerful chocolate industry, the Menier family closed down their lumber operation on the island. In 1926, Anticosti was sold for $6.5 million to the Anticosti Corp., a consolidated venture of three Canadian pulp and paper companies. Over the years, the furnishings of the mansion were sold or transported to company holdings on the mainland. Château Menier fell into such disrepair that the structure was considered a hazard, particularly to local children who would wander on the site. Orders were issued to burn it down in 1953.

New Developments – The Anticosti Corp. engaged in forestry activities and brought prosperity to the island for a brief period after the Menier era. In 1974 the Quebec Government acquired Anticosti for the sum of $23.78 million. Citizens were allowed to purchase land and residences in 1983, and a municipal government was established. Most of the island is now part of the Anticosti Reserve, covering 4,575sq km/1,766sq mi.

SIGHTS

PORT-MENIER AREA

See map above.

The only road crossing the island is surfaced between Port-Menier and the airport (7km/4.3mi), but then turns into a gravel track. Dirt roads connect Port-Menier to the hunting and fishing lodges and the camps on the Jupiter River. The island can be visited only by using a suitable vehicle.

Port-Menier

The only remaining village on the island, Port-Menier was established at the turn of the 19C as the island's deep-water port. A general store, bank, post office and laundromat are housed in the village center, and a grocery store is nearby.

Baie-Sainte-Claire

15km/9.3mi west of Port-Menier.

Originally known as English Harbour, the village was renamed by Henri Menier in honor of his mother. The site was first settled in the mid-19C by fishermen from Newfoundland and the Maritimes. The Forsyth Company attempted unsuccessfully to develop the village, and when George Martin-Zédé arrived there on behalf of Menier in 1895, he found only 11 families in residence. The village was transformed into a viable planned community, but was eventually abandoned in favor of the new village of Port-Menier. By 1931, Baie-Sainte-Claire lay in ruins.

In 1985 a lime kiln was rebuilt to the west of the village site. The original kiln had been used for nine years under Menier, producing slake lime for mortar and whitewash. Laws prohibiting hunting at Baie-Sainte-Claire make it an ideal spot to observe the unafraid **white-tailed deer**, which can sometimes be seen in herds of up to a hundred.

Pointe de l'Ouest (West Point)

1km/.6mi south of Baie-Sainte-Claire.

Despite the many lighthouses along the Anticosti shore, shipwrecks were numerous. Since the early 18C, more than 200 ships have sunk near the island. Remains of the **Calou**, which shipwrecked in 1982, can be seen from this point.

The first lighthouse built on this site (1858) was one of the most powerful on the St. Lawrence; its light could be seen for 50km/31mi in clear weather.

DRIVING TOUR

PORT-MENIER TO BAIE DE LA TOUR

169km/105mi on map p430–431.

Chutes de Kalimazoo (Kalimazoo Falls)

65km/40mi. Access to the falls is 1.7km/1mi from the main road.

Follow signs to the Kalimazoo Falls. Take the trail on the right down to the stream, cross it, then turn left to get a good view of the falls.

The falls cascade into a small, clear pond flanked by limestone cliffs.

Baie MacDonald (MacDonald Bay)

36km/22mi.

This scenic bay with its sandy beach was named for a fisherman from Nova Scotia, Peter MacDonald—popularly known as Peter the Hermit—who settled on Anticosti in the late 19C. After some time, his wife returned to Nova Scotia, but the fisherman stayed on, living as a hermit. According to legend, Martin-Zédé coaxed MacDonald into coming to Baie-Sainte-Claire when he became ill, but after his recuperation, the feisty old fellow (aged 87) made the trip home, traveling some 120km/74mi through the forests on snowshoes.

Pointe Carleton

6km/3.7mi east of Baie McDonald.

The road passes along sandy beaches offering good views of the sea. The picturesque lighthouse on the point was built in 1918. Lodging is available here at the Wilcox Campground.

GETTING THERE

BY AIR – From Montreal, Quebec City, Sept-Îles or Mont-Joli: *℘418-535-0156; www.sepaq.com.* Other regular airlines offering flights from Havre-Saint-Pierre and Sept-Îles: ExactAir *℘418-538-2332; www.exactair.ca.*

BY BOAT – Relais Nordik Inc. Sailings depart Rimouski on Tue at 12.30pm. *℘418-723-8787;* from Sept-Îles *℘418-968-4707,* or from Havre-Saint-Pierre *℘418-538-3533. www.relaisnordik.com.*

GETTING AROUND

BY CAR – Car rental available from Sauvageau. *℘418-535-0157, 1-866-728-8243; www.sauvageau.qc.ca* To visit the island, a radio-equipped, four-wheel-drive motor vehicle is essential.

Anticosti is crossed from west to east by route Henri-Menier, also known as "la route TransAnticostienne," a dirt road to which several secondary roads are connected. A long distance may separate your place of accommodation from the attraction that you wish to visit, whether in or outside the National Park. Take these distances into account when you plan your outings. Route Henri-Menier is the only road traversing the island from west to east. It is paved between Port-Menier and the airport (7km/4.3mi), but elsewhere has a gravel surface. Dirt roads link Port-Menier to deer hunting and fishing lodges and camps on the Jupiter River.

For information, contact SÉPAQ Anticosti. ℘418-890-0863 or 1-800-463-0863; www.sepaq.com.

Wilcox Shipwreck

Near Pointe Carleton, at the mouth of La Patate River, the beached hull of the *M.V. Wilcox* lies exposed to the pounding surf. This former minesweeper wrecked here in June 1954.

Caverne à la Patate (La Patate Cavern)

12km/7.5mi.

Turn off the main road approximately 3km/1.8mi beyond the two bridges that cross La Patate River and one of its tributaries.
With a four-wheel-drive vehicle, it is possible to continue on the forest road for about 2km/1.2mi. Then, on foot, follow the path indicated by colored ribbons for approximately 1hr to reach the entrance to the cavern.
It is advisable to bring along a safety helmet when visiting the cavern.

Discovered in 1981, the cavern was explored and mapped by a team of geographers the following year. The entrance to the cavern measures 10m/33ft high and about 7m/23ft wide. The total length of the passages is 625m/683.5yd.

Chute et Canyon de la Vauréal★★ (Vauréal Falls and Canyon)

The trail to the waterfall begins 24km/15mi east of La Patate Cavern. To reach the canyon, return to the main road and turn back toward Pointe Carleton. The turn-off is at 1.5km/1mi.

The Vauréal River was originally called Morsal in honor of a descendant of the Huguenots who arrived on Anticosti in 1847 and spent 45 years near the river. Menier renamed it Vauréal after one of his properties in the Oise region of France.
The one-hour hike along the riverbed to the base of the waterfall offers spectacular scenery. The grayish limestone walls, sometimes patterned with red and green schists, are carved into an undulating pattern by the forces of nature. Along the way, the steep walls are dotted with crevasses and caves. The waterfall plunges 76m/249ft into the canyon.

Baie de la Tour★★ (Tour Bay)

Turn left off the main road 10km/6.2mi beyond Vauréal Falls.

Continue on the secondary road for 14km/8.7mi.

Limestone cliffs dramatically plummeting into the sea create a breathtaking view from the sandy beach of the bay.

Return to the main road.

Detour to Cap Sandtop (Cape Sandtop)

172km/107mi round-trip. The road ends at Cape Sandtop. A dirt road stretches over this part of the island; in poor weather, deep ruts can sometimes make driving difficult.

The Natiscotec River marks the boundary of the SÉPAQ nature reserve. Low, sparse vegetation characterizes the marshlands found on this part of the island. The Renard River leads back into the SÉPAQ nature reserve. Renard Bay was once the site of an early settlement, where the Menier family eventually established a lobster-packing plant. A bird sanctuary is nestled in the small inlet between La Chute River and Innommée Bay.

Return to Port-Menier by the same road.

ADDRESSES

STAY

SÉPAQ Anticosti organizes vacation packages that include airfare from Mont-Joli (on the Gaspé Peninsula), lodging in cottages, board, and rental of a four-wheel-drive.

For example, the Family package (3 nights and air transportation from Quebec City or Montreal) allow you to stay at either **Galiotte or Chicotte cabin** on the seashore. In an air-conditioned mini-bus, a guide will take you to the Vauréal Falls, the Observation Canyon and the Wilcox shipwreck. You'll discover Baie-Sainte-Claire and the ruins of the Château Menier, and you'll visit the Ecomuseum. SÉPAQ packages extend to 14 days.

In addition to vacations organized by SÉPAQ are private outfitters (like *Pourvoirie du lac Geneviève* and its chalets not far from the Port-Menier airport *418-535-0294 and 1-800-463-1777. www.anticostiplg.com*).

Another lodging option is **Hôtel de l'Île**, a basic, friendly accommodation, now part of SÉPAQ, with 15 rooms (⊖⊖) in Port-Menier *418-890-0863.*

WHERE TO PITCH A TENT

At Wilcox campground, on the north shore of the island, near Pointe Fortune. For information, contact *418 535-0156 or SÉPAQ Anticosti and 1-800-463-0863.*

EAT

Meals are included in most packages sold by private outfitters and SÉPAQ. However, both simple and more elaborate dishes are served in Port-Menier hotel restaurants:

⊖ **Hôtel de l'Île** – *In the village of Port-Menier. 418-890-0863.* Casual restaurant serving fast food, pizza and simple meaty dishes. Loads of calories to fuel your explorations.

⊖ **Visitor Center** – *In the village of Port-Menier. 418-890-0863.* A new Discovery and Visitor Center has replaced the old Auberge Port Menier, which was destroyed in a fire, and is set to open in the summer of 2015. The visitor center will have a reception and restaurant and bar services, a gift shop, and a museum dedicated to the Anticosti National Park. Operated by SÉPAQ.

ACTIVITIES

There are plenty of leisure activities: walking or cycling, camping, sea kayaks, scuba diving, horseback riding, or swimming, and in winter, naturally, snowmobiles, hunting, and fishing. For hunting and fishing, you should contact the various outfitters organizing these activities on the island to find out the requirements. *Information: 418-535-0311.*

Écomusée d'Anticosti – Museum on the history of Anticosti and its natural wonders. *In the village of Port-Menier. Late Jun–late Aug daily 8am–5pm* (*free admission*). *418-535-0250. www.ile-anticosti.com.*

Northern and Western Areas

From the far western territories and the immense and historical fur-trading and mining-rich tracts surrounding Abitibi-Témiscamingue where aboriginal settlements were the only habitation until the 20C, this gargantuan region extends to the even larger and less populated Baie-James hinterlands (an area covering over 350,000sq km/135,000sq mi with only 30,000 residents). It includes the Inuit-dominated Nunavik region of the northern Hudson's Bay and eastern Ungava Bay. The wildlife, harsh weather, and aboriginal communities here continue to attract global visitors in any season to a variety of sights, activities, and cultural treasures unlike any other place on the planet.

Abitibi-Témiscamingue

The Algonquin First Nations People introduced Europeans to the beaver, fox, and mink fur trade in this region, and only in the last century did prospectors discover gold and other precious metals now so dominant here.

Travelers can still uncover the compelling story of the British versus French fur trade epoch at Fort Témiscamingue, where multimedia presentations cover the 17C through the 19C with artifacts from both major fur trading players: the Hudson's Bay Company and the Northwest Company.

Highlights

1. The gold mining town of **Val d'Or** (p464)
2. Canoe trips and wild camping in the **Réserve faunique La Vérendrye** (p465)
3. Scenic views from the **Aménagement Robert-Bourassa** (p471)
4. The incredible views from the **Torngat Mountains** (p458)
5. **Pingualuit National Park** at Kangiqsujuaq (p479)

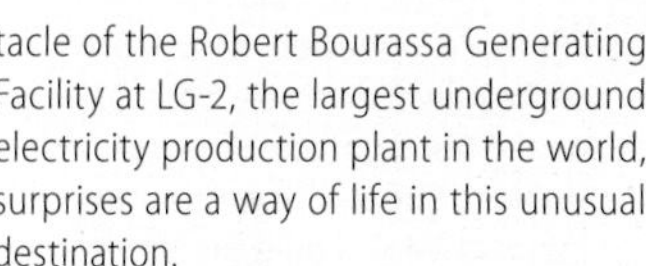

Natural Splendor

Recent times have seen the formation of large preserved areas of this pristine environment by Parks Canada. D'Aiguebelle National Park and La Vérendrye Wildlife Reserve are both veritable cornucopias of flora and fauna.

This is the land of the legendary coureur-de-bois (17C woodlands' fur trader and adventurer), and the thousands of rivers and lakes are testament to the wilderness European explorers, loggers, and fur traders faced upon their arrival here. Very little has changed since then.

Baie-James/Eeyou Istchee

This magical land of the Northern Lights is a continuous chain of tundra, accented by a stunning coastal expanse into Hudson's Bay, and a land speckled with rivers and lakes as far as the horizon.

Crossing the 49th parallel, guests will note the hospitality imbued in all the communities throughout this region.

From a humble sunrise ceremony riverside with a shaman in Wemindji, to the spectacle of the Robert Bourassa Generating Facility at LG-2, the largest underground electricity production plant in the world, surprises are a way of life in this unusual destination.

Ancestors of the current Cree residents, who make up about 40 percent of the population (Jamesian non-natives making up the balance), have occupied this land for more than 5,000 years.

The indigenous bedrock of the Baie-James region undergirded the post-WWII mining industry's ability to build roads and explore for precious metals. Harnessing the natural resources of the robust lakes and rivers would create a rich harvest of electricity for cities, and a decade-long confrontation with locals.

Nunavik

The far northern expanse of the province is home to mostly Inuit communities. It is an Arctic zone populated by exceptional wildlife species adapted to the harsh climate. The world's largest caribou herd

Northern and Western Areas

Teepee, Wemindji, Baie-James

©Gregory B. Gallagher/Michelin

Museums in the Region

For those interested in the story of the mining industry, Val d'Or on the trans-Canada Highway is home to Cité de l'Or, celebrating the discovery of gold there in 1923, and the subsequent operation of the Lamaque Gold Mines. Continue west to the town of Malartic, where you will discover Musée minéralogique de l'Abitibi-Témiscamingue, and more about area geology.

is here, plus healthy families of musk-ox, snowy owl, fox, Canada geese, walrus, seals, whales, and the iconic polar bear, perhaps never more challenged as global warming threatens its habitat.

Pingualuit National Park

The first national park in the region is centered on a mammoth meteor crater (3.4km/2mi diameter) and features crystal-clear blue water. Inuit elders from nearby Kangiqsujuaq (Wakeham Bay) continue to use the area as their summer camp for hunting and fishing.

Torngat Mountains

From the Innuktitut word meaning "spirits," Inuit people believe the spirit world overlaps the physical world in this dramatic land. Protected by provincial status as Kuururjuaq National Park, the Torngat Mountains are formed by some of the oldest rocks in the world; they are home to caribou, black bear, ptarmigan, and many other northern species, but very few people. They are the second-highest peaks in Canada, and the highest in eastern North America.

A Glimpse of Summer

Winter is what most people think about when they think of Nunavik. Snow begins in September and continues often until June, leaving a small window of opportunity to visit and explore in summer. Suppliers and service companies advise reservations far in advance for excursions, flights, equipment, etc. for the Far North. Planning is key to enjoyment and survival in the land of the midnight sun.

Abitibi

This region of the Canadian Shield stretches along the border with Ontario, between the Ottawa River and the Eastmain Plain, to the south of James Bay. Further south, a loop in the Ottawa River forms the border of the Témiscamingue region, known for its dairy farms tucked away amidst hills covered in spruce trees.

- **Info: Amos:** 892 Rte. 111 east, 1-800-670-0499, www.ville.amos.qc.ca. **Rouyn-Noranda:** 1675 av Larivière, 819-797-3195 or 1-888-797-3195, www.tourismerouyn-noranda.ca. **Ville-Marie:** 1, rue Industrielle, 819-723-2500, http://tourismetemiscamingue.ca; **Val d'Or:** 1070, 3rd ave East, 819-824-9646 or 1-877-582-5367 www.tourismevaldor.com.
- **Location:** The 200km/125mi-region is approx. 600km/300mi NW of Montreal.
- **Don't Miss:** Pageau Refuge, a unique insight into Northern Canada's wildlife, Amos. Cité de l'Or in Val d'Or.

SIGHTS

AMOS

Originally called Harricana for the river that flows through its center, the town was later renamed Amos in honor of Alice Amos, wife of Lomer Gouin, premier of Quebec in the early 1900s. Amos is the cradle of the Abitibi region. The "agriculturalist" movement promoted by French-Canadian religious and political leaders, who painted a return to the land as a panacea for the economic crisis of the 1930s, brought settlers to the area. The Catholic Church played a major role in the development of the region; in addition to providing moral and at times political support, priests acted as social mediators. Agriculture, mining and forestry remain the region's main industries.

Cathédrale Sainte-Thérèse d'Avila (Cathedral of St. Teresa of Avila)

11 Blvd Monsignor-Dudemaine. Open year-round daily 9am–5pm. 819-732-2110.

Located in the heart of town, this cathedral (1923) is a rare example of the Romano-Byzantine style in North America. The structure features a circular floor plan crowned by a spectacular dome. Noteworthy decorative elements include a 2.75m/9ft painted dove adorning the dome's interior, pink Italian marble, and stained-glass windows imported from France.

An **art gallery** *(centre d'exposition d'Amos, 571 1re Rue)* showcases and sells artwork and handicrafts from artists and artisans of the Abitibi region.

Pikogan Village

4km/2.5mi north of Amos. Turn left on Rue Principale, left again on 1ère Ave. Ouest and then right on 6e Rue Ouest, which becomes Rte. 109. Continue for 2km/1.2mi.

All the residents of this Algonquin village are originally from the Lake Abitibi region. Founded in 1954, the village is now administered solely by indigenous people, reflecting their desire to reclaim their culture. All the services of a vibrant community exist here, including classes in the Algonquian language at the school. The Saint-Catherine **church★** (open May–Sept, Mon–Fri 9am–5pm; rest of the year and holidays by appointment only; 514-844-1924) of the St. Catherine's Mission, built in 1967, is reminiscent of a wigwam, a native architectural form. The church's interior is decorated in the local Algonquin style.

Refuge Pageaus (Pageau Refuge)

8km/5mi east of Amos. Take Rte. 111 East toward Val-d'Or, and turn left on Rang Dix, at Figuery, toward Saint-Maurice (4241 chemin Croteau). Open year-round daily. Guided tours ().

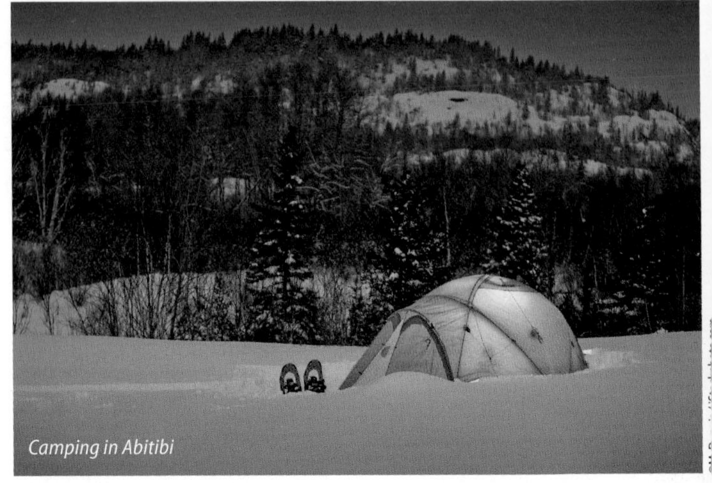
Camping in Abitibi

Mon–Fri 1:30pm, Sat 10:30am & 1:30pm. ⊛$15. ♿ P ✆819-732-8999. www.refugepageau.ca.
Formerly a trapper, owner Michel Pageau has been an animal lover for more than 30 years. Forest rangers and hunters direct him to injured, mistreated, and abandoned animals, which he then cares for. Once nursed back to health, the animals are set free; those

Rouyn-Noranda: A Brief History

Colonization of the region began in 1853 when lumbering laid bare large tracts of farmland. In 1863, the Oblate Fathers took up residence in the Old Fort Mission (Mission du Vieux Fort), located south of Fort Témiscamingue. In 1887 they moved to Baie des Pères, Ville-Marie's former appellation. The Grey Nuns followed shortly thereafter. Since their arrival in the region, both orders have pursued their religious mission in the realms of education and culture. Nicknamed "the father of agriculture in Témiscamingue," Brother Joseph Moffet (1852–1932), from the Old Fort Mission, was a well-known organizer and negotiator as well as an intermediary between the settlers and lumber company officials. He also negotiated with produce buyers from Ontario, located on the other side of Lake Témiscamingue.

To this day, the region has retained its agricultural vocation while diversifying its forest industry and services. The town boasts golf and tennis facilities and organizes an international regatta on Pères Bay every July.

As its name indicates, Rouyn-Noranda is the result of a merger between the towns of Noranda and Rouyn. Although both are mining towns, their history is quite different. Noranda owed its creation to Ontarian interests and was primarily anglophone: The town's name is a contraction of the words north and Canada. In its early days, it was essentially a residential town, administered exclusively by the Noranda mine. The town of Rouyn was named for Sieur de Rouyn, a captain of the Royal Roussillon regiment, famed for his battle against the English at Sainte-Foy, near Quebec City. Rouyn was originally a meeting place for adventurers in search of a quick fortune; at that time, it was known as the "street of pleasures" *(rue des plaisirs)*. The town is truly a product of the gold rush (which in fact became a copper rush) of 1923. Primarily francophone, it was home to most of the miners and is today the business district of the city.

unable to survive in the wild remain at the refuge. Michel Pageau and the refuge have become synonymous with northern Canada's wildlife. A **zoo** (♟♟), with cages tagged with the Algonquian, French, and English names of the animals, delights youngsters.

Preissac Village

35km/22mi SW of Amos by Rte. 395.

Lost in time, the village of Preissac is nestled in a rural setting on the edge of the Kinojévis River. Next to the bridge over the rapids is a fine spot for a picnic. Just before reaching the Lake Preissac outfitter (*approximately 15km/9.3mi from Rte. 117*), a lookout point on Rte. 95 affords a splendid **view★** overlooking the lake. Fishing and tourism services, a marina and a campground are located on the shores of the lake.

Le Dispensaire de la Garde

In La Corne, 26km/16mi southeast of Amos on Rte. 111. Open mid-Jun–early Sept daily 9am–5pm. Rest of the year by appointment. $6. 819-799-2181. www.dispensairedelagarde.com.

Experience the history of colonization, the early days of rural clinics, the social role and personal life of nurses in this house. Guides dressed as nurses lead visitors through the multimedia presentation that brings rural medicine to life.

ROUYN-NORANDA

Located in the heart of the Abitibi region, directly on the watershed line and astride the most mineral-rich portion of the Cadillac Fault, Rouyn-Noranda is both the regional capital of the Abitibi region and its main population center. Abitibi, a relatively uncultivated region of forest, rock, lakes, and rivers, takes its name from an Algonquian term meaning "watershed line." The region rests on a peneplain, or flat land surface created by erosion, gently sloping toward James Bay, carrying along the waters of Lake Abitibi and the Harricana River.

Not just another mining town, the city is the region's cultural center, boasting an international film festival and vibrant artistic community. In order to counteract the negative aesthetic effect of mining, residents are dedicated to the development of parks and their prize flower gardens. Rouyn-Noranda proudly claims Richard Desjardins, the popular singer, poet, and activist, as its native son.

Maison Dumulon★ (Dumulon House)

191 Ave. du Lac. Approaching from the direction of Val-d'Or, turn left off Rte. 117 onto Ave. du Lac and continue to Lake Osisko, where a tourist information booth is located. Open mid-Jun–late Aug daily 8.30am–5pm; rest of the year Wed–Sun noon–6pm. Admission free; guided tours $7. 819-797-7125. www.maison-dumulon.ca.

This reconstructed log house re-creates the atmosphere of the 1920s, when it served as Rouyn's first general store and post office. Photographs and various objects reminiscent of bygone days trace the history of the town.

The local tourism office is located in the building.

In **Parc des Pionniers** (Pioneer Park) next to Dumulon House, the Tremoy promenade leads along Lake Osisko to the Centre nautique de Rouyn-Noranda.

Église orthodoxe russe Saint-Georges (Saint-Georges Russian Orthodox Church)

201 Rue Taschereau Ouest; turn left off Rue Larivière. Open mid-Jun–mid-Aug daily 8:30am–5pm. Admission free; guided tour is $7. 819-797-7125. www.maison-dumulon.ca.

Among the wave of immigrants arriving after World War II to work as miners were about 20 Russian families; to serve them, Father Ustuchenko erected this small church according to the principles of Russian Orthodoxy. The two superimposed cupolas are intended to represent God embracing the earth. The church has been transformed into a small but extensively documented **museum**, full of picturesque details that lead the visitor to the heart of the Russian soul.

Théâtre du Cuivre (Copper Theater)

145 Rue Taschereau East.

In 1987 this eminently contemporary building, topped by a copper roof, won the prestigious Felix award for best theater in the province. It hosts movies, plays, and concerts, as well as the popular Abitibi-Témiscamingue *Festival du cinéma international.*

Noranda Metallurgie

1 rue Cartier. 819-797-3195 or 1-888-797-3195.

The discovery of this mine led to the rush of 1923. In 1927, the mine started operations with the help of American and Canadian investors. A total of 51 million tons of high-grade copper and gold ore were mined (on average, five tons of ore are required to produce one ounce of gold). A smelter now occupies the site of the former mine.

Fonderie Horne (Horne Smelter)

101 Ave. Portelance. Visit by guided tour (2hrs) only, by reservation, late Jun–early Sept daily 9am–3pm. Rest of the year by appointment. 819-979-3195.

The exhibit here focuses on the entire copper mining and refining process: From extraction to the production of an anode, a large 99 percent copper ingot weighing about 290kg/639lbs. After touring the home of Edmund Horne, discoverer of the Noranda Mine, visitors enter a railway compartment where a film on mining and the history of the region is presented. Finally, everyone is invited to don helmets and boots to visit the surface installations of the smelter.

Parc botanique à Fleur d'Eau

325 av. Principale. Open year round. Julienne-Cliche visitor center open mid-Jun–Aug daily 9:30am–6:30pm. 819-762 3178. www.corpodesfetes.ca.

This botanical garden is set around Lac Édouard, which is surrounded by magnificent trees and landscaped gardens, and is a favorite destination for the region's ducks.

Angliers

From Rouyn-Noranda head west on Rte. 117. Past Arntfield, turn off Rte. 117 and go south on Rte. 101. About 5km/3mi south of the village of Rollet, turn left onto Rte. 391 to Angliers.

This peaceful village is home to the old **T.E. Draper**, a tugboat used to haul lumber when rivers were the only way to transport materials and reach remote areas (open Jun–early Sept daily 10am–6pm; $6; 819-949-4431; www.tedraper.ca). The vessel was in service from 1929 through 1972, dropping off passengers at the southern end of Lake Témiscamingue. You can also tour the Gédéon logging site, a reconstructed logging camp.

Parc national d'Aiguebelle

50km/31mi northeast of Rouyn-Noranda (Rtes. 117 and 101). 1702 Rang Hudon, Mont-Brun. Open all year round; another visitor center at Taschereau (78km/48mi from Rouyn on Route 111) open mid-May–eary Sept. $6.50. 819-637-7322. www.sepaq.com.

The Aiguebelle national park is an amazing place. You can observe the traces left by glaciers, or lava flows and rocks dating back 2.7 billion years, cross a 64m/210ft walkway suspended 22m/72ft above Lac La Haie, scan the horizon from a fire lookout tower, or climb down a cliff face on a spiral staircase.

Farm in Ville-Marie

VILLE-MARIE

This small, yet vibrant community is the capital of the remote Témiscamingue region, on a vast and fertile plain that runs next to Lake Témiscamingue (an Algonquian word meaning "deep waters"). While farming continues as the town's economic mainstay, forestry and services also figure prominently in the local economy.

Grotte Notre-Dame-de-Lourdes

Rue Notre-Dame-de-Lourdes.

This mountain **site★** reveals a splendid view overlooking Lake Témiscamingue. The pleasant park is dotted with walking trails, picnic areas, and Stations of the Cross. On the corner of Rues Dollard and Notre-Dame-de-Lourdes stands the Medieval-style **town hall**. A school of agriculture from 1939 through 1965, it bears the name of the famed pioneer Brother Moffet. *See box p460.*

Maison du Frère-Moffet (Brother Moffet's House)

7 Rue Notre-Dame-de-Lourdes, by the lake. Open late Jun–early Sept daily 10am–6pm. $2. 819-629-3533.

The oldest house (1881) in the community holds a small museum that presents various objects from the colonization period recounting the unique history of Ville-Marie and Témiscamingue.

Facing the house, a small park affords good **views** of the vast and deep (up to 210m/688ft) Lake Témiscamingue. Stretching over 103km/64mi, the lake forms a border between Quebec and Ontario.

Fort Témiscamingue National Historic Site of Canada★

8km/5mi S of Ville-Marie, at 824 chemin du Vieux-Fort. Turn right off Rte. 101 to Témiscamingue. Open late Jun–early Sept daily 10am–5pm; rest of the year by appointment only. $4.90. 819-629-3222. www.pc.gc.ca.

In 1679 the French established a fur-trading post on this site; the post was later abandoned. A second post was erected in 1720, and remained active for nearly two centuries. The post changed hands several times as a result of political and commercial fluctuations, passing from the Northwest Company to that company's rival, the Hudson's Bay Company. Today several structures testify to what may have been the region's earliest fur-trading post.

The site's **interpretation center** (♟♟) offers a glimpse of life at a fur-trading post during the 18C and 19C. Various types of furs and trade items are displayed; the center also houses exhibits on the *voyageurs*.

Visitors can relax at the site's large **beach★**, picnic grounds, and recreational areas.

Forêt enchantée★ (Enchanted Forest)

This unusual natural site covers most of the site's 4ha/9.8 acres. Here the visitor can admire oddly shaped stands of silverberry, Eastern white cedar, and red pine. It is said that strong northerly winds sweep over the forest at the onset of winter, bending the trees under the forceful gales. Caught by a sudden frost, the small trees stay bent under their cover of snow during the entire winter and retain an irregular shape even after the late thaw. A trail runs alongside the lake, leading to the ruins of old chimneys, remains of the original fort. Tombstones mark the graves of early European settlers.

Route 101 meanders near Lake Témiscamingue, which in some places is visible beyond a forest of oak, beech, maple, poplar, and white or red pine.

A few rest areas with picnic grounds and facilities are located along the road.

Témiscaming

Rte. 101 to the Ontario border ends in this small village, 90km/56mi south of Ville-Marie.

In 1917 the Riordon Company, a pulp and paper plant, was established in this charming town, which fostered a prosperous lumber industry. The picturesque main road, known as the **Kipawa**

Route, runs along the hillside to the southern end of Lake Témiscamingue, where it meets the Ottawa River.

VAL-D'OR★

Situated in the heart of the Abitibi region, the area around Val-d'Or was the exclusive domain of Algonquin and Crees prior to the arrival of Catholic missionaries and trappers in the 17C. The history of the city itself covers less than a century. The town was created in 1922 during the great gold rush that followed the discovery of major mineral deposits in Rouyn-Noranda.

Located on the easternmost portion of the Cadillac Fault, Val-d'Or (meaning valley of gold) was the most important gold producer in the region during the 1929 economic crisis.

Today it remains an active mining town in the Abitibi region, with extraction of gold, copper and silver at boom levels since 2006. A thriving logging industry also supports the local economy. In summer, the many saloons, bars, and restaurants light up the Rue Principale with the colorful neon signs reminiscent of 1950s and 1960s western towns.

Cité de l'Or – Village Minier de Bourlamaque (Mining Village)

South of 3e Ave. Upon entering Val-d'Or, take Rue Saint-Jacques, directly opposite the tourist information booth, up to Rue Perreault.

Merged with Val-d'Or in 1965, this mining village was named for François-Charles de Bourlamaque, an aide of French General Montcalm. The village, which was declared a historic district in 1979, was administered exclusively by the Lamaque Mine, one of the main employers on the Cadillac Fault. The mine shaft, hospital and residence of the mine executives are intact, and the solid log cabins that housed the mine employees are still inhabited.

The **Cité de l'Or** provides guided tours (👣) of the village; for an additional fee, visitors can see the surface buildings of the Lamaque Mine and descend some 91m/300ft into an authentic mine **tunnel** (open late Jun–early Sept daily 9am–5pm; rest of the year by appointment; ⊛$25.25 for 2hr village tour, or $38 for 4hr tour of village, surface and underground; tickets available at 90 Ave. Perreault; ♿ ✆819-825-1274, 1-877-582-5367; www.citedelor.com).

Tour d'observation (Rotary Observation Tower)

Rue Sabourin at Rue des Pins. Open year-round daily.

Rising above an attractive forest setting, this tower (18m/59ft) in Belvédère Park overlooks the town and surrounding area, which has been nicknamed the "country of one hundred thousand lakes" (*le pays aux cent mille lacs*).

MALARTIC

25km/15mi west of Val-d'Or, on Rte. 117.

This mining and industrial town was created as a "mushroom city" in 1922, and flourished during the mid-20C, with seven active gold mines. Along the Avenue Royal, false-front buildings recall the city's gold-rush days.

Musée minéralogique de l'Abitibi-Témiscamingue★

Arriving from Val-d'Or, turn right on Rue de la Paix (no. 650). 👣Visit by guided tour (1hr 30min) only, mid-Jun–mid-Sept daily 9am–5pm; rest of the year, Mon–Fri 9am–noon, 1pm–5pm, weekends by appointment. ⊛$9. ♿ 🅿 ✆819-757-4677. www.museemalartic.qc.ca.

This museum was established as a tribute to the mining heritage of the Abitibi-Témiscamingue region. It features a fine collection of mineral samples from the region and from around the world (and the Moon), as well as an avant-garde exhibit that takes visitors on a simulated journey to the core of the ore.

Réserve faunique La Vérendrye

North entrance is 57km/35.4mi southeast of Val-d'Or on Rte. 117; south entrance is 275km/171mi from Montreal on Rte. 117. △✕♿🅿. Visitor centers

open May–Sept. Free. 819-354-4392. www.sepaq.com.
This vast wildlife reserve (12,589sq km /7,822sq mi) is the second largest in Quebec after the Lacs Albanel-Mistassini-et-Waconichi reserve (*see opposite*). It spans two tourist regions: Abitibi-Témiscamingue to the north and the Outaouais region. It was named for the illustrious explorer of the Rocky Mountains, Pierre Gaultier de Varennes, Sieur de La Vérendrye, and has been delighting visitors since 1939.
Its lakes, rivers, and streams, which feed into the Ottawa and Gatineau rivers, are inhabited by some 100 kinds of birds and fish, including pike, walleye, perch, and brook trout. The immense conifer forests that cover the territory host all kinds of mammals, from moose to beavers, deer, black bears, wolves, and foxes.
A main road, Route 117 (180km/111mi), passes through the reserve—you will come across Lac Jean-Péré, one of the biggest draws in the park, the Cabonga reservoir, which controls the flow to the Gatineau River, and the Dozois reservoir, which regulates the course of the Ottawa River (further on, the road also crosses the dam over the river).
Canoe enthusiasts can enjoy some 800km/500mi of routes equipped with wild camping areas and portages. The preferred departure point is Lac Jean-Péré, which offers relatively easy circuits for beginners. Canoes and fishing boats can be rented.

Chibougamau

Baie James region

The region around the town of Chibougamau is a vast expanse of lakes and forests, bordered by Lakes Mistassini, Chibougamau and Aux Dorés. The name Chibougamau is derived from the Cree word *shabogamaw,* meaning "lake traversed by a river."
The indigenous population in this region consisted of nomadic hunters and gatherers who separated into small multifamily groups for the long winter and reassembled into large bands at various strategic meeting places during the summer. Today half the town's inhabitants are francophones of European descent, and half are Cree, who live mostly around lakes and rivers, drawing their livelihood primarily from the immense boreal forest that is divided into familial hunting territories.

- **Population:** 7,541.
- **Info:** 1252 Rte. 167 Sud. 418-748-8140 or 1-888-748-8140. www.tourismebaiejames.com.
- **Location:** Chibougamau is located 700km/434mi north of Montreal by Rtes. 40, 55, 155 and 167 (starting at Lake Saint-Jean). One daily flight departs from Montreal on Air Creebec 800-567-6567; for schedules www.aircreebec.ca.
- **Don't Miss:** The Albanel-Mistassini-and-Waconichi Lakes Wildlife Reserve for a real wilderness camping experience.
- **Timing:** Allow at least 10hrs to drive from Montreal to Chibougamau via Lac St-Jean on Rte. 167, or 13hrs via Mont-Laurier on Rte. 117. If you intend to camp or fish, be sure to make your reservations before you leave.

A BIT OF HISTORY

Lake Chibougamau is situated along the northern route traveled by early European explorers. Among these were Sieur des Groseilliers (1618–96) and Radisson (1636–1710), followed closely by Father Charles Albanel (1616–96). Trading posts gave way to the mining town of Chibougamau, built in the midst of the boreal forest on a sandy plain near Gilman Lake, 15km/9mi north of Lake Chibougamau.

Traces of ore were first discovered in the 1840s. Several companies in the mining industry recognized the area's great mineral wealth. Prospectors, mining engineers, promoters, and geologists flooded the area. It was not until 1950, with the completion of a 240km/149mi winter road between Saint-Félicien and Chibougamau, that mining companies established themselves here permanently.

The first copper, zinc and gold mine opened in 1951 on the site of Chapais, 44km/27mi west of Chibougamau.

Today's residents are mainly miners and forest workers. Several sawmills and working mines remain. Prospecting continues chiefly within the Lake Aux Dorés complex. Both copper and gold are mined in this area. Once the extracted rock has passed through the local concentrators, it is shipped by train to Chapais and then on to the Noranda smelter in Rouyn-Noranda.

SIGHTS

Réserves fauniques des Lacs-Albanel-Mistassini-et-Waconichi (Albanel-Mistassini and-Waconichi Lakes Wildlife Reserves)

Open Jun–early Sept daily 7am–7pm. Fee applies. The entrance is located 3km/1.8mi from Chibougamau on Rte. 167. Welcome center in Rupert (Rte. 167), 18km/11mi north of Chibougamau. ⚠ ✆1-800-665-6527 and 418-748-7748. www.sepaq.com. ⚠Wilderness camping is limited to 14 consecutive days. All waste must be packed out. Self-guided overnight canoe trips: one-month advance notice is required. Rowboats may be rented by reservation only; no guide services available.

This immense expanse of wilderness, stretching over 25,225sq km/9,652sq mi, is covered with forests of black spruce and fir. A multitude of lakes, including Lake Mistassini—the largest lake in the province (2,019sq km/780sq mi)—make this a haven for fishing enthusiasts.

Waconichi Reserve

Named for the hills to the west of Lake Waconichi that protect Native encampments from the frosty northwest winds, the reserve includes a tourist complex with fishing facilities. Recently built log cabins (30km/18.8mi from Rupert welcome center; reservations required ✆1-800-665-6527) are located on a lovely **site★**.

Mistassini

From the Rupert welcom center, drive 67km/41.6mi on Rte. 167 and turn left toward Mistassini (Baie-du-Poste); continue 16km/10mi.

Mistassini is located on the old fur-trading route leading to Fort Rupert (Waskaganish), on Hudson Bay. A Cree community, known as the Mistassini, already inhabited the area in 1640. The Hudson's Bay Company (HBC) maintained a trading post at Fort Rupert for 100 years, but competition from the Northwest Company eventually forced the HBC to move inland.

In order to intercept the furs before they arrived at Fort Rupert, the French established their own trading post in Mistassini in 1674, after Father Charles Albanel's visit to the area. The first trading post at Neoskweskau, on the Eastmain River, was moved to the north of Lake Mistassini in 1800 and to the south of the lake, where Mistassini is now located, in 1835.

Église Saint-Marcel (St. Marcel's Church)

This striking edifice was constructed during the 1960s. The roof, with its openwork center, is composed of two concrete shells thrust upward in opposing curves; the resulting design evokes the form of a fish, an ancient Christian symbol. From a great distance, it is an amazing architectural sight.

EXCURSION

Oujé-Bougoumou

58km/36mi west of Chibougamau. Access via Rte. 167, Rte. 113, then a gravel road. 418-745-2573. www.creetourism.ca.

After being dispossessed of its villages and its means of survival, the Cree community of Oujé-Bougoumou developed a new site and a new way of living combining the ancient and modern.

You can stay at the village, which offers accommodation in a teepee, a lodge or a guesthouse. Besides touring the traditional village, visitors can participate in numerous activities, such as canoeing, snowshoeing and dogsledding, and try Native dishes in the on-site restaurant.

Activities

Canoes, pedal boats and sailboards can be rented at the beach in the center of town, on the shore of Lake Gilman. A campground is located at the town entrance, behind the tourist information booth. Mt. Chalko, on Rte. 167, offers skiing in winter and hiking trails in summer.

DRIVING TOUR

CHIBOUGAMAU TO VAL-D'OR

About 413km/250mi southwest on Rtes. 167, 113 and 117.

44km/27mi from Chibougamau by Rtes. 167 and 113.

Chapais

The town was named in honor of the politician and historian Sir Thomas Chapais. The first major ore deposit in the Chibougamau-Chapais region was discovered on this site in 1929 by Leo Springner. In 1989, the Chapais sawmill was awarded a prize as the largest lumber producer in Eastern Canada. A thermal mill converts wood residue into electric energy.

Waswanipi

Like Mistassini, Waswanipi has been designated an Indian and wildlife reserve. Many Cree who live in this area are employed in the mines at Desmaraisville and Miquelon, south of Waswanipi; others work on reforestation projects in the region.

120km/74mi from Waswanipi.

Lebel-sur-Quévillon

In 1965 the shores of Lake Quévillon, fed by the Bell River, were still pristine wilderness. Since then, a small, vibrant community has developed.

Located at the edge of town on Blvd Quévillon are a municipal campground and beach with watersport equipment rental and charted walking trails.

Senneterre

Situated at the town's three entry points are three sculptures representing the forestry and railway industries and the Canadian armed forces. They serve as reminders of a difficult but glorious past, while instilling hope for the future of this dynamic little forestry community.

Take access road N-806 for 45km/28mi.

Lac Faillon

Lake Faillon offers visitors a lovely setting enhanced by the unspoiled beauty of the Mégiscane River. Recreational activities on the lake include swimming, boating, canoeing, and fishing.

Baie-James★

Baie-James region

Covering an area of 350,000sq km/135,135sq mi between the 49th and 55th parallels, the James Bay territory makes up 20 percent of Quebec's total land area. A wilderness of innumerable lakes, mighty rivers, and coniferous forests of spindly black spruce and gray pine, the region is home to some 40 species of mammals including caribou, moose, black bear, beaver, lynx, beluga whales, and seals, and a multitude of waterfowl and fish.

- **Info:** 1252 Rte. 167 Sud. ℘418-748-8140 or ℘1-888-748-8140. www.tourismebaiejames.com.
- **Location:** Radisson (La Grande) is located 1,448km/899.7mi northwest of Montreal and 625km/388mi north of Matagami by the James Bay Rd. At 381km/236.7mi, there is a 24hr gas station with a mechanic on duty during regular working hours, and a snack cafeteria. Flights are available between Montreal, Quebec City, Val-d'Or, and Radisson on Air Inuit (www.airinuit.com), and Air Creebec (www.aircreebec.ca). Accommodation is available in Radisson.
- **Don't Miss:** A visit to the Robert Bourassa Generating Facility.
- **Timing:** From Matagami, the only service station is 381km/236.7mi farther north, so stock up and make your reservations for the tour of the power plants. Allow a full 4hrs for the tour of the generating facilities near Radisson. Take the paved road west to just past Chisasibi to look out onto James Bay before returning south. While it is possible to drive 582km/361.6mi east from Km 544 along the Trans-Taiga road to Hydro-Québec's service center at Brisay, it is a very remote gravel road with no towns or services.

A BIT OF HISTORY

Cree Population – The Crees of Quebec are part of the large Algonquian linguistic family. Their spoken language is Cree. In 2007 the sedentary population numbered approximately 13,000 people, living in nine villages: Whapmagoostui (Kuujjuarapik–Poste-de-la-Baleine), Chisasibi, Wemindji, Eastmain and Waskaganish, on the east coast of James Bay and Hudson Bay; and Nemaska, Mistassini, Oujé-Bougoumou and Waswanipi, farther inland. Native to the northern forests, the Crees have hunted (moose, caribou, beaver, and geese) and fished in the region for thousands of years. In 1950 the federal government became more involved in the region, establishing a compulsory English-language educational system. Since the mid-1970s, the Crees have exercised a strong degree of autonomy, governing their own school system, health and social services as well as housing and economic development programs.

Each community is administered by a local band council. The Crees have established numerous organizations and companies, such as Air Creebec.

James Bay and Northern Quebec Agreement (Convention de la baie James et du Nord québécois) – In 1971 the provincial government passed a law to develop Quebec's northern territory and created corporations to oversee the developmental, technical and financial aspects of the Hydro-Québec project. The energy project immediately raised legal questions regarding Native rights not taken into account by the provincial

Baie-James

© Gregory B. Gallagher / Michelin

government. The Inuit and Cree nations obtained an injunction and eventually entered into negotiations with the federal and provincial governments and three corporations to resolve the issue of territorial claims. On November 11, 1975, all parties, including the Grand Council of the Crees of Quebec and the Northern Quebec Inuit Assn., signed the James Bay and Northern Quebec Agreement. It was the first modern-day settlement of Native claims in Canada. Under the agreement, the Inuit and Cree yielded certain claims and rights. In return, they were awarded exclusive hunting, fishing, and trapping rights in designated areas; ownership of certain lands (16 percent of the claimed territory); the creation of aboriginal councils to oversee community and regional affairs and to participate in decisions concerning the various phases of the James Bay project; and financial compensation. In addition, programs for health care, education, and economic development were implemented.

James Bay Energy Project – Envisioned to exploit the vast hydroelectric potential of Quebec's remote northern reaches, this ambitious long-term project originally called for the construction of 19 power plants grouped in three distinct complexes: La Grande, Grande-Baleine (Great Whale) and Nottaway-Broadback-Rupert. To this day, only the **La Grande complex** is nearing completion. The first phase of the project extended from May 1973 through December 1985, at a cost of almost $14 billion, and led to the construction of 2,000km/1,242.7mi of roads linking the area with the south, five airports, and five working camps.

This colossal undertaking required the construction of 215 earth-and-rockfill dams and dikes, displacing enormous amounts of gravel, rock and sand—enough, in fact, to construct the Great Pyramid of Cheops 80 times over!

The three power plants house a total of 37 generator sets and have a combined capacity of 10,282 megawatts (1 megawatt=1,000,000 watts). During the second phase of the project, between 1988 and 1996, construction of La Grande-1, La Grande-2-A, La Forge-1, La Forge-2 and Brisay was completed, bringing the total capacity of the La Grande complex to over 16,000 megawatts—more than half the electricity produced in Quebec. The third phase, begun in 2002, provides for the creation of three new plants.

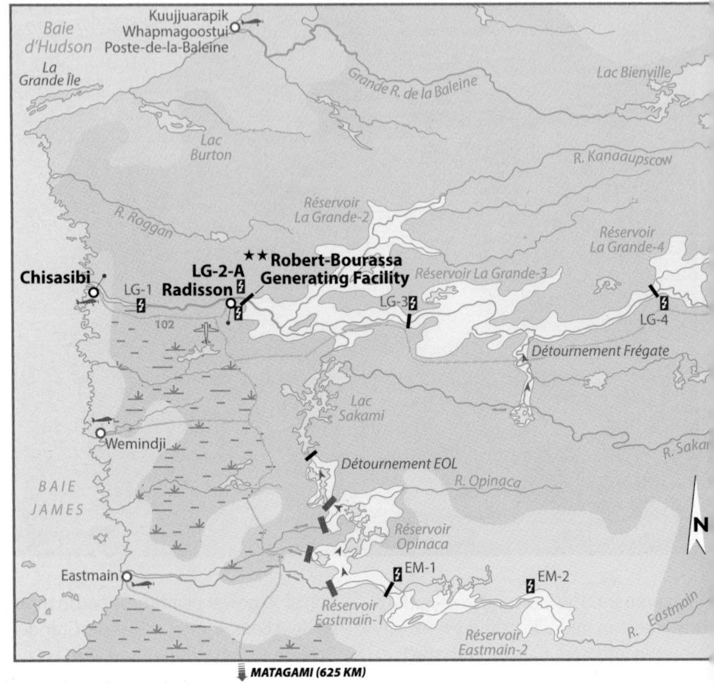

VISIT

LA GRANDE COMPLEX Radisson

Of the five temporary villages established during the construction of the La Grande complex, Radisson is the only one that remains as a permanent settlement. It is located on the south shore of the La Grande River, just east of the Matagami Road and 5km/3mi west of the Robert Bourassa power plant.

The hub of the village is the Pierre-Radisson community center; it houses shops, a post office and recreational facilities including a gymnasium and a swimming pool. Living quarters for employees of Hydro-Québec and a hotel are connected to the center by enclosed passageways.

Aménagement Robert-Bourassa★★ (Robert Bourassa Generating Facility)

Visit by guided tour (3.5hr) only, mid-Jun–late Aug daily at 1pm (2pm Tue) in French (English tours available on request). Rest of the year Mon and Fri 8.30am, Wed 1pm. Reservations required 48hrs in advance. Hydro-Québec in Radisson 1-800-291-8486. www.hydroquebec.com.

The guided tour includes a documentary about the construction and operation of the complex, explanations of the production of electricity, and a visit to the power plant. The most powerful hydroelectric facility in Quebec, the Robert Bourassa power plant has an installed capacity of 7,722 megawatts. The reservoir covers an area of 2,835sq km/1,094sq mi and is contained by one dam and 31 dikes.

Spillway

Used to release excess water accumulated in the reservoir during exceptionally strong floods, the spillway is extended in a "**giant's staircase★**" made up of 10 steps, each 10m/33ft high and 122m/400ft wide. Carved out of rock, it is a visible testimony to the feats of engineering achieved at the La Grande complex.

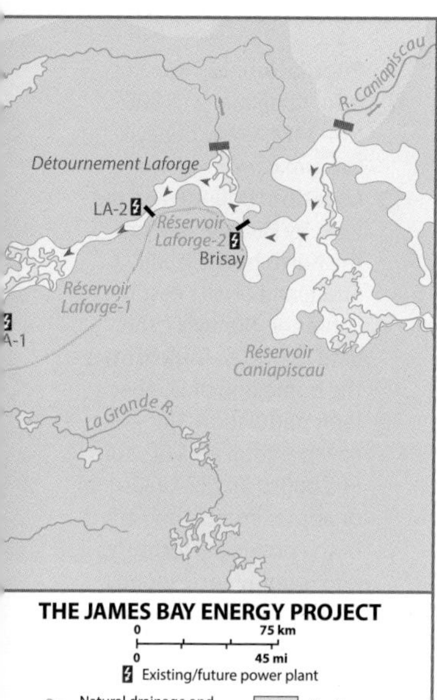

Activities

The Chisasibi Mandow Agency (*819-855-3373; www.creetourism.ca)* offers a variety of activities, including guided tours of the village. James Bay is located 15km/9.3mi from the center of Chisasibi. To reach the shores of James Bay, leave the center, turn right and continue straight toward the La Grande River for 2km/1.2mi. Turn left and follow the road for another 2km/1.2mi. At the fork, turn left and continue for 11km/6.8mi.

Robert Bourassa Power Plant

The Centrale Robert-Bourassa is located 137m/450ft underground in an immense granite cavern, 0.5km/0.3mi in length, equipped with 16 generator sets. It is the largest underground power plant in the world and among the most productive power plants in North America.

La Grande-2-A Power Plant

Located less than a kilometer west of the Robert Bourassa Power Plant, the **La Grande 2-A** power plant began operations at the end of 1992. Its six generating units function to produce additional power during peak consumption periods.

La Grande-1 Power Plant

This power plant, situated an hour's drive west of Radisson, is a more conventional river dam.

Driving Tour of the Facility

Depart from the Hydro-Québec information center (in the Pierre-Radisson community center in Radisson), which provides a free map and information about the tour.

This pleasant drive, dotted with informative panels, winds for some 30km/18.6mi around the dikes of the Robert Bourassa reservoir and offers scenic views of the surrounding area.

EXCURSION

Chisasibi

From Radisson, head south on the Baie James road for 20km/12.4mi. Turn right and continue west on the asphalt road for 82km/51mi.

The hydroelectric development of the territory caused a sharp increase in the flow of the La Grande River as it empties into James Bay. In 1981 the Crees residing in the community of Fort George, on an island at the river's mouth, demanded (by way of referendum) that their village be relocated to a site 8km/5mi upstream. The new village was called Chisasibi, meaning "Great River."

Tours of the village and other activities in the area are arranged by the Chisasibi Mandow Agency (*see box above*).

Nunavik★★

In recent years, Nunavik has become a choice destination for adventurous travelers eager to explore one of the world's few remaining frontiers. The region's spectacular expanses of natural wonders offer a unique experience, but visitors must be well equipped to cope with harsh conditions (nearly all visitors to Nunavik avail themselves of the services of an outfitter and/or guide).

- **Population:** 12,707.
- **Info:** Kuujjuaq. ℘1-888-594-3424. www.nunavik-tourism.com.
- **Location:** Bounded on the west by Hudson Bay, on the north by the Hudson Strait, and on the east by Labrador, Nunavik ("the land to live" in **Inuktitut**) is the homeland of Quebec's Inuit population. Nunavik covers a total area of some 505,000sq km/194,980sq mi or approximately one-third of the provincial territory, and roughly corresponds to the region formerly known as Nouveau-Québec and still referred to as the "Grand Nord" or Far North.
- **Timing:** May to October.

NUNAVIK TODAY

The socio-cultural region of Nunavik was designated by referendum in the Inuit villages in 1986 and officially accepted by the provincial government two years later. Much of Nunavik's continental territory is situated within **Kativik**, the administrative region created by the James Bay and Northern Quebec Agreement in 1975 to represent the municipalities north of the 55th parallel. Today modern achievements have considerably transformed the Inuit lifestyle, but the traditional values and heritage of the people survive.

GEOGRAPHICAL NOTES

The dominant feature of Nunavik's geography is the long, jagged coastline of the **Ungava Peninsula**, which juts north from the interior of the Quebec-Labrador peninsula, a subcontinental part of the Precambrian Canadian Shield. Most of Nunavik's **14 modern villages** are located along this coast.

The northern half of the Ungava Peninsula is divided by the **Povungnituk Mountains**. This range stretches from east to west and includes the Nouveau-Québec Crater, thought to have been created by a meteorite 1.4 million years ago. The **Torngat Mountains** in the east, dominated by Quebec's highest peak, **Mount Iberville** (1,662m/5,451ft), form the boundary between Quebec and Labrador.

Nunavik is a land of myriad lakes and rivers. These waterways, draining into Ungava Bay and Hudson Bay, have long been used by the Inuit to transport resources and raw materials such as wood, steatite and walrus ivory. In the 1950s the Labrador Trough, a mineral-rich geological fault between Kangirsuk in the north and Schefferville/Labrador City/Gagnon in the south, became a major center for iron-ore mining.

Flora – Nunavik comprises three distinct zones of vegetation: To the north, the open **tundra** zone, which is a treeless area rich with lichens, mosses and shrubs; to the south, the northern woodlands or **taiga**, dotted with small stands of black spruce and jack pine; and in between, the **forest tundra**, characterized by spruce, larch and pine trees. The tree line separating these environments extends from Umiujaq in the west to Tasiujaq, Kuujjuaq and Kangiqsualujjuaq in the northeast. Most of the Ungava Peninsula is under permafrost reaching 275m/902ft in depth at Salluit. Discontinuous permafrost (permafrost that appears in patches) occurs throughout Nunavik.

© Theo van Rijn / age fotostock

View from the end of Douglas Harbour, Wakeham Bay

Climate – The climate of Nunavik is determined by the opposing influences of the cold continental landmass and the warmer Atlantic Ocean. The winters are long and cold; the summers are in general cool, but temperatures can reach up to 30°C/86°F. Spring usually provides long, beautiful days, but—similar to the fall—can be marked by strong storms and unstable weather. Temperatures, which vary between the interior and the coast, range from -40°C/-40°F in January to 20°C/68°F in July. Snowfall is generally high (more than 2m/78.7in) and snow cover can be expected between October and June. The coastal areas are locked in by sea ice between November and June depending on the location, allowing for only a very short boating and shipping season. Nunavik's northern location gives it long days in the summer (about 20 hours of light in June) and short ones in the winter (about five hours in December). In recent years, global warming has had the dramatic effect of accelerating the melting of the permafrost and thereby impacting the Inuit way of life.

A BIT OF HISTORY

Early Inhabitants – The Inuit (*Inuit* means "the People": *Inu* means "human being"; *it* means "many") are the aboriginal population of arctic Canada. Some 15,000 or more years ago, hunters from Asia crossed the land bridge that spanned the Bering Strait and settled in Alaska's coastal areas. In about 2000 BC, these hunters began migrating eastward, leading to the creation of a second culture that developed along the Labrador Coast, toward Cape Dorset, south of Baffin Island. The so-called "Dorset People" are credited with introducing the igloo to the area. A third culture, known as Thule, developed in Alaska about AD 1000 and invaded the territory of the Dorset People, who eventually disappeared. The present-day Inuit are descendants of the Thule branch.

Like their ancestors, the early Inuit hunted marine mammals (seals, walruses, and whales) along the coast and on the nearby islands. They also ventured inland along rivers and lakes to fish and hunt musk ox, caribou, and waterfowl. Organized in small family groups, they traveled from camp to camp by dogsleds, kayaks, umiaks (large, open boats made from seal skins), or on foot, living in skin tents and sod houses in summer and in igloos in winter. Known for their keen navigational skills, the Inuit were able to travel great distances without the use of maps.

With the growth of the fur trade, the age-old rivalry between the Inuit and Native peoples living to the south escalated. Having been introduced to firearms before the Inuit, Algonquin

Indians forced the Inuit to abandon part of their territory.

Arrival of Europeans – About AD 1000, Vikings appeared on the east coast of Canada. Their visits were brief, however, and for several centuries Europe appeared to have forgotten the existence of the American continent, with the exception of Basque, English, and French fishermen who frequented the fish-laden waters of North America. After the early 15C, European explorers probably found their way to the Arctic, but contact with the Inuit remained limited. In 1610, in his quest for the Northwest Passage, Henry Hudson, the British navigator and namesake of the immense bay off the western shores of Nunavik, met the Inuit in what later became known as the Hudson Strait.

In 1670, Charles II of England granted a charter to the **Hudson's Bay Company** (HBC), allowing exclusive trading rights in the immense territory surrounding Hudson Bay. Named Rupert's Land in honor of Prince Rupert, cousin of Charles II, this remote expanse was virtually controlled by the HBC, which long dominated the lucrative North American fur trade. After 1750, the Inuit homeland became known to outsiders through subsequent explorations by the HBC. In 1870 Rupert's Land was legally transferred to the young Canadian Confederation in return for certain compensations.

Protestant Moravian missionaries arrived in the early 1810s, and Canadian scientific expeditions took place between the 1880s and 1900. In the early 20C, the French fur company, **Révillon Frères**, established trading posts in the region, thereby competing with the well-established HBC. In 1936, the HBC reaffirmed its economic supremacy in the area by buying out its French competitor. The arrival of European traders and missionaries in the region dramatically transformed the local lifestyle: The economic organization of the indigenous populations shifted from a hunter-gatherer to a barter system, and the religious orders—Protestant, and later, Catholic—introduced European values and education. To a great degree the traders and missionaries brought about the abandonment of the semi-nomadic, self-sufficient existence of the indigenous peoples and the development of permanent, coastal settlements. American whale ships, which frequented the Hudson Strait after 1845, introduced the practice of remuneration, as well as rifles and wooden boats, which led the Inuit to abandon their traditional harpoons and seal-skin kayaks. The new, more efficient hunting methods brought walruses and whales near to extinction, and the Inuit were forced to hunt on land to survive. The last whale ship was seen in 1915.

20C Transformations – In 1912 the Canadian government divided the former Rupert's Land among Manitoba, Ontario, and Quebec. The Quebec border was moved up from the Eastmain River to the Hudson Strait, some 1,100km/683.5mi farther north. Federal laws confirming the new border included a clause requiring the province to buy the land belonging to the indigenous peoples. In the 1940s, the Canadian and Quebec governments and the American army began establishing facilities (Fort Chimo, or present-day Kuujjuaq, and Poste-de-la-Baleine, or Kuujjuarapik), and developing mineral and hydroelectric projects in the area. Modern villages with schools and wooden buildings were established by the Canadian federal government as part of its legal obligation toward the local population. Between 1950 and 1963, Inuit family groups became somewhat more sedentary, leaving their hunting and fishing camps for the new villages.

In the 1960s, Hydro-Québec launched a monumental hydroelectric project, made effective by the subsequent **James Bay and Northern Quebec Agreement (JBNQA)**, signed in 1975. This historic accord required the native population to surrender certain claims

Art and the Community

As in the past, the Inuit culture finds expression in art and family, and in community festivals. In addition, the Inuit have created projects and organizations to preserve their cultural heritage, such as the **Avataq Cultural Institute** in Inukjuak, which was established in 1980. An active **cooperative movement** has been another characteristic of the community since 1959. Today, the 12 co-ops, under the umbrella of the Fédération des Coopératives du Nouveau-Québec, hold an important position in regional commerce. Each one owns a general store on the local level and regulates the commercialization of crafts, ensuring a livelihood for the many artists, painters, sculptors, and engravers.

but enabled them to gain other rights (*see BAIE-JAMES*).
Since 1975, all 14 coastal villages have experienced major expansions in housing. In addition, airports, health care, and schooling facilities have been upgraded. The HBC operated stores in many of the villages until the mid-1980s; currently these stores are operated by the Northwest Company, and are called Northern Stores. The Inuit have established commercial activities, creating employment opportunities in the villages. These enterprises range from commercial fishing and mining through construction and hotel management. The Inuit-owned Makivik Corporation manages the compensation packages established by the Agreement and has created a variety of subsidiaries, including Air Inuit and First Air airlines.

Nunavik Today – The 1986 grassroots referendum that created the socio-cultural region of Nunavik sent out a clear signal throughout Quebec for wider acceptance of the distinct cultural identity of the Inuit. Two years later, Nunavik was officially recognized by the provincial government. Today the vast majority of Inuit live in modern, prefabricated houses, and can obtain schooling and professional training. Some Inuit study and have jobs in Montreal or other places outside their homeland. TV, video, telephone, fax machines, and high-speed internet connection (through satellite dishes) are available in all villages. A wide variety of vehicles (motor boats and snowmobiles, for example) have made travel easier and faster.
Despite their settlement in the new coastal villages, the Inuit have generally maintained their traditional economic activities, such as fishing and hunting. The Inuit hope to reap financial benefit from projects undertaken in Nunavik, such as the controversial James Bay project.

Current Population – Nunavik's population today consists of four different groups: The **Inuit** (about 10,000), occupying some 14 coastal villages; the **Naskapi** (at Kawawachikamach) and the **Cree** (at Whapmagoostui); and the **nonindigenous** or Caucasian, primarily francophones, most of whom reside

Ungava Bay

© Gregory B. Gallagher / Michelin

in Kuujjuaq, the region's administrative center. The Inuit of Nunavik today are geographically and culturally divided into those living in the northern and western Hudson Strait/Bay area and those in the eastern Ungava Bay area, who have ties with the Inuit on the Labrador coast. The Inuit of Canada have kept their language (some 66 percent still speak Inuktitut), although English and French have become important languages in schools and public life in Nunavik. Since 1978, in accordance with the conditions of the James Bay and Northern Quebec Agreement, the Inuit have created their own school board, and Inuktitut is now taught in all schools.

VISIT

EAST COAST

The villages described in this section are designated by their official names. Former names are given in parentheses and current population figures are shown for the villages. See the opposite page and last page of the chapter for practical information about getting there, accommodations and activities.

Nunavut

The people maintain strong ties with other Inuit in Canada, Greenland, Alaska and Russia through cultural exchanges and political activities under the **Inuit Circumpolar Conference**, which was founded in 1977 and is recognized as a non-governmental agency by the United Nations. In late 1992 the Canadian government announced the creation of **Nunavut** ("our land" in Inuktitut), a 2,000,000sq km/770,000sq mi Inuit homeland carved out of the vast eastern expanses of the Northwest Territories, stretching from the Saskatchewan-Manitoba provincial border to Greenland. In 1999 administration of this new nation passed to the Inuit.

Kuujjuaq★ (Fort Chimo)

2132 inhabitants.

Located on the western shore of the Koksoak River on flat, sandy land some 50km/31mi upstream from Ungava Bay, this regional administrative center is also Nunavik's largest village. Officially named Kuujjuaq, meaning "the great river" in Inuktitut, the settlement has retained its popular name, Fort Chimo. Upon first meeting Europeans, the Inuit would say "Saïmuk! Saïmuk!," which meant "Shake hands!" However, the Europeans understood "Chimo" and so it remained the name of the first post they established. The original fort was founded on the opposite shore of the Koksoak as the first HBC trading post in northern Quebec. The settlement was transferred to its present site in 1945. The traditional red and white buildings of the post have been transported piece by piece to their new location on the western shore of the **Koksoak River** (guided tours are available through local guides; 819-964-2943).

As the administrative center of Kativik, Kuujjuaq is the seat of regional government offices, health services and a hospital, and a base for Air Inuit. A US Air Force base operated here between 1942 and 1949. Today its two major airfields are part of the current North Warning Systems, and the village serves as the transportation hub for northern Quebec, with several private air charter companies operating here. The present settlement was established around the base in the 1950s. The village has a hotel, restaurants, stores, banks, and art shops. Between the 1960s and 1980s the provincial government maintained a musk-ox farm here; the animals were released in 1985 and now roam Nunavik.

Environs

A number of outfitters are available to arrange wilderness outings around Kuujjuaq for the Arctic traveler (char and salmon fishing, as well as caribou hunting). A limited road system (*8km/5mi*) allows travel onto the tundra and to the tree line, in the vicin-

GETTING THERE

Nunavik is accessible only by airplane *(for more details on airline routes* *see PLANNING YOUR TRIP)*.

First Air *(1-800-267-1247; https://firstair.ca)* offers daily jet service between Kuujjuaq and Montreal for entry into Nunavik; plus connections between 30 Far North communities.

Air Inuit *(1-800-361-2965; www.airinuit.com)*, based in Kuujjuaq and Kuujjuarapik, offers service from Montreal to Kuujjuaq, Kuujjuarapik, Inukjuak and Puvirnituq (with or without stops). Air Inuit also flies to the region's villages on a regular basis. On both the Hudson and Ungava coasts, several **airline charter** companies offer service in the region according to your schedule.

GENERAL INFORMATION

The villages in the Arctic and subarctic regions of Quebec offer limited facilities to tourists, and traveling in these northern areas requires careful preparation. Reserving the services of outfitters in advance is highly recommended.

Four different types of travel for individuals or groups are offered: Nature, culture, hunting and fishing, and adventure. Due to government regulations, hunters and anglers must employ the services of a licensed outfitter. A listing can be found on the Nunavik Tourism website. The cost for one week is about $3,000-$4,500 per person, all-inclusive. Contact the Nunavik Tourism office for exact information on the availability of accommodations and on different packages offered by adventure operators and outfitters.

Nunavik Tourism Association, *P.O. Box 779, Kuujjuaq, QC J0M 1C0. 819-964-2876 or 1-888-594-3424; www.nunavik-tourism.com.*

Inform appropriate people about your movements in the area (location, routes, means of transportation, and times). Never leave villages alone. When going on hikes and/or trips, take along sufficient provisions, proper clothing, shelter, and emergency equipment.

Be aware of rapidly changing **weather conditions** depending on the season and area. When exploring the region during the Arctic winter, it is strongly recommended that you hire a guide acquainted with the area. Nunavik's weather and temperatures have nothing in common with the rest of the world. In summer, come prepared for bright sunshine, wind, rain, and perhaps, even snow; pack long underwear and sunscreen. Outdoor activities are impossible without complete snow attire, including mittens rather than gloves.

Northern Lights

Aurora is, *arsaniit* in Inuktitut, "aurore boréale" in French, and Northern Lights in English, all describe one of the most spectacular shows in the natural world. Only in the Far North can you see clearly and regularly a wide rippling green, sometimes red and purple, arc across the night sky (from August through March in Nunavik).

View over the Hudson Strait

©Gregory B. Gallagher/Michelin

ity of the settlement. These outings take travelers into isolated forested patches on a plateau of rolling hills between 80m/262ft and 250m/820ft in altitude. A highlight of the region is the Koksoak River, a tidal river whose character changes continuously with the ebb and flow of the tides. The tides reaching upstream into the river create a variety of fascinating and ever-changing landscapes.

Kangiqsualujjuaq

874 inhabitants.

This village is located on the eastern shore of **George River**, 25km/15.5mi south of Ungava Bay. It is situated in the shadow of an imposing granite outcrop in a narrow valley at the north end of a bay. Formerly known as George River and Port-Nouveau-Québec, Kangiqsualujjuaq, meaning "very large bay" in Inuktitut, is the northeasternmost permanent settlement in Nunavik. It was established on the initiative of local Inuit, who founded the first co-op in Nunavik, a char fishery, on this site in 1962. In the 1830s, an HBC post operated south of the contemporary village; it closed in the mid-20C.

The settlement hangs on the tree line, and a small lumber (spruce) mill operated here in the 1960s. The area appeals to canoeists, who ride the George River, and to anglers attracted by the Atlantic salmon populating the river. The George River is also the feeding area of one of Northern Quebec's largest caribou herds. Outfitter camps are found upriver at the beautiful **Helen Falls** (*64km/39.7mi*).

Kuururjuaq National Park

Open year-round; visitor center open Mon– Fri 9am– noon and 1pm–5pm. Make reservations six weeks in advance. ⊛$5.65. ✆819-337-5454. www.nunavikparks.ca.

Established in 2009 and still under development, the park covers 4,461sq km/1,722sq mi and is intended to protect the banks of the Koroc River and the Torngat Mountains, where the river originates. The best time to tour is mid-June through mid-September and March to May.

Tasiujaq (Leaf Bay, Baie-aux-Feuilles)

303 inhabitants.

This small settlement, whose name means "that which resembles a lake" in Inuktitut, is located on low-lying marshy flatland bordering the **Baie-aux-Feuilles**, the westernmost extension of Ungava Bay. The bay is noteworthy for its exceptional tidal range (up to 17m/56ft), which is considered the highest in the world.

Founded in the 1960s on the western shore of the Bérard River, the settlement was established in the vicinity of early 20C trading posts established by the HBC and the Révillon Frères. Later, its economy was bolstered by mineral exploration that took place in the north-

Kangiqsujuaq

© Gregory B. Gallagher / Michelin

ern section of the Labrador Trough. Several outfitters' camps provide char, lake trout and brook trout fishing. Herds of caribou annually pass close to the village on their autumnal trek south.

Aupaluk

195 inhabitants.

This village is located on the southern shores of **Hopes Advance Bay**, an inlet on the western coast of Ungava Bay. Aupaluk owes its name, meaning "red place" in Inuktitut, to the reddish color of the soil—the result of the high iron-ore content of the northern reaches of the Labrador Trough.

Originally a traditional hunting camp, Aupaluk was established in 1980 when Inuit from Kangirsuk and some other villages relocated to this area, which is renowned for its abundance of caribou, fish and marine mammals. Aupaluk is the first Arctic village in Canada whose town site was planned by the Inuit themselves. It obtained the status of a Northern Village in 1981 and quickly opened its own co-operative store.

Kangirsuk (Payne Bay, Bellin)

549 inhabitants.

Situated on the northern shore of Arnaud River, 13km/8mi upstream from Ungava Bay, Kangirsuk ("the bay" in Inuktitut) began when trading and mission posts were established here in the late 1880s. The HBC established a trading post in 1925. Government services were first introduced in the 1950s, and the village developed during the following decades.

Quaqtaq (Koartac)

376 inhabitants.

The village is located in a small valley on the eastern coast of Diana Bay at Cape Hopes Advance, which protrudes into the Hudson Strait. Frequented by the Inuit and their ancestors for 4,000 years, this region is rich in archeological sites. Marine resources remain a mainstay of the Inuit to this day. Various trading posts existed here between 1930 and 1960, and a government weather station operated in the vicinity between 1927 and 1969. The local co-op store was founded in 1974. Quaqtaq lies on the Arctic barrens with rugged mountains to the north and short rocky hills to the south and east. The valleys and other protected places show a little vegetation in summer: Moss, lichens, minuscule flowers in bright colors, berry bushes.

Diana Bay

The region around Diana Bay ("Tuvaaluk" in Inuktitut) is renowned for its rich hunting grounds, where abound land mammals (arctic fox, otter, rabbit, and sometimes the polar bear, which travels on ice for about 80km/50mi from the island of Akpatok) and sea mammals (various species of seals, walruses, beluga whales, and some narwhals). Species of bird found here include the partridge; snow, Canada and barnacle geese (Quaqtaq is on their flyway); and the eider duck. Among the most common fish are the gray, red, and speckled trout, and the Arctic char. Nature enthusiasts might see musk-ox, the legendary snowy owl or the loon.

Kangiqsujuaq (Wakeham Bay, Maricourt)

696 inhabitants.

Occupying an exceptional **site★★** in a valley on the southeastern shore of Wakeham Bay, Kangiqsujuaq was established on the site of an early 20C trading post. In the 1930s the Oblate mission founded a station here. Government services were introduced in the 1960s, and today the village has a Northern Store, a co-op and two churches.

The village is located 88km/55mi northeast of the famous **Nouveau-Québec Crater★**, measuring 3km/1.8mi in diameter and 267m/876ft deep. Outfitters arrange snowmobile excursions to the crater and surrounding **Pingualuit National Park** *(℘ 819-338-3282l; www.nunavikparks.ca)* in winter, and elders still maintain summer camps to hunt caribou and fish during summer.

Salluit (Saglouc, Sugluk)

1,347 inhabitants.

Located on the narrow **Sugluk Fjord**, about 10km/6.2mi from the Hudson Strait, this village is one of the largest settlements in northern Nunavik. Salluit is known for the beauty of its **site★★**, surrounded by high, rugged mountains and cliffs rising to 500m/1,640ft.

East of Salluit, asbestos mining at Purtuniq (Asbestos Hills) and **Deception Bay** introduced industrial activities and a modern infrastructure (jet airfield and harbor) in the early 1970s. Full-scale mining and shipping were abandoned in the 1980s. Nature observation tours afford possibilities for viewing walrus herds, polar bears and caribou.

Ivujivik

370 inhabitants.

Located in a cove south of Digges Sound, in a mountainous region near Cape Wolstenholme, Ivujivik is the northernmost settlement in the entire province; its name means "place where ice accumulates during ice break" in Inuktitut. After 1947, the Inuit of the neighboring shores gradually settled in the small village established around the Catholic mission, which was founded in 1938 and closed in the 1960s. Shortly thereafter, government services were introduced and the co-op began operations in 1967. The Inuit of Ivujivik have not signed the James Bay and Northern Quebec Agreement of 1975. Instead, these dissenters have allied themselves with Inuit from Puvirnituq and Salluit to form the Inuit-Tungavingat-Nunamini movement. These groups administer their own schools, under the supervision of a locally elected committee. **Digges Island**, north of Ivujivik in the Hudson Strait, was the site of the first recorded encounter between Inuit from the Quebec-Labrador peninsula and Europeans. The historic event took place in 1610 during one of Henry Hudson's expeditions in search of a Northwest Passage to Asia.

Avataq Cultural Institute

Inukjuak is the seat of the head officer of the Avataq Cultural Institute, a non-profit organization devoted to the preservation and development of the linguistic and cultural heritage of the Inuit in Nunavik. Activities linked to toponymy, history, literature, games, traditional music, etc., are offered. The Institute also collects various Inuit pieces from other museums and sponsors the annual Conference of the Inuit Elders, whose goal is to collect and preserve oral traditions and knowledge for the benefit of future generations. *For more information, www.avataq.qc.ca.*

WEST COAST

Akulivik (Cape Smith)

615 inhabitants.

Akulivik is located on a peninsula bordered on the north by a deep water port, and on the south by the mouth of the Illukotat River. Its name, meaning "middle part of a leister (fishing spear)," refers to the geographical aspect of the site. Just off the coast lies the island of **Cape Smith**, on which the HBC operated a post between 1924 and 1951. Akulivik was founded by the Inuit in 1976 on the site that served as the summer camp of the Qikirtajuarmiut Inuit group before they moved to Puvirnituq in 1955.

Puvirnituq (Puvirnituuq)

1,692 inhabitants.

The village is situated on the northern shore of the Puvirnituq River, 4km/2.5mi east of Povungnituk Bay. The name Puvirnituq, meaning "place where there is a smell of putrefied meat," refers to a tragic episode in the short history of the village: An epidemic ravaged the settlement, and all the villagers died, leaving no one to bury the dead. When friends and family arrived from nearby camps in the spring, the stench of decaying bodies permeated the air.

As in other villages of the Far North, Puvirnituq developed after the establishment of a HBC fur-trading post (1921). The Inuit who came to live in this post after 1951 had occupied, up to that time, summer camps near Akulivik and winter camps on the island of Cape Smith.

In 1975 the citizens of Puvirnituq were joined by those of Ivujivik and 49 percent of those of Salluit in refusing to sign the James Bay and Northern Quebec Agreement. The position taken on this issue has instilled a strong sense of solidarity within the community.

The Hudson Bay Hospital Center, a modern health facility serving the villages of the Hudson Bay coast, is located here. Originating as the Carving Association, created in 1950 by Father André Steinman, a French Oblate missionary, the **Cooperative Association of Puvirnituq** is among the most dynamic co-ops of Nunavik. The association operates a retail store and a hotel, and manages the community's fuel supply. Several local artists have achieved international recognition.

Inukjuak (Port Harrison)

1,597 inhabitants.

Nunavik's second-largest village, Inukjuak, is located at the mouth of the Innuksuac River near the **Hopewell Islands**. Non-natives arrived in the area in 1909 when the French fur company, Révillon Frères, installed a fur-trading post on the site, which they called Port Harrison. The HBC, however, established a post here in 1920 and eventually bought out the French company in 1936. The HBC's monopoly on fur trade with the Inuit continued until 1958. The Anglican Mission arrived in 1927, and in 1935 a postal service for the Far North was established.

Life in Inukjuak maintains a strong link with traditional activities. An important deposit of steatite, stone used for sculptures, was discovered here. The find has encouraged the growth of the arts.

Older buildings near the Co-op Hotel include the Anglican Mission, the Northern Store, the co-op store and the carving shop. The newer constructions of the village are concentrated along the route leading to the airport. On the eastern shore of the river, remnants of the old trading post, settlement, and cemetery can be seen.

Musée Daniel Weetaluktuk

In the lobby of the modern, brick schoolhouse, a series of bas-relief sculptures depicting everyday life in a traditional Inuit community demonstrates the skills of village carvers. The collection of hunting and fishing objects and practical cutting and scraping tools was assembled by a young Inuit archeologist from Inukjuak, Daniel Weetaluktuk (1951–82), who during his short career greatly contributed to Arctic anthropology.

Environs

The gently rolling rock formations dominating the landscape around the village provide a **panorama★** of the village and port of Inukjuak, the river, the **Hopewell Islands** and Hudson Bay, and the mountains lying to the north.

A **walk** along the shore of the Innuksuac River toward the airport offers the possibility of discovering many varieties of the tiny wildflowers that miraculously survive in the Arctic climate. The clear waters of the meandering river form cascades and pools along the way.

Umiujaq

444 inhabitants.

This village was created for the Inuit of Kuujjuarapik who decided to relocate, believing that phase 2 of the James Bay project would necessitate profound changes to their way of life. Archeological, environmental, and settlement-planning studies were conducted, and construction began during the summer of 1985. At this time, several hundred of the Inuit of Kuujjuarapik moved to the area and lived in temporary quarters until their homes were completed in 1986.

Umiujaq (meaning "which resembles a boat" in Inuktitut, because of a hill that looks like an *umiak,* a large open boat made from seal skins) is set on a tranquil site near Lake Guillaume-Delisle (Richmond Bay), remarkable for its escarpments along the seashore. A municipal building houses the FM radio station, town hall, an Air Inuit bureau and the post office. A **museum** in the town hall displays a collection of tools, household items and other artifacts that were unearthed by archeologists and village elders during the excavation of the site. Beside the municipal building stands the modern and well-equipped clinic, and the co-op, which also contains the carving shop.

Outfitters offer sightseeing trips to nearby islands and excursions on the Nastapoka River.

Kuujjuarapik

1,517 inhabitants.

Located on Hudson Bay, 172km/106mi north of Radisson, Kuujjuarapik ("little great river") was established as a fur-trading post by the Hudson's Bay Company in 1813. The Anglican mission arrived in 1882, but the village did not become a permanent settlement until 1901.

The first contacts with Catholic missionaries occurred in 1924. The French fur company, Révillon Frères, set up a post in 1908, at the mouth of the Little Whale River, to trade with the Cree and Inuit living along the coast of the region. In the 1920s, the village was relocated to the mouth of the Great Whale River.

A weather station was established in 1895, but most government services did not reach the village until after 1949. From 1954 through 1959, Kuujjuarapik became a communication center for northern Quebec through the construction of a series of radar stations known as the "mid-Canada line," between the Atlantic coast and Hudson Bay, north of the 55th parallel. The headquarters was established at Poste-de-la-Baleine. At this time the region around Kuujjuarapik experienced its greatest population growth. In 1965, the installation was evacuated and turned over to the province of Quebec.

A Multi-ethnic Community

Today the village of Kuujjuarapik is home to Inuit, Cree and non-Native populations. The post and village have gone through a number of name changes: First Great Whale River in English, then Poste-de-la-Baleine in

Inuit Sculpture

The first Inuit works were traditionally made from materials like whalebone, caribou antlers, or ivory, but after the arrival of steel tools, stone became one of the materials of choice. Although many Inuit sculptures are carved from soapstone (steatite), the majority are made from serpentine. There are also sculptures in other types of stone, such as basalt, marble, or quartz. The subject matter also varies from one community to the next, but Inuit art is above all based on observation, with animals, hunting scenes and people forming the most common subjects. Inukjuak-born Johnny Inukpuk is an internationally renowned artist.

Stone and Ivory Sculpture by George Kopak Tayarak

© R. Corbel / Michelin

French, Kuujjuarapik ("the little big river") in Inuktitut and Whapmagoostui ("Whale River") in Cree. The last three have gained official recognition, making the village one of the few places in Canada with three names.

The Inuit community is located near the mouth of Great Whale River, while the Cree community has settled farther upstream. The Inuit and Cree have separate schools, infirmaries and municipal organizations. The Anglican Church holds services in Inuktitut and Cree. In the **old church** is a fresco by Eddie Weetaluktuk of Christ walking on the waters of the Great Whale River. The **Asimautaq school** has a superb collection of Inuit carvings as well as Eddie Weetaluktuk's paintings.

The village is bordered on the west by the airstrip which lies parallel to the Hudson Bay. Government offices and non-native housing are located near the airport in the former radar station complex. A research center of the Université Laval (see *QUEBEC CITY*) is also located here.

Environs

A wide, **sandy beach** stretches from the mouth of the Great Whale River to the opposite side of the village where high dunes provide good views of the Hudson Bay and the area around Kuujjuarapik, Nunavik's southernmost village.

Approximately 12km/7.4mi upstream from the village, a scenic **Amitapanuch waterfall** is accessible by boat in summer or snowmobile in winter.

ADDRESSES

STAY

It is highly advisable to arrange all accommodations in advance. The *Nunavik Tourist Guide,* available from Nunavik Tourism Association, lists accommodations for Akulivik, Aupaluk, Inukjuak, Ivujivik, Kangiqsualujjuaq, Kangiqsujuaq, Kangirsuk, Kuujjuaq, Kuujjuarapik, Puvirnituq, Quaqtaq, Salluit and Umiujaq. Guest quarters in local homes are sometimes available. Double occupancy rates in hotels and inns range from $190 to $350; private bathrooms are not always available. For reservations, contact Arctic Adventures, *19950 Rue Clark-Graham, Baie D'Urfé, QC H9X 3R8. 514-457-6580 and 1-800-465-9474* (outfitting services at the same number); *www.arcticadventures.ca.*

EAT

Most restaurants serve American fast food. Tourists generally buy and cook their own provisions, as most hotels are equipped with kitchenettes. The local diet consists of caribou, char, and other fish, seal, and canned foods; fresh fruits and vegetables are scarce.

Good to know – Each village has at least one cooperative where you can buy basic goods. You can pay with a credit or debit card almost everywhere. Local specialties include caribou and seal meat, fish (including smoked Arctic char), and canned food, given the scarcity of fresh fruit and vegetables!

SHOPPING

Artisan boutiques are to be found at **Kuujjuarapik** *(sculptures)*; **Kuujjuaq** (in addition to the cooperative, the establishments 'I'Innivik Arts and Craft shop and Tivi Galleries display some superb art); and at **Kangiqsualujjuaq** *(clothes).*

ACTIVITIES

Adventure Canada – *905-271-4000 and 1-800-363-7566. www.cruisenorthexpeditions.com.* This company offers expeditions in the Arctic and visits to the communities of Nunavik by boat.

Arctic Adventures – *19950 Rue Clark-Graham, Baie D'Urfé, QC H9X 3R8. 514-457-6580 and 1-800-465-9474. www.arcticadventures.ca.* Arctic Adventures specializes in organizing hunting and fishing activities in Nunavik.

Arctic Wind Riders – *514-233-6093 www.arcticwindriders.ca.* Arctic Wind Riders recently introduced the new sport of kite-skiing in Nunavik. Programs are offered for all levels.

A

B

D

J

K

L

M

Q

T

STAY

EAT

Thematic Maps

Maps and Plans

★★★ **Highly recommended**
★★ **Recommended**
★ **Interesting**

Sight symbols

Recommended itineraries with departure point

	Church, chapel – Synagogue		Building described
	Town described		Other building
AZ B	Map co-ordinates locating sights		Small building, statue
	Other points of interest		Fountain – Ruins
	Mine – Cave		Visitor information
	Windmill – Lighthouse		Ship – Shipwreck
	Fort – Mission		Panorama – View

Other symbols

80 Interstate highway (USA) — 225 US highway — 180 Other route

Trans-Canada highway — 401 Canadian highway — 9 Mexican federal highway

	Highway, bridge		Major city thoroughfare
	Toll highway, interchange		City street with median
	Divided highway		One-way street
	Major, minor route		Pedestrian Street
15	Distance in kilometers		Tunnel
655	Pass, elevation *(meters)*		Steps – Gate
△ *1917*	Mtn. peak, elevation *(meters)*		Drawbridge – Water tower
	Airport – Airfield		Parking – Main post office
	Ferry: Cars and passengers		University – Hospital
	Ferry: Passengers only		Train station – Bus station
	Waterfall – Lock – Dam		Subway station
	International boundary		Observatory
	Provincial boundary, state boundary		Cemetery – Swamp
	Winery		Long lines

Recreation

	Gondola, chairlift		Stadium – Golf course
	Tourist or steam railway		Park, garden
	Harbor, lake cruise – Marina		Wildlife reserve
	Surfing – Windsurfing		Wildlife/Safari park, zoo
	Diving – Kayaking		Walking path, trail
	Ski area – Cross-country skiing		Hiking trail

Sight of special interest for children

Abbreviations and special symbols

	National Park		Subway station (Montréal)
	Interpretation centre		Calvary, sanctuary
	Hydroelectric plant		Ghost town
	National historic site		Covered bridge

Amerindian reservation

All maps are oriented north, unless otherwise indicated by a directional arrow.

North America Road Atlas

A geographically organized atlas with extensive detailed coverage of the USA, Canada and Mexico. Includes 246 city maps, distance chart, state and provincial driving requirements and a climate chart.

- Comprehensive city and town index
- Easy to follow "Go-to" pointers

Map 583 Northeastern USA/Eastern Canada

Large-format map providing detailed road systems; includes driving distances, interstate rest stops, border crossings and interchanges.

- Comprehensive city and town index
- Scale 1:2,400,000

(1 inch = approx. 38 miles)

Internet

Michelin is pleased to offer a route-planning service on the Internet:
www.travel.viamichelin.com
www. viamichelin. com

Choose the shortest route, a route without tolls, or the Michelin recommended route to your destination; you can also access information about hotels and restaurants from The Michelin Guide, and tourist sights from The Green Guide.

Useful Words and Phrases

The following phrases denote translations between English and **French**, the official language of Quebec and better known as Québécois in the wider world.

SIGHTS

	Translation
Abbaye	Abbey
Chapelle	Chapel
Cimetière	Cemetery
Couvent	Convent
Écluse	Lock (Canal)
Église	Church
Jardin	Garden
Maison	House
Marché	Market
Monastère	Monastery
Moulin	Windmill
Musée	Museum
Place	Square *(In Quebec Place can designate commercial centers)*
Pont	Bridge
Port	Port/harbor
Quai	Quay
Remparts	Ramparts
Rue	Street

NATURAL SITES

	Translation
Barrage	Dam
Belvédère	Viewpoint
Cascade	Waterfall
Col	Pass
Corniche	Ledge
Côte	Coast, Hillside
Forêt	Forest
Plage	Beach
Rivière	River
Ruisseau	Stream

ON THE ROAD

	Translation
Stationnement	Car parking
Diesel/gazole	Diesel
Permis de conduire	Driving license
Est	East
Gauche	Left
Autoroute	Motorway
Nord	North
Essence	Petrol/gas
Droite	Right
Sud	South
Feu tricolore	Traffic lights
Pneu	Tire
Sans Plomb	Unleaded
Ouest	West
Pedestre	Pedestrian

TIME

	Translation
Aujourd'hui	Today
Demain	Tomorrow

Hier	Yesterday
Hiver	Winter
Printemps	Spring
Été	Summer
Automne	Autumn/fall
Semaine	Week
Lundi	Monday
Mardi	Tuesday
Mercredi	Wednesday
Jeudi	Thursday
Vendredi	Friday
Samedi	Saturday
Dimanche	Sunday

NUMBERS

	Translation
zéro	0
un	1
deux	2
trois	3
quatre	4
cinq	5
six	6
sept	7
huit	8
neuf	9
dix	10
vingt	20
trente	30
quarante	40
cinquante	50
soixante	60
soixante-dix	70
quatre-vingt	80
quatre-vingt-dix	90
cent	100
mille	1000

SHOPPING

	Translation
Antiseptique	Antiseptic
Banque	Bank
Boulangerie	Bakery
Grand	Big
Librairie	Bookstore
Boucherie	Butcher's
Pharmacie	Chemist's
Fermé	Closed
Sirop pour la toux	Cough mixture
Cachets pour la gorge	Cough sweets
Entrée	Entrance
Sortie	Exit
Poissonnerie	Fishmonger's
Épicerie	Grocer's
Maison de la Presse	Newsagent's
Ouvert	Open
Analgésique	Painkiller
Pansement Adhésif	Plaster (Adhesive)
Poste	Post office
Livre	Pound (Weight)
Magasin	Shop
Petit	Small
Timbres	Stamps

FOOD AND DRINK

	Translation
Bœuf	Beef
Bière	Beer
Beurre	Butter
Pain	Bread
Petit-déjeuner	Breakfast
Fromage	Cheese
Poulet	Chicken
Dîner	Dinner
Canard	Duck
Poisson	Fish
Fourchette	Fork
Verre	Glass
Raisin	Grape
Salade verte	Green salad
Jambon	Ham
Crème Glacée	Ice cream
Pichet de vin	Jug of wine
Couteau	Knife

Agneau	Lamb
Déjeuner	Lunch
Sirop d'érable	Maple syrup
Viande	Meat
Eau minérale	Mineral water
Salade composée	Mixed salad
Jus d'orange	Orange juice
Assiette	Plate
Vin rouge	Red wine
Sel	Salt
Eau gazeuse	Sparkling water
Cuillère	Spoon
Eau plat	Still water
Sucre	Sugar
Légumes	Vegetables
De l'eau	Water
Vin blanc	White Wine

PERSONAL DOCUMENTS AND TRAVEL

	Translation
Aéroport	Airport
Carte de crédit	Credit Card
Douane	Customs
Passeport	Passport
Voie, Quai	Platform
Gare	Railway station
Navette	Shuttle
Valise	Suitcase
Billet de train/d'avion	Train/plane ticket
Portefeuille	Wallet

CLOTHING

	Translation
Manteau	Coat
Pull	Jumper
Imperméable	Raincoat
Chemise	Shirt
Chaussures	Shoes
Chaussettes	Socks
Bas	Stockings
Costume/tailleur	Suit
Collant	Tights
Pantalon	Trousers

USEFUL PHRASES

	Translation
Au Revoir	Goodbye
Bonjour	Hello
Bonsoir	Good evening
Comment	How
Excusez-moi	Excuse me
Merci	Thank you
Oui/non	Yes/no
Pardon	I am sorry
Pourquoi	Why
Quand	When
S'il vous plaît	Please

Do you speak English? Parlez-vous anglais?

I don't understand Je ne comprends pas

Talk slowly Parlez lentement

Where's...? Où est...?

When does the ... leave? À quelle heure part...?

When does the ... arrive? À quelle heure arrive...?

When does the museum open? À quelle heure ouvre le musée?

When is the show? À quelle heure est la spectacle?

When is breakfast served? À quelle heure sert-on le petit-déjeuner?

What does it cost? Ça coûte combien?

Where can I buy a newspaper in English? Où puis-je acheter un journal en anglais?

Where is the nearest petrol/ gas station? Où se trouve la station essence la plus proche?

Where can I change travelers' checks? Où puis-je échanger des travelers' checks?

Where are the toilets? Où sont les toilettes?

Do you accept credit cards? Acceptez-vous les cartes de crédit?

I need a receipt Je voudrais une facture, s'il vous plaît.

YOU ALREADY KNOW THE GREEN GUIDE,
NOW FIND OUT ABOUT THE MICHELIN GROUP

The Michelin Adventure

It all started with rubber balls! This was the product made by a small company based in Clermont-Ferrand that André and Edouard Michelin inherited, back in 1880. The brothers quickly saw the potential for a new means of transport and their first success was the invention of detachable pneumatic tires for bicycles. However, the automobile was to provide the greatest scope for their creative talents. Throughout the 20th century, Michelin never ceased developing and creating ever more reliable and high-performance tires, not only for vehicles ranging from trucks to F1 but also for underground transit systems and airplanes.

From early on, Michelin provided its customers with tools and services to facilitate mobility and make traveling a more pleasurable and more frequent experience. As early as 1900, the Michelin Guide supplied motorists with a host of useful information related to vehicle maintenance, accommodation and restaurants, and was to become a benchmark for good food. At the same time, the Travel Information Bureau offered travelers personalised tips and itineraries.

The publication of the first collection of roadmaps, in 1910, was an instant hit! In 1926, the first regional guide to France was published, devoted to the principal sites of Brittany, and before long each region of France had its own Green Guide. The collection was later extended to more far-flung destinations, including New York in 1968 and Taiwan in 2011.

In the 21st century, with the growth of digital technology, the challenge for Michelin maps and guides is to continue to develop alongside the company's tire activities. Now, as before, Michelin is committed to improving the mobility of travelers.

MICHELIN TODAY

WORLD NUMBER ONE TIRE MANUFACTURER

- 70 production sites in 18 countries
- 111,000 employees from all cultures and on every continent
- 6,000 people employed in research and development

Moving for a world

Moving forward means developing tires with better road grip and shorter braking distances, whatever the state of the road.

CORRECT TIRE PRESSURE

- Safety
- Longevity
- Optimum fuel consumption

- Durability reduced by 20% (- 8,000 km)

- Risk of blowouts
- Increased fuel consumption
- Longer braking distances on wet surfaces

forward together
where mobility is safer

It also involves helping motorists take care of their safety and their tires. To do so, Michelin organises "Fill Up With Air" campaigns all over the world to remind us that correct tire pressure is vital.

WEAR

DETECTING TIRE WEAR

The legal minimum depth of tire tread is 1.6mm. Tire manufacturers equip their tires with tread wear indicators, which are small blocks of rubber moulded into the base of the main grooves at a depth of 1.6mm.

Tires are the only point of contact between the vehicle and road.

The photo below shows the actual contact zone.

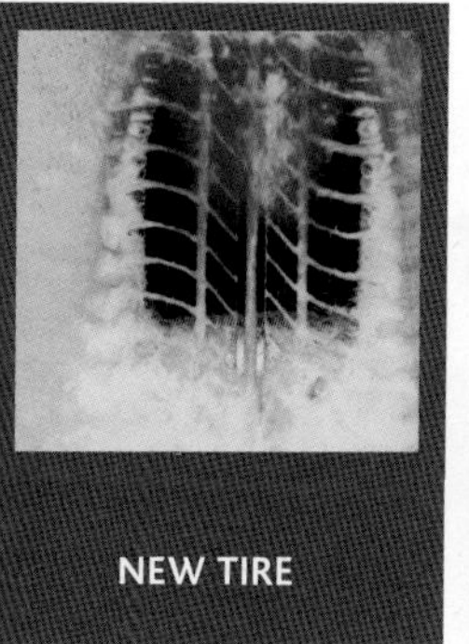

NEW TIRE

WORN TIRE
(1,6 mm tread)

If the tread depth is less than 1.6mm, tires are considered to be worn and dangerous on wet surfaces.

Moving forward means sustainable mobility

INNOVATION AND THE ENVIRONMENT

By 2050, Michelin aims to cut the quantity of raw materials used in its tire manufacturing process by half and to have developed renewable energy in its facilities. The design of MICHELIN tires has already saved billions of litres of fuel and, by extension, billions of tons of CO2.

Similarly, Michelin prints its maps and guides on paper produced from sustainably managed forests and is diversifying its publishing media by offering digital solutions to make traveling easier, more fuel efficient and more enjoyable!

The group's whole-hearted commitment to eco-design on a daily basis is demonstrated by ISO 14001 certification.

Like you, Michelin is committed to preserving our planet.

Chat with Bibendum

Go to
www.michelin.com/corporate/en
Find out more about
Michelin's history and the
latest news.

QUIZ

Michelin develops tires for all types of vehicles.
See if you can match the right tire with the right vehicle…

Solution : A-6 / B-4 / C-2 / D-1 / E-3 / F-7 / G-5

THEGREENGUIDE **MONTREAL & QUEBEC CITY**

Editorial Director	Cynthia Clayton Ochterbeck
Project Manager	Gwen Cannon
Editor	Brent Hannon
Contributing Writers	Rick Charette, Ilona Kauremszky, Rochelle Lash, Linda Lee, Margaret Lemay
Production Manager	Natasha George
Cartography	Peter Wrenn
Photo Editor	Yoshimi Kanazawa
Proofreader	Sheila Wong
Interior Design	Jonathan P. Gilbert, Natasha George
Cover Design	Chris Bell, Christelle Le Déan
Layout	Sean Sachon, Nicole D. Jordan
Cover Layout	Michelin Travel Partner, Natasha George

Contact Us

Michelin Travel and Lifestyle North America
One Parkway South
Greenville, SC 29615
USA
travel.lifestyle@us.michelin.com
www.michelintravel.com

Michelin Travel Partner
Hannay House
39 Clarendon Road
Watford, Herts WD17 1JA
UK
℘01923 205240
travelpubsales@uk.michelin.com
www.ViaMichelin.com

Special Sales

For information regarding bulk sales, customized editions and premium sales, please contact us at:
travel.lifestyle@us.michelin.com
www.michelintravel.com

Note to the reader Addresses, phone numbers, opening hours and prices published in this guide are accurate at the time of press. We welcome corrections and suggestions that may assist us in preparing the next edition. While every effort is made to ensure that all information printed in this guide is correct and up-to-date, Michelin Travel Partner accepts no liability for any direct, indirect or consequential losses howsoever caused so far as such can be excluded by law.

Michelin Travel Partner

Société par actions simplifiées au capital de 11 288 880 EUR
27 cours de l'Ile Seguin - 92100 Boulogne Billancourt (France)
R.C.S. Nanterre 433 677 721

No part of this publication may be reproduced in any form without the prior permission of the publisher.

© Michelin Travel Partner

ISBN 978-2-067204-20-1
Printed: June 2015
Printed and bound in France : Imprimerie CHIRAT, 42540 Saint-Just-la-Pendue - N° 201506.0075

Although the information in this guide was believed by the authors and publisher to be accurate and current at the time of publication, they cannot accept responsibility for any inconvenience, loss, or injury sustained by any person relying on information or advice contained in this guide. Things change over time and travelers should take steps to verify and confirm information, especially time-sensitive information related to prices, hours of operation, and availability.